Programming ASP.NET

Programming ASP.NET

Jesse Liberty and Dan Hurwitz

O'REILLY®

Beijing · Cambridge · Farnham · Köln · Paris · Sebastopol · Taipei · Tokyo

Programming ASP.NET
by Jesse Liberty and Dan Hurwitz

Published by O'Reilly & Associates, Inc., 1005 Gravenstein Highway North, Sebastopol, CA 95472.

O'Reilly & Associates books may be purchased for educational, business, or sales promotional use. Online editions are also available for most titles *(safari.oreilly.com)*. For more information, contact our corporate/institutional sales department: (800) 998-9938 or *corporate@oreilly.com*.

Editors:	Ron Petrusha and Valerie Quercia
Production Editor:	Catherine Morris
Cover Designer:	Emma Colby
Interior Designer:	David Futato

Printing History:

February 2002:	First Edition.

ISBN: 0-596-00171-1

[M]

Table of Contents

Preface

ASP.NET is the successor to "classic" ASP technology, the world's leading web development tool. ASP.NET solves many of the problems associated with ASP and provides an integrated and consistent approach to software development that builds on the libraries and languages of the .NET platform.

About This Book

This book will teach you all you need to know to be effective with ASP.NET. We assume you have some background with either C# or Visual Basic .NET (VB.NET), or sufficient programming experience to pick up what you need to know from the examples shown. Experience with "classic" ASP will help, but it is not required.

ASP.NET is not difficult. All of the concepts are straightforward, and the Visual Studio .NET environment greatly simplifies building powerful web applications. The difficulty in ASP.NET is only that it is so complete and flexible that there are many pieces that must be woven together to build a robust, scalable, and efficient application.

Since there are two authors' names on this book, you might be concerned that the tone will be uneven. Every possible measure has been taken to avoid this. Although each chapter was initially written by one author, all chapters were then edited by both authors. Then every chapter was extensively edited and rewritten by Jesse Liberty to give the book a single voice. And if that weren't enough, the chapters were subsequently edited by the O'Reilly editors, and then again by the authors. The bottom line is that while two authors wrote this book, you should find that it reads as if written by a single author.

How This Book Is Organized

Chapter 1, *ASP.NET and the .NET Framework*, is an introduction to ASP.NET and the .NET platform.

Chapter 2, *Hello World*, gives you the simplest possible application you might build with ASP.NET. It also introduces ASP.NET development within the Visual Studio .NET environment.

The next three chapters—Chapter 3, *Events*, Chapter 4, *Controls*, and Chapter 5, *ASP Control Details*—provide complete coverage of HTML Server Controls and ASP Controls. (Note that Chapter 10, 13, and 14 round out the extensive discussion of controls in ASP.NET.)

Chapter 6, *Programming Web Forms*, covers several fundamental concepts crucial to building powerful web applications, including code segregation, state management, control life cycle, and the usage of Visual Studio .NET.

Chapter 7 examines *Tracing, Debugging, and Error Handling* in ASP.NET.

Chapter 8 looks at *Validation*. ASP.NET provides extensive support for data validation, including range checking, ensuring that a choice has been made, checking that values are within a range and matching regular expressions. The ASP.NET Framework will automatically and invisibly take advantage of the capabilities of up-level browsers (e.g., IE6) to do the data validation at the client, while still providing server-based validation for down-level browsers.

Chapter 9 looks at *Data Binding*, the powerful ability to bind complex user interface controls to database tables and other data structures.

Chapter 10 examines the *List-Bound Controls, Part I*, including the incredibly powerful data grid. This chapter also looks at the event-driven nature of ASP.NET controls.

Chapter 11 focuses on *Accessing Data with ADO.NET* and the new technology for interacting with back-end databases. ADO.NET is built on a disconnected data set that provides a subset of the database, complete with multiple tables and full encapsulation of the relationships among the tables. ADO.NET is, essentially, an object-oriented model of your data.

Chapter 12, *ADO Data Updates*, looks at the support provided in ADO.NET for updating your data and ensuring data integrity in the presence of concurrency issues. This chapter also explains a variety of techniques for supporting transactions

Chapter 13, *List-Bound Controls, Part II*, explores advanced techniques integrating these powerful tools with the ADO.NET technology.

Chapter 14, *Custom and User Controls*, covers the powerful yet easy to use technology that allows you to extend ASP.NET to create controls customized for your specific problem domain.

Chapter 15 is a *Web Services Overview*, which are essentially web applications without a user interface. Web services allow you to provide services, potentially for a fee, to other web sites or applications. Chapter 16, *Creating Web Services*, and Chapter 17, *Consuming Web Services*, complete the comprehensive discussion of this subject.

Chapter 18 looks at *Caching and Performance*, focusing on issues related to building fast, scalable applications.

Chapter 19 examines *Security* and the tremendous support provided by the .NET Framework for building secure applications.

Chapter 20 covers *Controlling, Configuring, and Deploying Applications*. The .NET platform greatly simplifies building ASP.NET applications, with text file configuration and XCOPY deployment.

Appendix A provides a crash course in *Relational Database Technology*, and Appendix B is a reference to *Bug Database Architecture*.

Who This Book Is For

This book was written for programmers and web developers who want to build web applications using Microsoft's powerful new ASP.NET platform. Many readers will have experience with "classic" ASP or other web development platforms, though that is not required. Many developers will have read a primer on C# (see Jesse Liberty's *Programming C#*, second edition, O'Reilly & Associates) or VB.NET (see Dave Grundgeiger's *Programming Visual Basic .NET*, O'Reilly & Associates). Other experienced VB, Java, or C++ developers may decide they can pick up what they need to know about the languages just by working through the exercises in this book.

Conventions Used in This Book

The following font conventions are used in this book:

Italic
> Used for pathnames, filenames, program names, Internet addresses, such as domain names and URLs, and new terms where they are defined.

`Constant Width`
> Used for command lines and options that should be typed verbatim, and names and keywords in program examples. Also used for parameters, attributes, expressions, statements, and values.

`Constant Width Italic`
> Used for replaceable items, such as variables or optional elements, within syntax lines or code.

`Constant Width Bold`
> Used for emphasis within program code.

Pay special attention to notes set apart from the text with the following icons:

 This is a tip. It contains useful supplementary information about the topic at hand.

 This is a warning. It helps you solve and avoid annoying problems.

Support: A Note from Jesse Liberty

As part of my responsibilities as author, I provide ongoing support for my books through my web site. You can also obtain the source code for all of the examples in *Programming ASP.NET* at my site:

> *http://www.LibertyAssociates.com*

On this web site, you'll also find access to a book-support discussion group and a section set aside for questions about *Programming ASP.NET*. Before you post a question, however, please check my web site to see if there is an FAQ (Frequently Asked Questions) list or an errata file. If you check these files and still have a question, then please go ahead and post to the discussion center. The most effective way to get help is to ask a very precise question or even to create a very small program that illustrates your area of concern or confusion. You may also want to check the various newsgroups and discussion centers on the Internet. Microsoft offers a wide array of newsgroups, and Developmentor (*http://www.develop.com*) has a wonderful .NET email discussion list, as does Charles Carroll at *http://www.asplists.com*.

We have tested and verified the information in this book to the best of our ability, but you may find that features have changed (or even that we have made mistakes!). Please let us know about any errors you find, as well as your suggestions for future editions, by sending email to *jliberty@libertyassociates.com*.

We'd Like to Hear from You

If you would like to provide feedback or suggestions to the editors, please write to:

> O'Reilly & Associates, Inc.
> 1005 Gravenstein Highway North
> Sebastopol, CA 95472
> (800) 998-9938 (in the U.S. or Canada)
> (707) 829-0515 (international/local)
> (707) 829-0104 (fax)

You can also send messages electronically. To be put on the mailing list or request a catalog, send email to:

info@oreilly.com

To comment on the book, send email to:

bookquestions@oreilly.com

For more information about this book and others, as well as additional technical articles and discussion on ASP.NET and the .NET Framework, see the O'Reilly & Associates web site:

http://www.oreilly.com/

and the O'Reilly .NET DevCenter:

http://www.oreillynet.com/dotnet

Acknowledgments

From Jesse Liberty:

John Osborn signed me to O'Reilly, for which I will forever be in his debt. Ron Petrusha, Valerie Quercia, Claire Cloutier, and Tatiana Diaz helped make this book better than what we'd written. Rob Romano created a number of the illustrations and improved the others. And Daniel Creeron did an excellent job with his technical review of the manuscript.

This book is dedicated to the folks fighting to keep us free, and to those working to protect us at home.

From Dan Hurwitz:

In addition to the O'Reilly people mentioned by Jesse, I would like to thank Charles Carroll for running the excellent ASP Friends list server (*www.aspfriends.com/aspfriends*). The help and insight provided by the people responding on his lists was invaluable. I especially want to thank my wife for being so supportive of this project and making it possible.

ASP.NET and the .NET Framework

Microsoft first announced ASP.NET (then called ASP+) and the .NET platform in July, 2000. .NET is, in essence, a new development framework that provides a fresh application programming interface to the services and APIs of classic Windows operating systems, especially Windows 2000, while bringing together a number of disparate technologies that emerged from Microsoft during the late 1990s. Among the latter are COM+ component services, a commitment to XML and object-oriented design, support for new web services protocols such as SOAP, WSDL, and UDDI, and a focus on the Internet, all integrated within the DNA architecture.

ASP.NET represents a significant enhancement to and extension of classic ASP. ASP programmers will be very pleased by how easy the transition to ASP.NET is, yet there is tremendous power and flexibility in the new development platform. ASP and ASP.NET applications can run side by side, allowing for easy migration of legacy applications.

This chapter introduces both ASP.NET and the .NET platform, notably the .NET Framework.

The .NET Framework

The .NET Framework sits on top of the operating system, which can be any flavor of Windows,* and consists of a number of components. Currently, the .NET Framework consists of:

- Four official languages: C#, Visual Basic .NET, Managed C++, and JScript .NET.
- The *Common Language Runtime* (CLR), an object-oriented platform for Windows and web development that all these languages share.

---

* Because of the architecture of the Common Language Runtime, the operating system can be potentially any flavor of Unix or any other operating system.

- A number of related class libraries, collectively known as the *Framework Class Library* (FCL).

Figure 1-1 breaks down the .NET Framework into its system architectural components.

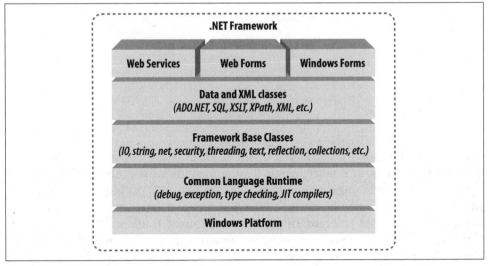

Figure 1-1. .NET Framework architecture

The Common Language Runtime (CLR) executes your program on your web server. The CLR activates objects, performs security checks on them, lays them out in memory, executes them, and handles garbage collection.

In Figure 1-1, the layer on top of the CLR is a set of framework base classes, followed by an additional layer of data and XML classes, plus another layer of classes intended for web services and forms, and Windows forms. Collectively, these classes are known as the Framework Class Library (FCL). With more than 5,000 classes, the FCL facilitates rapid development of ASP.NET applications. This same class library is used for desktop applications as well.

Microsoft .NET supports a *Common Language Specification* (CLS) that allows you to choose the syntax with which you are most comfortable. You can write classes in C# and derive from them in VB.NET. You can throw an exception in VB.NET and catch it in a C# class. Suddenly the choice of language is a personal preference rather than a limiting factor in your application's development.

The set of framework base classes support rudimentary input and output, string manipulation, security management, network communication, thread management, text manipulation, reflection, and collections functionality, etc.

Above the base class level are classes that support data management and XML manipulation. The data classes support persistent management of data that is maintained on backend databases. These classes include the Structured Query Language

(SQL) classes to let you manipulate persistent data stores through a standard SQL interface. Additionally, a set of classes called ADO.NET allows you to manipulate persistent data. There are classes optimized for the Microsoft SQL Server relational database, and there are generic classes for interacting with OLE DB compliant databases. The .NET Framework also supports a number of classes to let you manipulate XML data and perform XML searching and translations. The data handling aspects of the .NET Framework are covered in Chapter 8 through 13.

Extending the framework base classes and the data and XML classes is yet another tier of classes, an applications level. This tier of classes is geared towards three different technologies:

Windows Forms
> Allows the development of Windows desktop applications with rich and flexible user interfaces. These "traditional" desktop applications can interact with other computers on the local network or over the Internet through the use of web services.

Web Forms
> Allows the development of robust, scalable web pages and web sites. Server controls enable many new features, such as validation, event-driven programmatic manipulation of the web pages, state maintenance, and more. Web forms are covered in detail in Chapter 6.

Web Services
> Allows the development of applications that provide method calls over the Internet. Web services include a number of classes that support the development of lightweight distributed components, which will work even in the face of firewalls and NAT software. Because web services employ standard HTTP and SOAP as underlying communications protocols, these components support plug-and-play across cyberspace. Web services are covered specifically in Chapter 15, 16, and 17.

ASP.NET

ASP.NET is the name Microsoft has given to the combination of its two web development technologies: Web Forms and Web Services. Using ASP.NET, it is easier than ever to create web applications that are dynamic and data-driven, that scale well, and that work well across a broad range of browsers without any custom coding by the developer.

Used in conjunction with Visual Studio .NET, Web Forms allow you to apply Rapid Application Development techniques to building web applications. Simply drag and drop controls onto your form, double-click on a control, and write the code to respond to the associated event.

Generally speaking, web services are web applications without a user interface that allow you to provide services to other web sites or applications. As you'll see in later chapters, ASP.NET allows you to create web services using a simple text editor or faciliate the process by using Visual Studio .NET.

ASP.NET Versus ASP

The key differences between ASP.NET and ASP are:

- ASP.NET is much more event-driven, with the event handlers running on the server.
- ASP.NET separates code from HTML.
- The code in ASP.NET is compiled, not interpreted.
- Configuration and deployment are greatly simplified.

There are many other minor differences, but these four are the key changes, and they change everything. The event-driven model in ASP.NET is very powerful and is explored in detail in Chapter 3. The separation of HTML from code, and the fact that the code is compiled rather than interpreted, allows for the creation of larger, easier to scale, easier to maintain web sites. The configuration and deployment simplifications make working with ASP.NET web sites, both large and small, much easier.

Languages: C# and VB.NET

You can program ASP.NET in any language that supports the .NET Common Language Specification. The examples in this book will be given in both C# and VB. NET. It is a theme of this book that C# and VB.NET are sufficiently similar, at least as used in ASP.NET, so if you know one you will have no problem with examples shown in the other. That said, we do offer the examples in both languages to simplify the process of learning the technology.

Visual Studio .NET

Since all the ASP.NET source files are plain text, you can develop all your web applications using your favorite text editor. In fact, many of the examples in this book are presented just that way. However, Visual Studio .NET, the integrated development environment that is being released in conjunction with the .NET Framework, offers many advantages and productivity gains. These include:

- Visual development of web pages
- Drag-and-drop web form design
- IntelliSense and automatic code completion

- Integrated debugging
- Automated build and compile
- Integration with the Visual SourceSafe source control program
- Fully-integrated, dynamic help

CHAPTER 2
Hello World

The previous chapter introduced the ASP.NET architecture. In future chapters, you will learn all about creating web applications with ASP.NET. The current chapter presents a whirlwind tour by creating a simple web page to show you how easy it can be.

It is a long-standing tradition among programmers to begin the study of a new language by writing a program that prints "Hello World" to the screen. In deference to tradition, our first web page will do just that.

The tool you are most likely to use when developing ASP.NET applications is an integrated development environment (IDE), such as Visual Studio .NET. You may use any editor you like, however—even the venerable text editor Notepad.

There are a number of advantages to using an IDE such as Visual Studio .NET. The Visual Studio .NET editor provides indentation and color coding of your source code, the IntelliSense feature helps you choose the right commands and attributes, and the integrated debugger helps you find and fix errors in your code.

The disadvantage of using an IDE, however, is that it may do so much work for you that you don't get a good feel for what is going on in your application. It is like bringing your car in to the mechanic; he does all the work for you, but you never really learn how your engine works.

As a beginner, you may be better off doing more of the work yourself, giving up the support of the IDE in exchange for the opportunity to see how things really work. In this chapter, you will use a simple text editor to create the source code for the first several iterations. At the end of the chapter, you will use Visual Studio .NET to create the same web page. (For the remainder of the book, you will find both examples that are created using a text editor and examples that are developed in Visual Studio .NET.)

Back in the old days, before ASP and ASP.NET, web pages were created with simple HTML. To better appreciate the features of ASP.NET, you will first create the Hello World web page in HTML, then convert it to ASP, and finally convert it to ASP.NET.

A Word About the Samples in This Book

In real life, web sites run from a web server, which is typically a separate machine (or machines) running a web server program, such as Microsoft Internet Information Server (IIS). In that case, a browser makes a request to the server, which processes the request and sends HTML back to the browser.

If you have a web server available, you could certainly put the samples from this book on the server and run them that way. Suppose the server domain name is *MyServer.com* and the web page you want to test is *HelloWorld.htm*, which is located in the virtual root directory of the web server. The URL to be entered in your browser would be:

```
www.MyServer.com/HellowWorld.htm
```

It is often easier to do all your development and testing on a single machine, then deploy to a web server for final testing and production. To do so, you must have IIS set up on your local machine.

IIS (the name has evolved to Internet Information Services) is included with Windows 2000 Professional and Windows XP Professional. It is not installed by default, although it can be installed if a custom Win2K/WinXP installation is performed. It can also be installed at any time by going to Control Panel, selecting Add/Remove Programs, and clicking on the Add/Remove Windows Components button.

In order to access the virtual root of a local copy of IIS, the URL should refer to *localhost*. By default, *localhost* points to the physical directory *c:\inetpub\wwwroot*.

Typically, you will define other *virtual directories* using Internet Services Manager (found in Control Panel → Administrative Tools). These virtual directories can be subdirectories anywhere on the local machine. If you have a directory defined on your C drive named *c:\myProjects*, you can define a virtual directory named *projects* that you "point" to that directory. If your *HelloWorld.htm* file is located in *c:\myProjects*, then the URL to enter in your browser would be:

```
localhost/projects/HelloWorld.htm
```

For now, you will create a subdirectory called *c:\projects\Programming ASP.NET*. Then you will use Internet Services Manager to define a virtual directory, called *ProgAspNet*, pointing to that location. If the HTML file you want to run, *HelloWorld.htm*, is in that directory, then the URL to enter in your browser will be:

```
localhost/ProgAspNet/HelloWorld.htm
```

The HTML Version

Straight HTML provides a means of creating and presenting static web pages. This book is not a tutorial on how to write HTML, and we assume you know enough HTML to follow the simple examples provided. (For background reading, see *HTML: The Definitive Guide*, by Chuck Musciano and Bill Kennedy, published by O'Reilly.) To get started, create a very simple Hello World HTML file, as shown in Example 2-1, and call it *HelloWorld1.htm*. The output is shown in Figure 2-1.

Example 2-1. Code listing for HelloWorld1.htm

```
<html>
   <body>

      <h1>Hello World</h1>

   </body>
</html>
```

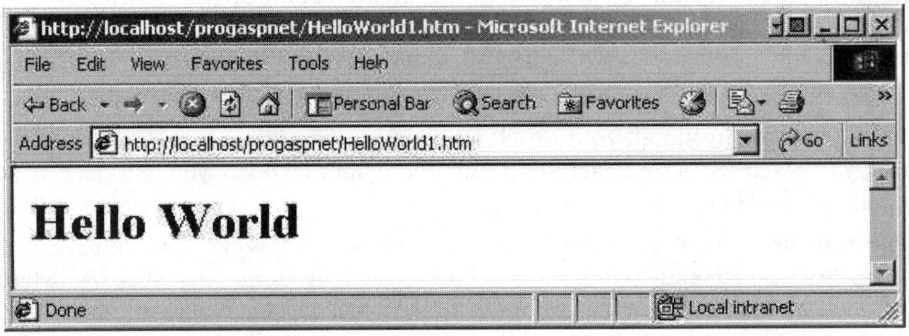

Figure 2-1. Output from Example 2-1

The HTML page displays the static text, using the HTML heading1 format. If you want to include dynamic content, such as the results of a query against a database, or even the current time, then a static HTML page is not the thing to use. For that you need some sort of server processing. There are a number of alternatives; we will focus on ASP and then on ASP.NET.

The ASP Version

ASP allows the programmer to intersperse scripting code snippets within the HTML code. This scripting code can be written in a scripting language such as JavaScript or VBScript. Adding embedded script to your sample web page allows you to insert dynamic content. Modify the previous code listing, converting it to ASP, by changing the filename extension to *.asp* and adding VBScript to display the current time, as shown in Example 2-2. The output is shown in Figure 2-2.

Example 2-2. Code listing for HelloWorld1.asp

```
<html>
   <body>

      <h1>Hello World</h1>
      <br/>
      <h2>The date and time is <% =Now%>.</h2>

   </body>
</html>
```

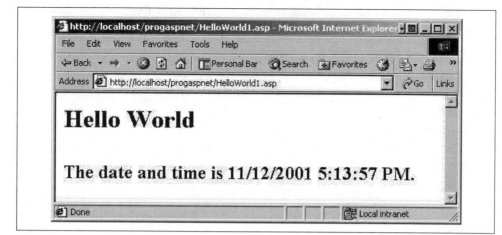

Figure 2-2. Output from Example 2-2

It may not look like much, but this represents a vast improvement over static HTML. ASP allows you to create web sites full of rich and dynamic content. The scripting allows for queries, reads and writes against databases, implementation of programming logic, control of the appearance of web pages in response to user actions or returned data, and a host of other features.

Hello World the ASP.NET Way

You will complete this evolutionary journey by changing your Hello World web page from ASP to ASP.NET. A key difference in ASP.NET is that you no longer use interpreted languages but instead use compiled languages. Typically, ASP.NET applications are built using either C# or VB.NET. In either case, the performance will be a great improvement over script.

 A significant theme of this book is that the choice between C# and VB.NET is purely syntactic; you can express any ASP.NET programming idea in either language. We suggest you write in whichever language you're more comfortable with. The transition from VBScript to VB.NET may be slightly easier than to C#, but much of the Microsoft and third-party documentation is in C#. In this book we will show most examples in both languages, though we confess to a slight preference for C# because it is a bit more terse.

For a full exploration of VB.NET, see *Programming Visual Basic .NET*, by Dave Grundgeiger (O'Reilly), and for C#, see *Programming C#*, by Jesse Liberty (O'Reilly).

Example 2-3 shows *vbHelloWorld1.aspx* in VB.NET, and Example 2-4 shows the same program in C#.

Example 2-3. Code listing for vbHelloWorld1.aspx

```
<%@ Page Language="VB" %>
<html>
   <body>

      <h1>Hello World</h1>
      <h1>ASP.NET Style</h1>
      <h2>Using VB .NET</h2>

      <br/>
      <h2>The date and time is <% =DateTime.Now( ) %>.</h2>

   </body>
</html>
```

Example 2-4. Code listing for csHelloWorld1.aspx

```
<%@ Page Language="C#" %>
<html>
   <body>

      <h1>Hello World</h1>
      <h1>ASP.NET Style</h1>
      <h2>Using C#</h2>

      <br/>
      <h2>The date and time is <% =DateTime.Now.ToString( ) %>.</h2>

   </body>
</html>
```

Note that the changes required to convert the ASP page to ASP.NET are minimal:

1. Rename the file, changing the extension from *.asp* to *.aspx*.
2. Add a first line to the code, called a *page directive*, which tells the compiler which language to use for all in-line code. Page directives can also be used to pass a variety of configuration settings to the compiler and will be discussed in more detail later.
3. Change the script code to code written in the desired language.

The output from these changes is shown in Figure 2-3.

The ASP.NET version uses compiled code (either C# or VB.NET), which gives it a performance advantage. That advantage is meaningless in this simple example but can be very significant with larger and more complex programs.

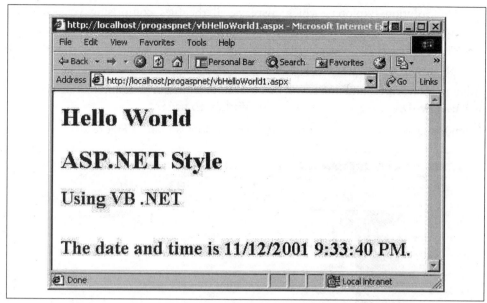

Figure 2-3. Output from Example 2-3

Hello World Using Visual Studio .NET

Visual Studio .NET is a full-featured IDE that provides all sorts of productivity tools for developing .NET applications, both for the Windows desktop and for the Web. These features include:

- A Start page, which allows you to set user preferences for IDE behavior and provides easy access to new and existing projects.

- Dynamic, context-sensitive help, which allows you to view topics and samples relevant to your current selection. You can also search the MSDN library from within the IDE.

- IntelliSense technology and code completion, which allow you to enter code with fewer errors and much less typing. Syntax errors are flagged immediately, allowing you to fix problems as they are entered.

- The tabbed document interface, which provides convenient access to multiple design and code windows.

- All the languages use the same code editor for a shortened learning curve. Each language can have specialized features, but all benefit from features such as incremental search, code outlining, collapsing text, line numbering, and color-coded keywords.

- The HTML editor, which provides both Design and HTML views that update each other in real time.

- The Solution Explorer, which displays all the files comprising your solution (which is a collection of projects) in a hierarchical, visual manner.
- The integrated Debugger, which allows you to set breakpoints and step through code, even across multiple languages.

All of these features, and more, will be covered in subsequent chapters. For now, you will use the IDE to create a simple Hello World web page.

Open Visual Studio .NET. You should see a window similar to Figure 2-4.

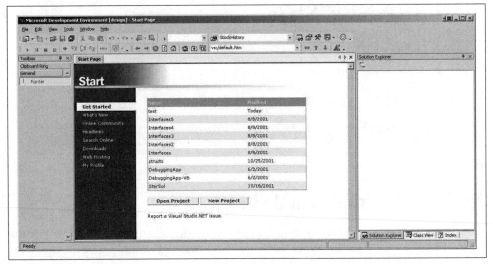

Figure 2-4. Start page in Visual Studio .NET

Click on the New Project button in the middle of the screen. This brings up the New Project dialog box shown in Figure 2-5.

The left side of this dialog box allows you to choose the type of project. In Figure 2-5, Visual C# Projects is selected. You could click on Visual Basic Projects or Visual C++ Projects if you would rather work in either of those languages. The example will be shown in C# and VB.NET; as you will see, it is virtually identical in both languages.

The right side of the dialog box lists the various project templates to choose from. Select ASP.NET Web Application.

The Name and Location edit fields will contain default values. Change the Name, by editing the Location field, from WebApplication1 to HelloWorld. As you do so, you will see the label below the Location edit field change to:

```
Project will be created at HTTP://localhost/HelloWorld.
```

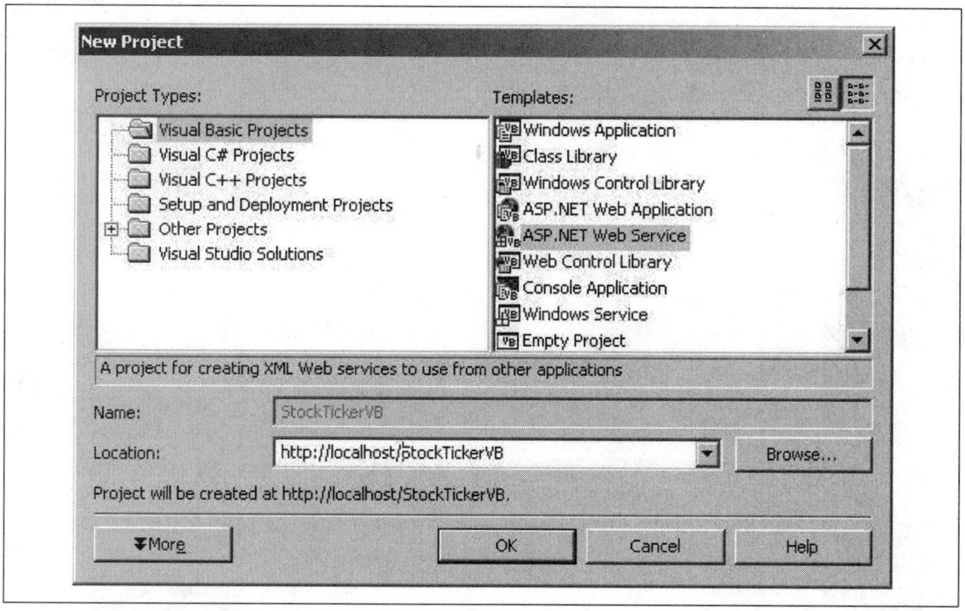

Figure 2-5. New Project dialog box in Visual Studio .NET

By default, localhost corresponds to the physical directory *c:\inetpub\wwwroot*. This line tells you that it will create this new web application in the physical directory *c:\inetpub\wwwroot\HelloWorld*. Click OK.

Visual Studio .NET will now present a design surface in the middle of the screen. Before proceeding any further, change the pageLayout mode from GridLayout to FlowLayout. This will make the resulting HTML simpler and more in line with our previous examples. To do so, click anywhere on the design surface. The Properties Window, visible in the lower right of the screen, should be visible with the word DOCUMENT showing in the edit field at the top of the Properties Window. If the Properties Window is not visible, choose Properties Window from the View menu or press F4.

In the Properties Window, slide down until the pageLayout property is visible. Click on the displayed value, GridLayout. A drop-down arrow will appear. Click on it and select FlowLayout. Immediately, the design surface changes appearance. The results will look something like Figure 2-6.

Now you want to add some labels. Notice that the Toolbox on the left edge of the screen currently displays Web Forms controls. You will use those in a moment. For now, you want to place some HTML controls, so click on the HTML button near the bottom of the Toolbox.

Click on the Label control and drag it to the design surface. It will automatically go to the upper-left corner of the design surface and contain the word Label. Click on

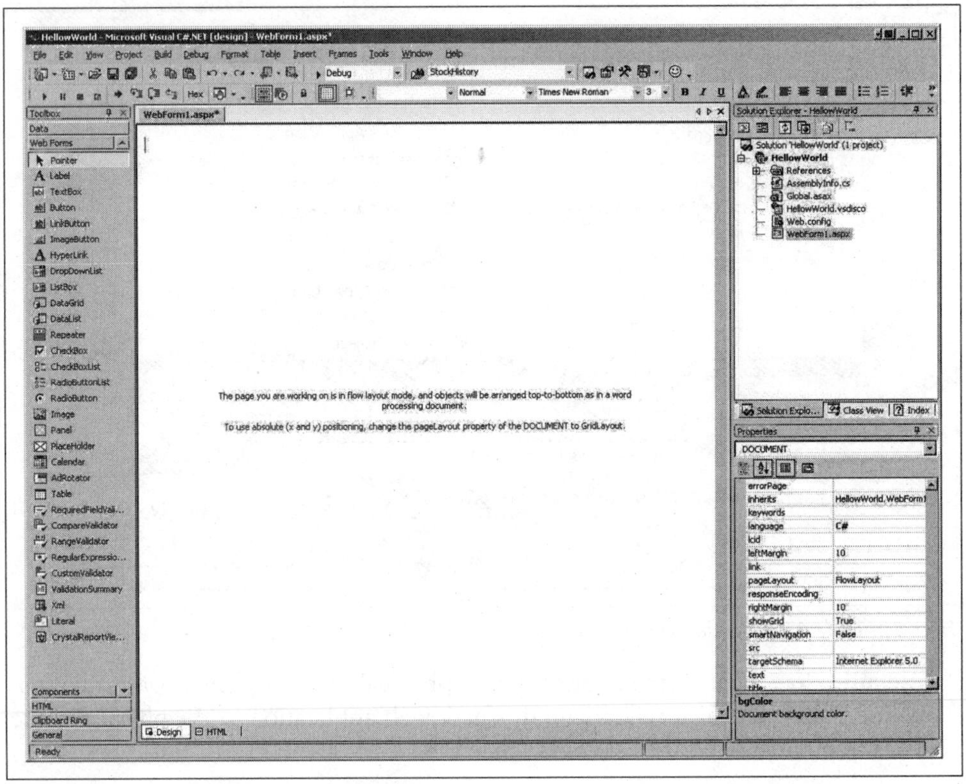

Figure 2-6. Setting FlowLayout in Visual Studio .NET

the control, backspace over the word Label, and type the words Hello World. It will look something like Figure 2-7.

Notice the drop-down lists in the toolbar just above the design surface, one of which displays the word Normal. These are part of the Formatting menu. If they are not visible, choose Toolbars from the View menu and click on Formatting.

The drop-down containing the word Normal displays the available block formats. Click on the down arrow and select Heading 1. Then click and drag on the resizing handles to stretch the control so that the phrase does not wrap. The screen should look something like Figure 2-8.

> If you want to see or edit the HTML directly, click on the HTML tab at the bottom of the design surface. The Design and HTML tabs allow you to toggle between graphical design and code-editing modes.

Now add two more HTML labels. To get to the next line on the design surface, click on the design surface outside the Hello World label and press the Enter key. The cursor will move to the next line.

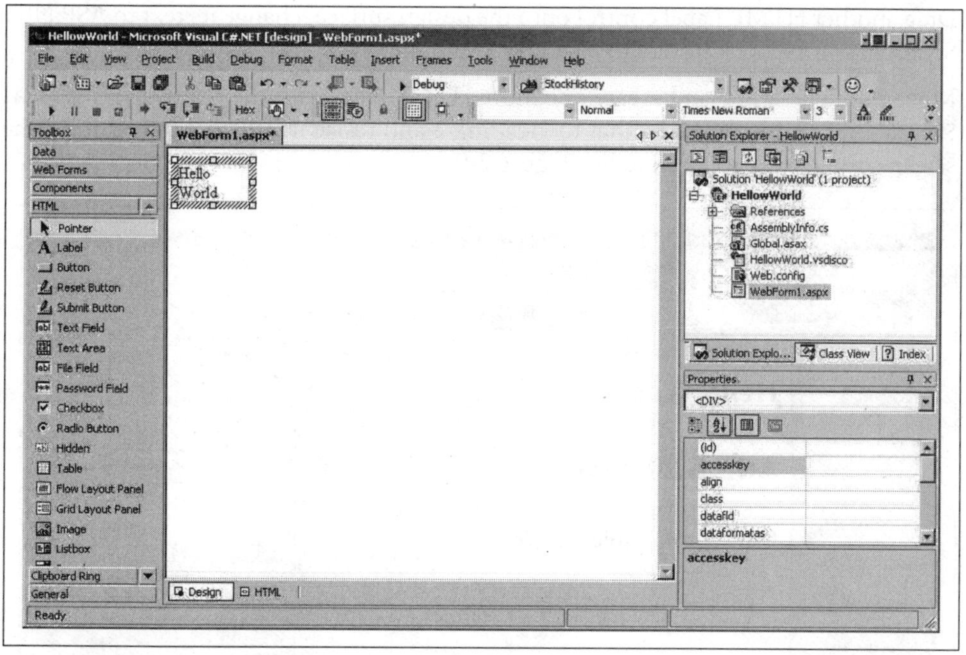

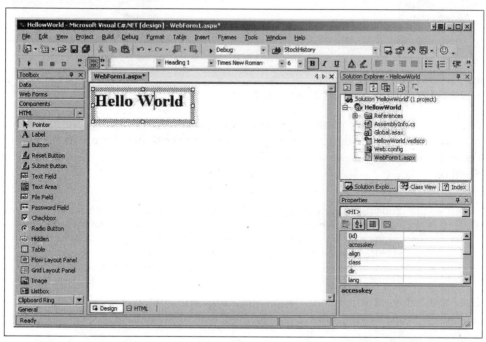

Figure 2-7. Placing an HTML label in Visual Studio .NET

Figure 2-8. Resizing an HTML label in Visual Studio .NET

Drag another HTML Label control onto the design surface, change its text to ASP.NET Style, change its block format to Heading 1, and then resize it.

Move to the next line and create one more HTML label with the words Using Visual Studio .NET. Set its block format to Heading 2 and resize it. When you are done, the screen should look something like Figure 2-9.

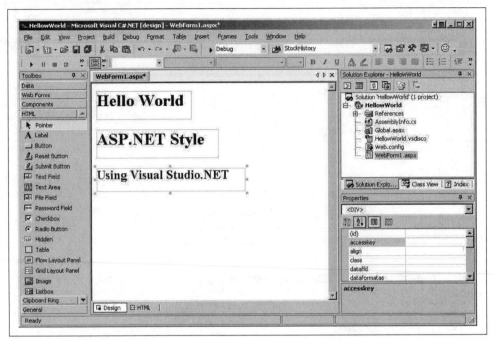

Figure 2-9. HTML labels in Visual Studio .NET

Now it's time to place a control that will display the date and time. To do this, move to the next line on the design surface by clicking on the design surface at the end of the last control and pressing Enter. Then click on the Web Forms button on the Toolbox.

 You are probably wondering about the differentiation between HTML controls and Web Forms controls. The reasons and details for this will fill the next several chapters. For now, suffice it to say that "classic" HTML controls are more resource-efficient, but the controls contained in the Web Forms toolbox allow for server-side processing.

Drag a Label control onto the design surface. It will contain the text Label. If you look at the Properties Window, the object will have an ID of Label1.

Look at the Solution Explorer on the right side of the screen. If the Solution Explorer is not visible, choose Solution Explorer from the View menu, or press Ctrl+Alt+L.

Right-click on WebForm1.aspx and select View Code. A code window will appear where the design surface was. The tab at the top of the code window will be labeled `WebForm1.aspx.cs*`.

 If you are working in Visual Basic .NET, the tab will be labeled `WebForm1.aspx.vb*`. In either case, the asterisk indicates that the file has not yet been saved.

Slide down the code window until you see the Page_Load method. In C#, this will look like:

```
private void Page_Load(object sender, System.EventArgs e)
{
    // Put user code to initialize the page here
}
```

and in VB.NET, it will look like:

```
Private Sub Page_Load(ByVal sender As System.Object, _
                ByVal e As System.EventArgs) Handles MyBase.Load
    'Put user code to initialize the page here
End Sub
```

Put your cursor at the end of the comment line (after the word here) and press the Enter key. This will move the cursor to the beginning of the next line, properly indented, ready to type. If you are working in C#, enter the following lines of code:

```
Label1.Text = "The date and time is " +
    DateTime.Now.ToString( );
```

If you are working in VB.NET, enter these lines of code:

```
Label1.Text = "The data and time is " & _
    DateTime.Now.ToString( )
```

When you type the period after `Label1`, you see a drop-down of all the possible methods and properties that are valid in this context. (If you don't see the drop-down list, verify that the label name is spelled properly and, if using C#, that the casing is correct.) This is the IntelliSense technology at work.

You can either scroll down and select the proper method or function by pressing Tab or any other key, or start typing the desired method or function to narrow the search. When you get to the desired selection, press Tab or any other key. The Tab key enters that selection into your code without your having to type the entire word; pressing any other key enters the selection into your code followed by the key you pressed.

The completed Page_Load method in the code window should look like the following in C#:

```csharp
private void Page_Load(object sender, System.EventArgs e)
{
    // Put user code to initialize the page here
    Label1.Text = "The date and time is " +
        DateTime.Now.ToString();
}
```

and like this in VB.NET:

```vbnet
Private Sub Page_Load(ByVal sender As System.Object, _
                      ByVal e As System.EventArgs) Handles MyBase.Load
    'Put user code to initialize the page here
    Label1.Text = "The date and time is " & _
        DateTime.Now.ToString()
End Sub
```

Press F5 to run the web application. When either the C# or VB.NET version is run it will look like the browser shown in Figure 2-10.

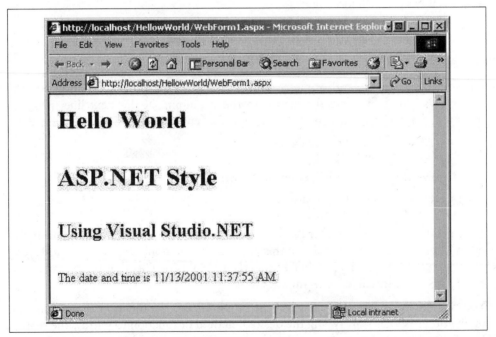

Figure 2-10. Hello World in Visual Studio .NET

Although the code is nearly identical between the two languages, there are some differences worth noting:

- C# code is case-sensitive while VB.NET is not.

- All C# statements must end with a semicolon.

- While both languages mostly ignore whitespace outside of quotes, VB.NET statements cannot span multiple lines without using a line-continuation character (the underscore preceded by a space). C# statements can span multiple lines.

You have now learned how to write an extremely simple ASP.NET web application. The remaining chapters will show you, in greater detail, how to develop rich, robust web applications using many of the controls and tools available from ASP.NET.

CHAPTER 3
Events

In Chapter 2, you saw just a glimpse of ASP.NET. Now you might be asking your-self (especially if you're a developer experienced in classic ASP), "What's the big deal?" One of the significant differences between ASP.NET and classic ASP is that ASP.NET is event-driven.

In order to talk about events, you need to understand controls. In order to talk about controls, you must first know about events. We'll solve this classic chicken-and-egg problem by providing just enough information in this chapter about controls to understand events. The next two chapters will cover controls in depth.

Event Model

There are two models of program execution, which are not necessarily mutually exclusive: *linear* and *event-driven*.

Linear programs move in a linear fashion from step 1 to step 2 and so on to the end of all the steps. Flow control structures within the code, such as loops, if state-ments, or function or subroutine calls, may redirect the flow of the program, but essentially, once program execution begins, it runs its course unaffected by anything the user or system may do. Prior to the advent of GUI environments, most computer programs were linear.

In contrast, event-driven programming responds to events. An event is generated (or *raised*) when "something happens," such as the user pressing a button. Often events are generated by user action, but events can also be generated by the system starting or finishing work. For example, the system might raise an event when a file that you open for reading has been read into memory or when your battery's power is run-ning low.

Windows is an event-driven program. The operating system is relatively quiescent until it detects an event such as the user clicking the mouse on a button. The click raises an event, which must be handled. The method that responds to the event is called the *event handler*. When the event is raised, the event handler, if one exists, is automatically executed by Windows.

In ASP.NET, objects may raise events and may have assigned event handlers. For example, a button may raise the Click event and may have an OnClick method that handles the event.

The event handler name is formed by prepending the word "On" to the event name, so in the case of a Click event, the event handler is called OnClick. Table 3-1 lists some of the more commonly used events and the names of their event handlers.

Table 3-1. Common events and their event handler names

Event name	Event handler name	Applies to
BubbleEvent	OnBubbleEvent	All controls
CheckedChanged	OnCheckedChanged	CheckBox
Click	OnClick	Button, LinkButton, ImageButton
DataBinding	OnDataBinding	All controls
Init	OnInit	All controls
ItemCreated	OnItemCreated	Repeater
ItemDataBound	OnItemDataBound	Repeater
Load	OnLoad	All controls
PreRender	OnPreRender	All controls
SelectedIndexChanged	OnSelectedIndexChanged	DataGrid, DataList, CheckBoxList, DropDownList, ListBox, RadioButtonList
TextChanged	OnTextChanged	TextBox
Unload	OnUnload	All controls

ASP Versus ASP.NET Events

ASP was primarily a linear programming model. It had six events, of which only four were commonly used. These were:

- Application_OnStart, which was fired when the application started
- Application_OnEnd, which was fired when the application terminated
- Session_OnStart, which was fired at the beginning of each session
- Session_OnEnd, which was raised when the session ended

ASP.NET, on the other hand, is primarily an event-driven programming model. The application has events, each session has events, and the page and most of the server controls can also raise events. All ASP.NET events are handled on the server. Some events cause an immediate posting to the server, while other events are simply stored until the next time the page is posted back to the server.

Because they are handled on the server, ASP.NET events are somewhat different from events in traditional client applications, in which both the event itself and the event handler occur on the client. In ASP.NET applications, however, an event is typically raised on the client but handled on the server.

Consider a classic ASP web page with a button control on it. A Click event is raised when the button is clicked. This event is handled by the client (i.e., the browser), which responds by posting the form to the server. No event handling occurs server-side.

Now consider an ASP.NET web page with a similar button control. The difference between an ASP.NET button control and a classic HTML button control is primarily that the ASP.NET button has an attribute, runat=server, that adds server-side processing to all the normal functionality of an HTML button.

When the click event is raised, once again, the browser handles the client-side event by posting the page to the server. This time, however, an event message is also transmitted to the server. The server determines if the click event has an event handler associated with it, and, if so, the event handler is executed on the server.

An event message is transmitted to the server via an HTTP POST. ASP.NET automagically (that's a technical term) handles all the mechanics of capturing the event, transmitting it to the server, and processing the event. As the programmer, all you have to do is create your event handlers.

Many events, such as MouseOver, are not eligible for server-side processing because they kill performance. All server-side processing requires a postback, and you do not want to post the page every time there is a MouseOver event. If these events are handled at all, it is on the client side.

One of the broad categories of controls available in ASP.NET applications is HTML server controls (described in Chapter 4). These are identical to the classic HTML controls, except that they enable server-side processing. In addition, they are still used for implementing client-side event handling.

 If you want a client-side event handler to perform scripted functions, you must supply your own scripting in either JavaScript or VBScript called from the appropriate event handler. For this to work properly, the client browser must support scripting. (Client-side scripting is outside the scope of this book.)

As far as ASP.NET is concerned, events are handled on the server, and the result of an event that posts back to the server is that the page is modified and redelivered to the browser.

Event Arguments

Events are handled by *delegates*. Essentially, a delegate is an object that encapsulates the description of a method to which you may delegate responsibility for handling the event.

 For a complete discussion of delegates, see *Programming C#* by Jesse Liberty (O'Reilly).

Event handlers must always take two parameters and return nothing (in VB.NET, use a Sub, in C# return void). The first parameter represents the object raising the event. The second, called the *event argument*, contains information specific to the event, if any. For most events, the event argument is of type EventArgs, which does not expose any properties. So the general prototype for an event in Visual Basic is:

```
Private Sub EventName(ByVal sender As Object, _
                 ByVal e As EventArgs)
```

and the general prototype for an event in C# is:

```
private void EventName (object sender, EventArgs e)
```

For some controls, the event argument may be of a type derived from EventArgs and may expose properties specific to that event type. For example, the AdRotator control's AdCreated event handler receives an argument of type AdCreatedEventArgs, which has the properties AdProperties, AlternateText, ImageUrl, and NavigateUrl. The specifics of the event argument for each control are detailed in the section of Chapter 5 describing the control.

Note that when using Visual Studio .NET, the IDE often inserts qualifying namespaces in front of parameter types in event handler declarations. These are redundant, as long as the relevant namespace is already referenced in the project using a using statement in C# or an Imports statement in VB.NET. For example, the default Page_Load event handler in VB.NET inserted by Visual Studio .NET looks like:

```
Private Sub Page_Load(ByVal sender As System.Object, _
                 ByVal e As System.EventArgs) Handles MyBase.Load
```

The following declaration works equally as well, since the System namespace is automatically imported into ASP.NET applications:

```
Private Sub Page_Load(ByVal sender As Object, _
                 ByVal e As EventArgs) Handles MyBase.Load
```

The default Page_Load event handler in C# inserted by Visual Studio .NET looks like:

```
private void Page_Load(object sender, System.EventArgs e)
```

while all that is strictly necessary is:

```
private void Page_Load(object sender, EventArgs e)
```

Application and Session Events

ASP.NET supports the Application and Session events familiar to ASP programmers. An Application_Start event is raised when the application first starts. This is a good time to initialize resources that will be used throughout the application, such as database connection strings (but not the database connection itself). An Application_End event is raised when the application ends. This is the time to close resources and do any other housekeeping that may be necessary. Note that garbage collection will automatically take care of freeing up memory, but if you allocated unmanaged resources, such as components created with languages that are not compliant with the .NET Framework, you must clean them up yourself.

Likewise there are session events. A session starts when a user first requests a page from your application and ends when the application closes the session or the session times out. A Session_Start event is raised when the session starts, at which time you can initialize resources that will be specific to the session, such as opening a database connection. When the session ends, there will be a Session_End event.

Page and Control Events

The page and controls all have a number of events that are derived from the Control class (or the TemplateControl class, in the case of the Error event). All pass an event argument of type EventArgs that exposes no properties. Some of these events are listed in Table 3-2.

Table 3-2. Some common page and control events

Event name	Description
DataBinding	Occurs when control binds to a data source
Disposed	Occurs when control is released from memory
Error	For the page only, occurs when an unhandled exception is thrown
Init	Occurs when the control is initialized
Load	Occurs when the control is loaded to the Page object
PreRender	Occurs when the control is about to be rendered
Unload	Occurs when the control is unloaded from memory

 Binding a control to a data source means that the control and the data source are tied together so that the control knows to use that data source for populating itself. For a complete description of controls and data binding, see Chapter 9.

IsPostBack

Both the page and controls expose the IsPostBack property. This is a read-only Boolean property that indicates if the page or control is being loaded for the first time, or if it is being loaded in response to a client postback. Many expensive operations, such as getting data from a database or populating ListItems, need to be performed only the first time the page or control is loaded. If the page is posted to the server and then reloaded, there is no need to repeat the operation. By testing the value of IsPostBack, you can skip the expensive operation, as in the code snippets in Examples 3-1 and 3-2.

Example 3-1. Testing for IsPostBack in VB.NET

```
sub Page_Load(ByVal Sender as Object, _
            ByVal e as EventArgs)
    if not IsPostBack then
        '  Do the expensive operations only the
        '  first time the page is loaded.
    end if
end sub
```

Example 3-2. Testing for IsPostBack in C#

```
void Page_Load(Object sender, EventArgs e)
{
    if (! IsPostBack)
    {
        // Do the expensive operations only the
        // first time the page is loaded.
    }
}
```

Postback Versus Non-Postback Events

Postback events cause the form to be posted back to the server immediately. These include click-type events, such as Button.Click. In contrast, many events, typically change events, are considered *non-postback* because the event is not posted back to the server immediately. Instead, these events are cached by the control until the next time a post occurs. Controls with non-postback events can be forced to behave in a postback manner by setting their AutoPostBack property to true.

Table 3-3 summarizes the controls with postback and non-postback events.

Table 3-3. Controls with postback and non-postback events

Postback	Non-postback
Button	CheckBox
Calendar	CheckBoxList

Table 3-3. Controls with postback and non-postback events (continued)

Postback	Non-postback
DataGrid	DropDownList
DataList	ListBox
ImageButton	RadioButtonList
LinkButton	RadioButton
Repeater	TextBox

Comparing ASP.NET to ASP

Classic ASP is not event driven in the way that ASP.NET is. To see the difference, consider the following application: you want to open the NorthWind database, supplied with both Microsoft SQL Server and Microsoft Access, and read through the Customers table. For each customer you want to display the company name, customer ID, the name and title of the contact person and the phone number. If the contact person is the owner, you want to display the title in red so that it is easy to see.

This example contains a great deal of complexity that will be covered in future chapters, including all the issues surrounding database access, but the fundamentals are straightforward. In classic ASP you would open a connection to the database, perform a query, and get back a RecordSet. You then iterate over the RecordSet, adding each record to an HTML table. If the current record's ContactTitle column is "Owner," you set the display to red. The code to accomplish this in classic ASP is shown in Example 3-3.

Example 3-3. Populating a table in classic ASP

```
<% Response.Expires=0 %>
<HTML>
<HEAD>
<META NAME="GENERATOR" Content="Microsoft FrontPage 4.0">
<META HTTP-EQUIV="Content-Type" content="text/html; charset=iso-8859-1">
<TITLE>List Log</TITLE>
<STYLE>
BODY,TD, TH {font-family:Verdana;font-size:8pt}
.controls {font-family:Verdana;font-size:8pt}
#owner {color:red}
</STYLE>
</HEAD>
<BODY>
<%


    dim DBConn, rs
    set DBConn = Server.CreateObject("ADODB.Connection")
```

Example 3-3. Populating a table in classic ASP (continued)

```
DBConn.open "Driver={SQL Server};server=YourServer; uid=sa; pwd=YourPw;
            database=northwind;"

set rs = DBConn.Execute("select * from Customers")

%>
<table bgcolor = "lavender">
    <tr>
        <th>Company Name</th>
        <th>Customer ID</th>
        <th>Contact</th>
        <th>Title</th>
        <th>Phone</th>
    </tr>
<% while not rs.eof %>
    <tr bgColor="lightsteelblue">
        <td><% =rs("CompanyName") %></td>
        <td><% =rs("CustomerID") %> </td>
        <td><%=rs("ContactName") %></td>
        <td
            <% if rs("ContactTitle") = "Owner" then %>
            id = owner
            <% end if %>
            > <% = rs("ContactTitle") %> </td>
        <td><%=rs("Phone") %></td>
    </tr>

<%
    rs.moveNext
      wend
%>
</Table>
```

In Example 3-3, as with all classic ASP applications, the HTML is intermingled with the script code. You add all the records in a while loop:

```
<% while not rs.eof %>
```

When it is time to create the <td> tag for the title, place the if statement, which tests if the ContactTitle is an Owner, inside the code for writing the tag:

```
<td
    <% if rs("ContactTitle") = "Owner" then %>
    id = owner
    <% end if %>
    >
```

The logic here is to open the <td> tag, then switch to script that tests the value of the ContactTitle field for the current row. If it matches Owner, you then set the id attribute; otherwise you do not. You then close the <td> tag.

The code is a bit tangled, but it certainly works, as shown in Figure 3-1.

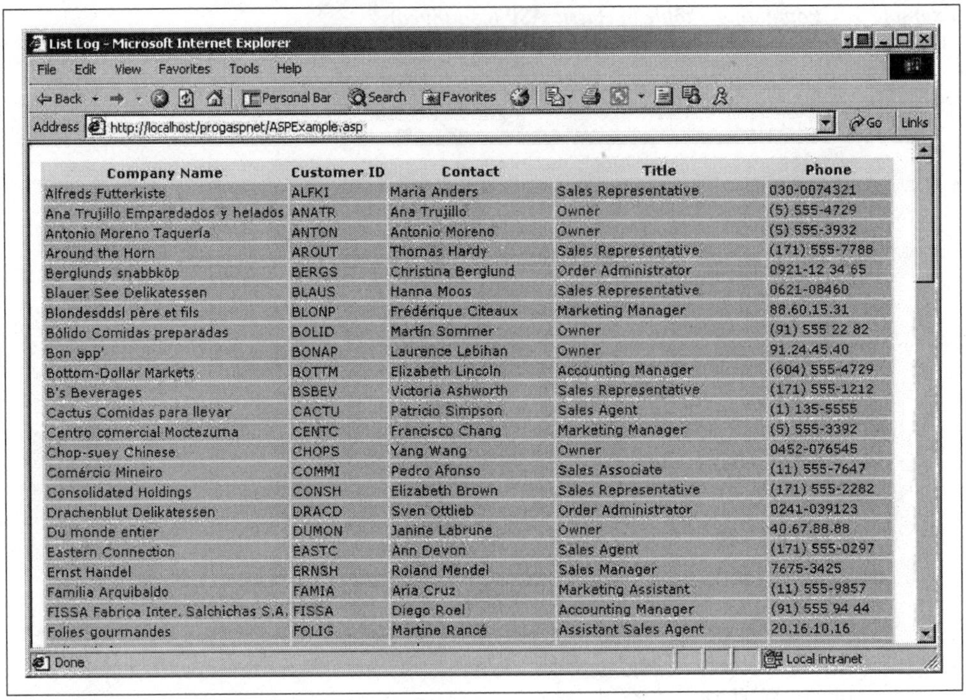

Figure 3-1. ASP version of event-driven data table

To write this same application in ASP.NET, you would take a very different approach. First, to make this demonstration easier, you'll use a DataGrid rather than a table. Here are the steps:

1. Open Visual Studio .NET and create a new ASP.NET web application project using either VB.NET or C#. Name it EventDrivenGrid.

2. Right-click on the grid and choose Properties. Set the Page Layout to FlowLayout and click OK.

3. Drag a DataGrid onto the form from the Toolbar and widen it. Set the grid's ID to dgCustomers.

4. Right-click on the grid and choose View Code.

5. At the top of the code page add:

   ```
   using System.Data.SqlClient;
   ```

   if you are using C#, or:

   ```
   imports System.Data.SqlClient
   ```

   if you are using VB.NET.

6. Modify the Page_Load event by adding the code shown in Example 3-4 for a VB.NET project or the code shown in Example 3-5 for a C# project.

There are many details to the code in Examples 3-4 and 3-5 that will be explained in future chapters. The essence is that you are retrieving the data you need from the database into a DataSet and then binding the appropriate table from the DataSet to the DataGrid.

Example 3-4. Populating a table in ASP.NET using VB.NET

```
Private Sub Page_Load(ByVal sender As System.Object, _
                      ByVal e As System.EventArgs) _
                      Handles MyBase.Load
    'Put user code to initialize the page here
    if not IsPostBack then
        '  create the connection string
        dim strConnection as String = _
            "server=YourServer; uid=sa; pwd=YourPw; database=northwind"

        '  create the command string
        dim strCommand as String = _
            "select * from customers"

        '  create the dataset command object and dataset
        dim dataAdapter as new SqlDataAdapter(strCommand, strConnection)
        dim ds as New DataSet( )

        '  fill the dataset
        dataAdapter.Fill(ds, "Products")
        dim bldr as New SqlCommandBuilder(dataAdapter)

        '  get the table
        dim dt as DataTable = ds.Tables(0)
        dgCustomers.DataSource = dt
        dgCustomers.DataBind( )
    End If
End Sub
```

Example 3-5. Populating a table in ASP.NET using C#

```
private void Page_Load(Object Source System.EventArgs E)
{
if (!IsPostBack)
    {
        // create the connection string
        string strConnection =
            "server=YourServer; uid=sa; pwd=YourPW; database=northwind";

        // create the command string
        string strCommand = "Select * from Customers";

        // create the data set command object and dataset
        SqlDataAdapter dataAdapter =
            new SqlDataAdapter(strCommand, strConnection);
```

Example 3-5. Populating a table in ASP.NET using C# (continued)

```
    DataSet dataSet = new DataSet();

    // fill the dataset
    dataAdapter.Fill(dataSet,"Products");
    SqlCommandBuilder bldr = new SqlCommandBuilder(dataAdapter);

    // get the table
    DataTable dataTable = dataSet.Tables[0];
    dgCustomers.DataSource = dataTable;
    dgCustomers.DataBind( );
  }
}
```

7. Return to the Designer and click on the HTML tab. Add these attributes to the DataGrid:

```
    HeaderStyle-BackColor="Yellow"
    BorderWidth ="5"
    BorderColor ="#000099"
    AlternatingItemStyle-BackColor="LightGrey"
    HeaderStyle-Font-Bold
    AutoGenerateColumns="False"
```

8. Add Columns and BoundColumn elements to the DataGrid:

```
    <Columns>
        <asp:BoundColumn DataField ="CompanyName" HeaderText="Company Name" />
        <asp:BoundColumn DataField ="ContactName" HeaderText="Contact" />
        <asp:BoundColumn DataField ="ContactTitle" HeaderText="Title" />
        <asp:BoundColumn DataField ="Phone" HeaderText="Phone" />
    </Columns>
```

The complete DataGrid declaration should look something like Example 3-6.

Example 3-6. DataGrid HTML

```
<asp:DataGrid
    id="dgCustomers"
    runat="server"
    Width="466px"
    Height="278px"
    HeaderStyle-BackColor="Yellow"
    BorderWidth="5"
    BorderColor="#000099"
    AlternatingItemStyle-BackColor="LightGrey"
    HeaderStyle-Font-Bold
    AutoGenerateColumns="False"  >
    <COLUMNS>
        <asp:BoundColumn HeaderText="Company Name"
            DataField="CompanyName"></asp:BoundColumn>
        <asp:BoundColumn HeaderText="Contact"
            DataField="ContactName"></asp:BoundColumn>
        <asp:BoundColumn HeaderText="Title"
```

Example 3-6. DataGrid HTML (continued)

```
            DataField="ContactTitle"></asp:BoundColumn>
        <asp:BoundColumn HeaderText="Phone"
            DataField="Phone"></asp:BoundColumn>
    </COLUMNS>
</asp:DataGrid>
```

Run the application. You have a DataGrid populated by the data in the Customer's table, as shown in Figure 3-2.

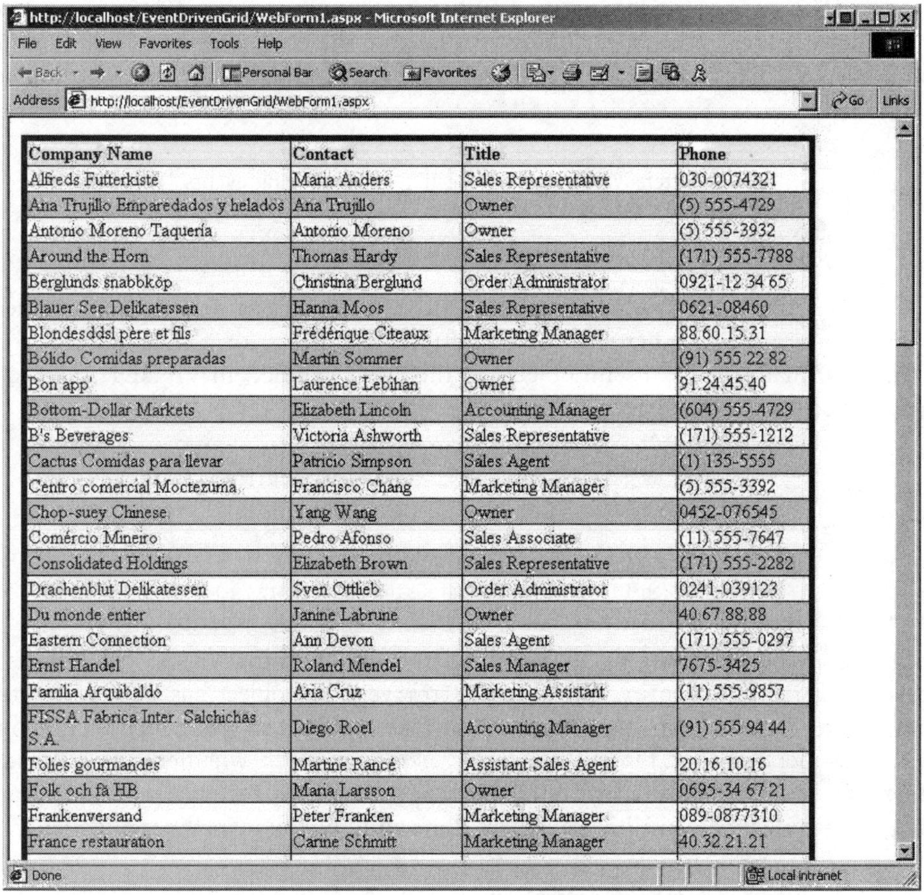

Figure 3-2. DataGrid populated without events

You've populated the table very nicely, but you have not set the Owner to be red. And how can you if you are not iterating over the data at any time? You are simply handing the table to the grid and telling the grid to bind to the data.

The DataGrid publishes a number of useful events that you can choose to handle. In this case, the event you care about is the ItemDataBound event that is raised every time an item is bound to the grid. You should write a handler for this event that will give you the opportunity to examine the data and decide if you need to change the way it is displayed.

To do this, add an attribute to the DataGrid. Return to the Designer and click on the HTML tab. Add the following attribute to the DataGrid:

```
OnItemDataBound="OnItemDataBoundEventHandler"
```

You are now ready to implement the handler for that event. This is done using code you will add to the code page. You can get back to the code page by clicking on the tab labeled WebForm1.aspx.vb or WebForm1.cs, depending on the language you are using.

 There is extensive support in the IDE for managing events. This will be shown in subsequent chapters.

The event handler takes two parameters. One is an object that represents the object raising the event. The other is an object of type EventArgs (or a class derived from EventArgs) that provides useful objects to the event handler. In VB.NET, the event handler declaration looks like:

```
public sub OnItemDataBoundEventHandler(ByVal sender as System.Object, _
            ByVal e as System.Web.UI.WebControls.DataGridItemEventArgs)
```

and in C# it looks like:

```
public void OnItemDataBoundEventHandler(object sender,
            System.Web.UI.WebControls.DataGridItemEventArgs e)
{
```

In this case, the first thing to do is test whether the item that raised the event is a Header, Separator, or Footer. The DataGridItemEventArgs object has a property Item that returns the data item. You can ask that Item for its ItemType, which will be one of the enumerated ListItemType constants. You can check whether it is a Header, Separator, or Footer. If it is any of these types, you can return, since you don't want to process those items. In VB.NET, this is done with the following lines of code:

```
dim itemType as ListItemType = CType(e.Item.ItemType,ListItemType)
if (itemType = ListItemType.Header) or _
   (itemType = ListItemType.Separator) or _
   (itemType = ListItemType.Footer) then
   exit Sub
End If
```

and in C# with this code snippet:

```
ListItemType itemType = (ListItemType) e.Item.ItemType;
if (itemType == ListItemType.Header ||
```

```
    itemType == ListItemType.Separator ||
    itemType == ListItemType.Footer)
return;
```

Assuming you do not have a Header, Separator, or Footer, you are ready to get the DataItem as a DataRowView. You can then index into that DataRowView using the name of the column (ContactTitle) to get the particular column you want. If you call ToString on that column, you get back the value of the column, which you can assign to a string variable. In VB.NET, the code is:

```
dim drv as DataRowView = CType(e.Item.DataItem,DataRowView)
dim title as String = drv("ContactTitle").ToString( )
```

and in C#, it's:

```
DataRowView dataRowView = (DataRowView)e.Item.DataItem;
string title = dataRowView["contactTitle"].ToString( );
```

You can combine these two lines into a single statement, if you like terser but harder to debug code, as in this C# code snippet:

```
string title = ((DataRowView)e.Item.DataItem)["ContactTitle"].ToString( );
```

In any case, with the title in hand, you can compare it to the string "Owner." In VB.NET, this is done using:

```
if title = "Owner" then
```

and in C#:

```
if (title == "Owner")
{
```

If you get a match, you can extract the cell you want to color by asking the DataGridItemEventArgs object passed in as a parameter for the current Item. You can then index into the Controls collection of the Item to get the particular cell you care about. In VB.NET:

```
dim ownerCell as TableCell=CType(e.Item.Controls(2), TableCell)
```

and in C#:

```
TableCell ownerCell = (TableCell)e.Item.Controls[2];
```

You can now set the foreground color of that cell to red by calling the static (or shared) FromName method on the Color class, passing in the string "Red." In VB.NET, the code is:

```
ownerCell.ForeColor = Color.FromName("Red")
```

and in C#, it's:

```
ownerCell.ForeColor = Color.FromName("Red");
```

The complete OnItemDataBoundEventHandler is shown in Example 3-7 using VB.NET and in Example 3-8 using C#.

Example 3-7. OnItemDataBoundEventHandler in VB.NET

```
public sub OnItemDataBoundEventHandler(ByVal sender as System.Object, _
            ByVal e as System.Web.UI.WebControls.DataGridItemEventArgs)
    dim itemType as ListItemType = CType(e.Item.ItemType,ListItemType)
    if (itemType = ListItemType.Header) or _
       (itemType = ListItemType.Separator) or _
       (itemType = ListItemType.Footer) then
        exit Sub
    End If

    dim drv as DataRowView = CType(e.Item.DataItem,DataRowView)
    dim title as String = drv("ContactTitle").ToString()
    if title = "Owner" then
        dim ownerCell as TableCell=CType(e.Item.Controls(2), TableCell)
        ownerCell.ForeColor = Color.FromName("Red")
    End If
End Sub
```

Example 3-8. OnItemDataBoundEventHandler in C#

```
public void OnItemDataBoundEventHandler(object sender,
            System.Web.UI.WebControls.DataGridItemEventArgs e)
{
    ListItemType itemType = (ListItemType) e.Item.ItemType;
    if (itemType == ListItemType.Header ||
        itemType == ListItemType.Separator ||
        itemType == ListItemType.Footer)
        return;

    DataRowView dataRowView = (DataRowView)e.Item.DataItem;
    string title = dataRowView["contactTitle"].ToString();
    if (title == "Owner")
    {
        TableCell ownerCell = (TableCell)e.Item.Controls[2];
        ownerCell.ForeColor = Color.FromName("Red");
    }
}
```

When the web page utilizing the event handler shown in either Example 3-7 or 3-8 is run, you get a web page similar to Figure 3-3. It is the same as the web page in Figure 3-2, except that all instances in which the Title is Owner are displayed in red. (Since your book is printed in black and white, you will have to actually run the project to see this.)

The event-driven model as shown in this simple example isn't easier than the non-event driven model in ASP, but it does scale well. As programs become more complex, having a more object-oriented event-driven model makes for code that is easier to maintain.

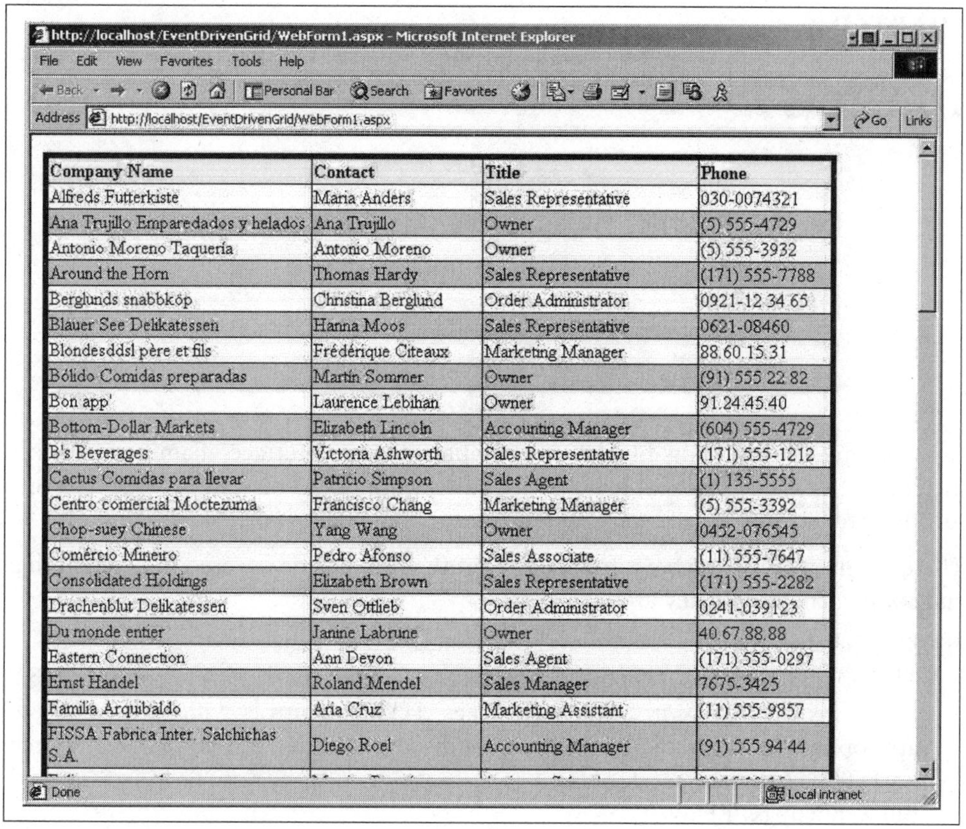

Company Name	Contact	Title	Phone
Alfreds Futterkiste	Maria Anders	Sales Representative	030-0074321
Ana Trujillo Emparedados y helados	Ana Trujillo	Owner	(5) 555-4729
Antonio Moreno Taquería	Antonio Moreno	Owner	(5) 555-3932
Around the Horn	Thomas Hardy	Sales Representative	(171) 555-7788
Berglunds snabbköp	Christina Berglund	Order Administrator	0921-12 34 65
Blauer See Delikatessen	Hanna Moos	Sales Representative	0621-08460
Blondesddsl père et fils	Frédérique Citeaux	Marketing Manager	88.60.15.31
Bólido Comidas preparadas	Martín Sommer	Owner	(91) 555 22 82
Bon app'	Laurence Lebihan	Owner	91.24.45.40
Bottom-Dollar Markets	Elizabeth Lincoln	Accounting Manager	(604) 555-4729
B's Beverages	Victoria Ashworth	Sales Representative	(171) 555-1212
Cactus Comidas para llevar	Patricio Simpson	Sales Agent	(1) 135-5555
Centro comercial Moctezuma	Francisco Chang	Marketing Manager	(5) 555-3392
Chop-suey Chinese	Yang Wang	Owner	0452-076545
Comércio Mineiro	Pedro Afonso	Sales Associate	(11) 555-7647
Consolidated Holdings	Elizabeth Brown	Sales Representative	(171) 555-2282
Drachenblut Delikatessen	Sven Ottlieb	Order Administrator	0241-039123
Du monde entier	Janine Labrune	Owner	40.67.88.88
Eastern Connection	Ann Devon	Sales Agent	(171) 555-0297
Ernst Handel	Roland Mendel	Sales Manager	7675-3425
Familia Arquibaldo	Aria Cruz	Marketing Assistant	(11) 555-9857
FISSA Fabrica Inter. Salchichas S.A.	Diego Roel	Accounting Manager	(91) 555 94 44

Figure 3-3. DataGrid populated with events

CHAPTER 4

Controls

Controls are the building blocks of a graphical user interface. Familiar controls include buttons, checkboxes, list boxes, and so forth. Controls can provide a means for a user to indicate a preference, enter data, or make selections.

There are five types of web controls; each but the first will be covered in detail in this and coming chapters. They are:

HTML controls
> The original controls available to any HTML page. These all work in ASP.NET exactly as they work in other web pages. HTML controls will be used where appropriate in this book, but will not be discussed in detail. For a good resource on HTML controls, see *HTML: The Definitive Guide*, by Chuck Musciano and Bill Kennedy (O'Reilly).

HTML server controls
> Based on original HTML controls, but enhanced to enable server-side processing.

Web (ASP) server controls
> Server-side controls providing the same functionality as HTML server controls but integrated into the ASP.NET programming model.

Validation controls
> Provide a full range of built-in form validation capability. Validation controls are covered in Chapter 8.

User controls and custom controls
> Controls created by the developer. User and custom controls are covered in Chapter 14.

HTML server controls and ASP controls both offer significant improvements over the old-style HTML controls. These include:

- The ability to automatically maintain state, covered in detail in Chapter 6.
- Browser independence. ASP.NET detects the level of the target browser. Up-level DHTML browsers are sent script for client-side processing. On downlevel

standard browsers, all processing is done on the server. The appropriate HTML is generated for each browser.

- Use of a compiled language instead of interpreted script, resulting in better performance.

- The ability to bound HTML server controls and ASP controls to a data source, as discussed in Chapter 9.

HTML Server Controls

Normal HTML controls such as <h1>, <a>, and <input> are not processed by the server, but are sent directly to the browser for display. Standard HTML controls can be exposed to the server and made available for server-side processing by turning them into HTML server controls. Server-side processing allows for data binding, programmatic response to events, and the ability to use a fully featured and compiled coding language rather than a scripting language.

In order to convert an HTML control to an HTML server control, simply add the attribute runat="server". In addition, you will probably want to add an id attribute, so that contents of the control can be accessed and controlled programmatically. If you start with a simple input control:

```
<input type="text" size="40">
```

you can convert it to an HTML server control by adding the id and runat attributes, as follows:

```
<input type="text" id="BookTitle" size="40" runat="server">
```

There are several benefits to converting an HTML control to an HTML server control:

- Once a control is converted to a server control, it can be referred to in code. For example, in Example 4-1 and 4-2 you can read or set the value of the text box by referring to lblBookName.Value or txtBookName.Value.

- Server controls retain state during round trips to the server (more on this in Chapter 6).

- Server controls generate events, which your code can then handle.

- Server controls are aware of the client browser level and generate HTML appropriate to the target browser.

Example 4-1 and Example 4-2 demonstrate the use of HTML server controls in C# and VB.NET, respectively. In these listings, a text box is used to prompt the user to enter a book name. When the Button control is clicked, it fires an event that fills a second text box with the contents of the first text box and also changes its size.

Example 4-1. Code listing for csHTMLServerControls.aspx

```
<%@ Page Language="C#" %>
<html>

<script runat="server">
    void btnBookName_Click(Object Source, EventArgs E)
    {
        lblBookName.Value = txtBookName.Value;
        lblBookName.Size = 80;
    }
</script>

    <body>
    <form runat=server>

        <h1>HTML Server Controls</h1>

        <br/>
        <h2>The date and time is <% =DateTime.Now.ToString( ) %>.</h2>

        <br/>

        <h2>HTML Server Control</h2>
        Book Name:   
        <input type="text"
            id="txtBookName"
            size="40"
            value="Enter book name."
            runat="server" />

        <br/>
        <br/>
        <br/>

        <input type="submit"
            id="btnBookName"
            value="Book Name"
            onServerClick="btnBookName_Click"
            runat="server" />
        <br/>
        <br/>
        <input type="text" id="lblBookName" size="40" runat="server" />

    </form>
    </body>
</html>
```

Example 4-2. Code listing for vbHTMLServerControls.aspx

```
<%@ Page Language="VB" %>
<html>

<script runat="server">
    Sub btnBookName_Click(ByVal Sender as Object, _
                          ByVal e as EventArgs)

        lblBookName.Value = txtBookName.Value
        lblBookName.Size = 80
    End Sub
</script>

    <body>
    <form runat=server>

        <h1>HTML Server Controls</h1>

        <br/>
        <h2>The date and time is <% =DateTime.Now( ) %>.</h2>

        <br/>

        <h2>HTML Server Control</h2>
        Book Name:   
        <input type=text
            id="txtBookName"
            size="40"
            value="Enter book name."
            runat="server" />

        <br/>
        <br/>
        <br/>

        <input type="submit"
            id="btnBookName"
            value="Book Name"
            onServerClick="btnBookName_Click"
            runat="server" />

        <br/>
        <br/>
        <input type="text" id="lblBookName" size="40" runat="server"/>

    </form>
    </body>
</html>
```

The very first line of code in both listings:

```
<%@ Page Language="C#" %>
```

```
<%@ Page Language="VB" %>
```

is a *page directive,* which tells the compiler that any script found in this page is written using the C# or VB language, respectively. Immediately following the opening <HTML> tag in Example 4-1 and Example 4-2 is a script block, written in C# or VB.NET, respectively, as indicated by the page directive. It contains a routine called btnBookName_Click, which is the event handler for the Click event of the btn-BookName button. This method takes two parameters and returns nothing (as indicated by the void keyword in C# and the Sub keyword in VB.NET). These parameters are typical for all event handler methods in ASP.NET, as discussed in Chapter 3. In C# the parameter list is of the form:

```
(Object Source, EventArgs E)
```

and in VB.NET:

```
(ByVal Sender as Object, ByVal e as EventArgs)
```

Note that within the body of the routine, the HTML server controls are referred to by their id attribute, for example lblBookName and txtBookName.

The Submit button:

```
<input type="submit"
```

is prototypical of converting HTML controls to server controls. It has an id attribute and the runat attribute:

```
id="btnBookName"
runat="server"
```

Rather than the traditional onClick attribute used in conventional HTML or ASP pages, the Submit button has an onServerClick attribute, telling the server what function to call when the Click event occurs:

```
onServerClick="btnBookName_Click"
```

 If you want the control to handle the event on the client side, you should use the onClick attribute. In this case, you must provide client-side scripting to handle the event. You cannot have both an onClick and onServerClick attribute for the same control.

Figure 4-1 shows the page that results from running the code in either Example 4-1 or 4-2, filling in a book name, and clicking the Book Name button.

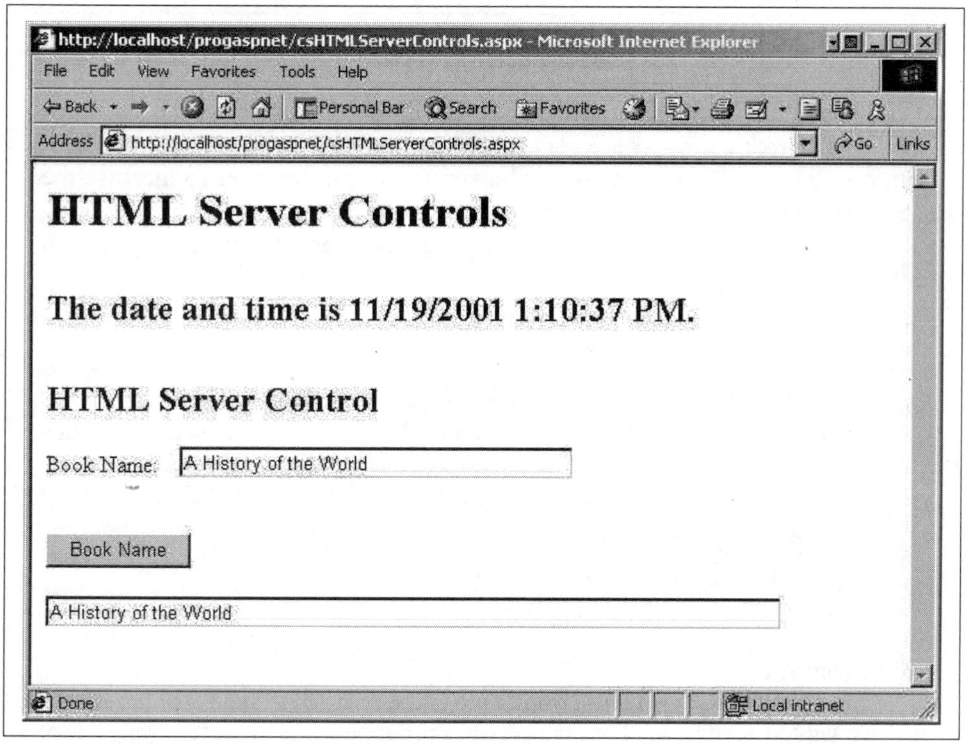

Figure 4-1. Output from Example 4-1 or 4-2

HTML controls are divided into two categories: *input* and *container*. HTML input controls do not require a closing tag (although to be well-formed, they should be made self-closing with a trailing /) and have Name, Value, and Type attributes, which may be accessed and controlled programmatically.

HTML container controls are required to have either a trailing / or a closing tag. They do not have Name, Value, or Type attributes. Instead, the content found between opening and closing tags may be accessed programmatically using the InnerHtml or Inner-Text property. The difference between these two properties is that InnerText provides automatic HTML encoding and decoding of special characters, such as < or >. If the InnerHtml property is used, these characters are interpreted as being part of the HTML and will not display in the final output.

Examples 4-3 and 4-4 show both input controls and HTML server container controls in C# and VB.NET, respectively, and demonstrate the use of the InnerHtml property.

Well-Formed HTML

Well-formed HTML (sometimes called XHTML) conforms to the rules for XML. Many web browsers are very forgiving, and ill-formed HTML will work fine, but the world is moving toward a stricter syntax in order to increase the robustness of the Web. Well-formed code has a huge benefit for authoring tools and is worthwhile when hand coding as well, since it decreases confusion and ambiguity.

Among the rules of well-formed HTML are these:

Close all tags

Several HTML tags, such as <p>, <tr>, and <td>, are routinely left unclosed. In well-formed HTML, there will always be a closing tag, such as </td>. Many tags, such as <br>, <hr>, <input>, and <img>, can be made self-closing by putting the closing forward slash within the tag itself. This makes it well-formed. For example:

```
<input type="submit"
id="btnBookName"
value="Book Name"
onServerClick="btnBookName_Click"
runat="server" />.
```

No overlapping tags

Some browsers are tolerant of overlapping tags, but well-formed HTML requires that tags do not overlap. For example, the overlapping tags in the following line of HTML:

```
<b>This is <i>the year</b>for the Red Sox.</i>
```

can instead be expressed as:

```
<b>This is</b> <i><b>the year</b>for the Red Sox.</i>
```

Case-sensitivity

Like all HTML and ASP pages, ASP.NET is generally not case-sensitive. The one glaring exception is that C#, when it is used, is always case-sensitive. That said, it should be noted that script components are actually XML files, and as such should follow XML Version 1.0 conventions. According to these conventions, element types and attributes are case-sensitive. This will usually only matter if you use an XML editing tool to work with the script components or if you are creating an XML file, such as an advertisement file for use with the AdRotator control, described in Chapter 5. However, it is good practice to follow the XML guidelines. Element types and attributes are usually lowercase, except multipart names, such as onServerClick, which use camel notation, with initial lowercase. For other HTML tags, being well-formed requires that start and end tags have matching case. This book will generally use lowercase for all HTML tags.

—continued—

Quotation marks

In well-formed HTML, all attributes are enclosed in quotation marks.

Single root

The top-level element in a page must be <html>. Remember to close it at the end with </html>.

Reserved characters

There are only five built-in character entities in XML. They are:

```
&lt;      <
&gt;      >
&amp;     &
&quot;    "
&apos;    '
```

If any of these characters is used in script, then it must be "escaped" by using the above character entity, or by enclosing the entire script block in a CDATA section. (CDATA is an XML type.)

Example 4-3. Input and container HTML server controls using C#, csHTMLServerControls2.aspx

```
<%@ Page Language="C#" %>

<script runat="server">
   void Page_Load(Object Source, EventArgs E)
   {
      string strHtml = "";
      strHtml += txtName.Value + "<br/>";
      strHtml += txtStreet.Value + "<br/>";
      strHtml += txtCity.Value + ", " + txtState.Value;
      tdInnerHtml.InnerHtml = strHtml;
   }
</script>

<html>
   <body>
   <form runat="server">

      <h1>HTML Server Controls</h1>
      <h2>InnerHTML</h2>

      <table>
        <tr>
          <td>Name:</td>
          <td>
              <input type="text"
                 id="txtName"
                  runat="server"/>
          </td>
        </tr>
```

```
            <tr>
               <td>Street:</td>
               <td>
                   <input type="text"
                       id="txtStreet"
                         runat="server"/>
               </td>
            </tr>
            <tr>
               <td>City:</td>
               <td>
                   <input type="text"
                       id="txtCity"
                         runat="server"/>
                </td>
            </tr>
            <tr>
               <td>State:</td>
               <td>
                   <input type="text"
                       id="txtState"
                         runat="server"/>
               </td>
            </tr>
            <tr>
               <td></td>
               <td id="tdInnerHtml" runat="server" />
            </tr>
         </table>

         <input type=submit value="Do It!">

      </form>
   </body>
</html>
```

Example 4-4. Input and container HTML server controls using VB.NET, vbHTMLServerControls2. aspx

```
<%@ Page Language="VB" %>

<script runat="server">
   sub Page_Load(ByVal Sender as Object, _
               ByVal e as EventArgs)
      dim strHtml as string
      strHtml = txtName.Value & "<br/>"
      strHtml = strHtml & txtStreet.Value & "<br/>"
      strHtml = strHtml & txtCity.Value & ", " & txtState.Value
      tdInnerHtml.InnerHtml = strHtml
   end sub
</script>
```

Example 4-4. Input and container HTML server controls using VB.NET, vbHTMLServerControls2. aspx (continued)

```
<html>
    <body>
    <form runat="server">

        <h1>HTML Server Controls</h1>
        <h2>InnerHTML</h2>

        <table>
            <tr>
                <td>Name:</td>
                <td>
                    <input type="text"
                        id="txtName"
                            runat="server"/>
                </td>
            </tr>
            <tr>
                <td>Street:</td>
                <td>
                    <input type="text"
                        id="txtStreet"
                            runat="server"/>
                </td>
            </tr>
            <tr>
                <td>City:</td>
                <td>
                    <input type="text"
                        id="txtCity"
                            runat="server"/>
                </td>
            </tr>
            <tr>
                <td>State:</td>
                <td>
                    <input type="text"
                        id="txtState"
                            runat="server"/>
                </td>
            </tr>
            <tr>
                <td></td>
                <td id="tdInnerHtml" runat="server" />
            </tr>
        </table>

        <input type=submit value="Do It!">

    </form>
    </body>
</html>
```

In Example 4-3 and Example 4-4, there are two types of input controls: text fields and a button. Both happen to use the `<input>` HTML tag, although as you can see in Table 4-1, there are other input controls that do not use those tags.

Table 4-1. HTML tags and their categories

HTML tag	Category	HTML server control name	Description
`<input>`	Input	HtmlInputButton	\<input type=button | submit | reset>
		HtmlInputCheckBox	\<input type=checkbox>
		HtmlInputFile	\<input type=file>
		HtmlInputHidden	\<input type=hidden>
		HtmlInputImage	\<input type=image>
		HtmlInputRadioButton	\<input type=radio>
		HtmlInputText	\<input type=text | password>
`<img>`	Input	HtmlImage	Image
`<textarea>`	Input	HtmlTextArea	Multiline text entry
`<a>`	Container	HtmlAnchor	Anchor
`<button>`	Container	HtmlButton	Customizable output format, usable with IE 4.0 and above browsers
`<form>`	Container	HtmlForm	Maximum of one HtmlForm control per page; default method is POST
`<table>`	Container	HtmlTable	Table, which can contain rows, which can contain cells
`<td>`	Container	HtmlTableCell	Table cell
`<th>`			Table header cell
`<tr>`	Container	HtmlTableRow	Table row
`<select>`	Container	HtmlSelect	Pull-down menu of choices
	Container	HtmlGenericControl	Any HTML control not listed here

The table, which is a container control, is used in these examples primarily as a means of controlling the layout of the other controls on the page. It has not been converted to an HTML server control, since it does not have the `runat="server"` attribute. One of the cells, however, has been converted for server-side processing by the inclusion of that attribute. In addition, that cell has an id attribute so that it can be referred to programmatically in the Page_Load routine.

Looking at the Page_Load routine, which is executed every time the page is posted, i.e., every time the Do It! button is clicked, an HTML string is constructed containing the values of the input text fields, interspersed with some HTML to control line breaks. This string is then assigned to the InnerHtml property of the table cell with the tdInnerHtml id attribute:

```
tdInnerHtml.InnerHtml = strHtml
```

If the InnerText property is used instead of the InnerHtml property, then the resulting page would display the actual < and > symbols. As written, however, the resulting page will look something like Figure 4-2, after values are entered in the text fields and the button is clicked.

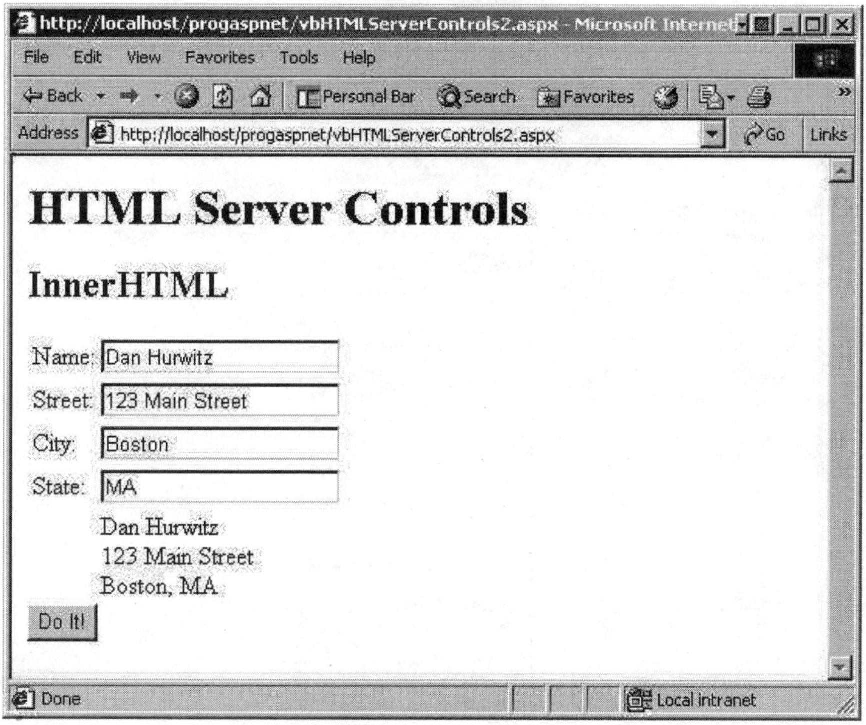

![Browser window screenshot showing HTML Server Controls page]

The browser window titled "http://localhost/progaspnet/vbHTMLServerControls2.aspx - Microsoft Internet" displays:

HTML Server Controls

InnerHTML

Name: Dan Hurwitz
Street: 123 Main Street
City: Boston
State: MA

Dan Hurwitz
123 Main Street
Boston, MA

[Do It!]

Figure 4-2. Output from Example 4-3 or 4-4

Table 4-1 lists HTML tags and the category to which they belong.

> You never actually use the name of HTML server control shown in Table 4-1 in any of your code. What goes in your HTML code is the HTML tag with the addition of the runat="server" attribute and usually with the addition of an id attribute.

Actually, any HTML control can be converted to server-side processing with the addition of the runat="server" attribute. If the control is not listed in Table 4-1, then it will be treated as an HtmlGenericControl. As with any other container control, this allows programmatic access to the control's inner HTML.

All the HTML server controls derive from the System.Web.UI.Control class and are contained in the System.Web.UI.HTMLControls namespace. Figure 4-3 shows the HTML server control hierarchy.

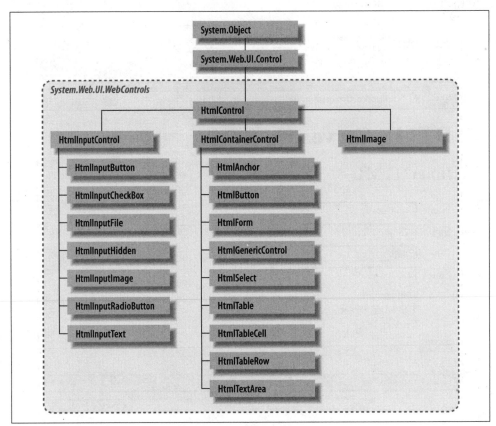

Figure 4-3. The HTML server control object hierarchy

ASP (Web Server) Controls

The third type of control is the *ASP control*, also known as the *ASP server control* or the *web server control*. In this book, we will refer to it as an ASP control, since the syntax used to implement it is of the form:

```
<asp:controlType
    id="ControlID"
    runat="server" />
```

where the control tag always begins with asp:. ASP controls offer a more consistent programming model than the analogous HTML server control. For example, in

HTML, the input tag (<input>) is used for buttons, single-line text fields, check-boxes, hidden fields, and passwords. For multiline text fields, you must use the <textarea> tag. With ASP controls, each different type of functionality corresponds to a specific control. For example, all text is entered using the TextBox control; the number of lines is specified using a property. In fact, for ASP controls in general, all the attributes correspond to properties of the control.

The ASP controls also include additional, rich controls, such as the Calendar and AdRotator.

Example 4-5 and Example 4-6 demonstrate the use of ASP controls in a web page analogous to the HTML server controls of Example 4-1 and Example 4-2. They show the use of the TextBox and Button ASP controls, rather than of the HTML controls.

Example 4-5. Code listing for csASPServerControls1.aspx

```
<%@ Page Language="C#" %>
<html>

<script runat="server">
    void btnBookName_Click(Object Source, EventArgs E)
    {
        lblBookName.Text = txtBookName.Text;
    }
</script>

    <body>
    <form runat="server">

        <h1>ASP Controls</h1>

        <br/>
        <h2>The date and time is <% =DateTime.Now.ToString( ) %>.</h2>

        <br/>

        <h2>ASP Control</h2>
        Book Name:   
        <asp:TextBox
            id="txtBookName"
            size="40"
            text="Enter book name."
            runat="server" />

        <br/>
        <br/>
        <br/>

        <asp:Button
            id="btnBookName"
```

Example 4-5. Code listing for csASPServerControls1.aspx (continued)

```
        text="Book Name"
        onClick="btnBookName_Click"
        runat="server" />
    <br/>
    <br/>
    <asp:Label id="lblBookName" text="" runat="server"/>

  </form>
  </body>
</html>
```

Example 4-6. Code listing for vbASPServerControls1.aspx

```
<%@ Page Language="VB" %>
<html>

<script runat="server">
    sub btnBookName_Click(ByVal Sender as Object, _
                          ByVal e as EventArgs)
        lblBookName.Text = txtBookName.Text
    end sub
</script>

    <body>
    <form runat="server">

        <h1>ASP Controls</h1>

        <br/>
        <h2>The date and time is <% =DateTime.Now.ToString( ) %>.</h2>

        <br/>

        <h2>ASP Control</h2>
        Book Name:   
        <asp:TextBox
           id="txtBookName"
           size="40"
           text="Enter book name."
           runat="server" />

        <br/>
        <br/>
        <br/>

        <asp:Button
           id="btnBookName"
           text="Book Name"
           onClick="btnBookName_Click"
           runat="server" />
        <br/>
        <br/>
```

Example 4-6. Code listing for vbASPServerControls1.aspx (continued)

```
        <asp:Label id="lblBookName" text="" runat="server"/>

    </form>
    </body>
</html>
```

The immediate difference between HTML server controls and ASP controls is how the control is referenced in code. In addition to the obvious fact that the controls have different names, the ASP controls are preceded by the ASP namespace. This is indicated by the asp: in front of each control name. For example:

<asp:TextBox

Another difference between the HTML server controls and the ASP controls is the slightly different attribute name used for the displayed text. In many HTML controls (including <input> tags), value is used to specify the text that will be displayed by the control. In ASP controls, text is always the attribute name used to specify the text that will be displayed.

In Example 4-5 and Example 4-6, this difference is seen in all three ASP controls used in the page, as well as in the btnBookName method, which makes reference to the text attribute for two of the controls.

As you will see later in this chapter and in Chapter 5, ASP controls offer a set of attributes for each control that is more consistent than the attributes available to HTML server controls. In actuality, the attributes are not really attributes, but rather properties of the ASP control, and they are programmatically accessible.

Just as with the HTML server controls, ASP controls have an attribute called onClick, which defines the event handler for the Click event. In the examples, it points to the method btnBookName_Click, defined in the script block at the top of the code.

Figure 4-4 shows the page that results from Example 4-5 and 4-6.

ASP.NET and Browsers

The browser never sees the ASP control. The server processes the ASP control and sends standard HTML to the browser.

ASP.NET considers browsers to be either *uplevel* or *downlevel*. Uplevel browsers support script Versions 1.2 (ECMA Script, JavaScript, JScript) and HTML 4.0; typical uplevel browsers would include Internet Explorer 4.0 and later releases. Downlevel browsers, on the other hand, support only HTML 3.2.

ASP.NET can tell you which browser is being used to display the page. This information is made available via the HttpRequest.Browser property. HttpRequest.Browser returns a HttpBrowserCapabilities object whose many properties include a number of Booleans, such as whether the browser supports cookies, frames, and so forth.

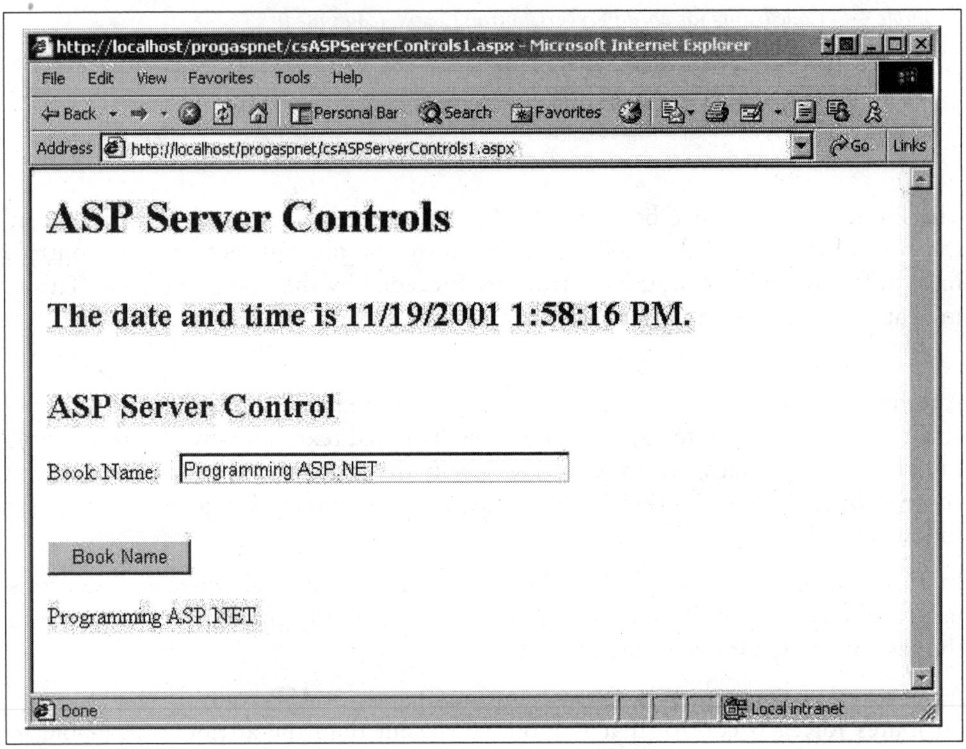

Figure 4-4. Output from Example 4-5 or 4-6

You will find that you don't often need to check the HttpBrowserCapabilities object because the server will automatically convert your HTML to reflect the capabilities of the client browser. For example, validation controls (considered in Chapter 8) can be used to validate customer data entry. If the user's browser supports client-side Java-Script, the validation will happen on the client. However, if the browser does not support client-side scripting, then the validation is done server-side.

Custom programming to support various browsers has been incorporated into the ASP.NET framework, freeing you to focus on the larger task at hand. From within your browser, view the source for the web page displayed in Figure 4-4, and originally coded in Example 4-5. This source is shown in Example 4-7. (The HTML output produced by Example 4-6 is comparable.) Notice that there are no ASP controls, but that all the controls have been converted to traditional HTML tags. Also, note that a hidden field with the name "__VIEWSTATE" has been inserted into the output. This is how ASP.NET maintains the state of the controls; when a page is submitted to the server and then redisplayed, the controls are not reset to their default values. State will be discussed in Chapter 6.

Example 4-7. Output HTML from csASPServerControls.aspx

```html
<html>

    <body>
    <form name="ctrl2" method="post" action="aspservercontrols.aspx" id="ctrl2">
<input type="hidden" name="__VIEWSTATE"
value="dDwtMTA4MDU5NDMzODtoPDtsPDE8Mj47PjtsPHQ8O2w8MTwwPjsxPDI+Oz47bDxoPHA8cDxsPFRleHQ7Pj
tsPFByb2dyYW1taW5nIEFTUC5ORVQ7Pj47PjtoPHA8cDxsPFRleHQ7PjtsPFByb2dyYW1taW5nIEFTUC5ORVQ
7Pj47Pjs7Pjs+Pjs+yvuEznOtPMOuYYSNQ+dcGDUzI3M=" />

        <h1>ASP Controls</h1>

        <br/>
        <h2>The date and time is 11/19/2001 1:58:16 PM.</h2>

        <br/>

        <h2>ASP Control</h2>
        Book Name:   
        <input name="txtBookName" type="text" value="Programming ASP.NET" id="txtBookName"
size="40" />

        <br/>
        <br/>
        <br/>

        <input type="submit" name="btnBookName" value="Book Name" id="btnBookName" />
        <br/>
        <br/>
        <span id="lblBookName">Programming ASP.NET</span>

    </form>
    </body>
</html>
```

ASP Control Hierarchy

All the ASP controls except for the Repeater (discussed in Chapter 13) derive from the WebControl class. The WebControl class and the Repeater class both derive from System.Web.UI.Control, which itself derives from System.Object. The Repeater class, the WebControl class, and all the controls that derive from WebControl are in the System.Web.UI.WebControls namespace. These relationships are shown in Figure 4-5.

All of the properties, events, and methods of WebControl and System.Web.UI.Control are inherited by the ASP controls. Table 4-2 lists many of the commonly used properties inherited by all the ASP controls. Where applicable, default values are indicated.

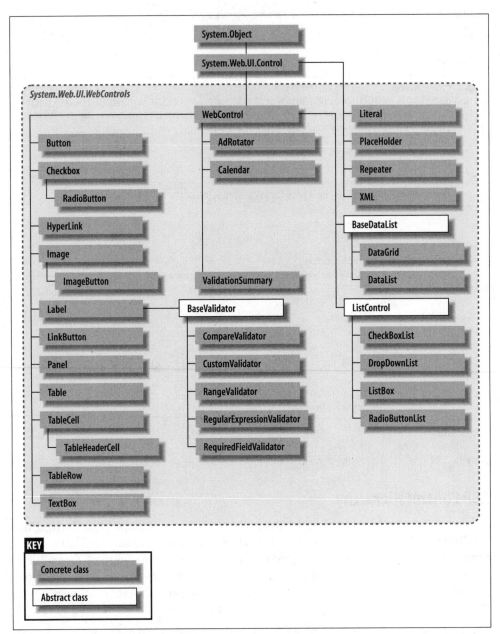

Figure 4-5. Relationships of controls in the System.Web.UI.WebControls namespace

Table 4-2. Properties inherited by all ASP controls

Name	BCL Type	Get	Set	Values	Description
AccessKey	String	x	x	Single-character string.	Pressing the Alt key in combination with this value moves focus to the control.
BackColor	Color	x	x	Azure, Green, Blue, etc.	Background color.
BorderColor	Color	x	x	Fuchsia, Aqua, Coral, etc.	Border color.
BorderStyle	BorderStyle	x	x	Dashed, Dotted, Double, NotSet, etc.	Border style. Default is NotSet.
BorderWidth	Unit	x	x	nn nnpt	Width of the border. If of the form nn, where nn is an integer, then in units of pixels. If of the form nnpt, where nn is an integer, then in units of points.
CausesValidation	Boolean	x	x	true, false	Indicates if entering control causes validation for controls that require validation. Default is true.
CssClass	String	x	x		CSS class.
Enabled	Boolean	x	x	true, false	If disabled, control is visible but grayed out and not operative. Contents are still selectable for copy and paste. Default is true.
Font	FontInfo	x	x		See Table 5-1 in Chapter 5.
ForeColor	Color	x	x	Lavender, LightBlue, Blue, etc.	Foreground color.
Height	Unit	x	x	nn nn%	If of the form nn, where nn is an integer, then in units of pixels. If of the form nn%, then it is a percentage of the width of the container. For downlevel browsers, will not render for Label, HyperLink, LinkButton, any validator controls, or for CheckBoxList, RadioButtonList, or DataList when their RepeatLayout property is Flow.
ID	String	x	x		Programmatic identifier for the control.
ToolTip	String	x	x		Text string displayed when the mouse hovers over the control; not rendered in downlevel browsers.
Visible	Boolean	x	x	true, false	If false, then control is not rendered; the default is true.

Table 4-2. Properties inherited by all ASP controls (continued)

Name	BCL Type	Get	Set	Values	Description
Width	Unit	x	x	nn nn%	If of the form *nn*, where *nn* is an integer, then in units of pixels. If of the form *nn*%, where nn is an integer, then it is a percentage of the width of the container. For downlevel browsers, will not render for Label, HyperLink, LinkButton, any validator controls, or for CheckBoxList, RadioButtonList, or DataList when their RepeatLayout property is Flow.

Comparing HTML and ASP Server Controls

The two types of server controls (HTML server controls and ASP controls) have nearly the same functionality. The advantages of each type are summarized in Table 4-3.

Table 4-3. Advantages of HTML server controls and ASP controls

Type of control	Advantages
Web server controls (ASP controls)	• Offer an event-driven programming model • Provide richer controls, such as calendar and ad rotator • Support event bubbling in nested controls • Automatically detect client browser level and generate correct HTML for both uplevel (HTML 4.0) and downlevel (HTML 3.2) browsers • Typed object model provides type safety and reduces programming errors
HTML server controls	• Provide transition from existing HTML pages • Offer a familiar HTML-like object model • Can be supported by any HTML design environment, since they map to HTML elements • Allow controls that will also interact with client script

ASP Control Details

The previous chapter briefly discussed the different types of controls available in ASP.NET. It went into some detail on HTML server controls and gave an introductory example of ASP server controls. While the latter are sometimes also referred to as web server controls, in the context of this book we call them, simply, *ASP controls*, to reflect the syntax used to implement them:

```
<asp:controlType
       id="ControlID"
       runat="server" />
```

Notice that the control tag always begins with `asp:`.

This chapter provides a wealth of detail about ASP controls. It covers the features and properties common to many of these controls and surveys the specific details of all the ASP controls included with the .NET Framework.

The Basics

In this section, you will create a simple web page, in either C# or VB.NET, in which you will explore many of the properties, events, and methods common to all ASP controls. Example 5-1 shows *csASPServerControlBasics1.aspx*, the first iteration in C#, and Example 5-2 shows *vbASPServerControlBasics1.aspx*, the equivalent file in VB.NET. These two examples demonstrate a Label control, an event handler, and properties being set for a control.

Example 5-1. Basic web page in C#, csASPServerControlBasics.aspx

```
<%@ Page Language="C#" %>
<script runat="server">
   void lblTime_Init(Object Source, EventArgs E)
   {
      lblTime.Font.Name = "Verdana";
      lblTime.Font.Size = 20;
      lblTime.Font.Underline = true;
```

Example 5-1. Basic web page in C#, csASPServerControlBasics.aspx (continued)

```
        lblTime.Font.Bold = true;
        lblTime.Font.Italic = true;
        lblTime.Font.Overline = true;
        lblTime.Font.Strikeout = true;
        lblTime.Text = DateTime.Now.ToString()
            + ". Font Name: "
            + lblTime.Font.Name;
    }
</script>

<html>
    <body>
    <form runat="server">

        <h1>ASP Controls</h1>
        <h2>Basics 1</h2>

        <asp:label
            id="lblTime"
            onInit="lblTime_Init"
            runat="server" />
    </form>
    </body>
</html>
```

Example 5-2. Basic web page in VB.NET, vbASPServerControlBasics1.aspx

```
<%@ Page Language="VB" %>
<script runat="server">
    Sub lblTime_Init(ByVal Sender as Object, _
                     ByVal e as EventArgs)
        lblTime.Font.Name = "Verdana"
        lblTime.Font.Size = new FontUnit(20)
        lblTime.Font.Underline = true
        lblTime.Font.Bold = true
        lblTime.Font.Italic = true
        lblTime.Font.Overline = true
        lblTime.Font.Strikeout = true
        lblTime.Text = DateTime.Now() _
            & ". Font Name: " _
            & lblTime.Font.Name
    End Sub
</script>

<html>
    <body>
    <form runat="server">

        <h1>ASP Controls</h1>
        <h2>Basics 1</h2>

        <asp:label
```

Example 5-2. Basic web page in VB.NET, vbASPServerControlBasics1.aspx (continued)

```
         id="lblTime"
         onInit="lblTime_Init"
         runat="server" />
    </form>
    </body>
</html>
```

This is a very simple web page with static text and an ASP Label control. The Label control has been assigned an `id` of lblTime, which allows the control to be referred to elsewhere in the code.

Of more interest is the `onInit` attribute, which defines an event handler for the Init event. The Init event, a member of the Control class, is called when a control is initialized. It is the first step in each control's lifecycle. All WebControls, since they are derived from Control, have an Init event.

The Init event in Example 5-1 and 5-2 is handled by a method called lblTime_Init, defined in the code block at the top of the *.aspx* file. lblTime_Init sets several properties of the label's font (Name, Size, etc.) and sets the value of the Text property. Notice that the Text property value is a concatenation of the current date and time, a literal string, and the name of the font used. Because the DateTime is a DateTime object, it must be converted to a string in the C# code. In VB.NET, the conversion is implicit (and occurs regardless of the VB Option Strict setting). Also notice the syntax required for setting the font size in VB.NET versus the syntax in C#. (Fonts and their properties will be covered in detail shortly.)

The results, shown in Figure 5-1, are not very pretty but are instructive. The figure shows how several text attributes—bold, italic, overline, underline, and strikeout—can be applied to a label.

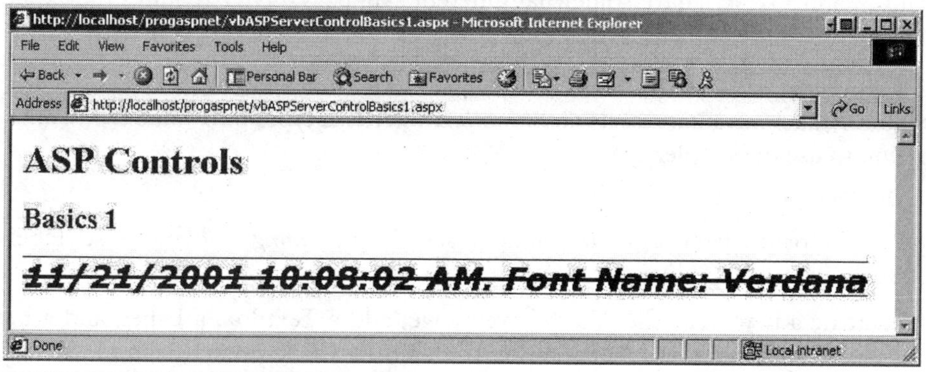

Figure 5-1. Output from Example 5-1 or 5-2

Fonts deserve special mention. Fonts contain *subproperties*, which are listed in Table 5-1. When used in HTML, subproperties are accessed declaratively in code in the form:

```
Font-Italic
```

When used in code blocks, subproperties are accessed programmatically in the form:

```
Font.Italic
```

Table 5-1. Subproperties of the Font object

SubProperty	Type	Values	Description
Bold	Boolean	true, false	Makes the text bold; the default is false.
Italic	Boolean	true, false	Italicizes the text; the default is false.
Name	String	Verdana, Courier, etc.	Primary font name. Automatically updates first item in Names property. Font must be installed and available to the client browser.
Names	String	Times, etc.	Ordered array of font names. Stores list of available font names. Name property automatically updated with first item in array.
Strikeout	Boolean	true, false	Puts a line through the text; the default is false.
Underline	Boolean	true, false	Puts a line under the text; the default is false.
Overline	Boolean	true, false	Puts a line over the text; the default is false. Will not render on downlevel browsers.
Size	FontUnit or String	Small, Smaller, Large, Larger, or an integer representing point size	Uses named sizes or integer point size. Named sizes only work declaratively as control attributes.

If you use points rather than named sizes for the font size, then it is worth noting that C# and VB.NET have somewhat different syntax. VB.NET requires the explicit instantiation of a FontUnit object, as in:

```
lblTime.Font.Size = New FontUnit(20)
```

while C# takes advantage of its ability to *box* reference types into value types, allowing you to use the simpler syntax:

```
lblTime.Font.Size = 20;
```

For a complete description of boxing, see *Programming C#* by Jesse Liberty (O'Reilly).

Now create a new *.aspx* file. To this web page, add a TextBox, a Label, and a Button, along with an event handler for the Button Click event. Example 5-3 and Example 5-4 show the code in C# and VB.NET, respectively. (Note that the C# code and the VB.NET code are very similar; there are differences in the Page directive and the syntax for defining methods.) When you enter something in the TextBox and click the Button, the contents of the TextBox are assigned to the Label.

Example 5-3. Another basic web page in C#, csASPServerControlBasics2.aspx

```
<%@ Page Language="C#" %>
<script runat="server">
    void btnBookName_Click(Object Source, EventArgs E)
    {
        lblBookName.Text = txtBookName.Text;
    }
</script>

<html>
    <body>
    <form runat="server">

        <h1>ASP Controls</h1>
        <h2>Basics 2</h2>

        Book Name:   
        <asp:textBox
            id="txtBookName"
            width="50%"
            maxlength="50"
            text="Enter book name."
            enabled= "true"
            readonly="false"
            toolTip="Enter book name here."
            runat="server" />

        <asp:button
            id="btnBookName"
            text="Book Name"
            onClick="btnBookName_Click"
            enabled= "true"
            visible="true"
            toolTip="Click here to post the book name."
            runat="server" />
        <br/>
        <br/>
        You entered:  
        <asp:label
            id="lblBookName"
            Font-Name="Courier"
            Font-Bold= "true"
            Font-Size="Large"
            runat="server"/>
    </form>
    </body>
</html>
```

Example 5-4. Another basic web page in VB.NET, vbASPServerControlBasics2.aspx

```
<%@ Page Language="VB" %>
<script runat="server">
    sub btnBookName_Click(Sender as Object, _
```

```
                              e as EventArgs)
      lblBookName.Text = txtBookName.Text
   End Sub
</script>

<html>
   <body>
   <form runat="server">

      <h1>ASP Controls</h1>
      <h2>Basics 2</h2>

      Book Name:   
      <asp:textBox
         id="txtBookName"
         width="50%"
         maxlength="50"
         text="Enter book name."
         enabled= "true"
         readonly="false"
         toolTip="Enter book name here."
         runat="server" />

      <asp:button
         id="btnBookName"
         text="Book Name"
         onClick="btnBookName_Click"
         enabled= "true"
         visible="true"
         toolTip="Click here to post the book name."
         runat="server" />

      <br/>
      <br/>
      You entered:  
      <asp:label
         id="lblBookName"
         Font-Name="Courier"
         Font-Bold= "true"
         Font-Size="Large"
         runat="server"/>
   </form>
   </body>
</html>
```

Three controls—a TextBox, a Button, and a Label control—and an additional event handler method have been added. Both the TextBox and the Button have several properties set in addition to their id and runat properties.

Figure 5-2 shows the results of running the code contained in Example 5-3 or Example 5-4.

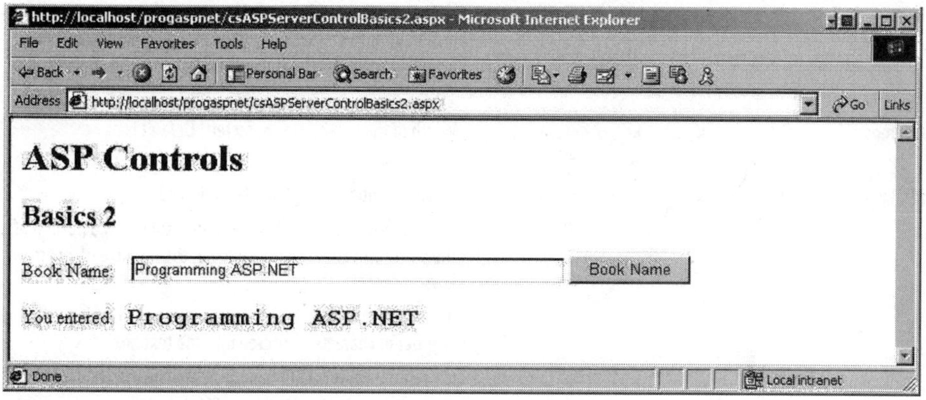

Figure 5-2. Output from Example 5-3 or 5-4

Label Control

A Label control is used to display text. The Label control's Text property contains the text string to be displayed by the label. Note that Text is the only Label control property that is not inherited from the WebControl class. The Label control has no events or methods that are not derived from WebControl.

You have already seen the Label control used in the previous code examples in this chapter. The Text and Font properties of the Label control can be set programmatically, as shown in Example 5-1 and Example 5-2, or declaratively, as demonstrated in Example 5-3 and Example 5-4.

TextBox Control

The TextBox control can be used for both user input and read-only text display. It can be configured to be any one of the following: single-line, multiline, or to accept passwords. If multiline, it automatically wraps, unless the Wrap property is set to false. The text it contains can exceed the length of the control displayed on the page.

Table 5-2 lists many of the common properties specific to the TextBox control. If any of these attributes are omitted from the control, then the default value will apply.

Table 5-2. Some properties specific to the TextBox control

Name	Type	Get	Set	Values	Description
AutoPost-Back	Boolean	x	x	true, false	Determines if automatic postback to server will occur if user changes contents of control. If false, postback to server will not occur until the page is posted, either by a button or another control with AutoPostBack set to true. Default is false.
Columns	Int32	x	x	0, 1, 2, etc.	Width of the text box in characters. Default is 0.
MaxLength	Int32	x	x	0, 1, 2, etc.	Maximum number of characters allowed. If MaxLength is greater than Columns, then only a portion of the string will display without using the home, end, or arrow keys. Its default value is 0, which does not impose a limit on the number of characters entered into the text box.
ReadOnly	Boolean	x	x	true, false	If true, content cannot be changed by user. Default is false, meaning content can still be changed programmatically.
Rows	Int32	x	x	0, 1, 2, etc.	Number of lines of text in a multiline text box. The default is 0, which imposes no limit on the number of lines.
Text	String	x	x		Content of the TextBox.
TextMode	TextBox-Mode	x	x	Single-Line, Multi-Line, Password	SingleLine, the default value, displays a single line of text. MultiLine allows multiple lines of text and displays a vertical scroll bar, even for Rows = 1. The text wraps automatically to fit the width of the box. The Enter key enters a CR/LF. The mouse or tab key causes focus to leave the box and initiates postback if AutoPostBack is true. Password displays content in asterisks, then clears the text box on posting. The value is not case-sensitive.
Wrap	Boolean	x	x	true, false	Indicates if text within a multiline text box should wrap. If false, then the text box will have a horizontal scrollbar. Default is true.

The TextBox control raises the TextChanged event, which is handled by the OnText-Changed event handler. This event handler is passed a standard EventArgs argument.

Button Controls

Buttons are controls that post the form back to the server, enabling server-side processing to commence. There are three types of button controls:

- Button
- LinkButton
- ImageButton

In addition to the properties, methods, and events inherited along with all the other ASP controls, all three button types have the following two events:

Click

> Raised when control is clicked and no command name is associated with the button (i.e., no value has been assigned to the Button control's CommandName property). The method is passed an argument of type EventArgs.

Command

> Raised when the control is clicked and a command name is associated with the button (i.e., a command name has been assigned to the Button control's CommandName property). The event is passed an argument of type CommandEventArgs, which has the following two members:

> *CommandName*
>> The name of the command

> *CommandArgument*
>> An optional argument for the command

The code in Example 5-5 and Example 5-6 creates a web page containing three buttons, one of each type. Each button performs the same task: transferring control to another web page. Example 5-5 shows the C# code, and Example 5-6 shows the same code in VB.NET. Figure 5-3 shows the web page that results from running the example code.

> In order for the code in Example 5-5 and 5-6 to work correctly, you need to have a target web page to link to. This can be any valid *.htm*, *.asp* or *.aspx* file. In these examples, the target page is hard-coded as *TargetPage.aspx*, located in the *ProgAspNet* virtual directory. In addition, you will need an image file for the ImageButton. These examples use a file called "Dan at vernal pool.jpg," also located in the ProgAspNet virtual directory, but you can use any jpg file you want.

Example 5-5. Buttons in C#, csASButtons.aspx

```
<%@ Page Language="C#" %>
<script runat="server">
   void btnLink_Click(Object Source, EventArgs E)
   {
      Response.Redirect("//localhost/progaspnet/TargetPage.aspx");
   }

   void imgLink_Click(Object Source, ImageClickEventArgs E)
   {
      Response.Redirect("//localhost/progaspnet/TargetPage.aspx");
   }
</script>

<html>
```

Example 5-5. Buttons in C#, csASButtons.aspx (continued)

```
<body>
<form runat="server">

    <h1>ASP Controls</h1>
    <h2>Buttons</h2>

    <asp:button
        id="btnLink"
        text="Link to Target Page"
        onClick="btnLink_Click"
        toolTip="Click here to go to Target Page."
        runat="server" />

    <asp:imageButton
        id="imgLink"
        imageURL="Dan at vernal pool.jpg "
        alternateText="Link to Target Page"
        onClick="imgLink_Click"
        toolTip="Click here to go to Target Page."
        runat="server" />

    <asp:linkButton
        id="lnkLink"
        text="LinkButton to Target Page"
        onClick="btnLink_Click"
        Font-Name="Comic Sans MS Bold"
        Font-Size="16pt"
        toolTip="Click here to go to Target Page."
        runat="server" />
</form>
</body>
</html>
```

Example 5-6. Buttons in VB.NET, vbASPButtons.aspx code

```
<%@ Page Language="VB" %>
<script runat="server">
    Sub btnLink_Click(ByVal Sender as Object, _
                    ByVal e as EventArgs)
        Response.Redirect("//localhost/progaspnet/TargetPage.aspx")
    End Sub

    Sub imgLink_Click(ByVal Sender as Object, _
                    ByVal e as ImageClickEventArgs)
        Response.Redirect("//localhost/progaspnet/TargetPage.aspx")
    End Sub
</script>

<html>
    <body>
    <form runat="server">
```

Example 5-6. Buttons in VB.NET, vbASPButtons.aspx code (continued)

```
<h1>ASP Controls</h1>
<h2>Buttons</h2>

<asp:button
    id="btnLink"
    text="Link to Target Page"
    onClick="btnLink_Click"
    toolTip="Click here to go to Target Page."
    runat="server" />

<asp:imageButton
    id="imgLink"
    imageURL=" Dan at vernal pool.jpg "
    alternateText="Link to Target Page"
    onClick="imgLink_Click"
    toolTip="Click here to go to Target Page."
    runat="server" />

<asp:linkButton
    id="lnkLink"
    text="LinkButton to Target Page"
    onClick="btnLink_Click"
    Font-Name="Comic Sans MS Bold"
    Font-Size="16pt"
    toolTip="Click here to go to Target Page."
    runat="server" />
</form>
</body>
</html>
```

The System.Web.UI.WebControls namespace offers three kinds of button-like ASP controls:

Button

> This is the standard button that we have seen earlier. The interesting thing about the Button control in Example 5-5 and Example 5-6 is that the onClick event handler calls the btnLink_Click method, which navigates to a new web page using:
>
> ```
> Response.Redirect("//localhost/progaspnet/TargetPage.aspx");
> ```
>
> The string in quotes can be any valid URL.

ImageButton

> The ImageButton control performs the same function as the standard button, except that an image bitmap takes the place of the button on the browser UI. For the ImageButton control, there is no Text attribute, but there is an AlternateText attribute, which specifies what text to display on non-graphical browsers.
>
> In addition, note that the event handler uses an ImageClickEventArgs event argument, which is slightly different than the event handlers for the Button and LinkButton controls.

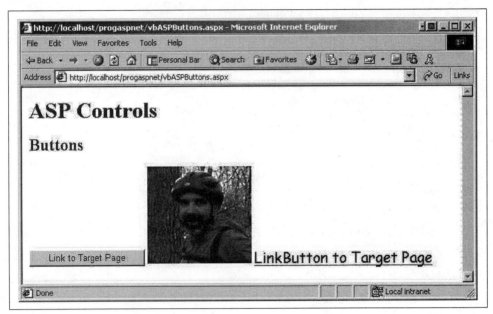

Figure 5-3. Button controls

LinkButton

The LinkButton control is sort of a cross between a standard button and a HyperLink control (described in the next section). A LinkButton appears to the user as a hyperlink, i.e., the text is colored and underlined. The big difference between a LinkButton control and a standard Button control is that the LinkButton's functionality is implemented using client-side scripting.

This is readily apparent if you look at the source code from your browser resulting from Example 5-5 or 5-6, an excerpt of which is shown in Example 5-7. Remember, this source code is output by ASP.NET, not written by you.

Example 5-7. Browser source segment from csASPButtons.aspx

```
<input type="submit" name="btnLink" value="Link to Target Page" id="btnLink" title="Click
here to go to Target Page." />

<input type="image" name="imgLink" id="imgLink" title="Click here to go to Target Page."
src="/progaspnet/Dan at vernal pool.jpg" alt="Link to Target Page" border="0" />

<a id="lnkLink" title="Click here to go to Target Page." href="javascript:__
doPostBack('lnkLink','')" style="font-family:Comic Sans MS Bold;font-size:16pt;">Link to
Target Page</a>

<script language="javascript">
<!--
    function __doPostBack(eventTarget, eventArgument) {
        var theform = document.ctrl0
        theform.__EVENTTARGET.value = eventTarget
```

Example 5-7. Browser source segment from csASPButtons.aspx (continued)

```
        theform.__EVENTARGUMENT.value = eventArgument
        theform.submit( )
    }
// -->
</script>
```

HyperLink Control

A HyperLink control looks similar to a LinkButton control. However, there is a fundamental difference: the HyperLink control only navigates to the target URL, while the LinkButton control posts the form and, if the event handler chooses, navigates to the target URL.

The HyperLink control has four specific attributes:

ImageURL

> The path to an image (rather than text) to display. If this attribute is used, the control appears to the user as identical to an ImageButton control, although the ImageButton control still posts the form and the HyperLink control only navigates.

NavigateURL

> The target URL to navigate to.

Text

> The text string that will be displayed on the browser as the link. If both the Text and ImageURL properties are set, the ImageURL takes precedence. The text is displayed if the image is unavailable.

> If the browser supports tool tips and the ToolTip property has not been set, then the Text value will display as a tool tip. If the ToolTip property has been set, then the ToolTip text string will display as a tool tip.

Target

> Defines the target window or frame that will load the linked page. The value is case insensitive and must begin with a character in the range of a to z, except for the special values shown in Table 5-3, all of which begin with an underscore.

Table 5-3. Special values of the Target attribute

Value	Description
_blank	Renders the content in a new unnamed window without frames.
_new	Not documented, but behaves the same as _blank.
_parent	Renders the content in the parent window or frameset of the window or frame with the hyperlink. If the child container is a window or top-level frame, it behaves the same as _self.
_self	Renders the content in the current frame or window with focus. This is the default value.
_top	Renders the content in the current full window without frames.

Example 5-8 and Example 5-9 demonstrate a hyperlink in C# and VB.NET, respectively.

Example 5-8. HyperLink in C#, csASPHyperLink.aspx

```
<%@ Page Language="C#" %>

<html>
   <body>
   <form runat="server">

      <h1>ASP Controls</h1>
      <h2>HyperLink</h2>

      <asp:hyperLink
         id="hypLink"
         NavigateURL="//localhost/progaspnet/TargetPage.aspx"
         Text="HyperLink to Target Page"
         target="_self"
         Font-Name="Impact"
         Font-Size="16pt"
         toolTip="Click here to go to Target Page."
         runat="server" />
   </form>
   </body>
</html>
```

Example 5-9. HyperLink in VB.NET, vbASPHyperLink.aspx

```
<%@ Page Language="VB" %>

<html>
   <body>
   <form runat="server">

      <h1>ASP Controls</h1>
      <h2>HyperLink</h2>

      <asp:hyperLink
         id="hypLink"
         NavigateURL="//localhost/progaspnet/TargetPage.aspx"
         Text="HyperLink to Target Page"
         target="_self"
         Font-Name="Impact"
         Font-Size="16pt"
         toolTip="Click here to go to Target Page."
         runat="server" />
   </form>
   </body>
</html>
```

The result of running Example 5-8 or Example 5-9 is shown in Figure 5-4.

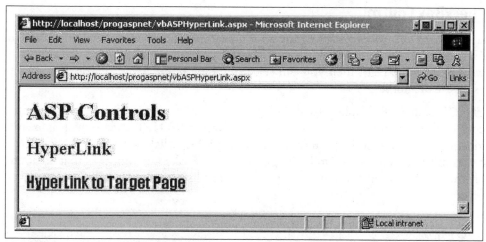

Figure 5-4. HyperLink control

The HyperLink control is rendered on the client browser as an HTML anchor tag, i.e., <a>. You can verify this by examining the source code for the web page on your browser.

Selecting Values

Several ASP controls allow the user to select a value or values:

CheckBox
> Allows selection of Boolean data

RadioButton
> Allows only a single option to be selected

CheckBoxList
> Group of CheckBox controls that can be dynamically created and bound to a data source

RadioButtonList
> Group of RadioButton controls that can be dynamically created and bound to a data source

ListBox
> Allows selection of one or more items from a predefined list

DropDownList
> Similar to a ListBox, but allows only a single selection

All of these controls derive from the WebControl class. The RadioButton derives further from the CheckBox class, and the last four controls, the List controls, all derive from the abstract ListControl class. Each of these controls is considered in detail in the upcoming sections.

CheckBox Control

A CheckBox control provides a means for a user to select Boolean data (i.e., Yes/No or True/False). If you have several checkboxes arranged together (not to be confused with a CheckBoxList), then you can select multiple options. No option is mutually exclusive of another.

The C# code in Example 5-10 shows the use of three independent CheckBoxes to control the appearance of a Label. (The equivalent VB.NET code, which is nearly identical to the C# code, is shown in Example 5-11.) Clicking on any of the checkboxes in these examples—Underline, Overline, or Strikeout—imposes that attribute on the text string in the Label control. The results of the C# code are shown in Figure 5-5.

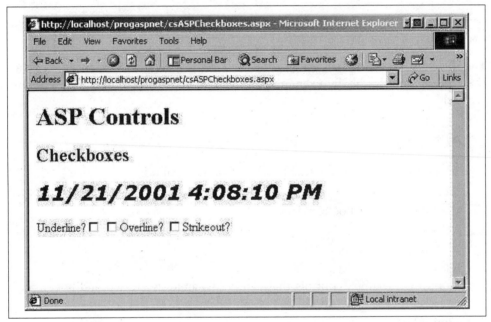

Figure 5-5. Checkboxes

Example 5-10. CheckBoxes in C#, csASPCheckboxes.aspx

```
<%@ Page Language="C#" %>

<script runat="server">
   void lblTime_Init(Object Source, EventArgs E)
   {
      lblTime.Font.Name = "Verdana";
      lblTime.Font.Size = 20;
      lblTime.Font.Bold = true;
      lblTime.Font.Italic = true;
```

Example 5-10. CheckBoxes in C#, csASPCheckboxes.aspx (continued)

```
        lblTime.Text = DateTime.Now.ToString( );
    }

    void chkUnderLine_CheckedChanged(Object Source, EventArgs E)
    {
        if (chkUnderLine.Checked )
            lblTime.Font.Underline = true;
        else
            lblTime.Font.Underline = false;
    }

    void chkOverLine_CheckedChanged(Object Source, EventArgs E)
    {
        if (chkOverLine.Checked )
            lblTime.Font.Overline = true;
        else
            lblTime.Font.Overline = false;
    }

    void chkStrikeout_CheckedChanged(Object Source, EventArgs E)
    {
        if (chkStrikeout.Checked )
            lblTime.Font.Strikeout = true;
        else
            lblTime.Font.Strikeout = false;
    }
</script>

<html>
    <body>
    <form runat="server">

        <h1>ASP Controls</h1>
        <h2>Checkboxes</h2>

        <asp:label
            id="lblTime"
            runat="server"
            onInit="lblTime_Init"/>

        <br/>
        <br/>

        <asp:checkBox
            id="chkUnderLine"
            autoPostBack="true"
            checked="false"
            text="Underline?"
            textAlign="left"
            onCheckedChanged="chkUnderLine_CheckedChanged"
            runat="server" />
```

Example 5-10. CheckBoxes in C#, csASPCheckboxes.aspx (continued)

```
    <asp:checkBox
        id="chkOverLine"
        autoPostBack="true"
        checked="false"
        text="Overline?"
        textAlign="right"
        onCheckedChanged="chkOverLine_CheckedChanged"
        runat="server" />

    <asp:checkBox
        id="chkStrikeout"
        autoPostBack="true"
        checked="false"
        text="Strikeout?"
        onCheckedChanged="chkStrikeout_CheckedChanged"
        runat="server" />
  </form>
  </body>
</html>
```

Example 5-11. CheckBoxes in VB.NET, vbASPCheckboxes.aspx

```
<%@ Page Language="VB" %>

<script runat="server">
    Sub lblTime_Init(ByVal Sender as Object, _
                     ByVal e as EventArgs)
        lblTime.Font.Name = "Verdana"
        lblTime.Font.Size = new FontUnit(20)
        lblTime.Font.Bold = true
        lblTime.Font.Italic = true
        lblTime.Text = DateTime.Now( )
    End Sub

    Sub chkUnderLine_CheckedChanged(ByVal Sender as Object, _
                                    ByVal e as EventArgs)
        if (chkUnderLine.Checked )
            lblTime.Font.Underline = true
        else
            lblTime.Font.Underline = false
        end if
    End Sub

    Sub chkOverLine_CheckedChanged(ByVal Sender as Object, _
                                   ByVal e as EventArgs)
        if (chkOverLine.Checked )
            lblTime.Font.Overline = true
        else
            lblTime.Font.Overline = false
        end if
    End Sub
```

Example 5-11. CheckBoxes in VB.NET, vbASPCheckboxes.aspx (continued)

```
    Sub chkStrikeout_CheckedChanged(ByVal Sender as Object, _
                                    ByVal e as EventArgs)
      if (chkStrikeout.Checked )
          lblTime.Font.Strikeout = true
      else
          lblTime.Font.Strikeout = false
      end if
    End Sub
</script>

<html>
   <body>
   <form runat="server">

       <h1>ASP Controls</h1>
       <h2>Checkboxes</h2>

       <asp:label
           id="lblTime"
           runat="server"
           onInit="lblTime_Init"/>

       <br/>
       <br/>

       <asp:checkBox
           id="chkUnderLine"
           autoPostBack="true"
           checked="false"
           text="Underline?"
           textAlign="left"
           onCheckedChanged="chkUnderLine_CheckedChanged"
           runat="server" />

       <asp:checkBox
           id="chkOverLine"
           autoPostBack="true"
           checked="false"
           text="Overline?"
           textAlign="right"
           onCheckedChanged="chkOverLine_CheckedChanged"
           runat="server" />

       <asp:checkBox
           id="chkStrikeout"
           autoPostBack="true"
           checked="false"
           text="Strikeout?"
           onCheckedChanged="chkStrikeout_CheckedChanged"
           runat="server" />
   </form>
```

Example 5-11. CheckBoxes in VB.NET, vbASPCheckboxes.aspx (continued)

```
    </body>
</html>
```

Like all controls derived from WebControl, CheckBoxes have an ID property. But as the sample code in Example 5-10 and 5-11 shows, there are several other properties and methods that are not inherited from WebControl. These members are listed in Table 5-4. Note, however, that some of these properties, such as AutoPostBack and Text, are common to several other controls.

Table 5-4. Members of the CheckBox class not inherited from the WebControl class

Name	Type	Get	Set	Values	Description
AutoPostBack	Boolean	x	x	true, false	Determines if automatic postback to the server will occur if the user changes the contents of the control. If false (the default), postback to the server will not occur until the page is posted, either by a button or another control with AutoPostBack set to true.
Checked	Boolean	x	x	true, false	Indicates if the CheckBox is checked. Default is false.
Text	String	x	x		The text label associated with the CheckBox.
TextAlign	TextAlign	x	x	Left, Right	Dictates if the text label is on the left or right of the CheckBox. Default is Right.
CheckedChanged	Event			Event-Args	This event is raised when the Checked property is changed. Note that this event will not immediately post back to the server unless AutoPostBack is set to true.

The CheckBox control can raise the CheckedChanged event, which is handled by the OnCheckedChanged event handler. This event passes a standard EventArgs argument, which does not expose any properties.

RadioButton Control

A RadioButton control is very similar to, and in fact is derived from, a CheckBox control. The only difference between the two classes is that RadioButtons are typically grouped using the GroupName property, and only one RadioButton in the group can be checked (that is, its Checked property is true) at one time. Changing the Checked property of one RadioButton control in the group to true changes the Checked property of all other controls in the group to false.

Example 5-12 is a C# version of a web page that contains three RadioButton controls to set the font size of a label. Example 5-13 provides the equivalent VB.NET version. Each of the radio buttons in Example 5-12 and Example 5-13 is part of the group grpSize. The result of running either Example 5-12 or Example 5-13 is shown in Figure 5-6.

Example 5-12. RadioButtons in C#, csASPRadioButtons.aspx

```
<%@ Page Language="C#" %>

<script runat="server">
   void lblTime_Init(Object Source, EventArgs E)
   {
      lblTime.Font.Name = "Verdana";
      lblTime.Font.Size = 20;
      lblTime.Font.Bold = true;
      lblTime.Font.Italic = true;
      lblTime.Text = DateTime.Now.ToString( );
   }

   void grpSize_CheckedChanged(Object Source, EventArgs E)
   {
      if (rdoSize10.Checked)
         lblTime.Font.Size = 10;
      else if (rdoSize14.Checked)
         lblTime.Font.Size = 14;
      else    lblTime.Font.Size = 16;
   }
</script>

<html>
   <body>
   <form runat="server">

      <h1>ASP Controls</h1>
      <h2>Radio Buttons</h2>

      <br/>
      <br/>

      <asp:label
         id="lblTime"
         runat="server"
         onInit="lblTime_Init"/>

      <br/>
      <br/>

      <asp:radioButton
         groupName="grpSize"
         id="rdoSize10"
         autoPostBack="true"
         checked="false"
         text="10pt"
         onCheckedChanged="grpSize_CheckedChanged"
         runat="server" />
      <asp:radioButton
         groupName="grpSize"
         id="rdoSize14"
         autoPostBack="true"
```

Example 5-12. RadioButtons in C#, csASPRadioButtons.aspx (continued)

```
            checked="false"
            text="14pt"
            onCheckedChanged="grpSize_CheckedChanged"
            runat="server" />
        <asp:radioButton
            groupName="grpSize"
            id="rdoSize16"
            autoPostBack="true"
            checked="false"
            text="16pt"
            onCheckedChanged="grpSize_CheckedChanged"
            runat="server" />
    </form>
    </body>
</html>
```

Example 5-13. RadioButtons in VB.NET, vbASPRadioButtons.aspx

```
<%@ Page Language="VB" %>

<script runat="server">
    Sub lblTime_Init(ByVal Sender as Object, _
                     ByVal e as EventArgs)
        lblTime.Font.Name = "Verdana"
        lblTime.Font.Size = new FontUnit(20)
        lblTime.Font.Bold = true
        lblTime.Font.Italic = true
        lblTime.Text = DateTime.Now( )
    End Sub

    Sub grpSize_CheckedChanged(ByVal Sender as Object, _
                               ByVal e as EventArgs)
        if (rdoSize10.Checked)
            lblTime.Font.Size = new FontUnit(10)
        else if (rdoSize14.Checked)
            lblTime.Font.Size = new FontUnit(14)
        else
            lblTime.Font.Size = new FontUnit(16)
        End If
    End Sub
</script>

<html>
    <body>
    <form runat="server">

        <h1>ASP Controls</h1>
        <h2>Radio Buttons</h2>

        <br/>
        <br/>
```

Example 5-13. RadioButtons in VB.NET, vbASPRadioButtons.aspx (continued)

```
        <asp:label
            id="lblTime"
            runat="server"
            onInit="lblTime_Init"/>

        <br/>
        <br/>

        <asp:radioButton
            groupName="grpSize"
            id="rdoSize10"
            autoPostBack="true"
            checked="false"
            text="10pt"
            onCheckedChanged="grpSize_CheckedChanged"
            runat="server" />
        <asp:radioButton
            groupName="grpSize"
            id="rdoSize14"
            autoPostBack="true"
            checked="false"
            text="14pt"
            onCheckedChanged="grpSize_CheckedChanged"
            runat="server" />
        <asp:radioButton
            groupName="grpSize"
            id="rdoSize16"
            autoPostBack="true"
            checked="false"
            text="16pt"
            onCheckedChanged="grpSize_CheckedChanged"
            runat="server" />
    </form>
    </body>
</html>
```

The CheckedChanged event, which is derived from CheckBox, is handled by the onCheckedChanged event handler, which points to the grpSize_CheckedChanged method. That method is a simple if..else block that changes the text size depending on which button is selected. In practice, it would probably be better to use a C# switch statement or a VB Select Case statement to make it easier to add additional radio buttons in the future.

Selecting from a List

ASP.NET provides four ASP controls for selecting either single or multiple items from a list:

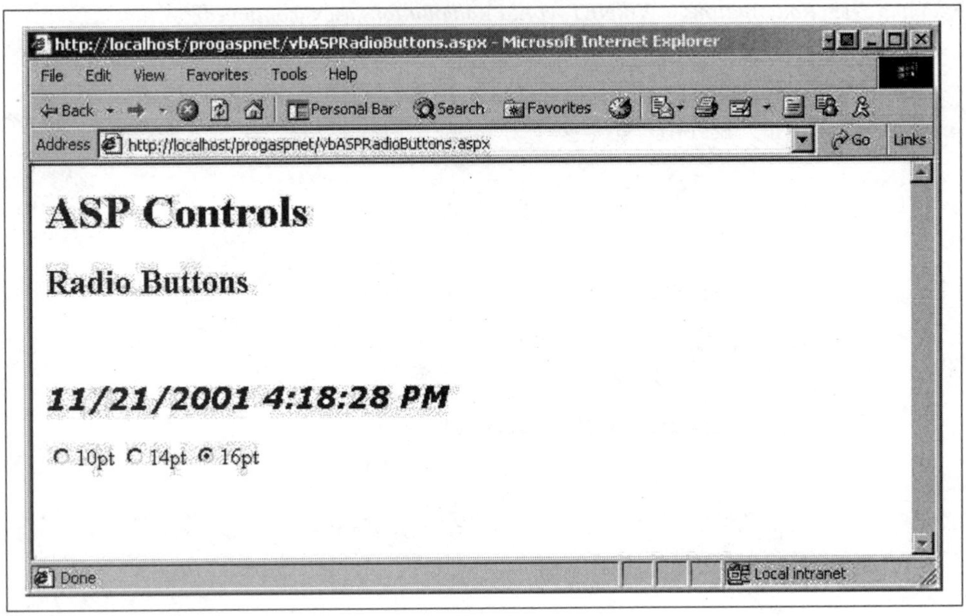

Figure 5-6. Radio buttons

- CheckBoxList
- RadioButtonList
- ListBox
- DropDownList

All of these controls are derived from ListControl and have much in common:

- ListItem (the information displayed by the list) works exactly the same way for all the ListControls, with a Value property and a Text property.
- Items can be added either statically, programmatically through the Add method, or from a data source.
- The SelectedIndex and SelectedItem properties point to the selected item with the lowest index.
- The Selected property is true for any item that is selected.
- All four controls raise and respond to the SelectedIndexChanged event.

The ListBox and DropDownList controls differ from the other two list controls (CheckBoxList and RadionButtonList) in that they appear to the user to be a single control—a list box or a drop-down list—rather than a collection of buttons or check-boxes. The ListBox and DropDownList controls lend themselves to longer lists because they scroll.

Table 5-5 summarizes the differences among the four list controls.

Table 5-5. Differences among the four list controls

Characteristic	CheckBox List	RadioButton List	DropDown List	ListBox
Single selection only		X	X	
Able to select one or more items	X			X
Displays the entire list	X	X		
Displays single item at a time, along with a button for seeing the entire list, using vertical scroll bar if necessary			X	
Displays multiple items, using vertical scroll bar if necessary				X
Best for short lists	X	X		
Best for long lists			X	X

The following sections describe the controls and objects related to selecting items from a list.

ListItem Object

There are four ASP controls that allow you to select from a list, all derived from the ListControl class. A ListControl control consists of a collection of ListItem objects. Each ListItem object has two properties, as Table 5-6 shows.

Table 5-6. Properties of the ListItem object

Name	Type	Get	Set	Description
Text	String	X	X	The text string displayed for a ListItem.
Value	String	X	X	A value associated with a ListItem. The value is not displayed, but is available programmatically.

When dealing with lists, it is very common to display one thing to the user, but to pass the selection to your code as something different. For example, if presenting your users with a list of states, the list might display state names, such as Massachusetts. But when they select an item, the program will pass the selected item as ma. Massachusetts would be the ListItem object's Text property, and ma would be the Value property.

The Text property can be specified in one of two ways:

Inner HTML content
> Text contained between the opening and closing tags of any control

Text attribute
> An attribute within the opening tag of the ListItem control

There can be either a closing tag with no inner HTML, or the opening tag can be self-closing. All three of the following lines are equivalent:

```
<asp:listItem >Item 7</asp:listItem>
<asp:listItem text="Item 7"></asp:listItem>
<asp:listItem text="Item 7"/>
```

If both a Text property and inner HTML content are specified, the inner HTML content will be displayed. For example, if the following line were used:

```
<asp:listItem text="Item 7">Item 8</asp:listItem>
```

then "Item 8" is what would be displayed on the web page.

The Value property can be set similarly to the Text property. So, for example, the lines of code presented previously could be modified to also set the value, as follows:

```
<asp:listItem value="7">Item 7</asp:listItem>
<asp:listItem text="Item 7" value="7"></asp:listItem>
<asp:listItem text="Item 7" value="7"/>
```

CheckBoxList Control

The CheckBoxList is a parent control containing a collection of CheckBox items. It is very similar to the group of CheckBox controls shown previously in Example 5-10 and Example 5-11, except that all the child checkboxes are handled as a group. The CheckBoxList control derives from ListControl rather than directly from WebControl.

The CheckBoxList control is better suited than individual checkboxes for creating a series of checkboxes out of data in a database, although either type of control can be bound to data. Data binding to a database will be covered in detail in Chapter 9.

There are three ways to add items to a CheckBoxList:

- Statically, using the ASP ListItem control tag
- Programmatically from an array
- Dynamically from a data source such as a database

Adding items statically

The web page shown in Example 5-14 demonstrates many of the properties of CheckBoxLists. The list items are added statically in the HTML code. The CheckBoxList control attributes specify the appearance and behavior of the control. (This code is the same for both C# and VB.) Figure 5-7 shows the resulting web page.

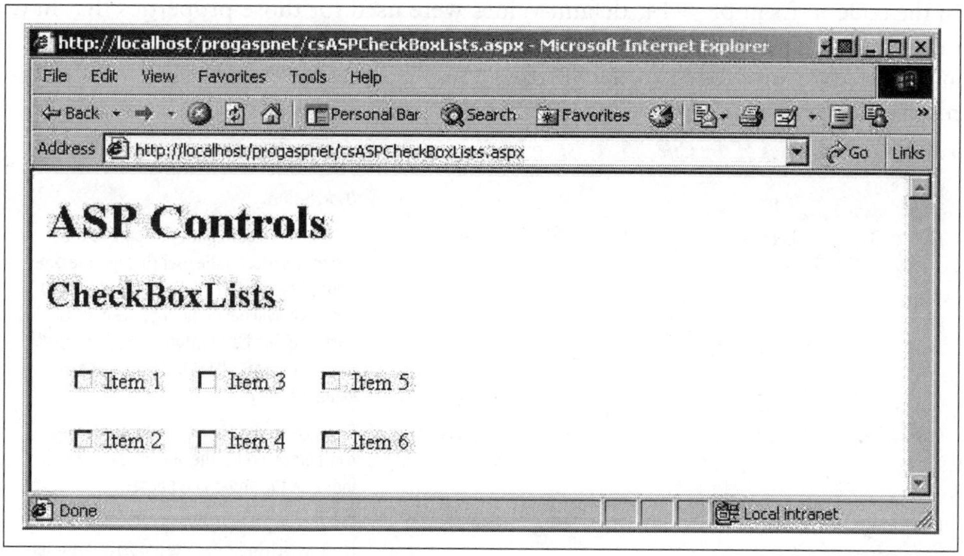

Figure 5-7. CheckBoxList statically added items

Example 5-14. CheckBoxLists, ASPCheckBoxList.aspx

```
<html>
    <body>
    <form runat="server">

        <h1>ASP Controls</h1>
        <h2>CheckBoxLists</h2>

        <asp:checkBoxList
            id="cblGenre"
            autoPostBack="true"
            cellPadding="5"
            cellSpacing="10"
            repeatColumns="3"
            repeatDirection="vertical"
            RepeatLayout="table"
            textAlign="right"
            runat="server">

        <asp:listItem> Item 1 </asp:listItem>
        <asp:listItem> Item 2 </asp:listItem>
        <asp:listItem> Item 3 </asp:listItem>
        <asp:listItem> Item 4 </asp:listItem>
        <asp:listItem> Item 5 </asp:listItem>
        <asp:listItem> Item 6 </asp:listItem>
    </asp:checkBoxList>
    </form>
    </body>
</html>
```

In the code in Example 5-14, default values were used for those properties that have defaults, as indicated in Table 5-7. By changing the RepeatDirection, RepeatLayout, and TextAlign properties to Horizontal, Flow, and Left, respectively, you get the results shown in Figure 5-8.

Table 5-7. Properties of the CheckBoxList control

Name	Type	Get	Set	Values	Description
AutoPostBack	Boolean	x	x	true, false	Determines if automatic postback to the server will occur if the user changes the contents of the control. If false, postback to the server will not occur until the page is posted, either by a button or another control with AutoPostBack set to true. Its default value is false.
CellPadding	Int32	x	x	Integers	Distance in pixels between the border and contents of a cell. The default is -1, which indicates the property is not set.
CellSpacing	Int32	x	x	Integers	Distance in pixels between cells. The default is -1, which indicates the property is not set.
DataSource	Object	x	x		Source that populates the control.
RepeatColumns	Integer	x	x	Integers	Number of columns to display.
RepeatDirection	RepeatDirection	x	x	Horizontal, Vertical	Horizontal specifies that items are loaded from left to right, then top to bottom.
					Vertical specifies that items are loaded top to bottom, then left to right. The default value is Vertical.
RepeatLayout	RepeatLayout	x	x	Flow, Table	Flow specifies that items are displayed without a table structure.
					Table specifies that items are displayed in a table structure. Default is Table.
Selected	Boolean	x	x	true, false	Indicates an item has been selected. Default is false.
TextAlign	TextAlign	x	x	Left, Right	Dictates if the text label is on the left or right of the checkboxes. Default is Right.

Adding items programmatically from an array

There are times when you do not know at compile time what checkboxes you want to create. For example, you may want to draw the choices from a database. In these cases, you need to be able to add items programmatically.

In Example 5-15 (in C#) and Example 5-16 (in VB.NET), ListItem objects are added both programmatically and also are hard-coded within the CheckBoxList tags, for purposes of illustration.

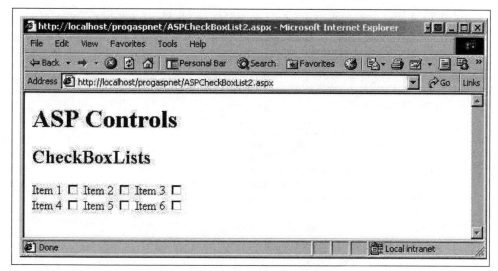

Figure 5-8. Static CheckBoxList modified to use non-default values

Example 5-15. Adding items from an array in C#, csASPCheckBoxListArray.aspx

```
<%@ Page Language="C#" %>
<script runat="server">
   void cblGenre_Init(Object Source, EventArgs E)
   {
      // create an array of items to add
      string[] Genre = {"SciFi","Novels", "Computers", "History", "Religion"};

      int i;
      for (i = 0; i < Genre.GetLength(0); i++)
      {
         this.cblGenre.Items.Add(new ListItem(Genre[i]));
      }
   }
</script>

<html>
   <body>
   <form runat="server">

      <h1>ASP Controls</h1>
      <h2>CheckBoxList</h2>
      <h3>Adding Items From An Array</h3>

      <asp:checkBoxList
         id="cblGenre"
         autoPostBack="true"
         cellPadding="5"
         cellSpacing="10"
```

```
            repeatColumns="3"
            repeatDirection="vertical"
            RepeatLayout="table"
            textAlign="right"
            onInit="cblGenre_Init"
            runat="server">

            <asp:listItem> Item 1 </asp:listItem>
            <asp:listItem> Item 2 </asp:listItem>
            <asp:listItem> Item 3 </asp:listItem>
            <asp:listItem> Item 4 </asp:listItem>
            <asp:listItem> Item 5 </asp:listItem>
            <asp:listItem> Item 6 </asp:listItem>
        </asp:checkBoxList>
    </form>
    </body>
</html>
```

Example 5-16. Adding items from an array in VB.NET, vbASPCheckBoxListArray.aspx

```
<%@ Page Language="VB" %>
<script runat="server">
    Sub cblGenre_Init(ByVal Sender as Object, _
                      ByVal e as EventArgs)
        ' create an array of items to add
        dim Genre() as string = {"SciFi", "Novels", "Computers", "History", "Religion"}

        dim i as integer
        For i = 0 To Genre.GetLength(0) - 1
            cblGenre.Items.Add(new ListItem(Genre(i)))
        Next
    End Sub
</script>

<html>
    <body>
    <form runat="server">

        <h1>ASP Controls</h1>
        <h2>CheckBoxList</h2>
        <h3>Adding Items From An Array</h3>

        <asp:checkBoxList
            id="cblGenre"
            autoPostBack="true"
            cellPadding="5"
            cellSpacing="10"
            repeatColumns="3"
            repeatDirection="vertical"
            RepeatLayout="table"
```

```
            textAlign="right"
            onInit="cblGenre_Init"
            runat="server">

            <asp:listItem> Item 1 </asp:listItem>
            <asp:listItem> Item 2 </asp:listItem>
            <asp:listItem> Item 3 </asp:listItem>
            <asp:listItem> Item 4 </asp:listItem>
            <asp:listItem> Item 5 </asp:listItem>
            <asp:listItem> Item 6 </asp:listItem>
        </asp:checkBoxList>
    </form>
    </body>
</html>
```

You add an attribute to the control tag that implements an event handler for control initialization:

```
    onInit="cblGenre_Init"
```

Then you add the cblGenre_Init method, called by onInit, to the script block at the beginning of the page. This method creates a string array of genres to add to the list of checkboxes. Then a for loop is used to iterate through the array, calling the Add method on each item to add a new ListItem object to the CheckBoxList control.

Notice the slight difference in the logic used in the for loops between the C# code and the VB.NET code. This is because the C# loop repeats while the second parameter is true, while the VB.NET loop repeats until the end value is exceeded. Therefore, in the VB.NET loop you have to subtract 1 from the end value.

When you run the web pages in Example 5-15 or Example 5-16, you get the results shown in Figure 5-9.

You can modify the code in Example 5-15 and Example 5-16 to add Value properties for some of the ListItems created in the CheckBoxList tag, as well as in all the ListItem objects created in the cblGenre_Init event procedure. Example 5-17 shows the code to do so in C#, and Example 5-18 shows the same code in VB.NET. Code lines that have been added or modified are shown in boldface.

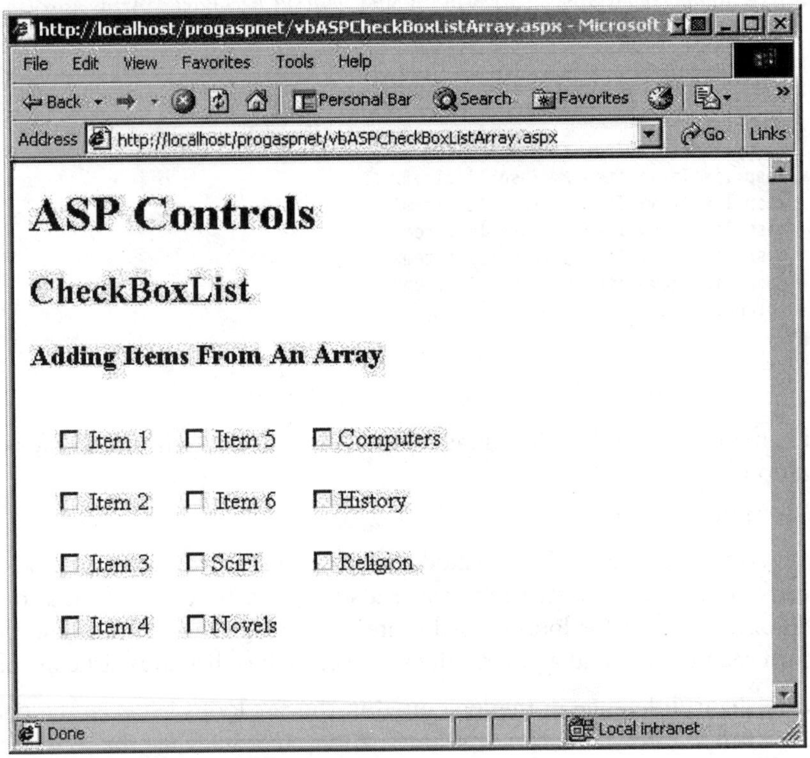

Figure 5-9. CheckBoxList with items added from array

Example 5-17. Adding items with values to CheckBoxList from array using C#,
csASPCheckBoxListArrayValue.aspx

```csharp
<%@ Page Language="C#" %>
<script runat="server">
   void cblGenre_Init(Object Source, EventArgs E)
   {
      // create arrays of items to add
      string[] Genre = {"SciFi","Novels", "Computers", "History", "Religion"};
      string[] Code = {"sf","nvl", "cmp", "his", "rel"};

      int i;
      for (i = 0; i < Genre.GetLength(0); i++)
      {
         //  Add both Text and Value
         this.cblGenre.Items.Add(new ListItem(Genre[i],Code[i]));
      }
   }
</script>

<html>
   <body>
```

Example 5-17. Adding items with values to CheckBoxList from array using C#,
csASPCheckBoxListArrayValue.aspx (continued)

```
    <form runat="server">

        <h1>ASP Controls</h1>
        <h2>CheckBoxList</h2>
        <h3>Adding Items From An Array With a Value</h3>

        <asp:checkBoxList
            id="cblGenre"
            autoPostBack="true"
            cellPadding="5"
            cellSpacing="10"
            repeatColumns="3"
            repeatDirection="vertical"
            RepeatLayout="table"
            textAlign="right"
            onInit="cblGenre_Init"
            runat="server">

            <asp:listItem value="1"> Item 1 </asp:listItem>
            <asp:listItem text="Item 2" value="2"></asp:listItem>
            <asp:listItem text="Item 3"/>
            <asp:listItem text="Item 4"> Inner Item 4 </asp:listItem>
            <asp:listItem value="5"></asp:listItem>
            <asp:listItem> Item 6 </asp:listItem>
        </asp:checkBoxList>
    </form>
    </body>
</html>
```

Example 5-18. Adding items with values to CheckBoxList from array using VB.NET,
vbASPCheckBoxListArrayValue.aspx

```
<%@ Page Language="VB" %>
<script runat="server">
    Sub cblGenre_Init(ByVal Sender as Object, _
                      ByVal e as EventArgs)
        ' create arrays of items to add
        dim Genre() as string = {"SciFi", "Novels", "Computers", "History", "Religion"}
        dim Code() as string = {"sf","nvl", "cmp", "his", "rel"}

        dim i as integer
        For i = 0 To Genre.GetLength(0) - 1
            ' Add both Text and Value
            cblGenre.Items.Add(new ListItem(Genre(i),Code(i)))
        Next
    End Sub
</script>

<html>
    <body>
    <form runat="server">
```

*Example 5-18. Adding items with values to CheckBoxList from array using VB.NET,
vbASPCheckBoxListArrayValue.aspx (continued)*

```
        <h1>ASP Controls</h1>
        <h2>CheckBoxList</h2>
        <h3>Adding Items From An Array With a Value</h3>

        <asp:checkBoxList
            id="cblGenre"
            autoPostBack="true"
            cellPadding="5"
            cellSpacing="10"
            repeatColumns="3"
            repeatDirection="vertical"
            RepeatLayout="table"
            textAlign="right"
            onInit="cblGenre_Init"
            runat="server">

            <asp:listItem value="1"> Item 1 </asp:listItem>
            <asp:listItem text="Item 2" value="2"></asp:listItem>
            <asp:listItem text="Item 3"/>
            <asp:listItem text="Item 4"> Inner Item 4 </asp:listItem>
            <asp:listItem value="5"></asp:listItem>
            <asp:listItem> Item 6 </asp:listItem>
        </asp:checkBoxList>
    </form>
    </body>
</html>
```

If the code in Example 5-17 or 5-18 is run, it will look as shown in Figure 5-10.

In cblGenre_Init, where you previously created a single string array to hold the Text
properties, there are now two string arrays: one for the Text properties, and one for
the Value properties. You now use the overloaded Add method that takes two arguments. The first argument is the Text property, and the second argument is the Value
property. In C#, this looks like:

```
    this.cblGenre.Items.Add(new ListItem(Genre[i],Code[i]));
```

while in VB.NET, it looks like:

```
    cblGenre.Items.Add(new ListItem(Genre(i),Code(i)))
```

An object may overload its methods, which means it may declare two
or more methods with the same name. The compiler differentiates
among these methods based on the number and type of parameters
provided.

For example, the ListItemCollection class overloads the Add method.
One version takes a string, and the second version takes a ListItem
object.

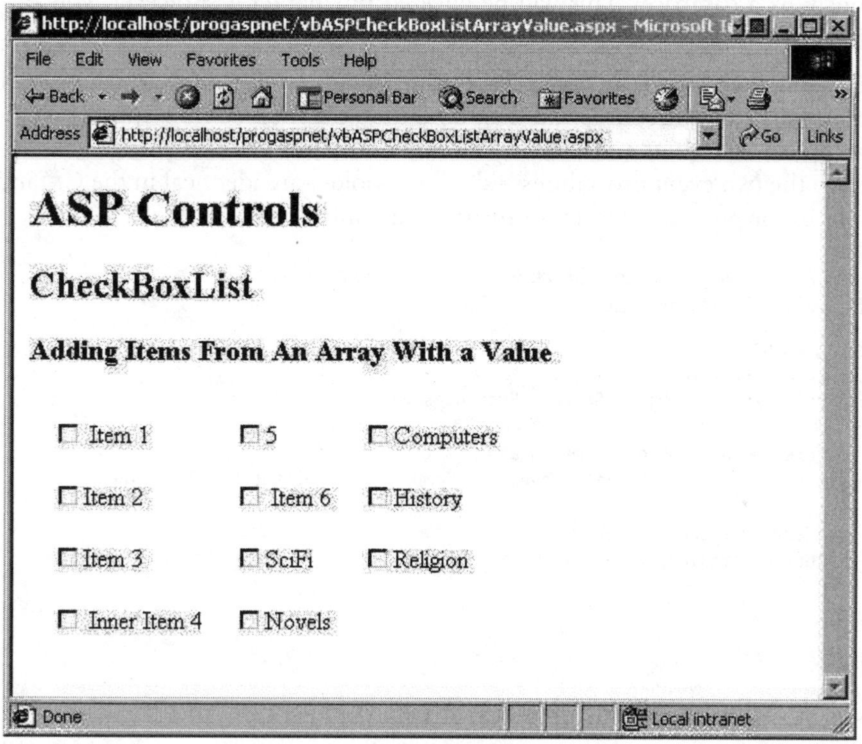

Figure 5-10. CheckBoxList with items and values added from array

In cblGenre_SelectedIndexChanged, you modified the string to include the Value property as well as the Text property. In C#, this looks like:

```
sb.Append("<br/>" + li.Value + " - " + li.Text);
```

while in VB.NET, it looks like:

```
sb.Append("<br/>" & li.Value & " - " & li.Text)
```

Finally, in creating the static ListItems, you used several different methods of creating Values and Text, including instances of missing Text (Item 5), missing Value (Item 3, Item 4, Item 6), and divergent Text property from inner HTML content (Item 4). The differences between Figure 5-9 and 5-10 can be seen in Items 4 and 5.

You can see that if the Value is missing, then the Text is displayed. If the Text is missing, then the Value is displayed. If the Text is different from the inner HTML content, then the inner HTML content is displayed.

Adding items from a data source

The real power of adding items programmatically comes when you can use a data source to populate the items in a CheckBoxList control. The ultimate data source, obviously, is a database. This will be covered in Chapter 9. However, you can use the array just created to demonstrate binding to a data source.

By replacing the for loop in cblGenre_Init in Example 5-15 and 5-16 with two lines, which specify the data source and then bind to it, the method now appears as shown in Example 5-19 for C# and 5-20 for VB. (Note that the lines of code that have been added to the two event procedures—shown in bold—are identical in the C# and VB versions of the program, except for the trailing semicolon in C#.)

Example 5-19. Adding items to a CheckBoxList from a data source using C#,
csASPCheckBoxListDataBind.aspx

```
<%@ Page Language="C#" %>
<script runat="server">
   void cblGenre_Init(Object Source, EventArgs E)
   {
      // create an array of items to add
      string[] Genre = {"SciFi","Novels", "Computers", "History", "Religion"};

      cblGenre.DataSource = Genre;
      cblGenre.DataBind( );
   }
</script>

<html>
   <body>
   <form runat="server">

      <h1>ASP Controls</h1>
      <h2>CheckBoxList</h2>
      <h3>Adding Items From An Array Using DataBinding</h3>

      <asp:checkBoxList
         id="cblGenre"
         autoPostBack="true"
         cellPadding="5"
         cellSpacing="10"
         repeatColumns="3"
         repeatDirection="vertical"
         RepeatLayout="table"
         textAlign="right"
         onInit="cblGenre_Init"
         runat="server">

         <asp:listItem> Item 1 </asp:listItem>
         <asp:listItem> Item 2 </asp:listItem>
         <asp:listItem> Item 3 </asp:listItem>
         <asp:listItem> Item 4 </asp:listItem>
         <asp:listItem> Item 5 </asp:listItem>
         <asp:listItem> Item 6 </asp:listItem>
      </asp:checkBoxList>
```

Example 5-19. Adding items to a CheckBoxList from a data source using C#,
csASPCheckBoxListDataBind.aspx (continued)

```
    </form>
    </body>
</html>
```

Example 5-20. Adding items to a CheckBoxList from a data source using VB.NET,
vbASPCheckBoxListDataBind.aspx

```
<%@ Page Language="VB" %>
<script runat="server">
    Sub cblGenre_Init(ByVal Sender as Object, _
                      ByVal e as EventArgs)
        '   create an array of items to add
        dim Genre() as string = {"SciFi", "Novels", "Computers", "History", "Religion"}

        cblGenre.DataSource = Genre
        cblGenre.DataBind( )
    End Sub
</script>

<html>
    <body>
    <form runat="server">

        <h1>ASP Controls</h1>
        <h2>CheckBoxList</h2>
        <h3>Adding Items From An Array Using DataBinding</h3>

        <asp:checkBoxList
            id="cblGenre"
            autoPostBack="true"
            cellPadding="5"
            cellSpacing="10"
            repeatColumns="3"
            repeatDirection="vertical"
            RepeatLayout="table"
            textAlign="right"
            onInit="cblGenre_Init"
            runat="server">

            <asp:listItem> Item 1 </asp:listItem>
            <asp:listItem> Item 2 </asp:listItem>
            <asp:listItem> Item 3 </asp:listItem>
            <asp:listItem> Item 4 </asp:listItem>
            <asp:listItem> Item 5 </asp:listItem>
            <asp:listItem> Item 6 </asp:listItem>
        </asp:checkBoxList>
    </form>
    </body>
</html>
```

You might expect the results to be unchanged from Figure 5-10, but that is not the case. Instead you get the results shown in Figure 5-11.

Figure 5-11. CheckBoxList with items added using DataBinding

In the previous example, using the for loop, ListItems were added by the Init method after the control was created. In this example, the pre-existing ListItem objects were replaced by the new data source. This is because the ListControl.Items collection is initialized by the data source, so any ListItem objects previously defined are lost.

Responding to user selections

When a user checks or unchecks one of the checkboxes in a CheckBoxList, the SelectedIndexChanged event is raised. This event passes an argument of type Event-Args, which does not expose any properties. By setting an attribute for handling this event and putting code in the event handler method, you can respond to the user clicking on one of the checkboxes. If AutoPostBack is set to true, the response occurs immediately. Otherwise, the response occurs the next time the form is posted to the server.

The additional code added to the previous examples, shown highlighted in Example 5-21 for C# and Example 5-22 for VB.NET, demonstrates responding to SelectedIndexChanged.

*Example 5-21. Responding to CheckBoxList User Action using C#, csASPCheckBoxListEvents.
aspx*

```
<%@ Page Language="C#" %>
<script runat="server">
    void cblGenre_Init(Object Source, EventArgs E)
    {
        // create arrays of items to add
        string[] Genre = {"SciFi","Novels", "Computers", "History", "Religion"};
        string[] Code = {"sf","nvl", "cmp", "his", "rel"};

        int i;
        for (i = 0; i < Genre.GetLength(0); i++)
        {
            //  Add both Text and Value
            this.cblGenre.Items.Add(new ListItem(Genre[i],Code[i]));
        }
    }

    void cblGenre_SelectedIndexChanged(Object Source, EventArgs E)
    {
        StringBuilder sb = new StringBuilder();
        foreach(ListItem li in cblGenre.Items)
        {
            if (li.Selected == true)
            {
                sb.Append("<br/>" + li.Value);
            }
        }

        if (sb.Length == 0)
            lblGenre.Text = "No genres selected.";
        else
            lblGenre.Text = sb.ToString();
    }
</script>

<html>
    <body>
    <form runat="server">

        <h1>ASP Controls</h1>
        <h2>CheckBoxList</h2>
        <h3>Responding to Events</h3>

        <asp:checkBoxList
            id="cblGenre"
            autoPostBack="true"
            cellPadding="5"
            cellSpacing="10"
            repeatColumns="3"
            repeatDirection="vertical"
```

Example 5-21. Responding to CheckBoxList User Action using C#, csASPCheckBoxListEvents.aspx (continued)

```
            RepeatLayout="table"
            textAlign="right"
            onInit="cblGenre_Init"
            onSelectedIndexChanged="cblGenre_SelectedIndexChanged"
            runat="server">

            <asp:listItem value="1"> Item 1 </asp:listItem>
            <asp:listItem text="Item 2" value="2"></asp:listItem>
            <asp:listItem text="Item 3"/>
            <asp:listItem text="Item 4"> Inner Item 4 </asp:listItem>
            <asp:listItem value="5"></asp:listItem>
            <asp:listItem> Item 6 </asp:listItem>
        </asp:checkBoxList>
        <asp:label id="lblGenre" runat="server" />
    </form>
    </body>
</html>
```

Example 5-22. Responding to CheckBoxList User Action using VB.NET-vbASPCheckBoxListEvents.aspx

```
<%@ Page Language="VB" %>
<script runat="server">
   Sub cblGenre_Init(ByVal Sender as Object, _
                     ByVal e as EventArgs)
      '  create arrays of items to add
      dim Genre() as string = {"SciFi", "Novels", "Computers", "History", "Religion"}
      dim Code() as string = {"sf","nvl", "cmp", "his", "rel"}

      dim i as integer
      For i = 0 To Genre.GetLength(0) - 1
         '  Add both Text and Value
         cblGenre.Items.Add(new ListItem(Genre(i),Code(i)))
      Next
   End Sub

   Sub cblGenre_SelectedIndexChanged(ByVal Sender as Object, _
                                     ByVal e as EventArgs)
     dim sb as new StringBuilder()
     dim li as ListItem
      for each li in cblGenre.Items
         if li.Selected then
            sb.Append("<br/>" & li.Value)
        end if
      next li

      if sb.Length = 0 then
         lblGenre.Text = "No genres selected."
```

```
      else
          lblGenre.Text = sb.ToString( )
      end if
   End Sub
</script>

<html>
   <body>
   <form runat="server">

      <h1>ASP Controls</h1>
      <h2>CheckBoxList</h2>
      <h3>Adding Items From An Array With a Value</h3>

      <asp:checkBoxList
          id="cblGenre"
          autoPostBack="true"
          cellPadding="5"
          cellSpacing="10"
          repeatColumns="3"
          repeatDirection="vertical"
          RepeatLayout="table"
          textAlign="right"
          onInit="cblGenre_Init"
          onSelectedIndexChanged="cblGenre_SelectedIndexChanged"
          runat="server">

          <asp:listItem value="1"> Item 1 </asp:listItem>
          <asp:listItem text="Item 2" value="2"></asp:listItem>
          <asp:listItem text="Item 3"/>
          <asp:listItem text="Item 4"> Inner Item 4 </asp:listItem>
          <asp:listItem value="5"></asp:listItem>
          <asp:listItem> Item 6 </asp:listItem>
      </asp:checkBoxList>
      <asp:label id="lblGenre" runat="server" />
   </form>
   </body>
</html>
```

Notice how the StringBuilder class is used in the method cblGenre_
SelectedIndexChanged to create the string, rather than just concate-
nating each string value onto the previous value, as in this line of (C#)
code:

```
str += "<br/>" + li.Text;
```

The StringBuilder class provides a much more efficient way of constructing strings, since it does not require that a new string be implicitly created with every change to the string.

In the code in Example 5-21 and Example 5-22, you add an attribute named OnSelectedIndexChanged to identify the event handler for the SelectedIndexChanged event. Like all event handlers, the name comes from prepending the word "On" to the event name. You also add a Label control to the form, lblGenre, to display the selected items.

The event handler points to a method in the script block at the top of the page called cblGenre_SelectedIndexChanged. In this event handler, you iterate through the collection of ListItems in the CheckBoxList. For each ListItem, you check to see if the Selected property is true. If it is, then you add the Value property of that item to the HTML string you are constructing, using the StringBuilder class. Finally, the length of the StringBuilder string is tested. If it is zero length, then an appropriate message is displayed, otherwise the StringBuilder string containing the selected values is displayed.

The results of Example 5-21 and Example 5-22 are shown in Figure 5-12, where several items have been selected.

RadioButtonList Control

The RadioButtonList control is very similar to the CheckBoxList control. They are both derived from the ListControl class and share all of the same properties, events, and methods. The only difference between the two is that the RadioButtonList control can have only one item selected at a time. When an item is selected, any other selected item is deselected.

The RadioButtonList and the CheckBoxList controls share the two properties inherited from ListControl that are shown in Table 5-8.

Table 5-8. Selection properties inherited from the ListControl class

Name	Type	Get	Set	Description
SelectedIndex	Integer	x	x	If equal to -1, then nothing has been selected.
SelectedItem	ListItem	x		

To demonstrate how these are used, modify the code in Example 5-12 and Example 5-13, replacing the three radio buttons controlling the font size in grpSize with a single RadioButtonList, calling it rblSize. Example 5-23 shows the resulting C# ASP.NET page, while Example 5-24 shows the ASP.NET page with VB.NET code.

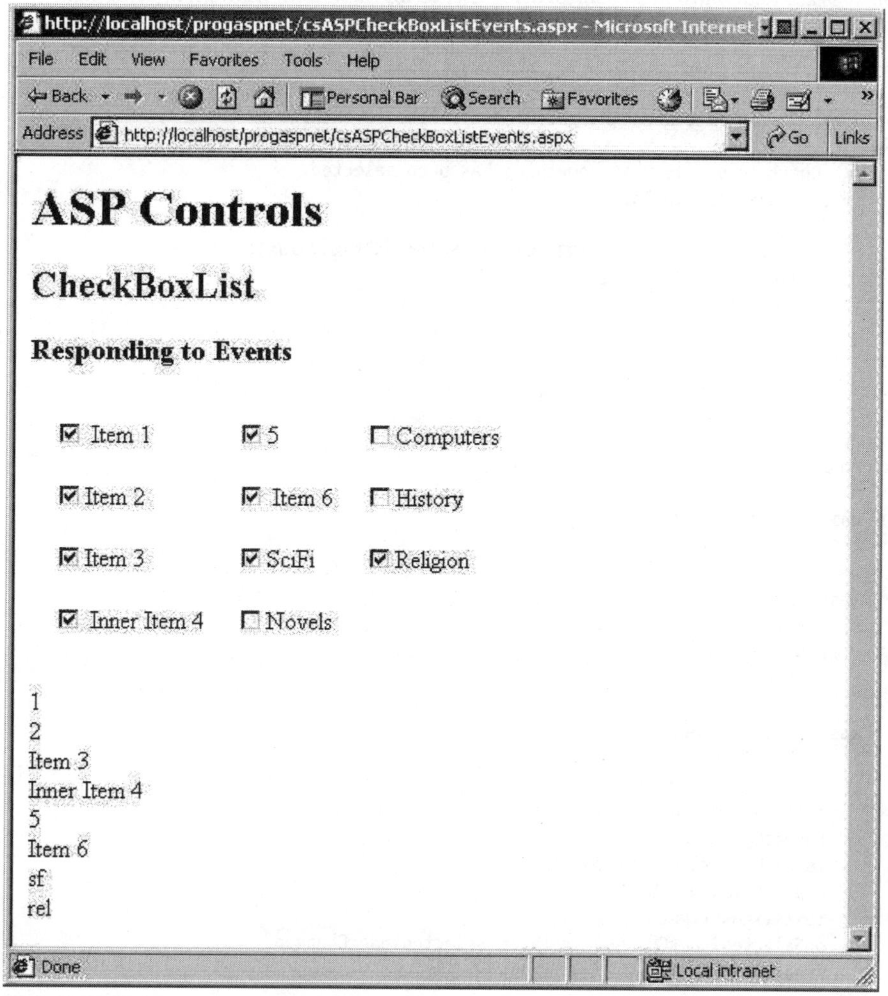

Figure 5-12. Responding to CheckBoxList user selections

Example 5-23. RadioButtonList control using C#, csASPRadioButtonList.aspx

```
<%@ Page Language="C#" %>

<script runat="server">
   void lblTime_Init(Object Source, EventArgs E)
   {
      lblTime.Font.Name = "Verdana";
      lblTime.Font.Size = 20;
      lblTime.Font.Bold = true;
      lblTime.Font.Italic = true;
```

```
        lblTime.Text = DateTime.Now.ToString( );
    }

    void rblSize_SelectedIndexChanged(Object Source, EventArgs E)
    {
        //  Check to verify that something has been selected.
        if (rblSize.SelectedIndex != -1)
        {
            int size = Convert.ToInt32(rblSize.SelectedItem.Value);
            lblTime.Font.Size = size;
        }
    }
</script>

<html>
    <body>
    <form runat="server">

        <h1>ASP Controls</h1>
        <h2>RadioButtonList</h2>

        <asp:label
            id="lblTime"
            runat="server"
            onInit="lblTime_Init"/>

        <asp:radioButtonList
            id="rblSize"
            autoPostBack="true"
            cellSpacing="20"
            repeatColumns="3"
            repeatDirection="horizontal"
            RepeatLayout="table"
            textAlign="right"
            onSelectedIndexChanged="rblSize_SelectedIndexChanged"
            runat="server">

            <asp:listItem text="10pt" value="10"/>
            <asp:listItem text="14pt" value="14"/>
            <asp:listItem text="16pt" value="16"/>
        </asp:radioButtonList>
    </form>
    </body>
</html>
```

Example 5-24. RadioButtonList control using VB.NET, vbASPRadioButtonList.aspx

```
<%@ Page Language="VB" %>

<script runat="server">
    Sub lblTime_Init(ByVal Sender as Object, _
                     ByVal e as EventArgs)
```

```
        lblTime.Font.Name = "Verdana"
        lblTime.Font.Size = new FontUnit(20)
        lblTime.Font.Bold = true
        lblTime.Font.Italic = true
        lblTime.Text = DateTime.Now( )
    End Sub

    Sub rblSize_SelectedIndexChanged(ByVal Sender as Object, _
                            ByVal e as EventArgs)
        '  Check to verify that something has been selected.
        if (rblSize.SelectedIndex <> -1) then
            dim size as integer = Convert.ToInt32(rblSize.SelectedItem.Value)
            lblTime.Font.Size = new FontUnit(size)
        end if
    End Sub
</script>

<html>
    <body>
    <form runat="server">

        <h1>ASP Controls</h1>
        <h2>RadioButtonList</h2>

        <asp:label
            id="lblTime"
            runat="server"
            onInit="lblTime_Init"/>

        <asp:radioButtonList
            id="rblSize"
            autoPostBack="true"
            cellSpacing="20"
            repeatColumns="3"
            repeatDirection="horizontal"
            RepeatLayout="table"
            textAlign="right"
            onSelectedIndexChanged="rblSize_SelectedIndexChanged"
            runat="server">

            <asp:listItem text="10pt" value="10"/>
            <asp:listItem text="14pt" value="14"/>
            <asp:listItem text="16pt" value="16"/>
        </asp:radioButtonList>
    </form>
    </body>
</html>
```

The results of Example 5-23 or Example 5-24 are shown in Figure 5-13. It doesn't look much different than the individual radio buttons, but it is much easier to populate from a data source.

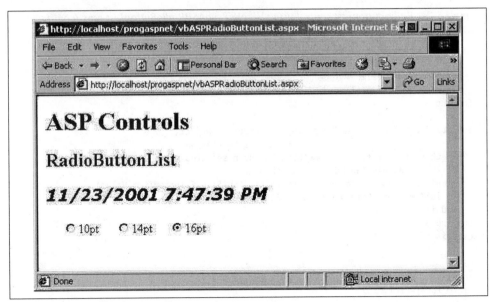

Figure 5-13. Using the RadioButtonList control

In Example 5-23 and Example 5-24, the original separate radio buttons are replaced by a RadioButtonList control. Note that each ListItem object has both a Text property and a Value property. The event handler, rblSize_SelectedIndexChanged, takes an integer value for the Font.Size property in the C# code:

```
int size = Convert.ToInt32(rblSize.SelectedItem.Value);
lblTime.Font.Size = size;
```

but requires a FontUnit type in VB.NET:

```
dim size as integer = Convert.ToInt32(rblSize.SelectedItem.Value)
lblTime.Font.Size = new FontUnit(size)
```

As described previously, in conjunction with Table 5-1, this is because C# supports automatic boxing of value types into reference types, but VB.NET does not.

The event handler method makes use of the SelectedIndex and SelectedItem properties mentioned previously. The SelectedIndex property represents the lowest integer value index of all the selected items. The SelectedItem property returns the Text property of the item pointed to by SelectedIndex. Since a RadioButtonList, by definition, can have at most a single selected item, then SelectedIndex and SelectedItem will tell us which item is selected. These properties of a CheckBoxList control or other ListControl control (which allow multi-selection) are more ambiguous.

Example 5-23 and Example 5-24 verify that at least one of the values has been selected. If no item has been selected, then the SelectedIndex property is equal to -1. If an item has been selected, you set the Font.Size property by converting the

SelectedItem.Value property to an integer in C# and by passing the SelectedItem. Value as an argument to the FontUnit class constructor in VB.

(Note that the following two lines of C# code in Example 5-23:

```
int size = Convert.ToInt32(rblSize.SelectedItem.Value);
lblTime.Font.Size = size;
```

could just as easily have been written as a single line:

```
lblTime.Font.Size = Convert.ToInt32(rblSize.SelectedItem.Value);
```

However, I often use the more verbose version in order to enhance readability and make the code easier to debug.)

DropDownList Control

DropDownList controls display a single item at a time with a button for dropping the list to display more selections. Only a single item can be selected. The code in Example 5-25 demonstrates a DropDownList control in C#, while the code in Example 5-26 shows the same in VB.NET. A two-dimensional string array is used to hold both the Text and Value properties. The array is then used to add the ListItem objects.

Example 5-25. DropDownList control using C#, csASPDropDownList.aspx

```
<%@ Page Language="C#"  %>
<script runat="server">
   void Page_Load(Object sender, EventArgs e)
   {
      if (! IsPostBack)
      {
         // Build 2 dimensional array for the lists
         // First dimension contains bookname
         // 2nd dimension contains ISBN number
         string[,] books = {
               {"Programming C#","0596001177"},
               {"Programming ASP.NET","0596001711"},
               {"WebClasses From Scratch","0789721260"},
               {"Teach Yourself C++ in 21 Days","067232072X"},
               {"Teach Yourself C++ in 10 Minutes","067231603X"},
               {"XML & Java From Scratch","0789724766"},
               {"Complete Idiot's Guide to a Career in Computer Programming", _
                     "0789719959"},
               {"XML Web Documents From Scratch","0789723166"},
               {"Clouds To Code","1861000952"},
               {"C++: An Introduction to Programming","1575760614"},
               {"C++ Unleashed","0672312395"}
            };

         // Now populate the list.
         int i;
         for (i = 0; i < books.GetLength(0); i++)
```

Example 5-25. DropDownList control using C#, csASPDropDownList.aspx (continued)

```csharp
            {
                //  Add both Text and Value
                ddl.Items.Add(new ListItem(books[i,0],books[i,1]));
            }
        }
    }

    void ddl_SelectedIndexChanged(Object Source, EventArgs E)
    {
        //  Check to verify that something has been selected.
        if (ddl.SelectedIndex != -1)
        {
            lblDdl.Text=ddl.SelectedItem.Text + " ---> ISBN: " +
                ddl.SelectedItem.Value;
        }
    }
</script>

<html>
    <body>
    <form runat="server">

        <h1>ASP Controls</h1>
        <h2>DropDownList</h2>

        <asp:dropDownList
            id="ddl"
            autoPostBack="true"
            onSelectedIndexChanged="ddl_SelectedIndexChanged"
            runat="server"/>

        <br/>
        <asp:label id="lblDdl" runat="server" />
    </form>
    </body>
</html>
```

Example 5-26. DropDownList control using VB.NET, vbASPDropDownList.aspx

```vbnet
<%@ Page Language="VB"  %>
<script runat="server">

    Sub Page_Load(ByVal Sender as Object, _
                ByVal e as EventArgs)
        if not IsPostBack then
            '  Build 2 dimensional array for the lists
            '  First dimension contains bookname
            '  2nd dimension contains ISBN number
            dim books(,) as string = { _
                {"Programming C#","0596001177"}, _
                {"Programming ASP.NET","1234567890"}, _
                {"WebClasses From Scratch","0789721260"}, _
```

```
                {"Teach Yourself C++ in 21 Days","067232072X"}, _
                {"Teach Yourself C++ in 10 Minutes","067231603X"}, _
                {"XML & Java From Scratch","0789724766"}, _
                {"Complete Idiot's Guide to a Career in Computer Programming",
                     "0789719959"}, _
                {"XML Web Documents From Scratch","0789723166"}, _
                {"Clouds To Code","1861000952"}, _
                {"C++: An Introduction to Programming","1575760614"}, _
                {"C++ Unleashed","0672312395"} _
            }

        '  Now populate the list.
        dim i as integer

        for i = 0 to books.GetLength(0) - 1
            '  Add both Text and Value
            ddl.Items.Add(new ListItem(books(i,0),books(i,1)))
        next
      end if
   End Sub


   Sub ddl_SelectedIndexChanged(ByVal Sender as Object, _
                            ByVal e as EventArgs)
      '  Check to verify that something has been selected.
      if ddl.SelectedIndex <> -1 then
         lblDdl.Text=ddl.SelectedItem.Text & " ---> ISBN: " & _
            ddl.SelectedItem.Value
      end if
   End Sub
</script>

<html>
   <body>
   <form runat="server">

      <h1>ASP Controls</h1>
      <h2>DropDownList</h2>

      <asp:dropDownList
         id="ddl"
         autoPostBack="true"
         onSelectedIndexChanged="ddl_SelectedIndexChanged"
         runat="server"/>

      <br/>
      <asp:label id="lblDdl" runat="server" />
   </form>
   </body>
</html>
```

The results of Example 5-25 or Example 5-26 are shown in Figure 5-14.

In Example 5-25 and Example 5-26, a DropDownList with the id of ddl is added. This control is populated when the page is first loaded, in the Page_Load event handler method.

In order to prevent this code running every time the page is reloaded, you test to see if the IsPostBack property is true. The IsPostBack property is false when the page is first loaded, but is set to true whenever the form is posted back to the server as a result of user action on one of the controls. In many applications, the contents of controls are filled from a database, which is a relatively expensive operation. Only hitting the database when necessary makes the implementation more efficient. In Example 5-17 and Example 5-26, you used two arrays to populate a CheckBoxList with both the Text and Value properties. In Example 5-25 and Example 5-26, you use a single two-dimensional array to accomplish the same thing. As before, you call the Items.Add method to add the ListItems to the control. In Chapter 9, you will see how to populate a ListControl from a database.

As with the other ListControls, the OnSelectedIndexChanged attribute points to the event handler method, ddl_SelectedIndexChanged. In that method, just as with the RadioButtonList control, you first check to see if something is selected by testing if the SelectedIndex property is not equal to -1. If an item has been selected, you display a concatenation of SelectedItem.Text and SelectedItem.Value in the label called lblDdl.

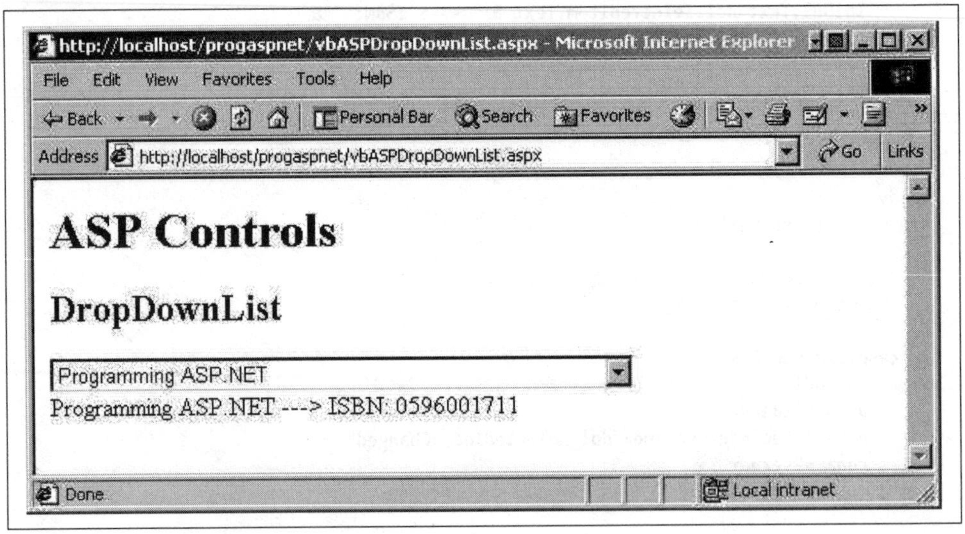

Figure 5-14. DropDownList control

ListBox Control

ListBox controls are very similar to DropDownList controls. Example 5-27 and Example 5-28 demonstrate two different ListBoxes—one using single selection, and one allowing multiple selection. As you will see, they are almost identical in implementation, with the only significant difference being the method used to identify the selected item(s).

The code in Example 5-27 and Example 5-28 for implementing ListBox controls is nearly identical to that in Example 5-25 and Example 5-26 for implementing DropDownLists. The differences, highlighted in Example 5-27 and Example 5-28, include the addition of the two DropDownList controls, modification to the Page_Load method to populate those controls, and the addition of event handlers for those two controls.

Example 5-27. ListBox control using C#, csASPListBox.aspx

```
<%@ Page Language="C#"  %>
<script runat="server">
   void Page_Load(Object sender, EventArgs e)
   {
      if (! IsPostBack)
      {
         //  Build 2 dimensional array for the lists
         //  First dimension contains bookname
         //  2nd dimension contains ISBN number
         string[,] books = {
               {"Programming C#","0596001177"},
               {"Programming ASP.NET","0596001711"},
               {"WebClasses From Scratch","0789721260"},
               {"Teach Yourself C++ in 21 Days","067232072X"},
               {"Teach Yourself C++ in 10 Minutes","067231603X"},
               {"XML & Java From Scratch","0789724766"},
               {"Complete Idiot's Guide to a Career in Computer Programming", _
                     "0789719959"},
               {"XML Web Documents From Scratch","0789723166"},
               {"Clouds To Code","1861000952"},
               {"C++: An Introduction to Programming","1575760614"},
               {"C++ Unleashed","0672312395"}
         };
         //  Now populate the lists.
         int i;
         for (i = 0; i < books.GetLength(0); i++)
         {
            //  Add both Text and Value
            lbSingle.Items.Add(new ListItem(books[i,0],books[i,1]));
            lbMulti.Items.Add(new ListItem(books[i,0],books[i,1]));
         }
      }
   }

   void lbSingle_SelectedIndexChanged(Object Source, EventArgs E)
   {
      //  Check to verify that something has been selected.
      if (lbSingle.SelectedIndex != -1)
      {
```

Example 5-27. ListBox control using C#, csASPListBox.aspx (continued)

```csharp
        lblLbSingle.Text=lbSingle.SelectedItem.Text + " ---> ISBN: " +
            lbSingle.SelectedItem.Value;
    }
}

void lbMulti_SelectedIndexChanged(Object Source, EventArgs E)
{
    string str = "";
    foreach(ListItem li in lbMulti.Items)
    {
        if (li.Selected == true)
        {
            str += "<br/>" + li.Text + " ---> ISBN: " +li.Value;
        }
    }

    if (str.Length == 0)
        lblLbMulti.Text = "No books selected.";
    else
        lblLbMulti.Text = str;
}
</script>

<html>
    <body>
    <form runat="server">

        <h1>ASP Controls</h1>
        <h2>ListBox</h2>

        <h3>ListBox - single selection</h3>
        <asp:ListBox
            id="lbSingle"
            autoPostBack="true"
            rows="6"
            selectionMode="single"
            onSelectedIndexChanged="lbSingle_SelectedIndexChanged"
            runat="server"/>

        <br/>
        <asp:label id="lblLbSingle" runat="server" />
        <br/>

        <h3>ListBox - multiple selection</h3>
        <asp:ListBox
            id="lbMulti"
            autoPostBack="true"
            selectionMode="multiple"
            onSelectedIndexChanged="lbMulti_SelectedIndexChanged"
            runat="server"/>

        <asp:label id="lblLbMulti" runat="server" />
```

Example 5-27. ListBox control using C#, csASPListBox.aspx (continued)

```
    </form>
    </body>
</html>
```

Example 5-28. ListBox control using VB.NET, vbASPListBox.aspx

```vb
<%@ Page Language="VB"  %>
<script runat="server">
   Sub Page_Load(ByVal Sender as Object, _
                 ByVal e as EventArgs)
      if not IsPostBack then
         '   Build 2 dimensional array for the lists
         '   First dimension contains bookname
         '   2nd dimension contains ISBN number
         dim books(,) as string = { _
               {"Programming C#","0596001177"}, _
               {"Programming ASP.NET","1234567890"}, _
               {"WebClasses From Scratch","0789721260"}, _
               {"Teach Yourself C++ in 21 Days","067232072X"}, _
               {"Teach Yourself C++ in 10 Minutes","067231603X"}, _
               {"XML & Java From Scratch","0789724766"}, _
               {"Complete Idiot's Guide to a Career in Computer Programming", _
                    "0789719959"}, _
               {"XML Web Documents From Scratch","0789723166"}, _
               {"Clouds To Code","1861000952"}, _
               {"C++: An Introduction to Programming","1575760614"}, _
               {"C++ Unleashed","0672312395"} _
            }
         '   Now populate the lists.
         dim i as integer

         for i = 0 to books.GetLength(0) - 1
            '   Add both Text and Value
            lbSingle.Items.Add(new ListItem(books(i,0),books(i,1)))
            lbMulti.Items.Add(new ListItem(books(i,0),books(i,1)))
         next
      end if
   End Sub

   Sub lbSingle_SelectedIndexChanged(ByVal Sender as Object, _
                                     ByVal e as EventArgs)
      '  Check to verify that something has been selected.
      if lbSingle.SelectedIndex <> -1 then
         lblLbSingle.Text=lbSingle.SelectedItem.Text & " ---> ISBN: " & _
            lbSingle.SelectedItem.Value
      end if
   End Sub

   Sub lbMulti_SelectedIndexChanged(ByVal Sender as Object, _
                                    ByVal e as EventArgs)
      dim sb as new StringBuilder( )
      dim li as ListItem
```

```
      for each li in lbMulti.Items
         if li.Selected then
            sb.Append("<br/>" & li.Text & " ---> ISBN: " & li.Value)
         end if
      next li

      if sb.Length = 0 then
         lblLbMulti.Text = "No books selected."
      else
         lblLbMulti.Text = sb.ToString( )
      end if
   End Sub
</script>

<html>
   <body>
   <form runat="server">

      <h1>ASP Controls</h1>
      <h2>ListBox</h2>

      <h3>ListBox - single selection</h3>
      <asp:ListBox
         id="lbSingle"
         autoPostBack="true"
         rows="6"
         selectionMode="single"
         onSelectedIndexChanged="lbSingle_SelectedIndexChanged"
         runat="server"/>

      <br/>
      <asp:label id="lblLbSingle" runat="server" />
      <br/>

      <h3>ListBox - multiple selection</h3>
      <asp:ListBox
         id="lbMulti"
         autoPostBack="true"
         selectionMode="multiple"
         onSelectedIndexChanged="lbMulti_SelectedIndexChanged"
         runat="server"/>

      <asp:label id="lblLbMulti" runat="server" />
   </form>
   </body>
</html>
```

ListBox controls have two properties in addition to those inherited from List-Control. These properties are shown in Table 5-9.

Table 5-9. Properties of ListBox controls not inherited from the ListControl control

Name	Type	Get	Set	Values	Description
SelectionMode	ListSelectionMode	x	x	Single, Multiple	Determines if a ListBox is in single selection mode or multiple selection mode. Default is Single.
Rows	Integer	x	x		Number of rows displayed. Default is 4.

The first ListBox added in Example 5-27 and Example 5-28, with an id of lbSingle, is a single selection list box. The Rows property has been set to 6, and 6 items are displayed. Since the control has been populated with more than 6 items, a vertical scrollbar automatically appears. If a second item is selected, the first item is deselected. As with most of the examples in this chapter, AutoPostBack has been set to true so that the effects of the change are visible immediately.

The second ListBox control, with an id of lbMultiple, is a multiple selection list box. The Rows property has not been set, so the default 4 rows are visible. Since it is multi-select, the standard Windows techniques of multi-selection can be used.

Windows Multi-Selection Techniques

Most Windows applications use the same techniques for selecting multiple items.

To add a *range of items* to the selected list, click on the first item to be selected, then hold down the Shift key while clicking on the last item to be selected. All the items between the two are highlighted for selection.

To add *non-contiguous items* to the selection, hold down the Ctrl key while clicking on items.

To deselect single items that have already been selected, hold down the Ctrl key while clicking on each item to toggle its selection status.

The event handlers for processing the selections of the two list boxes are very different. The event handler for the single selection list box is very similar to the one for the DropDownList control or any other single select ListControl, such as the RadioButtonList control.

The event handler for the multi-select list box, on the other hand, is more like that used for the CheckBoxList control. It iterates through the collection of ListItem objects, checking each to see if the Selected property is true. If it is true, then the Text and Value properties are added to the string for output to a label.

The result of running the web page in Example 5-27 or Example 5-28 is shown in Figure 5-15.

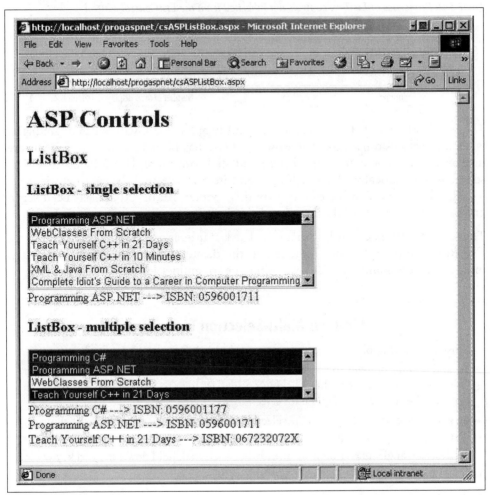

Figure 5-15. ListBox controls

Tables

Tables are very important in web page design, as they are one of the primary means of controlling the layout on the page. In pure HTML, there are several tags for creating and formatting tables, and many of those have analogs in ASP controls. If you don't need server-side capabilities, then you are just as well off using the static HTML tags. But when you need to control the table at runtime, then ASP controls are the way to go. (You could also use HTML Server controls, described earlier in this chapter, but they don't offer the consistency of implementation and object model that ASP controls offer.)

Table 5-10 summarizes the ASP controls used to create tables in web pages.

Table 5-10. ASP controls used to create tables in web pages

ASP control	HTML analog	Description
Table	`<table>`	Parent control for TableRow controls. The Rows property of the Table object is a collection of TableRow objects.
TableRow	`<tr>`	Parent control for TableCell controls. The Cells property of the TableRow object contains a collection of TableCell objects.
TableCell	`<td>`	Contains content to be displayed. The Text property contains HTML text. The Controls collection can contain other controls.
TableHeaderCell	`<th>`	Derived from the TableCell class. Controls the display of heading cell(s).

There is some overlap in the functionality of Table controls and the DataList controls, such as the Repeater, DataList, and DataGrid, covered in detail in Chapter 9. All can be used to display data in a table or list formatted layout. In fact, all of these controls render to the browser (or have the option to render) as HTML tables. (You can verify this by going to your browser and viewing the source of the page displayed.) Table 5-11 summarizes the differences between these four controls.

Table 5-11. Differences between the Table control and DataList controls

Control	Usage	Description
Table	General layout	• Can contain any combination of text, HTML, and other controls, including other tables. • Uses TableCell rather than templates to control appearance. • Not data bound, but can contain data bound controls.
Repeater	Read-only data	• Read-only. • Uses templates for the look. • Data bound. • No paging.
DataList	List output with editing	• Default layout is a table. • Can be extensively customized using templates and styles. • Editable. • Data bound. • No paging.
DataGrid	List output with editing	• Default look is a grid (i.e., a customizable table). • Must use templates. • Editable. • Data bound. • Supports paging and sorting.

Example 5-29 demonstrates most of the basic table functionality using C#. Example 5-30 does the same in VB.NET. In these examples, you will use a CheckBoxList control and a RadioButtonList control to set attributes of the font samples displayed in the table. Then a table that contains a sample of every font installed on your system is created. The finished product is shown in Figure 5-16.

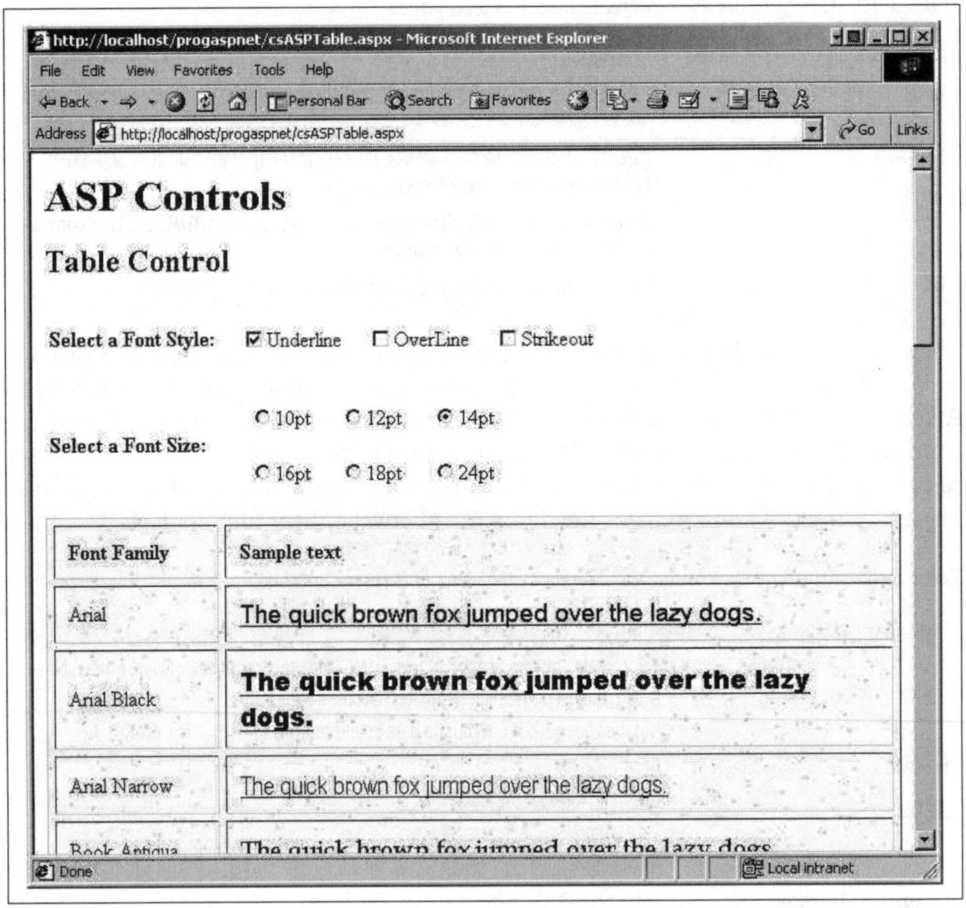

Figure 5-16. Table control

Example 5-29. Table control using C#, csAspTable.aspx

```
<%@ Page Language="C#" %>
<%@import namespace="System.Drawing" %>
<%@import namespace="System.Drawing.Text" %>

<script runat="server">
   void Page_Load(Object Source, EventArgs E)
   {
      string str = "The quick brown fox jumped over the lazy dogs.";
      int i = 0;

      //  Get the style checkboxes.
      bool boolUnder = false;
      bool boolOver = false;
      bool boolStrike = false;

      foreach(ListItem li in cblFontStyle.Items)
```

Example 5-29. Table control using C#, csAspTable.aspx (continued)

```
    {
        if (li.Selected == true)
        {
            switch (li.Value)
            {
                case "u":
                    boolUnder = true;
                    break;
                case "o":
                    boolOver = true;
                    break;
                case "s":
                    boolStrike = true;
                    break;
            }
        }
    }

    //  Get the font size.
    int size = Convert.ToInt32(rblSize.SelectedItem.Value);

    //  Get a list of all the fonts installed on the system
    //  Populate the table with the fonts and sample text.
    InstalledFontCollection ifc = new InstalledFontCollection( );
    foreach( FontFamily ff in ifc.Families )
    {
        TableRow r = new TableRow( );

        TableCell cFont = new TableCell( );
        cFont.Controls.Add(new LiteralControl(ff.Name));
        r.Cells.Add(cFont);

        TableCell cText = new TableCell( );
        Label lbl = new Label( );
        lbl.Text = str;

        //  ID not necessary here. This just to show it can be set.
        i++;
        lbl.ID = "lbl" + i.ToString( );

        //  Set the font name
        lbl.Font.Name = ff.Name;

        //  Set the font style
        if (boolUnder)
            lbl.Font.Underline = true;
        if (boolOver)
            lbl.Font.Overline = true;
        if (boolStrike)
            lbl.Font.Strikeout = true;

        //  Set the font size.
```

Example 5-29. Table control using C#, csAspTable.aspx (continued)

```
        lbl.Font.Size = size;

        cText.Controls.Add(lbl);
        r.Cells.Add(cText);

        tbl.Rows.Add(r);
    }
}

void cblFontStyle_Init(Object Source, EventArgs E)
{
    // create arrays of items to add
    string[] FontStyle = {"Underline","OverLine", "Strikeout"};
    string[] Code = {"u","o","s"};

    int i;
    for (i = 0; i < FontStyle.GetLength(0); i++)
    {
        //  Add both Text and Value
        this.cblFontStyle.Items.Add(new ListItem(FontStyle[i],Code[i]));
    }
}
}
</script>

<html>
    <body>
    <form runat="server">

        <h1>ASP Controls</h1>
        <h2>Table Control</h2>

        <table>
            <tr>
                <td>
                    <strong>Select a Font Style:</strong>
                </td>
                <td>
                    <asp:checkBoxList
                        id="cblFontStyle"
                        autoPostBack="true"
                        cellPadding="5"
                        cellSpacing="10"
                        repeatColumns="3"
                        textAlign="right"
                        onInit="cblFontStyle_Init"
                        runat="server">
                    </asp:checkBoxList>
                </td>
            </tr>
            <tr>
                <td>
                    <strong>Select a Font Size:</strong>
```

Example 5-29. Table control using C#, csAspTable.aspx (continued)

```
                </td>
                <td>
                    <asp:radioButtonList
                        id="rblSize"
                        autoPostBack="true"
                        cellSpacing="20"
                        repeatColumns="3"
                        textAlign="right"
                        repeatDirection="Horizontal"
                        runat="server">
                        <asp:listItem text="10pt" value="10"/>
                        <asp:listItem text="12pt" value="12" selected = "true"/>
                        <asp:listItem text="14pt" value="14"/>
                        <asp:listItem text="16pt" value="16"/>
                        <asp:listItem text="18pt" value="18"/>
                        <asp:listItem text="24pt" value="24"/>
                    </asp:radioButtonList>
                </td>
            </tr>
        </table>

        <asp:table
            id="tbl"
            backImageURL="Sunflower Bkgrd.jpg"
            font-Name="Times New Roman"
            Font-Size="12"
            GridLines="Both"
            CellPadding="10"
            CellSpacing="5"
            HorizontalAlign="Left"
            Width="100%"
            runat="server">

            <asp:TableRow
                horizontalAlign="Left">
                <asp:TableHeaderCell>
                    Font Family
                </asp:TableHeaderCell>
                <asp:TableHeaderCell  Width="80%">
                    Sample text
                </asp:TableHeaderCell>
            </asp:TableRow>
        </asp:table>
    </form>
    </body>
</html>
```

In Example 5-30, you can see the event handler methods in VB.NET. I have not included the HTML, since it is identical with that in Example 5-29.

Example 5-30. Event handlers for Table control using VB.NET, vbAspTable.aspx

```vb
<%@ Page Language="VB" %>
<%@import namespace="System.Drawing" %>
<%@import namespace="System.Drawing.Text" %>

<script runat="server">
   sub Page_Load(ByVal Sender as Object, _
                 ByVal e as EventArgs)
      dim str as string = "The quick brown fox jumped over the lazy dogs."
      dim i as integer = 0

      ' Get the style checkboxes.
      dim boolUnder as Boolean = false
      dim boolOver as Boolean = false
      dim boolStrike as Boolean = false

      dim li as ListItem
      for each li in cblFontStyle.Items
         if li.Selected then
            select case li.Value
               case "u"
                  boolUnder = true
               case "o":
                  boolOver = true
               case "s":
                  boolStrike = true
            end select
         end if
      next li

      ' Get the font size.
      dim size as integer = Convert.ToInt32(rblSize.SelectedItem.Value)

      ' Get a list of all the fonts installed on the system
      ' Populate the table with the fonts and sample text.
      dim ifc as InstalledFontCollection = new InstalledFontCollection()
      dim ff as FontFamily
      for each ff in ifc.Families
         dim r as TableRow = new TableRow()
         dim cFont as TableCell = new TableCell()
         cFont.Controls.Add(new LiteralControl(ff.Name))
         r.Cells.Add(cFont)

         dim cText as TableCell = new TableCell()
         dim lbl as Label = new Label()
         lbl.Text = str

         ' ID not necessary here. This just to show how it can be set.
         i = i + 1
         lbl.ID = "lbl" & i.ToString()

         ' Set the font name
         lbl.Font.Name = ff.Name
```

```
         '  Set the font style
         if boolUnder then
            lbl.Font.Underline = true
         end if
         if boolOver then
            lbl.Font.Overline = true
         end if
         if boolStrike then
            lbl.Font.Strikeout = true
         end if

         '  Set the font size.
         lbl.Font.Size = new FontUnit(size)

         cText.Controls.Add(lbl)
         r.Cells.Add(cText)

         tbl.Rows.Add(r)
      next ff
   end sub

   sub cblFontStyle_Init(ByVal Sender as Object, _
                     ByVal e as EventArgs)
      ' create arrays of items to add
      dim FontStyle() as string = {"Underline","OverLine", "Strikeout"}
      dim Code() as string= {"u","o","s"}

      dim i as integer
      for i = 0 to FontStyle.GetLength(0) -1
         '  Add both Text and Value
         cblFontStyle.Items.Add(new ListItem(FontStyle(i),Code(i)))
      next
   end sub
</script>
```

Example 5-29 and Example 5-30 begin with a few *directives:*

```
<%@ Page Language="C#" %>
<%@import namespace="System.Drawing" %>
<%@import namespace="System.Drawing.Text" %>
```

The first is a Page directive, one we have seen before—it tells the compiler that the language used is C# (or VB in the case of Example 5-30). The next two are Import directives, which import namespaces. These import directives perform the same function as the using statement in C# or the Imports statement in VB.NET. Directives are described in detail in Chapter 6.

Before delving into the script block in detail, hop down to the <body> of the page. After some opening headers, there is a standard, plain vanilla HTML table. This uses the familiar <table> tags enclosing table rows (<tr>), which enclose table cells (<td>).

Commenting Your Code

Commenting ASP.NET is particularly difficult. As an ASP.NET developer, you may be working with HTML, C#, VB.NET, JavaScript, VBScript, TransactSQL, among others. Each language has its own unique syntax for comments, and it is even possible for one language to overlap another.

Here is a summary of the different ways to comment:

HTML:

```
<!-- text to be commented goes in here  -->
```

JavaScipt:

```
// commented text follows


/* multiline
comment  */
```

C#:

```
// commented text follows


/* multiline
comment  */
```

VB.NET and VBScript:

```
' commented text follows
```

ASP controls: There is no comment within an ASP control. However, since any unrecognized attributes are ignored, some developers prepend any attributes they wish to comment out with XX.

Transact SQL:

```
-- commented text follows two dashes
```

There is nothing dynamic going on here, just the common technique of using a table to control the layout of the page.

The second cell of the first row contains an ASP CheckBoxList control, and the second cell of the second row contains an ASP RadioButtonList control, both of which have been discussed earlier in this chapter. Both of these controls have several things in common: an id attribute, the all-important runat attribute, and AutoPostBack set to true, so that any changes will take effect immediately. Both controls also have various other attributes to give the layout I wanted.

Notice that the CheckBoxList control has an event handler defined for initialization, onInit, which points to a method called cblFontStyle_Init. This method is in the script block at the top of the page. Here is the C# version:

```
void cblFontStyle_Init(Object Source, EventArgs E)
{
    string[] FontStyle = {"Underline","OverLine", "Strikeout"};
```

```
    string[] Code = {"u","o","s"};

    int i;
    for (i = 0; i < FontStyle.GetLength(0); i++)
    {
        this.cblFontStyle.Items.Add(new ListItem(FontStyle[i],Code[i]));
    }
}
```

and here is the VB.NET version:

```
sub cblFontStyle_Init(ByVal Sender as Object, _
                      ByVal e as EventArgs)
  ' create arrays of items to add
  dim FontStyle() as string = {"Underline","OverLine", "Strikeout"}
  dim Code() as string= {"u","o","s"}

  dim i as integer
  for i = 0 to FontStyle.GetLength(0) -1
    '  Add both Text and Value
    cblFontStyle.Items.Add(new ListItem(FontStyle(i),Code(i)))
  next
end sub
```

This code is very similar to Example 5-17 and Example 5-18. Here you create two string arrays, FontStyle and Code, to fill the ListItem properties Text and Value, respectively.

The RadioButtonList control, on the other hand, does not have an onInit event handler, but rather the ListItems it contains are defined right within the control itself. This example uses self-closing ListItem tags with attributes specifying both the Text property and the Value property. In the case of the 12pt radio button, the Selected property is set to true, which makes this the default value on initialization.

Notice that neither of these controls has any other event handler. Specifically, there is no event handler for OnSelectedIndexChanged, as there are in previous examples in this chapter. Yet, AutoPostBack is true. As you will see, the ASP Table control is rebuilt every time the page is loaded, which occurs every time either the CheckBox-List or the RadioButtonList control is changed. The current value for the font style is obtained from the CheckBoxList control, and the current font size is obtained from the RadioButtonList control.

The ASP Table control is the heart of this page:

```
<asp:Table
    id="tbl"
    backImageURL="Sunflower Bkgrd.jpg"
    font-Name="Times New Roman"
    Font-Size="12"
    GridLines="Both"
    CellPadding="10"
    CellSpacing="5"
    HorizontalAlign="Left"
```

```
      Width="100%"
      runat="server">

      <asp:TableRow>
          horizontalAlign="Left">
          <asp:TableHeaderCell>
              Font Family
          </asp:TableHeaderCell>
          <asp:TableHeaderCell  Width="80%">
              Sample text
          </asp:TableHeaderCell>
      </asp:TableRow>
   </asp:Table>
```

Like all ASP controls, the Table control inherits from WebControl and therefore has the standard set of properties, methods, and events from that class and the classes above it in the hierarchy. In addition, the Table control has properties of its own, which are listed in Table 5-12. Most of these properties are demonstrated in Example 5-29 and Example 5-30.

Table 5-12. Properties of the Table control not derived from other controls

Name	Type	Get	Set	Values	Description
BackImageURL	String	x	x		The URL of an image to display behind the table. If the image is smaller than the table, it will be tiled.
CellPadding	Integer	x	x		Distance, in pixels, between the border and the contents of a table cell.
CellSpacing	Integer	x	x		Distance, in pixels, between adjacent table cells.
GridLines	GridLines	x	x	Both, Horizontal, None, Vertical	Determines which, if any, gridlines will be drawn in the table. Default is None.
HorizontalAlign	HorizontalAlign	x	x	Center, Justify, Left, NotSet, Right	Specifies the horizontal alignment of the table within the page. Default is NotSet.

Note the following information about the ASP Table control in Example 5-29 and Example 5-30:

- The BackImageURL attribute in the ASP Table control points to an image file located in the same directory as the *.aspx* file itself, so the URL does not need to be fully qualified. In these code examples, I used *Sunflower Bkgrd.jpg*, which was copied from my *c:\Program Files\Common Files\Microsoft Shared\Stationery* directory. You can use any jpg file you want or simply omit the BackImageURL attribute.

- The syntax for font name and size attributes is Font-Name and Font-Size when declared as part of the ASP control using its HTML syntax, but Font.Name and Font.Size when declared in the script block.

- The Width attribute in the ASP Table control is set to 100%. This causes the table to dynamically size to the full width of the browser window. The percentage value can be any integer, including values greater than 100, in which case the table will be wider than the browser window.

  If the Width attribute is set as an integer with no units, it causes the table to be the specified number of pixels in width, irrespective of the width of the browser window. Again, the table can be made wider than the browser window.

  If the Width attribute is not specified, then the table will automatically be as wide as necessary to display the contents of the cells. If the browser window is not wide enough, the cell contents will wrap. Once the browser window is made wide enough that all the cells can display without wrapping, the table will not get any wider.

Nested inside the ASP Table control is a single ASP TableRow control. This row contains the header cells, as indicated by the fact that the ASP controls nested inside the TableRow control are ASP TableHeaderCell controls.

Table Rows

The ASP TableRow control is used to represent a single row in a Table control. It is derived from the WebControl class, just like the Table control. As Table 5-13 shows, it has only two properties that are not shared with all its other sibling controls.

Table 5-13. Properties of the TableRow control not shared by other ASP table controls

Name	Type	Get	Set	Values	Description
HorizontalAlign	HorizontalAlign	x	x	Center, Justify, Left, NotSet, Right	Specifies the horizontal alignment of the contents of all the cells in the row. Default is NotSet.
VerticalAlign	VerticalAlign	x	x	Bottom, Middle, NotSet, Top	Specifies the vertical alignment of the contents of all the cells in the row. Default is NotSet.

Table Cells

There are two types of table cell ASP controls: a TableCell control for the body of the table and a TableHeaderCell for header cells. Both are used in Example 5-29 and Example 5-30.

The ASP TableHeaderCell control represents a heading cell in a Table control. It is derived from the ASP TableCell control class. In fact, all of its properties, events, and methods are exactly the same as for the ASP TableCell control. The single difference between the TableCell and TableHeaderCell controls is that the TableHeaderCell control renders with a bold font, as can be seen in Figure 5-16.

Notice that none of these nested TableHeaderCell controls in this example have either an id or a runat attribute. These attributes are not necessary here, since these controls are not accessed programmatically elsewhere in the code.

Only a single row is defined statically. The rest of the rows are defined dynamically in the Page_Load method in the script block.

In Example 5-29 and 5-30, the content of the header cells is the literal text strings between the opening and closing control tags. Alternatively, you may use self-closing tags and specify the content as a Text property:

```
<asp:TableHeaderCell text="Font Family"/>
```

The ASP TableCell control is used to contain the actual content of the table. Like the Table and TableRow controls, it is derived from the WebControl class. The Table-Cell and the TableHeaderCell controls have the properties shown in Table 5-14, which are not shared with its siblings.

Table 5-14. Properties of the TableCell and TableHeaderCell controls not shared with other table controls

Name	Type	Get	Set	Values	Description
ColumnSpan	Integer	X	X		Number of columns in the Table that the cell spans.
HorizontalAlign	HorizontalAlign	X	X	Center, Justify, Left, NotSet, Right	Specifies the horizontal alignment of the content of the cell. Default is NotSet.
RowSpan	Integer	X	X		Number of rows in the Table that the cell spans.
Text	String	X	X		The text content of the cell.
VerticalAlign	VerticalAlign	X	X	Bottom, Middle, NotSet, Top	Specifies the vertical alignment of the contents of the cell. Default is NotSet.
Wrap	Boolean	X	X	true, false	If true (the default), the contents of the cell wraps. If false, contents do not wrap. Note that there is an interaction between the Wrap property and cell width.

You now have an ASP Table control containing a single TableRow object that contains a pair of TableHeaderCell objects. The script block's Page_Load method, which is run every time the page is loaded, creates the table dynamically.

Often times, the Page_Load method will examine the IsPostBack property to test if the page is being loaded for the first time. If the load is the result of a postback, you may not want certain code to execute, either because it is both unnecessary and expensive, or because you will lose or change state information.

In this example, however, you want the code to run every time the page loads. In fact, both the CheckBoxList and the RadioButtonList controls have their AutoPostBack properties set to true to force the page to post. This forces the table to be regenerated. Each time the table is regenerated, the font styles are obtained from the CheckBoxList control, and the font size is obtained from the RadioButtonList control.

The Page_Load method begins by initializing a couple of variables. In C#, the code is:

```
string str = "The quick brown fox jumped over the lazy dogs.";
int i = 0;
```

and in VB.NET:

```
dim str as string = "The quick brown fox jumped over the lazy dogs."
dim i as integer = 0
```

str is the text displayed in the table, and *i* is a counter used later on.

You get the style or styles from the CheckBoxList control. To do so, you initialize three Boolean variables to use as flags, one for each style. In C#, the code looks like:

```
bool boolUnder = false;
bool boolOver = false;
bool boolStrike = false;
```

and in VB.NET, it looks like:

```
dim boolUnder as Boolean = false
dim boolOver as Boolean = false
dim boolStrike as Boolean = false
```

Then, using a for each loop to test each of the ListItem objects in the cblFontStyle CheckBoxList in turn, you set the variable for each font style to true if that checkbox has been selected. That is done by testing to see if the Selected property of the ListItem object is true. In C#, you might write:

```
foreach(ListItem li in cblFontStyle.Items)
{
    if (li.Selected == true)
    {
        switch (li.Value)
        {
            case "u":
                boolUnder = true;
                break;
            case "o":
                boolOver = true;
                break;
            case "s":
                boolStrike = true;
                break;
        }
    }
}
```

and in VB.NET, you'd use:

```
dim li as ListItem
for each li in cblFontStyle.Items
    if li.Selected then
        select case li.Value
            case "u"
                boolUnder = true
            case "o":
                boolOver = true
            case "s":
                boolStrike = true
        end select
    end if
next li
```

Getting the font size selected in the RadioButtonList rblSize is much simpler, since all you have to do is get the Value property of the ListItem object returned by the SelectedItem property. You put that integer into the *size* variable. In C#, the code is:

```
int size = Convert.ToInt32(rblSize.SelectedItem.Value);
```

and in VB.NET, it's:

```
dim size as integer = Convert.ToInt32(rblSize.SelectedItem.Value)
```

Now comes the meat of the method. You need to get a list of all the fonts installed on the machine. To do this, instantiate a new InstalledFontCollection object. In C#, the code is:

```
InstalledFontCollection ifc = new InstalledFontCollection();
```

and in VB.NET, it's:

```
dim ifc as InstalledFontCollection = new InstalledFontCollection()
```

Iterate over that collection, using a for each loop, looking at each of the FontFamily objects in turn. In C#, you'd use:

```
foreach( FontFamily ff in ifc.Families )
```

and in VB.NET, the code is:

```
dim ff as FontFamily
for each ff in ifc.Families
```

For each font family in the collection of FontFamilies, you create a new TableRow object. In C#, this looks like:

```
TableRow r = new TableRow();
```

and in VB.NET, you'd have:

```
dim r as TableRow = new TableRow()
```

Within that TableRow object, you create two TableCell objects—one called cFont to hold the font name, and a second called cText to hold the sample text string defined earlier. In C#, the following code would suffice for the cFont cell:

```
TableCell cFont = new TableCell( );
cFont.Controls.Add(new LiteralControl(ff.Name));
r.Cells.Add(cFont);
```

and in VB.NET, you'd use:

```
dim cFont as TableCell = new TableCell( )
cFont.Controls.Add(new LiteralControl(ff.Name))
r.Cells.Add(cFont)
```

The cFont TableCell object makes use of an ASP control called the LiteralControl. This control is used to insert text and HTML elements into the page. The only property of the LiteralControl, other than those inherited from Control, is the Text property.

For the cell containing the sample text, you will use a slightly different technique, because you want to be able to manipulate the font and size properties of the text string. After instantiating a new TableCell object named cText, you also instantiate a Label control and assign the variable *str*, defined earlier, to its Text property. In C#, the code would be:

```
TableCell cText = new TableCell( );
Label lbl = new Label( );
lbl.Text = str;
```

and in VB.NET, you'd use:

```
dim cText as TableCell = new TableCell( )
dim lbl as Label = new Label( )
lbl.Text = str
```

You increment the counter defined earlier and use it by assigning an ID property to the Label control. In C#, the following lines would work:

```
i++;
lbl.ID = "lbl" + i.ToString( );
```

and in VB.NET, you'd use:

```
i = i + 1
lbl.ID = "lbl" & i.ToString( )
```

Actually, this step is not necessary, because nowhere in this example do you actually need to refer back to any specific cell, but this was added to demonstrate how it can be done.

You now assign the font name. In C#, this would look like:

```
lbl.Font.Name = ff.Name;
```

and in VB.NET, it would look like:

```
lbl.Font.Name = ff.Name
```

Notice the syntax used here is different from the syntax for setting the font name within the tags of an ASP control (Font.Name versus Font-Name).

Use the flags set earlier to set the font styles. In C#, the code is:

```
if (boolUnder)
    lbl.Font.Underline = true;
if (boolOver)
    lbl.Font.Overline = true;
if (boolStrike)
    lbl.Font.Strikeout = true;
```

and in VB.NET, it's:

```
if boolUnder then
    lbl.Font.Underline = true
end if
if boolOver then
    lbl.Font.Overline = true
end if
if boolStrike then
    lbl.Font.Strikeout = true
end if
```

Since the table is being recreated from scratch each time the page is loaded, and the defaults for each of these styles is no style (i.e., false), there is no need to set the properties explicitly to false.

Set the font size, add the TableCell object to the TableRow object, and add the TableRow object to the Table object. In C#, you'd use:

```
lbl.Font.Size = size;
cText.Controls.Add(lbl);
r.Cells.Add(cText);
tbl.Rows.Add(r);
```

and in VB.NET:

```
lbl.Font.Size = new FontUnit(size)
cText.Controls.Add(lbl)
r.Cells.Add(cText)
tbl.Rows.Add(r)
```

There you have it.

Cell Width

Controlling the width of the cells merits special mention. It is similar to controlling table width, but different enough to cause some confusion. Looking at the HTML portion of Example 5-29, you can see that the second cell in the header row has a Width attribute set to 80%:

```
<asp:TableHeaderCell Width="80%">
    Sample text
</asp:TableHeaderCell>
```

Browsers make all the cells in a column the same width. If none of the cells have any width specification, then the column will automatically size to best accommodate all the cells, taking into account any width specifications for the table and the size of the browser window.

If multiple cells in a column have a width specification, then the widest cell specification is used. For easiest readability, it is usually best to include a width specification in only one row, generally the first row of the table. Hence, the Width attribute appears in the header row of this example.

When the width is specified declaratively as part of an ASP control tag, it can be given either as a percentage of the entire table, as was done in this example, or it can be given as a fixed number of pixels, as in the following:

```
Width="400">
```

Cell width can also be specified programmatically, in which case the syntax is somewhat different. Furthermore, the syntax differs between C# and VB.NET. Consider the lines of code from Example 5-29 and Example 5-30 that instantiate the cells containing the sample text, reproduced here for convenience. In C#, the code is:

```
TableCell cText = new TableCell( );
```

and in VB.NET, it is:

```
TableCell cText = new TableCell( )
```

In either language, the variable cText, of type TableCell, is assigned to the cell instance. The Width property can be applied to this TableCell instance, either as pixels or a percentage of the table width. To specify the Width property as 80% of the table width, use the following line of code in C#:

```
cText.Width = Unit.Percentage(80);
```

and this line of code in VB.NET:

```
cText.Width = Unit.Percentage(80)
```

To specify a fixed number of pixels, use *either* of the following lines of code in C#:

```
cText.Width = Unit.Pixel(400);
cText.Width = 400;
```

In VB.NET, only this line of code will set the cell width to a fixed number of pixels:

```
dim cTest as TableCell = new TableCell()
```

There is an interaction between the cell Width property and the Wrap property. The default value for the Wrap property is true. If the Wrap property is set to false, one of the following situations will occur:

- If there is no Width property specified, then the contents of the cell does not wrap and the column width expands to accommodate the largest cell.
- If the Width property is set to a pixel value, the Wrap property is overridden and the cell contents wrap to honor the Width property.
- If the Width property is set to a percentage value, it is overridden and the column is made wide enough to preclude any wrapping.

Panel Control

The Panel control is used as a container for other controls. It serves several functions:

- To control the visibility of the controls it contains
- To control the appearance of the controls it contains
- To make it easier to generate controls programmatically

The Panel control is derived from WebControl and adds the properties shown in Table 5-15.

Table 5-15. Properties of the Panel control not inherited from WebControl

Name	Type	Get	Set	Values	Description
BackImageURL	String	x	x		The URL of an image to display behind the table. If the image is smaller than the table, it is tiled.
HorizontalAlign	HorizontalAlign	x	x	Center, Justify, Left, NotSet, Right	Specifies the horizontal alignment of the contents of all the cells in the row. Default is NotSet. Note there is no VerticalAlign property.
Wrap	Boolean	x	x	true, false	If true (the default), the contents of the cell wraps. If false, contents do not wrap.

Example 5-31 demonstrates how to control the appearance and visibility of child controls and add controls programmatically using C#. Example 5-32 shows the script block of the same program in VB.NET. The HTML section of the code is the same for both the VB.NET and C# versions; consequently, the HTML is shown only in the C# version.

Example 5-31. Panel control using C#, csAspPanel.aspx

```
<%@ Page Language="C#" %>
<script runat="server">
   void Page_Load(Object sender, EventArgs e)
   {
       // Show/Hide Panel Contents
       if (chkHide.Checked)
       {
           pnl.Visible=false;
       }
       else
       {
           pnl.Visible=true;
       }

       // Generate label controls
```

Example 5-31. Panel control using C#, csAspPanel.aspx (continued)

```
        int numlabels = Int32.Parse(ddlLabels.SelectedItem.Value);
        for (int i=1; i<=numlabels; i++)
        {
            Label lbl = new Label();
            lbl.Text = "Label" + (i).ToString();
            lbl.ID = "Label" + (i).ToString();
            pnl.Controls.Add(lbl);
            pnl.Controls.Add(new LiteralControl("<br>"));
        }

        // Generate textbox controls
        int numBoxes = Int32.Parse(ddlBoxes.SelectedItem.Value);
        for (int i=1; i<=numBoxes; i++)
        {
            TextBox txt = new TextBox();
            txt.Text = "TextBox" + (i).ToString();
            txt.ID = "TextBox" + (i).ToString();
            pnl.Controls.Add(txt);
            pnl.Controls.Add(new LiteralControl("<br>"));
        }
    }
}
</script>

<html>
<body>

    <form runat=server>
        <h1>ASP Controls</h1>
        <h2>Panel Control</h2>

        <asp:Panel
            id="pnl"
            BackColor="DeepPink"
            Height="250px"
            Width="80%"
            Font-Name="Impact"
            HorizontalAlign="Center"
            runat="server" >

            This is static content in the Panel.
        <p/>
        </asp:Panel>

    <table>
        <tr>
            <td>
                Number of Labels:
            </td>
            <td>
                    <asp:DropDownList
                        id=ddlLabels
```

Example 5-31. Panel control using C#, csAspPanel.aspx (continued)

```
                        runat="server">
                        <asp:ListItem text="0" value="0" />
                        <asp:ListItem text="1" value="1" />
                        <asp:ListItem text="2" value="2" />
                        <asp:ListItem text="3" value="3" />
                        <asp:ListItem text="4" value="4" />
                    </asp:DropDownList>
            </td>
        </tr>
        <tr>
            <td>
                Number of TextBoxes:
            </td>
            <td>
                    <asp:DropDownList
                        id=ddlBoxes
                        runat="server">
                        <asp:ListItem text="0" value="0" />
                        <asp:ListItem text="1" value="1" />
                        <asp:ListItem text="2" value="2" />
                        <asp:ListItem text="3" value="3" />
                        <asp:ListItem text="4" value="4" />
                    </asp:DropDownList>
            </td>
        </tr>
        <tr>
            <td colspan=2> </td>
        </tr>
        <tr>
            <td>
                <asp:CheckBox
                    id="chkHide"
                    text="Hide Panel"
                    runat="server"/>
            </td>
            <td>
                <asp:Button
                    text="Refresh Panel"
                    runat="server"/>
            </td>
        </tr>
    </table>
    </form>
</body>
</html>
```

This sample is very straightforward. Skipping over the script block at the beginning for the moment, look just past the start of the HTML form, where an ASP Panel control is defined:

```
        <asp:Panel
            id="pnl"
```

```
        BackColor="DeepPink"
        Height="250px"
        Width="80%"
        Font-Name="Impact"
        HorizontalAlign="Center"
        runat="server" >

    This is static content in the Panel.
<p/>
</asp:Panel>
```

In order to access the Panel control programmatically, like all ASP controls, it has the id and runat attributes set. You also define several attributes for the Panel, including BackColor, Height (in pixels), Width (in percentage of the browser window), the font name (Font-Name), and the horizontal alignment (HorizontalAlign). Note that this control does not have a property for vertical alignment.

The only acceptable value for the Height attribute is an integer representing the number of pixels. The px as part of the value is optional, but does serve to self-document. For example, the following two lines are equivalent:

```
Height="250px"
Height="250"
```

The Height attribute does not cause a browser or compiler error if a percentage sign (%) is used, but the Height attribute is ignored in that case. If the Height attribute is either ignored or missing, then the Panel control automatically sizes itself vertically to contain all of its children controls.

The Width attribute can be either an integer number of pixels or a percentage of the browser window. The latter is shown in this example. If the Width attribute is missing, then the Panel control will default to a width of 100%.

The Panel control in the example also contains static text and HTML before the closing tag.

A static HTML table is defined in the example to lay out the controls that will control the contents and visibility of the panel. This table contains two DropDownList controls, a CheckBox control, and a Button control.

Note that none of these controls has its AutoPostBack property set. Therefore, in order to see any of the changes take effect, you need to click the button, which posts the form. When the form is posted, the Page_Load method is run. In C# (reproduced here from Example 5-31), this code is:

```
void Page_Load(Object sender, EventArgs e)
{
    // Show/Hide Panel Contents
    if (chkHide.Checked)
    {
        pnl.Visible=false;
```

```
    }
    else
    {
        pnl.Visible=true;
    }

    // Generate label controls
    int numlabels = Int32.Parse(ddlLabels.SelectedItem.Value);
    for (int i=1; i<=numlabels; i++)
    {
        Label lbl = new Label( );
        lbl.Text = "Label" + (i).ToString( );
        lbl.ID = "Label" + (i).ToString( );
        pnl.Controls.Add(lbl);
        pnl.Controls.Add(new LiteralControl("<br>"));
    }

    // Generate textbox controls
    int numBoxes = Int32.Parse(ddlBoxes.SelectedItem.Value);
    for (int i=1; i<=numBoxes; i++)
    {
        TextBox txt = new TextBox( );
        txt.Text = "TextBox" + (i).ToString( );
        txt.ID = "TextBox" + (i).ToString( );
        pnl.Controls.Add(txt);
        pnl.Controls.Add(new LiteralControl("<br>"));
    }
}
```

Example 5-32 shows the code in VB.NET.

Example 5-32. Panel control script block using VB.NET, vbAspPanel.aspx

```
<%@ Page Language="VB" %>
<script runat="server">
    sub Page_Load(ByVal Sender as Object, _
                  ByVal e as EventArgs)
        ' Show/Hide Panel Contents
        if chkHide.Checked then
            pnl.Visible=false
        else
            pnl.Visible=true
        end if

        ' Generate label controls
        dim numlabels as integer = Int32.Parse(ddlLabels.SelectedItem.Value)
        dim i as integer
        for i=1 to numlabels
            dim lbl as Label = new Label( )
            lbl.Text = "Label" & (i).ToString( )
            lbl.ID = "Label" & (i).ToString( )
            pnl.Controls.Add(lbl)
            pnl.Controls.Add(new LiteralControl("<br>"))
```

```
        next

    ' Generate textbox controls
    dim numBoxes as integer = Int32.Parse(ddlBoxes.SelectedItem.Value)
    for i=1 to numBoxes
        dim txt as TextBox = new TextBox()
        txt.Text = "TextBox" & (i).ToString()
        txt.ID = "TextBox" & (i).ToString()
        pnl.Controls.Add(txt)
        pnl.Controls.Add(new LiteralControl("<br>"))
    next
    end sub
</script>
```

First an `if-else` statement turns on or off the visibility of the panel. Note that when the panel is not visible, its contents are not visible either. Likewise, when the panel is visible, all of its contents are visible.

The two for loops, one each for labels and text boxes, generate the contained controls. After converting the entry in the appropriate DropDownList control to an integer, the for loop iterates through the procedure the specified number of times.

The procedure is very similar in each of the two cases. A new control is instantiated, then the Text and ID properties assigned. The control is added to the Controls collection of the panel, and finally a LiteralControl containing some HTML is added to the collection as well.

The results are shown in Figure 5-17.

Note that the font name specified inside the `Panel` tags affected the static text and labels in the panel, but not the contents of the text boxes.

Images

There are two ASP controls for displaying images: the Image control and the AdRotator control.

Image Control

The Image control has very limited functionality—it is used for displaying an image on a web page or, alternatively, displaying some text if the image is not available. If you need to have button functionality (i.e., to capture mouse clicks), then you should use the ImageButton control, described earlier in this chapter.

In addition to the properties inherited from WebControl, the Image control has the properties shown in Table 5-16.

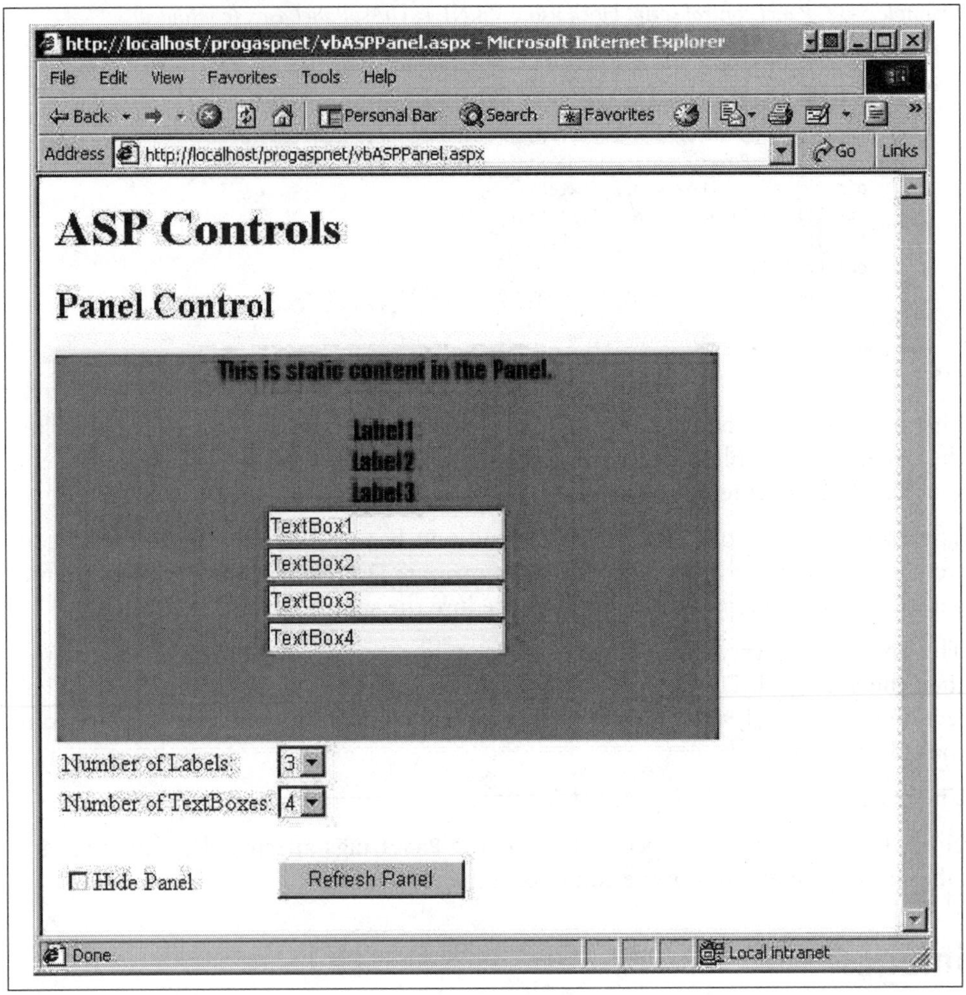

Figure 5-17. Panel control

Table 5-16. Properties of the Image control

Name	Type	Get	Set	Values	Description
AlternateText	String	x	x		The text displayed in the control if the image is unavailable. In browsers that support the ToolTips feature, this text is also displayed as a ToolTip.
ImageAlign	ImageAlign	x	x	See Table 5-17.	Alignment options relative to the text of the web page. See Table 5-17.
ImageURL	String	x	x		The URL pointing to the location of an image to display.

The ImageURL property can be either *relative* or *absolute*. A relative URL is the location relative to the location of the web page, without specifying a fully qualified path on the server. Using relative URLs makes it easier to move an entire site without modifying any of the code, as long as the image is in a subdirectory relative to the virtual root and the same directory structure is maintained. An absolute URL provides a fully qualified path. If the site is moved, then the code containing the absolute URL may need to be modified.

There are ten possible values for the ImageAlign property, as shown in Table 5-17. If you need better control of image and text placement, you will probably want to put the Image control in an HTML table.

Table 5-17. Members of the ImageAlign enumeration

Values	Description
NotSet	Not set. This is the default value.
AbsBottom	Aligns the lower edge of the image with the lower edge of the largest element on the same line.
AbsMiddle	Aligns the middle of the image with the middle of the largest element on the same line.
Top	Aligns the upper edge of the image with the upper edge of the highest element on the same line.
Bottom	Aligns the lower edge of the image with the lower edge of the first line of text. Same as Baseline.
Baseline	Aligns the lower edge of the image with the lower edge of the first line of text. Same as Bottom.
Middle	Aligns the middle of the image with the lower edge of the first line of text.
TextTop	Aligns the upper edge of the image with the upper edge of the highest text on the same line.
Left	Aligns the image on the left edge of the page with text wrapping on the right.
Right	Aligns the image on the right edge of the page with the text wrapping on the left.

In Example 5-33, you will see how the various ImageAlign values affect the appearance of a web page, using C#. Example 5-34 shows the script block using VB.NET. The web page produced by either example is shown in Figure 5-18.

 In order for the code in Example 5-33 and 5-34 to work correctly, you will need an image file for the ImageURL. These examples use "Dan at vernal pool.jpg," located in the ProgAspNet virtual directory. You can use any jpg file you want.

Example 5-33. Image alignment using C#, csAspImageAlign.aspx

```
<%@ Page Language="C#" %>

<script runat="server">
   void Page_Load(Object sender, EventArgs e)
   {
      switch(ddl.SelectedIndex)
      {
         case 0:
            img1.ImageAlign = ImageAlign.NotSet;
            img2.ImageAlign = ImageAlign.NotSet;
            break;
```

Example 5-33. Image alignment using C#, csAspImageAlign.aspx (continued)

```
          case 1:
              img1.ImageAlign = ImageAlign.AbsBottom;
              img2.ImageAlign = ImageAlign.AbsBottom;
              break;
          case 2:
              img1.ImageAlign = ImageAlign.AbsMiddle;
              img2.ImageAlign = ImageAlign.AbsMiddle;
              break;
          case 3:
              img1.ImageAlign = ImageAlign.Top;
              img2.ImageAlign = ImageAlign.Top;
              break;
          case 4:
              img1.ImageAlign = ImageAlign.Bottom;
              img2.ImageAlign = ImageAlign.Bottom;
              break;
          case 5:
              img1.ImageAlign = ImageAlign.Baseline;
              img2.ImageAlign = ImageAlign.Baseline;
              break;
          case 6:
              img1.ImageAlign = ImageAlign.Middle;
              img2.ImageAlign = ImageAlign.Middle;
              break;
          case 7:
              img1.ImageAlign = ImageAlign.TextTop;
              img2.ImageAlign = ImageAlign.TextTop;
              break;
          case 8:
              img1.ImageAlign = ImageAlign.Left;
              img2.ImageAlign = ImageAlign.Left;
              break;
          case 9:
              img1.ImageAlign = ImageAlign.Right;
              img2.ImageAlign = ImageAlign.Right;
              break;
          default:
              img1.ImageAlign = ImageAlign.NotSet;
              img2.ImageAlign = ImageAlign.NotSet;
              break;
      }
   }
</script>

<html>
<body>

   <form runat="server">

      <h1>ASP Controls</h1>
      <h2>Panel Control</h2>
      <h3>Image Alignment</h3>
```

Example 5-33. Image alignment using C#, csAspImageAlign.aspx (continued)

```
<font name="Garamond" size ="4">
This is a sample paragraph which is being used
to demonstrate the effects that various values
of ImageAlign has. As you will see, the effects
are sometimes difficult to pin down, and vary
depending on the width of the browser window.
</font>

<asp:Image id="img1"
    AlternateText="Dan"
    ImageAlign="NotSet"
    ImageUrl="Dan at Vernal Pool.jpg"
    runat="server" />

<hr/>
<hr/>

<asp:button
    Text="Sample Button"
    runat="server"/>

<asp:Image id="img2"
    AlternateText="Dan"
    ImageAlign="NotSet"
    ImageUrl="Dan at Vernal Pool.jpg"
    runat="server" />

<hr/>
<hr/>

Select Image Align: <br/>

<asp:DropDownList
    id="ddl"
    AutoPostBack="true"
    runat="server">
    <asp:ListItem text="NotSet" />
    <asp:ListItem text="AbsBottom" />
    <asp:ListItem text="AbsMiddle" />
    <asp:ListItem text="Top" />
    <asp:ListItem text="Bottom" />
    <asp:ListItem text="BaseLine" />
    <asp:ListItem text="Middle" />
    <asp:ListItem text="TextTop" />
    <asp:ListItem text="Left" />
    <asp:ListItem text="Right" />
    </asp:DropDownList>
    </form>
</body>
</html>
```

Example 5-34. Image alignment script block using VB.NET, vbAspImageAlign.aspx

```
<%@ Page Language="VB" %>
<script runat="server">
   sub Page_Load(ByVal Sender as Object, _
                 ByVal e as EventArgs)
      select case ddl.SelectedIndex
         case 0
            img1.ImageAlign = ImageAlign.NotSet
            img2.ImageAlign = ImageAlign.NotSet
         case 1
            img1.ImageAlign = ImageAlign.AbsBottom
            img2.ImageAlign = ImageAlign.AbsBottom
         case 2
            img1.ImageAlign = ImageAlign.AbsMiddle
            img2.ImageAlign = ImageAlign.AbsMiddle
         case 3
            img1.ImageAlign = ImageAlign.Top
            img2.ImageAlign = ImageAlign.Top
         case 4
            img1.ImageAlign = ImageAlign.Bottom
            img2.ImageAlign = ImageAlign.Bottom
         case 5
            img1.ImageAlign = ImageAlign.Baseline
            img2.ImageAlign = ImageAlign.Baseline
         case 6
            img1.ImageAlign = ImageAlign.Middle
            img2.ImageAlign = ImageAlign.Middle
         case 7
            img1.ImageAlign = ImageAlign.TextTop
            img2.ImageAlign = ImageAlign.TextTop
         case 8
            img1.ImageAlign = ImageAlign.Left
            img2.ImageAlign = ImageAlign.Left
         case 9
            img1.ImageAlign = ImageAlign.Right
            img2.ImageAlign = ImageAlign.Right
         case else
            img1.ImageAlign = ImageAlign.NotSet
            img2.ImageAlign = ImageAlign.NotSet
      end select
   end sub
</script>
```

AdRotator Control

This control is called an AdRotator because it is most often used to display advertisements on web pages. It displays an image randomly selected from a list stored in a separate XML file. The XML file contains image attributes, including the path to the image and a URL to link to when the image is clicked. The image changes every time the page is loaded.

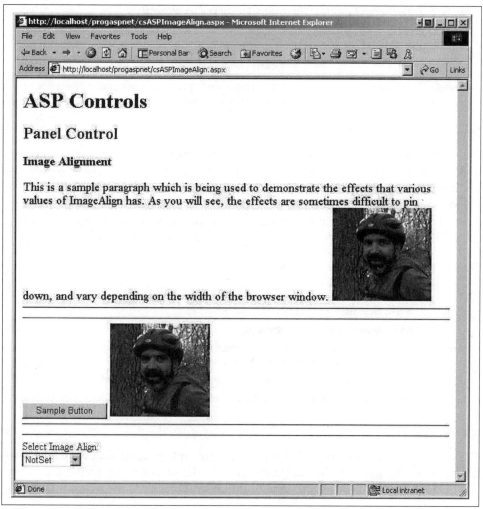

Figure 5-18. Image alignment

In addition to the properties inherited from WebControl, the AdRotator control has the properties and events listed in Table 5-18.

Table 5-18. Properties and events of the AdRotator control

Name	Type	Get	Set	Description
AdvertisementFile	String	x	x	The path to an XML file that contains the list of advertisements and their attributes. This file is described in detail below.
KeywordFilter	String	x	x	Filters ads displayed to include only those with the specified keyword in the AdvertisementFile.

Table 5-18. Properties and events of the AdRotator control (continued)

Name	Type	Get	Set	Description
Target	String	x	x	The browser window or frame that displays the contents of the page linked to when the AdRotator is clicked. See Table 5-19.
AdCreated	Event			Occurs once per round trip to the server after creation of the control, but before the page is rendered.

Target

The Target property is used to specify which browser window or frame is used to display the results of clicking on the AdRotator control. It dictates whether the resulting page displaces the current contents in the current browser window or frame, opens a new browser window, and so on. The values of the Target property must begin with any letter in the range of a to z, case insensitive, except for the special values shown in Table 5-19, which begin with an underscore.

Table 5-19. Special values of the Target property

Value	Description
_blank	Renders the content in a new, unnamed window without frames.
_new	Not documented, but behaves the same as _blank.
_parent	Renders the content in the parent window or frameset of the window or frame with the hyperlink. If the child container is a window or top-level frame, it behaves the same as _self.
_self	Renders the content in the current frame or window with focus. This is the default behavior.
_top	Renders the content in the current full window without frames.

Advertisement file

The *advertisement file* is an XML file that contains information about the advertisements to be displayed by the AdRotator control. Its location and filename is specified by the AdvertisementFile property of the control.

The advertisement file and the AdvertisementFile property are optional. If you want to create an advertisement programmatically, without the use of an advertisement file, put the code to display the desired elements in the AdCreated event.

As an XML file, the advertisement file is a structured text file with well defined tags delineating the data. Table 5-20 lists the standard tags, which are enclosed in angle brackets (< >) and require matching closing tags.

 Since this is XML and not HTML, it is much less forgiving of files that are not well-formed. These tags are case-sensitive: ImageUrl will work; ImageURL will not.

Table 5-20. XML tags used in the advertisement file

Tag	Description
Advertisements	Encloses the entire advertisement file.
Ad	Delineates each separate ad.
ImageUrl	The URL of the image to display. Required.
NavigateUrl	The URL of the page to navigate to when the control is clicked.
AlternateText	The text displayed in the control if the image is unavailable. In browsers that support the ToolTips feature, this text is also displayed as a ToolTip.
Keyword	The advertisement category. The keyword can be used to filter the advertisements displayed by the control by setting the AdRotator KeywordFilter property.
Impressions	A value indicating how often the ad is displayed relative to the other ads in the file.

In addition to the tags listed in Table 5-20, you can include your own custom tags in order to have custom attributes. In the sample advertisement file in Example 5-35, you create a custom attribute called Symbol, which will hold the stock symbol of each firm.

All the attribute tags in the advertisement file are parsed and placed in the adProperties dictionary. This dictionary can be used programmatically to access attributes, either standard or custom, by placing code in the onAdCreated event handler.

Example 5-35 shows a sample advertisement file that contains references to logos and web sites for several well-known companies.

Example 5-35. ads.XML, sample advertisement file

```
<Advertisements>

    <Ad>
        <ImageUrl>ms-banner.gif</ImageUrl>
        <NavigateUrl>http://www.microsoft.com</NavigateUrl>
        <AlternateText>Microsoft - Where do you want to go today?</AlternateText>
        <Keyword>Software</Keyword>
        <Impressions>50</Impressions>
        <Symbol>msft</Symbol>
    </Ad>

    <Ad>
        <ImageUrl>yahoo.gif</ImageUrl>
        <NavigateUrl>http://www.yahoo.com</NavigateUrl>
        <AlternateText>Do you Yahoo?</AlternateText>
        <Keyword>Portal</Keyword>
        <Impressions>50</Impressions>
        <Symbol>yhoo </Symbol>
    </Ad>

    <Ad>
```

Example 5-35. ads.XML, sample advertisement file (continued)

```
        <ImageUrl>hpLogo.gif</ImageUrl>
        <NavigateUrl>http://www.hp.com</NavigateUrl>
        <AlternateText>HP - Invent</AlternateText>
        <Keyword>Hardware</Keyword>
        <Impressions>40</Impressions>
        <Symbol>hwp</Symbol>
    </Ad>

    <Ad>
        <ImageUrl>dellLogo.jpg</ImageUrl>
        <NavigateUrl>http://www.dell.com</NavigateUrl>
        <AlternateText>Easy as Dell.</AlternateText>
        <Keyword>Hardware</Keyword>
        <Impressions>40</Impressions>
        <Symbol></Symbol>
    </Ad>

</Advertisements>
```

Now all you need is a web page with an AdRotator control to utilize this advertisement file, as shown in Example 5-36 in C# and in Example 5-37 in VB.NET.

Example 5-36. AdRotator control using C#, csASPAdRotator.aspx

```
<%@ Page Language="C#" %>
<script runat="server">
    void AdCreated(Object sender, AdCreatedEventArgs e)
    {
        if ((string)e.AdProperties["Symbol"] != "")
            lblSymbol.Text = (string)e.AdProperties["Symbol"];
        else
            lblSymbol.Text = "n.a.";
    }
</script>

<html>
    <body>
    <form runat="server">

        <h1>ASP Controls</h1>
        <h2>AdRotator Control</h2>

        <asp:AdRotator
            id="ad"
            target="_blank"
            AdvertisementFile="ads.xml"
            onAdCreated="AdCreated"
            runat="server" />

        <table>
            <tr>
                <td>
```

```
                    Stock Symbol:
                </td>
                <td>
                    <asp:Label
                        id="lblSymbol"
                        runat="server"/>
                </td>
            </tr>
        </table>
    </form>
    </body>
</html>
```

Example 5-37. AdRotator control using VB.NET, vbASPAdRotator.aspx

```
<%@ Page Language="VB" %>
<script runat="server">
    sub AdCreated(ByVal Sender as Object, _
                    ByVal e as AdCreatedEventArgs)
        if CStr(e.AdProperties("Symbol")) <> "" then
            lblSymbol.Text = CStr(e.AdProperties("Symbol"))
        else
            lblSymbol.Text = "n.a."
        end if

    end sub
</script>

<html>
    <body>
    <form runat="server">

        <h1>ASP Controls</h1>
        <h2>AdRotator Control</h2>

        <asp:AdRotator
            id="ad"
            target="_blank"
            AdvertisementFile="ads.xml"
            onAdCreated="AdCreated"
            runat="server" />

        <table>
            <tr>
                <td>
                    Stock Symbol:
                </td>
                <td>
                    <asp:Label
                        id="lblSymbol"
                        runat="server"/>
                </td>
```

```
            </tr>
          </table>
      </form>
      </body>
</html>
```

The results of the code in Example 5-36 and Example 5-37 are shown in Figure 5-19. In order to see the images cycle through, simply refresh the view on your browser.

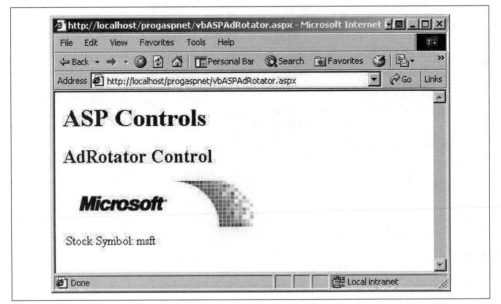

Figure 5-19. AdRotator control

In Example 5-36 and Example 5-37, an AdRotator control is created with an id of ad. The Target attribute is _blank, which has the effect of opening a new browser window when the user clicks on the image. You can play with the other values of the Target attribute. The AdvertisementFile attribute points to the advertisement file shown in Example 5-35.

This control raises an AdCreated event, which occurs on every round trip to the server after the control is created but before the page is rendered. There is an event handler called onAdCreated that defines the event procedure to execute whenever the event fires. The event handler is passed an argument of type AdCreatedEventArgs, which has the properties listed in Table 5-21.

The AdRotator tag in Example 5-36 and Example 5-37 includes an onAdCreated attribute that defines the AdCreated method as the handler for the AdCreated event. Every time the ad is changed, i.e., every time the page is reloaded, this event fires and updates the Label control contained in the static HTML table. Note that AdCreated first tests to be certain there is a value in the Symbol attribute. If not, then n.a. (for "not available") is displayed.

Table 5-21. Properties of the AdCreateEventArgs class

Property	Description
AdProperties	Gets a dictionary object that contains all the advertisement properties contained in the advertisement file.
AlternateText	The alternate text displayed by the browser when the advertisement image is not available. If the browser supports ToolTips, then this text is displayed as a ToolTip.
ImageUrl	The URL of an image to display.
NavigateUrl	URL of the web page to display when the control is clicked.

AdProperties returns a Dictionary object. When the AdProperties property is invoked, it implicitly calls the Item method of the Dictionary object, which returns the value corresponding to the dictionary entry whose key is Symbol. This value is then cast, or converted, to a string. In C#, this is done with the following syntax:

```
(string)e.AdProperties["Symbol"]
```

while in VB.NET the syntax is:

```
CStr(e.AdProperties("Symbol"))
```

Calendar

The ASP Calendar control is a rich web control that provides several capabilities:

- Displays a calendar showing a single month
- Allows the user to select a day, week, or month
- Allows the user to select a range of days
- Allows the user to move to the next or previous month
- Allows all aspects of the appearance of the calendar to be customized either at design time or under program control
- Programmatically controls the display of specific days

The Calendar control is extremely customizable, with a large variety of properties and events. Before digging into all the detail, look at a bare bones *.aspx* file showing a simple Calendar control, along with the resulting web page. Example 5-38 contains the code, and Figure 5-20 shows the results. Since there is no script block in this code, there is no need for equivalent C# and VB.NET versions.

Example 5-38. Simple Calendar control, Calendar-Simple.aspx

```
<html>
  <body>
  <form runat="server">
```

Example 5-38. Simple Calendar control, Calendar-Simple.aspx (continued)

```
    <h1>ASP Controls</h1>
    <h2>Calendar Demonstration</h2>

    <asp:Calendar
        id="cal"
        runat="server" >
    </asp:Calendar>
  </form>
  </body>
</html>
```

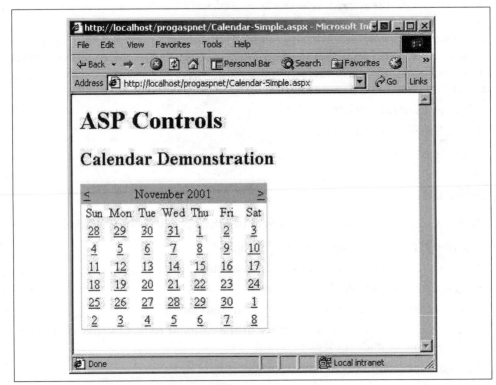

Figure 5-20. Results of Example 5-38 (calendar)

Pretty spiffy. Very few lines of code yield a web page with a working calendar that displays the current month. The user can select a single day (although at this point nothing happens when a day is selected, other than it being highlighted) and move through the months by clicking on the ≤ and ≥ navigation symbols on either side of the month name.

In addition to the properties inherited by all the ASP controls that derive from Web-Control, the Calendar has many properties of its own, which are listed in Table 5-22.

Table 5-22. Properties of the Calendar control

Name	Type	Get	Set	Values	Description
CellPadding	Integer	x	x	0, 1, 2, etc.	Distance in pixels between the border and contents of a cell. Applies to all the cells in the calendar and to all four sides of each cell. Default is 2.
CellSpacing	Integer	x	x	0, 1, 2, etc.	Distance in pixels between cells. Applies to all the cells in the calendar. Default is 0.
DayNameFormat	DayNameFormat	x	x	Full, Short, FirstLetter, FirstTwo-Letters	Format of days of the week. Values are self-explanatory, except Short, which is first three letters. Default is Short.
FirstDayOfWeek	FirstDayOf-Week	x	x	Default, Sunday, Monday, ... Saturday	Day of week to display in first column. Default (the default) specifies system setting.
NextMonthText	String	x	x		Text for next month navigation control. The default is &gt, which renders as the greater than sign (>). Only applies if ShowNextPrev-Month property is true.
NextPrevFormat	NextPrevFor-mat	x	x	CustomText, FullMonth, ShortMonth	To use CustomText, set this property and specify the actual text to use in NextMonth-Text and PrevMonthText.
PrevMonthText	String	x	x		Text for previous month navigation control. Default is "<", which renders as less than sign (<). Only applies if ShowNextPrev-Month property is true.
SelectedDate	DateTime	x	x		A single selected date. Only the Date is stored; the time is set to null (nothing in VB. NET).
SelectedDates	DateTime	x	x	DateTime	Collection of DateTime objects when multiple dates selected. Only the Date is stored; the time is set to null (Nothing in VB.NET).
SelectionMode	Calendar-SelectionMode	x	x		Described below.
SelectMonthText	String	x	x		Text for month selection element in the selector column. Default is ">>", which renders as two greater than signs (>). Only applies if SelectionMode set to DayWeekMonth.
ShowDayHeader	Boolean	x	x	true, false	Indicates if days of week heading shown. Default is true.
ShowGridLines	Boolean	x	x	true, false	Indicates if grid lines between cells shown. Default is false.
ShowNextPrev-Month	Boolean	x	x	true, false	Indicates if next and previous month navigation elements are shown. Default is true

Table 5-22. Properties of the Calendar control (continued)

Name	Type	Get	Set	Values	Description
ShowTitle	Boolean	x	x	true, false	Indicates if title is shown. If false, then next and previous month navigation elements also hidden. Default is true
TitleFormat	TitleFormat	x	x	Month, MonthYear	Indicates whether title is month only or month and year. Default is MonthYear.
TodaysDate	DateTime	x	x		Today's date.
VisibleDate	DateTime	x	x		Any date in the month to display.

If you want to give the user the ability to select either a single day, an entire week, or an entire month, then you must set the SelectionMode property. Table 5-23 lists the legal values for the SelectionMode property.

Table 5-23. Members of the CalendarSelectionMode enumeration

SelectionMode	Description
Day	Allows the user to select a single day. This is the default value.
DayWeek	Allows user to select either a single day or an entire week.
DayWeekMonth	Allows user to select either a single day, an entire week, or an entire month.
None	Nothing on the Calendar can be selected.

Example 5-39 modifies the code in Example 5-38 to add the SelectionMode property. The resulting Calendar, with the entire month selected, looks like Figure 5-21.

Example 5-39. Simple Calendar control with SelectionMode property, Calendar-Simple2.aspx

```
<html>
   <body>
   <form runat="server">

      <h1>ASP Controls</h1>
      <h2>Calendar Demonstration</h2>
      <h3>Selection Property</h3>

      <asp:Calendar
         id="cal"
         SelectionMode="DayWeekMonth"
         runat="server" />
   </form>
   </body>
</html>
```

When the SelectionMode property is set to DayWeek, an extra column containing the ≥ symbol is added to the left side of the calendar. Clicking on one of those symbols selects that entire week.

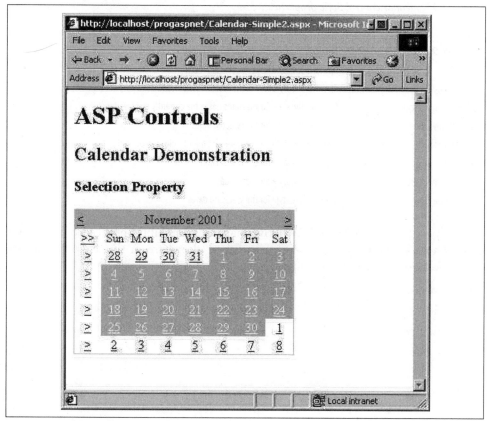

Figure 5-21. Calendar with month selected

Similarly, when the SelectionMode property is set to DayWeekMonth, in addition to the week selection column, a ≥ ≥ symbol is added to the left of the day names row. Clicking on that symbol selects the entire month, as is shown in Figure 5-21.

There are a number of properties that control the style for each part of the calendar. These properties are listed in Table 5-24 and demonstrated in Example 5-40.

Note that there are two different syntaxes for using these style properties. The first puts the style attribute inside the Calendar control tags, using the convention of hyphenating the style name and property, as in the following:

```
DayHeaderStyle-BackColor="Black"
```

The second syntax, used for most of the style examples here, encloses each style within its own HTML tag, rather than including it with other properties within the asp:Calendar tag:

```
<DayStyle
    BackColor="White"
    ForeColor="Black"
    Font-Name="Arial" />
```

Table 5-24. Calendar control Style properties

Name	Description
DayHeaderStyle	Specifies the style for the days of the week
DayStyle	Specifies the style for the dates
NextPrevStyle	Specifies the style for the month navigation controls
OtherMonthDayStyle	Specifies the style for the dates not in the currently displayed month
SelectedDayStyle	Specifies the style for the selected dates
SelectorStyle	Specifies the style for the week and month selection column
TitleStyle	Specifies the style for the title section
TodayDayStyle	Specifies the style for today's date
WeekendDayStyle	Specifies the style for the weekend dates

The properties listed in Table 5-24 derive many of their subproperties from the Style class. Those properties have all been described elsewhere in this chapter and are mostly self-explanatory. These include:

- BackColor
- BorderColor
- BorderStyle
- CssClass
- Font
- ForeColor
- Height
- HorizontalAlign
- VerticalAlign
- Width
- Wrap

In addition, there are four Boolean properties that control various aspects of the calendar. They are shown in Table 5-25.

Table 5-25. Boolean properties controlling various aspects of the Calendar control's appearance

Property	Default	Description
ShowDayHeader	true	Controls visibility of the names of the days of the week
ShowGridLines	false	Controls visibility of the grid lines between the days of the month
ShowNextPrevMonth	true	Controls visibility of the month navigation controls
ShowTitle	true	Controls visibility of the title section

Example 5-40 shows a basic calendar control with many of the Style properties set. The resulting calendar is shown in Figure 5-22.

Example 5-40. Calendar control with Styles, Calendar-Simple3.aspx

```
<html>
   <body>
   <form runat="server">

       <h1>ASP Controls</h1>
       <h2>Calendar Demonstration</h2>
       <h3>Styles</h3>

       <asp:Calendar
          id="cal"
          SelectionMode="DayWeekMonth"
          ShowGridLines="true"
          ShowNextprevMonth="true"
          CellPadding="7"
          CellSpacing="5"
          DayNameFormat="FirstTwoLetters"
          FirstDayOfWeek="Monday"
          NextPrevFormat="CustomText"
          NextMonthText="Next >"
          PrevMonthText="< Prev"
          DayHeaderStyle-BackColor="Black"
          DayHeaderStyle-ForeColor="White"
          DayHeaderStyle-Font-Name="Arial Black"
          runat="server" >

          <DayStyle
             BackColor="White"
             ForeColor="Black"
             Font-Name="Arial" />
          <NextPrevStyle
             BackColor="DarkGray"
             ForeColor="Yellow"
             Font-Name="Arial" />
          <OtherMonthDayStyle
             BackColor="LightGray"
             ForeColor="White"
             Font-Name="Arial" />
          <SelectedDayStyle
             BackColor="CornSilk"
             ForeColor="Blue"
             Font-Name="Arial"
             Font-Bold="true"
             Font-Italic="true"/>
          <SelectorStyle
             BackColor="CornSilk"
             ForeColor="Red"
             Font-Name="Arial" />
          <TitleStyle
```

```
            BackColor="Gray"
            ForeColor="White"
            HorizontalAlign="Left"
            Font-Name="Arial Black" />
         <TodayDayStyle
            BackColor="CornSilk"
            ForeColor="Green"
            Font-Name="Arial"
            Font-Bold="true"
            Font-Italic="false">
         </TodayDayStyle>
         <WeekendDayStyle
            BackColor="LavenderBlush"
            ForeColor="Purple"
            Font-Name="Arial"
            Font-Bold="false"
            Font-Italic="false"/>
      </asp:Calendar>
   </form>
   </body>
</html>
```

In the code in Example 5-40, notice that the DayHeaderStyles are contained within the Calendar tag, while all the other styles use their own tag. This is strictly a matter of personal preference. Notice also that the TodayDayStyle uses a separate closing tag, while all the other styles are self-closing. This too is a matter of personal preference.

Programming the Calendar Control

The ASP Calendar control provides three events and one method that are not inherited from other control classes and are of particular interest. By providing event handlers for the events, you can exercise considerable control over how the calendar behaves. These are:

- SelectionChanged event
- DayRender event
- VisibleMonthChanged event
- SelectRange method

The following sections describe each of these in detail.

SelectionChanged event

The SelectionChanged event fires when the user makes a selection—either a day, a week, or an entire month—in the Calendar control. The event is not fired if the

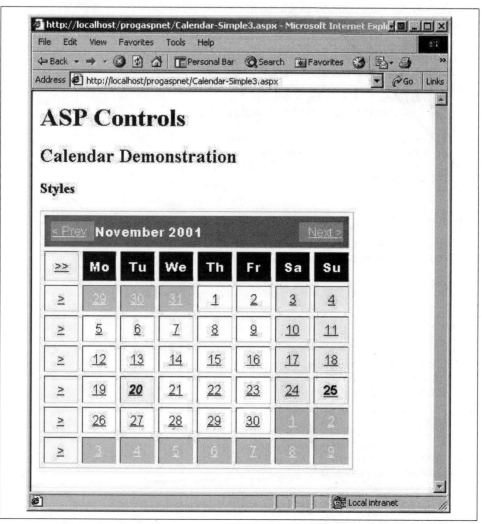

Figure 5-22. Calendar with Styles

selection is changed programmatically. The event handler is passed an argument of type EventArgs.

Example 5-41 demonstrates handling the SelectionChanged event in C#, and Example 5-42 demonstrates the same thing in VB.NET. (The VB.NET example, however, includes only the script block, since its HTML is identical to that in Example 5-41.) Whenever you select a new date, it displays text strings with today's date, the selected date, and number of days selected.

Example 5-41. Calendar control with SelectionChanged event in C#,
csASPCalendarSelectionChanged.aspx

```
<%@ Page Language="C#" %>
<script  runat="server">
   void SelectionChanged(Object sender, EventArgs e)
   {
      lblTodaysDate.Text = "Today's Date is " +
            cal.TodaysDate.ToShortDateString( );

      if (cal.SelectedDate != DateTime.MinValue)
         lblSelected.Text = "The date selected is " +
               cal.SelectedDate.ToShortDateString( );
      lblCountUpdate( );
   }

   void lblCountUpdate( )
   {
      lblCount.Text = "Count of Days Selected:   " +
            cal.SelectedDates.Count.ToString( );
   }
</script>

<html>
   <body>
   <form runat="server">

      <h1>ASP Controls</h1>
      <h2>Calendar Control</h2>
      <h2>SelectionChanged Event</h2>

      <asp:Calendar
         id="cal"
         SelectionMode="DayWeekMonth"
         ShowGridLines="true"
         ShowNextprevMonth="true"
         CellPadding="7"
         CellSpacing="5"
         DayNameFormat="FirstTwoLetters"
         FirstDayOfWeek="Monday"
         NextPrevFormat="CustomText"
         NextMonthText="Next &gt;"
         PrevMonthText="&lt; Prev"
         onSelectionChanged="SelectionChanged"
         DayHeaderStyle-BackColor="Black"
         DayHeaderStyle-ForeColor="White"
         DayHeaderStyle-Font-Name="Arial Black"
         runat="server" >

         <DayStyle
            BackColor="White"
            ForeColor="Black"
```

```
                    Font-Name="Arial" />
            <NextPrevStyle
                BackColor="DarkGray"
                ForeColor="Yellow"
                Font-Name="Arial" />
            <OtherMonthDayStyle
                BackColor="LightGray"
                ForeColor="White"
                Font-Name="Arial" />
            <SelectedDayStyle
                BackColor="CornSilk"
                ForeColor="Blue"
                Font-Name="Arial"
                Font-Bold="true"
                Font-Italic="true"/>
            <SelectorStyle
                BackColor="CornSilk"
                ForeColor="Red"
                Font-Name="Arial" />
            <TitleStyle
                BackColor="Gray"
                ForeColor="White"
                HorizontalAlign="Left"
                Font-Name="Arial Black" />
            <TodayDayStyle
                BackColor="CornSilk"
                ForeColor="Green"
                Font-Name="Arial"
                Font-Bold="true"
                Font-Italic="false"/>
            <WeekendDayStyle
                BackColor="LavenderBlush"
                ForeColor="Purple"
                Font-Name="Arial"
                Font-Bold="false"
                Font-Italic="false"/>
        </asp:Calendar>

        <br/>
        <asp:Label id="lblCount" runat="server" />
        <br/>
        <asp:Label id="lblTodaysDate" runat="server" />
        <br/>
        <asp:Label id="lblSelected" runat="server" />
    </form>
    </body>
</html>
```

Example 5-42. Calendar control with SelectionChanged event script block in VB.NET, vbASPCalendarSelectionChanged.aspx

```
<%@ Page Language="VB"%>
<script  runat="server">
   sub SelectionChanged(ByVal Sender as Object, _
                          ByVal e as EventArgs)
      lblTodaysDate.Text = "Today's Date is " & _
          cal.TodaysDate.ToShortDateString()

      if (cal.SelectedDate <> DateTime.MinValue) then
         lblSelected.Text = "The date selected is " & _
             cal.SelectedDate.ToShortDateString()
      end if

      lblCountUpdate()
   end sub

   sub lblCountUpdate()
      lblCount.Text = "Count of Days Selected:   " & _
          cal.SelectedDates.Count.ToString()
   end sub
</script>
```

Skipping over the script block at the beginning of Example 5-41 for a moment, you can see that this example adds the onSelectionChanged event handler to the Calendar control. This event handler points to the SelectionChanged method in the script block. Three ASP Label controls are also added after the Calendar control. The first of these labels, named lblCount, is used to display the number of days selected. The other two labels, named lblTodaysDate and lblSelected, are used to display today's date and the currently selected date, respectively.

All three of these labels have their Text property set in the SelectionChanged event handler method. Looking at that method in either Example 5-41 or 5-42, you can see that the label containing today's date is filled by getting the Calendar control's TodaysDate property. In C#, this is done using code similar to:

```
lblTodaysDate.Text = "Today's Date is " +
    cal.TodaysDate.ToShortDateString();
```

and in VB.NET, the code looks like:

```
lblTodaysDate.Text = "Today's Date is " & _
    cal.TodaysDate.ToShortDateString()
```

The id of the Calendar control is cal. TodaysDate is a property of the Calendar control that returns an object of type System.DateTime. In order to assign this to a Text property, which is an object of type String, you must convert the DateTime to a String. This is done with the ToShortDateString method. The DateTime object has a variety of methods for converting a DateTime object to other formats, including those shown in Table 5-26.

Table 5-26. Methods for converting a DateTime object to a string

Method name	Description
ToFileTime	Converts to the format of the local file system
ToLongDateString	Converts to a long date string
ToLongTimeString	Converts to a long time string
ToShortTimeString	Converts to a short time string
ToString	Converts to a string

Although not specific to ASP.NET, the DateTime class is very useful for obtaining all sorts of date and time information. Some of the read-only properties available from this class include those listed in Table 5-27.

Table 5-27. DateTime read-only properties

Property name	Description
Date	Returns the date component
Day	Returns the day of the month
DayOfWeek	Returns the day of the week
DayOfYear	Returns the day of the year
Hour	Returns the hour component
Millisecond	Returns the millisecond component
Minute	Returns the minute component
Month	Returns the month component
Second	Returns the second component
Ticks	Returns the number of 100 nanosecond ticks representing the date and time
TimeOfDay	Returns the time of day
Year	Returns the year component

In order to detect if any date has been selected, you test to see if the currently selected date, cal.SelectedDate, is equal to DateTime.MinValue. DateTime.Min-Value is a constant representing the smallest possible value of DateTime and is the default value for the SelectedDate property if nothing has been selected yet. Min-Value has the literal value of 12:00:00 AM, 1/1/0001 CE. There is also a MaxValue that has the literal value of 11:59:59 PM, 12/31/9999 CE.

 CE, which stands for the Common Era, is the scientific notation for the span of years referred to as AD (Anno Domini) on the Gregorian calendar. BCE (Before Common Era) is the scientific equivalent to BC (Before Christ).

If a date has been selected by the user, the Text property of the Label control is set to the string value of the SelectedDate property. In both C# and VB.NET, the code that accomplishes this is the same (except for the semicolon in C#):

```
cal.SelectedDate.ToShortDateString( )
```

The lblCount label displays the number of days selected. The SelectionChanged event procedure calls the lblCountUpdate method, which sets the Text property of the lblCount Label control. To set that control, you must determine how many dates were selected. The Calendar control has a SelectedDates property that returns a SelectedDates collection. SelectedDates is a collection of DateTime objects representing all the dates selected in the Calendar control. Count is a property of the Selected-DatesCollection object that returns an integer containing the number of dates in the collection. Since the Count property is an integer, you must use the ToString method to convert it to a string so that it can be assigned to the Text property. Once again, the code to do this in C# and in VB.NET is identical (although in VB.NET the call to the ToString method is optional):

```
cal.SelectedDates.Count.ToString( )
```

Although SelectedDates (the collection of selected dates) and SelectedDate (the single selected date) both contain DateTime objects, only the Date value is stored. The time value for these objects is set to a null reference in C# and to Nothing in VB. NET.

The range of dates in the SelectedDates collection is sorted in ascending order by date. When the SelectedDates collection is updated, the SelectedDate property is automatically updated to contain the first object in the SelectedDates collection.

The result of the ASP.NET pages in Example 5-41 and Example 5-42 is shown in Figure 5-23.

The user can navigate from month to month by clicking on the month navigation controls to either side of the month title. The user can also select a single day by clicking on that day, or an entire week by clicking on the week selector control, or the entire month by clicking on the month selector control. However, you can give the user much more flexibility than this. To demonstrate, you will add several controls and methods.

To enable the user to navigate directly to any month in the current year, add a Drop-DownList containing all the months of the year. You also add a button, labeled TGIF, which selects all the Fridays in the currently viewed month. The code for these two additions is shown in Example 5-43 in C# and Example 5-44 in VB.NET. The VB.NET version shows code only; its HTML content is the same as in Example 5-43. Lines that have been added are shown in boldface.

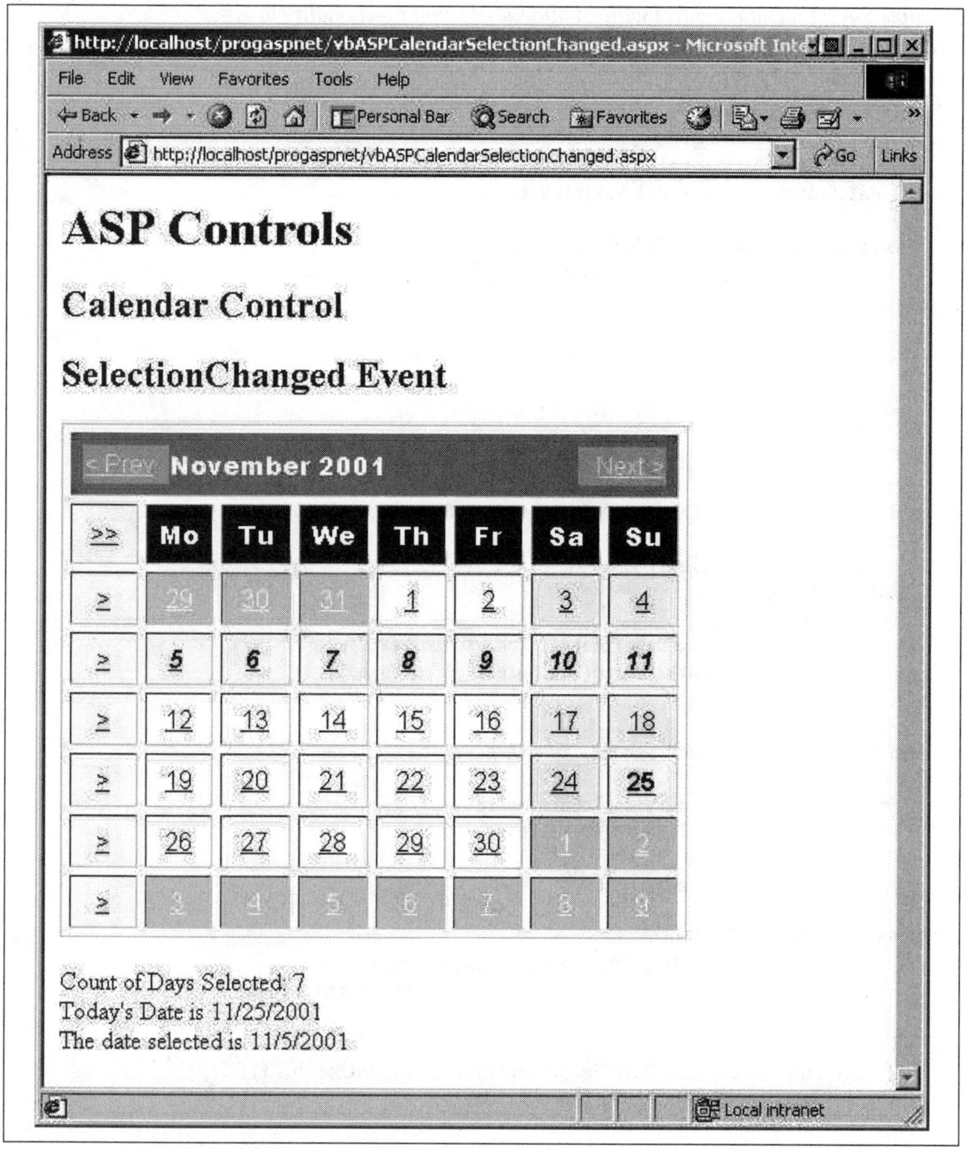

Figure 5-23. Calendar with SelectedDate

Example 5-43. Calendar control with additional selection functionality in C#,
csASPCalendarMoreSelections.aspx

```
<%@ Page Language="C#" %>
<script runat="server">
   // This Page_Load makes the selected days visible first time
   // the TGIF button is clicked by initializing the VisibleDate
   // property.
   void Page_Load(Object sender, EventArgs e)
```

```csharp
{
   if (!IsPostBack)
   {
     cal.VisibleDate = cal.TodaysDate;
     ddl.SelectedIndex = cal.VisibleDate.Month - 1;
   }
   lblTodaysDate.Text = "Today's Date is " +
         cal.TodaysDate.ToShortDateString( );
}

void SelectionChanged(Object sender, EventArgs e)
{
   lblSelectedUpdate( );
   lblCountUpdate( );
}

void ddl_SelectedIndexChanged(Object sender, EventArgs e)
{
   cal.SelectedDates.Clear( );
   lblSelectedUpdate( );
   lblCountUpdate( );
   cal.VisibleDate = new DateTime(cal.TodaysDate.Year,
                     Int32.Parse(ddl.SelectedItem.Value), 1);
}

void btnTgif_Click(Object sender, EventArgs e)
{
   int currentMonth = cal.VisibleDate.Month;
   int currentYear = cal.VisibleDate.Year;

   cal.SelectedDates.Clear( );

   for (int i = 1;
           i <= System.DateTime.DaysInMonth(currentYear,
                                            currentMonth);
           i++ )
   {
     DateTime date = new DateTime(currentYear, currentMonth, i);
     if (date.DayOfWeek == DayOfWeek.Friday)
        cal.SelectedDates.Add(date);
   }

   lblSelectedUpdate( );
   lblCountUpdate( );
}

void lblCountUpdate( )
{
   lblCount.Text = "Count of Days Selected:   " +
         cal.SelectedDates.Count.ToString( );
}
```

```csharp
    void lblSelectedUpdate( )
    {
        if (cal.SelectedDate != DateTime.MinValue)
            lblSelected.Text = "The date selected is " +
                    cal.SelectedDate.ToShortDateString( );
        else
            lblSelected.Text = "";
    }
</script>

<html>
    <body>
    <form runat="server">

        <h1>ASP Controls</h1>
        <h2>Calendar Control</h2>
        <h2>More Selections</h2>

        <asp:Calendar
            id="cal"
            SelectionMode="DayWeekMonth"
            ShowGridLines="true"
            ShowNextprevMonth="true"
            CellPadding="7"
            CellSpacing="5"
            DayNameFormat="FirstTwoLetters"
            FirstDayOfWeek="Monday"
            NextPrevFormat="CustomText"
            NextMonthText="Next &gt;"
            PrevMonthText="&lt; Prev"
            onSelectionChanged="SelectionChanged"
            DayHeaderStyle-BackColor="Black"
            DayHeaderStyle-ForeColor="White"
            DayHeaderStyle-Font-Name="Arial Black"
            runat="server" >

            <DayStyle
                BackColor="White"
                ForeColor="Black"
                Font-Name="Arial" />
            <NextPrevStyle
                BackColor="DarkGray"
                ForeColor="Yellow"
                Font-Name="Arial" />
            <OtherMonthDayStyle
                BackColor="LightGray"
                ForeColor="White"
                Font-Name="Arial" />
            <SelectedDayStyle
                BackColor="CornSilk"
```

```
            ForeColor="Blue"
            Font-Name="Arial"
            Font-Bold="true"
            Font-Italic="true"/>
    <SelectorStyle
        BackColor="CornSilk"
        ForeColor="Red"
        Font-Name="Arial" />
    <TitleStyle
        BackColor="Gray"
        ForeColor="White"
        HorizontalAlign="Left"
        Font-Name="Arial Black" />
    <TodayDayStyle
        BackColor="CornSilk"
        ForeColor="Green"
        Font-Name="Arial"
        Font-Bold="true"
        Font-Italic="false"/>
    <WeekendDayStyle
        BackColor="LavenderBlush"
        ForeColor="Purple"
        Font-Name="Arial"
        Font-Bold="false"
        Font-Italic="false"/>
</asp:Calendar>

<br/>
<asp:Label id="lblCount" runat="server" />
<br/>
<asp:Label id="lblTodaysDate" runat="server" />
<br/>
<asp:Label id="lblSelected" runat="server" />
<br/>
<table>
    <tr>
        <td>
            Select a month:
        </td>
        <td>
            <asp:DropDownList
                id= "ddl"
                AutoPostBack="true"
                onSelectedIndexChanged = "ddl_SelectedIndexChanged"
                runat="server">

                <asp:ListItem text="January" value="1" />
                <asp:ListItem text="February" value="2" />
                <asp:ListItem text="March" value="3" />
                <asp:ListItem text="April" value="4" />
                <asp:ListItem text="May" value="5" />
```

Example 5-43. Calendar control with additional selection functionality in C#,
csASPCalendarMoreSelections.aspx (continued)

```
                    <asp:ListItem text="June" value="6" />
                    <asp:ListItem text="July" value="7" />
                    <asp:ListItem text="August" value="8" />
                    <asp:ListItem text="September" value="9" />
                    <asp:ListItem text="October" value="10" />
                    <asp:ListItem text="November" value="11" />
                    <asp:ListItem text="December" value="12" />

              </asp:DropDownList>
          </td>
          <td>
              <asp:Button
                  id="btnTgif"
                  text="TGIF"
                  onClick="btnTgif_Click"
                  runat="server" />
          </td>
        </tr>
      </table>
   </form>
   </body>
</html>
```

Example 5-44. Calendar control with additional selection functionality in VB.NET (script block
only), vbASPCalendarMoreSelections.aspx

```
<%@ Page Language="VB"%>
<script  runat="server">
    '  This Page_Load makes the selected days visible first time
    '  the TGIF button is clicked by initializing the VisibleDate
    '  property.
    sub Page_Load(ByVal Sender as Object, _
                  ByVal e as EventArgs)
       if not IsPostBack then
          cal.VisibleDate = cal.TodaysDate
          ddl.SelectedIndex = cal.VisibleDate.Month - 1
       end if

       lblTodaysDate.Text = "Today's Date is " & _
             cal.TodaysDate.ToShortDateString( )
    end sub

    sub SelectionChanged(ByVal Sender as Object, _
                          ByVal e as EventArgs)
       lblSelectedUpdate( )
       lblCountUpdate( )
    end sub

    sub ddl_SelectedIndexChanged(ByVal Sender as Object, _
                                  ByVal e as EventArgs)
       cal.SelectedDates.Clear( )
```

```
        lblSelectedUpdate()
        lblCountUpdate()
        cal.VisibleDate = new DateTime(cal.TodaysDate.Year, _
                            Int32.Parse(ddl.SelectedItem.Value), 1)
    end sub

    sub btnTgif_Click(ByVal Sender as Object, _
                     ByVal e as EventArgs)
        dim currentMonth as integer = cal.VisibleDate.Month
        dim currentYear as integer = cal.VisibleDate.Year

        cal.SelectedDates.Clear()

        dim i as integer
        for i = 1 to System.DateTime.DaysInMonth(currentYear, currentMonth)
            dim dt as DateTime = new DateTime(currentYear, currentMonth, i)
            if dt.DayOfWeek = DayOfWeek.Friday then
                cal.SelectedDates.Add(dt)
            end if
        next

        lblSelectedUpdate()
        lblCountUpdate()
    end sub

    sub lblCountUpdate()
        lblCount.Text = "Count of Days Selected:   " & _
            cal.SelectedDates.Count.ToString()
    end sub

    sub lblSelectedUpdate()
        if (cal.SelectedDate <> DateTime.MinValue) then
            lblSelected.Text = "The date selected is " & _
                cal.SelectedDate.ToShortDateString()
        else
            lblSelected.Text = ""
        end if
    end sub
</script>
```

The DropDownList control and the TGIF button are in a static HTML table so that you can easily control the layout of the page.

The ListItem objects in the dropdown contain the names of the months for the Text properties and the number of the month for the Value properties.

The SelectionChanged method has been modified by having the bulk of its code moved into a separate method named lblSelectedUpdate, which updates the Text property of the lblSelected label. This method is then called from SelectionChanged, as well as several other places throughout the code.

The ddl_SelectedIndexChanged event handler method begins by clearing the SelectedDates collection. This is the same in C# and VB.NET except for the closing semicolon in C#:

```
cal.SelectedDates.Clear();
```

A call is made to the lblSelectedUpdate method to clear the Label control containing the first selected date and to the lblCountUpdate method to clear the Label control containing the count of selected dates. Then the VisibleDate property of the Calendar control is set to the first day of the newly selected month. This is the same in C# and VB.NET except for the closing semicolon in C#:

```
cal.VisibleDate = new DateTime(cal.TodaysDate.Year,
                Int32.Parse(ddl.SelectedItem.Value), 1);
```

The VisibleDate property is of type DateTime; a new DateTime is instantiated. The DateTime object, like many objects in the .NET Framework, uses an *overloaded constructor*. An object may have more than one constructor; each must be differentiated by having different types of arguments or a different number of arguments.

In this case, you want to instantiate a DateTime object that contains only the date. To do so requires three integer parameters—year, month, and day. The first parameter, *cal.TodaysDate.Year*, and the last parameter, 1, are both inherently integers. However, the month parameter comes from the Value property of the selected item in the DropDownList control. Recall that the Value property is a string, not an integer, even though the characters it contains *look* like an integer. Therefore it must be converted to an integer using the statement (the same for C# and VB.NET):

```
Int32.Parse(ddl.SelectedItem.Value)
```

The TGIF button is named btnTgif and has an event handler for the Click event, btnTgif_Click. This method iterates over all the days of the currently visible month and tests to see if it is Friday. If so, then it will add that date to the collection of SelectedDates.

First the btnTgif_Click method gets the month and year of the currently visible month, using the VisibleDate property of the Calendar control, which is a DateTime object, and the Month and Year properties of the DateTime object. This is the same in C# and VB.NET except for the closing semicolon in C#:

```
int currentMonth = cal.VisibleDate.Month;
int currentYear = cal.VisibleDate.Year;
```

Then it clears all the currently selected dates:

```
cal.SelectedDates.Clear();
```

Now it does the iteration. The limit part of the for loop is the number of days in the month, as determined by the DaysInMonth property of the DateTime object. The month in question is specified by the currentYear and currentMonth variables:

```
System.DateTime.DaysInMonth(currentYear, currentMonth)
```

Once inside the for loop, a DateTime variable called *date* (in the C# code) or *dt* (in the VB.NET code) is assigned to each day. Again, the DateTime object is instantiated with parameters for year, month, and day. Then the crucial question: Is the day of the week for this day a Friday? If so, then TGIF and add it to the collection of SelectedDates. In C#, this would be done:

```
DateTime date = new DateTime(currentYear, currentMonth, i);
if (date.DayOfWeek == DayOfWeek.Friday)
    cal.SelectedDates.Add(date);
```

and in VB.NET, you'd use:

```
dim dt as DateTime = new DateTime(currentYear, currentMonth, i)
if dt.DayOfWeek = DayOfWeek.Friday then
    cal.SelectedDates.Add(dt)
end if
```

 The reason that the two languages use a different variable name in this instance is a consequence of the fact that C# is case-sensitive, while VB.NET is not. In VB.NET, date is equivalent to Date, either of which is a keyword and so cannot be used as a variable name, unless it is enclosed in brackets every time it is used. However, in C#, while Date is a keyword, date is not, so the latter can be used as a variable name.

Finally, after iterating over all the days of the month, call the lblSelectedUpdate method to update the label showing the first selected date and call the lblCountUpdate method to update the label showing the number of days selected.

You will notice that there is now a Page_Load method in the script block. As the comment in the code explains, this makes the page behave correctly the first time the TGIF button is clicked, even before the month is changed. Without this Page_Load event procedure, the page behaves correctly for the TGIF button only after the month has been changed at least once. The btnTgif_Click method uses the Visible-Date property to set the current month and year variables. If that property is not initialized during the initial page load, then the values assigned to those variables will not correspond to the visible month.

In addition, the code to update the label displaying today's data has been moved from the SelectionChanged method to the Page_Load method, because it makes more sense to have it there.

The results of these changes and additions are shown in Figure 5-24.

The Calendar control also allows the user to select a range of dates. You might expect to be able to use the standard Windows techniques of holding down the Ctrl or Shift keys while clicking on dates, but this does not work. However, you can put controls on the page to select a starting day and ending day. In Example 5-45 (in C#)

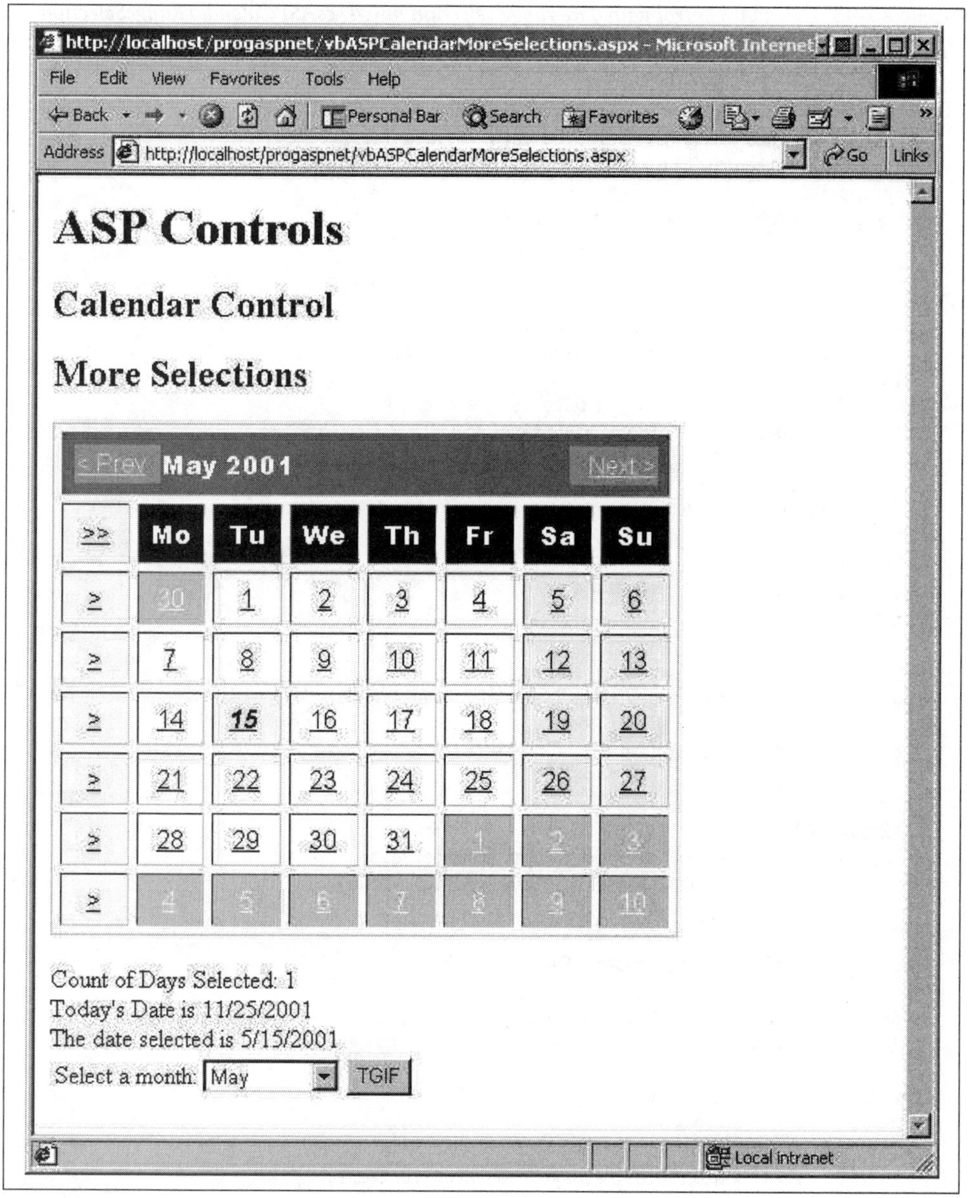

Figure 5-24. Calendar with month and Friday selection

and 5-46 (in VB.NET, script block only since the HTML is identical to that in Example 5-45), add a pair of TextBox controls to accept a starting day and an ending day for a range of dates. There is also a Button control to force the selection of the range of dates.

Example 5-45. Calendar control with date range selection in C#, csASPCalendarRangeSelection. aspx

```
<%@ Page Language="C#" %>
<script runat="server">
   //  This Page_Load makes the selected days visible first time
   //  the TGIF button is clicked by initializing the VisibleDate
   //  property.
   void Page_Load(Object sender, EventArgs e)
   {
     if (!IsPostBack)
     {
         cal.VisibleDate = cal.TodaysDate;
         ddl.SelectedIndex = cal.VisibleDate.Month - 1;
     }
     lblTodaysDate.Text = "Today's Date is " +
             cal.TodaysDate.ToShortDateString( );
   }

   void SelectionChanged(Object sender, EventArgs e)
   {
     lblSelectedUpdate( );
     lblCountUpdate( );
     txtClear( );
   }

   void ddl_SelectedIndexChanged(Object sender, EventArgs e)
   {
     cal.SelectedDates.Clear( );
     lblSelectedUpdate( );
     lblCountUpdate( );
     txtClear( );
     cal.VisibleDate = new DateTime(cal.TodaysDate.Year,
                       Int32.Parse(ddl.SelectedItem.Value), 1);
   }

   void btnTgif_Click(Object sender, EventArgs e)
   {
     int currentMonth = cal.VisibleDate.Month;
     int currentYear = cal.VisibleDate.Year;

     cal.SelectedDates.Clear( );

     for (int i = 1;
             i <= System.DateTime.DaysInMonth(currentYear,
                                                currentMonth);
             i++ )
     {
       DateTime date = new DateTime(currentYear, currentMonth, i);
       if (date.DayOfWeek == DayOfWeek.Friday)
          cal.SelectedDates.Add(date);
     }

     lblSelectedUpdate( );
```

```
        lblCountUpdate( );
        txtClear( );
    }

    void btnRange_Click(Object sender, EventArgs e)
    {
        int currentMonth = cal.VisibleDate.Month;
        int currentYear = cal.VisibleDate.Year;
        DateTime StartDate = new DateTime(currentYear, currentMonth,
                            Int32.Parse(txtStart.Text));
        DateTime EndDate = new DateTime(currentYear, currentMonth,
                            Int32.Parse(txtEnd.Text));

        cal.SelectedDates.Clear( );
        cal.SelectedDates.SelectRange(StartDate, EndDate);

        lblSelectedUpdate( );
        lblCountUpdate( );
    }

    void lblCountUpdate( )
    {
        lblCount.Text = "Count of Days Selected:  " +
            cal.SelectedDates.Count.ToString( );
    }

    void lblSelectedUpdate( )
    {
        if (cal.SelectedDate != DateTime.MinValue)
            lblSelected.Text = "The date selected is " +
                cal.SelectedDate.ToShortDateString( );
        else
            lblSelected.Text = "";
    }

    void txtClear( )
    {
        txtStart.Text = "";
        txtEnd.Text = "";
    }
</script>

<html>
    <body>
    <form runat="server">

        <h1>ASP Controls</h1>
        <h2>Calendar Control</h2>
        <h2>Range Selection</h2>

        <asp:Calendar
```

```
id="cal"
SelectionMode="DayWeekMonth"
ShowGridLines="true"
ShowNextprevMonth="true"
CellPadding="7"
CellSpacing="5"
DayNameFormat="FirstTwoLetters"
FirstDayOfWeek="Monday"
NextPrevFormat="CustomText"
NextMonthText="Next &gt;"
PrevMonthText="&lt; Prev"
onSelectionChanged="SelectionChanged"
DayHeaderStyle-BackColor="Black"
DayHeaderStyle-ForeColor="White"
DayHeaderStyle-Font-Name="Arial Black"
runat="server" >

<DayStyle
    BackColor="White"
    ForeColor="Black"
    Font-Name="Arial" />
<NextPrevStyle
    BackColor="DarkGray"
    ForeColor="Yellow"
    Font-Name="Arial" />
<OtherMonthDayStyle
    BackColor="LightGray"
    ForeColor="White"
    Font-Name="Arial" />
<SelectedDayStyle
    BackColor="CornSilk"
    ForeColor="Blue"
    Font-Name="Arial"
    Font-Bold="true"
    Font-Italic="true"/>
<SelectorStyle
    BackColor="CornSilk"
    ForeColor="Red"
    Font-Name="Arial" />
<TitleStyle
    BackColor="Gray"
    ForeColor="White"
    HorizontalAlign="Left"
    Font-Name="Arial Black" />
<TodayDayStyle
    BackColor="CornSilk"
    ForeColor="Green"
    Font-Name="Arial"
    Font-Bold="true"
    Font-Italic="false"/>
<WeekendDayStyle
```

```
        BackColor="LavenderBlush"
        ForeColor="Purple"
        Font-Name="Arial"
        Font-Bold="false"
        Font-Italic="false"/>
    </asp:Calendar>

    <br/>
    <asp:Label id="lblCount" runat="server" />
    <br/>
    <asp:Label id="lblTodaysDate" runat="server" />
    <br/>
    <asp:Label id="lblSelected" runat="server" />
    <br/>
    <table>
        <tr>
            <td>
                Select a month:
            </td>
            <td>
                <asp:DropDownList
                    id= "ddl"
                    AutoPostBack="true"
                    onSelectedIndexChanged = "ddl_SelectedIndexChanged"
                    runat="server">

                    <asp:ListItem text="January" value="1" />
                    <asp:ListItem text="February" value="2" />
                    <asp:ListItem text="March" value="3" />
                    <asp:ListItem text="April" value="4" />
                    <asp:ListItem text="May" value="5" />
                    <asp:ListItem text="June" value="6" />
                    <asp:ListItem text="July" value="7" />
                    <asp:ListItem text="August" value="8" />
                    <asp:ListItem text="September" value="9" />
                    <asp:ListItem text="October" value="10" />
                    <asp:ListItem text="November" value="11" />
                    <asp:ListItem text="December" value="12" />

                </asp:DropDownList>
            </td>
            <td>
                <asp:Button
                    id="btnTgif"
                    text="TGIF"
                    onClick="btnTgif_Click"
                    runat="server" />
            </td>
        </tr>
        <tr>
            <td colspan="2"> </td>
```

Example 5-45. Calendar control with date range selection in C#, csASPCalendarRangeSelection.
aspx (continued)

```
            </tr>
            <tr>
               <td colspan="2"><b>Day Range</b></td>
            </tr>
            <tr>
               <td>Starting Day</td>
               <td>Ending Day</td>
            </tr>
            <tr>
               <td>
                  <asp:TextBox
                     id= "txtStart"
                     Size="2"
                     MaxLength="2"
                     runat="server" />
               </td>
               <td>
                  <asp:TextBox
                     id= "txtEnd"
                     Size="2"
                     MaxLength="2"
                     runat="server" />
               </td>
               <td>
                  <asp:Button
                     id="btnRange"
                     text="Apply"
                     onClick="btnRange_Click"
                     runat="server" />
               </td>
            </tr>
         </table>
      </form>
      </body>
</html>
```

Example 5-46. Calendar control with date range selection in VB.NET (script block only),
vbASPCalendarRangeSelection.aspx

```
<%@ Page Language="VB"%>
<script runat="server">
    '  This Page_Load makes the selected days visible first time
    '  the TGIF button is clicked by initializing the VisibleDate
    '  property.
    sub Page_Load(ByVal Sender as Object, _
                  ByVal e as EventArgs)
       if not IsPostBack then
          cal.VisibleDate = cal.TodaysDate
          ddl.SelectedIndex = cal.VisibleDate.Month - 1
       end if
```

```
      lblTodaysDate.Text = "Today's Date is " & _
            cal.TodaysDate.ToShortDateString( )
   end sub

   sub SelectionChanged(ByVal Sender as Object, _
                        ByVal e as EventArgs)
      lblSelectedUpdate( )
      lblCountUpdate( )
      txtClear( )
   end sub

   sub ddl_SelectedIndexChanged(ByVal Sender as Object, _
                                ByVal e as EventArgs)
      cal.SelectedDates.Clear( )
      lblSelectedUpdate( )
      lblCountUpdate( )
      txtClear( )
      cal.VisibleDate = new DateTime(cal.TodaysDate.Year, _
                        Int32.Parse(ddl.SelectedItem.Value), 1)
   end sub

   sub btnTgif_Click(ByVal Sender as Object, _
                     ByVal e as EventArgs)
      dim currentMonth as integer = cal.VisibleDate.Month
      dim currentYear as integer = cal.VisibleDate.Year

      cal.SelectedDates.Clear( )

      dim i as integer
      for i = 1 to System.DateTime.DaysInMonth(currentYear, _
                                               currentMonth)
         dim dt as DateTime = new DateTime(currentYear, _
                                           currentMonth, _
                                           i)
         if dt.DayOfWeek = DayOfWeek.Friday then
            cal.SelectedDates.Add(dt)
         end if
      next

      lblSelectedUpdate( )
      lblCountUpdate( )
      txtClear( )
   end sub

   sub btnRange_Click(ByVal Sender as Object, _
                      ByVal e as EventArgs)
      dim currentMonth as integer = cal.VisibleDate.Month
      dim currentYear as integer = cal.VisibleDate.Year
      dim StartDate as DateTime = new DateTime(currentYear, _
                                               currentMonth, _
                                               Int32.Parse(txtStart.Text))
```

```
        dim EndDate as DateTime = new DateTime(currentYear, _
                                               currentMonth, _
                                               Int32.Parse(txtEnd.Text))
    cal.SelectedDates.Clear( )
    cal.SelectedDates.SelectRange(StartDate, EndDate)

    lblCountUpdate( )
end sub

sub lblCountUpdate( )
    lblCount.Text = "Count of Days Selected:   " & _
        cal.SelectedDates.Count.ToString( )
end sub

sub lblSelectedUpdate( )
   if (cal.SelectedDate <> DateTime.MinValue) then
      lblSelected.Text = "The date selected is " & _
          cal.SelectedDate.ToShortDateString( )
   else
      lblSelected.Text = ""
   end if
end sub

sub txtClear( )
   txtStart.Text = ""
   txtEnd.Text = ""
end sub
</script>
```

This UI is admittedly somewhat limiting because you cannot span multiple months. You could almost as easily provide three independent Calendar controls—one for the start date, one for the end date, and one for the range. Also, the day range does not apply after the month changes without reapplying the selection because the VisibleMonthChanged event is not trapped. (See the section "VisibleMonthChanged event" later in this chapter.)

The controls for selecting the range are in the same static HTML table as the controls described previously for selecting the month and all the Fridays. There are two text boxes, one named txtStart for the start day and one named txtEnd for the end day. In this example, the TextBox controls' Size and MaxLength attributes provide limited control over the user input. In a production application you will want to add validation controls as described in Chapter 8.

A new method, txtClear, is provided to clear out the day range selection boxes. This method is called at appropriate points in the other methods.

The Apply button is named btnRange, with the Click event handled by the method btnRange_Click. In btnRange_Click, you set integer variables to hold the current month and year. In C#, the code is:

```
int currentMonth = cal.VisibleDate.Month;
int currentYear = cal.VisibleDate.Year;
```

and in VB.NET, it is:

```
dim currentMonth as integer = cal.VisibleDate.Month
dim currentYear as integer = cal.VisibleDate.Year
```

Set two DateTime variables to hold the start date and the end date. In C#, you would write:

```
DateTime StartDate = new DateTime(currentYear, currentMonth,
                                  Int32.Parse(txtStart.Text));
DateTime EndDate = new DateTime(currentYear, currentMonth, Int32.Parse(txtEnd.Text));
```

and in VB.NET, the code is:

```
dim StartDate as DateTime = new DateTime(currentYear, _
            currentMonth, _
            Int32.Parse(txtStart.Text))
dim EndDate as DateTime = new DateTime(currentYear, _
            currentMonth, _
            Int32.Parse(txtEnd.Text))
```

Similarly to the month DropDownList described previously, the DateTime object requires the year, month, and day. You already have the year and month as integers; all you need is the day. You get the day by converting the text entered in the appropriate text box to an integer.

 This is not very robust code. If the user enters non-numeric data in one of the text boxes, or a value greater than the number of days in the month, an ugly error will result. If the start date is later than the end date, no error message will result, but neither will anything be selected. In a real application, you will want to use validation controls as described in Chapter 8.

Once the method has the start and end dates as DateTime objects, it clears any currently selected dates and uses the SelectRange method to add the range of dates to the SelectedDates collection. This is the same in both C# and VB.NET, except for the trailing semicolon in C#:

```
cal.SelectedDates.Clear();
cal.SelectedDates.SelectRange(StartDate, EndDate);
```

The SelectRange method requires two parameters: the start date and the end date.

The result of adding the selection tools to the page is shown in Figure 5-25.

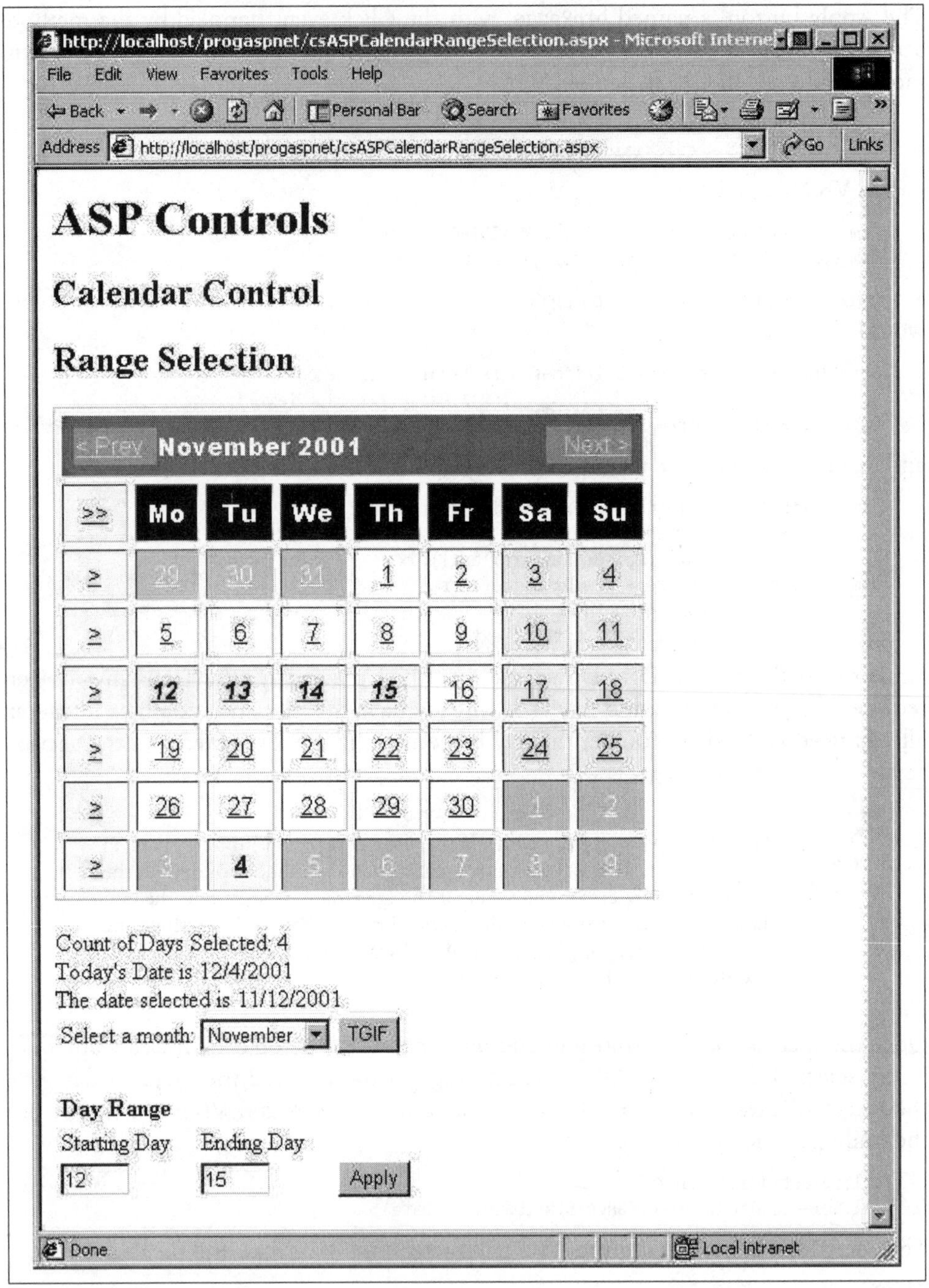

Figure 5-25. Calendar with range selection

DayRender event

Data binding is not supported directly for the Calendar control. However, you can modify the content and formatting of individual date cells. This allows you to retrieve values from a database, process those values in some manner, and place them in specific cells.

Before the Calendar control is actually rendered to the client browser, all of the components that comprise the control are created. As each date cell is created, it raises the DayRender event. This event can be handled.

The DayRender event handler receives an argument of type DayRenderEventArgs. This object has two properties that may be programmatically read:

Cell

TableCell object that represents the cell being rendered

Day

CalendarDay object that represents the day being rendered in that cell.

The code in Example 5-47 and Example 5-48 demonstrates how this event can be used. All the weekend days will have their background color changed and a New Year's greeting will be displayed for January 1.

Example 5-47 shows the complete *.aspx* page with script written in C# while Example 5-48 shows only the VB code, since its HTML content is the same as Example 5-47. The examples are modified versions of Examples 5-45 and 5-46, with added lines shown in boldface.

Example 5-47. DayRender event in C#, csASPCalendarDayRender.aspx

```
<%@ Page Language="C#" %>
<script  runat="server">
   // This Page_Load makes the selected days visible first time
   // the TGIF button is clicked by initializing the VisibleDate
   // property.
   void Page_Load(Object sender, EventArgs e)
   {
      if (!IsPostBack)
      {
         cal.VisibleDate = cal.TodaysDate;
         ddl.SelectedIndex = cal.VisibleDate.Month - 1;
      }
      lblTodaysDate.Text = "Today's Date is " +
            cal.TodaysDate.ToShortDateString( );
   }

   void SelectionChanged(Object sender, EventArgs e)
   {
      lblSelectedUpdate( );
      lblCountUpdate( );
      txtClear( );
```

Example 5-47. DayRender event in C#, csASPCalendarDayRender.aspx (continued)

```csharp
    }

    void ddl_SelectedIndexChanged(Object sender, EventArgs e)
    {
        cal.SelectedDates.Clear( );
        lblSelectedUpdate( );
        lblCountUpdate( );
        txtClear( );
        cal.VisibleDate = new DateTime(cal.TodaysDate.Year,
                            Int32.Parse(ddl.SelectedItem.Value), 1);
    }

    void btnTgif_Click(Object sender, EventArgs e)
    {
        int currentMonth = cal.VisibleDate.Month;
        int currentYear = cal.VisibleDate.Year;

        cal.SelectedDates.Clear( );

        for (int i = 1;
                i <= System.DateTime.DaysInMonth(currentYear,
                                                currentMonth);
                i++ )
        {
            DateTime date = new DateTime(currentYear, currentMonth, i);
            if (date.DayOfWeek == DayOfWeek.Friday)
                cal.SelectedDates.Add(date);
        }

        lblSelectedUpdate( );
        lblCountUpdate( );
        txtClear( );
    }

    void btnRange_Click(Object sender, EventArgs e)
    {
        int currentMonth = cal.VisibleDate.Month;
        int currentYear = cal.VisibleDate.Year;
        DateTime StartDate = new DateTime(currentYear, currentMonth,
                            Int32.Parse(txtStart.Text));
        DateTime EndDate = new DateTime(currentYear, currentMonth,
                            Int32.Parse(txtEnd.Text));

        cal.SelectedDates.Clear( );
        cal.SelectedDates.SelectRange(StartDate, EndDate);

        lblSelectedUpdate( );
        lblCountUpdate( );
    }

    void DayRender(Object sender, DayRenderEventArgs e)
    {
```

```
      //  Notice that this overrides the WeekendDayStyle.
      if (!e.Day.IsOtherMonth && e.Day.IsWeekend)
         e.Cell.BackColor=System.Drawing.Color.LightGreen;

      //  Happy New Year!
      if (e.Day.Date.Month == 1 && e.Day.Date.Day == 1)
         e.Cell.Controls.Add(new LiteralControl("<br/>Happy New Year!"));
   }

   void lblCountUpdate( )
   {
      lblCount.Text = "Count of Days Selected:   " +
           cal.SelectedDates.Count.ToString( );
   }

   void lblSelectedUpdate( )
   {
      if (cal.SelectedDate != DateTime.MinValue)
         lblSelected.Text = "The date selected is " +
              cal.SelectedDate.ToShortDateString( );
      else
        lblSelected.Text = "";
   }

   void txtClear( )
   {
      txtStart.Text = "";
      txtEnd.Text = "";
   }
</script>

<html>
   <body>
   <form runat="server">

      <h1>ASP Controls</h1>
      <h2>Calendar Control</h2>
      <h2>DayRender</h2>

      <asp:Calendar
         id="cal"
         SelectionMode="DayWeekMonth"
         ShowGridLines="true"
         ShowNextprevMonth="true"
         CellPadding="7"
         CellSpacing="5"
         DayNameFormat="FirstTwoLetters"
         FirstDayOfWeek="Monday"
         NextPrevFormat="CustomText"
         NextMonthText="Next &gt;"
         PrevMonthText="&lt; Prev"
         onSelectionChanged="SelectionChanged"
```

Example 5-47. DayRender event in C#, csASPCalendarDayRender.aspx (continued)

```
    onDayRender="DayRender"
    DayHeaderStyle-BackColor="Black"
    DayHeaderStyle-ForeColor="White"
    DayHeaderStyle-Font-Name="Arial Black"
    runat="server" >

    <DayStyle
        BackColor="White"
        ForeColor="Black"
        Font-Name="Arial" />
    <NextPrevStyle
        BackColor="DarkGray"
        ForeColor="Yellow"
        Font-Name="Arial" />
    <OtherMonthDayStyle
        BackColor="LightGray"
        ForeColor="White"
        Font-Name="Arial" />
    <SelectedDayStyle
        BackColor="CornSilk"
        ForeColor="Blue"
        Font-Name="Arial"
        Font-Bold="true"
        Font-Italic="true"/>
    <SelectorStyle
        BackColor="CornSilk"
        ForeColor="Red"
        Font-Name="Arial" />
    <TitleStyle
        BackColor="Gray"
        ForeColor="White"
        HorizontalAlign="Left"
        Font-Name="Arial Black" />
    <TodayDayStyle
        BackColor="CornSilk"
        ForeColor="Green"
        Font-Name="Arial"
        Font-Bold="true"
        Font-Italic="false"/>
    <WeekendDayStyle
        BackColor="LavenderBlush"
        ForeColor="Purple"
        Font-Name="Arial"
        Font-Bold="false"
        Font-Italic="false"/>
</asp:Calendar>

<br/>
<asp:Label id="lblCount" runat="server" />
<br/>
<asp:Label id="lblTodaysDate" runat="server" />
<br/>
```

```
<asp:Label id="lblSelected" runat="server" />
<br/>
<table>
  <tr>
     <td>
        Select a month:
     </td>
     <td>
        <asp:DropDownList
           id= "ddl"
           AutoPostBack="true"
           onSelectedIndexChanged = "ddl_SelectedIndexChanged"
           runat="server">

           <asp:ListItem text="January" value="1" />
           <asp:ListItem text="February" value="2" />
           <asp:ListItem text="March" value="3" />
           <asp:ListItem text="April" value="4" />
           <asp:ListItem text="May" value="5" />
           <asp:ListItem text="June" value="6" />
           <asp:ListItem text="July" value="7" />
           <asp:ListItem text="August" value="8" />
           <asp:ListItem text="September" value="9" />
           <asp:ListItem text="October" value="10" />
           <asp:ListItem text="November" value="11" />
           <asp:ListItem text="December" value="12" />

        </asp:DropDownList>
     </td>
     <td>
        <asp:Button
           id="btnTgif"
           text="TGIF"
           onClick="btnTgif_Click"
           runat="server" />
     </td>
  </tr>
  <tr>
     <td colspan="2"> </td>
  </tr>
  <tr>
     <td colspan="2"><b>Day Range</b></td>
  </tr>
  <tr>
     <td>Starting Day</td>
     <td>Ending Day</td>
  </tr>
  <tr>
     <td>
        <asp:TextBox
           id= "txtStart"
           Size="2"
```

```
                MaxLength="2"
                runat="server" />
        </td>
        <td>
            <asp:TextBox
                id= "txtEnd"
                Size="2"
                MaxLength="2"
                runat="server" />
        </td>
        <td>
            <asp:Button
                id="btnRange"
                text="Apply"
                onClick="btnRange_Click"
                runat="server" />
        </td>
     </tr>
   </table>
  </form>
  </body>
</html>
```

Example 5-48. DayRender event in VB.NET, vbASPCalendarDayRender.aspx

```
<%@ Page Language="VB"%>
<script  runat="server">
   '  This Page_Load makes the selected days visible first time
   '  the TGIF button is clicked by initializing the VisibleDate
   '  property.
   sub Page_Load(ByVal Sender as Object, _
                 ByVal e as EventArgs)
     if not IsPostBack then
        cal.VisibleDate = cal.TodaysDate
       ddl.SelectedIndex = cal.VisibleDate.Month - 1
     end if

     lblTodaysDate.Text = "Today's Date is " & _
           cal.TodaysDate.ToShortDateString( )
   end sub


   sub SelectionChanged(ByVal Sender as Object, _
                        ByVal e as EventArgs)
     lblSelectedUpdate( )
     lblCountUpdate( )
     txtClear( )
   end sub


   sub ddl_SelectedIndexChanged(ByVal Sender as Object, _
                                ByVal e as EventArgs)
     cal.SelectedDates.Clear( )
     lblSelectedUpdate( )
```

```
      lblCountUpdate( )
      txtClear( )
      cal.VisibleDate = new DateTime(cal.TodaysDate.Year, _
                       Int32.Parse(ddl.SelectedItem.Value), 1)
   end sub

   sub btnTgif_Click(ByVal Sender as Object, _
                     ByVal e as EventArgs)
      dim currentMonth as integer = cal.VisibleDate.Month
      dim currentYear as integer = cal.VisibleDate.Year

      cal.SelectedDates.Clear( )

      dim i as integer
      for i = 1 to System.DateTime.DaysInMonth(currentYear, _
                                               currentMonth)
         dim dt as DateTime = new DateTime(currentYear, _
                                           currentMonth, _
                                           i)
         if dt.DayOfWeek = DayOfWeek.Friday then
            cal.SelectedDates.Add(dt)
         end if
      next

      lblSelectedUpdate( )
      lblCountUpdate( )
      txtClear( )
   end sub

   sub btnRange_Click(ByVal Sender as Object, _
                      ByVal e as EventArgs)
      dim currentMonth as integer = cal.VisibleDate.Month
      dim currentYear as integer = cal.VisibleDate.Year
      dim StartDate as DateTime = new DateTime(currentYear, _
                                               currentMonth, _
                                               Int32.Parse(txtStart.Text))
      dim EndDate as DateTime = new DateTime(currentYear, _
                                             currentMonth, _
                                             Int32.Parse(txtEnd.Text))
      cal.SelectedDates.Clear( )
      cal.SelectedDates.SelectRange(StartDate, EndDate)

      lblCountUpdate( )
   end sub

   sub DayRender(ByVal Sender as Object, _
                 ByVal e as DayRenderEventArgs)
      ' Notice that this overrides the WeekendDayStyle.
      if (not e.Day.IsOtherMonth and e.Day.IsWeekend) then
         e.Cell.BackColor=System.Drawing.Color.LightGreen
      end if
```

```
   ' Happy New Year!
   if (e.Day.Date.Month = 1 and e.Day.Date.Day = 1) then
      e.Cell.Controls.Add(new LiteralControl("<br/>Happy New Year!"))
   end if
end sub

sub lblCountUpdate( )
   lblCount.Text = "Count of Days Selected:  " & _
         cal.SelectedDates.Count.ToString( )
end sub

sub lblSelectedUpdate( )
   if (cal.SelectedDate <> DateTime.MinValue) then
      lblSelected.Text = "The date selected is " & _
            cal.SelectedDate.ToShortDateString( )
   else
      lblSelected.Text = ""
   end if
end sub

sub txtClear( )
   txtStart.Text = ""
   txtEnd.Text = ""
end sub
</script>
```

In Example 5-47 and Example 5-48, an event handler, onDayRender, was added to the Calendar control. This event handler points to the DayRender method, contained in the script block.

The first thing the DayRender method does is color the weekends LightGreen. Recall that there is a WeekendDayStyle property set for this control that colors the weekends LavenderBlush. The DayRender method overrides the WeekendDayStyle. (The distinction may not be readily apparent in the printed book, but you will see the colors when the web page is run.)

The event handler method is passed two parameters. In C#, this is accomplished with:

```
void DayRender(Object sender, DayRenderEventArgs e)
```

and in VB.NET, the code is:

```
sub DayRender(ByVal Sender as Object, _
            ByVal e as DayRenderEventArgs)
```

DayRenderEventArgs contains properties for the Day and the Cell. The Day is tested to see if it is both the current month and also a weekend day. In C#, the code is:

```
(!e.Day.IsOtherMonth && e.Day.IsWeekend)
```

and in VB.NET, it's:

```
(not e.Day.IsOtherMonth and e.Day.IsWeekend)
```

The Day property is a member of the CalendarDay class, which has the properties shown in Table 5-28 (all of which are read-only except IsSelectable).

Table 5-28. Properties of the CalendarDay class

Property	Type	Description
Date	DateTime	Date represented by this Day. Read-only.
DayNumberText	String	String representation of the day number of this Day. Read-only.
IsOtherMonth	Boolean	Indicates this Day is in a different month than the month currently displayed by the Calendar. Read-only.
IsSelectable	Boolean	Indicates if Day can be selected. Not read-only.
IsSelected	Boolean	Indicates if Day is selected.
IsToday	Boolean	Indicates if Day is today's date.
IsWeekend	Boolean	Indicates if Day is a weekend date.

If the date is both in the current month and is also a weekend day, then the Cell. BackColor property is assigned a color. This is the same in C# and VB.NET except for the trailing semicolon in C#:

```
e.Cell.BackColor=System.Drawing.Color.LightGreen;
```

Example 5-47 and Example 5-48 then test to see if the selected date is New Year's day. Again, the Day property of the DayRenderEventArgs object is tested to see if the month of the Date is 1 and the Day of the Date is 1. In C#, this is done using the code:

```
if (e.Day.Date.Month == 1 && e.Day.Date.Day == 1)
```

and in VB.NET, the code is:

```
if (e.Day.Date.Month = 1 and e.Day.Date.Day = 1) then
```

If so, a LiteralControl is added to the cell that adds an HTML break tag and a greeting. This is the same in C# and VB.NET except for the trailing semicolon in C#:

```
e.Cell.Controls.Add(new LiteralControl("<br/>Happy New Year!"));
```

The thing to remember here is that, like all ASP controls, what is actually sent to the browser is HTML. Thus, a Calendar is rendered on the browser as an HTML table. Each of the selectable components of the calendar has an anchor tag associated with it, along with some JavaScript that accomplishes the postback. (This is evident when you hover the cursor over any clickable element of the calendar—the status line of the browser will display the name of the JavaScript function that will be executed if the link is clicked.) Using a LiteralControl inserts the text in its argument as a control into the HTML cell as-is. A look at a snippet from the source code visible on the browser confirms this:

```
<td align="Center" style="color:Black;background-color:White;
                  font-family:Arial;width:12%;">
```

```
<a href="javascript:__doPostBack('cal','selectDay7')" style="color:Black">
1
</a>
<br/>Happy New Year!
</td>
```

When the code from Example 5-47 or Example 5-48 is run, you get the results shown in Figure 5-26.

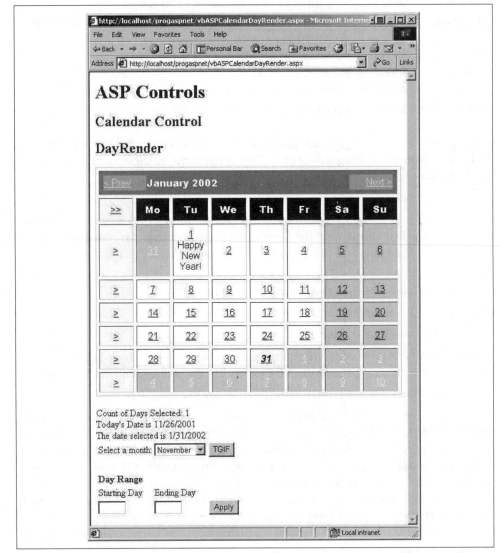

Figure 5-26. Calendar with DayRender event

VisibleMonthChanged event

The Calendar control also provides an event to indicate that the user has changed months. In Example 5-49, you add an event handler in C# for the VisibleMonth-Changed event. Example 5-50 shows the same event handler in VB.NET.

Example 5-49. VisibleMonthChanged event in C#, csASPCalendarVisibleMonth.aspx

```
<%@ Page Language="C#" %>
<script  runat="server">
   // This Page_Load makes the selected days visible first time
   //  the TGIF button is clicked by initializing the VisibleDate
   //  property.
   void Page_Load(Object sender, EventArgs e)
   {
      if (!IsPostBack)
    {
         cal.VisibleDate = cal.TodaysDate;
        ddl.SelectedIndex = cal.VisibleDate.Month - 1;
      }
      lblTodaysDate.Text = "Today's Date is " +
            cal.TodaysDate.ToShortDateString( );
   }

   void SelectionChanged(Object sender, EventArgs e)
   {
      lblSelectedUpdate( );
      lblCountUpdate( );
      txtClear( );
   }

   void ddl_SelectedIndexChanged(Object sender, EventArgs e)
   {
      cal.SelectedDates.Clear( );
      lblSelectedUpdate( );
      lblCountUpdate( );
      txtClear( );
      cal.VisibleDate = new DateTime(cal.TodaysDate.Year,
                     Int32.Parse(ddl.SelectedItem.Value), 1);
   }

   void btnTgif_Click(Object sender, EventArgs e)
   {
      int currentMonth = cal.VisibleDate.Month;
      int currentYear = cal.VisibleDate.Year;

      cal.SelectedDates.Clear( );

      for (int i = 1;
              i <= System.DateTime.DaysInMonth(currentYear,
                                        currentMonth);
```

```
            i++ )
   {
      DateTime date = new DateTime(currentYear, currentMonth, i);
      if (date.DayOfWeek == DayOfWeek.Friday)
         cal.SelectedDates.Add(date);
   }

   lblSelectedUpdate( );
   lblCountUpdate( );
   txtClear( );
}

void btnRange_Click(Object sender, EventArgs e)
{
   int currentMonth = cal.VisibleDate.Month;
   int currentYear = cal.VisibleDate.Year;
   DateTime StartDate = new DateTime(currentYear, currentMonth,
                        Int32.Parse(txtStart.Text));
   DateTime EndDate = new DateTime(currentYear, currentMonth,
                      Int32.Parse(txtEnd.Text));

   cal.SelectedDates.Clear( );
   cal.SelectedDates.SelectRange(StartDate, EndDate);

   lblSelectedUpdate( );
   lblCountUpdate( );
}

void DayRender(Object sender, DayRenderEventArgs e)
{
   //  Notice that this overrides the WeekendDayStyle.
   if (!e.Day.IsOtherMonth && e.Day.IsWeekend)
      e.Cell.BackColor=System.Drawing.Color.LightGreen;

   //  Happy New Year!
   if (e.Day.Date.Month == 1 && e.Day.Date.Day == 1)
      e.Cell.Controls.Add(new LiteralControl("<br/>Happy New Year!"));
}

void VisibleMonthChanged(Object sender, MonthChangedEventArgs e)
{
   if (e.NewDate.Year > e.PreviousDate.Year) |
      ((e.NewDate.Year == e.PreviousDate.Year) &
      (e.NewDate.Month > e.PreviousDate.Month)))
      lblMonthChanged.Text = "My future's so bright...";
   else
      lblMonthChanged.Text = "Back to the future!";

   cal.SelectedDates.Clear( );
   lblSelectedUpdate( );
```

```csharp
      lblCountUpdate( );
      txtClear( );
   }

   void lblCountUpdate( )
   {
      lblCount.Text = "Count of Days Selected:   " +
            cal.SelectedDates.Count.ToString( );
   }

   void lblSelectedUpdate( )
   {
      if (cal.SelectedDate != DateTime.MinValue)
         lblSelected.Text = "The date selected is " +
               cal.SelectedDate.ToShortDateString( );
      else
         lblSelected.Text = "";
   }

   void txtClear( )
   {
      txtStart.Text = "";
      txtEnd.Text = "";
   }
</script>

<html>
   <body>
   <form runat="server">

      <h1>ASP Controls</h1>
      <h2>Calendar Control</h2>
      <h2>VisibleMonthChanged Event</h2>

      <asp:Label id="lblMonthChanged" runat="server" />

      <asp:Calendar
         id="cal"
         SelectionMode="DayWeekMonth"
         ShowGridLines="true"
         ShowNextprevMonth="true"
         CellPadding="7"
         CellSpacing="5"
         DayNameFormat="FirstTwoLetters"
         FirstDayOfWeek="Monday"
         NextPrevFormat="CustomText"
         NextMonthText="Next &gt;"
         PrevMonthText="&lt; Prev"
         onSelectionChanged="SelectionChanged"
```

```
        onDayRender="DayRender"
        onVisibleMonthChanged="VisibleMonthChanged"
        DayHeaderStyle-BackColor="Black"
        DayHeaderStyle-ForeColor="White"
        DayHeaderStyle-Font-Name="Arial Black"
        runat="server" >

        <DayStyle
            BackColor="White"
            ForeColor="Black"
            Font-Name="Arial" />
        <NextPrevStyle
            BackColor="DarkGray"
            ForeColor="Yellow"
            Font-Name="Arial" />
        <OtherMonthDayStyle
            BackColor="LightGray"
            ForeColor="White"
            Font-Name="Arial" />
        <SelectedDayStyle
            BackColor="CornSilk"
            ForeColor="Blue"
            Font-Name="Arial"
            Font-Bold="true"
            Font-Italic="true"/>
        <SelectorStyle
            BackColor="CornSilk"
            ForeColor="Red"
            Font-Name="Arial" />
        <TitleStyle
            BackColor="Gray"
            ForeColor="White"
            HorizontalAlign="Left"
            Font-Name="Arial Black" />
        <TodayDayStyle
            BackColor="CornSilk"
            ForeColor="Green"
            Font-Name="Arial"
            Font-Bold="true"
            Font-Italic="false"/>
        <WeekendDayStyle
            BackColor="LavenderBlush"
            ForeColor="Purple"
            Font-Name="Arial"
            Font-Bold="false"
            Font-Italic="false"/>
    </asp:Calendar>

    <br/>
    <asp:Label id="lblCount" runat="server" />
```

```
<br/>
<asp:Label id="lblTodaysDate" runat="server" />
<br/>
<asp:Label id="lblSelected" runat="server" />
<br/>
<table>
  <tr>
    <td>
        Select a month:
    </td>
    <td>
        <asp:DropDownList
            id= "ddl"
            AutoPostBack="true"
            onSelectedIndexChanged = "ddl_SelectedIndexChanged"
            runat="server">

            <asp:ListItem text="January" value="1" />
            <asp:ListItem text="February" value="2" />
            <asp:ListItem text="March" value="3" />
            <asp:ListItem text="April" value="4" />
            <asp:ListItem text="May" value="5" />
            <asp:ListItem text="June" value="6" />
            <asp:ListItem text="July" value="7" />
            <asp:ListItem text="August" value="8" />
            <asp:ListItem text="September" value="9" />
            <asp:ListItem text="October" value="10" />
            <asp:ListItem text="November" value="11" />
            <asp:ListItem text="December" value="12" />

        </asp:DropDownList>
    </td>
    <td>
        <asp:Button
            id="btnTgif"
            text="TGIF"
            onClick="btnTgif_Click"
            runat="server" />
    </td>
  </tr>
  <tr>
    <td colspan="2"> </td>
  </tr>
  <tr>
    <td colspan="2"><b>Day Range</b></td>
  </tr>
  <tr>
    <td>Starting Day</td>
    <td>Ending Day</td>
  </tr>
  <tr>
```

```
            <td>
                <asp:TextBox
                    id= "txtStart"
                    Size="2"
                    MaxLength="2"
                    runat="server" />
            </td>
            <td>
                <asp:TextBox
                    id= "txtEnd"
                    Size="2"
                    MaxLength="2"
                    runat="server" />
            </td>
            <td>
                <asp:Button
                    id="btnRange"
                    text="Apply"
                    onClick="btnRange_Click"
                    runat="server" />
            </td>
        </tr>
    </table>
  </form>
  </body>
</html>
```

Example 5-50. VisibleMonthChanged event in VB.NET (script block only),
vbASPCalendarVisibleMonth.aspx

```
<%@ Page Language="VB"%>
<script  runat="server">
    ' This Page_Load makes the selected days visible first time
    ' the TGIF button is clicked by initializing the VisibleDate
    ' property.
    sub Page_Load(ByVal Sender as Object, _
                ByVal e as EventArgs)
        if not IsPostBack then
            cal.VisibleDate = cal.TodaysDate
            ddl.SelectedIndex = cal.VisibleDate.Month - 1
        end if

        lblTodaysDate.Text = "Today's Date is " & _
                cal.TodaysDate.ToShortDateString()
    end sub

    sub SelectionChanged(ByVal Sender as Object, _
                        ByVal e as EventArgs)
        lblSelectedUpdate()
        lblCountUpdate()
        txtClear()
```

```
    end sub

    sub ddl_SelectedIndexChanged(ByVal Sender as Object, _
                                 ByVal e as EventArgs)
        cal.SelectedDates.Clear()
        lblSelectedUpdate()
        lblCountUpdate()
        txtClear()
        cal.VisibleDate = new DateTime(cal.TodaysDate.Year, _
                         Int32.Parse(ddl.SelectedItem.Value), 1)
    end sub

    sub btnTgif_Click(ByVal Sender as Object, _
                      ByVal e as EventArgs)
        dim currentMonth as integer = cal.VisibleDate.Month
        dim currentYear as integer = cal.VisibleDate.Year

        cal.SelectedDates.Clear()

        dim i as integer
        for i = 1 to System.DateTime.DaysInMonth(currentYear, _
                                                 currentMonth)
            dim dt as DateTime = new DateTime(currentYear, _
                                              currentMonth, _
                                              i)
            if dt.DayOfWeek = DayOfWeek.Friday then
                cal.SelectedDates.Add(dt)
            end if
        next

        lblSelectedUpdate()
        lblCountUpdate()
        txtClear()
    end sub

    sub btnRange_Click(ByVal Sender as Object, _
                       ByVal e as EventArgs)
        dim currentMonth as integer = cal.VisibleDate.Month
        dim currentYear as integer = cal.VisibleDate.Year
        dim StartDate as DateTime = new DateTime(currentYear, _
                                                 currentMonth, _
                                                 Int32.Parse(txtStart.Text))
        dim EndDate as DateTime = new DateTime(currentYear, _
                                               currentMonth, _
                                               Int32.Parse(txtEnd.Text))
        cal.SelectedDates.Clear()
        cal.SelectedDates.SelectRange(StartDate, EndDate)

        lblCountUpdate()
```

```
    end sub

    sub DayRender(ByVal Sender as Object, _
                  ByVal e as DayRenderEventArgs)
      ' Notice that this overrides the WeekendDayStyle.
      if (not e.Day.IsOtherMonth and e.Day.IsWeekend) then
          e.Cell.BackColor=System.Drawing.Color.LightGreen
      end if

      ' Happy New Year!
      if (e.Day.Date.Month = 1 and e.Day.Date.Day = 1) then
          e.Cell.Controls.Add(new LiteralControl("<br/>Happy New Year!"))
      end if
    end sub

    sub VisibleMonthChanged(ByVal Sender as Object, _
                            ByVal e as MonthChangedEventArgs)
      if e.NewDate.Year > e.PreviousDate.Year Or _
         ((e.NewDate.Year == e.PreviousDate.Year) And _
         (e.NewDate Month > e.PreviousDate.Month)) Then
          lblMonthChanged.Text = "My future's so bright..."
      else
          lblMonthChanged.Text = "Back to the future!"
      end if

      cal.SelectedDates.Clear()
      lblSelectedUpdate()
      lblCountUpdate()
      txtClear()
    end sub

    sub lblCountUpdate()
      lblCount.Text = "Count of Days Selected:   " & _
            cal.SelectedDates.Count.ToString()
    end sub

    sub lblSelectedUpdate()
      if (cal.SelectedDate <> DateTime.MinValue) then
          lblSelected.Text = "The date selected is " & _
              cal.SelectedDate.ToShortDateString()
      else
          lblSelected.Text = ""
      end if
    end sub

    sub txtClear()
      txtStart.Text = ""
      txtEnd.Text = ""
    end sub
</script>
```

The onVisibleMonthChanged event handler calls the VisibleMonthChanged method, which is in the script block. A Label control named lblMonthChanged was added just before the Calendar control.

The VisibleMonthChanged event handler method receives an argument of type MonthChangedEventArgs. This argument contains two properties that may be read programmatically:

NewDate

    Represents the month currently displayed by the Calendar

PreviousDate

    Represents the month previously displayed by the Calendar

These values are tested in the VisibleMonthChanged method to see which came first. Depending on the results, one of two text strings is assigned to the Text property of lblMonthChanged.

Finally, the selected dates are cleared from the calendar, the text strings below the calendar are updated, and the day range edit boxes are cleared with the following lines of code (which are the same in C# and VB.NET, except for the trailing semicolons in C#):

```
cal.SelectedDates.Clear( )
lblSelectedUpdate( )
lblCountUpdate( )
txtClear( )
```

The results of running the pages in Example 5-49 and Example 5-50 can be seen in Figure 5-27.

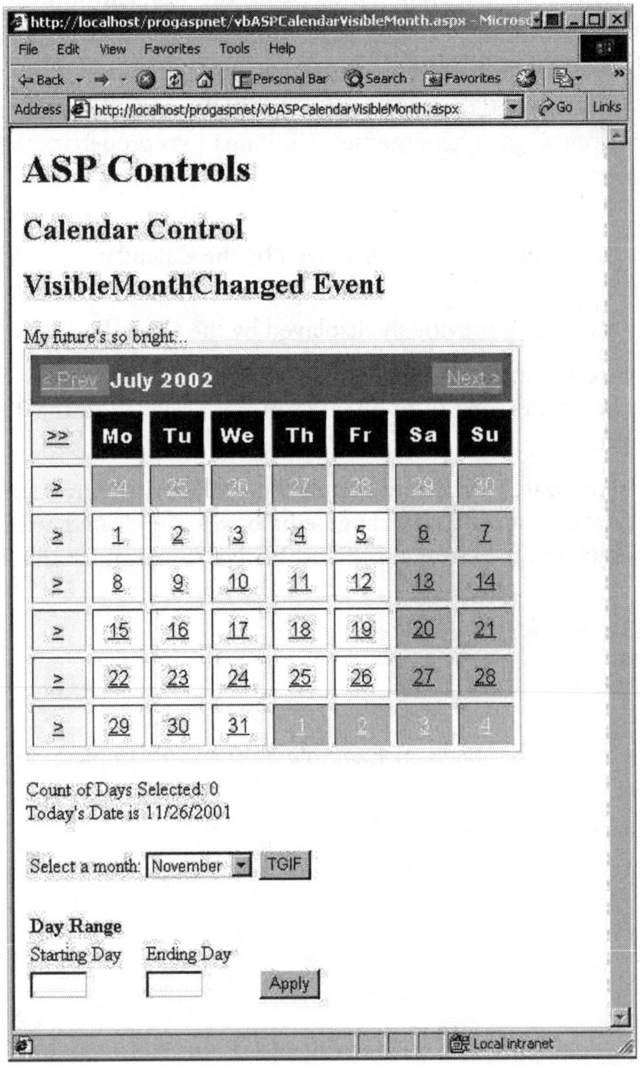

Figure 5-27. Calendar with VisibleMonthChanged event

CHAPTER 6

Programming Web Forms

In the previous chapter, you learned many of the details about using ASP server controls in Web Forms. In this chapter, you will learn techniques that will help you utilize the full power of ASP.NET in creating Web Forms, including:

- Using code-behind to segregate the presentation code from the logic
- Understanding the control lifecycle of a web page
- Managing state in ASP.NET
- Using Visual Studio .NET as a development tool

Code-Behind

In traditional ASP, the interweaving of script with HTML can produce source control nightmares and difficult-to-maintain ASP pages. ASP.NET addresses this problem by giving programmers the ability to separate the executable code from the presentation code. You write the HTML in a page file (with a *.aspx* extension), and you write the C# or VB.NET code in the *code-behind* file (with a *.cs* or *.vb* extension, depending on its language), which is another way of saying the "code file behind the form."

In the code-behind file, you create a class, which can be any class derived from the Page class, that serves as the base class for the web page you create in the *.aspx* file. This relationship between your class and the web page is established by a Page directive at the top of the *.aspx* file:

```
<%@ Page inherits="CodeBehindDemo" %>
```

The inherits attribute identifies the class created in the code-behind file from which this *.aspx* file will derive.

When a web form is compiled, its page is parsed and a new class is generated and compiled. This new class derives from the class identified in the inherits keyword, which in turn derives from System.Web.UI.Page.

Now the only question is: "How does the compiler know where to find this code-behind file class to derive from?" The answer depends on whether or not you are working in the Visual Studio .NET (VS.NET) IDE or using a text editor to work directly with the source files.

If you're working in the VS.NET IDE, then the development environment will automatically pre-compile the class in the code-behind file and use the inherits attribute to point to that class. The *.dll* that is created is placed in the \bin subdirectory in the application virtual directory.

You will notice that VS.NET also puts a codebehind attribute in the Page directive, which points to the code-behind file. The codebehind attribute is used to keep track of the code-behind file so that as you make changes to the page, VS.NET can make the appropriate changes to the code-behind file. Using VS.NET will be covered in more detail later in this chapter.

If you are not using a development environment such as VS.NET, but rather editing the files directly in a text editor, then you need to include the src attribute in the Page directive to identify the file containing the class specified in the inherits attribute for the JIT compiler:

```
<%@ Page inherits="CodeBehindDemo"  src="CodeBehind.cs"  %>
```

If the src string does not include a fully qualified path, then it is assumed that the file is in the same directory as the *.aspx* file. If the src attribute is missing, then the compiler will look in the \bin subdirectory of the application virtual directory for a *.dll* that contains the class marked with the inherits attribute.

In order to convert an *.aspx* file from in-line code to code-behind, you need to make modifications both to the *.aspx* file as well as to the code-behind file, as follows:

Modifications to the .aspx file

> The *.aspx* file needs to have its Page directive modified to include the inherits attribute.

> Optionally, the Page directive must be modified to include the src attribute.

Modifications to the code-behind file

> The code-behind file does not automatically inherit the common namespaces used in web forms. The code-behind file itself must tell the compiler which namespaces it needs with the using keyword in C# and the Imports keyword in VB.NET.

> The class you create must inherit from the System.Web.UI.Page class.

> Every control in the *.aspx* file referred to by name (id) in the code-behind file must have an accessible variable (declared using either the public or protected access modifier) defined in the code-behind class. The variable type must be the same as the control type, and the variable name must match the control name.

All methods in the code-behind class that are called directly from the *.aspx* file must be declared as either public or protected methods (i.e., using the public or protected access modifiers).

Access Modifiers

The keywords public, protected, private, and internal (in C#) or friend (in VB) are access modifiers. An access modifier determines which class methods can see and use a member variable or method. Table 6-1 summarizes the access modifiers.

The default accessibility of members of a class is private. Thus, if there is no access modifier provided for a class member, then it will be a private member. Regardless of this circumstance, it is always a good idea to explicitly specify the access modifier in order to enhance the readability of the code.

Table 6-1. Access modifiers

Access modifier	Restrictions
public	No restrictions. Members marked public are visible to any method of any class.
private	The members in class A that are marked private are accessible only to methods of class A.
protected	The members in class A that are marked protected are accessible to methods of class A and also to methods of classes derived from class A.
internal (C#) Friend (VB)	The members in class A that are marked internal or friend are accessible to methods of any class in A's assembly.
protected internal (C#) Protected friend (VB)	The members in class A that are marked protected internal or protected friend are accessible only to methods of class A and also to methods of classes derived from class A, and also to any class in A's assembly. This is effectively protected or internal.

To better understand code-behind, modify one of the Calendar examples from Chapter 5 (Example 5-43 in C# or 5-44 in VB.NET) to use code-behind. These modifications will entail removing the entire script block and changing the Page directive in the *.aspx* file, and creating a code-behind file that essentially contains the excised script block.

The easiest way to accomplish this is to copy the *.aspx* file twice: once to the file to use for the new *.aspx* file and once to the file to use for the code-behind file. Then edit each of those new files. In this example, the original Calendar example *.aspx* files will be copied and renamed as shown in Table 6-2.

It is important that the code-behind file have the correct file extension. This tells the framework which compiler to use to compile the code-behind file. Valid file extensions are:

- *.cs* for C#
- *.vb* for VB.NET
- *.js* for JavaScript

Table 6-2. Example filenames

Original filename	New filename	Purpose
csASPCalendarMoreSelections.aspx	csCodeBehind.aspx	Contains the HTML for the C# version
"	CodeBehind.cs	Contains the C# version of the code-behind class
vbASPCalendarMoreSelections.aspx	vbCodeBehind.aspx	Contains the HTML for the VB.NET version
"	CodeBehind.vb	Contains the VB.NET version of the code-behind class

Example 6-1 shows the *.aspx* file modified to use code-behind for C#. Since the HTML is exactly the same in both C# and VB.NET, Example 6-2 shows only the Page directive for the VB.NET version.

Example 6-1. Code-behind page using C#, csCodeBehind.aspx

```
<%@ Page inherits="CodeBehindDemo"  src ="CodeBehind.cs" %>

<html>
   <body>
   <form runat="server">

      <h1>ASP Controls</h1>
      <h2>Calendar Control</h2>
      <h2>More Selections</h2>

      <asp:Calendar
         id="cal"
         SelectionMode="DayWeekMonth"
         ShowGridLines="true"
         ShowNextprevMonth="true"
         CellPadding="7"
         CellSpacing="5"
         DayNameFormat="FirstTwoLetters"
         FirstDayOfWeek="Monday"
         NextPrevFormat="CustomText"
         NextMonthText="Next &gt;"
         PrevMonthText="&lt; Prev"
         onSelectionChanged="SelectionChanged"
         DayHeaderStyle-BackColor="Black"
         DayHeaderStyle-ForeColor="White"
         DayHeaderStyle-Font-Name="Arial Black"
         runat="server" >

         <DayStyle
            BackColor="White"
            ForeColor="Black"
            Font-Name="Arial" />
```

Example 6-1. Code-behind page using C#, csCodeBehind.aspx (continued)

```
        <NextPrevStyle
            BackColor="DarkGray"
            ForeColor="Yellow"
            Font-Name="Arial" />
        <OtherMonthDayStyle
            BackColor="LightGray"
            ForeColor="White"
            Font-Name="Arial" />
        <SelectedDayStyle
            BackColor="CornSilk"
            ForeColor="Blue"
            Font-Name="Arial"
            Font-Bold="true"
            Font-Italic="true"/>
        <SelectorStyle
            BackColor="CornSilk"
            ForeColor="Red"
            Font-Name="Arial" />
        <TitleStyle
            BackColor="Gray"
            ForeColor="White"
            HorizontalAlign="Left"
            Font-Name="Arial Black" />
        <TodayDayStyle
            BackColor="CornSilk"
            ForeColor="Green"
            Font-Name="Arial"
            Font-Bold="true"
            Font-Italic="false"/>
        <WeekendDayStyle
            BackColor="LavenderBlush"
            ForeColor="Purple"
            Font-Name="Arial"
            Font-Bold="false"
            Font-Italic="false"/>
</asp:Calendar>

<br/>
<asp:Label id="lblCount" runat="server" />
<br/>
<asp:Label id="lblTodaysDate" runat="server" />
<br/>
<asp:Label id="lblSelected" runat="server" />
<br/>
<table>
    <tr>
        <td>
            Select a month:
        </td>
        <td>
            <asp:DropDownList
                id= "ddl"
```

Example 6-1. Code-behind page using C#, csCodeBehind.aspx (continued)

```
                    AutoPostBack="true"
                    onSelectedIndexChanged = "ddl_SelectedIndexChanged"
                    runat="server">

                    <asp:ListItem text="January" value="1" />
                    <asp:ListItem text="February" value="2" />
                    <asp:ListItem text="March" value="3" />
                    <asp:ListItem text="April" value="4" />
                    <asp:ListItem text="May" value="5" />
                    <asp:ListItem text="June" value="6" />
                    <asp:ListItem text="July" value="7" />
                    <asp:ListItem text="August" value="8" />
                    <asp:ListItem text="September" value="9" />
                    <asp:ListItem text="October" value="10" />
                    <asp:ListItem text="November" value="11" />
                    <asp:ListItem text="December" value="12" />

                </asp:DropDownList>
            </td>
            <td>
                <asp:Button
                    id="btnTgif"
                    text="TGIF"
                    onClick="btnTgif_Click"
                    runat="server" />
            </td>
        </tr>
    </table>
  </form>
  </body>
</html>
```

Example 6-2. Code-behind page directive using VB.NET, vbCodeBehind.aspx

```
<%@ Page inherits="CodeBehindDemo"  src ="CodeBehind.vb" %>
```

In Example 6-1 and Example 6-2, the only changes necessary from the original *.aspx* file are to remove the script block entirely and modify the Page directive. The Page directive modifications are intended to:

1. Remove the Language attribute.

2. Add an inherits attribute for the code-behind class.

3. Add the appropriate value to the src attribute that points to the correct code-behind file.

> You remove the Language attribute because there is no longer any code other than HTML in the page file. If you keep script in the page file, the Language attribute would have to remain.

Example 6-3 shows the code-behind file for C#.

Example 6-3. CodeBehind.cs

```csharp
using System;
using System.Web;
using System.Web.UI;
using System.Web.UI.WebControls;

public class CodeBehindDemo : Page
{
    protected Calendar cal;
    protected Label lblCount;
    protected Label lblTodaysDate;
    protected Label lblSelected;
    protected DropDownList ddl;

    // This Page_Load makes the selected days visible first time
    // the TGIF button is clicked by initializing the VisibleDate
    // property.
    protected void Page_Load(Object sender, EventArgs e)
    {
        if (!IsPostBack)
        {
            cal.VisibleDate = cal.TodaysDate;
            ddl.SelectedIndex = cal.VisibleDate.Month - 1;
        }
        lblTodaysDate.Text = "Today's Date is " +
            cal.TodaysDate.ToShortDateString( );
    }

    protected void SelectionChanged(Object sender, EventArgs e)
    {
        lblSelectedUpdate( );
        lblCountUpdate( );
    }

    protected void ddl_SelectedIndexChanged(Object sender, EventArgs e)
    {
        cal.SelectedDates.Clear( );
        lblSelectedUpdate( );
        lblCountUpdate( );
        cal.VisibleDate = new DateTime(cal.TodaysDate.Year,
                        Int32.Parse(ddl.SelectedItem.Value), 1);
    }

    protected void btnTgif_Click(Object sender, EventArgs e)
    {
        int currentMonth = cal.VisibleDate.Month;
        int currentYear = cal.VisibleDate.Year;

        cal.SelectedDates.Clear( );

        for (int i = 1;
```

Example 6-3. CodeBehind.cs (continued)

```
                i <= System.DateTime.DaysInMonth(currentYear,
                                                  currentMonth);
                i++ )
   {
      DateTime date = new DateTime(currentYear, currentMonth, i);
      if (date.DayOfWeek == DayOfWeek.Friday)
         cal.SelectedDates.Add(date);
   }

   lblSelectedUpdate( );
   lblCountUpdate( );
}

private void lblCountUpdate( )
{
   lblCount.Text = "Count of Days Selected:   " +
         cal.SelectedDates.Count.ToString( );
}

private void lblSelectedUpdate( )
{
   if (cal.SelectedDate != DateTime.MinValue)
      lblSelected.Text = "The date selected is " +
            cal.SelectedDate.ToShortDateString( );
   else
      lblSelected.Text = "";
   }
}
```

Example 6-3 shows several changes from the original code in the in-line script block:

- There are several using statements at the beginning of the C# code-behind file to reference the needed namespaces. These were not required in the in-line code because they were automatically included by the compiler when it compiled the *.aspx* file.

- The class declaration for the CodeBehindDemo class inherits from the base class System.Web.UI.Page. (It is not actually necessary to fully qualify the Page object because you have included the System.Web.UI namespace in a using statement.)

- Variables are declared for each of the controls referred to in the code-behind file. Note that there is no declaration for the btnTgif control, since that control is not referenced anywhere in the code-behind file, although there is an event handler for the Click event.

  Remember that the *.aspx* file is compiled into a class that derives from the code-behind class, CodeBehindDemo. Because these variables must be visible to the *.aspx* class, they have to be declared as either public or protected. Good object-oriented programming practice recommends using protected to hide data as much as possible.

- All of the methods that are called directly from the *.aspx* file have the protected keyword added to their declaration. (These are all the methods except lblCount-Update and lblSelectedUpdate, which are declared private.)

  As with the variables, the program will work if the methods use the keyword public, but protected gives better encapsulation.

Example 6-4 shows the code-behind file for VB.NET. It makes the same functional changes as for the C# file, with only syntactic changes.

Example 6-4. CodeBehind.vb

```
Imports System
Imports System.Web
Imports System.Web.UI
Imports System.Web.UI.WebControls


public class CodeBehindDemo
Inherits Page

    protected cal as Calendar
    protected lblCount as Label
    protected lblTodaysDate as Label
    protected lblSelected as Label
    protected ddl as DropDownList

    '  This Page_Load makes the selected days visible first time
    '  the TGIF button is clicked by initializing the VisibleDate
    '  property.
    protected sub Page_Load(ByVal Sender as Object, _
                ByVal e as EventArgs)
        if not IsPostBack then
            cal.VisibleDate = cal.TodaysDate
        ddl.SelectedIndex = cal.VisibleDate.Month - 1
        end if

        lblTodaysDate.Text = "Today's Date is " & _
                cal.TodaysDate.ToShortDateString( )
    end sub

    protected sub SelectionChanged(ByVal Sender as Object, _
                    ByVal e as EventArgs)
        lblSelectedUpdate( )
        lblCountUpdate( )
    end sub

    protected sub ddl_SelectedIndexChanged(ByVal Sender as Object, _
                        ByVal e as EventArgs)
        cal.SelectedDates.Clear( )
        lblSelectedUpdate( )
        lblCountUpdate( )
        cal.VisibleDate = new DateTime(cal.TodaysDate.Year, _
```

Example 6-4. CodeBehind.vb (continued)

```vb
                                Int32.Parse(ddl.SelectedItem.Value), 1)
    end sub

    protected sub btnTgif_Click(ByVal Sender as Object, _
                    ByVal e as EventArgs)
        dim currentMonth as integer = cal.VisibleDate.Month
        dim currentYear as integer = cal.VisibleDate.Year

        cal.SelectedDates.Clear()

        dim i as integer
        for i = 1 to System.DateTime.DaysInMonth(currentYear, currentMonth)
            dim dt as DateTime = new DateTime(currentYear, currentMonth, i)
            if dt.DayOfWeek = DayOfWeek.Friday then
                cal.SelectedDates.Add(dt)
            end if
        next

        lblSelectedUpdate()
        lblCountUpdate()
    end sub

    private sub lblCountUpdate()
        lblCount.Text = "Count of Days Selected:  " & _
                cal.SelectedDates.Count.ToString()
    end sub

    private sub lblSelectedUpdate()
        if (cal.SelectedDate <> DateTime.MinValue) then
            lblSelected.Text = "The date selected is " & _
                    cal.SelectedDate.ToShortDateString()
        else
            lblSelected.Text = ""
        end if
    end sub
end class
```

When either Example 6-1 or 6-2 is run, it looks exactly the same as the example using in-line code, shown here in Figure 6-1.

State

State is the current value of all the controls and variables for the current user in the current session. The web is inherently a *stateless* environment, which means that every time a page is posted to the server and then sent back to the browser, the page is recreated from scratch. Unless you explicitly preserve the state of all the controls before the page is posted, the state is lost and all the controls are created with default values. One of the great strengths of ASP.NET is that it automatically maintains state

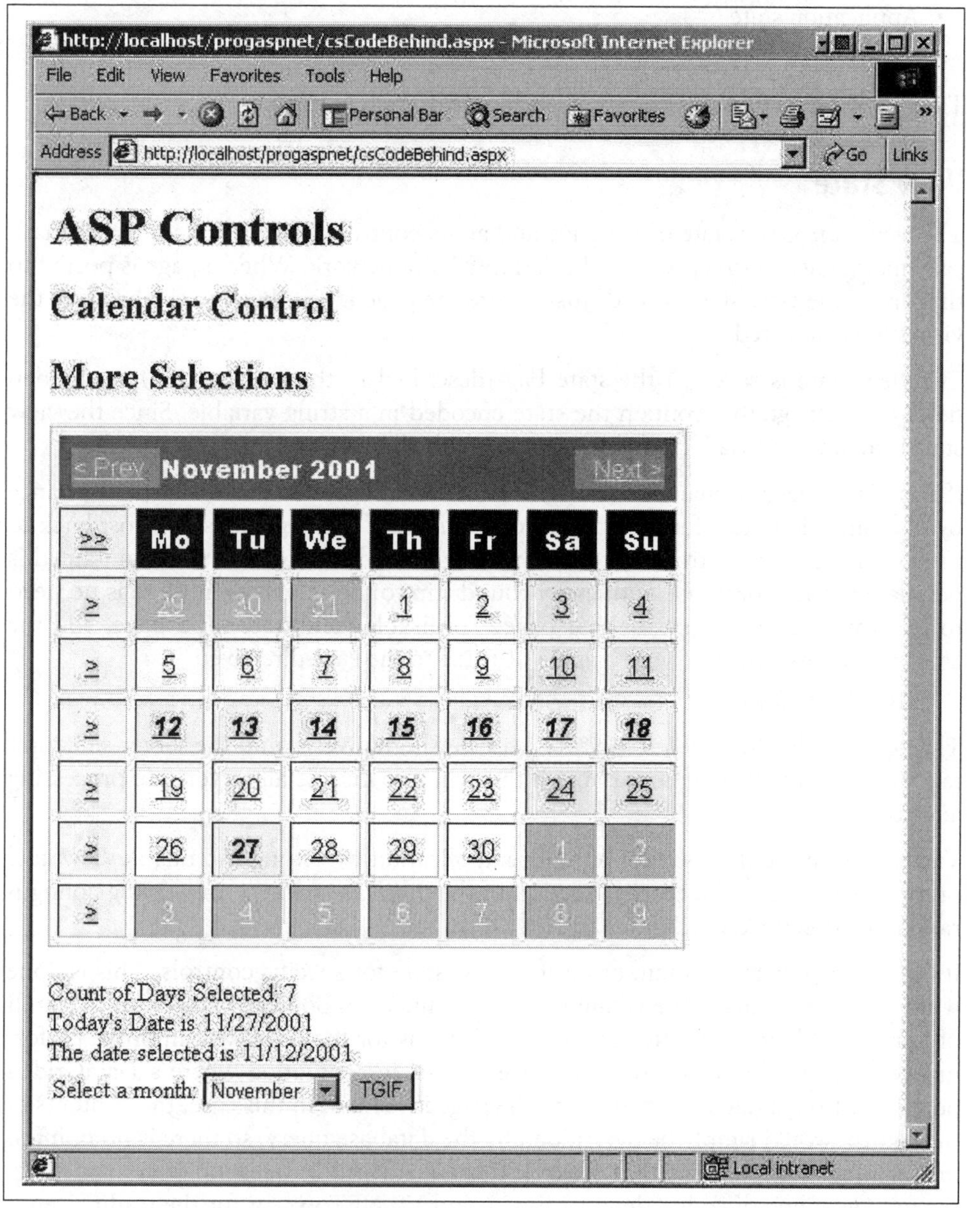

Figure 6-1. Code-behind from Example 6-1 or 6-2

for server controls—both HTML and ASP. This section will explore how that is done and how you can use the ASP.NET state management capabilities.

ASP.NET manages three types of state:

- View state (which is saved in the state bag)

- Application state
- Session state

The following sections will examine each type of state in turn.

View State

The *view state* is the state of the page and all its controls. The view state is automatically maintained across posts by the ASP.NET Framework. When a page is posted to the server, the view state is read. Just before the page is sent back to the browser the view state is restored.

The view state is saved in the state bag (described in the next section) via hidden fields on the page that contain the state encoded in a string variable. Since the view state is maintained via form fields, it works with all browsers.

If there is no need to maintain the view state for a page, you can boost performance by disabling view state for that page. For example, if the page does not post back to itself or if the only control on a page that might need to have its state maintained is populated from a database with every round trip to the server, then there is no need to maintain the view state for that page. To disable view state for a page, add the EnableViewState attribute with a value of false to the Page directive:

```
<%@ Page Language="C#"  EnableViewState="false" %>
```

The default value for EnableViewState is true. Alternatively, omit the server-side form tag (<form runat="server">), although this will also disable all server-side processing and controls.

View state can be disabled for an entire application by setting the EnableViewState property to false in the <pages> section of the *machine.config* or *web.config* configuration file (described in Chapter 20).

It is also possible to maintain or disable view state for specific controls. This is done with the Control.EnableViewState property, which is a Boolean value with a default of true. Disabling view state for a control, just as for the page, will improve performance. This would be appropriate, for example, in a situation where a DataGrid is populated from a database every time the page is loaded. In this case, the contents of the control would simply be overridden by the database query, so there is no point in maintaining view state for that control. If the DataGrid in question were named dg, the following line of code (identical in C# and VB.NET except for the trailing semicolon in C#) would disable its view state:

```
dg.EnableViewState = false
```

There are some situations where view state is not the best place to store data. If there is a large amount of data to be stored, then view state is not an efficient mechanism, since the data is transferred back and forth to the server with every page post. If there are security concerns about the data and it is not otherwise being displayed on the page, then including the data in view state increases the security exposure. Finally, view state is optimized only for strings, integers, Booleans, arrays, ArrayLists, and hashtables. Other .NET types may be serialized and persisted in view state, but will result in degraded performance and a larger view state footprint.

In some of these instances, session state might be a better alternative; on the other hand, view state does not consume any server resources and does not time out, as does session state.

State Bag

If there are values that are not associated with any control and you wish to preserve these values across round trips, you can store these values in the page's *state bag*. The *state bag* is a data structure containing attribute/value pairs, stored as strings associated with objects. The valid objects are the primitive data types—integers, bytes, strings, Booleans, etc. The state bag is implemented using the StateBag class, which is a dictionary object. You add or remove items from the state bag as with any dictionary object. (For a complete discussion of dictionary objects in C#, see *Programming C#* by Jesse Liberty, and in VB.NET see *VB.NET Language in a Nutshell* by Steven Roman, Ron Petrusha, and Paul Lomax, both published by O'Reilly.)

The state bag is maintained using the same hidden fields as the view state. You can set and retrieve values of things in the state bag using the ViewState keyword, as shown in Example 6-5 in C# and in Example 6-6 in VB.NET. These examples set up a counter that is maintained as long as the session is active. Every time the Increment Counter button is clicked, the page is reloaded, which causes the counter to increment.

Example 6-5. Using the StateBag using C#, csStateBagDemo.aspx

```
<%@ Page Language="C#" %>
<html>

<script runat="server">

   void Page_Load(Object sender, EventArgs e)
   {
      lblCounter.Text = Counter.ToString( );
      Counter++;
   }

   public int Counter
   {
      get
      {
         if (ViewState["intCounter"] != null )
         {
            return ((int)ViewState["intCounter"]);
         }
```

```
        return 0;
    }

    set
    {
        ViewState["intCounter"] = value;
    }
  }
</script>

  <body>
  <form runat="server">

      <h1>ASP.NET State</h1>
      <br/>
      <h2>csStateBagDemo.aspx</h2>
      <br/>

      Counter:
      <asp:Label
          id="lblCounter"
          runat="server" />

      <asp:Button
          id="btn"
          text = "Increment Counter"
          runat="server" />

  </form>
  </body>
</html>
```

Example 6-6. Using the StateBag using VB.NET, vbStateBagDemo.aspx

```
<%@ Page Language="VB" Strict="true" %>
<html>

<script runat="server">

  sub Page_Load(ByVal Sender as Object, _
                ByVal e as EventArgs)
    lblCounter.Text = Counter.ToString( )
    Counter += 1
  end sub

  public property Counter( ) as integer
    get
        if not (ViewState("intCounter") is Nothing) then
              return CInt(ViewState("intCounter"))
        else
           return 0
        end if
```

```
      end get

      set
          ViewState("intCounter") = value
      end set
   end property
</script>

   <body>
   <form runat="server">

      <h1>ASP.NET State</h1>
      <br/>
      <h2>vbStateBagDemo.aspx</h2>
      <br/>

      Counter:
      <asp:Label
          id="lblCounter"
          runat="server" />

      <asp:Button
          id="btn"
          text = "Increment Counter"
          runat="server" />

   </form>
   </body>
</html>
```

In both Example 6-5 and Example 6-6, a Counter property is created that returns an integer. In C#, shown in Example 6-5, this is implicit in the class constructor by the use of the get and set keywords. In VB.NET, shown in Example 6-6, the Property keyword makes this explicit.

In the get block, the contents of the state bag named intCounter are tested to see if anything is there. In C#, this is accomplished with the line:

```
if (ViewState["intCounter"] != null )
```

and in VB.NET with the line:

```
if not (ViewState("intCounter") is Nothing) then
```

If the intCounter state bag is empty, then zero is returned. Otherwise, the value is retrieved and returned. The state bag returns an object that is not implicitly recognized as an integer so it must be cast as an integer before the method returns the value. In C# the syntax is:

```
return ((int)ViewState["intCounter"]);
```

while in VB.NET the code is:

```
return CInt(ViewState("intCounter"))
```

In the VB.NET code examples, the Page directive includes the Strict attribute:

```
<%@ Page Language="VB" Strict="true" %>
```

This attribute tells the compiler to disallow any implicit narrowing data conversion, which could possibly result in data loss. In these cases, you must explicitly cast, i.e., convert, from one data type to another.

If the Strict attribute were omitted or set to false (its default value), then your code would not be forced to use type-safe behavior, allowing late binding of variable types. While on the one hand this would be a convenience, it would also represent a significant performance hit. If the Strict attribute were set to false, you would not have to cast your objects explicitly. You could replace the following lines:

```
if not ViewState("intCounter") is Nothing then
    return CInt(ViewState("intCounter"))
```

with these lines:

```
if (ViewState("intCounter") <> Nothing ) then
    return ViewState("intCounter")
```

In the set block, the intCounter value is set. In C#, the code is:

```
ViewState["intCounter"] = value;
```

and in VB.NET, it is:

```
ViewState("intCounter") = value
```

where value is a keyword used in the property set block to represent the implicit variable containing the value being passed in.

Then in the Page_Load, Counter is called twice—once to retrieve the counter value in order to set the value of the Label control's Text property and once to increment itself. In C# this is done with:

```
lblCounter.Text = Counter.ToString( );
Counter++;
```

and in VB.NET:

```
lblCounter.Text = Counter.ToString( )
Counter += 1
```

Application State

A web *application* consists of all the web pages, files, components, code, and images that reside in a virtual directory or its subdirectories.

The file *global.asax* contains global code for the web application. The *global.asax* file resides in the virtual root directory of the application. This file will be covered in detail in Chapter 20. For now, only the aspects relating to application state and session state will be covered.

Among other things, the *global.asax* file contains event handlers for the Application_ Start, Application_End, Session_Start, and Session_End events. When the application receives the first user request, the Application_Start event is fired. If the *global. asax* file is edited and the changes are saved, then all current pending requests are completed, the Application_End event is fired, and the application is restarted. This sequence effectively *reboots* the application, flushing all state information. The rebooting of the application is transparent to any users, however, since it occurs only after satisfying any pending requests and before any new requests are accepted. When the next request is received, the application starts over again raising another Application_Start event.

Information can be shared *globally* across your application via a dictionary of objects, each object associated with a key value. This is implemented using the intrinsic Application property of the HttpApplicationState class. The Application property allows access to the *Contents* collection, whose contents have been added to the Application state directly through code.

Example 6-7 and Example 6-8 each show a *global.asax* file, using C# and VB.NET, respectively.

Example 6-7. A global.asax file using C#

```
<%@ Application  Language="C#"%>
<script runat="server">

   protected void Application_Start(Object sender, EventArgs e)
   {
      Application["strStartMsg"] =  "The application has started.";
      Application["strDSN"] =
               "SERVER=Zeus;DATABASE=Pubs;UID=sa;PWD=secret;";

      string[] Books = {"SciFi","Novels", "Computers",
                     "History", "Religion"};
      Application["arBooks"] = Books;

      WriteFile("Application Starting");
   }

   protected void Application_End(Object sender, EventArgs e)
   {
      Application["strEndMsg"] =  "The application is ending.";
      WriteFile("Application Ending");
   }

   void WriteFile(string strText)
   {
      System.IO.StreamWriter writer = new
                     System.IO.StreamWriter(@"C:\test.txt",true);
      string str;
      str = DateTime.Now.ToString() + "  " + strText;
      writer.WriteLine(str);
```

Example 6-7. A global.asax file using C# (continued)

```
    writer.Close( );
  }
</script>
```

Example 6-8. A global.asax file using VB.NET

```
<%@ Application  Language="VB"%>
<script runat="server">

   protected sub Application_Start(ByVal Sender as Object, _
                                   ByVal e as EventArgs)
      Application("strStartMsg") = "The application has started."
      Application("strDSN") = _
                  "SERVER=Zeus;DATABASE=Pubs;UID=sa;PWD=secret;"

      dim Books( ) as string = {"SciFi","Novels", "Computers", _
                                "History", "Religion"}
      Application("arBooks") = Books

      WriteFile("Application Starting")
   end sub

   protected sub Application_End(ByVal Sender as Object, _
                                 ByVal e as EventArgs)
      Application("strEndMsg") = "The application is ending."
      WriteFile("Application Ending")
   end sub

   sub WriteFile(strText as string)
      dim writer as System.IO.StreamWriter = new _
                    System.IO.StreamWriter("C:\\test.txt",true)
      dim str as string
      str = DateTime.Now.ToString( ) & "  " & strText
      writer.WriteLine(str)
      writer.Close( )
   end sub

</script>
```

A *global.asax* file is very similar to a normal *.aspx* file in that there is a directive on the first line followed by a script block in the language specified in the directive. In these cases, the directive is not the Page directive of a normal page, but an *Application directive*. In C#, these two lines look like this:

```
<%@ Application  Language="C#"%>
<script runat="server">
```

and in VB.NET, the lines are:

```
<%@ Application  Language="VB"%>
<script runat="server">
```

You can see that the file has two event handlers—one each for Application_Start and Application_End. To see how this works, create a file called *global.asax* in your application virtual directory. (This book has been using the physical directory *e:\ Projects\Programming ASP.NET* assigned to the virtual directory *ProgAspNet* for all the examples so far.) Depending on your language preference, edit the file so that it contains the code of either Example 6-7 or 6-8.

 There can only be a single *global.asax* file in any application virtual directory. Each *global.asax* file must utilize a single language.

As mentioned previously, every time the *global.asax* file is modified, the .NET Framework detects this and automatically stops and restarts the application.

Now run any of the web pages in that virtual directory, such as one of the examples from earlier in this chapter. At the instant the server receives and begins to process the page request, the application starts and the Application_Start event handler is called.

If you now open another browser and call some other *.aspx* file located in the same virtual directory, the application doesn't start again; it is already running. In fact, closing all your browsers and then opening a page will still not fire the Application_ Start event. The application must first be ended, as described later in the explanation for Example 6-11.

Here is the Application_Start method in C#, reproduced from Example 6-7:

```
protected void Application_Start(Object sender, EventArgs e)
{
   Application["strStartMsg"] = "The application has started.";
   Application["strDSN"] =
           "SERVER=Zeus;DATABASE=Pubs;UID=sa;PWD=secret;";

   string[] Books = {"SciFi","Novels", "Computers",
                     "History", "Religion"};
   Application["arBooks"] = Books;

   WriteFile("Application Starting");
}
```

The Application property exposes a dictionary of objects linked to keys. In the Application_Start event handler in Example 6-7 and Example 6-8, three objects are entered in the Application dictionary: two strings and one string array. Then a call is made to the WriteFile method, which is coded further down in the script block. WriteFile writes a simple text log to the root of Drive C. If the file does not exist, it is created, and, if it does exist, the strings are appended to the end of the file.

Finally, the Application_End event handler of *global.asax* puts another string object in the Application dictionary, then makes a log entry.

The web pages in Example 6-9 and Example 6-10 show how these Application dictionary entries are used as global variables. Although the *global.asax* file is an excellent place to initialize global Application objects, it is not the only place. Application objects can be set from anywhere in the application, including any web page or code-behind file. The benefit of using the *global.asax* file is that you can be certain the global application objects will be set when the application first starts, regardless of which component of the application is accessed first. On the other hand, if the application design is such that a specific web page is always accessed first, then it would be perfectly reasonable to have that web page, or its associated code-behind file, perform any initialization.

Example 6-9. Application state example using C#, csApplicationState.aspx

```
<%@ Page Language="C#" %>
<html>

<script runat="server">

    void Page_Load(Object Source, EventArgs E)
    {
        Response.Write((string)Application["strStartMsg"] + "<br/>");
        Response.Write((string)Application["strDSN"] + "<br/>");
        Response.Write((string)Application["strEndMsg"]);

        string[] arTest = (string[])Application["arBooks"];
        Response.Write(arTest[1]);    }

</script>

    <body>
    <form runat="server">

        <h1>Application State Demo</h1>
        <br/>
        <br/>

    </form>
    </body>
</html>
```

Example 6-10. Application state example using VB.NET, vbApplicationState.aspx

```
<%@ Page Language="VB" Strict="true" %>
<html>

<script runat="server">

    sub Page_Load(ByVal Sender as Object, _
               ByVal e as EventArgs)
        Response.Write(Cstr(Application("strStartMsg")) & "<br/>")
        Response.Write(Cstr(Application("strDSN")) & "<br/>")
        Response.Write(Cstr(Application("strEndMsg")))
```

```
    dim arTest() as string = CType(Application("arBooks"), String())
    Response.Write(arTest(1))

  end sub

</script>

  <body>
  <form runat="server">

    <h1>Application State Demo</h1>
    <br/>
    <br/>

  </form>
  </body>
</html>
```

The Application dictionary objects are retrieved as any other property would be, then cast to the appropriate type for use in the Response.Write method.

> As mentioned previously in the section "State Bag," the VB.NET Page directive in Example 6-10 has set Strict equal to true, which enforces Option Strict. If this were omitted or set to false, then it would not be necessary to explicitly cast the type:
>
> ```
> dim arTest( ) as string = CType(Application("arBooks"), _
> string( ))
> ```
>
> Instead you could use this line:
>
> ```
> dim arTest( ) as string = Application("arBooks")
> ```
>
> (The *CType* function is used in VB.NET to generically convert any expression to any type.)

Note that for backwards compatibility with traditional ASP, you can refer to the Contents subproperty of the Application object. Thus, the following two lines of C# code are equivalent:

```
Response.Write((string)Application["strDSN"] + "<br/>");
Response.Write((string)Application.Contents["strDSN"] + "<br/>");
```

as are the following two lines of VB.NET code:

```
Response.Write(Cstr(Application("strDSN")) & "<br/>")
Response.Write(Cstr(Application.Contents("strDSN")) & "<br/>")
```

The results of running *csApplicationState.aspx* are shown in Figure 6-2.

The application ends whenever *global.asax* is edited. (It also ends when IIS or the physical server is restarted, or when one of the application configuration files, such as *web.config*, is edited. The use of these configuration files will be covered in

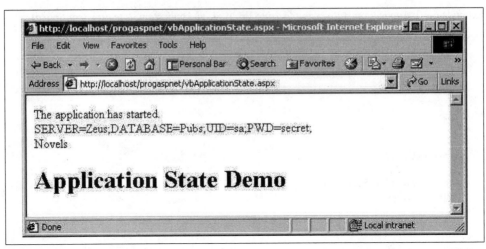

Figure 6-2. Application state demo

Chapter 20.) Furthermore, the results of this effective rebooting of the application is invisible to the end users, since all pending requests are filled before the application shuts down. This can be seen if you force the application to end by making a minor change to *global.asax* and saving the file, then looking at the resulting log file, *c:\test. txt*, in Notepad, as shown in Example 6-11.

Example 6-11. Test.txt

```
5/25/2001 11:09:59 AM  Application Starting
5/25/2001 11:10:41 AM  Application Starting
5/25/2001 11:10:57 AM  Application Ending
5/25/2001 11:11:22 AM  Application Starting
5/25/2001 11:13:32 AM  Application Ending
5/25/2001 11:13:47 AM  Application Starting
5/25/2001 2:37:18 PM   Application Ending
5/25/2001 2:53:23 PM   Application Starting
5/25/2001 2:55:51 PM   Application Ending
5/25/2001 2:55:54 PM   Application Starting
5/25/2001 3:27:13 PM   Application Ending
5/25/2001 3:35:14 PM   Application Starting
5/25/2001 3:37:05 PM   Application Ending
```

As soon as any page in the virtual directory is accessed by a browser, another line appends itself to the log, containing the words Application Starting. However, you will *never* see the contents of the strEndMsg Application property (which was set in the Application_End event handler of *global.asax* as shown in Example 6-7 or 6-8) displayed in your browser because the application always ends between browser requests.

When using the application state, keep in mind the following considerations:

Concurrency and application locking

Concurrency refers to two or more pages accessing the same Application dictionary object simultaneously. As long as an Application dictionary object is read-only, this is not a problem. However, if you are going to allow clients to modify objects held in application state, then great care must be exercised (you'll see why in a moment). You must use the Lock and Unlock methods of the HttpApplicationState class to control access to the application state objects. If you fail to lock the application state object, one client may corrupt the data used by a second client. For example, consider the following code snippet in VB.NET, which increments an Application dictionary object called Counter:

```
Dim iCtr As Integer = CInt(Application("Counter"()
iCtr += 1
Application("Counter") = iCtr
```

It is possible for this code to be called by two clients at just about the same time. This code works by reading the Application ("Counter") variable, adding 1 to it, and writing it back. Suppose that client A and B both read the counter when its value is 5. Client A increments and writes back 6. Client B increments and also writes back 6, which is not what you want—you've lost track of Client A's increment. If you are keeping track of inventory, that would be a serious bug. You can solve this problem by locking and unlocking the critical code:

```
Application.Lock
Dim iCtr As Integer = CInt(Application("Counter"()
iCtr += 1
Application("Counter") = iCtr
Application.Unlock
```

Now when Application A reads the counter, it locks it. When Application B comes along, it is blocked by the lock until A unlocks. Thus, the value is properly incremented at the cost of a potential performance bottleneck.

You should always call the Unlock method as soon as possible to prevent blocking other users. If you forget to call Unlock, the lock will be automatically removed by .NET when the request completes or times out, or when an unhandled error occurs that causes the request to fail, thus minimizing prolonged deadlocks.

Simple locks like this are fraught with danger. For example, suppose that you have two resources controlled by locks: Counter and ItemsOnHand. Application A locks Counter and then tries to lock ItemsOnHand. Unfortunately, ItemsOnHand is locked, so A must wait, holding its lock on Counter. It turns out that Application B is holding the lock on ItemsOnHand waiting to get the lock on Counter. Application B must block waiting for A to let go of Counter, while A waits for B to let go of ItemsOnHand. This is called a *deadlock* or a *deadly embrace*. It is deadly to your application, which grinds to a halt.

Locks are particularly dangerous with web applications that have to scale up quickly. Use application locking with extreme caution. By extension, you should also use read-write application state with extreme caution.

Scalability

The issue of concurrency has a direct effect on scalability. Unless all the Application dictionary objects are read-only, you are liable to run into severe performance issues as the number of simultaneous requests increases, due to locks blocking other processes from proceeding.

Memory

This is a consideration for scalability also, since every Application dictionary object takes up memory. Whether you have a million short string objects or a single DataSet that takes up 50 MB, you must be cognizant of the potential memory usage of Application state.

Persistence and survivability

Application state objects will not survive if the application is halted—whether intentionally due to updates to *global.asax* or a planned shutdown, or due to unanticipated system crashes (when is a crash ever anticipated?). If it is important to persist a global application state, then you must take some measure to save it, perhaps to a database or other permanent file on disk.

Expandability to web farms and web gardens

The Application state is specific to a single process on a single processor. Therefore, if you are running a *web farm* (multiple servers) or a *web garden* (multiple processors in a single server), then any global values in the Application state will not be global across all the servers or processors, and so will not be truly global. As with persistence and survivability, if this is an issue, then you should get and set the value(s) from a central store accessible to all the processes, such as a database or data file.

One additional way of providing information globally across the application is through the use of static objects. These objects are declared in the *global.asax* file, described more fully in Chapter 20. Once declared with the Scope attribute set to Application, the objects are accessible by name anywhere within the application code.

Session State

While an application is running, there will be many *sessions*. A session is a series of requests coming from a single browser client in a more or less continuous manner. If there are no requests from that client within a specified period of time, the timeout period, then the session ends. The default timeout period is 20 minutes.

As has been stated before, the Web is an inherently stateless environment. The HTTP protocol has no means of identifying which requests should be grouped together as belonging to the same session. A session must be imposed on top of HTTP. ASP.NET provides session-state with the following features:

- Works with browsers that have had cookies disabled.

- Identifies if a request is part of an existing session.

- Stores session-scoped data for use across multiple requests. This data persists across IIS restarts and works in multi-processor (web garden) and multi-machine (web farm) environments, as well as in single-processor, single-server situations.

- Raises session events such as Session_Start and Session_End, which can be handled either in the *global.asax* file or in other application code.

- Automatically releases session resources if the session ends or times out.

Session state is stored in server memory separately from the ASP.NET process. This means that if the ASP.NET process crashes or is restarted, the session state is not lost. In addition to unplanned outages, ASP.NET periodically performs a preventative restart of each process every 5000 requests by default. (This number is configurable in *machine.config* and/or *web.config*; see Chapter 20 for a complete discussion of configuration.) This periodic purge greatly improves availability and stability. Session state is preserved even across these restarts.

Sessions are identified and tracked with a 120-bit SessionID that is passed from client to server and back using either an HTTP cookie or a modified URL, depending on how the application is configured. The SessionID is handled automatically by the .NET Framework; there is no need to manipulate it programmatically. The SessionID consists of URL-legal ASCII characters that have two important characteristics:

- They are unique, so that there is no chance of two different sessions having the same SessionID.

- They are random, so that it is difficult to guess the value of another session's SessionID after learning the value of an existing session's SessionID.

Session state is implemented using the Contents collection of the SessionState class. This collection is a key-value dictionary containing all the session state dictionary objects that have been directly added using code. The dictionary objects are set and retrieved using the Session keyword, as shown in Example 6-12 (using C#) and Example 6-13 (using VB.NET). These examples present a set of radio buttons. Selecting one of the radio buttons and clicking on the Submit button sets three session dictionary objects—two strings and a string array. These session dictionary objects are then used to populate a label control and a drop-down list control.

Example 6-12. Session state using C#, csSessionState.aspx

```
<%@ Page Language="C#" %>
<script runat="server">
   void btn_Click(Object Source, EventArgs E)
   {
```

Example 6-12. Session state using C#, csSessionState.aspx (continued)

```
    if (rbl.SelectedIndex == -1)
    {
        lblMsg.Text = "You must select a book category.";
    }
    else
    {
        StringBuilder sb = new StringBuilder( );
        sb.Append("You have selected the category ");
        sb.Append((string)Session["cattext"]);
        sb.Append(" with code \"");
        sb.Append((string)Session["catcode"]);
        sb.Append("\".");

        lblMsg.Text = sb.ToString( );

        ddl.Visible = true;

        string[] CatBooks = (string[])Session["books"];

        //  Populate the DropDownList.
        int i;
        ddl.Items.Clear( );
        for (i = 0; i < CatBooks.GetLength(0); i++)
        {
            ddl.Items.Add(new ListItem(CatBooks[i]));
        }
    }
}

void rbl_SelectedIndexChanged(Object Source, EventArgs E)
{
    if (rbl.SelectedIndex != -1)
    {
        string[] Books = new string[3];

        Session["cattext"] = rbl.SelectedItem.Text;
        Session["catcode"] = rbl.SelectedItem.Value;

        switch (rbl.SelectedItem.Value)
        {
        case "n":
            Books[0] = "Programming C#";
            Books[1] = "Programming ASP.NET";
            Books[2] = "C# Essentials";

            break;

        case "d":
            Books[0] = "Oracle & Open Source";
            Books[1] = "SQL in a Nutshell";
            Books[2] = "Transact-SQL Programming";
```

Example 6-12. Session state using C#, csSessionState.aspx (continued)

```
            break;

        case "h":
            Books[0] = "PC Hardware in a Nutshell";
            Books[1] = "Dictionary of PC Hardware and Data Communications Terms";
            Books[2] = "Linux Device Drivers";

            break;
        }

        Session["books"] = Books;
        }
    }
</script>

<html>
    <body>
    <form runat="server">

        <h1>Session State Demo</h1>
        <br/>
        <br/>

        <h3>Select a Book Category</h3>
        <asp:radioButtonList
            id="rbl"
            autoPostBack="false"
            cellSpacing="20"
            repeatColumns="3"
            repeatDirection="horizontal"
            RepeatLayout="table"
            textAlign="right"
            onSelectedIndexChanged="rbl_SelectedIndexChanged"
            runat="server">

            <asp:listItem text=".NET" value="n"/>
            <asp:listItem text="Databases" value="d"/>
            <asp:listItem text="Hardware" value="h"/>

        </asp:radioButtonList>

        <asp:button
            id="btn"
            text="Submit"
            onClick="btn_Click"
            runat="server"/>

        <br/>
        <br/>
        <hr/>

        <asp:label
```

Example 6-12. Session state using C#, csSessionState.aspx (continued)

```
        id="lblMsg"
        runat="server"/>

   <br/>
   <br/>

   <asp:dropDownList
      id="ddl"
      autoPostBack="false"
    visible= "false"
      runat="server"/>

  </form>
  </body>
</html>
```

Example 6-13 shows only the Visual Basic script block, since the HTML portion of the *.aspx* file is identical to that in Example 6-12.

Example 6-13. Session state example using VB.NET, vbSessionState.aspx

```
<%@ Page Language="VB" Strict="true"%>
<script runat="server">

   sub btn_Click(ByVal Sender as Object, _
               ByVal e as EventArgs)
      if (rbl.SelectedIndex = -1) then
         lblMsg.Text = "You must select a book category."
      else
         dim sb as StringBuilder = new StringBuilder( )
         sb.Append("You have selected the category ")
         sb.Append(Cstr(Session("cattext")))
         sb.Append(" with code """)
         sb.Append(Cstr(Session("catcode")))
         sb.Append(""".")

         lblMsg.Text = sb.ToString( )

         ddl.Visible = true

         dim CatBooks() as string= CType(Session("books"), string( ))

         '  Populate the DropDownList.
         dim i as integer
         ddl.Items.Clear( )
         for i = 0 to CatBooks.GetLength(0) - 1
            ddl.Items.Add(new ListItem(CatBooks(i)))
         next
      end if
   end sub

   sub rbl_SelectedIndexChanged(ByVal Sender as Object, _
```

```
                            ByVal e as EventArgs)
     if (rbl.SelectedIndex <> -1) then

        dim Books(3) as string

        Session("cattext") = rbl.SelectedItem.Text
        Session("catcode") = rbl.SelectedItem.Value

        Select Case (rbl.SelectedItem.Value)
           Case "n"
              Books(0) = "Programming C#"
              Books(1) = "Programming ASP.NET"
              Books(2) = "C# Essentials"

           Case "d":
              Books(0) = "Oracle & Open Source"
              Books(1) = "SQL in a Nutshell"
              Books(2) = "Transact-SQL Programming"

           Case "h":
              Books(0) = "PC Hardware in a Nutshell"
              Books(1) = "Dictionary of PC Hardware and Data Communications Terms"
              Books(2) = "Linux Device Drivers"

        end select
        Session("books") = Books
     end if
  end sub
</script>
```

As usual, the first line of either the C# or the VB.NET *.aspx* file consists of a Page directive. In C#, this looks like:

```
<%@ Page Language="C#" %>
```

and in VB.NET, it looks like:

```
<%@ Page Language="VB" Strict="true"%>
```

Jumping over the script block for a moment, the HTML contains a RadioButtonList and a Submit button on the top portion of the code, and a Label and an invisible DropDownList on the bottom portion of the code.

In the script block are two event handlers—one for trapping a change in value to the RadioButtonList, and one for catching the button click.

Look first at rbl_SelectedIndexChanged, the RadioButtonList event handler. This method populates the Session dictionary objects whenever the user selects a different radio button.

After testing to ensure that something is selected, rbl_SelectedIndexChanged defines a string array to hold the lists of books in each category. Then it assigns the selected item Text and Value properties to two Session dictionary objects. In C#, this is done as follows:

```
Session["cattext"] = rbl.SelectedItem.Text;
Session["catcode"] = rbl.SelectedItem.Value;
```

and in VB.NET, the code is:

```
Session("cattext") = rbl.SelectedItem.Text
Session("catcode") = rbl.SelectedItem.Value
```

rblSelectedIndexChanged next uses a switch statement in C# or a Select Case statement in VB.NET to fill the previously declared string array with a list of books, depending on the book category selected.

Finally, the method assigns the string array to a Session dictionary object. In C#, this is done using:

```
Session["books"] = Books;
```

and in VB.NET, the line is:

```
Session("books") = Books
```

This example stores only strings and an array in the session dictionary objects. However, you can store any object that inherits from ISerializable. These include all the primitive data types and arrays comprised of primitive data types, as well as the DataSet, DataTable, HashTable, and Image objects. This would allow you to store query results, for example, or a collection of items in a user's shopping cart.

The other event handler method, btn_Click, is called whenever the user clicks on the Submit button. It first tests to verify that a radio button has been selected. If not, then the Label is filled with a warning message. In C#, the code that does this is:

```
if (rbl.SelectedIndex == -1)
{
    lblMsg.Text = "You must select a book category.";
}
```

and in VB.NET, the code is:

```
if (rbl.SelectedIndex = -1) then
    lblMsg.Text = "You must select a book category."
```

The else clause of the if statement is the meat of this page. It retrieves the session dictionary objects and uses the StringBuilder class to concatenate the strings together to make a single string for display in the Label control. In C#, this is done as follows:

```
StringBuilder sb = new StringBuilder();
sb.Append("You have selected the category ");
sb.Append((string)Session["cattext"]);
sb.Append(" with code \"");
sb.Append((string)Session["catcode"]);
sb.Append("\".");

lblMsg.Text = sb.ToString();
```

and in VB.NET:

```
dim sb as StringBuilder = new StringBuilder( )
sb.Append("You have selected the category ")
sb.Append(Cstr(Session("cattext")))
sb.Append(" with code """)
sb.Append(Cstr(Session("catcode")))
sb.Append(""".")

lblMsg.Text = sb.ToString( )
```

The btn_Click method also unhides the DropDownList that was created and made invisible in the HTML portion of the page. The method then retrieves the string array from the session dictionary object and populates the DropDownList. In C#, the code is:

```
ddl.Visible = true;

string[] CatBooks = (string[])Session["books"];

// Populate the DropDownList.
int i;
ddl.Items.Clear( );
for (i = 0; i < CatBooks.GetLength(0); i++)
{
    ddl.Items.Add(new ListItem(CatBooks[i]));
}
```

and in VB.NET:

```
ddl.Visible = true

dim CatBooks() as string= CType(Session("books"), string( ))

' Populate the DropDownList.
dim i as integer
ddl.Items.Clear( )
for i = 0 to CatBooks.GetLength(0) - 1
    ddl.Items.Add(new ListItem(CatBooks(i)))
next
```

Because the Page directive in the VB.NET example sets Strict="true", it is necessary to explicitly cast the session dictionary object containing the string array back to a string array using the *CType* function. The results of both the C# and VB.NET examples look the same, as shown in Figure 6-3.

As you examine this example, you might wonder what advantage is gained here by using session state, rather than just using the programmatically accessible control values. The answer in this case is that since this particular example is fairly trivial, no advantage is gained. However, in a real life application with many different pages, session state provides an easy method for values and objects to be passed from one page to the next, with all the advantages listed at the beginning of this section.

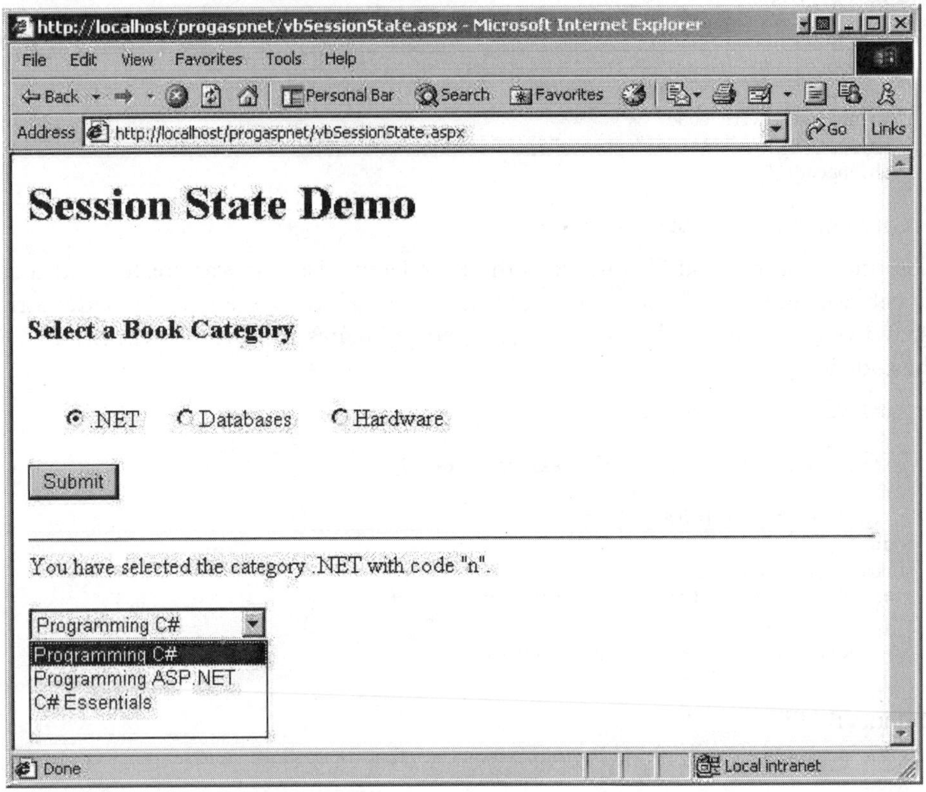

Figure 6-3. Session state demo

Session state configuration

The configuration of session state is controlled on a page by page basis by entries in the Page directive at the top of the page. On an application-wide basis, it is controlled by a file called *web.config*, typically located in the virtual root directory of the application. (Page directives will be covered in detail later in this chapter, and configuration files will be covered in detail in Chapter 20.)

Session state is enabled by default. You can enable session state for a specific page by adding the EnableSessionState attribute to the Page directive, as in the following VB Page directive:

```
<%@ Page Language="VB" Strict="true" EnableSessionState="true"%>
```

To disable session state for the page you would use:

```
<%@ Page Language="VB" Strict="true" EnableSessionState="false"%>
```

To enable session state in a read-only mode—i.e., values can be read but not changed—use the ReadOnly value of EnableSessionState, as in:

```
<%@ Page Language="VB" Strict="true" EnableSessionState="ReadOnly"%>
```

(All of the values for EnableSessionState are case-insensitive.) The reason for either disabling session state or making it read-only is performance. If you know that you will not be using session state on a page, you can gain a performance boost by disabling it.

The real configuration of session state occurs in the *web.config* file. This file is typically located in the virtual root directory, in which case the configuration values it contains will apply to the entire application. If there is a *web.config* file in a subdirectory of the virtual root, then that copy will apply to all the pages in that subdirectory and the subdirectories under it.

Keep in mind that *web.config* is an XML file and as such it must be well-formed. (Well-formed XML files are described in the sidebar "Well-Formed HTML" in Chapter 4.) The values are case-sensitive, and the file consists of sections delimited by tags. The session state configuration information is contained within the <system.web> section, which is contained within the <configuration> section. Thus, a typical session state configuration snippet will look something like Example 6-14.

Example 6-14. Code snippet from web.config

```
<?xml version="1.0" encoding="utf-8" ?>
<configuration>

  <system.web>
  .
  .
  .
  <sessionState
          mode="InProc"
          cookieless="false"
          timeout="20"
          stateConnectionString="tcpip=127.0.0.1:42424"
          sqlConnectionString="data source=127.0.0.1;userid=sa;password="
  />
```

There are five possible attributes for the sessionState section:

mode

> Specifies whether the session state is disabled for all the pages controlled by this copy of *web.config*, and, if enabled, where the session state is stored. Table 6-3 lists the permissible values.

Table 6-3. Possible values for the mode attribute

Values	Description
Off	Session state is disabled.
Inproc	Session state is stored in process on the local server. This is the default value.
StateServer	Session state is stored on a remote server. If this attribute is used, then there must also be an entry for stateConnectionString, which specifies which server to use to store the session state.

Table 6-3. Possible values for the mode attribute (continued)

Values	Description
SqlServer	Session state is stored on a SQL Server. If this attribute is used, then there must also be an entry for sqlConnectionString, which specifies how to connect to the SQL Server. The SQL Server used can either be on the local or a remote machine.

Storing the session state Inproc is the fastest and is well-suited to small amounts of volatile data. However, it is susceptible to crashes and is not suitable for web farms (multiple servers) or web gardens (multiple processors on a single machine). For these cases, you should use either StateServer or SqlServer. SqlServer is the most robust for surviving crashes and restarts.

cookieless

Cookies are used with session state to store the SessionID so that the server knows which session it is connected to. The permissible values of cookieless are true and false, with false being the default. In other words, the default behavior is to use cookies. However, if the client browser either does not support cookies or has had cookie support turned off by the user, then any attempt at saving and retrieving session state will be lost. To prevent this, set cookieless to true.

If cookieless is set to true, then the SessionID is persisted by adding a value to the URL, as shown in the address bar in Figure 6-4.

timeout

Specifies the number of minutes of inactivity before a session times out and is abandoned by the server. The default value is 20.

stateConnectionString

Specifies the server and port used to save the session state. It is required if mode is set to StateServer. Use of a specific server for saving state enables easy and effective session state management in web farm or web garden scenarios. An example of a stateConnectionString is:

```
stateConnectionString="tcpip=127.0.0.1:42424"
```

In this example, a server with an IP address of 127.0.0.1 would be used. This happens to be *localhost*, or the local machine. The port is 42424. In order for this to work, the server being specified must have the ASP.NET State service started (accessible via Control Panel/Administrative Tools/Services) and must have the specified port available for communications (i.e., not disabled or blocked by a firewall or other security measure).

sqlConnectionString

Specifies a connection string to a running instance of SQL Server. It must be set if mode is set to SqlServer. Similar to stateConnectionString in that it lends itself to use with web farms and gardens, it also will persist despite crashes and shutdowns. The session state is saved in SQL tables indexed by SessionID.

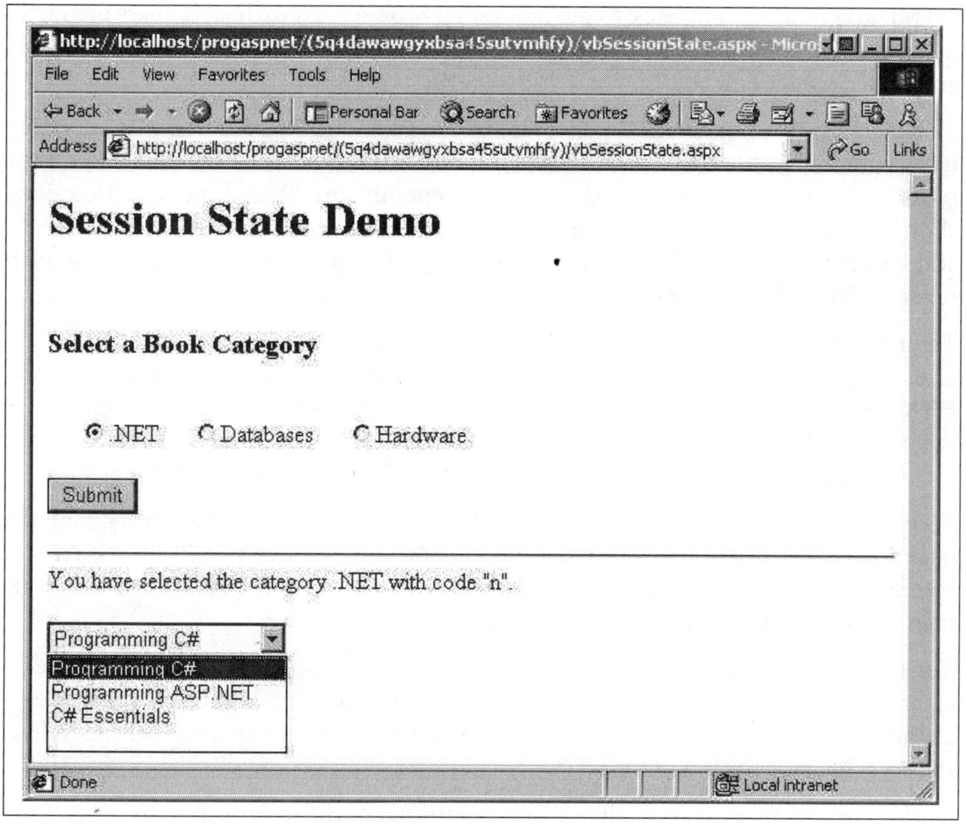

Figure 6-4. Session state demo in cookieless mode

Session scoped application objects

One additional way of providing information across the session is through the use of static objects, which are declared in the *global.asax* file (described in Chapter 20). Once declared with the Scope attribute set to Session, the objects are accessible by name to the session anywhere within the application code.

Lifecycle

A user sits at her browser and types in a URL. A web page appears, with text and images and buttons and so forth. She fills in a text box and clicks on a button. What is going on behind the scenes?

Every request made of the web server initiates a sequence of steps. These steps, from beginning to end, constitute the *lifecycle* of the page.

When a page is requested, it is loaded, processed, sent to the user, and unloaded. From one end of the lifecycle to the other, the goal of the page is to render appropriate

HTML and other output back to the requesting browser. At each step, there are methods and events available to let you override the default behavior or add your own programmatic enhancements.

In order to fully understand the lifecycle of the page and its controls, it is necessary to recognize that the Page class creates a hierarchical tree of all the controls on the page. All the components on the page, except for any Page directives (described shortly), are part of this *control tree*. You can see the control tree for any page by adding trace="true" to the Page directive. (Page directives are described in the next section of this chapter. Tracing is described in detail in Chapter 7.)

The Page itself is at the root of the tree. All the named controls are included in the tree, referenced by control ID. Static text, including whitespace, NewLines, and HTML tags, are represented in the tree as LiteralControls. The order of controls in the tree is strictly hierarchical. Within a given hierarchy level, the controls are ordered in the tree using the same sequence in which they appear in the page file.

Web components, including the Page, go through the entire lifecycle every time the page is loaded. (This involves a fair amount of performance overhead, which you can reduce by caching; this is covered in Chapter 18.) Events fire first on the Page, then recursively on every object in the control tree.

The following is a detailed description of each of the phases of the component lifecycle in a web form. There are two slightly different sequences of events in the lifecycle: on the first loading of the page and on subsequent postbacks. This lifecycle is shown schematically in Figure 6-5.

During the first page load, the lifecycle is composed of the following steps:

1. Initialization

   The *initialization* phase is the first phase in the lifecycle for any page or control. The control tree is built during the initialization phase. In this phase, you can initialize any values needed for the duration of the request.

   The initialize phase is modified by handling the Init event with the OnInit method.

2. Load

   User code runs and the form controls show client-side data.

   The load phase can be modified by handling the Load event with the OnLoad method.

3. PreRender

   This is the phase just before the output is rendered. CreateChildControls is called, if necessary, to create and initialize server controls in the control tree. Modifications are made via the PreRender event, using the OnPreRender method.

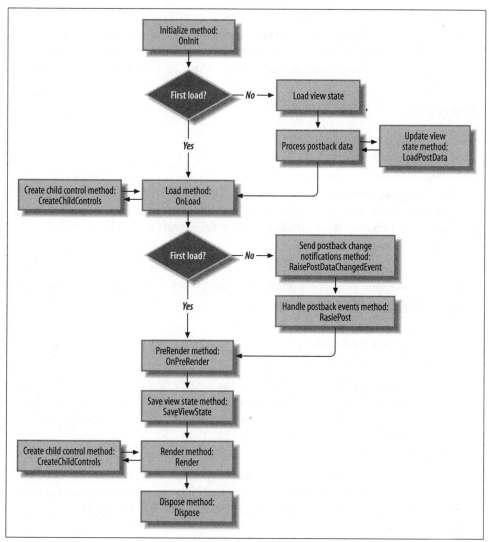

Figure 6-5. Web Form lifecycle

4. Save ViewState

   The view state is saved to a hidden variable on the page, persisting as a string object that will complete the round trip to the client. This can be overridden using the SaveViewState method.

5. Render

   The page and its controls are rendered as HTML. You can override using the Render method. Within Render, CreateChildControls is called, if necessary, to create and initialize server controls in the control tree.

6. Dispose

This is the last phase of the lifecycle. It gives you an opportunity to do any final cleanup and release references to any expensive resources, such as database connections. This is important for scalability. It can be modified using the Dispose method.

During postback, the lifecycle is:

1. Initialization

Same as on first load.

2. Load ViewState

The ViewState property of the control is loaded from a hidden variable on the page, as described in the "View State" section earlier in this chapter. You can modify this behavior by overriding the LoadViewState method.

3. Postback Data is loaded

During this phase, the data sent to the server via the POST method is processed. Any updates to the view state necessitated by the postback are performed via the LoadPostData method.

4. Load

Same as on first load.

5. Change events are raised

If there are any state changes between the current state and the previous state, change events are raised via the RaisePostDataChangedEvent method. Again, the events are raised for the controls in the order in which the controls appear in the control tree.

6. Handle postback events

Exactly one user action caused the postback. That user action is handled now, after all the change events have been handled. The original client-side event that instigated the postback is handled in the RaisePostBackEvent method.

7. PreRender

Same as on first load.

8. Save ViewState

Same as on first load.

9. Render

Same as on first load.

10. Dispose

Same as on first load.

Directives

Directives are used to pass optional settings to the ASP.NET pages and compilers. They typically have the following syntax:

```
<%@ directive attribute=value [attribute=value] %>
```

There are many valid types of directives, which will be described in detail in the following sections. Each directive can have one or more attribute/value pairs, unless otherwise noted. Attribute/value pairs are separated by a space character. Be careful *not* to have any space characters surrounding the equal sign (=) between the attribute and its value.

Directives are typically located at the top of the appropriate file, although that is not a strict requirement. For example, Application directives are at the top of the *global.asax* file, and Page directives are at the top of the *.aspx* files.

Application Directive

The Application directive is used to define application-specific attributes. It is typically the first line in the *global.asax* file, which is described fully in Chapter 20.

Here is a sample Application directive:

```
<%@ Application Language="C#" Codebehind="Global.asax.cs" Inherits="WebApplication1.
Global" %>
```

There are four possible attributes for use in the Application directive, which are outlined in Table 6-4.

Table 6-4. Possible attributes for the Application directive

Attribute	Description
CodeBehind	Used by Visual Studio .NET to identify a code-behind file.
Inherits	The name of the class to inherit from.
Description	Text description of the application. This is ignored by the parser and compiler.
Language	Identifies the language used in any code blocks. Valid values are "C#", "VB", and "JS". As other languages adopt support for the .NET Framework, this list will be expanded.

Assembly Directive

The Assembly directive links an assembly to the application or page at parse-time. It is analogous to the /reference: command-line switch used by the C# and VB.NET command-line compilers.

The Assembly directive is contained in either the *global.asax* file, for application-wide linking, or in a page (*.aspx*) or user control (*.ascx*) file, for linking to a specific page or user control. There can be multiple Assembly directives in any file. Each Assembly directive can have multiple attribute/value pairs.

Assemblies located in the \bin subdirectory under the application's virtual root are automatically linked to the application and do not need to be included in an Assembly directive. There are two permissible attributes, listed in Table 6-5.

Table 6-5. Attributes for the Assembly directive

Attribute	Description
Name	The name of the assembly to link to the application or page. Does not include a filename extension. Assemblies usually have a dll extension.
Src	Path to a source file to dynamically compile and link.

For example, the following Assembly directives link to the assembly or assemblies contained in the *MyAssembly.dll* file, and compile and link to a C# source code file named *SomeSource.cs*:

```
<%@ Assembly Name="MyAssembly" %>
<%@ Assembly Src="SomeSource.cs" %>
```

This directive is often used in conjunction with the Import directive, described later in this chapter.

Control Directive

The Control directive is used only with user controls and is contained in user control files *(.ascx)*. There can only be a single Control directive per *.ascx* file. Here is an example:

```
<%@ Control Language="VB" EnableViewState="false" %>
```

The Control directive has many possible attributes. Some of the more common attributes appear in Table 6-6.

Table 6-6. Attributes for the Control directive

Attribute	Values	Description
AutoEventWireup	true, false	Enables or disables event auto wiring. Default is true.
ClassName	any valid class name	The class name for the page that will be compiled dynamically.
Debug	true, false	Enables or disables compiling with debug symbols. Default is false.
Description	string	Text description of the page, ignored by the parser.
EnableViewState	true, false	Indicates if view state is maintained across page requests. Default is true.

Table 6-6. Attributes for the Control directive (continued)

Attribute	Values	Description
Explicit	true, false	If language is VB, tells compiler to use Option Explicit mode. Default is false.
Inherits	class name	Name of code-behind or other class for the page to inherit.
Language	VB, C#, JS	Programming language used for in-line code and script blocks. As other languages adopt support for the .NET Framework this list will be expanded.
Src	filename	Relative or fully qualified filename containing code-behind class.
Strict	true, false	If language is VB, tells compiler to use Option Strict mode. Default is false.

Implements Directive

The Implements directive is used in page (*.aspx*) and user control (*.ascx*) files or associated code-behind files. It specifies a COM+ interface that the current page implements. This allows a page or user control to declare the interface's events, methods, and properties.

For example, the following Implements directive allows access to a custom IDataAccess interface contained in a custom ProgrammingASPNET namespace:

```
<%@ Implements Interface="ProgrammingASPNET.IDataAccess" %>
```

Import Directive

The Import directive imports a namespace into a page, user control, or application, making all the classes and namespaces of the imported namespace available. It is analogous to the using statement in C# and the Imports statement in VB.NET. Imported namespaces can either be part of the .NET Framework Class Library or custom.

If the Import directive is contained in *global.asax*, then it applies to the entire application. If it is in a page (*.aspx*) or user control (*.ascx*) file, then it only applies to that page or user control.

Each Import directive can have only a single namespace attribute. If you need to import multiple namespaces, use multiple Import directives.

The following namespaces are automatically imported into all pages and user controls and do not need to be included in Import directives:

System
System.Collections
System.Collections.Specialized
System.Configuration
System.IO
System.Text

```
System.Text.RegularExpressions
System.Web
System.Web.Caching
System.Web.Security
System.Web.SessionState
System.Web.UI
System.Web.UI.HtmlControls
System.Web.UI.WebControls
```

The following two lines import the System.Drawing namespace from the .NET Base Class Library and a custom namespace:

```
<%@import namespace="System.Drawing" %>
<%@import namespace="ProgrammingASPNET" %>
```

OutputCache Directive

The OutputCache directive controls output caching for a page or user control. Caching and the use of the OutputCache directive will be covered in Chapter 18.

Page Directive

The Page directive is used to define attributes for the page parser and compiler specific to the page (.aspx) file. There can be no more than one Page directive for each page file. Each Page directive can have multiple attributes.

The Page directive has many possible attributes. Some of the more common attributes of the Page directive are listed in Table 6-7.

Table 6-7. Attributes for the Page directive

Attribute	Values	Description
AutoEventWireup	true, false	Enables or disables event auto wiring. Default is true.
Buffer	true, false	Enables or disables HTTP response buffering. Default is true.
ClassName	Any valid class name	The class name for the page that will be compiled dynamically.
ClientTarget	Any valid user-agent value or alias	Targets user agent that server controls should render content for.
CodeBehind	filename	Used by Visual Studio .NET to indicate the name of the code-behind file.
Debug	true, false	Enables or disables compiling with debug symbols. Default is false.
Description	string	Text description of the page, ignored by the parser.
EnableSessionState	true, false, ReadOnly.	Enables, disables, or makes SessionState read-only. Default is true.
EnableViewState	true, false	Enables or disables maintenance of view state across page requests. Default is true.

Table 6-7. Attributes for the Page directive (continued)

Attribute	Values	Description
ErrorPage		Targets URL for redirection if an unhandled page exception occurs.
Explicit	true, false	If language is VB, tells compiler to use Option Explicit mode. Default is false.
Inherits	class name	Name of code-behind or other class
Language	VB, C#, JS	Programming language used for in-line code.
Src	filename	Relative or fully qualified filename containing code behind class.
Strict	true, false	If language is VB, tells compiler to use Option Strict mode. Default is false.
Trace	true, false	Enables or disables tracing. Default is false.
TraceMode	SortByTime, SortByCategory	Indicates how trace messages are to be displayed. Default is SortByTime.
Transaction	NotSupported, Supported, Required, RequiresNew	Indicates if transactions supported on this page. Default is NotSupported.

The following code snippet is a Page directive specifying the language, a class to inherit, and a code-behind source file:

```
<%@ Page Language="C#" inherits="CodeBehindDemo"  src="codebehind.cs" %>
```

Reference Directive

The Reference directive can be included in a page file (*.aspx*). It indicates that another page or user control should be compiled and linked to the current page, giving you access to the controls on the linked page or user control as part of the ControlCollection object.

There are two permissible attributes: Page and Control. For either, the allowable value is a relative or fully qualified filename. For example:

```
<%@ Reference page="AnotherPage.aspx" %>
```

Register Directive

The Register directive is used in custom server controls and user controls to associate aliases with namespaces. Custom server controls and user controls are covered in Chapter 14.

Using the IDE

The Visual Studio .NET (VS.NET) integrated development environment (IDE) offers a rich feature set with tremendous productivity aids, such as:

- IntelliSense, which pops up with help on every method and function call as you type
- Integrated dynamic help
- Integrated build and compile support
- Integrated support for source control software
- Built-in task list
- A modern interface with a tabbed page metaphor for code and layout screens, dockable toolbars, a Solution Explorer, and Properties windows
- WYSIWYG (What You See Is What You Get) design of Windows and Web Forms
- Drag-and-drop form design, which allows you to drag controls from the Toolbox and position them on the design surface

Visual Studio .NET will save you a great deal of typing and will generate a tremendous amount of boiler plate code. This can be a mixed blessing, however, because the generated code can add a lot of clutter to your files.

In addition, VS.NET creates solutions and projects with directories and files in a number of places on your hard disk, and it can be confusing sorting out where everything is. Because VS.NET creates projects and file relationships for you and "saves" you from the details, it can be difficult at first to understand what all the files are and how they relate to one another. This is the chronic problem with helpful systems: if you want to do what they anticipate you will want to do, it is very easy; but if you want to do something unusual, it can be terribly difficult to find your way through the black box.

In this section, you will make the transition from hand-coding ASP.NET applications in a text editor to using the VS.NET IDE. This section will show some of the strong points of the IDE and guide you around some of the pitfalls.

Getting Started with the IDE

If you have not yet installed the .NET Framework and VS.NET, you should do so now.

In this section you will rewrite the calendar from Example 5-49 and Example 5-50 in Chapter 5, this time using the Visual Studio .NET IDE. The goal is shown in Figure 6-6.

When you open VS.NET, you are presented with a Get Started screen. This screen has a main panel with a list of previously opened projects, an Open Project button for opening a pre-existing project not listed, and a New Project button.

Click on the New Project button. It brings up a dialog box, as shown in Figure 6-7.

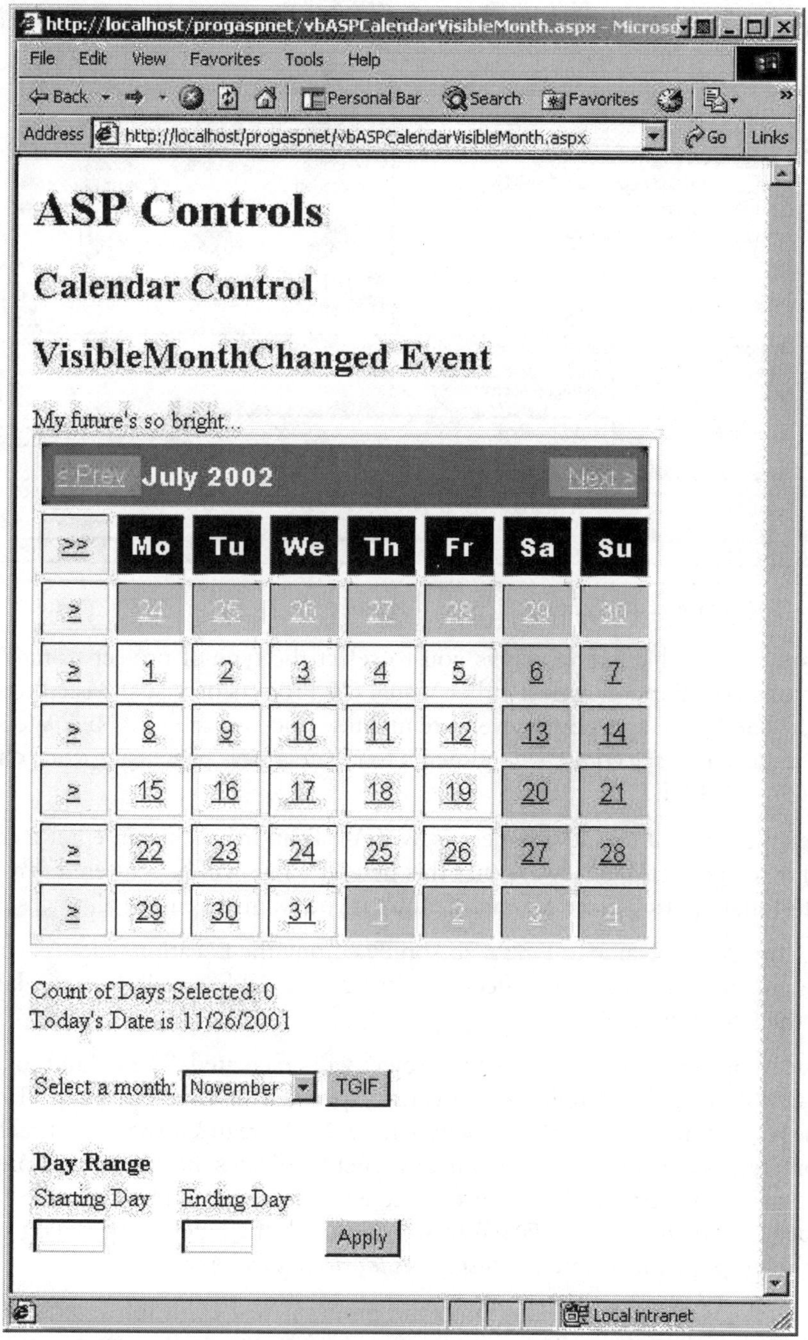

Figure 6-6. Calendar demonstration, hand-coded

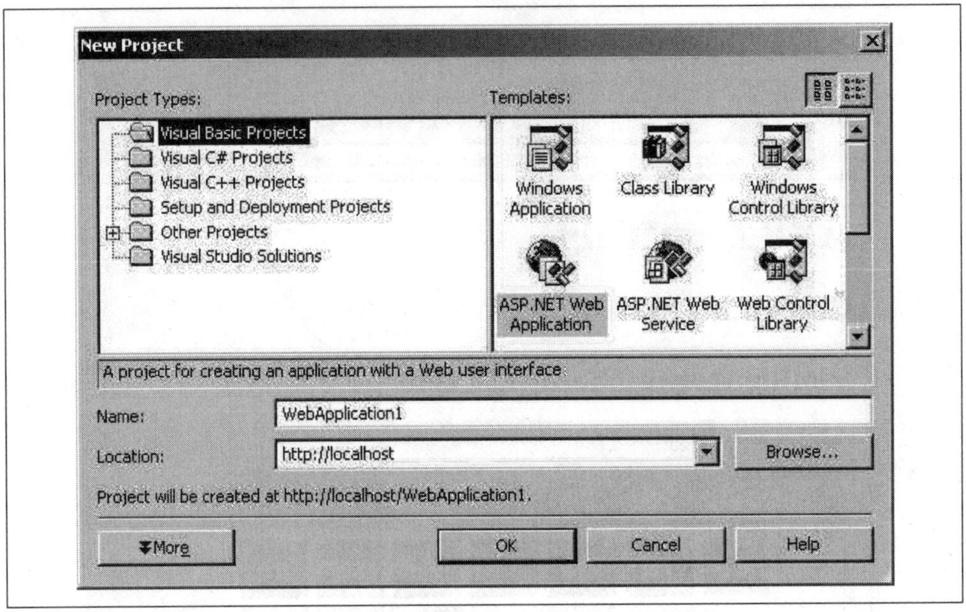

Figure 6-7. New Project dialog box

You can see that this dialog allows you to select the type of project from VB, C#, C++, and so on. For now, select either Visual C# Projects or Visual Basic Projects. In the right-hand pane are shown several templates. Click on the ASP.NET Web Application icon. These selections will allow us to create a web page using your choice of either C# or VB.NET.

The default name of the new project is WebApplication1. You can enter a different name for the project, but beware that this default name will be scattered throughout the solution, requiring some manual cleanup if you want to remove all traces of it.

Change the Project Name to FirstWebApp by editing the Location field. As you enter the new name, you will see it reflected in the Name field as well as in the label just below the Location field.

The Location field tells you where the project will be created. The default location is in localhost, i.e., the virtual root directory specified in your IIS setup. Typically, localhost is defined as *c:\inetpub\wwwroot*. VS.NET creates a separate directory for each project, as the label below the Location field indicates. Because you changed the project name to FirstWebApp, the project will actually be created in the physical directory *c:\inetpub\wwwroot\FirstWebApp*, although the label in the dialog box will show the project being created in *http://localhost/FirstWebApp*.

After clicking OK on this dialog box, the program will cook for several moments while it creates the project. Then it will bring you into the design screen, as shown in Figure 6-8.

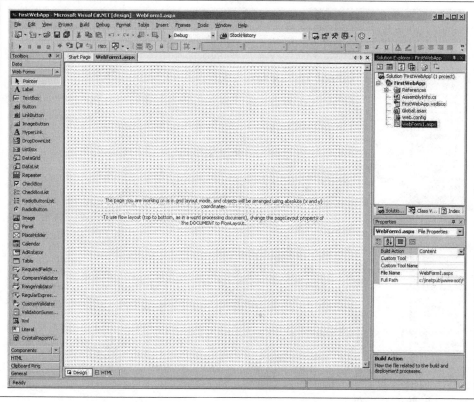

Figure 6-8. New Project design screen

Make certain the Toolbox is visible on the screen and that the WebForms tools are displayed. Either Click on the Label tool and drag it out onto the page Design screen or double click on the Label tool. It will now look like the word "Label" surrounded by six small gray handles with a tiny green icon in the upper-left corner. If you click anywhere off of the Label, the gray handles disappear until you click on the Label again to select it.

You can move the Label by selecting it, placing the cursor over the top of the Label until the cursor turns into a four headed arrow, and dragging the control. You can also resize the control by dragging on any of the six handles.

Select the Label. You will see that the Properties box in the lower-right corner of the screen now refers to Label1. Click on the Text field in the Properties box, highlight the existing value, Label, and replace it with the text string: ASP Control Using the IDE. While you're in the Properties box, change the Font to Bookman Old Style, Bold, Size X-Large. Finally, drag the control handles so that the now larger text string fits on one line. When you are done, the screen should look something like that in Figure 6-9.

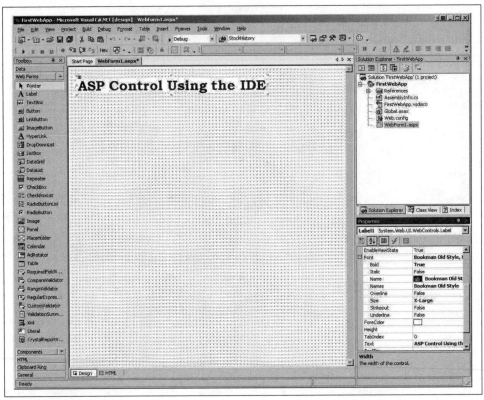

Figure 6-9. First label control

Double-click on the Calendar tool, then move it into position by dragging it with the mouse. Resize it by dragging on one of the corner handles. Rename the calendar's ID from Calendar1 to cal, to correspond with the code from Example 5-49 and Example 5-50. Now you need to essentially duplicate all the attributes applied to the Calendar control in Example 5-49 and Example 5-50. There are several ways to do this:

- You can change properties by entering values in the Properties box.

- In either C# or VB.NET projects, you can enter events by double-clicking on the control. This will open the code-behind page with the code for the default event handler already in place. Once you are looking at the code-behind page, you enter or move to different events differently, depending on the current language:

  — In C# projects, you can enter events by clicking on the Events icon (✎) in the toolbar at the top of the Properties box. Note that the available properties and icons will change depending on which control is currently selected.

  — In VB.NET projects, you can enter events by selecting the control from the drop-down list at the top left of the code-behind page, then selecting the event from the drop-down list at the top right of the code-behind page.

- You can enter the code directly in the HTML by clicking on the HTML tab at the bottom of the screen.

 If you are unhappy with the way VS.NET reformats your code you can turn reformatting off. From the menu, choose Tools/Options. In the dialog box under Text Editor:

- All Languages → Tabs. Change the Indenting to Block. Change both Tab Size and Indent Size to 3. Click on Insert spaces.
- Basic → VB Specific. Uncheck "Pretty listing (reformatting) of code."
- C# → Formatting. Uncheck Automatically format completed constructs and pasted source.
- HTML/XML → Format. Uncheck all the Automatic Formatting Options checkboxes.

Looking through all the options, there are probably other options you will want to change.

Enter all the properties of the Calendar control in the Properties box. To do this, click on the Calendar control so that the Properties window is showing the properties for Calendar. Then set all the control properties shown in the HTML portion of Example 5-49, listed here in Table 6-8. A typical view of the Properties window is shown in Figure 6-10.

Table 6-8. Calendar properties from Example 5-49

Property	Subproperty	Values
CellPadding		7
CellSpacing		5
DayNameFormat		FirstTwoLetters
FirstDayOfWeek		Monday
NextMonthText		Next >
NextPrevFormat		CustomText
PrevMonthText		< Prev
SelectionMode		DayWeekMonth
ShowGridLines		true
ShowNextPrevMonth		true
DayHeaderStyle	BackColor	Black
	Font-Name	Arial Black
	ForeColor	White
DayStyle	BackColor	White
	ForeColor	Black
	Font-Name	Arial

Table 6-8. Calendar properties from Example 5-49 (continued)

Property	Subproperty	Values
NextPrevStyle	BackColor	DarkGray
	ForeColor	Yellow
	Font-Name	Arial
OtherMonthDayStyle	BackColor	LightGray
	ForeColor	White
	Font-Name	Arial
SelectedDayStyle	BackColor	CornSilk
	ForeColor	Blue
	Font-Name	Arial
	Font-Bold	true
	Font-Italic	true
SelectorStyle	BackColor	CornSilk
	ForeColor	Red
	Font-Name	Arial
TitleStyle	BackColor	Gray
	ForeColor	White
	Font-Name	Arial Black
	HorizontalAlign	Left
TodayDayStyle	BackColor	CornSilk
	ForeColor	Green
	Font-Name	Arial
	Font-Bold	true
	Font-Italic	false
WeekendDayStyle	BackColor	LavenderBlush
	ForeColor	Purple
	Font-Name	Arial
	Font-Bold	false
	Font-Italic	false

When choosing colors, you have the choice of custom, web, or system colors. Custom colors will result in a six digit hexadecimal number that represents the red, green, and blue (RGB) components of the color. To ensure compatibility with the widest range of displays, this example uses predefined colors from the Web tab.

Note that the default value for the NextMonthText property is >, which displays the greater than symbol (>). Similarly, the PrevMonthText property default value is <, which displays the less than symbol (<). In the hand-coded example, these properties were set to "Next >" and "< Prev", respectively. If you enter those exact

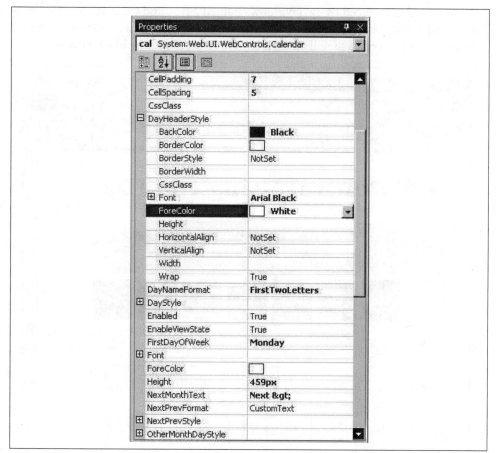

Figure 6-10. Properties window

literals in the Property box, it displays correctly in Design view, but the HTML view indicates a syntax problem. In order to avoid this, you should enter Next > for the NextMonthText property and < Prev for the PrevMonthText property.

Building the Project

Before going any further, build and run the project. There are three possible ways to do this:

- Click on the Start icon on the VS.NET toolbar.
- Click on the Debug/Start menu item.
- Press F5 on your keyboard.

Any of these actions causes VS.NET to build and run the project. A Build window appears at the bottom of the screen with build information. If there are no errors, it goes away and is replaced by two windows named Autos and Call Stack. The use of these windows will be described in Chapter 7. At the same time, a browser window representing your web page will open. It should look something like Figure 6-11.

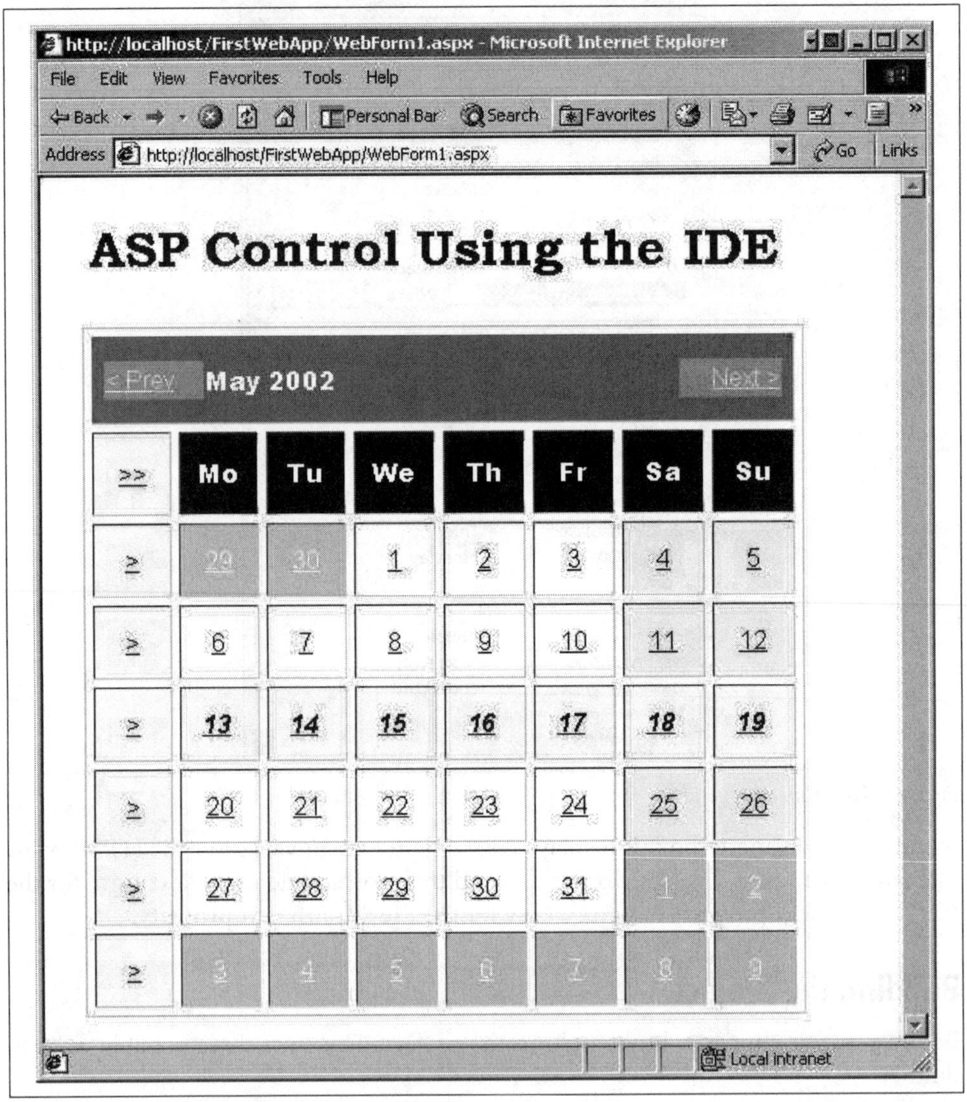

Figure 6-11. Calendar control, part 1

This is a fully functional, if somewhat limited, calendar. Click on any of the selection links and you will see that the appropriate day(s) are highlighted. Click on the Previous or Next links and the month changes. Very cool, considering that you have not yet written a single line of code. To see how this works, open the code-behind file.

The code-behind editing window is initially hidden from you. Looking back to Figure 6-9, you see a tab for the page file, *WebForm1.aspx*, above the design window. Nowhere is there a tab for a code-behind file.

At the bottom of the design window are two tabs, one for Design view (i.e., a graphical layout mode) and one for HTML view (i.e., a text editor). Click on the HTML tab and look at the first line of code. It should look similar to the following default Page directive:

```
<%@ Page language="c#" Codebehind="WebForm1.aspx.cs" AutoEventWireup="false"
Inherits="FirstWebApp.WebForm1" %>
```

Notice the Codebehind attribute pointing to the file *WebForm1.aspx.cs* (or *WebForm1.aspx.vb* if you chose VB.NET as your development language). This code-behind file has already been created by VS.NET and in fact resides in the same directory as the page file, *localhost\FirstWebApp*, which typically corresponds to the physical directory (*c:\inetpub\wwwroot\FirstWebApp*). As described in previous sections, this attribute is used by VS.NET to keep track of which code-behind file to update when changes are made to the page file. The Inherits attribute tells the compiler the name of the class that is being created in the code-behind file.

You can verify that this code-behind file already exists by looking on your hard drive. If you are really curious, open it in Notepad.

To open the code-behind file in VS.NET, do either of the following:

- Right-click on the web form in either Design mode or HTML editor mode. Select View Code from the menu.

- Click on the Design tab to see the page in Design mode, then double-click anywhere on the web form.

The C# code-behind file, *WebForm1.aspx.cs,* should look something like Example 6-15, after all the code regions have been expanded by clicking on the little gray plus signs down the left edge of the code. The equivalent code-behind file in VB. NET will look something like Example 6-16.

As you go back and forth between the Design page and the HTML editor, any changes automatically cause the corresponding change in the code-behind page.

Example 6-15. C# code-behind file, WebForm1.aspx.cs

```
using System;
using System.Collections;
using System.ComponentModel;
using System.Data;
using System.Drawing;
using System.Web;
using System.Web.SessionState;
using System.Web.UI;
using System.Web.UI.WebControls;
using System.Web.UI.HtmlControls;
```

Example 6-15. C# code-behind file, WebForm1.aspx.cs (continued)

```csharp
namespace FirstWebApp
{
    /// <summary>
    /// Summary description for WebForm1.
    /// </summary>
    public class WebForm1 : System.Web.UI.Page
    {
        protected System.Web.UI.WebControls.Calendar Cal;
        protected System.Web.UI.WebControls.Label Label1;

        public WebForm1( )
        {
            Page.Init += new System.EventHandler(Page_Init);
        }

        private void Page_Load(object sender, System.EventArgs e)
        {
            // Put user code to initialize the page here
        }

        private void Page_Init(object sender, EventArgs e)
        {
            //
            // CODEGEN: This call is required by the ASP.NET Windows Form Designer.
            //
            InitializeComponent( );
        }

        #region Web Form Designer generated code
        /// <summary>
        /// Required method for Designer support - do not modify
        /// the contents of this method with the code editor.
        /// </summary>
        private void InitializeComponent( )
        {
            this.Load += new System.EventHandler(this.Page_Load);

        }
        #endregion
    }
}
```

Visual Studio .NET has created a namespace based on your project name.

```csharp
namespace FirstWebApp
{
    .
    .
    .
}
```

The set of braces in C# indicates that everything contained within the braces is part of the FirstWebApp namespace.

Example 6-16. VB.NET code-behind file, WebForm1.aspx.vb

```
Public Class WebForm1
    Inherits System.Web.UI.Page
      Protected WithEvents Label1 As System.Web.UI.WebControls.Label
      Protected WithEvents Calendar1 As System.Web.UI.WebControls.Calendar

#Region " Web Form Designer Generated Code "

    'This call is required by the Web Form Designer.
    <System.Diagnostics.DebuggerStepThrough()> Private Sub InitializeComponent()

    End Sub

    Private Sub Page_Init(ByVal sender As System.Object, _
                        ByVal e As System.EventArgs) _
                        Handles MyBase.Init
        'CODEGEN: This method call is required by the Web Form Designer
        'Do not modify it using the code editor.
        InitializeComponent()
    End Sub

#End Region

    Private Sub Page_Load(ByVal sender As System.Object, _
                        ByVal e As System.EventArgs) _
                        Handles MyBase.Load
        'Put user code to initialize the page here
    End Sub

End Class
```

Notice that there are no Imports statements (equivalent to using statements in C#) in the VB.NET version, nor is a default namespace defined.

In both languages, the WebForm1 class is created, which inherits from System.Web. UI.Page. In C#, this looks like:

```
public class WebForm1 : System.Web.UI.Page
{
```

and in VB.NET, the code is:

```
Public Class WebForm1
    Inherits System.Web.UI.Page
```

Some of the lines of code in these examples from Visual Studio .NET are too long to show on the printed page without wrapping. Because line breaks generally do not affect the program in C#, lines are broken arbitrarily for readability in the C# examples. By contrast, line continuation characters are used in the VB.NET examples (although in Visual Studio .NET, the lines are actually single long lines).

You will recall that in the *.aspx* file the Inherits Page directive contains an attribute that identifies this WebForm1 class.

Visual Studio has created all the initialization code necessary to display the calendar and provide it with default behavior.

To flesh out this example, add the missing controls and then wire up the event handlers. Return to the Design form and add the controls in Table 6-9 to the form.

Table 6-9. Label controls

ID	Type (ASP control unless noted otherwise)	Text	Location
lblMonthChanged	Label		Above the calendar control
lblCount	Label		Immediately below the Calendar control
lblTodaysDate	Label		Immediately below lblCount
lblSelected	Label		Immediately below lblTodaysDate
	HTML Label	Select a month	Below lblSelected
ddl	DropDownList		To the right of label
btnTGIF	Button	TGIF	To the right of ddl
	HTML Label	Date Range	Below month label
	HTML Label	Start Date	Below Date Range label
	HTML Label	End Date	To right of Start Date label
txtStart	TextBox		Below Start Date label
txtEnd	TextBox		Below End Date label
btnRange	Button	Apply	To right of txtEnd

Be sure to set the Text property of each of the Labels as indicated in Table 6-9. If the label is an ASP control (from the Web Forms tab of the Toolbox), then the Text property is set in the Properties window. On the other hand, if the label is an HTML Label control (from the HTML tab of the Toolbox), the text is entered directly on the control, not in the Properties window (which identifies the type of control as DIV).

When adding the DropDownList control, set the AutoPostBack property to True. Also, you need to add all the ListItems. Click on the Items property and a build button (...) appears. Click on that and a ListItem Collection Editor dialog box pops up, as shown in Figure 6-12.

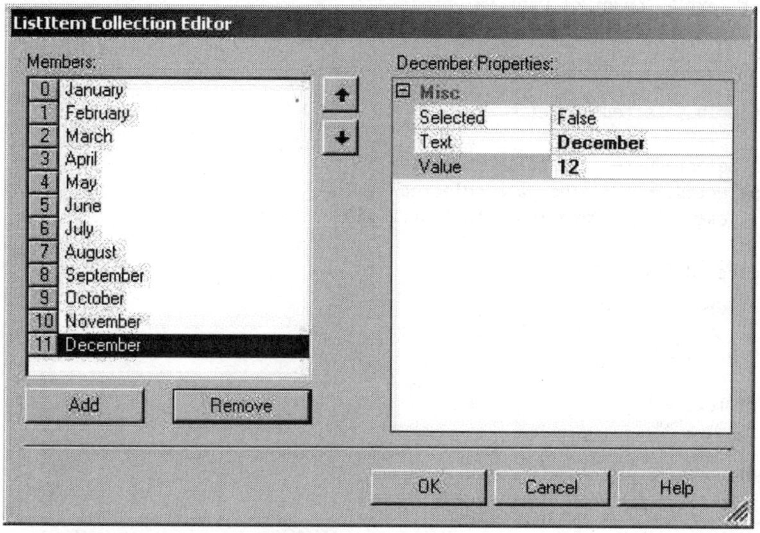

Figure 6-12. ListItem Collection Editor dialog box

Click the Add button to add each of the months of the year, along with a value. The values to use are 1 through 12, corresponding to the number of the month.

All the other controls are very straightforward. Be sure to use the correct ID so that the event handlers you are going to copy in will work.

Once all the controls are added to the page, open the code-behind file. You should see that there are protected member variables for each of the controls you've added to the form.

In order to make this web page fully functional, however, the Page_Load method needs to be coded and all the relevant controls need to have event handlers. Specifically, the calendar needs to respond to selecting a different day, to rendering each of the cells containing a day, and to changing the month. Also, the drop-down list needs to respond to a month being selected, and the two buttons need to respond to clicks. Copy the necessary code from Example 5-49 in C#, and 5-50 in VB.NET, that provided these event handlers.

Before creating any of the event handlers, copy the private helper methods shown in Example 6-17 (C#) and Example 6-18 (VB.NET)—taken from Example 5-49 and Example 5-50, respectively—to the code-behind page.

Example 6-17. C# helper methods

```csharp
private void lblCountUpdate( )
{
    lblCount.Text = "Count of Days Selected:   " +
        cal.SelectedDates.Count.ToString( );
}

private void lblSelectedUpdate( )
{
    if (cal.SelectedDate != DateTime.MinValue)
        lblSelected.Text = "The date selected is " +
            cal.SelectedDate.ToShortDateString( );
    else
        lblSelected.Text = "";
}

private void txtClear( )
{
    txtStart.Text = "";
    txtEnd.Text = "";
}
```

Example 6-18. VB.NET helper methods

```vbnet
private sub lblCountUpdate( )
    lblCount.Text = "Count of Days Selected:   " & _
        cal.SelectedDates.Count.ToString( )
end sub

private sub lblSelectedUpdate( )
    if (cal.SelectedDate <> DateTime.MinValue) then
        lblSelected.Text = "The date selected is " & _
            cal.SelectedDate.ToShortDateString( )
    else
        lblSelected.Text = ""
    end if
end sub

private sub txtClear( )
    txtStart.Text = ""
    txtEnd.Text = ""
end sub
```

Next, copy the contents of the Page_Load method from Example 5-49 (C#) and Example 5-50 (VB.NET) to the code-behind page. Notice that the code-behind page already has a shell of the Page_Load method. You should copy only the code within the shell. When completed, the Page_Load method should look like Example 6-19 in C# and Example 6-20 in VB.NET.

Example 6-19. Page_Load in C#

```csharp
private void Page_Load(object sender, System.EventArgs e)
{
    // Put user code to initialize the page here
    if (!IsPostBack)
    {
        cal.VisibleDate = cal.TodaysDate;
        ddl.SelectedIndex = cal.VisibleDate.Month - 1;
    }
    lblTodaysDate.Text = "Today's Date is " +
            cal.TodaysDate.ToShortDateString();
}
```

Example 6-20. Page_Load in VB.NET

```vbnet
Private Sub Page_Load(ByVal sender As System.Object, _
                        ByVal e As System.EventArgs) Handles MyBase.Load
    'Put user code to initialize the page here
    if not IsPostBack then
        cal.VisibleDate = cal.TodaysDate
        ddl.SelectedIndex = cal.VisibleDate.Month - 1
    end if

    lblTodaysDate.Text = "Today's Date is " & _
            cal.TodaysDate.ToShortDateString()
End Sub
```

Now it is time to hook up the event handlers. Double-click on the calendar control in the Design view. This creates an event handler for the SelectionChanged event in the code-behind page and places the cursor inside the shell for that event handler method. Then copy the code for the SelectionChanged event handler method from Example 5-49 (C#) and Example 5-50 (VB.NET) to inside the method shell created in the code-behind page. When you are finished, the cal_SelectionChanged method should look like Example 6-21 in C# and Example 6-22 in VB.NET.

Example 6-21. cal_SelectionChanged method in C#

```csharp
private void cal_SelectionChanged(object sender, System.EventArgs e)
{
    lblSelectedUpdate();
    lblCountUpdate();
    txtClear();
}
```

Example 6-22. cal_SelectionChanged method in VB.NET

```vbnet
Private Sub cal_SelectionChanged(ByVal sender As System.Object, _
                            ByVal e As System.EventArgs) _
                            Handles cal.SelectionChanged
    lblSelectedUpdate()
    lblCountUpdate()
```

Example 6-22. cal_SelectionChanged method in VB.NET (continued)

```
    txtClear( )
End Sub
```

You also need to hook up two other events for the calendar control: DayRender and VisibleMonthChanged. This is done differently in C# and VB.NET.

To hook up the events in C#, click on the Calendar control in the Design window, then click on the Events icon (pictured previously in the section "Getting Started with the IDE") in the toolbar at the top of the Properties box. All the possible events for the Calendar control are listed. Click on the DayRender event. Type in the name of the event handler method to use. In this example, type in cal_DayRender. Then go to the code-behind page. You will see that a shell has been created for that method. Copy in the contents of the DayRender method from Example 5-49. (Notice that you are using slightly different method names here than were used in Example 5-49. The actual names are not important, as long as they are consistent within each example.)

Do the same thing for the VisibleMonthChanged event, entering the method name cal_VisibleMonthChanged. Again, copy the contents of the VisibleMonthChanged method from Example 5-49.

When you are finished, the two methods in Visual Studio .NET should look like the code in Example 6-23.

Example 6-23. Calendar DayRender and VisibleMonthChanged methods in C#

```csharp
private void cal_DayRender(object sender,
              System.Web.UI.WebControls.DayRenderEventArgs e)
{
   // Notice that this overrides the WeekendDayStyle.
   if (!e.Day.IsOtherMonth && e.Day.IsWeekend)
      e.Cell.BackColor=System.Drawing.Color.LightGreen;

   // Happy New Year!
   if (e.Day.Date.Month == 1 && e.Day.Date.Day == 1)
      e.Cell.Controls.Add(new LiteralControl("<br/>Happy New Year!"));
}

private void cal_VisibleMonthChanged(object sender,
              System.Web.UI.WebControls.MonthChangedEventArgs e)
{
   if (e.NewDate.Month > e.PreviousDate.Month)
      lblMonthChanged.Text = "My future's so bright...";
   else
      lblMonthChanged.Text = "Back to the future!";

   cal.SelectedDates.Clear();
   lblSelectedUpdate();
   lblCountUpdate();
   txtClear();
}
```

The remaining events are hooked up similarly. You can either double-click on each control, which automatically creates the event handler method shell in the code-behind page, or use the Events icon from the Properties window for each control. In either case, you need to add the methods for the controls listed in Table 6-10. For each event handler, copy the code from the corresponding event handler method in Example 5-49. When you are done, the event handler methods should like the code in Example 6-24.

Table 6-10. Controls and methods for Example 6-24 (C#)

Control	Event handler method
ddl	ddl_SelectedIndexChanged
btnTGIF	btnTGIF_Click
btnRange	btnRange_Click

Example 6-24. Remaining event handling methods in C#

```csharp
private void ddl_SelectedIndexChanged(object sender, System.EventArgs e)
{
    cal.SelectedDates.Clear( );
    lblSelectedUpdate( );
    lblCountUpdate( );
    txtClear( );
    cal.VisibleDate = new DateTime(cal.TodaysDate.Year,
                    Int32.Parse(ddl.SelectedItem.Value), 1);
}

private void btnTGIF_Click(object sender, System.EventArgs e)
{
    int currentMonth = cal.VisibleDate.Month;
    int currentYear = cal.VisibleDate.Year;

    cal.SelectedDates.Clear( );

    for (int i = 1;
            i <= System.DateTime.DaysInMonth(currentYear,
                                            currentMonth);
            i++ )
    {
        DateTime date = new DateTime(currentYear, currentMonth, i);
        if (date.DayOfWeek == DayOfWeek.Friday)
            cal.SelectedDates.Add(date);
    }

    lblSelectedUpdate( );
    lblCountUpdate( );
    txtClear( );
}

private void btnRange_Click(object sender, System.EventArgs e)
{
```

Example 6-24. Remaining event handling methods in C# (continued)

```
    int currentMonth = cal.VisibleDate.Month;
    int currentYear = cal.VisibleDate.Year;
    DateTime StartDate = new DateTime(currentYear, currentMonth,
                        Int32.Parse(txtStart.Text));
    DateTime EndDate = new DateTime(currentYear, currentMonth,
                      Int32.Parse(txtEnd.Text));

    cal.SelectedDates.Clear();
    cal.SelectedDates.SelectRange(StartDate, EndDate);

    lblSelectedUpdate();
    lblCountUpdate();
}
```

The procedure to hook up the remaining events in VB.NET is different than in C# because Visual Studio .NET does not have an Events icon for VB.NET. Instead, you follow these steps:

1. Move to the code-behind page by clicking on the *WebForm1.aspx.vb* tab.

2. Click on the drop-down at the top left of the code page to see a list of all the controls on the page.

3. Select the control to which you want to add an event handler.

4. Click on the drop-down at the top right of the code page. This will list all the possible events for that control.

5. Select the desired event. A code shell will be created in the code page, ready to accept the code to handle the event.

6. Copy the code for the event handler method from Example 5-50 to the code page.

Perform these steps for each of the controls and event handler methods listed in Table 6-11. When you are finished, the code for all these methods should look like Example 6-25.

Table 6-11. Controls and methods for Example 6-25 (VB.NET)

Control	Event handler method
cal	cal_DayRender
cal	cal_VisibleMonthChanged
ddl	ddl_SelectedIndexChanged
btnTGIF	btnTGIF_Click
btnRange	btnRange_Click

Example 6-25. Remaining event handling methods in VB.NET

```
Private Sub cal_DayRender(ByVal sender As Object, _
        ByVal e As System.Web.UI.WebControls.DayRenderEventArgs) _
```

Example 6-25. Remaining event handling methods in VB.NET (continued)

```
            Handles cal.DayRender
   ' Notice that this overrides the WeekendDayStyle.
   if (not e.Day.IsOtherMonth and e.Day.IsWeekend) then
      e.Cell.BackColor=System.Drawing.Color.LightGreen
   end if

   ' Happy New Year!
   if (e.Day.Date.Month = 1 and e.Day.Date.Day = 1) then
      e.Cell.Controls.Add(new LiteralControl("<br/>Happy New Year!"))
   end if
End Sub

Private Sub cal_VisibleMonthChanged(ByVal sender As Object, _
      ByVal e As System.Web.UI.WebControls.MonthChangedEventArgs) _
      Handles cal.VisibleMonthChanged
   if (e.NewDate.Month > e.PreviousDate.Month) then
      lblMonthChanged.Text = "My future's so bright..."
   else
      lblMonthChanged.Text = "Back to the future!"
   end if

   cal.SelectedDates.Clear( )
   lblSelectedUpdate( )
   lblCountUpdate( )
   txtClear( )
End Sub

Private Sub ddl_SelectedIndexChanged(ByVal sender As Object, _
         ByVal e As System.EventArgs) _
         Handles ddl.SelectedIndexChanged
   cal.SelectedDates.Clear( )
   lblSelectedUpdate( )
   lblCountUpdate( )
   txtClear( )
   cal.VisibleDate = new DateTime(cal.TodaysDate.Year, _
                  Int32.Parse(ddl.SelectedItem.Value), 1)
End Sub

Private Sub btnTGIF_Click(ByVal sender As Object, _
         ByVal e As System.EventArgs) _
         Handles btnTGIF.Click
   dim currentMonth as integer = cal.VisibleDate.Month
   dim currentYear as integer = cal.VisibleDate.Year

   cal.SelectedDates.Clear( )

   dim i as integer
   for i = 1 to System.DateTime.DaysInMonth(currentYear, _
                           currentMonth)
      dim dt as DateTime = new DateTime(currentYear, _
                              currentMonth, _
                              i)
```

Example 6-25. Remaining event handling methods in VB.NET (continued)

```
        if dt.DayOfWeek = DayOfWeek.Friday then
            cal.SelectedDates.Add(dt)
        end if
    next

    lblSelectedUpdate( )
    lblCountUpdate( )
    txtClear( )
End Sub

Private Sub btnRange_Click(ByVal sender As Object, _
                ByVal e As System.EventArgs) _
                Handles btnRange.Click
    dim currentMonth as integer = cal.VisibleDate.Month
    dim currentYear as integer = cal.VisibleDate.Year
    dim StartDate as DateTime = new DateTime(currentYear, _
                                    currentMonth, _
                                    Int32.Parse(txtStart.Text))
    dim EndDate as DateTime = new DateTime(currentYear, _
                                    currentMonth, _
                                    Int32.Parse(txtEnd.Text))
    cal.SelectedDates.Clear( )
    cal.SelectedDates.SelectRange(StartDate, EndDate)

    lblCountUpdate( )
End Sub
```

Visual Studio .NET automatically inserts some additional code to enable the event handlers to be properly hooked up with the controls. This code differs in C# and VB.NET.

In the C# code-behind page, there is a method called InitializeComponent, shown here in Example 6-26.

Example 6-26. Event handler hookup in C# code-behind file

```
private void InitializeComponent( )
{
    this.btnTGIF.Click +=
            new System.EventHandler(this.btnTGIF_Click);
    this.cal.DayRender +=
            new System.Web.UI.WebControls.DayRenderEventHandler(
                this.cal_DayRender);
    this.cal.VisibleMonthChanged +=
            new System.Web.UI.WebControls.MonthChangedEventHandler(
                this.cal_VisibleMonthChanged);
    this.cal.SelectionChanged +=
            new System.EventHandler(this.cal_SelectionChanged);
    this.ddl.SelectedIndexChanged +=
            new System.EventHandler(this.ddl_SelectedIndexChanged);
    this.btnRange.Click += new System.EventHandler(this.btnRange_Click);
```

Example 6-26. Event handler hookup in C# code-behind file (continued)

```
    this.Load += new System.EventHandler(this.Page_Load);
}
```

For VB.NET, the equivalent code is found near the top of the class declaration, as shown in Example 6-27.

Example 6-27. Event handler hookups in VB.NET code-behind

```
Protected WithEvents Label1 As System.Web.UI.WebControls.Label
Protected WithEvents lblMonthChanged As System.Web.UI.WebControls.Label
Protected WithEvents lblCount As System.Web.UI.WebControls.Label
Protected WithEvents lblTodaysDate As System.Web.UI.WebControls.Label
Protected WithEvents lblSelected As System.Web.UI.WebControls.Label
Protected WithEvents ddl As System.Web.UI.WebControls.DropDownList
Protected WithEvents btnTGIF As System.Web.UI.WebControls.Button
Protected WithEvents txtStart As System.Web.UI.WebControls.TextBox
Protected WithEvents txtEnd As System.Web.UI.WebControls.TextBox
Protected WithEvents btnRange As System.Web.UI.WebControls.Button
Protected WithEvents cal As System.Web.UI.WebControls.Calendar
```

Run the form (F5) and verify that everything works. Be sure to save everything either by clicking on the Save All icon on the toolbar or clicking on File/All from the VS. NET menu.

Close VS.NET and run your new form by opening a browser and entering the following URL:

```
http://localhost/FirstWebApp/WebForm1.aspx
```

You should then see something like Figure 6-13.

If you compare the operation of the hand-coded web page shown in Figure 6-13 with that created in VS.NET, you'll notice one small difference. When the hand-coded page first appears in the browser, before you click on anything, the space between the month DropDownList and the Calendar control is closed up. Although there are three Label controls there, they are empty and do not take up any space. In the VS.NET created page, however, those labels take up space, even when empty.

This is caused by a fundamental difference in the way the two pages are laid out. The hand-coded page uses no absolute positioning but rather strategically placed break (<br/>) and paragraph (<p/>) tags, as well as an HTML table. In the VS.NET-produced page, all the controls have a style attribute that includes positioning information.

If you want the page layout in the Designer to not use absolute positioning but rather to use paragraph tags (<p>) as in the hand-coded version, then change the page-Layout property of the Document in Design mode from GridLayout (the default) to FlowLayout.

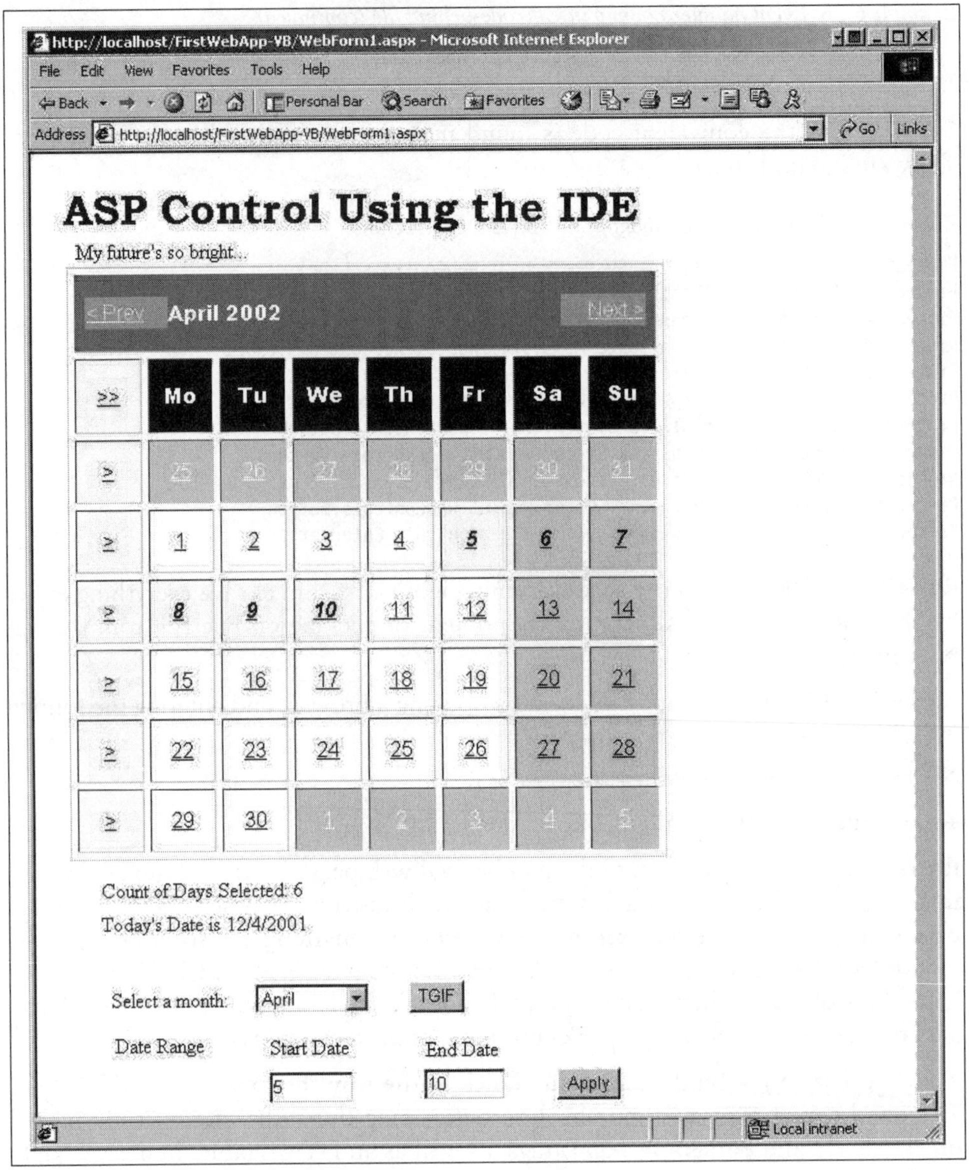

Figure 6-13. Completed calendar web page

CHAPTER 7

Tracing, Debugging, and Error Handling

Every computer programmer has run into bugs. It comes with the territory. Many bugs are found during the coding process. Others pop up only when an end user performs a specific and unusual sequence of steps or the program receives unexpected data. It is highly desirable to find bugs early in the development process, and very important to avoid having end users find your bugs for you. Countless studies have shown that the earlier you find a bug, the easier and less expensive it is to fix.

In the event that your program does run into a problem, you will want to recover quickly and invisibly, or, at worst, fail gracefully. ASP.NET provides tools and features to help reach these goals, including:

Tracing

You can easily trace program execution at either the page or application level. ASP.NET provides an extensible trace log with program lifecycle information.

Symbolic debugging

You can step through your program, set breakpoints, examine and modify variables and expressions, and step into and out of classes, even those written in other languages.

Error handling

You may handle standard or custom errors at either the application or page level. You can also show different error pages for different errors.

To get started exploring the ASP.NET debugging tools, you should first create a simple project to which you will add tracing code. You will then introduce bugs into the program and use the debugger to find and fix the bugs.

Creating the Sample Application

To start, create a new C# or VB.NET web application project in Visual Studio .NET and name it DebuggingApp. This project will consist of a single web page containing a header label, a DropDownList with a label below it to display the selected item, and a hyperlink.

Change the pageLayout property of the document from the default GridLayout to FlowLayout. Put a Label control on the top of the page and set the text (its Text property) to:

```
Tracing, Debugging & Error Handling Demo
```

Change its Font.Name property to Arial Black, its Font.Size property to Large, and its Font.Bold property to true.

Place a DropDownList control on the form. Name it ddlBooks. Change its AutoPost-Back property to true. The drop-down list's event handling code needs to be added. The exact steps for doing so are different in C# than in VB.NET.

In C#, click on the Events icon at the top of the Properties box, click on the field next to SelectedIndexChanged, and type in the event handler name ddlBooks_SelectedIndexChanged.

In VB.NET, display the code-behind source code window by clicking on the code-behind file tab at the top of the source code window. At the top of the window are two drop-down lists. The list on the left contains all the objects on the page. Select ddlBooks from that list. The drop-down on the right will contain all the available events. Select SelectedIndexChanged. Alternatively, double-click on the control in the Design view of the *.aspx* file. In either case, this will immediately open the code-behind page with the cursor inside the event handler method with that name, ready for you to add the event handling code.

Type or paste in the code in Example 7-1, if you're programming in C#, or Example 7-2, if you're programming in VB.NET. These examples are excerpted from Example 5-25 and Example 5-26, respectively.

Example 7-1. SelectedIndexChanged event handler in C#

```csharp
private void ddlBooks_SelectedIndexChanged(object sender,
                                   System.EventArgs e)
{
    // Check to verify that something has been selected.
        if (ddlBooks.SelectedIndex != -1)
        {
            lblDdl.Text=ddlBooks.SelectedItem.Text + " ---> ISBN: " +
            ddlBooks.SelectedItem.Value;
        }
}
```

Example 7-2. SelectedIndexChanged event handler in VB.NET

```vbnet
Sub ddlBooks_SelectedIndexChanged(ByVal Sender as Object, _
                        ByVal e as EventArgs)
    ' Check to verify that something has been selected.
```

Example 7-2. SelectedIndexChanged event handler in VB.NET (continued)

```
    if ddlBooks.SelectedIndex <> -1 then
        lblDdl.Text=ddlBooks.SelectedItem.Text & " ---> ISBN: " & _
            ddlBooks.SelectedItem.Value
    end if
End Sub
```

Add the code shown in Example 7-3, if you're using C#, or Example 7-4, if you're programming in VB, to replace the Page_Load event. (Again, these examples are excerpted from Example 5-25 and Example 5-26, respectively.)

Example 7-3. Page_Load event handler in C#

```
private void Page_Load(object sender, System.EventArgs e)
{
    // Put user code to initialize the page here
    if (! IsPostBack)
    {
        //  Build 2 dimensional array for the lists
        //  First dimension contains bookname
        //  2nd dimension contains ISBN number
        string[,] books = {
                {"Programming C#","0596001177"},
                {"Programming ASP.NET","1234567890"},
                {"WebClasses From Scratch","0789721260"},
                {"Teach Yourself C++ in 21 Days","067232072X"},
                {"Teach Yourself C++ in 10 Minutes","067231603X"},
                {"XML & Java From Scratch","0789724766"},
                {"Complete Idiot's Guide to a Career in Computer Programming","0789719959"},
                {"XML Web Documents From Scratch","0789723166"},
                {"Clouds To Code","1861000952"},
                {"C++: An Introduction to Programming","1575760614"},
                {"C++ Unleashed","0672312395"}
            };

        // Now populate the lists.
        int i;
        for (i = 0; i < books.GetLength(0); i++)
        {
            //  Add both Text and Value
            ddlBooks.Items.Add(new ListItem(books[i,0],books[i,1]));
        }
    }
}
```

Example 7-4. Page_Load event handler in VB.NET

```
Private Sub Page_Load(ByVal sender As System.Object, _
                    ByVal e As System.EventArgs) Handles MyBase.Load
    'Put user code to initialize the page here
    if not IsPostBack then
        ' Build 2 dimensional array for the lists
        ' First dimension contains bookname
```

Example 7-4. Page_Load event handler in VB.NET (continued)

```
'   2nd dimension contains ISBN number
dim books(,) as string = { _
    {"Programming C#","0596001177"}, _
    {"Programming ASP.NET","1234567890"}, _
    {"WebClasses From Scratch","0789721260"}, _
    {"Teach Yourself C++ in 21 Days","067232072X"}, _
    {"Teach Yourself C++ in 10 Minutes","067231603X"}, _
    {"XML & Java From Scratch","0789724766"}, _
    {"Complete Idiot's Guide to a Career in Computer Programming", _
            "0789719959"}, _
    {"XML Web Documents From Scratch","0789723166"}, _
    {"Clouds To Code","1861000952"}, _
    {"C++: An Introduction to Programming","1575760614"}, _
    {"C++ Unleashed","0672312395"} _
}

'   Now populate the lists.
dim i as integer

for i = 0 to books.GetLength(0) - 1
    '   Add both Text and Value
    ddlBooks.Items.Add(new ListItem(books(i,0),books(i,1)))
next

    end if
End Sub
```

Add a label below the DropDownList called lblDdl. Set the Text property so that it is empty.

Finally, add a HyperLink control below lblDdl. Name it hplTest. Change the Text property to Link To and change the NavigateUrl property to *TestLink.aspx*. Note that no page with this name actually exists. This is an intentional error to demonstrate error handling later in the chapter.

Run the web page and select one of the items in the drop-down list; you should see something like Figure 7-1.

Tracing

Tracing is an easy way to find out what is going on in your program. Back in the days of classic ASP, the only way to trace what was happening in your code was to insert Response.Write statements in strategic places. This allowed you to see that you had reached a known point in the code, and perhaps to display the value of some variables. The big problem with this hand-tracing technique, aside from the amount of work involved, was that you had to laboriously remove or comment out all those statements before the program went into production.

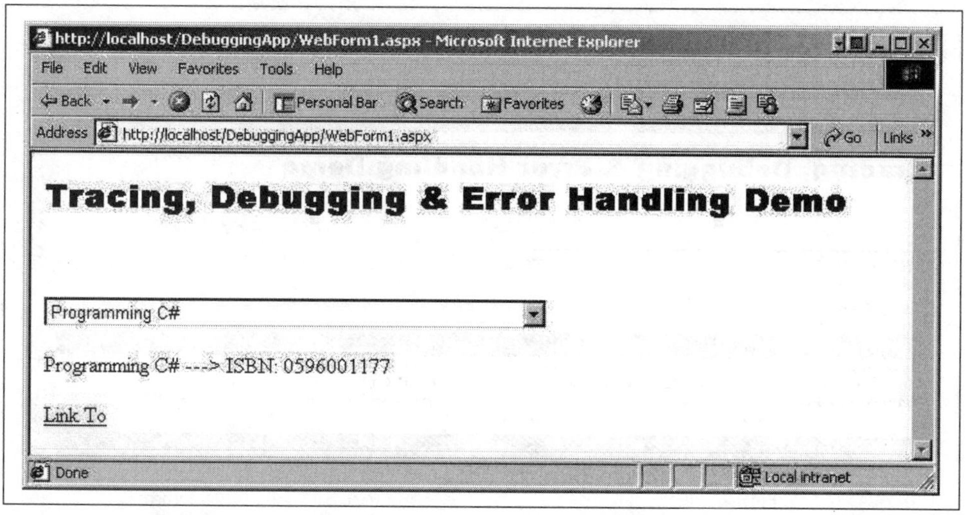

Figure 7-1. Sample page for tracing, debugging, and error handling

ASP.NET provides better ways of gathering the trace information. You can add tracing at the application level or at the page level. With *application-level tracing*, every page is traced, while with *page-level tracing,* you choose the pages to which to add tracing.

Page-Level Tracing

To add page-level tracing, modify the Page directive at the top of the *.aspx* page, by adding a Trace attribute and setting its value to true, as follows:

```
<%@ Page language="c#" Codebehind="WebForm1.aspx.cs" AutoEventWireup="false"
    Inherits="DebuggingApp.WebForm1" Trace="true" %>
```

When you view this page, there will now be tables at the bottom that contain a wealth of information about your web application. Select a book from the drop-down list and you will see something like Figure 7-2.

The top section, labeled Request Details, shows basic information, including the SessionID, the Time of Request, Request Type, and Status Code. Every time the page is posted to the server, this information is updated. If you change the selection (remember that AutoPostBack is set to true), you will see that the Time of Request is updated, but the SessionID remains constant.

The next section, labeled Trace Information, is the *trace log*, which provides lifecycle information. This includes elapsed times, in seconds, since the page was initialized (the From First(s) column) and since the previous event in the lifecycle (the From Last(s) column). You can add custom trace information to the trace log, as explained later in this chapter.

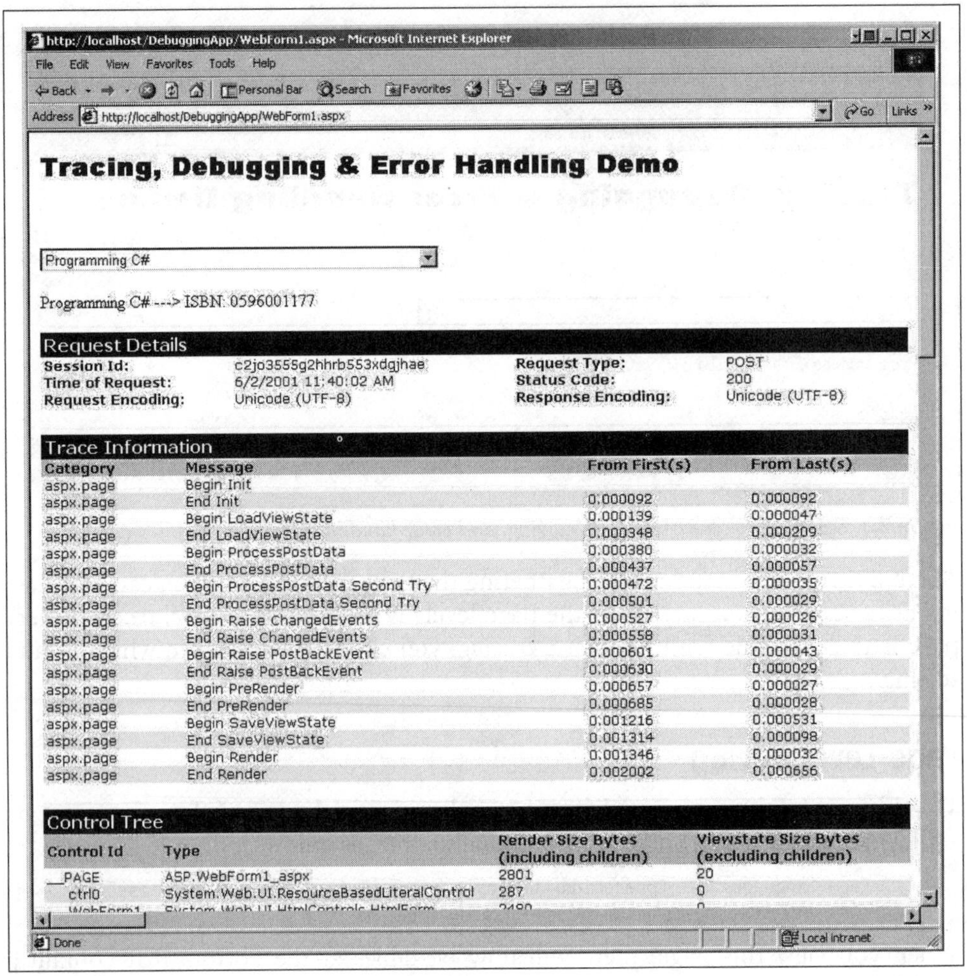

Figure 7-2. Trace results

Status Codes

The *status code*, which is shown in the Request Details section, is a three-digit code that is defined as part of the Hypertext Transfer Protocol HTTP/1.1. Table 7-1 lists some of the most common codes. You can find a complete listing at the web site *http://www. w3.org/Protocols/rfc2616/rfc2616-sec10.HTML.*

Table 7-1. Status codes

Category	Number	Description
Informational (100-199)	100	Continue
	101	Switching protocols
Successful (200-299)	200	OK
	204	No Content
Redirection (300-399)	301	Moved permanently
	305	Use proxy
	307	Temporary redirect
Client Errors (400-499)	400	Bad request
	402	Payment required
	404	Not found
	408	Request timeout
	417	Expectation failed
Server Errors (500-599)	500	Internal server error
	503	Service unavailable
	505	HTTP version not supported

The next section in the trace lists all the controls on the page in a hierarchical manner, including the name of the control, its type, and its size in bytes, both on the page and in the ViewState state bag.

This is followed by itemizations of the Cookies and Headers collections. Finally there is a list of all the server variables.

Inserting into the Trace Log

You can add custom information to the trace output by writing to the Trace object. This object exposes two methods for putting your own statements into the trace log, Write and Warn. The only difference between the two methods is that Warn writes to the log in red. The Warn and Write methods are overloaded to take either a single string, two strings, or two strings and an exception object. The following cases illustrate:

Trace.Warn("Warning Message")
Inserts a record into the trace log with the message passed in as a string.

Trace.Warn("Category","Warning Message")
Inserts a record into the trace log with the category and message you pass in.

Trace.Warn("Category","Warning Message", excp)
Inserts a record into the trace log with a category, warning message, and exception.

Example 7-5 contains the C# source code, and Example 7-6 contains the VB.NET source code for the Page_Load and ddlBooks_SelectedIndexChanged event procedures; this adds three messages to the trace. Changed lines of code are indicated in boldface.

Example 7-5. Writing to the Trace object in C#

```csharp
private void Page_Load(object sender, System.EventArgs e)
{
    // Put user code to initialize the page here
    Trace.Write("In Page_Load");
    if (! IsPostBack)
    {
        Trace.Write("Page_Load", "Not Postback.");
        //  Build 2 dimensional array for the lists
        //  First dimension contains bookname
        //  2nd dimension contains ISBN number
        string[,] books = {
            {"Programming C#","0596001177"},
            {"Programming ASP.NET","1234567890"},
            {"WebClasses From Scratch","0789721260"},
            {"Teach Yourself C++ in 21 Days","067232072X"},
            {"Teach Yourself C++ in 10 Minutes","067231603X"},
            {"XML & Java From Scratch","0789724766"},
            {"Complete Idiot's Guide to a Career in Computer Programming","0789719959"},
            {"XML Web Documents From Scratch","0789723166"},
            {"Clouds To Code","1861000952"},
            {"C++: An Introduction to Programming","1575760614"},
            {"C++ Unleashed","0672312395"}
                                };

        //  Now populate the lists.
        int i;
        for (i = 0; i < books.GetLength(0); i++)
        {
            //  Add both Text and Value
            ddlBooks.Items.Add(new ListItem(books[i,0],books[i,1]));
        }
    }
}

private void ddlBooks_SelectedIndexChanged(object sender, System.EventArgs e)
{
    // TestMethod( );
    try
    {
        int a = 0;
        int b = 5/a;
    }
    catch (System.Exception ex)
    {
```

Example 7-5. Writing to the Trace object in C# (continued)

```csharp
    Trace.Warn("UserAction","Calling b=5/a",ex);
  }

  //  Check to verify that something has been selected.
  if (ddlBooks.SelectedIndex != -1)
  {
     lblDdl.Text=ddlBooks.SelectedItem.Text + " ---> ISBN: " +
        ddlBooks.SelectedItem.Value;
  }
}
```

Example 7-6. Writing to the Trace object in VB.NET

```vbnet
Private Sub Page_Load(ByVal sender As System.Object, _
                      ByVal e As System.EventArgs) Handles MyBase.Load
   'Put user code to initialize the page here
   Trace.Write("In Page_Load")
   If Not IsPostBack Then
       '  Build 2 dimensional array for the lists
       '  First dimension contains bookname
       '  2nd dimension contains ISBN number
       Trace.Write("Page_Load", "Not Postback.")
       Dim books(,) As String = { _
          {"Programming C#", "0596001177"}, _
          {"Programming ASP.NET", "1234567890"}, _
          {"WebClasses From Scratch", "0789721260"}, _
          {"Teach Yourself C++ in 21 Days", "067232072X"}, _
          {"Teach Yourself C++ in 10 Minutes", "067231603X"}, _
          {"XML & Java From Scratch", "0789724766"}, _
          {"Complete Idiot's Guide to a Career in Computer Programming", _
                  "0789719959"}, _
          {"XML Web Documents From Scratch", "0789723166"}, _
          {"Clouds To Code", "1861000952"}, _
          {"C++: An Introduction to Programming", "1575760614"}, _
          {"C++ Unleashed", "0672312395"} _
       }

       '  Now populate the lists.
       Dim i As Integer

       For i = 0 To books.GetLength(0) - 1
          '  Add both Text and Value
          ddlBooks.Items.Add(New ListItem(books(i, 0), books(i, 1)))
       Next

   End If
End Sub

Private Sub ddlBooks_SelectedIndexChanged(ByVal sender As System.Object, _
      ByVal e As System.EventArgs) Handles ddlBooks.SelectedIndexChanged
   ' TestMethod( )
```

Example 7-6. Writing to the Trace object in VB.NET (continued)

```
Try
    Dim a As Integer = 0
    Dim b As Integer = 5 / a
Catch ex As System.Exception
    Trace.Warn("UserAction", "Calling b=5/a", ex)
End Try

' Check to verify that something has been selected.
If ddlBooks.SelectedIndex <> -1 Then
    lblDdl.Text = ddlBooks.SelectedItem.Text & " ---> ISBN: " & _
                ddlBooks.SelectedItem.Value
End If
End Sub
```

The first message is added in the Page_Load method to signal that you've entered that method:

```
Trace.Write("In Page_Load");
```

The second message is added if the page is not a postback:

```
if (! IsPostBack)
{
    Trace.Write("Page_Load", "Not Postback.");
```

This second message is categorized as Page_Load; using a category can help you organize the trace output. The effect of these two Write statements is shown in Figure 7-3. Shading was added to make it easy to see these two statements.

Trace Information			
Category	Message	From First(s)	From Last(s)
aspx.page	Begin Init		
aspx.page	End Init	0.000914	0.000914
	In Page_Load	0.002307	0.001393
Page_Load	Not Postback.	0.002380	0.000073
aspx.page	Begin PreRender	0.002447	0.000067

Figure 7-3. Two Trace.Write statements

The third message is added to demonstrate the process of inserting an exception into the error log. The ddlBooks_SelectedIndexChanged event handler also contains code to force an exception by dividing by zero. The code catches that exception and logs the exception with a trace statement, as shown by the following code fragment:

```
try
{
    int a = 0;
    int b = 5/a;
}
catch (System.Exception ex)
{
    Trace.Warn("UserAction","Calling b=5/a",ex);
}
```

Exceptions are an advanced error handling technique that allows you to *try* potentially dangerous code and *catch* any exception objects thrown by the operating system or by other parts of your own code. You might use exceptions when reading a file; if the file cannot be opened, the system will throw an exception. Exception handling is beyond the scope of this book, but is covered in Jesse Liberty's book *Programming C#* (O'Reilly).

The output from this trace statement is shown in Figure 7-4.

Trace Information

Category	Message	From First (s)	From Last (s)
aspx.page	Begin Init		
aspx.page	End Init	0.000060	0.000060
aspx.page	Begin LoadViewState	0.000094	0.000034
aspx.page	End LoadViewState	0.000687	0.000593
aspx.page	Begin ProcessPostData	0.000731	0.000044
aspx.page	End ProcessPostData	0.000795	0.000065
	In Page_Load	0.000824	0.000029
aspx.page	Begin ProcessPostData Second Try	0.000851	0.000027
aspx.page	End ProcessPostData Second Try	0.000874	0.000022
aspx.page	Begin Raise ChangedEvents	0.000896	0.000023
UserAction	Calling b=5/a Attempted to divide by zero. at DebuggingApp.WebForm1.ddl_SelectedIndexChanged(Object sender, EventArgs e) in c:\inetpub\wwwroot\debuggingapp\webform1.aspx.cs:line 93	0.004339	0.003443
aspx.page	End Raise ChangedEvents	0.005174	0.000835

Figure 7-4. Trace statement output

Because this trace statement was written calling the Warn method rather than the Write method, the trace output appears in red onscreen (though not in your copy of this book). Notice that string you passed in, Calling b=5/a, is displayed, followed by an error message extracted automatically from the exception object.

Not only is it easy to implement trace statements, but when it is time to put your page into production, all these statements can remain in place. The only modification you need to make is to change the Trace attribute in the Page directive from true to false.

Application-Level Tracing

Application-level tracing applies to all the pages in a given application. It is configured through the *web.config* file, which will be described more fully in Chapter 20.

The *web.config* file is typically located in the virtual root directory of the application. If there is a *web.config* file in a subdirectory of the virtual root, then that copy will apply only to the pages in that subdirectory and in the subdirectories under it. If tracing is enabled application-wide from the root directory, tracing will be applied across the application uniformly. The exception is when a specific page has a contradictory page directive, which supersedes the application directive.

Web.config is an XML file that consists of sections delimited by tags. The trace configuration information is contained in the <trace> section within the <system.web> section, which is contained within the <configuration> section.

Web.config, like all XML documents, must consist of well-formed XML. The elements of a well-formed XML file are discussed in a sidebar in Chapter 4. Note that XML is case-sensitive.

A typical trace configuration snippet will look something like Example 7-7.

Example 7-7. Trace code snippet from web.config

```xml
<?xml version="1.0" encoding="utf-8" ?>
<configuration>

  <system.web>
.
.
.
    <trace
        enabled="true"
        requestLimit="10"
        pageOutput="false"
        traceMode="SortByTime"
        localOnly="true"
    />
```

You can easily edit the *web.config* file in VS.NET by double-clicking on the file in the Solution Explorer. (If the Solution Explorer is not visible, click on the View/Solution Explorer menu item.) Alternatively, this file can be edited in any text editor.

There are five possible properties in the `<trace>` section. These properties appear in Table 7-2. Several of these properties affect the trace viewer, which will be described in the following section.

Table 7-2. Trace section properties

Property	Values	Description
enabled	true, false	Enables or disables application-level tracing. Default is `false`. If enabled, then all pages in the application will display trace information unless a specific page has "Trace = false" in the `Page` directive.
requestLimit	Integer	Number of trace requests that will be stored on the server and visible in the trace viewer. Default is 10.
pageOutput	true, false	Dictates if trace information is displayed on both the application pages and in the trace viewer. Default is `false`. Pages with tracing enabled are not affected by this setting.
traceMode	SortByTime, SortByCategory	Dictates whether the trace log is sorted by Time or Category. Default is `TraceMode.SortByTime`.
localOnly	true, false	Indicates if the trace viewer is available only on the host web server. Default is true.

Trace Viewer

If application-level tracing is enabled, the trace log can be viewed directly from your browser for any application, even across multiple page requests. The trace facility provides a *trace viewer*, called *trace.axd*. Aim your browser toward *trace.axd* as though it were a page in the application, with the following URL, for example:

```
http://localhost/DebuggingApp/trace.axd
```

You will see a summary of all the entries in the trace log, as shown in Figure 7-5.

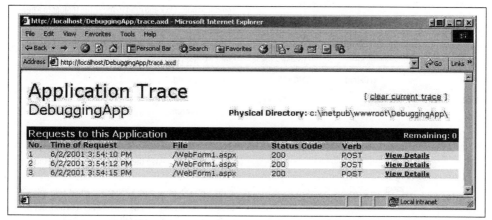

Figure 7-5. Trace viewer

Clicking on any of the View Details links will bring you to the same page as would be seen in page-level tracing for that page.

Debugging

Tracing provides you with a snapshot of the steps your code has taken after the code has run. At times, however, you'd probably like to monitor your code while it is running. What you want is more of a CAT scan than an autopsy. The code equivalent of a CAT scan is a symbolic debugger.

When you run your code in the debugger, you can literally watch your code work, step by step. As you walk through the code, you can see the variables change values, and you can watch as objects are created and destroyed.

This section will provide a brief introduction to the most important parts of the debugger that accompanies the Visual Studio .NET Integrated Development Environment (IDE). For complete coverage of how to use the Visual Studio .NET debugger, we urge you to spend time with the documentation and to experiment freely. The debugger is one of the most powerful tools at your disposal for learning ASP.NET.

The Debug Toolbar

There is a *Debug toolbar* available in the IDE. To make it visible, click on the View/ Toolbars menu commands, then click on Debug, if it is not already checked. Table 7-3 shows the icons that appear on the Debug toolbar.

Table 7-3. Debug toolbar icons

Icon	Debug menu equivalent	Keyboard shortcut	Description
			Toolbar handle. Click and drag to move the toolbar to a new location.
	Start / Continue	F5	Starts or continues executing the program.
	Break All	Ctrl+Alt+Break	Stops program execution at the currently executing line.
	Stop Debugging	Shift+F5	Stops debugging.
	Restart	Ctrl+Shift+F5	Stops the run currently being debugged and immediately begins a new run.
			Shows next statement.
	Step Into	F11	If the current line contains a call to a method or function, this icon will single-step the debugger into that method or function.
	Step Over	F10	If the current line contains a call to a method or function, this icon will not step into that method or function, but will go to the next line after the call.
	Step Out	Shift+F11	If the current line is in a method or function, that method or function will complete and the debugger will stop on the line after the method or function call.
Statement			Unit of debugger stepping. Possible values are `Line`, `Statement`, and `Instruction`.
Hex			Hexadecimal display toggle.
	Windows		Debug window selector.
			Toolbar options. Offers options for adding and removing buttons from all toolbars (Debug, Text Editor, etc.).

Breakpoints

> "The crux of the biscuit is the apostrophe."
>
> —Frank Zappa, *Apostrophe(')*

Breakpoints are at the heart of debugging. A breakpoint is an instruction to .NET to run to a specific line in your code and then to stop and wait for you to examine the current state of the application. While the execution is paused, you can:

- Examine and modify values of variables and expressions
- Single-step through the code

- Move into and out of methods and functions, even stepping into classes written in other CLR-compliant languages
- Perform any number of other debugging and analysis tasks

Setting a breakpoint

A breakpoint is set in the Source window (any Source window, such as page file, control file, or code-behind) by single-clicking on the gray vertical bar along the left margin of the window. A red dot will appear in the left margin and the line of code will be highlighted, as shown in Figure 7-6.

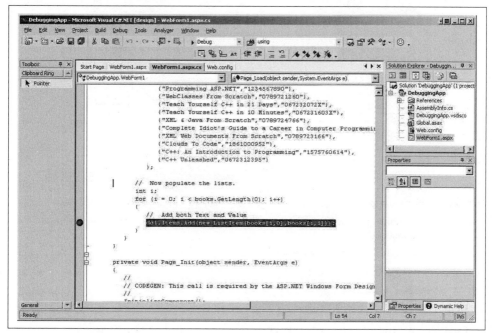

Figure 7-6. Breakpoint

An alternative to clicking in the left margin is to select the Debug/New Breakpoint... menu command. Clicking on the File tab will bring up the dialog shown in Figure 7-7. The text boxes will already be filled in with the current location of the cursor.

The four tabs in the dialog box in Figure 7-7 correspond to the four types of breakpoints, which are described in Table 7-4.

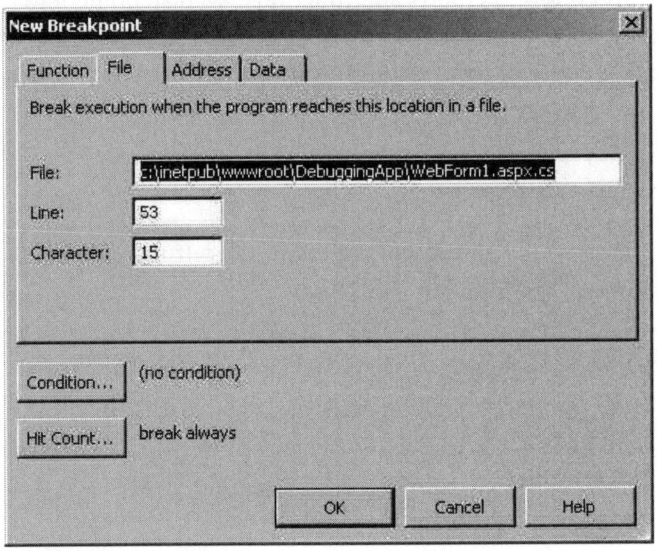

Figure 7-7. New breakpoint dialog box

Table 7-4. Four types of breakpoints

Type	Description
Function	Allows you to specify where, in which language, and in which method or function the break will occur.
File	Sets a breakpoint at a specific point in a source file. When you set a breakpoint by clicking in the left margin, a file breakpoint is being set.
Address	Sets a breakpoint at a specified memory address.
Data	Sets a breakpoint when the value of a variable changes.

Breakpoint window

You can see all the breakpoints currently set by looking at the *Breakpoint window*. To display the Breakpoint window, perform any one of the following actions:

- Press Ctrl+Alt+B.
- Select Breakpoints from the Debug/Windows menu command.
- Click on the Windows icon of the Debug toolbar and select Breakpoints.

A Breakpoint window is shown in Figure 7-8.

You can toggle a breakpoint between Enabled and Disabled by clicking on the corresponding checkbox in the Breakpoint window.

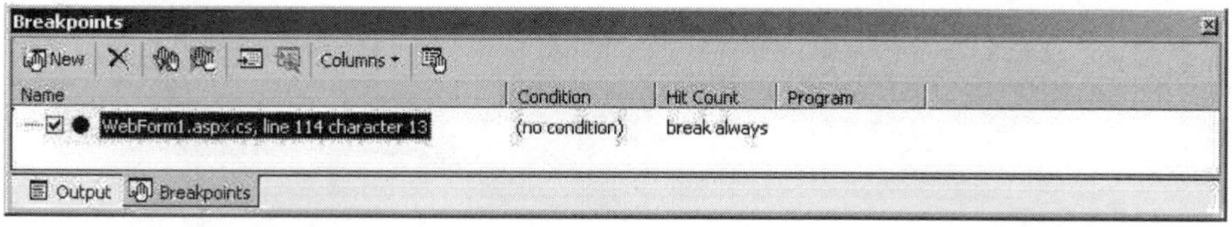

Figure 7-8. Breakpoint window

Breakpoint properties

Sometimes you don't want a breakpoint to stop execution every time the line is reached. VS.NET offers two properties that can be set to modify the behavior of a breakpoint. These properties can be set in either of two ways:

- Right-click on the breakpoint glyph in the left margin and select Breakpoint properties.

- Open the Breakpoint window, right-click on the desired breakpoint, and select Properties.

In either case, you will see the dialog box shown in Figure 7-9.

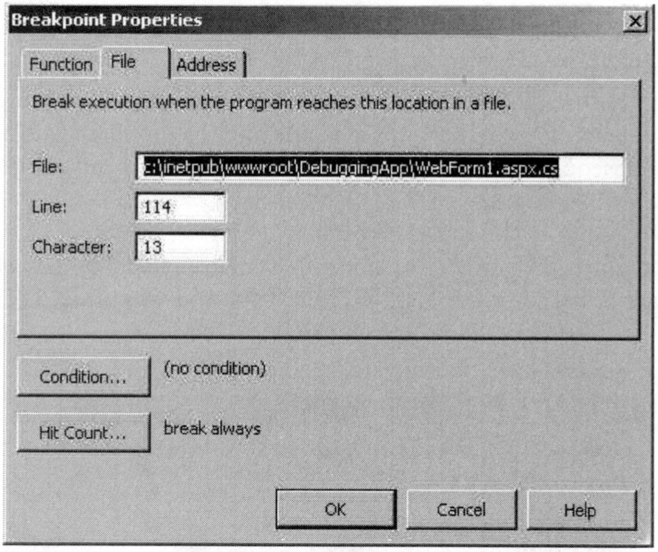

Figure 7-9. Breakpoint properties dialog box

The fields at the top of the Breakpoint Properties dialog box will default to the location of the current breakpoint. The two buttons allow access to the Condition and Hit Count properties.

Condition. The Condition button brings up the dialog shown in Figure 7-10.

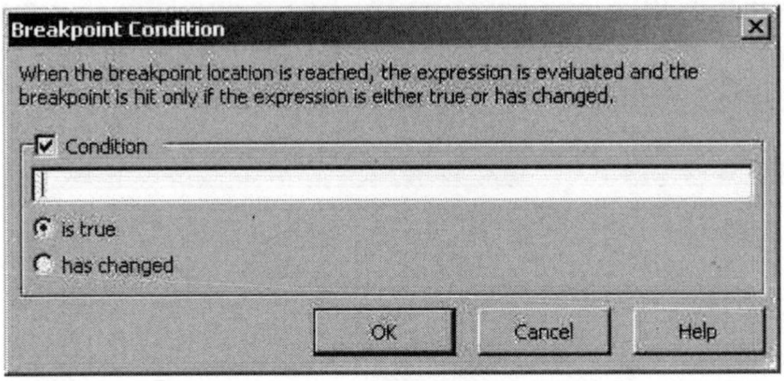

Figure 7-10. Breakpoint Condition dialog box

You can enter any valid expression in the edit field. This expression is evaluated when program execution reaches the breakpoint. Depending on which radio button is selected and how the Condition expression evaluates, the program execution will either pause or move on. The two radio buttons are labeled:

is true

> If the Condition entered evaluates to a Boolean true, then the program will pause.

has changed

> If the Condition entered has changed, then the program will pause. Note that on the first pass through the piece of code being debugged, the breakpoint will never pause execution because there is nothing to compare against. On the second and subsequent passes, the expression will have been initialized and the comparison will take place.

Hit count. *Hit count* is the number of times that spot in the code has been executed since either the run began or the Reset Hit Count button was pressed. The Hit Count button brings up the dialog shown in Figure 7-11.

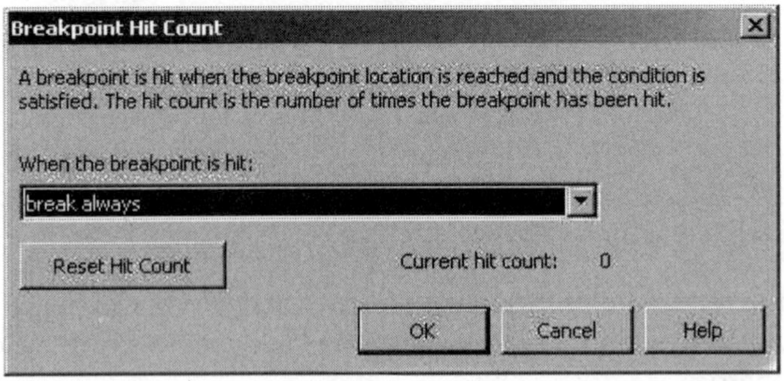

Figure 7-11. Breakpoint Hit Count dialog box

Clicking on the drop-down list presents the following options:

- Break always.
- Break always when the hit count is equal to . . .
- Break always when the hit count is a multiple of . . .
- Break always when the hit count is greater than or equal to . . .

If you click on any option other than "break always" (the default), the dialog box will add an edit field for you to enter a target hit count.

Suppose this is a breakpoint set in a loop of some sort. You selected "break when the hit count is a multiple of" and entered 5 in the edit field. Then the program will pause execution every fifth time it runs.

Breakpoint icons

There are several different breakpoint symbols, or glyphs, each conveying a different type of breakpoint. These glyphs appear in Table 7-5.

Table 7-5. Breakpoint icons

Icon	Type	Description
●	Enabled	A normal, active breakpoint. If breakpoint conditions or hit count settings are met, execution will pause at this line.
○	Disabled	Execution will not pause at this line until the breakpoint is re-enabled.
◖	Error	The location or condition is not valid.
❷	Warning	The code at this line is not yet loaded, so a breakpoint can't be set. If the code is subsequently loaded, then the breakpoint will become enabled.

Stepping through code

Go to the code-behind file in the example (either *WebForm1.aspx.cs* or *WebForm1. aspx.vb*, depending on your language). Place a breakpoint on the call to the Add method of the DropDownList control's Items collection, the line in the Page_Load method where the items are added to the DropDownList. Set the Hit Count to be a multiple of 5 (break always when hit count is a multiple of 5). Then run the program.

The breakpoint will be hit, and the program will stop execution at the line of code containing the breakpoint, which will turn yellow. The glyph in the left margin will have a yellow arrow on top of it. The VS.NET screen should look like Figure 7-12.

You can now move forward a single statement or line at a time, stepping into any methods or functions as you go, by using one of the following techniques:

- Select the Debug/Step Into menu command.
- Click on the Step Into icon (see Table 7-3, earlier in this chapter, for a picture of the icon).
- Press F11.

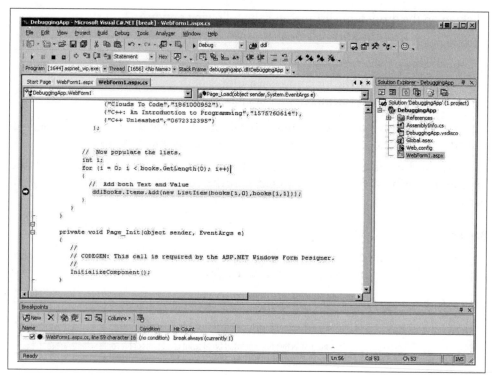

Figure 7-12. Breakpoint hit

You can step through the code without going through called functions or methods. That is, you can step over the calls rather than into the calls, using one of the following techniques:

- Select the Debug/Step Over menu item.
- Click on the Step Over icon (see Table 7-3 for a picture of the icon).
- Press F10.

Finally, if you are debugging in a called method or function, you can step out of that method or function call, using one of the following techniques:

- Select the Debug/Step Out menu command.
- Click on the Step Out icon (see Table 7-3 for a picture of the icon).
- Press Shift+F11.

To change the granularity of the stepping (i.e., step by Line, Statement, or Function), select a different value for Step By, either in the Debug Toolbar or at the Debug/Step By menu command.

Examining variables and objects

Once the program is stopped, you can examine the value of objects and variables currently in scope. This is incredibly intuitive and easy. Just place the mouse cursor over the top of any variable or object in the code, wait a moment, and a little pop-up window will appear with its current value

If the cursor is hovering over a variable, the pop-up will contain the type of variable, its value (if relevant), and any other properties it may have.

If the cursor is hovering over some other object, the pop-up window will contain information relevant to its type, including its full namespace and syntax, and a descriptive line of help.

Immediate window

The *Immediate window* allows you to type almost any variable, property, or expression and immediately see its value. To open the Immediate window, do any of the following:

- Press Ctrl+Alt+I.
- Select Immediate from the Debug/Windows menu commands.
- Click on the Windows icon of the Debug toolbar and select Immediate.

You can enter expressions for immediate execution in the Immediate window. If you want to see the value of an expression, prepend it with a question mark. For instance, if the breakpoint is on the line shown in Figure 7-12, you can see the value of the integer i by entering:

```
?i
```

in the Immediate window and pressing Enter. Figure 7-13 shows the result of that exercise; additionally, this figure shows the process of assigning a new value to the variable i and then viewing its value again.

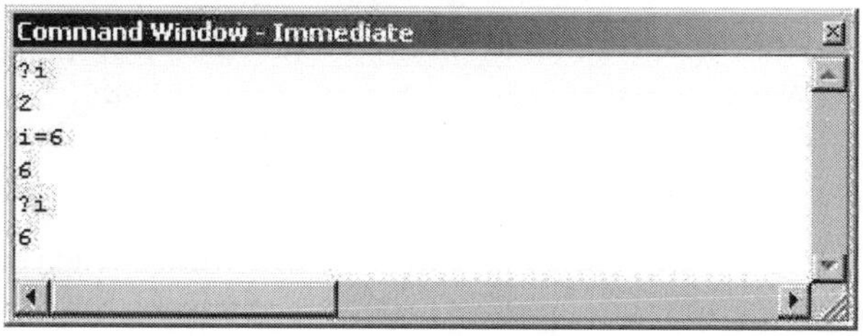

Figure 7-13. Immediate window

You can clear the contents of the Immediate window by right-clicking anywhere in the window and selecting Clear All. Close the window by clicking on the X in the upper-right corner. If you close the window and subsequently bring it back up in the same session, it will still have all the previous contents.

Autos window

The *Autos window* shows all the variables used in the current statement and the previous statement, displayed in a hierarchical table. To open the Autos window, do any of the following:

- Press Ctrl+Alt+V followed by A.
- Select Autos from the Debug/Windows menu commands.
- Click on the Windows icon of the Debug toolbar and select Autos.

A typical Autos window is shown in Figure 7-14.

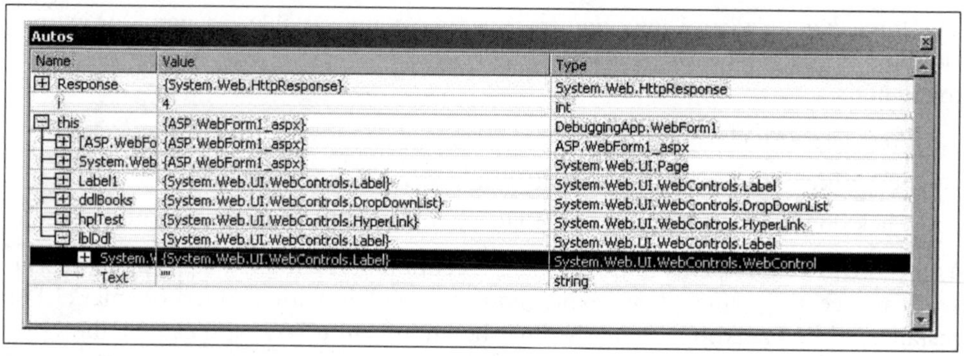

Figure 7-14. Autos window

There are columns for the name of the object, its value, and its type. A plus sign next to an object indicates that it has child objects that are not displayed while a minus sign indicates that its child objects are visible. Clicking on a plus symbol expands out the tree and shows any children, while clicking on a minus symbol contracts the tree and displays only the parent.

You can select and edit the value of any variable. The value will then display as red in the Autos window. Any changes to values take effect immediately.

Locals window

The *Locals window* is exactly the same as the Autos window, except that it shows variables local to the current context. By default, the current context is the method or function containing the current execution location.

To open a Locals window, do any of the following:

- Press Ctrl+Alt+V,L. (Press and hold Ctrl+Alt+V; release all three keys; then press L.)

- Select Locals from the Debug/Windows menu commands.
- Click on the Windows icon of the Debug toolbar and select Locals.

This/Me window

The C# *This* window and the VB.NET *Me* window are exactly the same as the Autos window, except that they show all objects pointed to by this in C# and Managed C++ and by Me in VB.NET.

To open a This/Me window, do any of the following:

- Press Ctrl+Alt+V,T/M. (Press and hold Ctrl+Alt+V; release all three keys; then press T for This or M for Me.)
- Select This or Me from the Debug/Windows menu commands.
- Click on the Windows icon of the Debug toolbar; select This or Me.

Watch window

The *Watch window* is exactly the same as the Autos window, except that it shows only variables, properties, or expressions that you enter into the Name field in the window or drag from another window. The advantage of using a Watch window is that it allows you to watch objects from several different source windows simultaneously. This overcomes the inability to add object types other than the specified type to any of the other debug windows.

To open a Watch window, do any of the following:

- Press Ctrl+Alt+W, followed by *n*, where *n* is either 1, 2, 3, or 4.
- Select Watch from the Debug/Windows menu commands.
- Click on the Windows icon of the Debug toolbar and select Watch.

In addition to typing in the name of the object you want to watch, you can also drag and drop variables, properties, or expressions from a Code window. Select the object in the code that you want to put in the Watch window, then drag it to the Name field in the open Watch window.

You can also drag and drop objects from any of the following windows into the Watch window:

- Locals
- Autos
- This/Me
- Disassembly

In order to drag something from one of these windows to the Watch window, both the source window and the Watch window must be open. Highlight a line in the source window, then drag it down over the Watch tab. The Watch window will come to the foreground. Continue dragging the object to an empty line in the Watch window.

Call Stack window

The *Call Stack window* displays the names of the methods and functions on the call stack, as well as their parameter types and values. You can control which information is displayed in the Call Stack window by right-clicking anywhere in the window and toggling field names that appear in the lower portion of the pop-up menu. To open a Call Stack window, do any of the following:

- Press Ctrl+Alt+C.
- Select Call Stack from the Debug/Windows menu commands.
- Click on the Windows icon of the Debug toolbar and select Call Stack.

Threads window

The *Threads window* allows you to examine and control threads in the program you are debugging. Threads are sequences of executable instructions. Programs can be either single-threaded or multithreaded. The whole topic of threading and multiprocess programming is beyond the scope of this book.

To open a Threads window, do any of the following:

- Press Ctrl+Alt+H.
- Select Threads from the Debug/Windows menu commands.
- Click on the Windows icon of the Debug toolbar and select Threads.

Modules window

The *Modules window* allows you to examine the *.exe* and *.dll* files that are being used by the program being debugged. To open a Modules window, do any of the following:

- Press Ctrl+Alt+U.
- Select Modules from the Debug/Windows menu commands.
- Click on the Windows icon of the Debug toolbar and select Modules.

A Modules window is shown in Figure 7-15.

By default, the modules are shown in the order in which they were loaded. You can re-sort the table by clicking on any of the column headers.

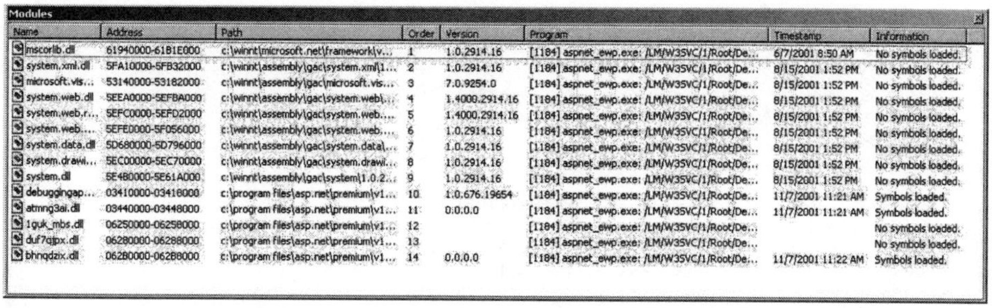

Figure 7-15. Modules window

Disassembly window

The *Disassembly window* shows the current program in assembly code. If you are debugging managed code, such as that which comes from VB.NET, C#, or Managed C++, this will correspond to Microsoft Intermediate Language (MSIL) code.

A Disassembly window is shown in Figure 7-16.

Unlike the previous windows discussed in this chapter, the Disassembly window displays as a tabbed item, as part of the main Source code window. You can set breakpoints anywhere in the window, just as for any other Source code window. To open a Disassembly window, do any of the following:

- Press Ctrl+Alt+D.
- Select Disassembly from the Debug/Windows menu commands.
- Click on the Windows icon of the Debug toolbar and select Disassembly.

Registers window

The *Registers window* allows you to examine the contents of the microprocessor's registers. Values that have changed recently are displayed in red. To open a Registers window, do any of the following:

- Press Ctrl+Alt+G.
- Select Registers from the Debug/Windows menu commands.
- Click on the Windows icon of the Debug toolbar and select Registers.

You can select which pieces of information to view by right-clicking anywhere in the Registers window and clicking on the information you would like displayed.

Memory windows

There are four *Memory windows* available for viewing memory dumps of large buffers, strings, and other data that will not display well in any other window. To open a Memory window, do any of the following:

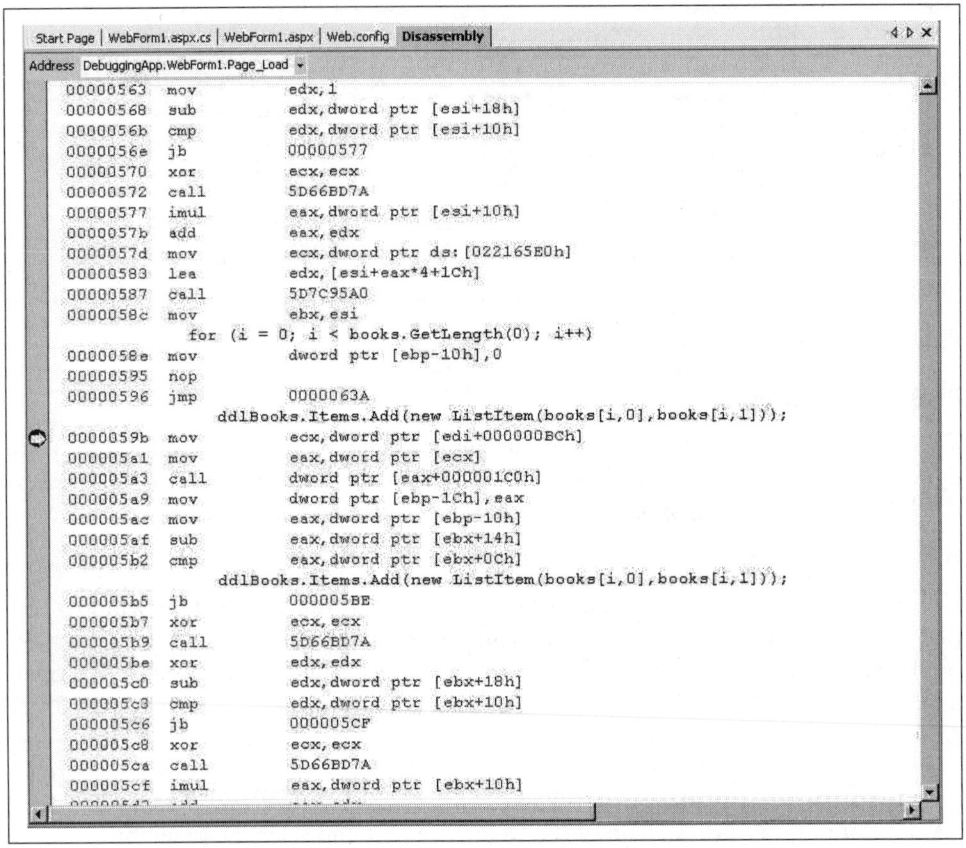

```
Start Page | WebForm1.aspx.cs | WebForm1.aspx | Web.config | Disassembly |          ◁ ▷ ✕
Address DebuggingApp.WebForm1.Page_Load ▾
   00000563  mov          edx,1
   00000568  sub          edx,dword ptr [esi+18h]
   0000056b  cmp          edx,dword ptr [esi+10h]
   0000056e  jb           00000577
   00000570  xor          ecx,ecx
   00000572  call         5D66BD7A
   00000577  imul         eax,dword ptr [esi+10h]
   0000057b  add          eax,edx
   0000057d  mov          ecx,dword ptr ds:[022165E0h]
   00000583  lea          edx,[esi+eax*4+1Ch]
   00000587  call         5D7C95A0
   0000058c  mov          ebx,esi
             for (i = 0; i < books.GetLength(0); i++)
   0000058e  mov          dword ptr [ebp-10h],0
   00000595  nop
   00000596  jmp          0000063A
             ddlBooks.Items.Add(new ListItem(books[i,0],books[i,1]));
   0000059b  mov          ecx,dword ptr [edi+000000BCh]
   000005a1  mov          eax,dword ptr [ecx]
   000005a3  call         dword ptr [eax+000001C0h]
   000005a9  mov          dword ptr [ebp-1Ch],eax
   000005ac  mov          eax,dword ptr [ebp-10h]
   000005af  sub          eax,dword ptr [ebx+14h]
   000005b2  cmp          eax,dword ptr [ebx+0Ch]
             ddlBooks.Items.Add(new ListItem(books[i,0],books[i,1]));
   000005b5  jb           000005BE
   000005b7  xor          ecx,ecx
   000005b9  call         5D66BD7A
   000005be  xor          edx,edx
   000005c0  sub          edx,dword ptr [ebx+18h]
   000005c3  cmp          edx,dword ptr [ebx+10h]
   000005c6  jb           000005CF
   000005c8  xor          ecx,ecx
   000005ca  call         5D66BD7A
   000005cf  imul         eax,dword ptr [ebx+10h]
   00000542  add          eax,edx
```

Figure 7-16. Disassembly window

- Press Ctrl+Alt+M followed by *n*, where *n* is either 1, 2, 3, or 4.
- Select Memory from the Debug/Windows menu commands.
- Click on the Windows icon of the Debug toolbar and select Memory.

Configuration

An application can be configured to either enable or disable debugging. This is done through the *web.config* file, which is described more fully in Chapter 20.

Web.config is an XML file, and as such it must be well-formed. The file consists of sections delimited by tags. The debugging configuration information is contained within the <compilation> section, within the <system.web> section, which in turn is contained within the <configuration> section. So a typical compilation configuration snippet will look something like Example 7-8.

Example 7-8. Debug configuration code snippet from web.config

```
<?xml version="1.0" encoding="utf-8" ?>
<configuration>

    <system.web>
.
.
.
    <compilation
        debug="true"
    />
```

Note that setting debug to false improves the runtime performance of the application.

Error Handling

You can and should avoid bugs, but there are runtime errors that cannot be avoided and must be handled. The simplest bugs to find and fix are *syntax* errors: violations of the rules of the language. For example, suppose you had the following line of code in your C# program:

```
intt i;
```

or this line in your VB.NET program:

```
dim i as intgr
```

In either case, when you try to compile the program, you will get a compiler error, because in each case, the keyword for integer is misspelled.

Syntax errors are reduced dramatically when using Visual Studio .NET. Depending on how VS.NET is configured, any code element that isn't recognized is underlined. If Auto List Members is turned on, the incidence of syntax errors is further reduced. Finally, because VB.NET doesn't necessarily require explicit variable declaration, you can turn Option Explicit on to eliminate typos as a source of syntax errors.

Should any syntax errors remain, or if you are using a different editor, then any syntax errors will be caught by the compiler every time you try to build the project. It is nearly impossible for a syntax error to slip by into production code.

 When the compiler finds a syntax error, an error message containing the location of the error and a terse explanation will be displayed in the Output window of VS.NET. If the error is caused by something such as an unbalanced parenthesis or bracket (or a missing semicolon in C#), then the actual error may not be on the exact line reported.

More problematic, and often more difficult to catch, are errors in *logic*. The program successfully compiles and may run perfectly well most of the time, yet still contain errors in logic. The very hardest bugs to find are those that occur least often. If you can't reproduce the problem, it is terribly difficult to find it.

While you will try to eliminate all the bugs from your code, you do want your program to react gracefully when a subtle bug rears its ugly head.

Unhandled Errors

In order to demonstrate what happens if there is no error handling in place, modify the sample project from this chapter to force some errors.

Go to the code-behind window. Find the for loop that populates the DropDownList in the Page_Load method. Change the test expression to intentionally cause an error at runtime. For example, in C#, change the line:

```
for (i = 0; i < books.GetLength(0); i++)
```

to:

```
for (i = 0; i < books.GetLength(0) + 2; i++)
```

In VB.NET, change the line:

```
for i = 0 to books.GetLength(0) - 1
```

to:

```
for i = 0 to books.GetLength(0) + 2
```

In either language, when this code runs it will try to add more items than have been defined in the books array, thus causing a runtime error. While this is not a subtle bug, it will serve to demonstrate how the system reacts to runtime errors.

Now run the program. As expected, an error is generated immediately, and the generic ASP.NET error page is displayed, as shown in Figure 7-17.

This error page is actually fairly useful to the developer or technical support person who will be trying to track down and fix any bugs. It tells you the type of error, the line in the code that is the approximate location of the error, and a stack trace to help in tracking down how that line of code was reached.

Application-wide Error Pages

The previous section showed the default error pages presented for unhandled errors. This is fine for a developer, but if the application is in production, it would be much more aesthetically pleasing if the user were presented with an error page that did not look so intimidating.

The goal is to intercept the error before it has a chance to send the generic error page to the client. This is done on an application-wide basis by modifying the *web.config* file, which will be described more fully in Chapter 20.

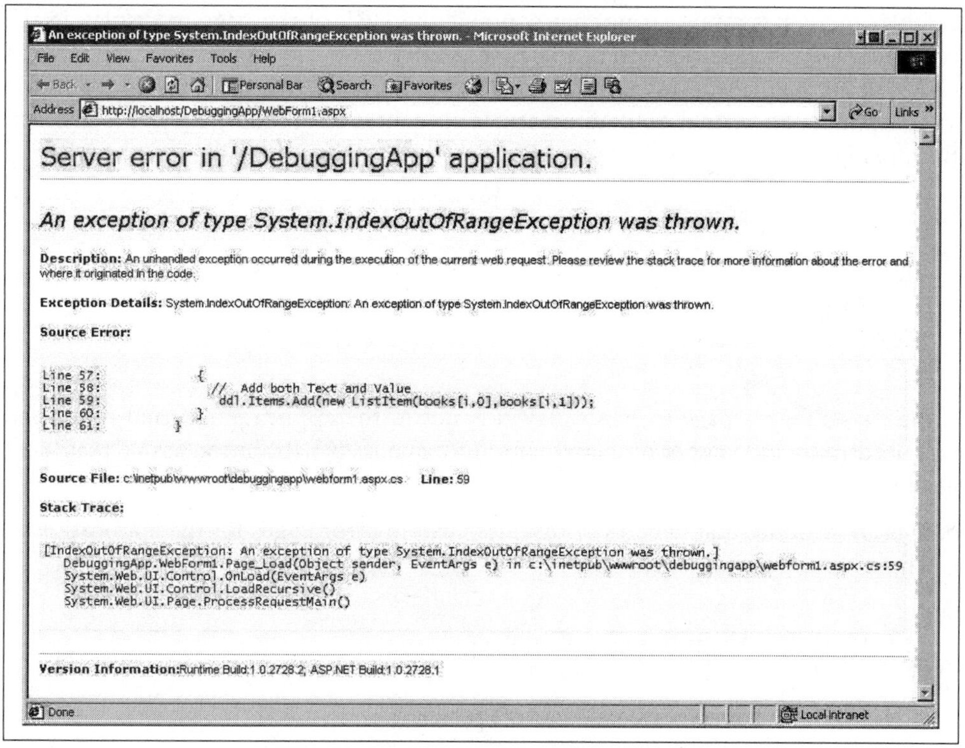

Figure 7-17. Generic error page

The error handling configuration information in *web.config* is contained within the
<customErrors> section within the <system.web> section, which is contained within
the <configuration> section. A typical <customErrors> section will look like
Example 7-9.

Example 7-9. Custom error code snippet from web.config

```xml
<?xml version="1.0" encoding="utf-8" ?>
<configuration>

   <system.web>
.
.
.
   <customErrors
      defaultRedirect="CustomErrorPage.htm"
      mode="On"
   />
```

There are two possible attributes for the <customErrors> section: defaultRedirect
and mode.

defaultRedirect is a text string that contains the URL of the page to display in the case of any error not otherwise handled. In Example 7-9, the defaultRedirect page is *CustomErrorPage.htm*. This example is a very simple HTML page contained in the same application virtual root directory. The contents of this page are shown in Example 7-10.

Example 7-10. CustomErrorPage.htm

```html
<html>
   <body>
      <h1>Sorry - you've got an error.</h1>
   </body>
</html>
```

If the custom error page to be displayed is not in the application virtual root, then you need to include either a relative or a fully qualified URL in the defaultRedirect attribute.

mode is an attribute that enables or disables custom error pages for the application. It can have three possible values:

On

> Enables custom errors for the entire application.

Off

> Disables custom errors for the entire application.

RemoteOnly

> Enables custom errors only for remote clients. Local clients will see the generic error page. In this way, developers can see all the possible error information, but end users will see the custom error page.

If you edit your *web.config* file to look like Example 7-9, then put *CustomErrorPage. htm* in your application virtual root and run the program. Instead of Figure 7-17, you will see something like Figure 7-18.

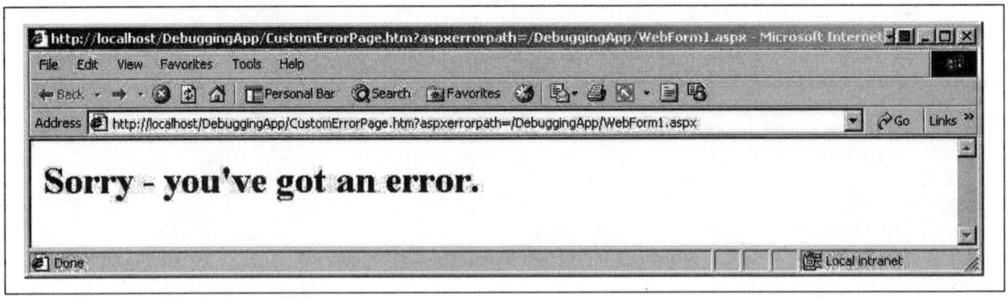

Figure 7-18. Custom error page

Obviously, you'll want to put more information on your custom error page, such as instructions or contact information, but you get the idea. It is also possible to show dynamic information about the error on the custom error page.

You can even use a different custom error page for different errors. To do this, you need to include one or more <error> subtags in the <customErrors> section of *web. config*. You might, for example, modify *web.config* to look like the code snippet in Example 7-11.

Example 7-11. Custom error code snippet with <error> subtags from web.config

```
<?xml version="1.0" encoding="utf-8" ?>
<configuration>

    <system.web>
.
.
.
    <customErrors
        defaultRedirect="CustomErrorPage.htm"
        mode="On" >

        <error statusCode="400" redirect="CustomErrorPage400.htm"/>
        <error statusCode="404" redirect="CustomErrorPage404.htm"/>
        <error statusCode="500" redirect="CustomErrorPage500.htm"/>

    </customErrors>
```

Copy *CustomErrorPage.htm* three times and rename the copies to the filenames in the <error> subtags in Example 7-11. Edit the files so that each displays a unique message.

Run the program again with the intentional error in the for loop still in place. You should see something like Figure 7-19.

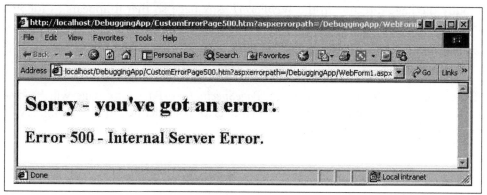

Figure 7-19. Custom error page for error 500

Fix the error in the for loop so that the program will at least load correctly. Then run the program and click on the hyperlink you put on the test page. Remember that that control is configured to link to a nonexistent *.aspx* file. You should see something like Figure 7-20.

Figure 7-20. Custom error page for error 404

Be aware that you can only display custom error pages for errors generated on *your* server. So, for example, if the hyperlink had been set to a nonexistent page, say, *http://TestPage.comx* (note the intentional misspelling of the extension), you will not see your custom error page for error 404. Instead you'll see whatever error page for which the remote server or your browser is configured. Also, you can only trap the 404 error if the page you are trying to link to has an extension of *.aspx*.

Page-Specific Error Pages

You can override the application-level error pages for any specific page by modifying the Page directive. (Page directives are covered fully in Chapter 6.)

Modify the Page directive in the *WebForm1.aspx* page so that it appears as follows (note the highlighted ErrorPage attribute, which has been added):

```
<%@ Page language="c#" Codebehind="WebForm1.aspx.cs" AutoEventWireup="false"
    Inherits="DebuggingApp.WebForm1" Trace="false" ErrorPage="PageSpecificErrorPage.
    aspx" %>
```

If there is an error on this page, the *PageSpecificErrorPage.aspx* page will be displayed. If there is an application-level custom error page defined in *web.config*, it will be overridden by the Page directive.

Validation

As we saw in Chapter 3, many web applications involve user input. The sad fact is, however, that users make mistakes: they skip required fields, they put in six digit phone numbers, and they return all manner of incorrectly formatted data to your application. Your database routines can choke on corrupted data, and orders can be lost if, for example, a credit card number is entered incorrectly or an address is omitted, so it is imperative that user input be validated.

Traditionally, it has taken a great deal of time and effort to validate user input. Each field must be checked and routines must be created for ensuring data integrity. In the event that bad data is found, error messages must be displayed so that the user knows how to correct the problem.

In a given application, you may choose to validate that certain fields have a value, that the values fall within a given range, or that the data is formatted correctly. For example, when processing an order, you may need to ensure that the user has input an address and phone number, that the phone number has the right number of digits (and no letters), and that the social security number entered is in the appropriate form of nine digits separated by hyphens.

Some applications require more complex validation, in which one field is validated to be within a range established by two other fields. For example, you might ask in one field what date the customer wishes to arrive at your hotel, and in a second field you might ask for the departure date. When the user books dinner, you'll want to ensure that the date is between the arrival and departure dates.

There is no limit to the complexity of the validation routines you may need to write. Credit cards have checksums built into their values, as do ISBN numbers. Zip and postal codes follow complex patterns, as do international phone numbers. You may need to validate passwords, membership numbers, dollar amounts, dates, runway choices, and launch codes.

In addition, it is very desirable for all of this validation to happen client-side so that you avoid the delay of repeated round trips to the server while the user tinkers with his input. In the past, this was solved by writing client-side JavaScript to validate the input, and then server-side script to handle input from browsers that don't support client-side programming. In addition, as a security check, you may want to do server-side validation even when you already have client-side validation, since it is extremely easy for users to circumvent validation code deliberately. Traditionally, this involved writing your validation code twice.

As you can see, in traditional Internet programming, validation requires extensive custom programming. The ASP.NET framework greatly simplifies this process by providing rich controls for validating user input that provide precise control over the validation routine while requiring far less custom coding. They also allow you to specify exactly how and where the error messages will be displayed; either in-line with the input controls, aggregated together in a summary report, or both. These controls can be used to validate input for both HTML and ASP controls.

You add validation controls to your ASP document just as you would add any other control. Within the declaration of the validation control, you specify which other control is being validated. You may freely combine the various validation controls, and you may write your own, as you'll see later in this chapter.

With uplevel browsers that support DHTML, such as Internet Explorer 4 or better, .NET validation is done client-side, avoiding the necessity of a round trip to the server. With downlevel browsers *your* code is unchanged, but the code sent to the client ensures validation at the server. Even when client-side validation is done, the values are validated server-side as well.

The validation is done client side (using DHTML) if the browser will support it; otherwise, the validation is done on the server. Note that even when the validation is done on the client, it is also done on the server as a security precaution.

Because client-side validation will prevent your server-side event handlers from ever running if the control is not valid, you may want to force server-side validation. In that case, set a page attribute:

```
<%@ Page language="c#" ClientTarget="downlevel"
Codebehind="WebForm1.aspx.cs"
AutoEventWireup="false"
Inherits="Validation04.WebForm1" %>
```

This directive will cause the validation to happen on the server even if your browser would have supported DHTML and client-side validation.

ASP.NET supports the following validation controls:

RequiredFieldValidator control
　　The simplest validation control, it ensures that the user does not skip over your input control. A RequiredFieldValidator can be tied to a text box to force input

---

into the text box. With selection controls, such as a drop-down or radio buttons, the RequiredFieldValidator ensures that the user makes a selection other than the default. The RequiredFieldValidator does not examine the validity of the data, but only makes sure that some data is entered or chosen.

RangeValidator control
Ensures that the value entered is within a specified lower and upper boundary. You can check the range within a pair of numbers (e.g., greater than 10 and less than 100), a pair of characters (e.g., greater than D and less than K) and a pair of dates (e.g., after 1/1/01 and before 2/28/01). The values you check can be constants that you create at design-time, or they can be derived from other controls on your page (greater than the value in textBox1 and less than the value in textBox2).

CompareValidator control
Compares the user's entry against another value. It can compare against a constant that you specify at design time, or against a property value of another control. It can also compare against a database value. The comparison must use one of the comparison operators such as less than, equal to, greater than, etc.

RegularExpressionValidator control
One of the most powerful validators, it compares the user's entry with a regular expression that you provide. You can use this validator to check for valid social security numbers, phone numbers, passwords, and so forth.

CustomValidator control
If none of these controls meets your needs, you can use the CustomValidator. This checks the user's entry against whatever algorithm you provide in a custom method.

In the remainder of this chapter, we'll examine how to use each of these controls to validate data in ASP.NET applications.

The RequiredFieldValidator

Let's start with one of the simpler validators: the RequiredFieldValidator, which ensures that the user provides a valid value for your control. You'll create the simple bug reporting form shown in Figure 8-1.

When the user presses the Submit Bug button, the form is validated to ensure that each field has been modified. If not, the offending field is marked with a red asterisk, as shown in Figure 8-2. If you prefer more meaningful data reports, you can specify a prompt for each error message, as shown in Figure 8-3. The choice of whether to use an asterisk or a meaningful error message is entirely up to you.

To create this form, you'll put the controls inside a simple table, building the drop-down list and button list with items added in the *.aspx* file.

Bug Report

Please report your bug here

Book   -- Please Pick A Book -- ▾

Edition:
- ○ 1st
- ○ 2nd
- ○ 3rd
- ○ 4th

Bug: [_____]

[Submit Bug]

Figure 8-1. The bug report

Bug Report

Please report your bug here

Book   -- Please Pick A Book -- ▾   *

Edition:
- ○ 1st
- ○ 2nd
- ○ 3rd
- ⊙ 4th

Bug: [_____]   *

[Submit Bug]

Figure 8-2. Indicating errors

You start by creating a form. Write the title (which will hold your updated message when the form is validated), and then create the table to hold the controls:

```
<body>
   <h3>
      <font face="Verdana">Bug Report</font>
   </h3>
   <form runat="server" ID="frmBugs">
      <table bgcolor=gainsboro cellpadding=10>
```

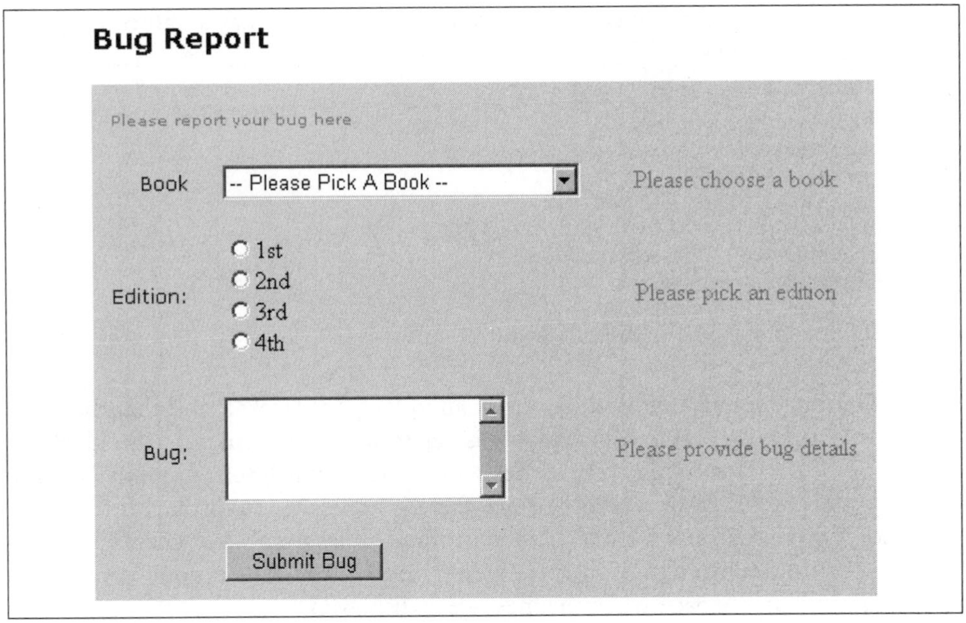

Figure 8-3. With error messages

Next, create the drop-down list in the first cell of the table to hold the book titles:

```
<td>
<!-- Drop down list with the books (must pick one) -->
   <ASP:DropDownList id=ddlBooks runat=server>
       <asp:ListItem>-- Please Pick A Book --</asp:ListItem>
       <asp:ListItem>Programming ASP.NET</asp:ListItem>
```

Each title is added and the list is ended:

```
       <asp:ListItem>Programming C#</asp:ListItem>
       <asp:ListItem>
           Teach Yourself C++ In 21 Days
       </asp:ListItem>
       <asp:ListItem>
           Teach Yourself C++ In 24 Hours
       </asp:ListItem>
       <asp:ListItem>TY C++ In 10 Minutes</asp:ListItem>
       <asp:ListItem>TY More C++ In 21 Days</asp:ListItem>
       <asp:ListItem>C++ Unleashed</asp:ListItem>
       <asp:ListItem>C++ From Scratch</asp:ListItem>
       <asp:ListItem>XML From Scratch</asp:ListItem>
       <asp:ListItem>Web Classes FS</asp:ListItem>
       <asp:ListItem>Beg. OO Analysis & Design</asp:ListItem>
       <asp:ListItem>Clouds To Code</asp:ListItem>
       <asp:ListItem>
           CIG Career Computer Programming
       </asp:ListItem>
   </ASP:DropDownList>
</td>
```

You then add, in the very next cell, the validator to ensure that a value is selected from the drop-down list:

```
<!-- Validator for the drop down -->
<td align=middle rowspan=1>
    <asp:RequiredFieldValidator
    id="reqFieldBooks"
    ControlToValidate="ddlBooks"
    Display="Static"
    InitialValue="-- Please Pick A Book --"
    Width="100%" runat=server>
        Please choose a book
    </asp:RequiredFieldValidator>
</td>
```

Notice that the RequiredFieldValidator has an id (reqFieldBooks), and that the value of the next attribute, ControlToValidate, is set to ddlBooks, which is the id of the book drop-down. The Display attribute is set to Static, which tells ASP.NET to allocate room for the validator whether or not there is a message to display. If this is set to Dynamic, space will not be allocated until (and unless) an error message is displayed. Dynamic allocation is very powerful, but it can cause your controls to bounce around on the page when the message is displayed.

In the example, if you set all the validation controls to dynamic no space will be allocated for them, and the browser will decide that your table is only two columns wide rather than three. That is, the table will not allocate any space for the validation messages, and will recognize only one column for the prompt, and the other for the controls. As Figure 8-4 and 8-5 illustrate, when you validate the controls (by pressing the Submit button) the table will widen, which can either be disconcerting or attractive, depending on how you manage the display.

The RequiredFieldValidator has an additional attribute, InitialValue, which is set to the initial value of the drop-down box. If the user presses Submit, this initial value will be compared with the value of the drop-down, and if they are the same, the error message will be displayed. This effectively forces the user to change the initial value, picking a particular book to report about.

The form continues with the radio buttons for the edition (1st, 2nd, etc.). These are added in a RadioButtonList, which allows you to programmatically add buttons just like you add items to a drop-down list:

```
<tr>
    <td align=right>
        <font face=Verdana size=2>Edition:</font>
    </td>
    <td>
        <ASP:RadioButtonList id=rblEdition
        RepeatLayout="Flow" runat=server>
            <asp:ListItem>1st</asp:ListItem>
            <asp:ListItem>2nd</asp:ListItem>
            <asp:ListItem>3rd</asp:ListItem>
```

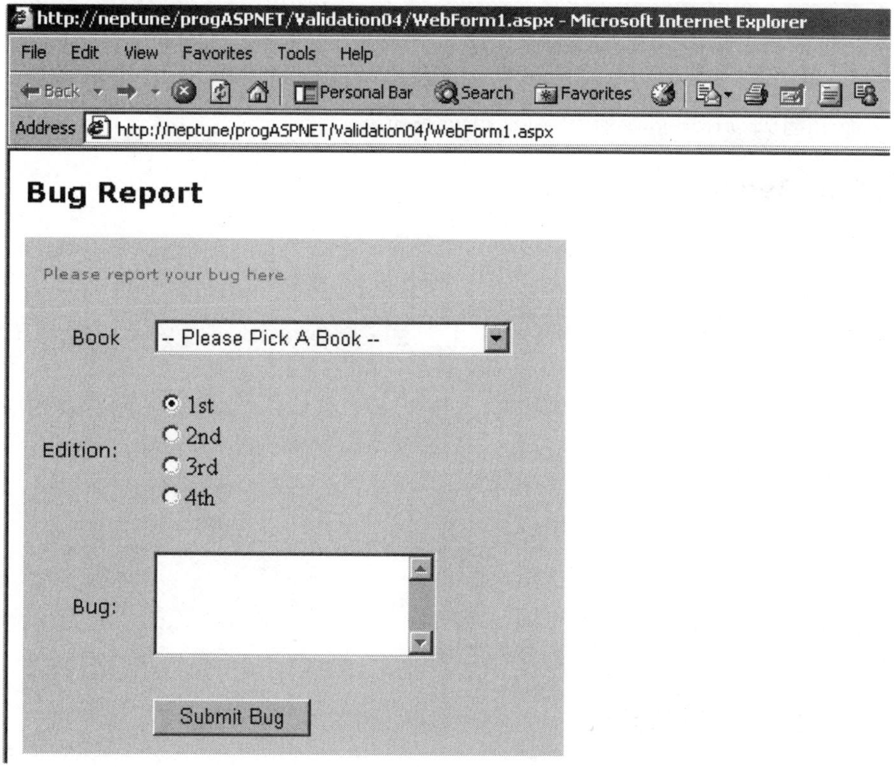

Figure 8-4. Before pressing Submit

```
            <asp:ListItem>4th</asp:ListItem>
        </ASP:RadioButtonList>
    </td>
```

With the buttons in place, you can add the RequiredFieldValidator, which ensures that a button is selected:

```
<!-- Validator for editions -->
<td align=middle rowspan=1>
   <asp:RequiredFieldValidator
   id="reqFieldEdition"
   ControlToValidate="rblEdition"
   Display="Static"
   InitialValue=""
   Width="100%" runat=server>
      Please pick an edition
   </asp:RequiredFieldValidator>
</td>
```

No need to indicate an initial value this time. Since the control is a radio button list, the validator knows that the user is simply required to pick one of the buttons; if any button is chosen, then the validation is satisfied.

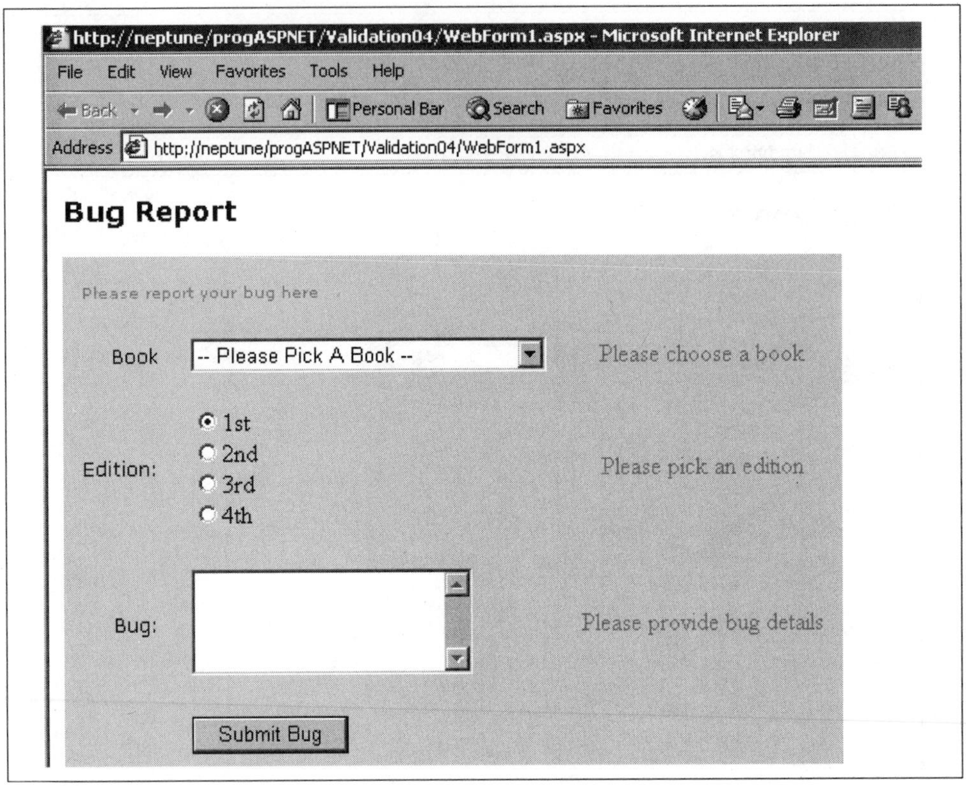

Figure 8-5. After pressing Submit

You could vary this example by setting the first button to selected

```
<asp:ListItem Selected="True">1st</asp:ListItem>
```

and setting the InitialValue to the text of the first radio button:

```
<td align=middle rowspan=1>
    <asp: RequiredFieldValidator
    id="reqFieldEdition"
    ControlToValidate="rblEdition"
    Display="Static"
    InitialValue="1st"
    Width="100%" runat=server>
        Please pick an edition
    </asp: RequiredFieldValidator>
```

In this case the form would open with the 1st edition chosen, and the user would be required to pick a different edition.

Finally, to complete the example, add a text box and require that the user enter some text into it. Start by adding the text box itself. The ASP text box control can handle single line (HTML text) or multi-line text boxes (HTML text areas). You'll ask for a multi-line text area:

```
<tr>
   <td align=right style="HEIGHT: 97px">
      <font face=Verdana size=2>Bug:</font>
   </td>
   <!-- Multi-line text for the bug entry -->
   <td style="HEIGHT: 97px">
      <ASP:TextBox id=txtBug runat=server width="183px"
      textmode="MultiLine" height="68px"/>
   </td>
```

The validator is straightforward; set the text box as the `ControlToValidate` and enter the error message to display if the box is left empty:

```
   <!-- Validator for the text box-->
   <td style="HEIGHT: 97px">
      <asp:RequiredFieldValidator
      id="reqFieldBug"
      ControlToValidate="txtBug"
      Display="Static"
      Width="100%" runat=server>
         Please provide bug details
      </asp:RequiredFieldValidator>
   </td>
</tr>
```

The complete source code is shown in Example 8-1.

Example 8-1. HTML source for the RequiredFieldValidator control example

```
<%@ Page language="c#" Codebehind="WebForm1.aspx.cs"
AutoEventWireup="false" Inherits="Validation04.WebForm1" %>

<HTML>
  <HEAD>

<!-- Demonstrate simple required field validation -->
      <meta name=vs_targetSchema content="Internet Explorer 5.0">
      <meta name="GENERATOR" Content="Microsoft Visual Studio 7.0">
      <meta name="CODE_LANGUAGE" Content="C#">
  </HEAD>
   <body>
      <h3>
         <font face="Verdana">Bug Report</font>
      </h3>
      <form runat="server" ID="frmBugs">
         <table bgcolor=gainsboro cellpadding=10>
            <tr valign="top">
               <td colspan=3>
                  <!-- Display error messages -->
                  <asp:Label ID="lblMsg"
                  Text="Please report your bug here"
                  ForeColor="red" Font-Name="Verdana"
                  Font-Size="10" runat=server />
                  <br>
               </td>
```

```
    </tr>
    <tr>
      <td align=right>
        <font face=Verdana size=2>Book</font>
      </td>
      <td>
      <!-- Drop down list with the books (must pick one) -->
        <ASP:DropDownList id=ddlBooks runat=server>
          <asp:ListItem>-- Please Pick A Book --</asp:ListItem>
          <asp:ListItem>Programming ASP.NET</asp:ListItem>
          <asp:ListItem>Programming C#</asp:ListItem>
          <asp:ListItem>
            Teach Yourself C++ In 21 Days
          </asp:ListItem>
          <asp:ListItem>
            Teach Yourself C++ In 24 Hours
          </asp:ListItem>
          <asp:ListItem>TY C++ In 10 Minutes</asp:ListItem>
          <asp:ListItem>TY More C++ In 21 Days</asp:ListItem>
          <asp:ListItem>C++ Unleashed</asp:ListItem>
          <asp:ListItem>C++ From Scratch</asp:ListItem>
          <asp:ListItem>XML From Scratch</asp:ListItem>
          <asp:ListItem>Web Classes FS</asp:ListItem>
          <asp:ListItem>Beg. OO Analysis & Design</asp:ListItem>
          <asp:ListItem>Clouds To Code</asp:ListItem>
          <asp:ListItem>
            CIG Career Computer Programming
          </asp:ListItem>
        </ASP:DropDownList>
      </td>
      <!-- Validator for the drop down -->
      <td align=middle rowspan=1>
        <asp:RequiredFieldValidator
        id="reqFieldBooks"
        ControlToValidate="ddlBooks"
        Display="Static"
        InitialValue="-- Please Pick A Book --"
        Width="100%" runat=server>
          Please choose a book
        </asp:RequiredFieldValidator>
      </td>
    </tr>
    <tr>
      <td align=right>
      <!-- Radio buttons for the edition -->
        <font face=Verdana size=2>Edition:</font>
      </td>
      <td>
        <ASP:RadioButtonList id=rblEdition
        RepeatLayout="Flow" runat=server>
          <asp:ListItem>1st</asp:ListItem>
          <asp:ListItem>2nd</asp:ListItem>
```

```
                <asp:ListItem>3rd</asp:ListItem>
                <asp:ListItem>4th</asp:ListItem>
            </ASP:RadioButtonList>
        </td>
        <!-- Validator for editions -->
        <td align=middle rowspan=1>
            <asp:RequiredFieldValidator
            id="reqFieldEdition"
            ControlToValidate="rblEdition"
            Display="Static"
            InitialValue=""
            Width="100%" runat=server>
                Please pick an edition
            </asp:RequiredFieldValidator>
        </td>
    </tr>
    <tr>
        <td align=right style="HEIGHT: 97px">
            <font face=Verdana size=2>Bug:</font>
        </td>
        <!-- Multi-line text for the bug entry -->
        <td style="HEIGHT: 97px">
            <ASP:TextBox id=txtBug runat=server width="183px"
            textmode="MultiLine" height="68px"/>
        </td>
        <!-- Validator for the text box-->
        <td style="HEIGHT: 97px">
            <asp:RequiredFieldValidator
            id="reqFieldBug"
            ControlToValidate="txtBug"
            Display="Static"
            Width="100%" runat=server>
                Please provide bug details
            </asp:RequiredFieldValidator>
        </td>
    </tr>
    <tr>
        <td>
        </td>
        <td>
            <ASP:Button id=btnSubmit
            text="Submit Bug" runat=server />
        </td>
        <td>
        </td>
    </tr>
    </table>
    </form>
</body>
</HTML>
```

The page in Example 8-1 uses a code-behind C# page. The only non–boiler-plate code on that page is the handler for the Submit button, which is shown in Example 8-2.

Example 8-2. Code-behind page for handling the Submit button

```csharp
protected void btnSubmit_Click(object sender, System.EventArgs e)
{
    if (Page.IsValid == true)
    {
        lblMsg.Text = "Page is Valid!";
    }
    else
    {
        lblMsg.Text = "Some of the required fields are empty";
    }
}
```

To get this code to work on your machine, follow these steps:

1. Open a new web form application
2. Copy the HTML code in Example 8-1 over the HTML code, starting at the opening <body> tag.
3. Switch to design view and look at the form. Double click on the Submit button and paste Example 8-2 over your event handler
4. Run the application

You can see that btnSubmit_Click is a very simple routine that checks to see if the IsValid flag for the page was set to true, in which case a validating message is displayed in the lblMsg label; otherwise, a warning message is displayed. The IsValid flag is set to true if all the validators report that they are valid.

Notice that if client-side validation is performed, the warning message will never display. This method only runs on the server, and the page will not be posted to the server if the data is not valid.

The same program in VB.NET looks like this:

```vbnet
Protected Sub btnSubmit_Click( _
    ByVal sender As System.Object, _
    ByVal e As System.EventArgs) _
    Handles btnSubmit.Click

    If Page().IsValid = True Then
        lblMsg().Text = "Page is Valid!"
    Else
        lblMsg().Text = "Some of the required fields are empty"
    End If
End Sub
```

The *.aspx* file is unchanged, except that the heading now appears as follows:

```
<%@ Page Language="vb" AutoEventWireup="false"
Codebehind="WebForm1.aspx.vb" Inherits="Validation04VB.WebForm1"%>
```

The Summary Validator

You have great control over how validation errors are reported. For example, rather than putting error messages alongside the control, you can summarize all the validation failures with a ValidationSummary control. This control can place a summary of the errors in a bulleted list, a simple list, or a paragraph that appears on the web page or in a popup message box.

Let's rewrite Example 8-1 to add a ValidationSummary control at the bottom of the page. This simply requires that you add the code shown in boldface after the </table> tag in Example 8-1:

```
</table>
<asp:ValidationSummary ID="ValSum" DisplayMode="BulletList"
runat="server" HeaderText="The following errors were found: "
ShowMessageBox="True" ShowSummary="True"></asp:ValidationSummary>
```

Here you've named the ValidationSummary control ValSum and set its DisplayMode property to BulletList. The HeaderText attribute holds the header that will be displayed only if there are errors to report. You can mix the ShowMessageBox and ShowSummary attributes to display the errors in the body of the HTML document (ShowSummary="true") or in a pop up message box (ShowMessageBox="true") or both.

To make this work, you'll need to add an ErrorMessage attribute to the other validation controls. For example, you might modify the first validation control as follows:

```
<td align=middle rowspan=1>
   <asp: RequiredFieldValidator
   id="reqFieldBooks"
   ControlToValidate="ddlBooks"
   Display="static"
   InitialValue="-- Please Pick A Book --"
   ErrorMessage ="You did not choose a book from the drop-down."
   Width="100%" runat=server
   NAME="reqFieldBooks">*</asp: RequiredFieldValidator>
</td>
```

The text in the ErrorMessage attribute will be displayed in the summary if this control reports a validation error. You've also modified the validator itself to display an asterisk, rather than the more complete error message; now that you have a summary, you need only flag the error. Similar changes can be made for each of the other RequiredFieldValidator controls.

Rather than choose which of the three types of summary reports (bulleted list, list, or summary paragraph) to provide, you'll let the user choose from a drop-down. You do this by inserting the following boldfaced code before the definition of the Submit button:

```
<tr>
    <td align="right">
        <font face=Verdana size=2>Display Report</font>
    </td>
    <td>
        <asp:DropDownList id="lstFormat"
        AutoPostBack=true
        OnSelectedIndexChanged="lstFormat_SelectedIndexChanged"
        runat=server >
            <asp:ListItem >List</asp:ListItem>
            <asp:ListItem Selected>Bulleted List</asp:ListItem>
            <asp:ListItem>Single Paragraph</asp:ListItem>
        </asp:DropDownList>
    </td>
</tr>
<tr>
<td>
</td>
<td>
<ASP:Button id=btnSubmit
```

This drop-down posts back the page so that you can update the display. You have assigned an event handler, lstFormat_SelectedIndexChanged, to handle the event when the user changes the current selection. The event handler code is very simple. Here it is in C#:

```
protected void lstFormat_SelectedIndexChanged(
    object sender, System.EventArgs e)
{
        ValSum.DisplayMode =
        (ValidationSummaryDisplayMode)
        lstFormat.SelectedIndex;
}
```

Here is the same code in VB.NET:

```
Protected Sub lstFormat_SelectedIndexChanged( _
    ByVal sender As System.Object, _
    ByVal e As System.EventArgs) _
    Handles lstFormat.SelectedIndexChanged

    ValSum( ).DisplayMode = _
        CType(lstFormat( ).SelectedIndex, _
        ValidationSummaryDisplayMode)

End Sub
```

The validation summary object (ValSum) has its DisplayMode set to the index of the selected item. This is a bit of a cheat. The ValidationSummary Display Mode is controlled by the ValidationSummaryDisplayMode enumeration, in which BulletList = 0,

List = 1, and SingleParagraph = 2. You take advantage of this and order your list so that the index of the selected item will equal the choice you want.

Similarly, you'll add a drop-down to allow the user to control whether the error report appears in the page or in a popup menu. To do this, insert the following code before the code that allows the user to choose the type of summary report:

```
<tr>
    <td align=right>
    <!-- Radio buttons for the error display -->
        <font face=Verdana size=2>Display Errors</font>
    </td>
    <td>
        <asp:DropDownList id="lstDisplay"
        AutoPostBack=true
        OnSelectedIndexChanged="lstDisplay_SelectedIndexChanged"
        runat=server >
            <asp:ListItem Selected>Summary</asp:ListItem>
            <asp:ListItem>Msg. Box</asp:ListItem>
        </asp:DropDownList>
    </td>
    <td>
    </td>
</tr>
```

Once again, this control posts back the page, and the changed selection event is handled in an event handler. The C# version is:

```
protected void lstDisplay_SelectedIndexChanged(
                    object sender, System.EventArgs e)
{
    ValSum.ShowSummary = lstDisplay.SelectedIndex == 0;
    ValSum.ShowMessageBox = lstDisplay.SelectedIndex == 1;
}
```

In VB.NET, this is:

```
Protected Sub lstDisplay_SelectedIndexChanged( _
    ByVal sender As System.Object, _
    ByVal e As System.EventArgs) _
    Handles lstDisplay.SelectedIndexChanged

    ValSum().ShowMessageBox = lstDisplay().SelectedIndex = 1
    ValSum().ShowSummary = lstDisplay().SelectedIndex = 0

End Sub
```

 To keep the example simple, we've allowed the order of the items in the drop-down to be tightly coupled with the event handling code. In a real application, these would be decoupled to make maintenance easier.

Figure 8-6 illustrates how the form looks to the user. Changing the first drop-down to Msg. Box and the second to List causes the message box shown in Figure 8-7 to appear on the user's screen.

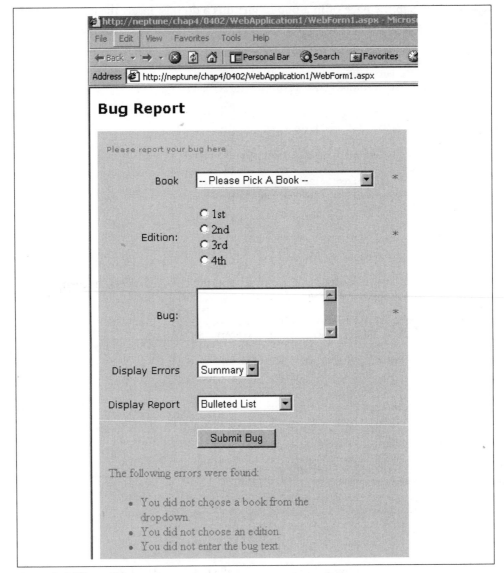

Figure 8-6. The summary

Figure 8-7. Message box

The Compare Validator

While ensuring that the user has made an entry is very useful, you will often want to validate that the content of the entry is within certain guidelines. One of the most common requirements for validation is to compare the user's input to a constant, the value of another control, or a database value.

For instance, to continue the example web page, you can add a new control to your bug reporting dialog that will ask the user how many copies of the book he purchased. The following code should be inserted immediately before the HTML source for the Display Errors drop-down:

```
<tr>
    <td>Number purchased:</td>
    <td><ASP:TextBox id="txtNumPurch" runat=server width="50px" /></td>
```

You can then add a required field validator to ensure that some number is entered:

```
<td>
<asp:RequiredFieldValidator
id="RequiredFieldValidatorNumPurch"
ControlToValidate="txtNumPurch"
ErrorMessage ="You did not enter the number purchased"
Width="100%" runat=server NAME="reqFieldBug">*
</asp:RequiredFieldValidator>
```

And finally you can add a compare validator to ensure that the number of books purchased is greater than zero:

```
<asp:CompareValidator
runat="server"
id="CompareValidatorNumPurch"
ControlToValidate="txtNumPurch"
ErrorMessage ="Invalid number purchased"
Type="Integer"
Operator="GreaterThan"
ValueToCompare=0>*</asp:CompareValidator>
</td></tr>
```

The Compare validator takes the name of the control to validate (in this case, your text field) as well as an error message to display in the summary if the validation fails.

In addition, the ValueToCompare attribute takes a constant, in this case zero. The Operator attribute determines how the comparison will be made—that is, how the input value must be related to the ValueToCompare.

The possible values for the Operator attribute are: Equal, NotEqual, GreaterThan, GreaterThanEqual, LessThan, LessThanEqual, and DataTypeCheck. In this example case, to be valid, the input value must be greater than the ValueToCompare constant.

You must use the Type attribute to tell the control what type of value it is working with. The Type attribute takes one of the ValidationDataType enumerated values: Currency, Date, Double, Integer, or String. In the example case, the values are compared as integers.

Checking the Input Type

Rather than checking that the number of books purchased is greater than zero, you might simply want to check that it is a number (rather than a letter or date). To do this, you make a minor change to the CompareValidator.

To accomplish this change, remove the ValueToCompare attribute and change the Operator attribute from GreaterThan to DataTypeCheck. Since the Type attribute is Integer, the control will report any integer value as valid. The following code should replace the code for the CompareValidator that you added in the last section:

```
<asp:CompareValidator
runat="server"
id="CompareValidatorNumPurch"
ControlToValidate="txtNumPurch"
ErrorMessage ="Invalid number purchased"
Type="Integer"
Operator="DataTypeCheck">*</asp:CompareValidator>
```

Comparing to Another Control

It is possible to compare a value in one control to the value in another control rather than to a constant. A classic use of this might be to ask the user to enter his password twice and then to validate that both entries are identical.

The common scenario is that you've asked the user to pick a new password. For security, when the password is entered, the text is disguised with asterisks, as shown in Figure 8-8. Because this will be the password the user will need for logging in, it is imperative you validate that the user entered the password as intended. The usual solution is to ask the user to re-enter the password, and then you validate that the same password was entered each time. The CompareValidator is perfect for this.

Start by asking for the password, setting the text field to TextMode="Password" so that the entry will be hidden. The following code can be inserted directly in front of the HTML source that defines the row containing the Display Errors drop-down list:

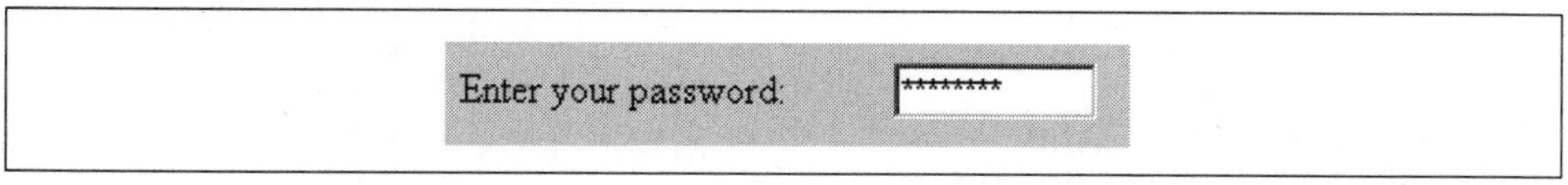

Figure 8-8. Entering a password

```
<tr>
    <td>Enter your password:</td>
    <td>
        <asp:TextBox id="txtPasswd1"
        runat=server
        TextMode="Password"
        Width="80"></asp:TextBox>
    </td>
</tr>
```

Next, add the second password field:

```
<tr>
    <td>Re-enter your password:</td>
    <td>
        <asp:TextBox id="txtPasswd2"
        runat=server
        TextMode="Password"
        Width="80"></asp:TextBox>
    </td>
```

All validators other than the RequiredFieldValidator consider a blank field to be valid. In fact, if one field has a value and the other field is blank, the comparison validator will return valid! To avoid this problem, add RequiredFieldValidators for both passwords:

```
<!-- Text fields for passwords -->
<tr>
    <td>Enter your password:</td>
    <td>
        <asp:TextBox id="txtPasswd1"
        runat=server
        TextMode="Password"
        Width="80"></asp:TextBox>
    </td>
    <td>
        <!-- required to enter the password -->
        <asp:RequiredFieldValidator
        id="ReqFieldTxtPassword1"
        ControlToValidate="txtPasswd1"
        ErrorMessage ="Please enter your password"
        Width="100%" runat=server>*</asp:RequiredFieldValidator>
    </td>
</tr>

<!-- Second password for comparison -->
<tr>
    <td>Re-enter your password:</td>
```

```
<td>
  <asp:TextBox id="txtPasswd2"
   runat=server
   TextMode="Password"
   Width="80"></asp:TextBox>
</td>

<td>
  <!-- Second password is required -->
  <asp:RequiredFieldValidator
  id="ReqFieldTxtPassword2"
  ControlToValidate="txtPasswd2"
  runat=server
  ErrorMessage ="Please re-enter your password"
  Width="100%" runat=server>*</asp:RequiredFieldValidator>

  <!-- Second password must match the first -->
  <asp:CompareValidator
  runat=server
  id="CompValPasswords"
  ControlToValidate="txtPasswd2"
  ErrorMessage ="Passwords do not match"
  Type="String"
  Operator="Equal"
  ControlToCompare="txtPasswd1">*</asp:CompareValidator>
</td>
</tr>
```

 If the controls you are comparing have a missing or invalid value, the values will be considered valid. The CompareValidator requires that values be present and valid.

You are now ready to validate that the entries in both text fields are identical. Add the comparison validator and its attributes to compare the first password field with the second, as shown in the following code fragment:

```
<asp:CompareValidator
runat=server
id="CompValPasswords"
ControlToValidate="txtPasswd2"
ErrorMessage ="Passwords do not match"
Type="String"
Operator="Equal"
ControlToCompare="txtPasswd1">*</asp:CompareValidator>
```

In this case you do not have a ValueToCompare attribute, but instead you have a ControlToCompare attribute, which takes the ID of the control against which you'll compare this value.

You've changed the Operator attribute to Equal, which indicates that the new value must be equal to the value in the control with which you're comparing it, and you've set the Type of the comparison to String. If you enter two different passwords, the error is reported, as shown in Figure 8-9.

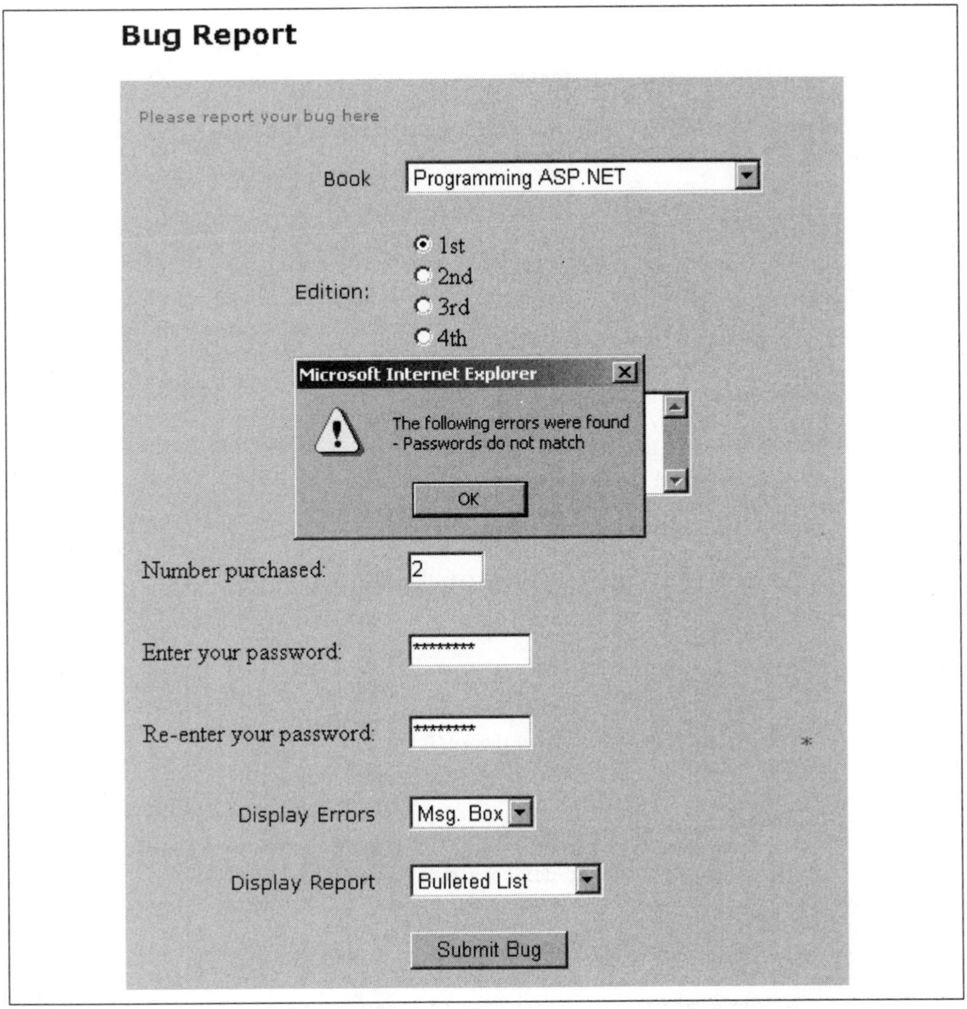

Figure 8-9. Comparing against a control

If the two passwords are identical, the ComparisonValidator is satisfied and the second password field is marked as valid. The complete source code is shown in Example 8-3.

Example 8-3. Compare validation

```
<%@ Page language="c#"
Codebehind="WebForm1.aspx.cs"
AutoEventWireup="false"
Inherits="WebApp0403.WebForm1" %>
```

Example 8-3. Compare validation (continued)

```
<HTML>
  <HEAD>

      <!-- Demonstrate comparison validation -->
      <meta name=vs_targetSchema content="Internet Explorer 5.0">
      <meta name="GENERATOR" Content="Microsoft Visual Studio 7.0">
      <meta name="CODE_LANGUAGE" Content="C#">
  </HEAD>

  <body>

    <H3><FONT face=Verdana>Bug Report</FONT> </H3>
      <form runat="server" ID="frmBugs">
        <table bgcolor=gainsboro cellpadding=10>
          <tr valign="top">
            <td colspan=3>
              <!-- Display error messages -->
              <asp:Label ID="lblMsg"
              Text="Please report your bug here"
              ForeColor="Red" Font-Name="Verdana"
              Font-Size="10px" runat=server
              font-names="Verdana">
              Please report your bug here</asp:Label>
              <br>
            </td>
          </tr>
          <tr>
            <td align=right>
              <font face=Verdana size=2>Book</font>
            </td>

            <td>
              <!-- Drop down list with the books (must pick one) -->
              <ASP:DropDownList id=ddlBooks runat=server>
<asp:ListItem Value="-- Please Pick A Book --">-- Please Pick A Book -
  </asp:ListItem>
<asp:ListItem Value="Programming ASP.NET">Programming
  ASP.NET</asp:ListItem>
<asp:ListItem Value="Programming C#">Programming C#</asp:ListItem>
<asp:ListItem Value="Teach Yourself C++ In 21 Days">Teach Yourself C++ In
  21 Days</asp:ListItem>
<asp:ListItem Value="Teach Yourself C++ In 24 Hours">Teach Yourself C++ In
  24 Hours</asp:ListItem>
<asp:ListItem Value="TY C++ In 10 Minutes">TY C++ In 10
  Minutes</asp:ListItem>
<asp:ListItem Value="TY More C++ In 21 Days">TY More C++ In 21
  Days</asp:ListItem>
<asp:ListItem Value="C++ Unleashed">C++ Unleashed</asp:ListItem>
<asp:ListItem Value="C++ From Scratch">C++ From Scratch</asp:ListItem>
<asp:ListItem Value="XML From Scratch">XML From Scratch</asp:ListItem>
<asp:ListItem Value="Web Classes FS">Web Classes FS</asp:ListItem>
```

Example 8-3. Compare validation (continued)

```
<asp:ListItem Value="Beg. OO Analysis &amp; Design">Beg. OO Analysis &amp;
    Design</asp:ListItem>
<asp:ListItem Value="Clouds To Code">Clouds To Code</asp:ListItem>
<asp:ListItem Value="CIG Career Computer Programming">CIG Career Computer
    Programming</asp:ListItem>
                </ASP:DropDownList>
                </td>

                <!-- Validator for the drop down -->
                <td align=center rowspan=1>
                  <asp:RequiredFieldValidator
                  id="reqFieldBooks"
                  ControlToValidate="ddlBooks"
                  InitialValue="-- Please Pick A Book --"
                  ErrorMessage ="You did not choose a book from the
                    drop-down"
                  Width="100%" runat=server >*</asp:RequiredFieldValidator>
                </td>
            </tr>

            <!-- Radio buttons for the edition -->
            <tr>
                <td align=right>
                    <font face=Verdana size=2>Edition:</font>
                </td>
                <td>
                    <ASP:RadioButtonList id=rblEdition
                    RepeatLayout="Flow" runat=server>
<asp:ListItem Value="1st">1st</asp:ListItem>
<asp:ListItem Value="2nd">2nd</asp:ListItem>
<asp:ListItem Value="3rd">3rd</asp:ListItem>
<asp:ListItem Value="4th">4th</asp:ListItem>
                </ASP:RadioButtonList>
                </td>

                <!-- Validator for editions -->
                <td align=center rowspan=1>
                  <asp:RequiredFieldValidator
                  id="reqFieldEdition"
                  ControlToValidate="rblEdition"
                  ErrorMessage ="You did not choose an edition"
                  Width="100%" runat=server NAME="reqFieldEdition">*
                  </asp:RequiredFieldValidator>
                </td>
            </tr>

            <!-- Multi-line text for the bug entry -->
            <tr>
                <td align=right style="HEIGHT: 97px">
                    <font face=Verdana size=2>Bug:</font>
                </td>
                <td style="HEIGHT: 97px">
```

Example 8-3. Compare validation (continued)

```
            <ASP:TextBox id=txtBug runat=server width="183px"
            textmode="MultiLine" height="68px"/>
        </td>

        <!-- Validator for the text box-->
        <td style="HEIGHT: 97px">
            <asp:RequiredFieldValidator
            id="reqFieldBug"
            ControlToValidate="txtBug"
            ErrorMessage ="You did not enter the bug text"
            Width="100%" runat=server>*</asp:RequiredFieldValidator>
        </td>
    </tr>

    <!-- Text box for number purchased -->
    <tr>
        <td>Number purchased:</td>
        <td><ASP:TextBox id="txtNumPurch" runat=server
         width="50px" /></td>
        <td>

            <!-- Required field validator for number purchased -->
            <asp:RequiredFieldValidator
            id="RequiredFieldValidatorNumPurch"
            ControlToValidate="txtNumPurch"
            ErrorMessage ="You did not enter the number purchased"
            Width="100%" runat=server>*</asp:RequiredFieldValidator>

            <!-- Validate at least one book purchased -->
            <asp:CompareValidator
            runat=server
            id="CompareValidatorNumPurch"
            ControlToValidate="txtNumPurch"
            ErrorMessage ="Invalid number purchased"
            Type="Integer"
            Operator="DataTypeCheck"
            ValueToCompare=0>*</asp:CompareValidator>
        </td>
    </tr>

    <!-- Text fields for passwords -->
    <tr>
        <td>Enter your password:</td>
        <td>
            <asp:TextBox id="txtPasswd1"
            runat=server
            TextMode="Password"
            Width="80"></asp:TextBox>
        </td>
        <td>
            <!-- required to enter the password -->
            <asp:RequiredFieldValidator
```

Example 8-3. Compare validation (continued)

```
                    id="ReqFieldTxtPassword1"
                    ControlToValidate="txtPasswd1"
                    ErrorMessage ="Please enter your password"
                    Width="100%" runat=server>*</asp:RequiredFieldValidator>
                </td>
            </tr>

            <!-- Second password for comparison -->
            <tr>
                <td>Re-enter your password:</td>
                <td>
                    <asp:TextBox id="txtPasswd2"
                      runat=server
                      TextMode="Password"
                      Width="80"></asp:TextBox>
                </td>

                <td>
                    <!-- Second password is required -->
                    <asp:RequiredFieldValidator
                    id="ReqFieldTxtPassword2"
                    ControlToValidate="txtPasswd2"
                    runat=server
                    ErrorMessage ="Please re-enter your password"
                    Width="100%" runat=server>*</asp:RequiredFieldValidator>

                    <!-- Second password must match the first -->
                    <asp:CompareValidator
                    runat=server
                    id="CompValPasswords"
                    ControlToValidate="txtPasswd2"
                    ErrorMessage ="Passwords do not match"
                    Type="String"
                    Operator="Equal"
                    ControlToCompare="txtPasswd1">*</asp:CompareValidator>
                </td>
            </tr>

        <!-- Drop down for the error display -->
        <tr>
            <td align=right>
                <font face=Verdana size=2>Display Errors</font>
            </td>
            <td>
                <asp:DropDownList id="lstDisplay"
                AutoPostBack=true
                OnSelectedIndexChanged="lstDisplay_SelectedIndexChanged"
                runat=server >
                        <asp:ListItem Selected>Summary</asp:ListItem>
                        <asp:ListItem>Msg. Box</asp:ListItem>
                </asp:DropDownList>
            </td>
```

Example 8-3. Compare validation (continued)

```
                <td>
                </td>
            </tr>

            <!-- Drop down for display report choice -->
            <tr>
                <td align="right">
                    <font face=Verdana size=2>Display Report</font>
                </td>
                <td>
                    <asp:DropDownList id="lstFormat"
                    AutoPostBack=true
                    OnSelectedIndexChanged="lstFormat_SelectedIndexChanged"
                    runat=server NAME="lstFormat">
                        <asp:ListItem >List</asp:ListItem>
                        <asp:ListItem Selected>Bulleted List</asp:ListItem>
                        <asp:ListItem>Single Paragraph</asp:ListItem>
                    </asp:DropDownList>
                </td>
            </tr>

            <!-- Submit button -->
            <tr>
                <td>
                </td>
                <td>
                    <ASP:Button id=btnSubmit
                    text="Submit Bug" runat=server />
                </td>
                <td>
                </td>
            </tr>
        </table>

        <!-- Validation Summary Report -->
        <asp:ValidationSummary ID="ValSum" runat="server"
         HeaderText="The following errors were found">
        </asp:ValidationSummary>
    </form>
  </body>
</HTML>
```

Range Checking

At times you'll want to validate that a user's entry falls within a range. That range
can be within a pair of numbers, characters, or dates. In addition, you can express
the boundaries for the range by using constants or by comparing its value with values found in other controls.

In this simple example, you'll prompt the user for a number between 10 and 20 and then validate his answer to ensure that it was entered properly. To do so, create a form with a prompt, a text box, and of course a RangeValidator control. The RangeValidator takes a number of attributes to designate the object to validate and the range within which its values must lie, as shown in the following HTML source:

```
<asp:RangeValidator ID="rangeValid"
runat="server"
type="Integer"
ControlToValidate="txtValue"
MinimumValue="10"
MaximumValue="20">Between 10 and 20 please</asp:RangeValidator>
```

The text Between 10 and 20 please will be displayed if the value is not within the range of values specified by the MinimumValue and MaximumValue attributes. The type attribute designates how the value should be evaluated, and may be any of the following types: Currency, Date, Double, Integer, String.

If there are no validation errors, the form can be submitted; otherwise, the range checking error message is displayed. The complete .aspx source is shown in Example 8-4.

Example 8-4. Range validation

```
<%@
Page language="c#"
Codebehind="WebForm1.aspx.cs"
AutoEventWireup="false"
Inherits="RangeValidation.WebForm1" %>
<HTML>
  <HEAD>
    <meta name=vs_targetSchema content="Internet Explorer 5.0">
    <meta name="GENERATOR" Content="Microsoft Visual Studio 7.0">
    <meta name="CODE_LANGUAGE" Content="C#">
  </HEAD>
  <body MS_POSITIONING="GridLayout">
    <form method="post" runat="server">
    <table>
      <tr>
        <td colspan="2">
          <h5>Enter a number between 10 and 20:</h5>
        </td>
      </tr>
      <tr>
        <td>
          <asp:TextBox  Width="30" ID="txtValue" Runat="server"/>
        </td>
        <td>
          <asp:RangeValidator ID="rangeValid"
          runat="server"
```

Example 8-4. Range validation (continued)

```
        type= "Integer"
        ControlToValidate="txtValue"
        MinimumValue="10"
        MaximumValue="20">Between 10 and 20 please</asp:RangeValidator>
    </td>
  </tr>
  <tr>
    <td colspan="2">
      <asp:Button Runat="server" Text="Validate"
        id=Button1></asp:Button>
    </td>
  </tr>
  <tr>
    <td>
      <asp:Label ID="lblMsg" Text="" runat="server"/>
    </td>
  </tr>
 </table>
 </form>
  </body>
</HTML>
```

Regular Expressions

Often a simple value or range check is insufficient; you must check that the *form* of the data entered is correct. For example, you may need to ensure that a zip code is five digits, an email address is in the form *name@place.com*, a credit card matches the right format, and so forth.

A regular expression validator allows you to validate that a text field matches a *regular expression*. Regular expressions are a language for describing and manipulating text. For more complete coverage of this topic, please see *Mastering Regular Expressions* by Jeffrey Friedl (O'Reilly).

A regular expression consists of two types of characters: *literals* and *metacharacters*. A literal is just a character you wish to match in the target string. A metacharacter is a special symbol that acts as a command to the regular expression parser. The parser is the engine responsible for understanding the regular expression. Consider this regular expression:

```
^\d{5}$
```

This will match any string that has exactly 5 numerals. The initial metacharacter, ^, indicates the beginning of the string. The second metacharacter, \d, indicates a digit. The third metacharacter, {5}, indicates exactly 5 of the digits, and the final metacharacter, $, indicates the end of the string. Thus, this regular expression matches five digits between the beginning and end of the line, and nothing else.

A slightly more sophisticated algorithm might accept either a 5 digit zip code or a 9 digit (plus 4) zip code in the format of 12345-1234. Rather than using the \d metacharacter, you could simply designate the range of acceptable values:

```
ValidationExpression="[0-9]{5}|[0-9]{5}-{0-9]{4}"
```

You create a RegularExpressionValidator much as you did the previous validators. The only new attribute is ValidationExpression, which takes a valid regular expression within quotes. For example, the following code fragment defines a regular expression validator to insure that the value entered into a text box is a five digit numeric zip code:

```
<asp:RegularExpressionValidator ID="regExVal"
 ControlToValidate="txtZip" Runat="server"
 ValidationExpression="^\d{5}$"
 display="Static">Please enter a valid 5 digit Zip code</asp:
RegularExpressionValidator>
```

If the control pointed to by ControlToValidate has a string that matches the regular expression, validation succeeds. The complete source is shown in Example 8-5.

Example 8-5. Regular expression validator

```
<%@ Page language="c#" Codebehind="WebForm1.aspx.cs" AutoEventWireup="false"
Inherits="RegularExpressionValidation.WebForm1" %>

<HTML>
  <HEAD>
<meta content="Internet Explorer 5.0" name=vs_targetSchema>
<meta content="Microsoft Visual Studio 7.0" name=GENERATOR>
<meta content=C# name=CODE_LANGUAGE>
  </HEAD>
<body MS_POSITIONING="GridLayout">
<form method=post runat="server">
    <table>
      <tr>
        <td colspan="2">
          <h5>Please enter your Zip Code</h5>
        </td>
      </tr>
      <tr>
        <td>
          <asp:TextBox width="60" ID="txtZip" runat="server" />
        </td>
        <td>
          <asp:RegularExpressionValidator ID="regExVal"
           ControlToValidate="txtZip" Runat="server"
           ValidationExpression="^\d{5}$"
           display="Static">Please enter a valid 5 digit Zip
           code</asp:RegularExpressionValidator>
        </td>
```

Example 8-5. Regular expression validator (continued)

```
      </tr>
      <tr>
        <td>
          <asp:Button ID="btnValidate" Text="Validate"
            Runat="server"></asp:Button>
        </td>
        <td>
          <asp:Label ID="lblMsg" Runat="server" Text=""/>
        </td>
      </tr>
    </table></FORM>
  </body>
</HTML>
```

> When you use a RegularExpressionValidator control with client-side validation, the regular expressions are matched using JScript. This may differ in small details from the regular expression checking done on the server.

Custom Validation

There are times when the validation of your data is so specific to your application that you will need to write your own validation method. The CustomValidator is designed to provide all the infrastructure support you need; you simply point to your validation method and have it return a Boolean value: true or false. The Custom-Validator control takes care of all the rest of the work.

Because validation can be done on the client or on the server, depending on the browser, the CustomValidator has attributes for specifying both a server-side and a client-side method for validation. The server-side method can be written in any .NET language, such as C# or VB.NET, while the client-side method must be written in a scripting language understood by the browser, such as VBScript or JavaScript.

You'll create a simple form that will request an even number from the user, and report the error if the number is not evenly divisible by 2. You can imagine, however, that you could perform a checksum on a credit card or ISBN or otherwise perform complex data checking.

The heart of this example is the CustomValidator control:

```
<asp:CustomValidator
id="cvEven"
controlToValidate="txtEven"
Display="Static"
runat="server"
ClientValidationFunction="ClientValidator"
OnServerValidate="ServerValidator">
Well, that's odd...
</asp:CustomValidator>
```

The CustomValidator takes many of the usual attributes, such as an ID, runat, ControlToValidate, and Display. In addition, this validator has an attribute that identifies the script method to run for client-side validation (ClientValidationFunction) and one that defines the method to run for server-side validation (OnServerValidate).

You'll provide JavaScript for the client-side validation:

```
<script language="javascript">
   function ClientValidator(source, value)
   {
      if (value % 2 == 0)
         return true;
      else
         return false;
   }
</script>
```

This simple function examines the value passed to the script by the validator, and if it is an even number, it returns true; otherwise, it returns false. You also need a server-side method:

```
Public Sub ServerValidator(ByVal source As Object, _
              ByVal e As ServerValidateEventArgs)
   Dim evenNumber As Int32 = Int32.Parse(value)

   If evenNumber Mod 2 = 0 Then
      e.IsValid = True
   Else
      e.IsValid = False
   End If

End Function
```

Or in C#:

```
public bool ServerValidator (object source, string value)
{
   try
   {
      int evenNumber = Int32.Parse(value);
      if (evenNumber % 2 == 0)
         return true;
   }
   catch (Exception)
   {
      // error handler here
   }
   return false;

}
```

This method does the same thing as the client-side validator, only in VB.NET or C# rather than in JavaScript. There are a few things to notice about these methods. First, the value that the CustomValidator is examining is passed to your routine as the string parameter *value*. You can convert that string to an int in C# or an Integer in VB.NET using the Base Class Library Int32 object's static Parse method, as shown. The C# example wraps the conversion in a try/catch block to handle any exception that might be thrown.

The complete *.aspx* file is provided in Example 8-6, with the code-behind file in Example 8-7.

Example 8-6. Custom validator

```
<%@ Page Language="C#" AutoEventWireup="false" Codebehind="WebForm1.aspx.cs"
Inherits="CustomValidatorVB.WebForm1" EnableSessionState="True"%>

<HTML>
  <HEAD>
    <meta name=vs_targetSchema content="Internet Explorer 5.0">
    <meta name="GENERATOR" Content="Microsoft Visual Studio 7.0">
    <meta name="CODE_LANGUAGE" Content="C#">
  </HEAD>
  <body MS_POSITIONING="GridLayout">

    <form method="post" runat="server" ID="Form1">
    <table>
      <tr>
        <td colspan="2">
          <h5>Please enter an even number</h5>
        </td>
      </tr>
      <tr>
        <td>
          <asp:TextBox Width="50" ID="txtEven"
           Runat="server" NAME="txtEven"/>
        </td>
        <td>
          <asp:CustomValidator
          id="cvEven"
          controlToValidate="txtEven"
          Display="Static"
          runat="server"
          ClientValidationFunction="ClientValidator"
          OnServerValidate="ServerValidator">
          Well, that's odd...
          </asp:CustomValidator>
        </td>
      </tr>
      <tr>
        <td>
          <asp:Button ID="btnValidate" Text="Validate"
           Runat="server"></asp:Button>
        </td>
        <td>
          <asp:Label ID="lblMsg" Text="" Runat="server"></asp:Label>
        </td>
```

Example 8-6. Custom validator (continued)

```
    </tr>
  </table>
  <script language="javascript">
    function ClientValidator(source, value)
    {
      if (value % 2 == 0)
        return true;
      else
        return false;
    }
  </script>
  </form>
 </body>
</HTML>
```

Example 8-7. C# code-behind file for Example 8-6

```
namespace CustomValidator
{
    using System;
    using System.Collections;
    using System.ComponentModel;
    using System.Data;
    using System.Drawing;
    using System.Web;
    using System.Web.SessionState;
    using System.Web.UI;
    using System.Web.UI.WebControls;
    using System.Web.UI.HtmlControls;

    public class WebForm1 : System.Web.UI.Page
    {
      protected System.Web.UI.WebControls.TextBox txtEven;
      protected System.Web.UI.WebControls.Button btnValidate;
      protected System.Web.UI.WebControls.Label lblMsg;

        public WebForm1()
        {
            Page.Init += new System.EventHandler(Page_Init);
        }

        protected void Page_Init(object sender, EventArgs e)
        {
            InitializeComponent();
        }

        #region Web Form Designer generated code
        /// <summary>
        ///     Required method for Designer support - do not modify
        ///     the contents of this method with the code editor.
        /// </summary>
      private void InitializeComponent()
```

Example 8-7. C# code-behind file for Example 8-6 (continued)

```csharp
    {
       this.btnValidate.Click += new
           System.EventHandler(this.btnValidate_Click);
       this.Load += new System.EventHandler(this.Page_Load);

    }
      #endregion

    private void Page_Load(object sender, System.EventArgs e)
    {

    }
    public void ServerValidator (object source, ServerValidateEventArgs e)
    {
       try
       {
          int evenNumber = Int32.Parse(e.value);
          if (evenNumber % 2 == 0)
             e.IsValid = true;
          else
             e.IsValid = false;
       }
       catch (Exception)
       {
          // error handler here
       }

    }

    protected void btnValidate_Click(object sender, System.EventArgs e)
    {
       if (Page.IsValid)
          lblMsg.Text = "Valid.";
       else
          lblMsg.Text = "Not Valid.";
    }
  }
}
```

CHAPTER 9

Data Binding

Nearly every ASP.NET application displays data of some sort, either from a database or from other data sources. *Data binding* allows you to create a relationship between a control (such as a list box or data grid) and a source of data (such as SQL Server). ASP.NET takes care of the details of displaying the data in your control.

You can bind to any data source, including such simple sources as properties, expressions, or the result of a method call, and such complex sources as arrays, collections, and databases. For controls that display a collection, such as a list box or data grid, you must bind to a source which implements the ICollection interface. This allows ASP.NET to iterate the collection and display each member in turn.

ArrayList

Later chapters will focus on binding to databases, since that is the common case for serious ASP.NET development. In order to focus on the mechanics of data-binding, however, this chapter starts simple, by binding controls to an ArrayList rather than to data from a database. Visual Basic .NET, C#, and most other programming language support the array, an ordered collection of objects, all of the same type. An ArrayList is a .NET Framework collection that acts as an expandable array.

In the previous chapter, you created a drop-down list box that contained the titles of some of my books on programming. The relevant portion of the HTML source appeared as follows:

```
                <ASP:DropDownList id=ddlBooks runat=server>
<asp:ListItem Value="-- Please Pick A Book --">-- Please Pick A Book -
    </asp:ListItem>
<asp:ListItem Value="Programming ASP.NET">Programming
    ASP.NET</asp:ListItem>
<asp:ListItem Value="Programming C#">Programming C#</asp:ListItem>
<asp:ListItem Value="Teach Yourself C++ In 21 Days">Teach Yourself C++ In
    21 Days</asp:ListItem>
<asp:ListItem Value="Teach Yourself C++ In 24 Hours">Teach Yourself C++ In
```

```
    24 Hours</asp:ListItem>
<asp:ListItem Value="TY C++ In 10 Minutes">TY C++ In 10
    Minutes</asp:ListItem>
<asp:ListItem Value="TY More C++ In 21 Days">TY More C++ In 21
    Days</asp:ListItem>
<asp:ListItem Value="C++ Unleashed">C++ Unleashed</asp:ListItem>
<asp:ListItem Value="C++ From Scratch">C++ From Scratch</asp:ListItem>
<asp:ListItem Value="XML From Scratch">XML From Scratch</asp:ListItem>
<asp:ListItem Value="Web Classes FS">Web Classes FS</asp:ListItem>
<asp:ListItem Value="Beg. OO Analysis &amp; Design">Beg. OO Analysis &amp;
    Design</asp:ListItem>
<asp:ListItem Value="Clouds To Code">Clouds To Code</asp:ListItem>
<asp:ListItem Value="CIG Career Computer Programming">CIG Career Computer
    Programming</asp:ListItem>
                </ASP:DropDownList>
```

The HTML source declares the DropDownList object, and then declares a ListItem
for each book title. Notice that the data here is hard-coded, which is not always optimal, particularly if you are displaying dynamic data. An alternative to declaring each
book is to add the books programmatically. To do so, create the DropDownList in
the WebForm, but do not add the items:

```
<tr>
    <td>
        Book
    </td>
    <td>
        <asp:DropDownList ID="ddlBooks" Runat="server">
        </asp:DropDownList>
    </td>
</tr>
```

Instead of adding ListItem objects, you'll fill the drop-down from a collection, in this
case an ArrayList object.

The first step is to create the ArrayList in the Page_Load event handler in the code-
behind page:

```
Private Sub Page_Load(ByVal sender As Object, ByVal e As System.EventArgs) _
                    Handles MyBase.Load

    ' declare the list
    Dim bookList As New ArrayList( )

    ' add the titles
    bookList.Add("Programming ASP.NET")
    bookList.Add("Programming C#")
    bookList.Add("Teach Yourself C++ In 21 Days")
    bookList.Add("Teach Yourself C++ In 24 Hours")
    bookList.Add("TY C++ In 10 Minutes")
    bookList.Add("TY More C++ In 21 Days")
    bookList.Add("C++ Unleashed")
```

```
bookList.Add("C++ From Scratch")
bookList.Add("XML From Scratch")
bookList.Add("Web Classes FS")
bookList.Add("Beg. OO Analysis & Design")
bookList.Add("Clouds To Code")
bookList.Add("CIG Career Computer Programming")
```

This ArrayList object is now ready to use. You can retrieve the titles using normal array syntax, but in this case you want to bind bookList to ddlbooks, the drop-down you created in the WebForm. You start by setting the DataSource property of ddlBooks to your new ArrayList:

```
ddlBooks.DataSource = bookList
```

When you set a data source, the data is not bound. You must explicitly bind the data, which you do by calling the DataBind method:

```
ddlBooks.DataBind( )
```

The advantage of requiring explicit binding is that you have complete control over when this action takes place. Since data binding can be an expensive operation (that is, it can take a lot of time and resources), having explicit control over the process can make your program more efficient.

Here is the same code in C#:

```csharp
protected void Page_Load(object sender, System.EventArgs e)
{
    // create the array list
    ArrayList bookList = new ArrayList( );

    // add all the books
    bookList.Add("Programming ASP.NET");
    bookList.Add("Programming C#");
    bookList.Add("Teach Yourself C++ In 21 Days");
    bookList.Add("Teach Yourself C++ In 24 Hours");
    bookList.Add("TY C++ In 10 Minutes");
    bookList.Add("TY More C++ In 21 Days");
    bookList.Add("C++ Unleashed");
    bookList.Add("C++ From Scratch");
    bookList.Add("XML From Scratch");
    bookList.Add("Web Classes FS");
    bookList.Add("Beg. OO Analysis & Design");
    bookList.Add("Clouds To Code");
    bookList.Add("CIG Career Computer Programming");

    // set the data source
    ddlBooks.DataSource=bookList;

    // bind to the data
    ddlBooks.DataBind( );
}
```

You will typically bind your data at two points while your program is running:

- When the Page.Load event procedure has fired, to initialize the values
- Again any time the data is changed

Once the data is bound, the drop-down list is filled with the contents of the array, as shown in Figure 9-1.

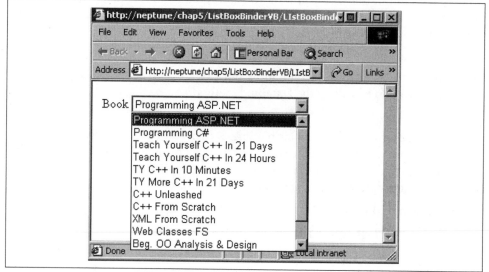

Figure 9-1. ArrayList bound to a list box

Data Binding and Postback

Extend the form to add a label that will display the selected book. Set the autopostback attribute of the drop-down control to true, so that when a selection is made, the page is posted back to the server and the label can be filled with the selected title.

```
<asp:DropDownList
ID="ddlBooks"
autopostback="True"
```

The problem you'll encounter is that when the page is reloaded the data will be reloaded as well, and your selection will be lost. You must protect against that by checking the page's IsPostBack property, which is set to true when the page is posted back, as shown in Example 9-1 (VB.NET) and Example 9-2 (C#).

 It is a recurring theme throughout this book that the differences between C# and VB.NET are syntactic sugar, and not terribly important. Even more interesting, if you know one language, the other is quite understandable. This example shows that quite clearly.

Example 9-1. Checking IsPostBack in VB.NET

```vb
Private Sub Form_Load(ByVal sender As object, _
            ByVal e As System.EventArgs) Handles MyBase.Load

   If Not IsPostBack( ) Then

      ' create the array list
      Dim bookList As New ArrayList( )

      ' add all the books
      bookList.Add("Programming ASP.NET")
      bookList.Add("Programming C#")
      bookList.Add("Teach Yourself C++ In 21 Days")
      bookList.Add("Teach Yourself C++ In 24 Hours")
      bookList.Add("TY C++ In 10 Minutes")
      bookList.Add("TY More C++ In 21 Days")
      bookList.Add("C++ Unleashed")
      bookList.Add("C++ From Scratch")
      bookList.Add("XML From Scratch")
      bookList.Add("Web Classes FS")
      bookList.Add("Beg. OO Analysis & Design")
      bookList.Add("Clouds To Code")
      bookList.Add("CIG Career Computer Programming")

      ' set the data source
      ddlBooks( ).DataSource = bookList

      ' bind to the data
      ddlBooks().DataBind( )
   Else
      lblMsg().Text = "Selected book: " & ddlBooks( ).SelectedItem.Text
   End If

End Sub
```

Example 9-2. Checking IsPostBack in C#

```csharp
private void Page_Load(object sender, System.EventArgs e)
{
   if (! Page.IsPostBack)
   {
      // create the array list
      ArrayList bookList = new ArrayList( );

      // add all the books
      bookList.Add("Programming ASP.NET");
      bookList.Add("Programming C#");
      bookList.Add("Teach Yourself C++ In 21 Days");
      bookList.Add("Teach Yourself C++ In 24 Hours");
      bookList.Add("TY C++ In 10 Minutes");
      bookList.Add("TY More C++ In 21 Days");
      bookList.Add("C++ Unleashed");
      bookList.Add("C++ From Scratch");
```

Example 9-2. Checking IsPostBack in C# (continued)

```
    bookList.Add("XML From Scratch");
    bookList.Add("Web Classes FS");
    bookList.Add("Beg. OO Analysis & Design");
    bookList.Add("Clouds To Code");
    bookList.Add("CIG Career Computer Programming");

    // set the data source
    ddlBooks.DataSource=bookList;

    // bind to the data
    ddlBooks.DataBind( );
  }
  else
  {
    lblMsg.Text = "Selected book: " + ddlBooks.SelectedItem.Text;
  }
}
```

In Example 9-1 and 9-2, the IsPostBack property is tested. If it returns true, then the page has been posted back to itself by a user taking an action, and the selected item is displayed. If the IsPostBack property returns false, then the book list is populated with data from the ArrayList.

Binding to a Class

In the previous example, you bound an ArrayList of strings to the list box. Often, you will want to bind objects more complex than strings. For example, you might imagine a Book class that has properties such as title, ISBN, and price, as shown in Example 9-3 (C#) and Example 9-4 (VB.NET).

Example 9-3. The Book class in C#

```
public class Book
{
    public Book(float price, string title, string ISBN)
    {
        this.price = price;
        this.title = title;
        this.isbn = ISBN;
    }

    public float Price { get {return price;} }
    public string Title { get {return title;} }
    public string ISBN { get {return isbn;} }

    private float price;
    private string title;
    private string isbn;

}
```

Example 9-4. The Book class in VB.NET

```
Public Class Book

    Private _Price As Double
    Private _Title As String
    Private _ISBN As String

    Public Sub New( _
        ByVal thePrice As Double, _
        ByVal theTitle As String, _
        ByVal theISBN as string)
        _Price = thePrice
        _Title = theTitle
        _ISBN = theISBN
    End Sub

    Public ReadOnly Property Price() As Double
        Get
            Return _Price
        End Get
    End Property

    Public ReadOnly Property Title() As String
        Get
            Return _Title
        End Get
    End Property

    Public ReadOnly Property ISBN() As String
        Get
            Return _ISBN
        End Get
    End Property

End Class
```

You add the new book objects to the ArrayList, just as you assigned the strings, shown here in C#. (The VB.NET code is the same except without the semicolons.)

```
bookList.Add(new Book(49.95f, "Programming ASP.NET","100000000"));
bookList.Add(new Book(49.95f,"Programming C#","0596001177"));
bookList.Add(new Book(34.99f,"Teach Yourself C++ In 21
            Days","067232072x"));
bookList.Add(new Book(24.95f,"Teach Yourself C++ In 24
            Hours","0672315165"));
bookList.Add(new Book(12.99f,"TY C++ In 10 Minutes","067231603X"));
```

If you are going to bind a collection of Book objects to the list box, you must tell the list box which property to bind to, so that it will know which property to display. You do this by adding the following lines indicated in boldface to the page's HTML source:

```
<asp:DropDownList
ID="ddlBooks"
autopostback="True"
```

```
DataTextField="Title"
DataValueField="ISBN"
Runat="server"></asp:DropDownList>
```

The DataTextField attribute assigns the property that will be displayed in the list box, while the DataValueField attribute assigns the property that will be held in the value attribute of the list box item. When you run this and examine the source through the browser, you find that ASP.NET has translated the ASP controls to the appropriate HTML as follows:

```
<option value="100000000">Programming ASP.NET</option>
<option value="100000000">Programming C#</option>
<option value="067232072x">Teach Yourself C++ In 21 Days</option>
```

Change the label to display the ISBN along with the title:

```
lblMsg.Text = "Selected: " + ddlBooks.SelectedItem.Text +
    "(" + ddlBooks.SelectedItem.Value + ")";
```

or in VB:

```
lblMsg.Text = "Selected book: " & ddlBooks().SelectedItem.Text _
& " (" & ddlBooks().SelectedItem.Value & ")"
```

The result is that the user selects a book and the book title and ISBN are displayed, as shown in Figure 9-2.

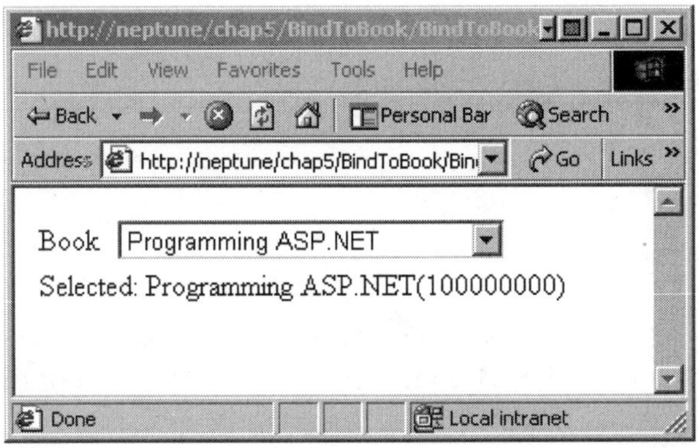

Figure 9-2. Binding an array of objects

Binding to Other Simple Controls

The simplest binding is to bind one control (for example a label) to another control (e.g., a list box). As a demonstration of data-binding one control to a second, add a new label to the form, and bind its contents to the drop-down selection:

```
<tr>
    <td>
        Chosen Book Title
```

```
    </td>
    <td>
       <asp:Label
       Text="<%# ddlBooks.SelectedItem.Text %>"
       Runat="server" />
    </td>
</tr>
```

This new label control is bound to the text value of the selected item in `ddlBooks`. The `<%# %>` tags accomplish the data binding. The only additional change to the code is in WebForm1_Load, where you bind the entire page, rather than a single control:

```
Page.DataBind( )
```

You could, of course, bind each of the controls individually rather than binding the entire page. In any case, the result, shown in Figure 9-3 is that the control is bound to the text of the control.

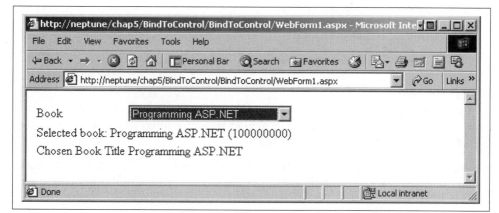

Figure 9-3. Data binding to a control

Binding Radio Buttons and Checkboxes

It is not uncommon to build your form dynamically; adding checkboxes, radio buttons, and other controls based on data extracted from a database. For example, you might like to add shipping methods (e.g., "first class", "next day", etc.) to the form. Typically you'd add these as radio buttons. To make the form flexible, you'd like to make it data-driven; getting the exact text for the radio buttons from a table in the database. That way, if you change from one delivery service to another, you do not need to change the web form; you just update the database and the form works.

As you saw in Chapter 3, ASP.NET offers a dynamic radio button control, Radio-ButtonList, which you can add to the form, deferring the content of the radio buttons (and even the number of buttons to create) until runtime. Begin the example with the following HTML source, which defines a RadioButtonList control named rbList:

```
<tr>
    <td>
        How should we ship?
    </td>
    <td>
        <asp:RadioButtonList
        RepeatDirection="Horizontal"
        id=rbList runat="server">
        </asp:RadioButtonList>
    </td>
</tr>
```

You'll look at how to fill the radio buttons with data in just a moment, but while you're building the form, add checkboxes to allow the customer to choose extras to go with his choice of books:

```
<tr>
    <td colspan="2">
        Please choose any "extras" you'd like: 
        <asp:CheckBoxList
        RepeatDirection="Horizontal"
        id="cbList"
        runat="server"></asp:CheckBoxList>
    </td>
</tr>
```

Normally, you'd fill the radio buttons and the checkboxes with data from the database. Database access is covered in the next chapter; for now, you'll keep things simple by extracting the data from array lists.

Create a new ArrayList, shippingMethods, in the Page_Load function in the codebehind page. Add the various shipping alternatives that you would otherwise extract from the database:

```
ArrayList shippingMethods = new ArrayList();
shippingMethods.Add("3rd Class");
shippingMethods.Add("1st Class");
shippingMethods.Add("Ground");
shippingMethods.Add("2nd Day");
shippingMethods.Add("Next Day");
```

With this ArrayList in hand, you can bind to the radio button list created in the HTML page. This is done in two steps: first you set the data source for the radio button list to the Array List:

```
rbList.DataSource=shippingMethods;
```

Second, and as a separate step, call the radio buttons list object's DataBind method:

```
rbList.DataBind( )
```

This separation is done for the reason explained earlier: by making the binding step explicit, you make the program more efficient, binding only when you invoke the DataBind method.

You'll do the same thing with the checkboxes, creating an ArrayList, setting the DataSource and calling DataBind:

```
ArrayList extras = new ArrayList( );
extras.Add("Gift Wrap");
extras.Add("Gift Card");
extras.Add("Book Mark");
extras.Add("Autographed copy");
extras.Add("Source Code");
cbList.DataSource=extras;
cbList.DataBind( );
```

That's all it takes; when the page is loaded, the checkboxes and radio buttons are created, based on the data in their data sources, as shown in Figure 9-4.

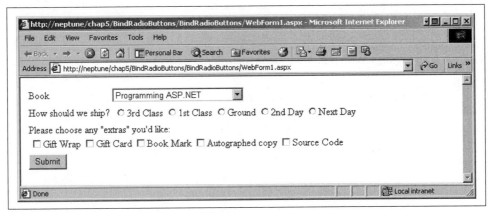

Figure 9-4. Binding to radio buttons and checkboxes

The user interface design is crude at best, and making this look nice is left as an exercise for the reader. While you are at it, you'll want to add a required field validator (see Chapter 8) to ensure that the user does select at least one shipping method.

In this example, a button has been added to the form, and the autopostback attribute has been removed from the drop-down; these additions are shown in boldface in the HTML source in Example 9-5. The user selects a shipping method and zero or more of the "extras", and the user's choice is reflected in a label placed below the Submit button, as shown in Figure 9-5. The code to support this is in the Page_Load method in the code-behind page and is shown in boldface in the code-behind in Example 9-6.

If the IsPostBack property is true, then the page has been submitted and you need to pick up the values from the radio buttons and checkboxes. This is accomplished by iterating the Items collection of the CheckBoxList and RadioButtonList controls. For example, to see which extras were chosen, you iterate the Items collection of cbList (the checkbox list on the form) as follows:

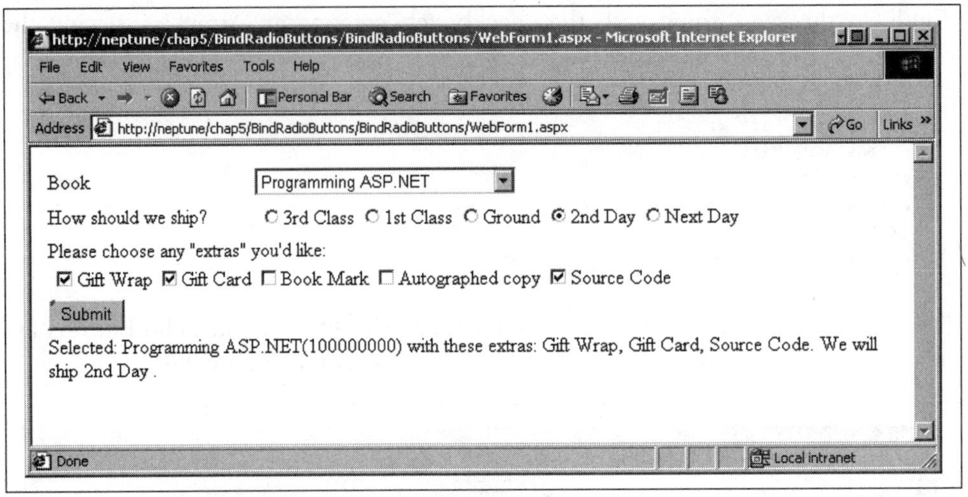

Figure 9-5. Displaying choices from data bound controls

```
int chosen = 0;
StringBuilder extrasChosen = new StringBuilder(" with these extras:");

for (int i = 0; i < cbList.Items.Count; i++)
{
    if (cbList.Items[i].Selected)
    {
        chosen++;
        if (chosen > 1)
            extrasChosen.Append(", ");
        extrasChosen.Append(cbList.Items[i].Text);

    }
}
```

> The for loop iterates the items collection. Inside the for loop, each
> item is tested to see if its Selected property evaluates to true. The line:
>
>   if (cbList.Items[i].Selected)
>
> can just as easily be written:
>
>   if (cbList.Items[i].Selected == true)
>
> In C# these two lines are identical. Similarly, in VB.NET the line:
>
>   If cbList.Items(i).Selected Then
>
> is identical to:
>
>   If cbList.Items(i).Selected = True Then

Each time a selected item is found, the local counter variable *chosen* is incremented, so that a comma can be placed after the first item. The extrasChosen StringBuilder object adds all the selected items so that they may be displayed in the lblMsg label.

Similar logic is applied to the radio buttons; however, you know in advance that only a single radio button can be selected:

```
for (int i = 0; i < rbList.Items.Count; i++)
    if (rbList.Items[i].Selected)
        shippingMethod.Append(rbList.Items[i].Text);
```

 In C#, if a for or if statement is followed by a single statement, there is no need to use braces. As far as the for statement is concerned, the if statement is a single statement.

Example 9-5 is the complete *.aspx* file, and Example 9-6 is the complete code-behind source file, both in C#.

Example 9-5. aspx file for radio button and checkbox dynamic controls

```
<%@ Page language="c#"
Codebehind="WebForm1.aspx.cs"
AutoEventWireup="false"
Inherits="BindRadioButtons.WebForm1" %>

<HTML>
  <HEAD>
<meta content="Internet Explorer 5.0" name=vs_targetSchema>
<meta content="Microsoft Visual Studio 7.0" name=GENERATOR>
<meta content=C# name=CODE_LANGUAGE>
  </HEAD>
<body MS_POSITIONING="GridLayout">
<form id=Form1 method=post runat="server">
<table>
  <tr>
    <td>Book </td>
    <td>
        <!-- the drop-down which will post back -->
        <asp:dropdownlist
        id=ddlBooks
        Runat="server"
        DataValueField="ISBN"
        DataTextField="Title">
        </asp:dropdownlist>
    </td>
  </tr>
  <! -- shipping method, radio buttons built dynamically -->
  <tr>
    <td>
      How should we ship?
    </td>
    <td>
        <asp:radiobuttonlist
        id=rbList runat="server"
        RepeatDirection="Horizontal">
        </asp:radiobuttonlist>
```

```
            </td>
        </tr>
        <! -- extra features. checkboxes built dynamically -->
        <tr>
            <td colspan="2">
                Please choose any "extras" you'd like: 
                <asp:CheckBoxList
                RepeatDirection="Horizontal"
                id="cbList"
                runat="server"></asp:CheckBoxList>
            </td>
        </tr>
        <tr>
            <td colspan="2">
                <asp:Button id="Submit" runat="server" Text="Submit">
                </asp:Button>
            </td>
        </tr>
        <tr>
            <!-- the lable to display the selection -->
            <td colspan="2">
                <asp:Label ID="lblMsg" Runat="server" Text="" />
            </td>
        </tr>
    </TABLE></FORM>
    </body>
</HTML>
```

Example 9-6. C# code-behind for dynamic radio buttons and checkboxes

```
namespace BindRadioButtons
{
    using System;
    using System.Collections;
    using System.ComponentModel;
    using System.Data;
    using System.Drawing;
    using System.Text;  // for string builder
    using System.Web;
    using System.Web.SessionState;
    using System.Web.UI;
    using System.Web.UI.WebControls;
    using System.Web.UI.HtmlControls;

    public class WebForm1 : System.Web.UI.Page
    {
        protected System.Web.UI.WebControls.DropDownList ddlBooks;
        protected System.Web.UI.WebControls.RadioButtonList rbList;
        protected System.Web.UI.WebControls.CheckBoxList cbList;
        protected System.Web.UI.WebControls.Button Submit;
        protected System.Web.UI.WebControls.Label lblMsg;
```

```csharp
public WebForm1( )
{
   Page.Init += new System.EventHandler(Page_Init);
}

protected void Page_Init(object sender, EventArgs e)
{
   //
   // CODEGEN: This call is required by the
   // ASP.NET Windows Form Designer.
   //
   InitializeComponent( );
}

#region Web Form Designer generated code
/// <summary>
///    Required method for Designer support - do not modify
///    the contents of this method with the code editor.
/// </summary>
private void InitializeComponent( )
{
   this.Load +=
      new System.EventHandler(this.Page_Load);

}
#endregion

public class Book
{
   public Book(float price, string title, string ISBN)
   {
      this.price = price;
      this.title = title;
      this.isbn = ISBN;
   }

   public float Price { get {return price;} }
   public string Title { get {return title;} }
   public string ISBN { get {return isbn;} }

   private float price;
   private string title;
   private string isbn;

}

private void Page_Load(object sender, System.EventArgs e)
{
   if (! Page.IsPostBack)
   {
      // create the array list
      ArrayList bookList = new ArrayList( );
```

Example 9-6. C# code-behind for dynamic radio buttons and checkboxes (continued)

```csharp
// add all the books
// (formatted to fit in margins)
bookList.Add(
    new Book(49.95f, "Programming ASP.NET",
        "100000000"));
bookList.Add(
    new Book(49.95f,"Programming C#",
        "100000001"));
bookList.Add(
    new Book(34.99f,"Teach Yourself C++ In 21 Days",
        "067232072x"));
bookList.Add(
    new Book(24.95f,"Teach Yourself C++ In 24 Hours",
        "0672315165"));
bookList.Add(
    new Book(12.99f,"TY C++ In 10 Minutes",
        "067231603X"));
bookList.Add(
    new Book(24.95f,"C++ Unleashed",
        "1199000663"));
bookList.Add(
    new Book(29.99f,"C++ From Scratch",
        "0789720795"));
bookList.Add(
    new Book(39.99f,"XML From Scratch",
        "0789723166"));

// set the data source
ddlBooks.DataSource=bookList;

// bind to the data
ddlBooks.DataBind();

// shippingMethods array list stands in for
// data retrieved from database
ArrayList shippingMethods = new ArrayList();
shippingMethods.Add("3rd Class");
shippingMethods.Add("1st Class");
shippingMethods.Add("Ground");
shippingMethods.Add("2nd Day");
shippingMethods.Add("Next Day");

// set the data source for the dynamic
// radio button list
rbList.DataSource=shippingMethods;

// bind the data
rbList.DataBind();

// extras array list stands in for
// data retrieved from database
```

```csharp
          ArrayList extras = new ArrayList( );
          extras.Add("Gift Wrap");
          extras.Add("Gift Card");
          extras.Add("Book Mark");
          extras.Add("Autographed copy");
          extras.Add("Source Code");

          // set the data source for the
          // dynamic checkbox list
          cbList.DataSource=extras;

          // bind the data
          cbList.DataBind( );
      }
      else     // is post-back, form was submitted
      {
          // string builders to hold text from controls
          StringBuilder extrasChosen =
             new StringBuilder(" with these extras: ");
          StringBuilder shippingMethod =
             new StringBuilder(" We will ship ");

          // build up string of choices. if more than one choice
          // make them comma delmited
          int chosen = 0;
          for (int i = 0; i < cbList.Items.Count; i++)
          {
             // if the item was selected
             if (cbList.Items[i].Selected == true)
             {
                // if this is not the first item
                // add a comma after the previous
                // before adding this one
                chosen++;
                if (chosen > 1)
                   extrasChosen.Append(", ");

                // add the item to the string builder
                extrasChosen.Append(cbList.Items[i].Text);

             }
          }

          // find the selected shipping method and add it
          // to the string builder
          for (int i = 0; i < rbList.Items.Count; i++)
             if (rbList.Items[i].Selected)
                shippingMethod.Append(rbList.Items[i].Text);


          // create the output text by concatenating the book title
          // isbn, the selected items and the shipping method
```

```
            lblMsg.Text = "Selected: " + ddlBooks.SelectedItem.Text +
                "(" + ddlBooks.SelectedItem.Value + ")" + extrasChosen +
                ".  " + shippingMethod + ".";

        } // end else
    }       // end page load
  }         // end class
}           // end namespace
```

There is complexity in the details here, but the essential idea remains quite simple: you bind a data source to a control. In this case the data source was an ArrayList, but typically the data source will be created with data from a database (see Chapter 11). In this example, you bound the data to a radio button list and to a checkbox list so that you could dynamically create the controls based on the data in the data source.

List-Bound Controls, Part I

ASP.NET offers three related list-bound controls: Repeater, DataList, and DataGrid. These controls support the display of repeating data such as database reports, shopping carts, menus, and query results. These are among the most powerful controls in ASP.NET and mastering them is key to creating viable commercial applications.

The Repeater is a lightweight control that derives directly from the base Control class. It is *lookless*, which means that there is no predefined user interface or style; the developer is free to provide virtually any look to the Repeater through the use of templates. Repeaters are ideal when the developer must maintain complete control over the look and feel of the control.

> *Templates* are HTML elements that define the content and rendering of a Repeater or other control. You create a template as you would any HTML element, for example:
>
> ```
> <template name="myTemplate">
>     Programming C#
> </template>
> ```
>
> Within the template you may nest other HTML elements such as labels and text. Templates are discussed in detail in Chapter 13.

The DataList control derives from the BaseDataList class, as does the DataGrid. The BaseDataList class derives in turn from the WebControl class, which derives from the Control class (see Figure 4-5 in Chapter 4, which depicts the relationship of controls in the System.Web.UI.WebControls namespace). The DataList displays either a columnar or a normal HTML flow layout. It also provides support for selection, editing, and deleting of items.

> *Flow layout* describes how the text on an HTML page will be displayed. In normal HTML the text is written across the page, in columnar layout the text is arranged in columns.

The DataGrid displays its data in a table of columns and rows. Like the DataList, the DataGrid provides style and appearance properties as well as selection and editing. The DataGrid also supports sorting of columns and paging through the data. Unlike the DataList, the DataGrid does not support template properties; the rows of the control cannot be controlled by templates. It is possible to add a TemplateColumn object to the DataGrid, however, which allows the use of templates within that column. We'll return to templates later in this chapter.

Table 10-1 illustrates the principal differences among the three list-bound controls.

Table 10-1. Features of the list-bound controls

Feature	Repeater	DataList	DataGrid
Column layout	No	Yes	No
Flow layout	Yes	Yes	No
Paging	No	No	Yes
Select/ Edit/Delete	No	Yes	Yes
Sort	No	No	Yes
Style properties	No	Yes	Yes
Table layout	No	No	Yes
Templates	Yes	Yes	Columns/ optional

If you examine this table closely, you find that Repeaters have no look to them, and offer only a flow layout. They are entirely controlled by templates. DataLists offer either flow or column layout, and their look is controlled by style properties and templates. DataLists also support selection, editing, and deletion, but not sorting and paging. DataGrids, finally, support table layout only; their look is controlled with style properties and optionally with column templates, and they support not only selection, editing, and deletion, but also sorting and paging.

This chapter will introduce and discuss the DataGrid control using an ArrayList as the data source. In Chapter 11, we'll explain how to access data in the database. Chapter 12 will cover updating data using ADO.NET. Then in Chapter 13, we'll return to the DataGrid control to bind to a database and continue the discussion of list-bound controls by examining the DataList and Repeater controls.

Shared Properties and Collections

Before delving into the specifics of each list-bound control, this chapter will examine the features all three controls share in common.

DataSource

All the list-bound controls have a DataSource property. This property defines the source for data binding, as you've seen earlier with other controls. A DataSource can be any object that implements the System.Collections.ICollection interface: an array, a dataset, or some other homogeneous collection of objects. Often, the data source will be a System.Data.Dataview object, as discussed in Chapter 11. For simplicity, in this chapter you will continue to use an ArrayList object, though you can use any object that implements System.Collections.ICollection, such as a HashTable or an Array object.

Items

The three list-bound controls also contain an Items property that returns a collection of objects representing an item (row) in the data source collection. You use the Items collection to manipulate the items in the list control programmatically.

 The Repeater control's Items property returns a collection of Repeater-Item objects, the DataList control's Items property returns a collection of DataListItem objects, and the DataGrid control's Items property returns DataGridItem objects.

The DataGridItem object has an ItemType property that returns an enumerated ListItemType. The members of the ListItemType enumeration are shown in Table 10-2.

Table 10-2. Members of the ListItemType enumeration

List item type	Purpose
AlternatingItem	Every other item
EditItem	Used for in-place editing; see Chapter 13
Footer	Display footer for control
Header	Display header information for control
Item	Displays information about data item
Pager	Display paging information
SelectedItem	The item the user has selected
Separator	Appears between items

Manipulation of the various types of members of the Items collection will be demonstrated throughout the rest of this chapter.

All of the list-bound controls follow the explicit binding method. When its Data-Bind method is called, the list-bound control enumerates its data source, creating DataListItems and initializing them from the DataSource items. The DataListItem objects are then added to the list-bound control's Items collection. Because this happens only on demand, there are fewer round trips to the server than might otherwise be expected.

The DataGrid Control

The problem with pre-designed user controls is typically that they are either simple and therefore too limited to do what you want, or they are powerful and therefore so complex that they are very difficult to learn. The DataGrid control attempts to overcome both of these constraints. Creating a simple DataGrid control couldn't be much easier, yet there is enough power and complexity to keep you quite busy tweaking and modifying the control to do exactly what you want.

To explore both the simplicity and the power of the DataGrid control, we'll use the process of successive approximation to get something working quickly and then to keep it working while we enhance it.

Version 1: Displaying Data

In the first iteration, you'll create a DataGrid object and display some simple data. To get started, you need a data source, in this case an ArrayList that you'll populate with Bug objects. You will define the Bug class, and each Bug object will represent a single bug report. For now to keep it simple, you'll give the Bug class a few fields to hold representative information about a given code bug. Example 10-1 is the definition of the Bug class in C#; Example 10-2 is the same definition in VB.NET.

Example 10-1. The Bug class in C#
```
public class Bug
{
    private int bugID;
    private string title;
    private string reporter;
    private string product;
    private string version;
    private string description;
    private DateTime dateCreated;

    public Bug(int bugID, string title, string reporter,
        string product, string version,
        string description, DateTime dateCreated)
    {
        this.bugID = bugID;
        this.title = title;
        this.reporter = reporter;
        this.product = product;
        this.version = version;
        this.description = description;
```

Example 10-1. The Bug class in C# (continued)

```
        this.dateCreated = dateCreated;
   }
   public int       BugID        { get { return bugID;        } }
   public string    Title        { get { return title;        } }
   public string    Reporter     { get { return reporter;     } }
   public string    Product      { get { return product;      } }
   public string    Version      { get { return version;      } }
   public string    Description  { get { return description;  } }
   public DateTime  DateCreated  { get { return dateCreated;  } }

}
```

Example 10-2. The Bug class in VB.NET

```
Public Class Bug
   Private _bugID As Int32
   Private _title As String
   Private _reporter As String
   Private _product As String
   Private _version As String
   Private _description As String
   Private _dateCreated As DateTime
   Private _severity As String

   Sub New(ByVal theID As Int32, _
   ByVal theTitle As String, _
   ByVal theReporter As String, _
   ByVal theProduct As String, _
   ByVal theVersion As String, _
   ByVal theDescription As String, _
   ByVal theDateCreated As DateTime, _
   ByVal theSeverity As String)

      _bugID = theID
      _title = theTitle
      _reporter = theReporter
      _version = theVersion
      _description = theDescription
      _dateCreated = theDateCreated
      _severity = theSeverity
   End Sub

   Public ReadOnly Property BugID() As Int32
      Get
         BugID = _bugID
      End Get
   End Property

   Public ReadOnly Property Title() As String
      Get
         Title = _title
      End Get
```

Example 10-2. The Bug class in VB.NET (continued)

```vb.net
    End Property

    Public ReadOnly Property Reporter( ) As String
        Get
            Reporter = _reporter
        End Get
    End Property

    Public ReadOnly Property Product( ) As String
        Get
            Product = _product
        End Get
    End Property

    Public ReadOnly Property Version( ) As String
        Get
            Version = _version
        End Get
    End Property

    Public ReadOnly Property Description( ) As String
        Get
            Description = _description
        End Get
    End Property

    Public ReadOnly Property DateCreated( ) As String
        Get
            DateCreated = _dateCreated
        End Get
    End Property

    Public ReadOnly Property Severity( ) As String
        Get
            Severity = _severity
        End Get
    End Property

End Class
```

The Bug class consists of nothing except a number of private members and read-only properties to retrieve these values. In addition, there is a constructor to initialize the values. The reporter member variable (_reporter) stores the name of the person reporting the bug, the product and version (_product and _version) are strings that represent the specific product that has the bug. The description field holds the full description of the bug, while title is a short summary to be displayed in the data grid.

The *.aspx* file simply creates a DataGrid within a form. The only attribute is the ID and, of course, runat="server", as you would expect in any ASP web control. The complete *.aspx* file is shown in Example 10-3.

Example 10-3. The .aspx file

```
<%@ Page language="c#"
Codebehind="WebForm1.aspx.cs"
AutoEventWireup="false"
Inherits="WebApplication1.WebForm1" %>

<html>
  <head>
      <meta name=vs_targetSchema content="Internet Explorer 5.0">
      <meta name="GENERATOR" Content="Microsoft Visual Studio 7.0">
      <meta name="CODE_LANGUAGE" Content="C#">
  </head>
  <body>
    <form runat="server" ID="Form1">
        <asp:DataGrid id="dataGrid1" runat="server" />
    </form>
  </body>
</html>
```

All that is left is to bind the data. This is accomplished in the Page_Load method in the code-behind file. If the page is not being posted back, you call a helper method, BindGrid.

BindGrid creates a new ArrayList named bugs and populates it with a couple of instances of the Bug class. It then sets dataGrid1's DataSource property to the bugs ArrayList object and calls BindGrid. The complete C# code-behind file is shown in Example 10-4, with the complete VB.NET code shown in Example 10-5.

Example 10-4. The code-behind file in C#

```
using System;
using System.Collections;
using System.ComponentModel;
using System.Data;
using System.Drawing;
using System.Web;
using System.Web.SessionState;
using System.Web.UI;
using System.Web.UI.WebControls;
using System.Web.UI.HtmlControls;

namespace DataGridBindAllColumnsBugs
{
    public class WebForm1 : System.Web.UI.Page
    {
        // declare the controls on the web page
        protected System.Web.UI.WebControls.DataGrid
            dataGrid1;

        public WebForm1( )
        {
            Page.Init +=
```

Example 10-4. The code-behind file in C# (continued)

```csharp
            new System.EventHandler(Page_Init);
    }

    private void Page_Load(
        object sender, System.EventArgs e)
    {
        // if this is the first time
        // the page is to be displayed
        // bind the data
        if (!IsPostBack)
        {
            BindGrid();
        }
    }

    private void Page_Init(
        object sender, EventArgs e)
    {
        InitializeComponent();
    }
    void BindGrid()
    {
        // create the data source
        // add a couple bug objects
        ArrayList bugs = new ArrayList();
        bugs.Add(
            new Bug(
            101,
            "Bad Property Value",
            "Jesse Liberty",
            "XBugs",
            "0.01",
            "Property values incorrect",
            DateTime.Now,
            "High"
            )       // end new bug
        );          // end add

        bugs.Add(
            new Bug(
            102,
            "Doesn't load properly",
            "Dan Hurwitz",
            "XBugs",
            "0.01",
            "The system fails with error x2397",
            DateTime.Now,
            "Medium"
            )       // end new bug
        );          // end add

        // assign the data source
```

Example 10-4. The code-behind file in C# (continued)

```
      dataGrid1.DataSource=bugs;

      // bind the grid
      dataGrid1.DataBind( );

   }
   #region Web Form Designer generated code
   /// <summary>
   /// Required method for Designer support - do not modify
   /// the contents of this method with the code editor.
   /// </summary>
   private void InitializeComponent( )
   {
      this.Load +=
          new System.EventHandler(this.Page_Load);

   }
   #endregion
}

// the Bug class
public class Bug
{
   // private instance variables
   private int bugID;
   private string title;
   private string reporter;
   private string product;
   private string version;
   private string description;
   private DateTime dateCreated;
   private string severity;

   // constructor
   public Bug(int id,
      string title,        // for display
      string reporter,     // who filed bug
      string product,
      string version,
      string description,  // bug report
      DateTime dateCreated,
      string severity)
   {
      bugID = id;
      this.title = title;
      this.reporter = reporter;
      this.product = product;
      this.version = version;
      this.description = description;
      this.dateCreated = dateCreated;
      this.severity = severity;
   }
```

Example 10-4. The code-behind file in C# (continued)

```
      // public read only properties
      public int      BugID
                { get { return bugID; }}
      public string    Title
                { get { return title; }}
      public string    Reporter
                { get { return reporter; }}
      public string    Product
                { get { return product;  }}
      public string    Version
                { get { return version;  }}
      public string    Description
                { get { return description; }}
      public DateTime   DateCreated
                { get { return dateCreated; }}
      public string    Severity
                { get { return severity; }}


   }
}
```

Example 10-5. The complete code-behind file in VB.NET

```
Public Class WebForm1
    Inherits System.Web.UI.Page
    Protected WithEvents dataGrid1 As System.Web.UI.WebControls.DataGrid


#Region " Web Form Designer Generated Code "

    'This call is required by the Web Form Designer.
    <System.Diagnostics.DebuggerStepThrough()> Private Sub InitializeComponent()

    End Sub

    Private Sub Page_Init(ByVal sender As System.Object _
                         ByVal e As System.EventArgs) _
                         Handles MyBase.Init
        'CODEGEN: This method call is required by the Web Form Designer
        'Do not modify it using the code editor.
        InitializeComponent()
    End Sub

#End Region

    Private Sub Page_Load(ByVal sender As System.Object, _
                         ByVal e As System.EventArgs) Handles MyBase.Load

       If Not IsPostBack Then
          BindGrid()
       End If
    End Sub
```

Example 10-5. The complete code-behind file in VB.NET (continued)

```
    Public Sub BindGrid( )
        Dim bugs As New ArrayList( )
        bugs.Add(New Bug(101, _
            "BadProperty Value", _
            "Jesse Liberty", _
            "XBugs", _
            "0.01", _
            "Property values incorrect", _
            DateTime.Now, _
            "High") _
        )
        bugs.Add( _
            New Bug( _
            102, _
            "Doesn't load properly", _
            "Dan Hurwitz", _
            "XBugs", _
            "0.01", _
            "The system fails with error x2397", _
            DateTime.Now, _
            "Medium") _
        )

        dataGrid1.DataSource = bugs
        dataGrid1.DataBind( )

    End Sub

End Class

Public Class Bug
    Private _bugID As Int32
    Private _title As String
    Private _reporter As String
    Private _product As String
    Private _version As String
    Private _description As String
    Private _dateCreated As DateTime
    Private _severity As String

    Sub New(ByVal theID As Int32, _
    ByVal theTitle As String, _
    ByVal theReporter As String, _
    ByVal theProduct As String, _
    ByVal theVersion As String, _
    ByVal theDescription As String, _
    ByVal theDateCreated As DateTime, _
    ByVal theSeverity As String)

        _bugID = theID
        _title = theTitle
```

Example 10-5. The complete code-behind file in VB.NET (continued)

```
        _reporter = theReporter
        _version = theVersion
        _description = theDescription
        _dateCreated = theDateCreated
        _severity = theSeverity
    End Sub

    Public ReadOnly Property BugID( ) As Int32
        Get
            BugID = _bugID
        End Get
    End Property

    Public ReadOnly Property Title( ) As String
        Get
            Title = _title
        End Get
    End Property

    Public ReadOnly Property Reporter( ) As String
        Get
            Reporter = _reporter
        End Get
    End Property

    Public ReadOnly Property Product( ) As String
        Get
            Product = _product
        End Get
    End Property

    Public ReadOnly Property Version( ) As String
        Get
            Version = _version
        End Get
    End Property

    Public ReadOnly Property Description( ) As String
        Get
            Description = _description
        End Get
    End Property

    Public ReadOnly Property DateCreated( ) As String
        Get
            DateCreated = _dateCreated
        End Get
    End Property

    Public ReadOnly Property Severity( ) As String
        Get
            Severity = _severity
```

Example 10-5. The complete code-behind file in VB.NET (continued)

```
    End Get
  End Property

End Class
```

When the page is loaded, Page_Load is called, which in turn calls BindGrid. In Bind-Grid, the bugs ArrayList object is created, and two instances of Bug are added, each representing a bug. The DataSource property of DataGrid1 is set, and DataBind is called. The data grid binds each of the properties in Bug to a column in the data grid. The result is shown in Figure 10-1.

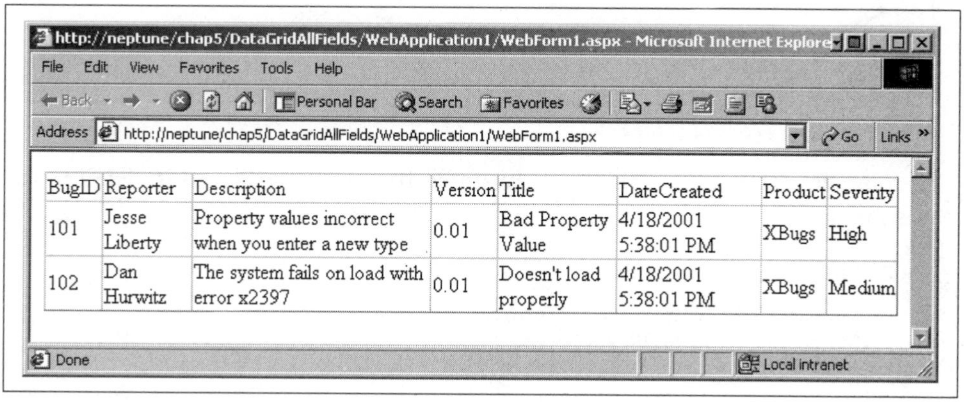

Figure 10-1. Displaying the bugs

This result is both spectacular and unacceptable. It is spectacular because you've done so little work to display this data from your data source. You did nothing more than bind the collection to the data grid, and ASP.NET took care of the rest. It is unacceptable because this is not how you want the grid to look: the columns are in the wrong order, there is data you don't want to display, there is no link to a detail record, and so forth.

Before you improve on this version of the Bug display page, however, take a close look at Figure 10-1. Notice that there is a header on each column! The data grid picked up the title for each column from the Bug object. The default column header is the name of the property.

Version 2: Controlling the Columns

In the next iteration of this program, you'll eliminate the Description column, add a link to a details page (where you can display the description), change the order of the columns, and color the Severity red if it is marked "high." Piece of cake. The result is shown in Figure 10-2.

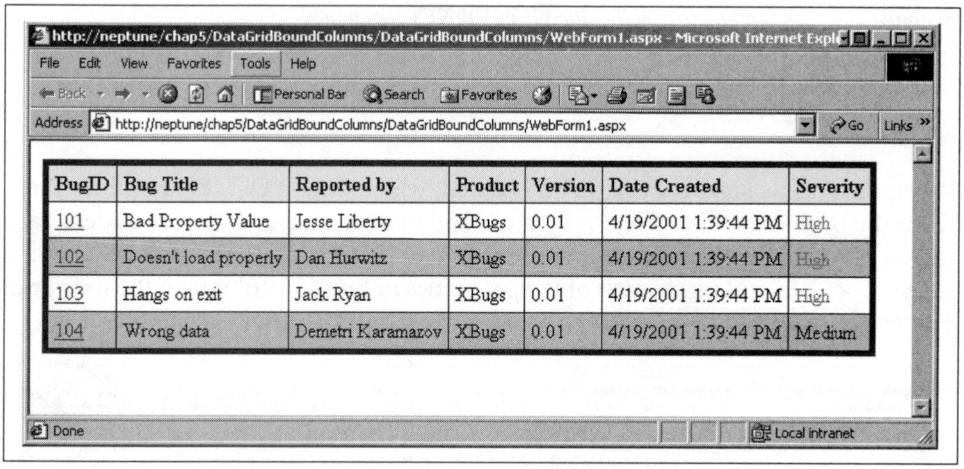

Figure 10-2. Taking control of the columns

The complete .aspx page is shown in Example 10-6 and is analyzed in detail in the pages that follow.

Example 10-6. Completed .aspx file in C#

```
<%@ Page language="c#" Codebehind="WebForm1.aspx.cs" AutoEventWireup="false"
Inherits="DataGridMasterDetailNew.WebForm1" %>
<!DOCTYPE HTML PUBLIC "-//W3C//DTD HTML 4.0 Transitional//EN" >

<html>
  <head>
    <meta name="GENERATOR" Content="Microsoft Visual Studio 7.0">
    <meta name="CODE_LANGUAGE" Content="C#">
    <meta name=vs_defaultClientScript content="JavaScript (ECMAScript)">
    <meta name=vs_targetSchema content="http://schemas.microsoft.com/intellisense/ie5">
  </head>
 <body MS_POSITIONING="GridLayout">

    <form runat="server" ID="Form1">
      <asp:DataGrid id="dataGrid1"
      OnItemDataBound="OnItemDataBoundEventHandler"
      AutoGenerateColumns="False"
      CellPadding="5"
      HeaderStyle-BackColor="PapayaWhip"
      BorderWidth="5px"
      BorderColor="#000099"
      AlternatingItemStyle-BackColor="LightGrey"
      HeaderStyle-Font-Bold="True"
      runat="server">
        <Columns>
          <asp:HyperLinkColumn HeaderText="Bug ID"
           DataTextField="BugID" DataNavigateUrlField="BugID"
           DataNavigateUrlFormatString="details.aspx?bugID={0}"  />
          <asp:BoundColumn DataField="Title" HeaderText="Bug Title" />
```

Example 10-6. Completed .aspx file in C# (continued)

```
            <asp:BoundColumn DataField="Reporter" HeaderText="Reported by" />
            <asp:BoundColumn DataField="Product" HeaderText="Product" />
            <asp:BoundColumn DataField="Version" HeaderText="Version" />
            <asp:BoundColumn DataField="DateCreated"
                HeaderText="Date Created" />
            <asp:BoundColumn DataField="Severity" HeaderText="Severity" />
        </Columns>
      </asp:DataGrid>
    </form>
  </body>
</html>
```

In the VB.NET version, do not include this line in the HTML:

```
        OnItemDataBound="OnItemDataBoundEventHandler"
```

The complete code-behind file in C# is shown in Example 10-7, and in VB.NET in Example 10-8.

Example 10-7. Implementing events with data grids in C#

```csharp
using System;
using System.Collections;
using System.ComponentModel;
using System.Data;
using System.Drawing;
using System.Web;
using System.Web.SessionState;
using System.Web.UI;
using System.Web.UI.WebControls;
using System.Web.UI.HtmlControls;

namespace DataGridMasterDetailNew
{
    public class WebForm1 : System.Web.UI.Page
    {

        protected System.Web.UI.WebControls.DataGrid dataGrid1;

        public WebForm1( )
        {
            Page.Init += new System.EventHandler(Page_Init);
        }

        private void Page_Load(object sender, System.EventArgs e)
        {
            if (!IsPostBack)
            {
                BindGrid( );
            }
```

Example 10-7. Implementing events with data grids in C# (continued)

```csharp
    }

    private void Page_Init(object sender, EventArgs e)
    {
        InitializeComponent();
    }

    // Handle the ItemDataBound event
    public void OnItemDataBoundEventHandler(Object sender, DataGridItemEventArgs e)
    {

        // Don't bother for header, footer and separator items
        ListItemType itemType = (ListItemType)e.Item.ItemType;
        if (itemType == ListItemType.Header ||
            itemType == ListItemType.Footer ||
            itemType == ListItemType.Separator)
            return;

        // e.Item.DataItem is the data for the item
        Bug bug = (Bug)e.Item.DataItem;

        // check the severity for this item
        // if it is high, set the cell to red
        if (bug.Severity == "High")
        {
            // this would make the entire entry red
            //   e.Item.ForeColor = Color.FromName("red");

            // get just the cell we want
            TableCell severityCell = (TableCell)e.Item.Controls[6];

            // set that cell's forecolor to red
            severityCell.ForeColor = Color.FromName("Red");
        }
    }
    void BindGrid()
    {
        ArrayList bugs = new ArrayList();
        bugs.Add(
            new Bug(
            101,
            "Bad Property Value",
            "Jesse Liberty",
            "XBugs",
            "0.01",
            "Property values incorrect when you enter a new type",
            DateTime.Now,
            "High"
            )
            );

        bugs.Add(
```

Example 10-7. Implementing events with data grids in C# (continued)

```
        new Bug(
        102,
        "Doesn't load properly",
        "Dan Hurwitz",
        "XBugs",
        "0.01",
        "The system fails on load with error x2397",
        DateTime.Now,
        "High"
        )
        );

    bugs.Add(
        new Bug(
        103,
        "Hangs on exit",
        "Jack Ryan",
        "XBugs",
        "0.01",
        "When you press close, it hangs",
        DateTime.Now,
        "High"
        )
        );

    bugs.Add(
        new Bug(
        104,
        "Wrong data",
        "Demetri Karamazov",
        "XBugs",
        "0.01",
        "The data does not match the DB",
        DateTime.Now,
        "Medium"
        )
        );

    dataGrid1.DataSource=bugs;
    dataGrid1.DataBind( );

}

#region Web Form Designer generated code
   /// <summary>
   /// Required method for Designer support - do not modify
   /// the contents of this method with the code editor.
   /// </summary>
   private void InitializeComponent( )
   {
      this.Load += new System.EventHandler(this.Page_Load);
```

Example 10-7. Implementing events with data grids in C# (continued)

```csharp
   }
  #endregion
}
public class Bug
{
   private int bugID;
   private string title;
   private string reporter;
   private string product;
   private string version;
   private string description;
   private DateTime dateCreated;
   private string severity;

   public Bug(int id, string title, string reporter,
      string product, string version,
      string description, DateTime dateCreated,
      string severity)
   {
      bugID = id;
      this.title = title;
      this.reporter = reporter;
      this.product = product;
      this.version = version;
      this.description = description;
      this.dateCreated = dateCreated;
      this.severity = severity;
   }
   public int       BugID        { get { return bugID;       }}
   public string    Title        { get { return title;       }}
   public string    Reporter     { get { return reporter;    }}
   public string    Product      { get { return product;     }}
   public string    Version      { get { return version;     }}
   public string    Description  { get { return description;}}
   public DateTime  DateCreated  { get { return dateCreated;}}
   public string    Severity     { get { return severity;   }}
   }
}
```

Example 10-8. Implementing events with data grids in VB.NET

```vbnet
Public Class WebForm1
   Inherits System.Web.UI.Page
   Protected WithEvents dataGrid1 As System.Web.UI.WebControls.DataGrid

#Region " Web Form Designer Generated Code "

   'This call is required by the Web Form Designer.
   <System.Diagnostics.DebuggerStepThrough()> Private Sub InitializeComponent()

   End Sub
```

Example 10-8. Implementing events with data grids in VB.NET (continued)

```
    Private Sub Page_Init(ByVal sender As System.Object, _
                           ByVal e As System.EventArgs) _
                           Handles MyBase.Init
        'CODEGEN: This method call is required by the Web Form Designer
        'Do not modify it using the code editor.
        InitializeComponent( )
    End Sub

#End Region

    Private Sub Page_Load(ByVal sender As System.Object _
                           ByVal e As System.EventArgs) _
                           Handles MyBase.Load
        If Not IsPostBack Then
            BindGrid( )
        End If
    End Sub

    Public Sub BindGrid( )
        Dim bugs As New ArrayList( )
        bugs.Add(New Bug(101, _
            "BadProperty Value", _
            "Jesse Liberty", _
            "XBugs", _
            "0.01", _
            "Property values incorrect", _
            DateTime.Now, _
            "High") _
        )
        bugs.Add( _
            New Bug( _
            102, _
            "Doesn't load properly", _
            "Dan Hurwitz", _
            "XBugs", _
            "0.01", _
            "The system fails with error x2397", _
            DateTime.Now, _
            "Medium") _
        )

        bugs.Add( _
            New Bug( _
            103, _
            "Hangs on exit", _
            "Jack Ryan", _
            "XBugs", _
            "0.01", _
            "When you press close, it hangs", _
            DateTime.Now, _
            "High") _
            )
```

Example 10-8. Implementing events with data grids in VB.NET (continued)

```vb
    bugs.Add( _
        New Bug( _
        104, _
        "Wrong data", _
        "Demetri Karamazov", _
        "XBugs", _
        "0.01", _
        "The data does not match the DB", _
        DateTime.Now, _
        "Medium") _
        )

    dataGrid1.DataSource = bugs
    dataGrid1.DataBind( )

End Sub

' handle the item data bound event
Private Sub dataGrid1_OnItemDataBoundEventHandler( _
ByVal sender As System.Object, _
ByVal e As System.Web.UI.WebControls.DataGridItemEventArgs) _
Handles dataGrid1.ItemDataBound

    '' Don't bother for the header, footer or separator type
    Dim itemType As ListItemType
    itemType = e.Item.ItemType
    If itemType = ListItemType.Header Or _
    itemType = ListItemType.Footer Or _
    itemType = ListItemType.Separator Then
        Exit Sub
    End If

    '' e.item.dataItem is the data for the item
    Dim theBug As Bug
    theBug = e.Item.DataItem

    '' check the severity of this item
    '' if it is high, set the cell to red
    If theBug.Severity = "High" Then
        Dim severityCell As TableCell

        '' just get the cell you want
        severityCell = e.Item.Controls(6)

        '' set the cell's foreground color to red
        severityCell.ForeColor = Color.FromName("Red")
    End If

    Dim linkCell As TableCell
    linkCell = e.Item.Controls(0)
    Dim h As HyperLink
```

Example 10-8. Implementing events with data grids in VB.NET (continued)

```
      h = linkCell.Controls(0)
      h.NavigateUrl = "details.aspx?bugID=" & theBug.BugID

   End Sub
End Class

Public Class Bug
   Private _bugID As Int32
   Private _title As String
   Private _reporter As String
   Private _product As String
   Private _version As String
   Private _description As String
   Private _dateCreated As DateTime
   Private _severity As String

   Sub New(ByVal theID As Int32, _
   ByVal theTitle As String, _
   ByVal theReporter As String, _
   ByVal theProduct As String, _
   ByVal theVersion As String, _
   ByVal theDescription As String, _
   ByVal theDateCreated As DateTime, _
   ByVal theSeverity As String)

      _bugID = theID
      _title = theTitle
      _reporter = theReporter
      _version = theVersion
      _description = theDescription
      _dateCreated = theDateCreated
      _severity = theSeverity
   End Sub

   Public ReadOnly Property BugID() As Int32
      Get
         BugID = _bugID
      End Get
   End Property

   Public ReadOnly Property Title() As String
      Get
         Title = _title
      End Get
   End Property

   Public ReadOnly Property Reporter() As String
      Get
         Reporter = _reporter
      End Get
```

Example 10-8. Implementing events with data grids in VB.NET (continued)

```
    End Property

    Public ReadOnly Property Product() As String
        Get
            Product = _product
        End Get
    End Property

    Public ReadOnly Property Version() As String
        Get
            Version = _version
        End Get
    End Property

    Public ReadOnly Property Description() As String
        Get
            Description = _description
        End Get
    End Property

    Public ReadOnly Property DateCreated() As String
        Get
            DateCreated = _dateCreated
        End Get
    End Property

    Public ReadOnly Property Severity() As String
        Get
            Severity = _severity
        End Get
    End Property
End Class
```

Data-bound columns

The key changes to the DataGrid declaration are to add two attributes: AutoGenerateColumns and (for the C# example) OnItemDataBound. In addition, a number of style attributes are set to make the DataGrid look a bit nicer. The following is the replacement DataGrid tag for the one shown in Example 10-2.

```
<asp:DataGrid id="dataGrid1"
AutoGenerateColumns="False"
OnItemDataBound="OnItemDataBoundEventHandler"
CellPadding="5"
HeaderStyle-BackColor="PapayaWhip"
BorderWidth ="5px"
BorderColor = "#000099"
AlternatingItemStyle-BackColor ="LightGrey"
HeaderStyle-Font-Bold
runat="server" >
```

AutoGenerateColumns is set to false, so that the data grid will not automatically add a column for every property it finds for the Bug object. You are now free to add bound columns for the data you do want to display, in whatever order you choose.

Bound columns are added within a Columns tag that acts as a subcontrol for the Data-Grid object, as follows:

```
<Columns>

</Columns>
```

Between the opening and the closing tags, you'll add the various bound columns:

```
<Columns>
    <asp:HyperLinkColumn HeaderText="Bug ID"
     DataTextField="BugID" DataNavigateUrlField="BugID"
     DataNavigateUrlFormatString="details.aspx?bugID={0}" />
    <asp:BoundColumn DataField="Title" HeaderText="Bug Title"/>
    <asp:BoundColumn DataField="Reporter" HeaderText="Reported by"/>
    <asp:BoundColumn DataField="Product" HeaderText="Product"/>
    <asp:BoundColumn DataField="Version" HeaderText="Version"/>
    <asp:BoundColumn DataField="DateCreated" HeaderText="Date Created"/>
    <asp:BoundColumn DataField="Severity" HeaderText="Severity"/>
</Columns>
```

Skip over the first column for now and look at the remaining ones, which are all simple BoundColumn elements. Each is given a DataField attribute to identify which property of the Bug object holds the data for that field, and a HeaderText attribute that defines a caption for that column's header.

Go back and look at the very first column that you skipped over previously.

```
<asp:HyperLinkColumn HeaderText="Bug ID"
 DataTextField="BugID" DataNavigateUrlField="BugID"
 DataNavigateUrlFormatString="details.aspx?bugID={0}" />
```

The job of the first column is not just to display the bug ID, but also to provide a link to the detail page for that bug. This is accomplished by creating an anchor tag using the HyperLinkColumn element.

The text to be displayed is taken from the data as defined by the DataTextField attribute. In this case, the text will be the value of the BugID property of the Bug object in the data grid's data source collection. The header to display for this column is set by the HeaderText attribute (in this case "Bug ID").

The link is created by the combination of the DataNavigateUrlField and DataNavigateUrlFormatString attributes. The {0} symbol is a *substitution parameter*. ASP.NET knows to substitute the value in the DataNavigateUrlField (the bug ID) for the parameter {0} in DataNavigateUrlFormatString If, for example, the current record's BugID is 101, the link created will be details.aspx?bugID=101.

Handling the ItemDataBound event

The ItemDataBound event is fired every time a data item is bound to a control. The OnItemDataBound attribute of the DataGrid control sets the method that will be called when the ItemDataBound event is fired, as the following fragment from the DataGrid tag shows:

```
OnItemDataBound="OnItemDataBoundEventHandler"
```

When the event fires, the event handler method is called. At that time, you can fix up the item in the data grid based on the contents of the data item. In this example, you'll set the value to display in red if the severity is High.

 Remember, the *item* is the element in the *data grid* and the *data item* is the data associated with that item from the collection that is the *data grid's data source.*

Your OnItemDataBoundEventHandler must take two parameters: an object, and a DataGridItemEventArgs type. You may of course name these arguments whatever you like. Visual Studio .NET will name them *sender* and *e*, respectively, when you declare the event handler.

The DataGridItemEventArgs object (*e*) has an Item property (e.Item) which returns the referenced item from the DataGrid control. That is, e.Item returns the item in the DataGrid that raised the event.

This item returned by e.Item is an object of type DataGridItem. As mentioned earlier, the DataGridItem class has an ItemType property (e.Item.ItemType) which returns a member of the ListItemType enumeration. You examine that value to see if it is equal to one of the enumerated types you want to ignore (Header, Footer, Separator), and if so, you return immediately, taking no further action on this item. In C#, this looks like:

```
ListItemType itemType = (ListItemType) e.Item.ItemType;
if (itemType == ListItemType.Header ||
    itemType == ListItemType.Footer ||
    itemType == ListItemType.Separator)
    return;
```

and in VB.NET, the code is:

```
Dim itemType As ListItemType
itemType = e.Item.ItemType
If itemType = ListItemType.Header Or _
            itemType = ListItemType.Footer Or _
            itemType = ListItemType.Separator Then
                Exit Sub
End If
```

Assuming you do have an item of a type you care about, you want to extract the actual data item that this row in the grid will represent. You go back to the object returned by the Item property, which you will remember is a DataGridItem object. The DataGridItem object has another property, DataItem, which gets us the actual Bug object from the collection that is this data grid's data source, as the following C# code fragment illustrates:

```
Bug bug = (Bug)e.Item.DataItem;
```

In VB.NET, the equivalent is:

```
Dim theBug As Bug
theBug = e.Item.DataItem
```

Bug is a class, and thus a reference object; therefore *bug* is a reference to the actual Bug object rather than a copy.

The relationships among the data grid objects can be a bit confusing and are worth a quick review. There are five objects involved in the previous scenario:

- The data grid (DataGrid1)
- The ArrayList (bugList), which acts as the data source to the data grid
- The DataGridItemEventArgs object, which is passed as the second parameter (*e*) to your designated event handler (OnItemDataBoundEventHandler) each time an item is added to the grid
- The DataGridItem object that raised the event and a reference to which you can get from the Item property of the DataGridItemEventArgs object (`e.Item`)
- The Bug that is being added to the data grid, which you can get to through the DataItem property of the DataGridItemEventArgs object (`e.Item.DataItem`)

Conditionally setting the severity color

Each time a data item is bound, the OnItemDataBoundEventHandler event handler is called, and you have an opportunity to examine the data and take action based on the specific data item being added. In this example, you'll check the severity of the bug, and if it is high, you'll set the color of that column to red.

To do so, you start with the Bug object, which in C# would be written:

```
Bug bug = (Bug)e.Item.DataItem;
```

The equivalent in VB.NET is:

```
Dim theBug As Bug
theBug = e.Item.DataItem
```

Severity is a property of the Bug object, illustrated here in C#:

```
if (bug.Severity == "High")
{
```

and in VB.NET:

```
If theBug.Severity = "High" Then
```

To set the entire row to red, just set the ForeColor property for the item:

```
e.Item.ForeColor = Color.FromName("red");.
```

FromName is a static method of the Color class, which in turn is a class provided by the System.Drawing namespace in the .NET Framework.

You've set the row red, but in this example you want to set only a single cell. The DataGridItem object has a Controls collection that represents all the child controls for that DataGrid item. Controls is of type ControlCollection and supplies a zero-based indexer that you can use like an array. The cell you want for the bugID is the seventh in the Controls collection, which in C# you specify using:

```
TableCell severityCell = (TableCell)e.Item.Controls[6];
```

Once you have that cell, you can set the properties of that TableCell object:

```
severityCell.ForeColor = Color.FromName("Red");
```

In VB.NET, these lines of code are:

```
Dim severityCell As TableCell
severityCell = e.Item.Controls(6)
severityCell.ForeColor = Color.FromName("Red")
```

Creating the hyperlink

In this example you have set the URL through the DataNavigateUrlField and the DataNavigateUrlFormatString attributes. It is possible, however, that you want to set the URL based not on a single attribute of the data item, but on a computation you'd like to make when the item is added to the grid. In that case, you can remove these two attributes from the declaration, and update the URL when you process the Item-DataBound event.

To set the anchor tag, you need the Hyperlink object within the first cell of the table. You start by getting the TableCell object, in this case the first cell in the row, which in C# looks like:

```
TableCell linkCell = (TableCell)e.Item.Controls[0];
```

In VB.NET, this is done using:

```
Dim linkCell As TableCell
linkCell = e.Item.Controls(0)
```

The table cell itself has child controls. The first child control is the hyperlink. The hyperlink was placed in that cell when the HyperLinkColumn was created in the *.aspx* file:

```
<asp:HyperlinkColumn  HeaderText="BugID" DataTextField="BugID"  />
```

You extract the HyperLink object from the TableCell by casting the first element in the collection to type HyperLink:

```
HyperLink h = (HyperLink) linkCell.Controls[0];
```

In VB.NET, this is done using:

```
Dim h As HyperLink
h = linkCell.Controls(0)
```

The HyperLink object has a NavigateUrl property. You can now set that to whatever string you like. For example, to accomplish the same work you did with the `DataNavigateUrlField` and the `DataNavigateUrlFormatString` attributes, you can set the NavigateUrl property in C# as follows:

```
h.NavigateUrl = "details.aspx?bugID=" + bug.BugID;
```

In VB.NET, use:

```
h.NavigateUrl = "details.aspx?bugID=" & theBug.BugID
```

Version 3: The Details Page

In the next version, you'll create the details page that the data grid links to. In addition, you'll add a footer to the data grid that summarizes how many bugs were found.

Example 10-9 is the modified C# code for the code-behind page, and Example 10-10 is the modified VB.NET code for the code-behind page. Detailed analysis follows the listings.

Example 10-9. Modified to handle footer and details page (C#)

```
using System;
using System.Collections;
using System.ComponentModel;
using System.Data;
using System.Drawing;
using System.Web;
using System.Web.SessionState;
using System.Web.UI;
using System.Web.UI.WebControls;
using System.Web.UI.HtmlControls;

namespace DataGridMasterDetailNew
{
    public class WebForm1 : System.Web.UI.Page
    {

        protected System.Web.UI.WebControls.DataGrid dataGrid1;

        public WebForm1( )
        {
            Page.Init += new System.EventHandler(Page_Init);
```

Example 10-9. Modified to handle footer and details page (C#) (continued)

```
   }

   private void Page_Load(object sender, System.EventArgs e)
   {
      if (!IsPostBack)
      {
         BindGrid( );
      }
   }

   private void Page_Init(object sender, EventArgs e)
   {
      InitializeComponent( );
   }
   public void OnItemCreatedEventHandler(
     Object sender, DataGridItemEventArgs e)
   {
      ListItemType itemType = (ListItemType)e.Item.ItemType;
      if (itemType == ListItemType.Footer)
      {
         // get the number of cells
         int numberOfCells = e.Item.Cells.Count;

         // remove all the cells except the last
         for (int i = 0; i < numberOfCells - 1; i++)
         {
            e.Item.Cells.RemoveAt(0);
         }

         // create string to report number
         // of bugs found
         int numberOfBugs = dataGrid1.Items.Count;
         string msg;
         if (numberOfBugs > 0 )
         {
            msg = "<b>" + numberOfBugs.ToString( ) + " bugs.</b>";
         }
         else
         {
            msg = "No bugs found.";
         }

         // get the one remaining cell
         TableCell msgCell = e.Item.Cells[0];
         msgCell.Text = msg;
         msgCell.ColumnSpan=numberOfCells;
         msgCell.HorizontalAlign = HorizontalAlign.Right;
      }
   }
   public void OnItemDataBoundEventHandler(
     Object sender, DataGridItemEventArgs e)
   {
```

Example 10-9. Modified to handle footer and details page (C#) (continued)

```csharp
    // Don't bother for header, footer and separator items
    ListItemType itemType = (ListItemType)e.Item.ItemType;
    if (itemType == ListItemType.Header ||
        itemType == ListItemType.Footer ||
        itemType == ListItemType.Separator)
        return;

    // e.Item.DataItem is the data for the item
    Bug bug = (Bug)e.Item.DataItem;

    // check the severity for this item
    // if it is high, set the cell to red
    if (bug.Severity == "High")
    {
        // this would make the entire entry red
        //   e.Item.ForeColor = Color.FromName("red");

        // get just the cell we want
        TableCell severityCell = (TableCell)e.Item.Controls[6];

        // set that cell's forecolor to red
        severityCell.ForeColor = Color.FromName("Red");
    }

    // get a reference to the HyperLink control in the first column
    TableCell linkCell = (TableCell)e.Item.Controls[0];

    // Controls[0]  the hyperlink
    HyperLink h = (HyperLink) linkCell.Controls[0];

    // create the link to the detail page
    h.NavigateUrl = "details.aspx?bugID=" + bug.BugID;
}
void BindGrid( )
{
    ArrayList bugs = new ArrayList( );
    bugs.Add(
        new Bug(
        101,
        "Bad Property Value",
        "Jesse Liberty",
        "XBugs",
        "0.01",
        "Property values incorrect when you enter a new type",
        DateTime.Now,
        "High"
        )
        );

    bugs.Add(
        new Bug(
```

Example 10-9. Modified to handle footer and details page (C#) (continued)

```csharp
            102,
            "Doesn't load properly",
            "Dan Hurwitz",
            "XBugs",
            "0.01",
            "The system fails on load with error x2397",
            DateTime.Now,
            "High"
            )
            );

        bugs.Add(
            new Bug(
            103,
            "Hangs on exit",
            "Jack Ryan",
            "XBugs",
            "0.01",
            "When you press close, it hangs",
            DateTime.Now,
            "High"
            )
            );

        bugs.Add(
            new Bug(
            104,
            "Wrong data",
            "Demetri Karamazov",
            "XBugs",
            "0.01",
            "The data does not match the DB",
            DateTime.Now,
            "Medium"
            )
            );

        dataGrid1.DataSource=bugs;
        dataGrid1.DataBind( );
        Session["bugList"] = bugs;

    }

#region Web Form Designer generated code
    private void InitializeComponent( )
    {
        this.Load += new System.EventHandler(this.Page_Load);

    }
#endregion
}
public class Bug
```

Example 10-9. Modified to handle footer and details page (C#) (continued)

```csharp
{
    private int bugID;
    private string title;
    private string reporter;
    private string product;
    private string version;
    private string description;
    private DateTime dateCreated;
    private string severity;

    public Bug(int id, string title, string reporter,
        string product, string version,
        string description, DateTime dateCreated,
        string severity)
    {
        bugID = id;
        this.title = title;
        this.reporter = reporter;
        this.product = product;
        this.version = version;
        this.description = description;
        this.dateCreated = dateCreated;
        this.severity = severity;
    }
    public int       BugID        { get { return bugID;   }}
    public string    Title        { get { return title;   }}
    public string    Reporter     { get { return reporter;}}
    public string    Product      { get { return product; }}
    public string    Version      { get { return version; }}
    public string    Description  { get { return description; }}
    public DateTime  DateCreated  { get { return dateCreated; }}
    public string    Severity     { get { return severity;  }}
}
}
```

Example 10-10. Modified to handle footer and details page (VB.NET)

```vbnet
Public Class WebForm1
    Inherits System.Web.UI.Page
    Protected WithEvents dataGrid1 As System.Web.UI.WebControls.DataGrid

#Region " Web Form Designer Generated Code "

    'This call is required by the Web Form Designer.
    <System.Diagnostics.DebuggerStepThrough()> Private Sub InitializeComponent()

    End Sub

    Private Sub Page_Init(ByVal sender As System.Object, _
                    ByVal e As System.EventArgs) _
                    Handles MyBase.Init
        'CODEGEN: This method call is required by the Web Form Designer
```

Example 10-10. Modified to handle footer and details page (VB.NET) (continued)

```
        'Do not modify it using the code editor.
        InitializeComponent()
    End Sub

#End Region

    Private Sub Page_Load(ByVal sender As System.Object, _
                          ByVal e As System.EventArgs) _
                          Handles MyBase.Load

        If Not IsPostBack Then
            BindGrid()
        End If
    End Sub

    Public Sub BindGrid()
        Dim bugs As New ArrayList()
        bugs.Add(New Bug(101, _
            "BadProperty Value", _
            "Jesse Liberty", _
            "XBugs", _
            "0.01", _
            "Property values incorrect", _
            DateTime.Now, _
            "High") _
        )
        bugs.Add( _
            New Bug( _
            102, _
            "Doesn't load properly", _
            "Dan Hurwitz", _
            "XBugs", _
            "0.01", _
            "The system fails with error x2397", _
            DateTime.Now, _
            "Medium") _
        )

        bugs.Add( _
            New Bug( _
            103, _
            "Hangs on exit", _
            "Jack Ryan", _
            "XBugs", _
            "0.01", _
            "When you press close, it hangs", _
            DateTime.Now, _
            "High") _
            )

        bugs.Add( _
            New Bug( _
```

```
            104, _
            "Wrong data", _
            "Demetri Karamazov", _
            "XBugs", _
            "0.01", _
            "The data does not match the DB", _
            DateTime.Now, _
            "Medium") _
            )

    dataGrid1.DataSource = bugs
    dataGrid1.DataBind( )
    Session("BugList") = bugs

End Sub

' Event handler for when items are created
Public Sub dataGrid1_OnItemCreatedEventHandler( _
ByVal sender As System.Object, _
ByVal e As System.Web.UI.WebControls.DataGridItemEventArgs) _
Handles dataGrid1.ItemCreated
    Dim itemType As ListItemType
    itemType = e.Item.ItemType
    If itemType = ListItemType.Footer Then

        ' get the number of cells
        Dim numberOfCells As Int32
        numberOfCells = e.Item.Cells.Count

        ' remove all cells except the last
        Dim i As Integer
        For i = 0 To numberOfCells - 2
            e.Item.Cells.RemoveAt(0)
        Next

        ' create string to report number
        ' of bugs found
        Dim numberOfBugs As Int32
        numberOfBugs = dataGrid1.Items.Count
        Dim msg As String
        If numberOfBugs > 0 Then
            msg = "<b>" & numberOfBugs.ToString & " bugs.</b>"
        Else
            msg = "No bugs found"
        End If

        ' get the one remaining cell
        ' fill it with number bugs found
        Dim msgCell As TableCell
        msgCell = e.Item.Cells(0)
        msgCell.Text = msg
        msgCell.ColumnSpan = numberOfCells
```

```
        msgCell.HorizontalAlign = HorizontalAlign.Right

    End If
End Sub

' handle item data bound event
Public Sub dataGrid1_OnItemDataBoundEventHandler( _
ByVal sender As System.Object, _
ByVal e As System.Web.UI.WebControls.DataGridItemEventArgs) _
Handles dataGrid1.ItemDataBound

    Dim itemType As ListItemType
    itemType = e.Item.ItemType

    ' don't bother for header footer or separator
    If itemType = ListItemType.Header Or _
    itemType = ListItemType.Footer Or _
    itemType = ListItemType.Separator Then
        Exit Sub
    End If

    'e.item.dataitem is the data for the item
    Dim theBug As Bug
    theBug = e.Item.DataItem

    ' if the severity is high, color it red
    If theBug.Severity = "High" Then
        Dim severityCell As TableCell
        severityCell = e.Item.Controls(6)
        severityCell.ForeColor = Color.FromName("Red")
    End If

    ' get a reference to the hyperlink control in the first oclumn
    Dim linkCell As TableCell
    linkCell = e.Item.Controls(0)

    ' get the hyperlink
    Dim h As HyperLink
    h = linkCell.Controls(0)

    ' create a link to the detail page
    h.NavigateUrl = "details.aspx?bugID=" & theBug.BugID

End Sub
End Class

Public Class Bug
    Private _bugID As Int32
    Private _title As String
    Private _reporter As String
    Private _product As String
    Private _version As String
```

```vb.net
Private _description As String
Private _dateCreated As DateTime
Private _severity As String

Sub New(ByVal theID As Int32, _
ByVal theTitle As String, _
ByVal theReporter As String, _
ByVal theProduct As String, _
ByVal theVersion As String, _
ByVal theDescription As String, _
ByVal theDateCreated As DateTime, _
ByVal theSeverity As String)

    _bugID = theID
    _title = theTitle
    _reporter = theReporter
    _version = theVersion
    _description = theDescription
    _dateCreated = theDateCreated
    _severity = theSeverity
End Sub

Public ReadOnly Property BugID( ) As Int32
    Get
        BugID = _bugID
    End Get
End Property

Public ReadOnly Property Title( ) As String
    Get
        Title = _title
    End Get
End Property

Public ReadOnly Property Reporter( ) As String
    Get
        Reporter = _reporter
    End Get
End Property

Public ReadOnly Property Product( ) As String
    Get
        Product = _product
    End Get
End Property

Public ReadOnly Property Version( ) As String
    Get
        Version = _version
    End Get
End Property
```

Example 10-10. Modified to handle footer and details page (VB.NET) (continued)

```
    Public ReadOnly Property Description( ) As String
        Get
            Description = _description
        End Get
    End Property

    Public ReadOnly Property DateCreated( ) As String
        Get
            DateCreated = _dateCreated
        End Get
    End Property

    Public ReadOnly Property Severity( ) As String
        Get
            Severity = _severity
        End Get
    End Property
End Class
```

Summary footer

To add the summary, you must tell the data grid to show its footer. This is set declaratively, as an attribute in the data grid declaration, as follows:

```
<form runat="server" ID="Form1">
    <asp:DataGrid id="dataGrid1"
        ShowFooter="True"
        FooterStyle-BackColor="Yellow"
```

To populate the footer you'll want to handle the ItemCreated event. This event is raised when an item in the data grid is created. You are particularly interested in the event that will be raised when the footer item is created, because you want to manipulate this item. For C#, you'll add an attribute to the DataGrid declaration for this event, just as you did for the ItemDataBound event. Here is the complete declaration of the data grid:

```
<asp:DataGrid id="dataGrid1"
OnItemDataBound="OnItemDataBoundEventHandler"
OnItemCreated="OnItemCreatedEventHandler"
AutoGenerateColumns="False"
CellPadding="5"
HeaderStyle-BackColor="Yellow"
BorderWidth="5px"
BorderColor="#000099"
AlternatingItemStyle-BackColor="LightGrey"
HeaderStyle-Font-Bold="True"
ShowFooter="True"
FooterStyle-BackColor="Yellow"
runat="server">
```

In VB.NET, you do not add this attribute, but you do add the event handler, as you do in C#. The first step is to check that the item is of type ListItemFooter. If so, then you want to remove all the cells in the footer except one, and set that cell's span to encompass the entire row. You'll then get the count of items in the grid and write a right-aligned message into the cell such as 4 bugs, thus displaying the message in the lower righthand corner of the grid.

ASP.NET has provided a programmatic interface to the attributes of the table cell in the DataGrid. This is just as if you had access to the <td> element and set its attributes accordingly, but you can do so dynamically at runtime, rather than statically at design time.

The event handler signature is just like the OnItemDataBoundEventHandler signature: it takes two parameters and returns void (or in VB.NET it is a Sub procedure). The parameters must be an Object and a DataGridItemEventArgs object, as shown in the following prototype in C#:

```
public void OnItemCreatedEventHandler(
    Object sender, DataGridItemEventArgs e)
{
```

In VB.NET, you implement the event handler with code that indicates that you are handling the ItemCreated event:

```
Public Sub dataGrid1_OnItemCreatedEventHandler( _
        ByVal sender As System.Object, _
        ByVal e As System.Web.UI.WebControls.DataGridItemEventArgs) _
        Handles dataGrid1.ItemCreated
```

You'll test the item type of the current item so that you take action only on the footer item, which in C# looks like:

```
ListItemType itemType = (ListItemType)e.Item.ItemType;
if (itemType == ListItemType.Footer)
{
```

And in VB.NET is:

```
Dim itemType As ListItemType
itemType = e.Item.ItemType
If itemType = ListItemType.Footer Then
```

You can determine the number of cells in the grid dynamically by asking the item for its Cells collection, which has a Count property. Once you know how many cells you have, you can remove all but one by calling the Cells collection's RemoveAt method, repeatedly removing the first cell until every one but the last has been removed. In C#, this looks like:

```
int numberOfCells = e.Item.Cells.Count;

// remove all the cells except the last
for (int i = 0; i < numberOfCells - 1; i++)
{
    e.Item.Cells.RemoveAt(0);
}
```

And in VB.NET:

```
Dim numberOfCells As Integer
numberOfCells = e.Item.Cells.Count

Dim i As Integer
For i = 0 To numberOfCells - 2
    e.Item.Cells.RemoveAt(0)
Next
```

You next ask the data grid for its Items collection, which you will remember is a collection of all the items in the grid. You can use the Count property of that collection to determine how many items there are in the entire grid, and formulate your output message accordingly:

```
int numberOfBugs = dataGrid1.Items.Count;
string msg;
if (numberOfBugs > 0 )
{
    msg = "<b>" + numberOfBugs.ToString( )
        + " bugs.</b>";
}
else
{
    msg = "No bugs found.";
}
```

In VB.NET, the code is:

```
Dim numberOfBugs As Integer = dataGrid1.Items.Count
Dim msg As String
If numberOfBugs > 0 Then
    msg = "<b>" & numberOfBugs.ToString & " bugs.</b>"
Else
    msg = "No bugs found"
End If
```

You are now ready to display the message in the cell. You obtain the TableCell object as you did in the previous example. The only remaining cell is the very first cell in the collection. You set that cell's Text property to the message you've created, and set its ColumnSpan property to the total number of cells that were in the row before you removed all the others. You then set the HorizontalAlign property to the enumerated value Right:

```
TableCell msgCell = e.Item.Cells[0];
msgCell.Text = msg;
msgCell.ColumnSpan=numberOfCells;
msgCell.HorizontalAlign = HorizontalAlign.Right;
```

The VB.NET code is:

```
Dim msgCell As TableCell
msgCell = e.Item.Cells(0)
msgCell.Text = msg
msgCell.ColumnSpan = numberOfCells
msgCell.HorizontalAlign = HorizontalAlign.Right
```

The result is to display the number of rows in the grid in the lower righthand side of the footer row, as shown in Figure 10-3.

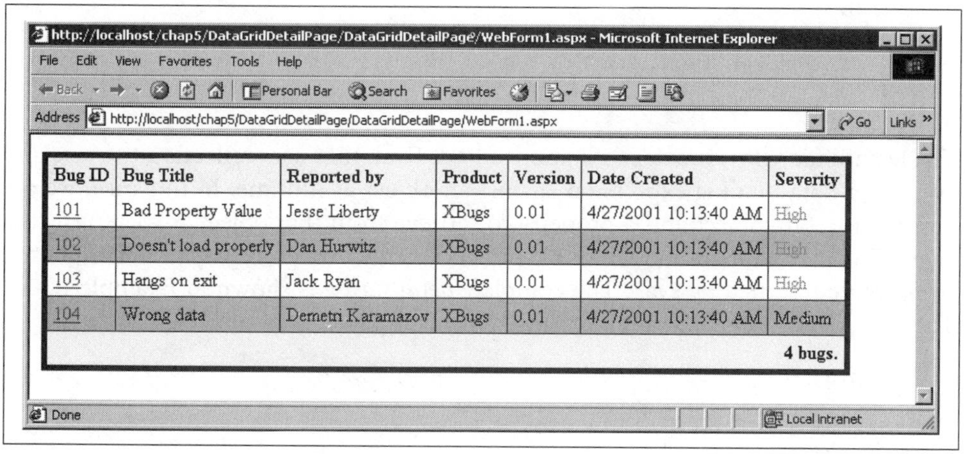

Figure 10-3. Summary in footer row

Creating the details page

In the previous example you created a link to the details page, but you did not implement that page. To do so, you'll create a new *.aspx* page, *details.aspx*, which will have a fairly simple table to display the details of the bug, as shown in Figure 10-4.

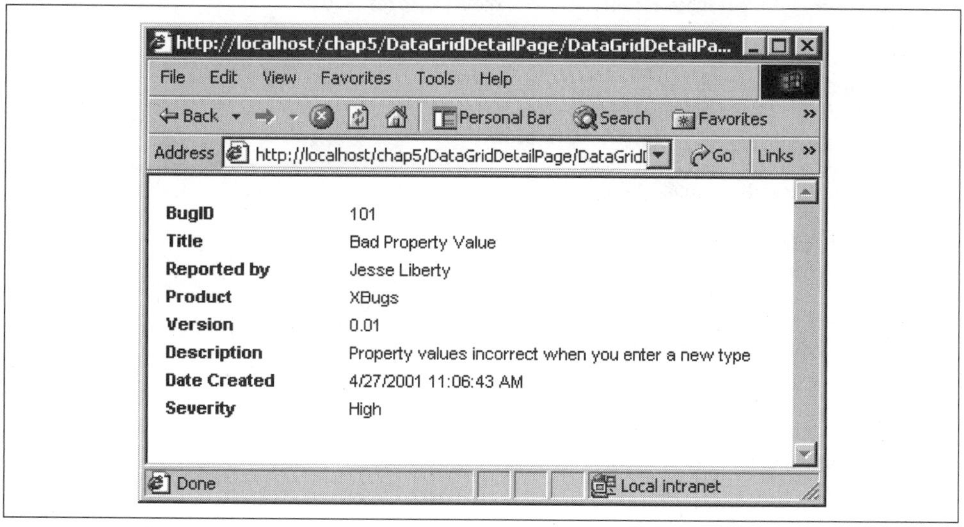

Figure 10-4. The details page

Each row will have two cells, one with a label in boldface, and the second with the data from the Bug object. The following code in the *.aspx* page creates a row:

```
<TR>
  <TD  width="30%">
    <b>BugID</b>
  </TD>
  <TD align=left>
    <%# DataBinder.Eval(CurrentBug, "BugID") %>
  </TD>
</TR>
```

The DataBinder class provides a static method, Eval, that uses reflection to parse and evaluate a data binding expression against an object at runtime. In this case, we are passing in a Bug object and a property to retrieve from that object; Eval returns the value. The <%# syntax in the ASP.NET page binds the text to display in the cell to the string value returned by Eval. The complete *details.aspx* is shown in Example 10-11. The subsequent rows have been collapsed to save space.

Example 10-11. details.aspx

```
<%@ Page language="c#"
Codebehind="details.aspx.cs"
AutoEventWireup="false"
Inherits="DataGridMasterDetailNew.details" %>

<HTML>
<HEAD>
    <meta name="GENERATOR" Content="Microsoft Visual Studio 7.0">
    <meta name="CODE_LANGUAGE" Content="C#">
    <meta name=vs_defaultClientScript content="JScript">
    <meta name=vs_targetSchema content="Internet Explorer 5.0">
</HEAD>
<body MS_POSITIONING="GridLayout">
<form id="details" method="post" runat="server">
<asp:Panel ID="BugDetailsPanel" Runat="server">
  <TABLE style="FONT-SIZE: 8pt; COLOR: black;
  FONT-FAMILY: Arial" cellSpacing=0
  cellPadding=2 width="100%" border=0>
    <TR>
        <TD  width="30%">
            <b>BugID</b>
        </TD>
        <TD align=left>
            <%# DataBinder.Eval(CurrentBug, "BugID") %>
        </TD>
    </TR>
    <tr><td><b>Title</b></td>
        <td><%# DataBinder.Eval(CurrentBug,"Title") %></td>
    </tr>
    <tr><td><b>Reported by</b></td>
        <td><%# DataBinder.Eval(CurrentBug,"Reporter") %></td>
    </tr><tr><td><b>Product</b></td>
        <td><%# DataBinder.Eval(CurrentBug,"Product") %></td>
    </tr>
    <tr><td><b>Version</b></td>
```

Example 10-11. details.aspx (continued)

```
        <td><%# DataBinder.Eval(CurrentBug,"Version") %></td>
    </tr>
    <tr><td><b>Description</b></td>
        <td><%# DataBinder.Eval(CurrentBug,"Description") %></td>
    </tr>
    <tr><td><b>Date Created</b></td>
        <td><%# DataBinder.Eval(CurrentBug,"DateCreated") %></td>
    </tr>
    <tr><td><b>Severity</b></td>
        <td><%# DataBinder.Eval(CurrentBug,"Severity") %></td>
    </tr>
  </TABLE>
</asp:Panel>
</form>
</body>
</HTML>
```

The page works only if the CurrentBug value is set properly. This is done in the code-behind page, specifically in the Page_Load method. Page_Load retrieves the Request. QueryString collection, which contains all the query strings passed in with the URL.

When you write a URL and append a question mark (?), the string elements that follow the question mark are considered to be query strings. Thus, if you write the URL as:

```
details.aspx?bugID=101
```

the first part, *details.aspx*, will be treated as the URL and the second part, bugID=101, will be considered the query string.

The complete C# source for the code-behind page for *details.aspx* is shown in C# in Example 10-12 and in VB.NET in 10-13.

Example 10-12. Code behind for details.aspx in C#

```
using System;
using System.Collections;
using System.ComponentModel;
using System.Data;
using System.Drawing;
using System.Web;
using System.Web.SessionState;
using System.Web.UI;
using System.Web.UI.WebControls;
using System.Web.UI.HtmlControls;

namespace DataGridMasterDetailNew
{
  public class details : System.Web.UI.Page
  {
      private object currentBug;
      protected System.Web.UI.WebControls.Panel BugDetailsPanel;
```

Example 10-12. Code behind for details.aspx in C# (continued)

```csharp
      public object CurrentBug { get { return currentBug; } }

   public details()
   {
     Page.Init += new System.EventHandler(Page_Init);
   }

   private void Page_Load(object sender, System.EventArgs e)
   {
       string bugID = Request.QueryString["BugID"];
       if (bugID != null)
       {
          SetCurrentBug(Convert.ToInt32(bugID));
          BugDetailsPanel.DataBind();
       }
   }

     private void SetCurrentBug(int bugID)
     {
       ArrayList bugs = (ArrayList) Session["bugList"];
       foreach (Bug theBug in bugs)
       {
          if(theBug.BugID == bugID)
             currentBug = theBug;
       }

     }
   private void Page_Init(object sender, EventArgs e)
   {
     InitializeComponent();
   }

   #region Web Form Designer generated code
   /// <summary>
   /// Required method for Designer support - do not modify
   /// the contents of this method with the code editor.
   /// </summary>
   private void InitializeComponent()
   {
       this.Load += new System.EventHandler(this.Page_Load);

   }
   #endregion
  }
}
```

Example 10-13. Code behind for details.aspx in VB.NET

```vb
Public Class details
   Inherits System.Web.UI.Page
   Protected BugDetailsPanel As System.Web.UI.WebControls.Panel
```

Example 10-13. Code behind for details.aspx in VB.NET (continued)

```
#Region " Web Form Designer Generated Code "

    'This call is required by the Web Form Designer.
    <System.Diagnostics.DebuggerStepThrough()> Private Sub InitializeComponent( )

    End Sub

    Private Sub Page_Init( _
    ByVal sender As System.Object, ByVal e As System.EventArgs) _
    Handles MyBase.Init
        InitializeComponent( )
    End Sub

#End Region

    Private Sub Page_Load( _
        ByVal sender As System.Object, _
        ByVal e As System.EventArgs) _
        Handles MyBase.Load

        Dim bugID As String
        bugID = Request.QueryString("BugID")
        If bugID <> "" Then
           SetCurrentBug(CInt(bugID))
           BugDetailsPanel.DataBind( )
        End If
    End Sub

    Private Sub SetCurrentBug(ByVal bugID As Int32)
        Dim bugs As ArrayList
        bugs = Session("bugList")
        Dim theBug As Bug
        For Each theBug In bugs
           If theBug.BugID = bugID Then
              _currentBug = theBug
           End If
        Next
    End Sub

    Private _currentBug As Object

    Public ReadOnly Property CurrentBug( ) As Object
        Get
            CurrentBug = _currentBug
        End Get
    End Property

End Class
```

ASP.NET wraps the HTTP request in a Request object (familiar to ASP programmers) and makes this object available to your methods. The Request object has a

QueryString property to retrieve the query strings. The QueryString property returns a NameValueCollection that can be treated like an array indexed on strings. Thus, you can retrieve the bugID queryString value (101) with this line of code:

```
string bugID = Request.QueryString["BugID"];
```

Or, in VB.NET:

```
Dim bugID As String
bugID = Request.QueryString("BugID")
```

If the bugID is not null, you will set a private variable, CurrentBug, to the value extracted (e.g., 101) and bind the data for display in the details page. In C#, the private variable CurrentBug is an int. In VB.NET, the private variable is an Integer named _currentBug. The value retrieved from Request.QueryString is a string, and so must be converted to an int, an operation performed by the following C# code fragment:

```
if (bugID != null)
{
    SetCurrentBug(Convert.ToInt32(bugID));
    BugDetailsPanel.DataBind();
}
```

In VB.NET, the equivalent is:

```
If bugID <> "" Then
    SetCurrentBug(CInt(bugID))
    BugDetailsPanel.DataBind()
End If
```

The private method SetCurrentBug is responsible for setting the private variable currentBug (_curentBug). In the example, it does so by iterating over the Bug objects in the ArrayList and finding the matching bug:

```
private void SetCurrentBug(int bugID)
{
    ArrayList bugs = (ArrayList) Session["bugList"];
    foreach (Bug theBug in bugs)
    {
        if(theBug.BugID == bugID)
            currentBug = theBug;
    }
}
```

In VB.NET:

```
Private Sub SetCurrentBug(ByVal bugID As Integer)
    Dim bugs As ArrayList
    bugs = Session("bugList")
    Dim theBug As Bug
    For Each theBug In bugs
        If theBug.BugID = bugID Then
            _currentBug = theBug
        End If
    Next
End Sub
```

Because currentBug is a private variable, it is not available to the dataGrid. You will therefore create a CurrentBug property that returns the value of currentBug:

```
public object CurrentBug {get {return currentBug;}}
```

In VB.NET:

```
Public ReadOnly Property CurrentBug() As Object
    Get
        CurrentBug = _currentBug
    End Get
End Property
```

 C# is case-sensitive, and so the name for the variable (currentBug) and the property (CurrentBug) are not considered to be the same. The property is in Pascal Notation (initial cap), and the name for the variable is in camel Notation (initial not capitalized).

VB.NET is not case-sensitive, so you use an underscore in front of the variable name.

Version 4: Sorting and Paging

In the next version of this program, you'll integrate the details panel into the page with the DataGrid, and you'll add the ability to sort the columns, as well as to page through the results.

Results on one page

In the previous version, you created a panel to hold the details and displayed that panel in a second *.aspx* page. In this version, you will paste that entire panel, and all the code created within the panel, into the same *.aspx* page as the data grid.

You will remember that the data grid page ends with this HTML:

```
    </form>
  </body>
</html>
```

Just after the close form tag, </form>, and before the close body tag, </body>, insert the panel from the details page. Hey! Presto! When you click on the details, they'll show in the panel (once you modify the code a bit). The complete *.aspx* page is shown in Example 10-14.

Example 10-14. .aspx page for sorting and paging

```
<%@ Page language="c#" Codebehind="WebForm1.aspx.cs" AutoEventWireup="false"
Inherits="DataGridDetailsInPage.WebForm1" %>
<!DOCTYPE HTML PUBLIC "-//W3C//DTD HTML 4.0 Transitional//EN" >

<html>
  <head>
    <meta name="GENERATOR" Content="Microsoft Visual Studio 7.0">
```

Example 10-14. .aspx page for sorting and paging (continued)

```
    <meta name="CODE_LANGUAGE" Content="C#">
    <meta name=vs_defaultClientScript content="JavaScript (ECMAScript)">
    <meta name=vs_targetSchema content="http://schemas.microsoft.com/intellisense/ie5">
  </head>
<body MS_POSITIONING="GridLayout">

    <form runat="server" ID="Form1">
    <asp:DataGrid id="dataGrid1"
    OnItemDataBound="OnItemDataBoundEventHandler"
     OnItemCreated ="OnItemCreatedEventHandler"
     OnSelectedIndexChanged="OnSelectedIndexChangedHandler"
     OnSortCommand="OnSortCommandHandler"
     OnPageIndexChanged ="OnPageIndexChangedHandler"
       AllowPaging="True"
     PageSize ="2"
     AllowSorting="True"
    AutoGenerateColumns="False"
    CellPadding="5"
    HeaderStyle-BackColor="Yellow"
    BorderWidth="5px"
    BorderColor="#000099"
    AlternatingItemStyle-BackColor="LightGrey"
    HeaderStyle-Font-Bold="True"
     ShowFooter="True"
     FooterStyle-BackColor="Yellow"
     DataKeyField="bugID"
    runat="server">

       <PagerStyle
       HorizontalAlign="Right"
       Mode="NextPrev">
       </PagerStyle>

      <Columns>
        <asp:ButtonColumn Text="Details" CommandName="Select"  />

        <asp:BoundColumn
        HeaderText="Title"
         DataField="Title"
         SortExpression="Title"
        />

        <asp:BoundColumn
        HeaderText="Reported by"
        Datafield="Reporter"
        SortExpression="Reporter"
        />


        <asp:BoundColumn DataField="Product" HeaderText="Product" />
        <asp:BoundColumn DataField="Version" HeaderText="Version" />
```

Example 10-14. .aspx page for sorting and paging (continued)

```
            <asp:BoundColumn
            HeaderText="Date Created"
            DataField="DateCreated"
            SortExpression="DateCreated"
            />

            <asp:BoundColumn DataField="Severity" HeaderText="Severity" />
        </Columns>
      </asp:DataGrid>
    </form>
<asp:Panel ID="BugDetailsPanel" Runat="server">
<TABLE style="FONT-SIZE: 8pt; COLOR: black; FONT-FAMILY: Arial" cellSpacing=0
cellPadding=2 width="100%" border=0>
  <TR>
    <TD width="15%"><B>BugID</B> </TD>
    <TD align=left><%# DataBinder.Eval(currentBug, "BugID") %></TD></TR>
  <TR>
    <TD><B>Title</B></TD>
    <TD><%# DataBinder.Eval(currentBug,"Title") %></TD></TR>
  <TR>
    <TD><B>Reported by</B></TD>
    <TD><%# DataBinder.Eval(currentBug,"Reporter") %></TD></TR>
  <TR>
    <TD><B>Product</B></TD>
    <TD><%# DataBinder.Eval(currentBug,"Product") %></TD></TR>
  <TR>
    <TD><B>Version</B></TD>
    <TD><%# DataBinder.Eval(currentBug,"Version") %></TD></TR>
  <TR>
    <TD><B>Description</B></TD>
    <TD><%# DataBinder.Eval(currentBug,"Description") %></TD></TR>
  <TR>
    <TD><B>Date Created</B></TD>
    <TD><%# DataBinder.Eval(currentBug,"DateCreated") %></TD></TR>
  <TR>
    <TD><B>Severity</B></TD>
    <TD><%# DataBinder.Eval(currentBug,"Severity") %></TD></TR></TABLE>
</asp:Panel>

  </body>

</html>
```

If you are building a VB.NET application, remove the following event
handlers from the data grid:

```
OnItemDataBound="OnItemDataBoundEventHandler"
OnItemCreated ="OnItemCreatedEventHandler"
OnSelectedIndexChanged="OnSelectedIndexChangedHandler"
OnSortCommand="OnSortCommandHandler"
OnPageIndexChanged = "OnPageIndexChangedHandler"
```

The complete source code for the C# version is shown in Example 10-15, and the VB.NET version is in Example 10-16.

Example 10-15. C# code-behind file for paging and sorting

```csharp
using System;
using System.Collections;
using System.ComponentModel;
using System.Data;
using System.Drawing;
using System.Web;
using System.Web.SessionState;
using System.Web.UI;
using System.Web.UI.WebControls;
using System.Web.UI.HtmlControls;

namespace DataGridDetailsInPage
{
    public class WebForm1 : System.Web.UI.Page
    {
        protected object currentBug;

        protected System.Web.UI.WebControls.DataGrid
            dataGrid1;
        protected System.Web.UI.WebControls.Panel
            BugDetailsPanel;

        public WebForm1( )
        {
            Page.Init += new System.EventHandler(Page_Init);
        }

        private void Page_Load(
            object sender, System.EventArgs e)
        {
            if (!IsPostBack)
            {
                BindGrid( );
                UpdateBugDetails( );
            }
        }

        private void Page_Init(object sender, EventArgs e)
        {
            InitializeComponent( );
        }

        // Property: which column is sorted
        protected string SortColumn
        {
            get
            {
                object o = ViewState["SortColumn"];
```

Example 10-15. C# code-behind file for paging and sorting (continued)

```
            if (o != null)
            {
                return (string) o;
            }
            return "Title"; // default
        }
        set
        {
            ViewState["SortColumn"] = value;
        }
    }

    // Property: are we sorting ascending (true)
    // or descending (false)
    protected bool SortAscend
    {
        get
        {
            object o = ViewState["SortAscend"];
            if (o != null)
                return (bool)o;
            return true; // default
        }
        set
        {
            ViewState["SortAscend"] = value;
        }
    }

    // handle new page request
    public void OnPageIndexChangedHandler(
        Object sender,
        DataGridPageChangedEventArgs e)
    {
        // set the new index
        dataGrid1.CurrentPageIndex = e.NewPageIndex;

        // rebind the data
        BindGrid();
        UpdateBugDetails();
    }

    // when a sort field title is clicked
    public void OnSortCommandHandler(
        Object sender,
        DataGridSortCommandEventArgs e)
    {
        // find out the current column being sorted
        string currentSortColumn = SortColumn;

        // set the property to the requested column
        SortColumn = e.SortExpression;
```

Example 10-15. C# code-behind file for paging and sorting (continued)

```
      // if the same column is clicked
      // reverse the sort
      if (currentSortColumn == SortColumn)
      {
         SortAscend = !SortAscend;
      }
      else  // otherwise sort ascending
      {
         SortAscend = true;
      }

      // rebind the data (sorted)
      BindGrid( );
      UpdateBugDetails( );
   }

   public void OnItemCreatedEventHandler(
      Object sender,
      DataGridItemEventArgs e)
   {
      ListItemType itemType =
         (ListItemType)e.Item.ItemType;

      if (itemType == ListItemType.Header)
      {
         Label sortSymbol = new Label( );
         sortSymbol.Text = SortAscend ? "5" : "6";
         sortSymbol.Font.Name = "Webdings";

         TableCell theCell = null;
         switch (SortColumn)
         {
            case "Title":
               theCell = e.Item.Cells[1];
               break;
            case "Reporter":
               theCell = e.Item.Cells[2];
               break;
            case "DateCreated":
               theCell = e.Item.Cells[5];
               break;
         }
         if (theCell != null)
            theCell.Controls.Add(sortSymbol);
      }

   }

   // the user has selected a row
   public void OnSelectedIndexChangedHandler(
      Object sender, EventArgs e)
```

Example 10-15. C# code-behind file for paging and sorting (continued)

```csharp
    {
        UpdateBugDetails( );
    }

    // If the user has selected a row
    // display the details panel
    private void UpdateBugDetails( )
    {
        // find out which bug selected
        UpdateSelectedBug( );

        // if there is a selected bug
        // display the details
        if (currentBug != null)
        {
            BugDetailsPanel.Visible=true;
            BugDetailsPanel.DataBind( );
        }
        else
        {
            BugDetailsPanel.Visible=false;
        }
    }

    // compare the selected row with
    // the array list of bugs
    // return the selected bug
    private void UpdateSelectedBug( )
    {
        int index = dataGrid1.SelectedIndex;
        currentBug = null;
        if (index != -1)
        {

            // get the bug id from the data grid
            int bugID = (int) dataGrid1.DataKeys[index];

            // recreate the arraylist from the session state
            ArrayList bugs = (ArrayList) Session["bugList"];

            // find the bug with the selected bug id
            foreach (Bug theBug in bugs)
            {
                if(theBug.BugID == bugID)
                    currentBug = theBug;
            }

        }
    }

    // when items are bound to the grid
    // examine them and set high status to red
```

Example 10-15. C# code-behind file for paging and sorting (continued)

```csharp
public void OnItemDataBoundEventHandler(
    Object sender, DataGridItemEventArgs e)
{

    // Don't bother for header, footer and separator items
    ListItemType itemType = (ListItemType)e.Item.ItemType;
    if (itemType == ListItemType.Header ||
        itemType == ListItemType.Footer ||
        itemType == ListItemType.Separator)
        return;

    // e.Item.DataItem is the data for the item
    Bug bug = (Bug)e.Item.DataItem;

    // check the severity for this item
    // if it is high, set the cell to red
    if (bug.Severity == "High")
    {
        // this would make the entire entry red
        //   e.Item.ForeColor = Color.FromName("red");

        // get just the cell we want
        TableCell severityCell = (TableCell)e.Item.Controls[6];

        // set that cell's forecolor to red
        severityCell.ForeColor = Color.FromName("Red");
    }

}

// create the bugs
// add them to the array list
// bind the data grid to the array list
void BindGrid()
{

    DateTime d1 = new DateTime(2002,7,10,13,14,15);
    DateTime d2 = new DateTime(2002,7,4,12,55,03);
    DateTime d3 = new DateTime(2002,8,5,13,12,07);
    DateTime d4 = new DateTime(2002,12,16,12,33,05);
    ArrayList bugs = new ArrayList();

    bugs.Add(
        new Bug(
        101,
        "Bad Property Value",
        "Jesse Liberty",
        "XBugs",
        "0.01",
        "Property values incorrect when you enter a new type",
        d1,
        "High")
```

Example 10-15. C# code-behind file for paging and sorting (continued)

```
        );

    bugs.Add(
        new Bug(
        102,
        "Doesn't load properly",
        "Dan Hurwitz",
        "XBugs",
        "0.01",
        "The system fails on load with error x2397",
        d2,
        "High")
        );

    bugs.Add(
        new Bug(
        103,
        "Hangs on exit",
        "Jack Ryan",
        "XBugs",
        "0.01",
        "When you press close, it hangs",
        d3,
        "High")
        );

    bugs.Add(
        new Bug(
        104,
        "Wrong data",
        "Demetri Karamazov",
        "XBugs",
        "0.01",
        "The data does not match the DB",
        d4,
        "Medium")
        );


    Bug.BugComparer c = Bug.GetComparer( );
    c.WhichField = SortColumn;
    c.Ascending = SortAscend;
    bugs.Sort(c);

    dataGrid1.DataSource=bugs;
    dataGrid1.DataBind( );
    Session["bugList"] = bugs;

}

#region Web Form Designer generated code
    /// <summary>
```

Example 10-15. C# code-behind file for paging and sorting (continued)

```csharp
        /// Required method for Designer support - do not modify
        /// the contents of this method with the code editor.
        /// </summary>
        private void InitializeComponent()
        {
            this.Load += new System.EventHandler(this.Page_Load);

        }
    #endregion
}


// The bug class.
// Implements IComparable for sorting
// Has nested IComparer class
public class Bug : IComparable
{
    private int bugID;
    private string title;
    private string reporter;
    private string product;
    private string version;
    private string description;
    private DateTime dateCreated;
    private string severity;

    public Bug(int id, string title, string reporter,
        string product, string version,
        string description, DateTime dateCreated,
        string severity)
    {
        bugID = id;
        this.title = title;
        this.reporter = reporter;
        this.product = product;
        this.version = version;
        this.description = description;
        this.dateCreated = dateCreated;
        this.severity = severity;
    }

    // static method returns dedicated IComparer
    public static BugComparer GetComparer()
    {
        return new Bug.BugComparer();
    }

    // implementing IComparable
    public int CompareTo(Object rhs)
    {
        Bug r = (Bug) rhs;
        return this.title.CompareTo(r.title);
    }
```

Example 10-15. C# code-behind file for paging and sorting (continued)

```csharp
// dedicated method for BugComparer to use
public int CompareTo(
    Bug rhs, string field, bool ascending)
{
    switch (field)
    {
        case "Title":
            if (ascending)
                return this.title.CompareTo(rhs.title);
            else
            {
                int retVal =
                    this.title.CompareTo(rhs.title);
                switch (retVal)
                {
                    case 1:
                        return -1;
                    case -1:
                        return 1;
                    default:
                        return 0;
                }
            }
        case "Reporter":
            if (ascending)
                return this.Reporter.CompareTo(
                    rhs.Reporter);
            else
            {
                int retVal = this.Reporter.CompareTo(
                    rhs.Reporter);
                switch (retVal)
                {
                    case 1:
                        return -1;
                    case -1:
                        return 1;
                    default:
                        return 0;
                }
            }

        case "BugID":
            if (this.bugID < rhs.BugID)
                return ascending ? -1 : 1;
            if (this.bugID > rhs.BugID)
                return ascending ? 1 : -1;
            return 0;
        case "DateCreated":
            if (this.dateCreated < rhs.dateCreated)
                return ascending ? -1 : 1;
```

Example 10-15. C# code-behind file for paging and sorting (continued)

```csharp
            if (this.dateCreated > rhs.dateCreated)
               return ascending ? 1 : -1;
            return 0;
      }
      return 0;
   }

   // nested specialized IComparer
   public class BugComparer : IComparer
   {
      public int Compare(object lhs, object rhs)
      {
         Bug l = (Bug) lhs;
         Bug r = (Bug) rhs;
         return l.CompareTo(r,whichField, ascending);
      }

      // Property: which field are we sorting
      public string WhichField
      {
         get
         {
            return whichField;
         }
         set
         {
            whichField=value;
         }
      }

      // Property: Ascending (true) or descending
      public bool Ascending
      {
         get
         {
            return ascending;
         }
         set
         {
            ascending = value;
         }

      }
      private string whichField;
      private bool ascending;
   }    // end nested class

   // Properties for Bugs
   public int      BugID       { get { return bugID;  }}
   public string   Title       { get { return title;  }}
   public string   Reporter    { get { return reporter; }}
   public string   Product     { get { return product;  }}
```

Example 10-15. C# code-behind file for paging and sorting (continued)

```
        public string     Version       { get { return version;     }}
        public string     Description   { get { return description; }}
        public DateTime   DateCreated   { get { return dateCreated; }}
        public string     Severity      { get { return severity;    }}

    }

}
```

Example 10-16. VB.NET code-behind file for paging and sorting

```
Public Class WebForm1
    Inherits System.Web.UI.Page
    Protected WithEvents dataGrid1 As System.Web.UI.WebControls.DataGrid
    Protected BugDetailsPanel As System.Web.UI.WebControls.Panel

#Region " Web Form Designer Generated Code "

    'This call is required by the Web Form Designer.
    <System.Diagnostics.DebuggerStepThrough()> Private Sub InitializeComponent( )

    End Sub

    Private Sub Page_Init(ByVal sender As System.Object, _
    ByVal e As System.EventArgs) _
    Handles MyBase.Init
        InitializeComponent( )
    End Sub

#End Region
    Private _currentBug As Object

    Private Sub Page_Load( _
    ByVal sender As System.Object, _
    ByVal e As System.EventArgs) _
    Handles MyBase.Load

        If Not IsPostBack Then
            BindGrid( )
            UpdateBugDetails( )
        End If
    End Sub

    Private Sub UpdateBugDetails( )
        UpdateSelectedBug( )
        If Not _currentBug Is Nothing Then
            BugDetailsPanel.Visible = True
            BugDetailsPanel.DataBind( )
        Else
            BugDetailsPanel.Visible = False
        End If
    End Sub
```

Example 10-16. VB.NET code-behind file for paging and sorting (continued)

```
Protected Property SortColumn( ) As String
    Get
        Dim o As Object
        o = ViewState("SortColumn")
        If Not o Is Nothing Then
            SortColumn = CStr(o)
        End If
    End Get
    Set(ByVal Value As String)
        ViewState("SortColumn") = Value
    End Set
End Property

Protected Property SortAscend( ) As Boolean
    Get
        Dim o As Object
        o = ViewState("SortAscend")
        If Not o Is Nothing Then
            SortAscend = CBool(o)
        End If

    End Get
    Set(ByVal Value As Boolean)
        ViewState("SortAscend") = Value
    End Set
End Property

Public ReadOnly Property CurrentBug( ) As Object
    Get
        CurrentBug = _currentBug
    End Get
End Property

Private Sub UpdateSelectedBug( )
    Dim index As Int32
    index = dataGrid1.SelectedIndex
    _currentBug = Nothing
    If index <> -1 Then
        Dim bugID As Int32
        bugID = dataGrid1.DataKeys(index)
        Dim bugs As ArrayList
        bugs = Session("bugList")
        Dim theBug As Bug
        For Each theBug In bugs
            If theBug.BugID = bugID Then
                _currentBug = theBug
            End If
        Next
    End If
End Sub
```

Example 10-16. VB.NET code-behind file for paging and sorting (continued)

```
Public Sub BindGrid( )
    Dim bugs As New ArrayList( )
    bugs.Add(New Bug(101, _
        "BadProperty Value", _
        "Jesse Liberty", _
        "XBugs", _
        "0.01", _
        "Property values incorrect", _
        DateTime.Now, _
        "High") _
    )
    bugs.Add( _
        New Bug( _
        102, _
        "Doesn't load properly", _
        "Dan Hurwitz", _
        "XBugs", _
        "0.01", _
        "The system fails with error x2397", _
        DateTime.Now, _
        "Medium") _
    )

    bugs.Add( _
        New Bug( _
        103, _
        "Hangs on exit", _
        "Jack Ryan", _
        "XBugs", _
        "0.01", _
        "When you press close, it hangs", _
        DateTime.Now, _
        "High") _
        )

    bugs.Add( _
        New Bug( _
        104, _
        "Wrong data", _
        "Demetri Karamazov", _
        "XBugs", _
        "0.01", _
        "The data does not match the DB", _
        DateTime.Now, _
        "Medium") _
        )

    Dim c As Bug.BugComparer = Bug.GetComparer( )
    c.WhichField = SortColumn
    c.Ascending = SortAscend
    bugs.Sort(c)
```

Example 10-16. VB.NET code-behind file for paging and sorting (continued)

```
        dataGrid1.DataSource = bugs
        dataGrid1.DataBind( )
        Session("BugList") = bugs

    End Sub

    Public Sub dataGrid1_OnItemCreatedEventHandler( _
    ByVal sender As System.Object, _
    ByVal e As System.Web.UI.WebControls.DataGridItemEventArgs) _
    Handles dataGrid1.ItemCreated
        Dim itemType As ListItemType
        itemType = e.Item.ItemType

        If itemType = ListItemType.Header Then
            Dim sortSymbol As New Label( )
            If SortAscend = True Then
                sortSymbol.Text = "5"
            Else
                sortSymbol.Text = "6"
            End If
            sortSymbol.Font.Name = "Webdings"

            Dim theCell As TableCell
            theCell = Nothing
            Select Case SortColumn
                Case "Title"
                    theCell = e.Item.Cells(1)
                Case "Reporter"
                    theCell = e.Item.Cells(2)
                Case "DateCreated"
                    theCell = e.Item.Cells(5)
            End Select
            ''If SortColumn = "Title" Then
            ''    theCell = e.Item.Cells(1)
            ''End If
            ''If SortColumn = "Reporter" Then
            ''    theCell = e.Item.Cells(2)
            ''End If
            ''If SortColumn = "DateCreated" Then
            ''    theCell = e.Item.Cells(5)
            ''End If
            If Not theCell Is Nothing Then
                theCell.Controls.Add(sortSymbol)
            End If

        End If
    End Sub

    Public Sub dataGrid1_OnItemDataBoundEventHandler( _
    ByVal sender As System.Object, _
    ByVal e As System.Web.UI.WebControls.DataGridItemEventArgs) _
    Handles dataGrid1.ItemDataBound
```

Example 10-16. VB.NET code-behind file for paging and sorting (continued)

```
    Dim itemType As ListItemType
    itemType = e.Item.ItemType

    If itemType = ListItemType.Header Or _
    itemType = ListItemType.Footer Or _
    itemType = ListItemType.Separator Then
        Exit Sub
    End If

    Dim theBug As Bug
    theBug = e.Item.DataItem
    If theBug.Severity = "High" Then
        Dim severityCell As TableCell
        severityCell = e.Item.Controls(6)
        severityCell.ForeColor = Color.FromName("Red")
    End If

    ''Dim linkCell As TableCell
    ''linkCell = e.Item.Controls(0)
    ''Dim h As HyperLink
    ''h = linkCell.Controls(0)
    ''h.NavigateUrl = "details.aspx?bugID=" & theBug.BugID

End Sub

Private Sub dataGrid1_PageIndexChanged( _
ByVal source As Object, _
ByVal e As System.Web.UI.WebControls.DataGridPageChangedEventArgs) _
Handles dataGrid1.PageIndexChanged
    dataGrid1.CurrentPageIndex = e.NewPageIndex
    BindGrid()
    UpdateBugDetails()
End Sub

Private Sub dataGrid1_SortCommand( _
ByVal source As Object, _
ByVal e As System.Web.UI.WebControls.DataGridSortCommandEventArgs) _
Handles dataGrid1.SortCommand
    Dim currentSortColumn As String = SortColumn
    SortColumn = e.SortExpression
    If currentSortColumn = SortColumn Then
        If SortAscend = True Then
            SortAscend = False
        Else
            SortAscend = True
        End If
    Else
        SortAscend = True
    End If
    BindGrid()
    UpdateBugDetails()
```

Example 10-16. VB.NET code-behind file for paging and sorting (continued)

```
    End Sub

    Private Sub dataGrid1_SelectedIndexChanged(ByVal sender As Object, _
                                        ByVal e As System.EventArgs) _
                                        Handles dataGrid1.SelectedIndexChanged
        UpdateBugDetails()
    End Sub
End Class


Public Class Bug : Implements IComparable

    Private _bugID As Int32
    Private _title As String
    Private _reporter As String
    Private _product As String
    Private _version As String
    Private _description As String
    Private _dateCreated As DateTime
    Private _severity As String

    Sub New(ByVal theID As Int32, _
    ByVal theTitle As String, _
    ByVal theReporter As String, _
    ByVal theProduct As String, _
    ByVal theVersion As String, _
    ByVal theDescription As String, _
    ByVal theDateCreated As DateTime, _
    ByVal theSeverity As String)

        _bugID = theID
        _title = theTitle
        _reporter = theReporter
        _version = theVersion
        _description = theDescription
        _dateCreated = theDateCreated
        _severity = theSeverity
    End Sub

    '' nested class
    Public Class BugComparer
        Implements IComparer

        Dim _whichField As String
        Dim _ascending As Boolean

        Public Function Compare( _
        ByVal lhs As Object, ByVal rhs As Object) _
        As Integer _
        Implements IComparer.Compare
            Dim l As Bug
            Dim r As Bug
            l = lhs
```

Example 10-16. VB.NET code-behind file for paging and sorting (continued)

```
        r = rhs
        Compare = l.CompareTo(r, _whichField, _ascending)
    End Function

    Public Property WhichField( ) As String
       Get
          WhichField = _whichField
       End Get
       Set(ByVal Value As String)
          _whichField = Value
       End Set
    End Property

    Public Property Ascending( ) As Boolean
       Get
          Ascending = _ascending
       End Get
       Set(ByVal Value As Boolean)
          _ascending = Value
       End Set
    End Property
End Class    '' end nested class

Public Shared Function GetComparer( ) As BugComparer
   GetComparer = New Bug.BugComparer( )
End Function

Public Function CompareTo(ByVal rhs As Object) As Integer _
Implements IComparable.CompareTo
   Dim r As Bug = rhs
   CompareTo = Me.Title.CompareTo(r.Title)
End Function

Public Function CompareTo( _
ByVal rhs As Bug, _
ByVal field As String, _
ByVal ascending As Boolean) As Int32
   CompareTo = 0
   Select Case field
      Case "Title"
         If ascending = True Then
            CompareTo = Me.Title.CompareTo(rhs.Title)
         Else
            Dim retVal As Int32
            retVal = Me.Title.CompareTo(rhs.Title)
            If retVal = 1 Then CompareTo = -1
            If retVal = -1 Then CompareTo = 1
         End If
      Case "Reporter"
         If ascending = True Then
            CompareTo = Me.Reporter.CompareTo(rhs.Reporter)
         Else
```

Example 10-16. VB.NET code-behind file for paging and sorting (continued)

```
            Dim retVal As Int32
            retVal = Me.Title.CompareTo(rhs.Reporter)
            If retVal = 1 Then CompareTo = -1
            If retVal = -1 Then CompareTo = 1
         End If
      Case "BugID"
         If Me.BugID < rhs.BugID Then
            If ascending = True Then
               CompareTo = -1
            Else
               CompareTo = 1
            End If
         End If
         If Me.BugID > rhs.BugID Then
            If ascending = True Then
               CompareTo = 1
            Else
               CompareTo = -1
            End If
         End If
      Case "DateCreated"
         If Me.DateCreated < rhs.DateCreated Then
            If ascending = True Then
               CompareTo = -1
            Else
               CompareTo = 1
            End If
         End If
         If Me.DateCreated > rhs.DateCreated Then
            If ascending = True Then
               CompareTo = 1
            Else
               CompareTo = -1
            End If
         End If
   End Select
End Function

Public ReadOnly Property BugID( ) As Int32
   Get
      BugID = _bugID
   End Get
End Property

Public ReadOnly Property Title( ) As String
   Get
      Title = _title
   End Get
End Property

Public ReadOnly Property Reporter( ) As String
   Get
```

Example 10-16. VB.NET code-behind file for paging and sorting (continued)

```
        Reporter = _reporter
    End Get
End Property

Public ReadOnly Property Product( ) As String
    Get
        Product = _product
    End Get
End Property

Public ReadOnly Property Version( ) As String
    Get
        Version = _version
    End Get
End Property

Public ReadOnly Property Description( ) As String
    Get
        Description = _description
    End Get
End Property

Public ReadOnly Property DateCreated( ) As String
    Get
        DateCreated = _dateCreated
    End Get
End Property

Public ReadOnly Property Severity( ) As String
    Get
        Severity = _severity
    End Get
End Property

End Class
```

You don't want the panel to be displayed if the user has not requested details on any particular bug. You'll create a method, UpdateBugDetails, that will set the panel's Visible property to false until the user selects a bug. When a bug is selected, UpdateBugDetails will set the panel's Visible property to true, and the panel will appear below the DataGrid. The following code shows the source code for the UpdateBugDetails method:

```
private void UpdateBugDetails( )
{
    UpdateSelectedBug( );

    if (currentBug != null)
    {
        BugDetailsPanel.Visible=true;
        BugDetailsPanel.DataBind( );
```

```
    }
    else
    {
        BugDetailsPanel.Visible=false;
    }
}
```

In VB.NET, the code is:

```
Private Sub UpdateBugDetails( )
    UpdateSelectedBug( )
    If Not _currentBug Is Nothing Then
        BugDetailsPanel.Visible = True
        BugDetailsPanel.DataBind( )
    Else
        BugDetailsPanel.Visible = False
    End If
End Sub
```

UpdateBugDetails starts by calling UpdateSelectedBug, whose job is to set the currentBug member variable to the Bug object the user has chosen, or to null if no bug has been chosen.

UpdateBugDetails tests the currentBug and, if it is not null, it displays the details panel and binds the data. The call to the panel's DataBind method causes the panel to evaluate the currentBug properties and display them, as seen earlier.

To set the current bug, UpdateSelectedBug gets the SelectedIndex property from the DataGrid control. This value will be -1 if the user has not selected an item, or it will be the item id of the selected item. You use that item id as an index into the DataKeys collection of the DataGrid to extract the BugID of the bug represented by the selected row in the grid.

The DataKeys collection is created by adding a DataKeyField attribute to the Data-Grid declaration in your *.aspx* file:

```
DataKeyField="bugID"
```

When the data grid is created and Bug objects are added, the DataGrid creates a DataKeys collection, populating it with the bugID for each bug for each row.

With the bugID, you can iterate over the ArrayList that represents your data and find the matching bug.

The following is the C# source code for the UpdateSelectedBug function:

```
private void UpdateSelectedBug( )
{
    int index = dataGrid1.SelectedIndex;
    currentBug = null;
    if (index != -1)
    {
        // get the bug id from the data grid
        int bugID = (int) dataGrid1.DataKeys[index];
```

```
    // recreate the arraylist from the session state
    ArrayList bugs = (ArrayList) Session["bugList"];

    // find the bug with the selected bug id
    foreach (Bug theBug in bugs)
    {
        if(theBug.BugID == bugID)
            currentBug = theBug;
    }
    }
}
```

In VB.NET, the code is:

```
Private Sub UpdateSelectedBug( )
    Dim index As Int32
    index = dataGrid1.SelectedIndex
    _currentBug = Nothing
    If index <> -1 Then
        Dim bugID As Int32
        bugID = dataGrid1.DataKeys(index)
        Dim bugs As ArrayList
        bugs = Session("bugList")
        Dim theBug As Bug
        For Each theBug In bugs
            If theBug.BugID = bugID Then
                _currentBug = theBug
            End If
        Next
    End If
End Sub
```

You also need to add the currentBug field to your class, along with its property:

```
private object currentBug;
public object CurrentBug { get { return currentBug;}}
```

In VB.NET, the equivalent is:

```
Private _currentBug As Object
Public ReadOnly Property CurrentBug( ) As Object
    Get
        CurrentBug = _currentBug
    End Get
End Property
```

Now that you can display the details of the bug on the same page as the data grid, let's take a look at how you sort the columns in the grid. To start, you must add a couple of attributes to the data grid itself:

```
AllowSorting="True"
OnSortCommand="OnSortCommandHandler"
```

The first tells the DataGrid to allow columns to be sorted, the second creates an event handler for the Sort command event. The Sort command event is fired by the user clicking on the header of a sortable column. You mark a column as sortable by adding a few attributes to the BoundColumn tag:

```
<asp:BoundColumn DataField="Title"
HeaderText="Title"
SortExpression="Title"
/>
```

HeaderText sets (or gets) the text displayed in the column header. DataField, as seen earlier, gets or sets the field in the data item to which this column will be bound.

SortExpression sets (or gets) the field to pass to the OnSortCommand method when a column is selected. By setting the SortExpression, the DataGrid knows to display the header as a link. Clicking on the link fires the SortCommand event, passing in the designated field.

Implementing the OnSortCommand event handler

The OnSortCommand event handler must evaluate whether the user has clicked on the currently selected column or another column. When a user clicks on a column, the items in that column are sorted. If the user clicks on the currently selected column, however, then the column is sorted in reverse order. That is, if you click on Title, the titles are sorted alphabetically in ascending order, but if you click on Title again, then the titles are sorted in descending order.

To manage this, you will create a property of the form named SortColumn, which will be responsible for knowing the currently selected column. This property will need to store the selection in view state so that the current selection will survive a round trip to the server. The C# code for the SortColumn property is:

```
protected string SortColumn
{
   get
   {
      object o = ViewState["SortColumn"];
      if (o != null)
      {
         return (string) o;
      }
         return "Title"; // default
   }
   set
   {
      ViewState["SortColumn"] = value;
   }
}
```

The VB.NET version is:

```
Protected Property SortColumn() As String
      Get
          Dim o As Object
```

```
        o = ViewState("SortColumn")
        If Not o Is Nothing Then
            SortColumn = CStr(o)
        End If
    End Get
    Set(ByVal Value As String)
        ViewState("SortColumn") = Value
    End Set
End Property
```

The logic of this property's Get method is to retrieve the value from view state. View state returns an object, as explained in Chapter 4. If that object is not null, you cast it to a string and return the string as the property; otherwise, you return Title as a default value for the property. The Set method adds the value to view state.

While you are at it, you'll create a second property, SortAscend, which will mark whether the current sort is in ascending order (SortAscend == true) or in descending order (SortAscend == false). The C# code for the SortAscent property is:

```
protected bool SortAscend
{
    get
    {
        object o = ViewState["SortAscend"];
        if (o != null)
            return (bool)o;
        return true; // default
    }
    set
    {
        ViewState["SortAscend"] = value;
    }
}
```

In VB.NET, the code is:

```
Protected Property SortAscend() As Boolean
    Get
        Dim o As Object
        o = ViewState("SortAscend")
        If Not o Is Nothing Then
            SortAscend = CBool(o)
        End If

    End Get
    Set(ByVal Value As Boolean)
        ViewState("SortAscend") = Value
    End Set
End Property
```

The logic is nearly identical: you attempt to get the current value from the ViewState. If no value is in view state, the object will be null and you return true; otherwise, you return the current value. The set logic is just to stash away the value assigned in the view state.

In the OnSortCommand event handler (dataGrid1_SortCommand in VB.NET), you first set a temporary string variable to the SortColumn property. You then set the SortColumn property to the value passed in via the DataGridSortCommandEventArgs object, which in C# is done as follows:

```
string currentSortColumn = SortColumn;
SortColumn = e.SortExpression;
```

In VB.NET, you write:

```
Dim currentSortColumn As String = SortColumn
SortColumn = e.SortExpression
```

You can now compare the current sort column value with the new sort column value, and if they are the same, you set the SortAscend property to the reverse of its current value; otherwise, you will sort the new column in ascending order. This is shown in the following C# code fragment:

```
if (currentSortColumn == SortColumn)
{
    SortAscend = !SortAscend;
}
else  // otherwise sort ascending
{
    SortAscend = true;
}
```

In VB.NET, the code is:

```
If currentSortColumn = SortColumn Then
    If SortAscend = True Then
        SortAscend = False
    Else
        SortAscend = True
    End If
Else
    SortAscend = True
End If
```

You are now ready to bind the DataGrid and update the details panel, as the following code shows:

```
BindGrid();
UpdateBugDetails();
```

Clearly something else must be going on; you've marked a couple of properties, but where did you actually sort the grid? You haven't yet; that work is delegated to the BindGrid method.

Inside BindGrid, just before you set the data source, you'll want to sort the array list. ArrayList implements the Sort method, but it wants you to pass in an object implementing IComparer. You will extend your Bug class to implement IComparable, and also to nest a class, BugComparer, which implements the IComparer class, as explained in the sidebar. You can then instantiate the BugComparer class, set its properties to sort on the appropriate field, and invoke Sort on the ArrayList object, passing in the BugComparer object:

```
Bug.BugComparer c = Bug.GetComparer( );
c.WhichField = SortColumn;
c.Ascending = SortAscend;
bugs.Sort(c);
```

In VB.NET, you'd write:

```
Dim c As Bug.BugComparer = Bug.GetComparer( )
c.WhichField = SortColumn
c.Ascending = SortAscend
bugs.Sort(c)
```

With the ArrayList object sorted, you are ready to set the DataSource for the Data-Grid and to call the DataBind method.

Adding a sort symbol

You may want to add a visible indication of the direction of the sort, as shown in Figure 10-5 and Figure 10-6. Clicking on the column not only reverses the sort, it changes the symbol, as shown in Figure 10-6.

Figure 10-5. The Title column when sorted in ascending order

Figure 10-6. The Title column when sorted in descending order

To accomplish this, you will implement the OnItemCreatedEventHandler, as you have in the past. This time, you will check to see if you are creating the header. If so, you will put this widget into the correct column, determined by checking the value of the SortColumn property.

You start by creating the label to add to the cell:

```
if (itemType == ListItemType.Header)
{
    Label sortSymbol = new Label( );
```

The VB.NET equivalent is:

```
If itemType = ListItemType.Header Then
    Dim sortSymbol As New Label( )
```

Implementing BugComparer

To allow the ArrayList to be sorted, you must ensure that it has sortable objects. In this case, you'll want to make your bugs be sortable, and to do so you will modify the Bug class so that it implements IComparable. The IComparable interface dictates that you must provide a CompareTo method so that two Bugs can be compared to one another to determine which comes first in a sort operation. One possible version of the code for our CompareTo method is:

```
public int CompareTo(Object rhs)
{
    Bug r = (Bug) rhs;
    return this.title.CompareTo(r.title);
}
```

In VB.NET, the code is:

```
Public Function CompareTo(ByVal rhs As Object) As Integer _
Implements IComparable.CompareTo
    Dim r As Bug = rhs
    CompareTo = Me.Title.CompareTo(r.Title)
End Function
```

In this implementation, you delegate the comparison to the CompareTo method of string, comparing the two titles. The titles are then sorted alphabetically.

This would be all you'd need to do if your Bugs were only to be compared by title. If you call the ArrayList object's Sort method with no parameters, the default behavior is to call the default IComparer object, which will call the IComparable implementation of the Bug object, and the Bugs will be sorted by Title in ascending order.

You would like to allow the DataGrid to sort your Bugs in any number of ways, however, and so you will need to implement a custom IComparer object that knows about Bugs. You'll call this new class BugComparer.

Since BugComparer is only needed to compare Bug objects, you'll nest the definition of BugComparer within the definition of Bug itself. When a client class needs an instance of BugComparer, it will call a method of Bug, GetComparer, that will return an instance of BugComparer:

```
public static BugComparer GetComparer()
{
    return new Bug.BugComparer();
}
```

In VB.NET, you'd write:

```
Public Shared Function GetComparer() As BugComparer
    GetComparer = New Bug.BugComparer()
End Function
```

—continued—

BugComparer will have just one method, Compare, which is required in any implementation of IComparer. In addition, BugComparer will have two properties: WhichField, which will hold the field to be compared as a string; and Ascending, which will hold the direction in which to sort as a Boolean. When you invoke Compare on BugComparer, it will call a special version of CompareTo on the Bug object, passing in the Bug to which the current Bug should be compared, as well as a string indicating which field to compare and a Boolean indicating whether to sort in ascending or descending order. The code for the Compare method is:

```
public int Compare(object lhs, object rhs)
{
    Bug l = (Bug) lhs;
    Bug r = (Bug) rhs;
    return l.CompareTo(r,whichField, ascending);
}
```

In VB.NET, the equivalent is:

```
Public Function Compare( _
  ByVal lhs As Object, ByVal rhs As Object) _
  As Integer _
  Implements IComparer.Compare
    Dim l As Bug
    Dim r As Bug
    l = lhs
    r = rhs
    Compare = l.CompareTo(r, _whichField, _ascending)
End Function
```

The Bug class must implement the specialized version of CompareTo and switch on the whichField parameter, setting the sort appropriately. The complete implementation, shown in Example 10-15 and 10-16, allows for sorting on any of four fields: Title, Reporter, BugID, or DateCreated.

The text to add to this label is the symbol itself, which is a Webding text symbol with the value of either 5 or 6 for ascending and descending, respectively:

```
sortSymbol.Text = SortAscend ? "5" : "6";
sortSymbol.Font.Name = "Webdings";
```

In VB.NET, the code is:

```
If SortAscend = True Then
    sortSymbol.Text = "5"
Else
    sortSymbol.Text = "6"
End If
sortSymbol.Font.Name = "Webdings"
```

You will add the label to the appropriate cell. To do so, you create an instance of a TableCell object:

```
TableCell theCell = null;
```

In VB.NET, the equivalent is:

```
Dim theCell As TableCell
theCell = Nothing
```

You will assign the correct cell to that variable, based on the value of the Sort-Column property:

```
switch (SortColumn)
{
    case "Title":
        theCell = e.Item.Cells[1];
        break;
    case "Reporter":
        theCell = e.Item.Cells[2];
        break;
    case "DateCreated":
        theCell = e.Item.Cells[5];
        break;
}
```

In VB.NET, use:

```
Select Case SortColumn
    Case "Title"
        theCell = e.Item.Cells(1)
    Case "Reporter"
        theCell = e.Item.Cells(2)
    Case "DateCreated"
        theCell = e.Item.Cells(5)
End Select
```

You must then test that you have a valid cell, and if so, add the label to that cell:

```
if (theCell != null)
    theCell.Controls.Add(sortSymbol);
```

In VB.NET, the code is:

```
If Not theCell Is Nothing Then
    theCell.Controls.Add(sortSymbol)
End If
```

As you will remember, each cell has a Controls collection. You don't care what is already in that collection (presumably, it contains the label for the header); you will simply add your label to the collection. When the cell is displayed the current contents are displayed and then your label is displayed.

Implementing paging

While the current version of this program uses an array list of Bug objects, a typical program will draw the objects from a database. It is possible that you may have a large number of Bug reports. (I apologize; you of course will never have a large number of bugs, but other, lowly, careless programmers may have a large number of bugs, and I explain this for their sake.)

Rather than filling the data grid with tens of thousands of bug reports (can you think of anything more depressing?), you'll want to add paging so that you are only forced to confront a limited number of bugs at any one time. To accomplish this, you add yet a few more attributes to your DataGrid declaration:

```
OnPageIndexChanged ="OnPageIndexChangedHandler"
AllowPaging="True"
PageSize ="2"
```

The `OnPageIndexChanged` attribute assigns the event handler to be called when the user clicks on the page navigation links. The `AllowPaging` attribute turns paging on, and the `PageSize` attribute sets the maximum number of items to be displayed in any single page. Because we have very few items in the array list, you'll set this to "2," although "10" is a more realistic real-world number.

You will add a new element to the DataGrid control: the `PagerStyle` element, which determines the style of paging the DataGrid will provide. Attributes to the `PagerStyle` element determine the alignment of the page navigation links and the *mode*. Two modes are supported: `NextPrev`, which provides two links, < to navigate backwards, and > to navigate forward; and `NumericPages`, which provides numeric values for each page. If you choose `NumericPages`, you'll want to add another attribute, `PageButtonCount`, which determines the maximum number of paging buttons to appear on the grid at one time.

 You will remember that we were previously filling the footer with the number of bugs found. You'll need to remove that code so that you can now fill the footer with the page navigation features.

Handling the event for page navigation

Each time the user clicks on the page navigation links, a PageIndexChanged event is raised, which is caught by your handler. The event handler is passed two arguments. The second is a DataGridPageChangedEventArgs object, which contains a NewPage-Index property that is the index of the selected page. You assign that value to the DataGrid object's CurrentPageIndex property and then redraw the page; the data grid takes care of the work of finding the right objects to display. The code for the OnPageIndexChangedHandler is the following:

```
public void OnPageIndexChangedHandler(
    Object sender, DataGridPageChangedEventArgs e)
{
    // set the new index
    dataGrid1.CurrentPageIndex = e.NewPageIndex;

    // rebind the data
    BindGrid();
    UpdateBugDetails();
}
```

In VB.NET, you'd write:

```
Private Sub dataGrid1_PageIndexChanged( _
 ByVal source As Object, _
 ByVal e As System.Web.UI.WebControls.DataGridPageChangedEventArgs) _
 Handles dataGrid1.PageIndexChanged
    dataGrid1.CurrentPageIndex = e.NewPageIndex
    BindGrid( )
    UpdateBugDetails( )
End Sub
```

The data grid uses the index value as an index into your complete set of data items (bugs, in the case of our example). For this to work, your data source must provide all the items, even though you will only display one page worth.

To avoid this, you can take explicit control over the page display by setting the Data-Grid object's AllowCustomPaging property to true (the default is false). With this set, you are responsible for telling the data grid the total number of values in your data source, which you do by setting the VirtualItemCount property. The advantage of custom paging is that you can minimize the number of values you retrieve in each query; you can get just the values for a single page.

Next Steps

The next steps with the Bug list are to provide in-place editing so that the user can click on a row and edit the record, and to add templates to control the display of the data. We'll defer this discussion until after Chapter 11, in which we will look at how to get data to and from a database, and how to update that data (Chapter 12). Once we have a database as a data source for the data grid, it will be easy to see how in-place editing is accomplished (Chapter 13).

Accessing Data with ADO.NET

So far in this book, we've used an ArrayList as the data source for data-bound controls. In most real-world applications, of course, the data source will be a database. ADO.NET provides a rich set of objects to manage database interaction.

ADO.NET looks, at first glance, very similar to ADO, its predecessor technology. The key difference, however, is that ADO.NET is modeled around a *disconnected* data architecture. Database connections are "expensive" (that is, they use a lot of resources), and it is difficult to have thousands (or tens of thousands) of simultaneous continuous connections. A disconnected architecture, on the other hand, is resource-frugal. Connections are used only briefly. Of course, ADO.NET does connect to the database to retrieve data, and connects again to update data when you've made changes. When not updating data to or from the database, the connection is broken. Most web applications spend most of their time simply reading through data and displaying it, and ADO.NET provides a disconnected subset of the data for your use while reading and displaying.

As you might imagine, disconnected datasets can have scale and performance problems of their own. There is overhead in creating and tearing down connections, and if you drop the connection each time you fill the database, and then must reestablish it each time you update the data, you will find that performance begins to degrade quickly. This problem is mitigated by the use of connection pooling. While it looks to your application like you are creating and destroying connections, you are actually borrowing and returning connections from a pool that ADO.NET manages on your behalf.

Bug Database Design

Imagine that you have been asked to create a tool to manage bugs for a large development effort. You will be supporting three developers who will work in C# and VB.NET, along with a user interface designer and a few quality control engineers.

You would like your design to be reasonably flexible so that you can reapply your bug tracking application to future projects.

Your first decision is that you will create a web application. This has the great advantage that all the participants will be able to access the application from their home computers. Since the developers work off-site, this is almost a necessity. You will, of course, develop your web application in ASP.NET.

You imagine that there will be a web page for entering bugs, as well as a page for reviewing and editing bugs. To support this, you will need to design a relational database, and for a number of reasons beyond the scope of this book, you decide to create that database using SQL Server.

You begin by thinking about the kinds of information you want to capture in the database, and how that information will be used. You will want to allow any user of the system to create a bug report. You'll also want certain users (e.g., developers and QA) to update the bug reports. Developers will want to be able to record progress in fixing a bug, or to mark a bug fixed. QA will want to check the fix and either close the bug or reopen it for further investigation. The original reporter of the bug will want to find out who is working on the bug, and track progress.

One requirement imposed early in the design process is that the bug database ought to provide an "audit trail." If the bug is modified you'll want to be able to say who modified it and when they did so. In fact, you'll want to be able to track all the changes to the bug, so that you can generate a report like the excerpt shown in Example 11-1.

Example 11-1. Excerpt from a bug report

```
Bug 101 - System crashes on login
101.1 - Reporter: Osborn
Date: 1/1/2002  Original bug filed
Description: When I login I crash.
Status: Open
Owner: QA

101.2 - Modified by: Smith
Date: 1/2/2002 Changed Status, Owner
Action: Confirmed bug.
Status: Assigned
Owner: Hurwitz

101.3 - Modified by Hurwitz
Date 1/2/2002 Changed Status
Action: I'll look into this but I don't think it is my code.
Status: Accepted
Owner: Hurwitz

101.4 - Modified by Hurwitz
Date 1/3/2002 Changed Status, Owner
```

Example 11-1. Excerpt from a bug report (continued)

```
Action: Fault lies in login code. Reassigned to Liberty
Status: Assigned
Owner: Liberty

101.5 - Modified by Liberty
Date: 1/3/2002 Changed Status
Action: Yup, this is mine.
Status: Accepted
Owner: Liberty

101.6 - Modified by Liberty
Date 1/4/2002 Changed Status, Owner
Action: Added test for null loginID in DoLogin( )
Status: Fixed
Owner: QA

101.7 - Modified by Smith
Date: 1/4/2002 Changed Status
Action: Tested and confirmed
Status: Closed
Owner: QA
```

To track this information you'll need to know the date and time of each modification, as well as who made the modification and what they did. There will probably be other information you'll want to capture as well, though this may become more obvious as you build the application (and as you use it!).

One way to meet these requirements is to create two tables to represent each Bug. Each record in the Bugs table will represent a single bug, but you'll need an additional table to keep track of the revisions. Call this second table BugHistory.

A Bug record will have a BugID and will include the information that is constant for the bug throughout its history. A BugHistory record will have the information specific to each revision.

The bug database design described in this chapter includes three significant tables: Bugs, BugHistory, and People. Bugs and BugHistory work together to track the progress of a bug. For any given bug, a single record is created in the Bugs table, and a record is created in BugHistory each time the bug is revised in any way. The People table tracks the developers, QA, and other personnel who might be referred to in a Bug report.

 This is a simplified design that meets the detailed specifications but which focuses on the key technologies; a robust professional design would necessarily be more complex. The complete database design as used in this book is shown in Appendix B. A crash course on relational database design is provided in Appendix A.

Figure 11-1 shows a snapshot of the Bugs table, while Figure 11-2 shows a snapshot of the BugHistory table.

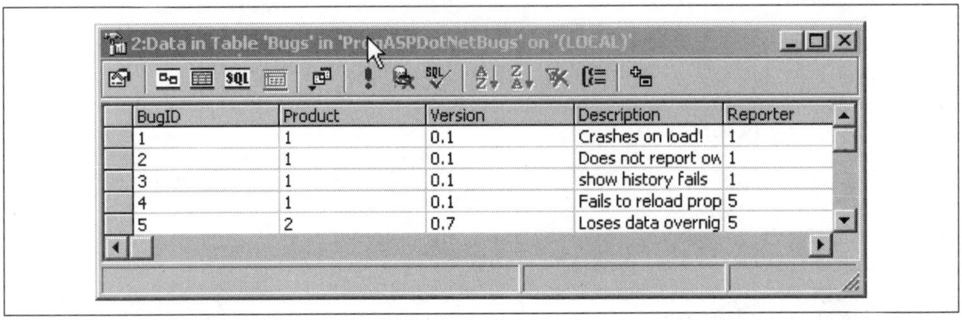

BugID	Product	Version	Description	Reporter
1	1	0.1	Crashes on load!	1
2	1	0.1	Does not report ow	1
3	1	0.1	show history fails	1
4	1	0.1	Fails to reload prop	5
5	2	0.7	Loses data overnig	5

Figure 11-1. The Bugs table

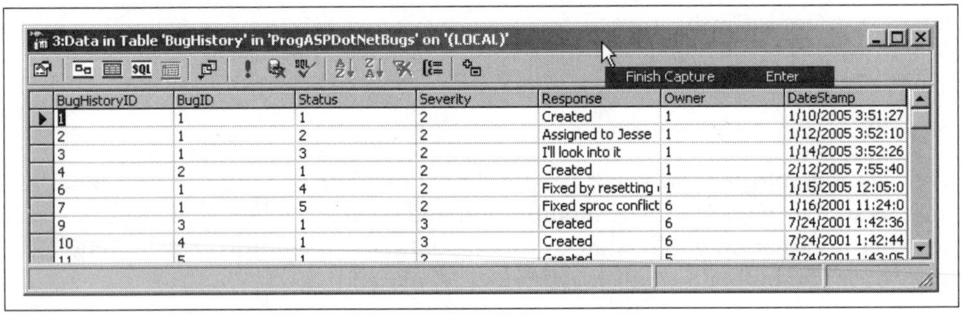

BugHistoryID	BugID	Status	Severity	Response	Owner	DateStamp
1	1	1	2	Created	1	1/10/2005 3:51:27
2	1	2	2	Assigned to Jesse	1	1/12/2005 3:52:10
3	1	3	2	I'll look into it	1	1/14/2005 3:52:26
4	2	1	2	Created	1	2/12/2005 7:55:40
6	1	4	2	Fixed by resetting	1	1/15/2005 12:05:0
7	1	5	2	Fixed sproc conflict	6	1/16/2001 11:24:0
9	3	1	3	Created	6	7/24/2001 1:42:36
10	4	1	3	Created	6	7/24/2001 1:42:44
11	5	1	2	Created	5	7/24/2001 1:43:05

Figure 11-2. The BugHistory table

When a bug is first entered, a record is created in each of the Bugs and BugHistory tables. Each time the bug is updated a record is added to BugHistory. During the evolution of a bug, the status, severity, and owner of a bug may change, but the initial description and reporter will not. Those items that are consistent for the entire bug are in the Bugs table; those that are updated as the bug is corrected are in the BugHistory table.

The reporter, for example, is the ID of the person who reported the bug. This is unchanged for the life of the bug and so is recorded in the Bugs table. The owner may be adjusted from time to time, and so is recorded in the BugHistory table. In both cases, however, what is actually recorded is just a PersonID, which acts as a foreign key into the People table. An excerpt from the People table is shown in Figure 11-3.

In addition to these three primary tables, there are a number of secondary tables which serve as look-up tables. For example, `lkStatus`, serves as a look-up table for the possible values of the `status` column in BugHistory.

Figure 11-3. The People table

The format for all of the look-up tables (lkStatus, lkProduct, lkRoles and lkSeverity) is the same: the ID followed by a text field. Each table will hold one row for each possible value. As an example, Figure 11-4 shows the various look-up tables.

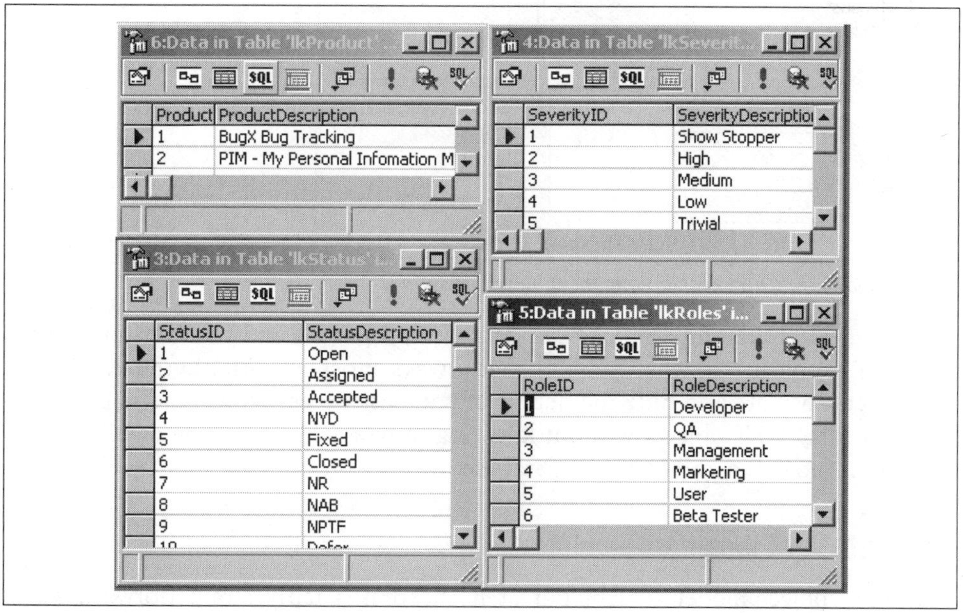

Figure 11-4. The look-up tables

Figure 11-5 illustrates the tables in their various relationships graphically.

The ADO.NET Object Model

The goal of ADO.NET is to provide a bridge between your objects in ASP.NET and your back end database. ADO.NET provides an object-oriented view into the

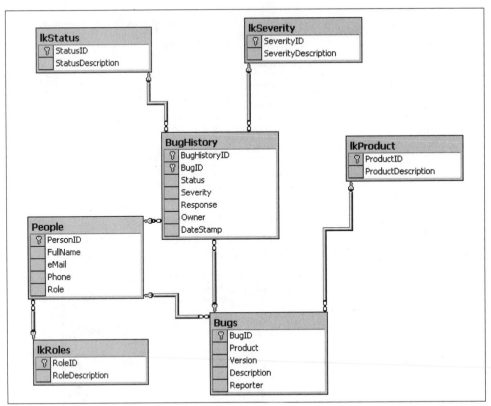

Figure 11-5. The relationship among the tables diagrammed

database, encapsulating many of the database properties and relationships within ADO.NET objects. Further, and in many ways most important, the ADO.NET objects encapsulate and hide the details of database access; your objects can interact with ADO.NET objects without knowing or worrying about the details of how the data is moved to and from the database.

The DataSet Class

The ADO object model is rich, but at its heart is a fairly straightforward set of classes. The key class is the DataSet, which is located in the System.Data namespace.

The dataset represents a rich subset of the entire database, cached on your machine without a continuous connection to the database. Periodically, you'll reconnect the dataset to its parent database, and update the database with changes to the dataset that you've made, and update the dataset with changes in the database made by other processes.

The dataset captures not just a few rows from a single table, but represents a set of tables with all the metadata necessary to represent the relationships and constraints among the tables recorded in the original database.

The dataset is comprised of DataTable objects as well as DataRelation objects. These are accessed as properties of the DataSet object. The most important methods and properties of the DataSet class are shown in Table 11-1.

Table 11-1. Important DataSet properties and methods

Class member	Description
DefaultViewManager property	Gets a view of the data in the dataSet that allows filtering, searching and navigation
HasErrors property	Gets a value indicating if there are any errors in any of the rows of any of the tables
Relations property	Gets the relations collection
Tables property	Gets the tables collection
AcceptChanges method	Accepts all the changes made since loaded or since last time AcceptChanges was called (see GetChanges)
Clear method	Clears the dataset of any data
GetChanges method	Returns a copy of the dataset containing all the changes made since loaded or since AcceptChanges was called
GetXML method	Gets the XML representation of the data in the dataset
GetXMLSchema method	Gets the XSD schema for the XML representation of the data in the dataset
Merge method	Merges the data in this dataset with another dataset
ReadXML method	Reads an XML schema and data into the dataset
ReadXMLSchema method	Reads an XML schema into the dataset
RejectChanges method	Rolls back to the state since last AcceptChanges (see AcceptChanges)
WriteXML method	Writes out the XML schema and data from the dataset
WriteXMLSchema method	Writes the structure of the dataset as an XML schema

The DataTable class

The DataSet object's Tables property returns a DataTableCollection collection, which in turn contains all the DataTable objects in the dataset. For example, the following line of code creates a reference to the first DataTable in the Tables collection of a DataSet object named myDataSet.

```
DataTable dataTable = myDataSet.Tables[0];
```

The DataTable has a number of public properties, including the Columns property, which returns the ColumnsCollection object, which in turn consists of DataColumn objects. Each DataColumn object represents a column in a table.

The DataRelation property returns a DataRelationCollection object, which contains DataRelation objects. Each DataRelation object represents a relationship between two tables, through DataColumn objects. For example, in the Bugs database, the Bugs table is in a relationship with the People table through the PersonID column. The nature of this relationship is parent/child—for any given Bug, there will be exactly one owner, but any given person may be represented in any number of Bugs. DataTables, DataColumns, and DataRelations are explored in more detail later in this chapter.

The most important methods and properties of the DataTable class are shown in Table 11-2.

Table 11-2. Important DataTable properties amd methods

Class member	Description
ChildRelations property	Gets the collection of child relations (see Relations object)
Columns property	Gets the columns collection
Constraints property	Gets the constraints collection
DataSet property	Gets the dataset this table belongs to
DefaultView property	Gets a view of the table for filtering
ParentRelations property	Gets the Parent Relations collection
PrimaryKey property	Gets or sets an array of columns as primary key for this table
Rows property	Gets the rows collection
AcceptChanges method	Commits all the changes since last AcceptChanges
Clear method	Clears the table of all data
GetChanges method	Gets a copy of the DataTable with all the changes since last AcceptChanges (see AcceptChanges)
NewRow method	Creates a new DataRow with the same schema as the table
RejectChanges method	Rolls back changes since last AcceptChanges (see AcceptChanges)
Select method	Gets an array of DataRow objects

The DataRow class

The Rows collection returns a set of rows for any given table. You use this collection to examine the results of queries against the database, iterating through the rows to examine each record in turn. Programmers experienced with classic ADO may be confused by the absence of the RecordSet, with its moveNext and movePrevious commands. With ADO.NET you do not iterate through the dataset; instead you access the table you need, and then you can iterate through the rows collection, typically with a foreach loop. You'll see this in the first example in this chapter.

The most important methods and properties of the DataRow class are shown in Table 11-3.

Table 11-3. Important DataRow properties and methods

Class member	Description
Item	Gets or sets the data stored in a specific column (in C# this is the indexer)
ItemArray	Gets or sets all the values for the row using an array
Table	Gets the table this row is owned by
AcceptChanges	Accepts all the changes since the last time AcceptChanges was called
GetChildRows	Gets the child rows for this row
GetParentRow	Gets the parent row of this row
RejectChanges	Rejects all the changes since the last time AcceptChanges was called (see AcceptChanges)

DBCommand and DBConnection

The DBConnection object represents a connection to a data source. This connection may be shared among different command objects.

The DBCommand object allows you to send a command (typically an SQL statement or the name of a stored procedure) to the database. Often DBCommand objects are implicitly created when you create your dataset, but you can explicitly access these objects, as you'll see in a subsequent example.

The DataAdapter Object

Rather than tie the DataSet object too closely to your database architecture, ADO.NET uses a DataAdapter object to mediate between the DataSet object and the database. This decouples the dataset from the database, and allows a single dataset to represent more than one database or other data source.

As of this writing, ASP.NET provides two different versions of the DataAdapter object; one for use with SQL Server, and the other for use with other OLE DB providers. If you are connecting to an SQL Server database you will increase the performance of your application by using SqlDataAdapter (from System.Data.SqlClient) along with SqlCommand and SqlConnection. If you are using another database, you will use OleDbDataAdapter (from System.Data.OleDb) along with OleDbCommand and OleDbConnection. The most important methods and properties of the DataAdapter class are shown in Table 11-4.

Table 11-4. Important DataAdapter properties and methods

Class member	Description
AcceptChangesDuringFill property	Indicates whether or not to call AcceptChanges on a DataRow after adding it to a DataTable.
Fill method	Fills a DataDatable by adding or updating rows in the dataset.

Table 11-4. Important DataAdapter properties and methods (continued)

Class member	Description
FillSchema method	Adds a DataTable object to the specified dataset. Configures the schema to the specified SchemaType.
Update method	Updates all the modified rows in the specified table of the DataSet.

The Data Reader

An alternative to the dataset is the DataReader object. The DataReader provides connected forward-only access to a recordset returned by executing an SQL statement or a stored procedure. DataReaders are light-weight objects ideally suited for filling a web page with data and then breaking the connection to the back-end database.

> Like DataAdapter, the DataReader class comes in two flavors: Sql-DataReader for use with SQL Server and OleDbDataReader for use with other databases.

The most important methods and properties of the DataReader class are shown in Table 11-5.

Table 11-5. Important DataReader properties and methods

Class member	Description
Close	Closes the data reader
NextResult	When reading the results of a batch SQL statement, advances to the next result set (set of records)

The DataReader is a very powerful object, but you don't often use many of its methods or properties. Most of the time, you simply use the DataReader to retrieve and iterate through the records that represent the result of your query.

> Note to ADO programmers: you do not issue a MoveNext command to the DataReader; by reading a record, you automatically move to the next record. This eliminates one of the most common bugs with recordsets: forgetting to move to the next record.

Getting Started with ADO.NET

In the coming examples, you'll create a more complex display with a DataGrid, and you'll display data from multiple tables, but to get started, you'll keep it as simple as possible. In this first example, you'll create a simple Windows Form with a single list box called lbBugs. You'll populate this list box with bits of information from the Bugs table in the ProgASPDotNetBugs database.

Create a new C# ASP.NET web application project named `SimpleBugListBox`. Drag a list box onto the form and name it lbBugs (that is, change the value of its ID property to lbBugs). The list box will size itself to fit the data, so you can leave its default size for now.

Example 11-2 is the complete source for the code-behind page; code lines that are not generated by Visual Studio automatically are shown in boldface. Analysis follows the listing.

Example 11-2. A simple ADO.NET example

```csharp
using System;
using System.Collections;
using System.ComponentModel;
using System.Data;
using System.Data.SqlClient;
using System.Drawing;
using System.Web;
using System.Web.SessionState;
using System.Web.UI;
using System.Web.UI.WebControls;
using System.Web.UI.HtmlControls;

namespace SimpleBugsListBox
{
    /// <summary>
    /// Summary description for WebForm1.
    /// </summary>
    public class WebForm1 : System.Web.UI.Page
    {
        protected System.Web.UI.WebControls.ListBox lbBugs;

        public WebForm1( )
        {
            Page.Init += new System.EventHandler(Page_Init);
        }

        private void Page_Load(object sender, System.EventArgs e)
        {
            // connect to the Bugs database
            string connectionString =
                "server=YourServer; uid=sa;
                 pwd=YourPassword; database=ProgASPDotNetBugs";

            // get records from the Bugs table
            string commandString =
                "Select BugID, Description from Bugs";

            // create the dataset  command object
            // and the DataSet
            SqlDataAdapter dataAdapter =
```

Example 11-2. A simple ADO.NET example (continued)

```
            new SqlDataAdapter(
            commandString, connectionString);

        DataSet dataSet = new DataSet();

        // fill the dataset object
        dataAdapter.Fill(dataSet,"Bugs");

        // Get the one table from the DataSet
        DataTable dataTable = dataSet.Tables[0];

        // for each row in the table, display the info
        foreach (DataRow dataRow in dataTable.Rows)
        {
            lbBugs.Items.Add(
                dataRow["BugID"] +
                ": " + dataRow["Description"]  );
        }
    }

    private void Page_Init(object sender, EventArgs e)
    {
        InitializeComponent();
    }

    #region Web Form Designer generated code
    private void InitializeComponent()
    {
        this.Load += new System.EventHandler(this.Page_Load);
    }
    #endregion
  }
}
```

With just about eight lines of code in the Page.Load event handler, you have extracted a set of data from the database and displayed it in the list box, as shown in Figure 11-6.

The eight lines accomplished the following tasks:

1. Created the string for the connection. The connection string is whatever string is needed to connect to the database, in the case of our example:

   ```
   string connectionString =
       "server=YourServer; uid=sa;
       pwd=YourPassword; database=ProgASPDotNetBugs";
   ```

2. Created the string for the select statement, which generates a table containing bug IDs and their descriptions:

   ```
   string commandString =
       "Select BugID, Description from Bugs";
   ```

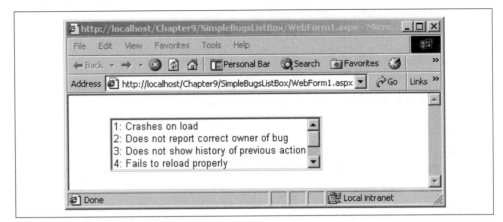

Figure 11-6. Displaying the list of bugs

3. Created the DataAdapter to extract the data from the SQL Server database and pass in the selection and connection strings:

```
SqlDataAdapter dataAdapter =
new SqlDataAdapter(
commandString, connectionString);
```

4. Created a new DataSet object:

```
DataSet dataSet = new DataSet( );
```

5. Filled the dataset with the data obtained from the SQL select statement using the DataAdapter:

```
dataAdapter.Fill(dataSet,"Bugs");
```

6. Extracted the data table from the DataTableCollection object:

```
DataTable dataTable = dataSet.Tables[0];
```

7. Iterated the rows in the data table to fill the list box:

```
foreach (DataRow dataRow in dataTable.Rows)
{
   lbBugs.Items.Add(
     dataRow["BugID"] +
     ": " + dataRow["Description"]  );
}
```

The Visual Basic .NET Page_Load equivalent is shown in Example 11-3.

Example 11-3. Page_Load in VB.NET

```
Private Sub Page_Load(ByVal sender As System.Object, _
                    ByVal e As System.EventArgs) _
                    Handles MyBase.Load
  Dim connectionString As String
  connectionString = _
      "Server=Neptune; uid=sa; pwd=oWenmEany; database=ProgASPDotNetBugs"

  Dim commandString As String
```

Example 11-3. Page_Load in VB.NET (continued)

```
commandString = "Select BugID, Description from Bugs"

Dim myDataAdapter As New System.Data.SqlClient.SqlDataAdapter(commandString, _
    connectionString)

Dim myDataSet As New DataSet( )

myDataAdapter.Fill(myDataSet, "Bugs")

Dim myDataTable As DataTable
myDataTable = myDataSet.Tables(0)

Dim theRow As DataRow
For Each theRow In myDataTable.Rows
    lbBugs.Items.Add(theRow("BugID") & ": " & theRow("Description"))
Next

End Sub
```

Managed Providers

The previous example used one of the two managed providers initially available with ADO.NET: the SQL Managed provider. The SQL Managed provider is optimized for SQL Server, but it is restricted to working with SQL Server databases. The more general solution is the OLE DB managed provider, which will connect to any OLE DB provider, including Access.

You can rewrite Example 11-3 to work with the Bugs database using Access rather than SQL Server with just a few small changes. First, of course, you need to create a new Access database. Name the new database SimpleBugListBoxAccessDB. Example 11-4 assumes you will save your database to the root directory on your C drive, but you may save it anywhere else that is convenient for you as long as you adjust the connection string.

Use the File → Import menu option in Access to import the data from the SQL database. This will create tables in Access that reflect the structure and content of the data in the SQL database. Notice that the Bugs database is now named dbo_Bugs in Access.

Create a new ASP web application project named SimpleBugListboxAccess and once again drag a list box onto the form and name it lbBugs. Copy the code from Example 11-3, but make the following changes:

1. Change the connection string to:

```
string connectionString =
    "provider=Microsoft.JET.OLEDB.4.0; "
    + "data source = c:\\simpleBugListAccessDB.mdb";
```

This will connect to the database you just created.

---

2. Change the `DataAdapter` object to be an `OleDbDataAdapter` rather than a Sql-DataAdapter:

```
OleDbDataAdapter DataAdapter =
    new OleDbDataAdapter (commandString, connectionString);
```

3. Replace the `System.Data.SqlClient` with the `using` statement for the `OleDb` namespace:

```
using System.Data.OleDb;
```

This design pattern continues throughout working with the two managed providers; for every object whose class name begins with `Sql`, there is a corresponding class beginning with `OleDb`. Example 11-4 is the complete OLE DB version of Example 11-3.

Example 11-4. Using ADO.NET with Access

```
using System;
using System.Collections;
using System.ComponentModel;
using System.Data;
using System.Data.OleDb;
using System.Drawing;
using System.Web;
using System.Web.SessionState;
using System.Web.UI;
using System.Web.UI.WebControls;
using System.Web.UI.HtmlControls;

namespace SimpleBugListBoxAccess
{
    /// <summary>
    /// Summary description for WebForm1.
    /// </summary>
    public class WebForm1 : System.Web.UI.Page
    {
        protected System.Web.UI.WebControls.ListBox lbBugs;

        public WebForm1( )
        {
            Page.Init += new System.EventHandler(Page_Init);
        }

        private void Page_Load(object sender, System.EventArgs e)
        {
            // connect to the Bugs database
            string connectionString =
                "provider=Microsoft.JET.OLEDB.4.0; "
                + "data source = c:\\simpleBugListAccessDB.mdb";

            // get records from the Bugs table
            string commandString =
                "Select BugID, Description from dbo_Bugs";
```

Example 11-4. Using ADO.NET with Access (continued)

```
            // create the dataset  command object
            // and the DataSet
            OleDbDataAdapter  dataAdapter =
               new OleDbDataAdapter (
               commandString, connectionString);

            DataSet dataSet = new DataSet( );

            // fill the dataset  object
            dataAdapter.Fill(dataSet,"Bugs");

            // Get the one table from the DataSet
            DataTable dataTable = dataSet.Tables[0];

            // for each row in the table, display the info
            foreach (DataRow dataRow in dataTable.Rows)
            {
               lbBugs.Items.Add(
                  dataRow["BugID"] +
                  ": " + dataRow["Description"]  );
            }
         }

         private void Page_Init(object sender, EventArgs e)
         {
            InitializeComponent( );
         }

         #region Web Form Designer generated code
         private void InitializeComponent( )
         {
            this.Load += new System.EventHandler(this.Page_Load);

         }
         #endregion
      }
}
```

Before you run this program, edit the description of the first bug to include the word Access; this will help you ensure that you are looking at the correct data. The output, which is shown in Figure 11-7, is identical to that from the previous example (except for the change you've made to the description of the first bug).

The OLE DB managed provider is more general than the SQL managed provider and can, in fact, be used to connect to SQL Server as well as to any other OLE DB object. Because the SQL Server provider is optimized for SQL Server, it will be more efficient to use the SQL Server-specific provider when working with SQL Server. In time, there will be any number of specialized managed providers available.

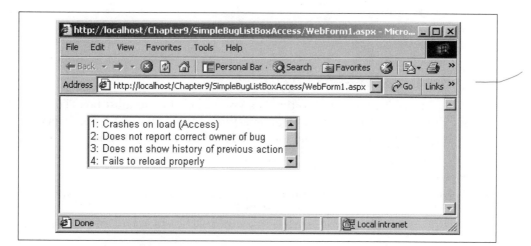

Figure 11-7. Using the ADO provider

Creating a Data Grid

You are now ready to return to the data grid examples from Chapter 10 and recode them by accessing the database. You will remember that in Examples 10-7 and 10-8, you created a simple data grid, and then populated it with data from an ArrayList object. You can recreate that now using ADO.NET to get bug data from the database.

To start, create a new C# project, SimpleADODataGrid. Drag a DataGrid control onto the form, Visual Studio will name it DataGrid1. Accept all the default attributes as offered.

In the code-behind page's Page_Load method, you get the Bugs table from the database, just as you did in Example 11-3:

```
string connectionString =
   "server=YourServer; uid=sa;
   pwd=YourPassword; database=ProgASPDotNetBugs";

// get records from the Bugs table
string commandString =
   "Select BugID, Description from Bugs";

// create the dataset  command object
// and the DataSet
SqlDataAdapter dataAdapter =
   new SqlDataAdapter(
   commandString, connectionString);

DataSet dataSet = new DataSet();
```

```
// fill the dataset  object
dataAdapter.Fill(dataSet,"Bugs");

// Get the one table from the DataSet
DataTable dataTable = dataSet.Tables[0];
```

This time, however, you'll bind to the data grid rather than to a list box. To do so, you set the DataGrid control's DataSource property to dataTable, the DataTable object you get from the dataset, and then call DataBind on the data grid:

```
DataGrid1.DataSource=dataTable;
DataGrid1.DataBind();
```

When you run the page, hey! presto! the data grid is connected, as shown in Figure 11-8.

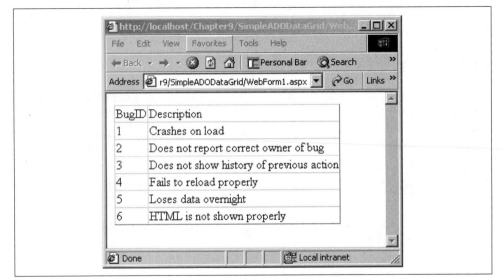

Figure 11-8. A simple data grid

Notice that the columns in the data grid have titles. These are the names of the columns from the Bugs table. Unless you tell it otherwise, the data grid picks up the titles from the columns in the database. You'll see how to modify this in a later example.

Displaying Relational Data

If you change the commandString in Example 11-2 from:

```
string commandString =
    "Select BugID, Description from Bugs";
```

to:

```
string commandString =
    "Select * from Bugs";
```

to get all the fields in the table, the output (shown in Figure 11-9) reflects the fact that some of the fields have numeric IDs that do not convey a lot of information to the user.

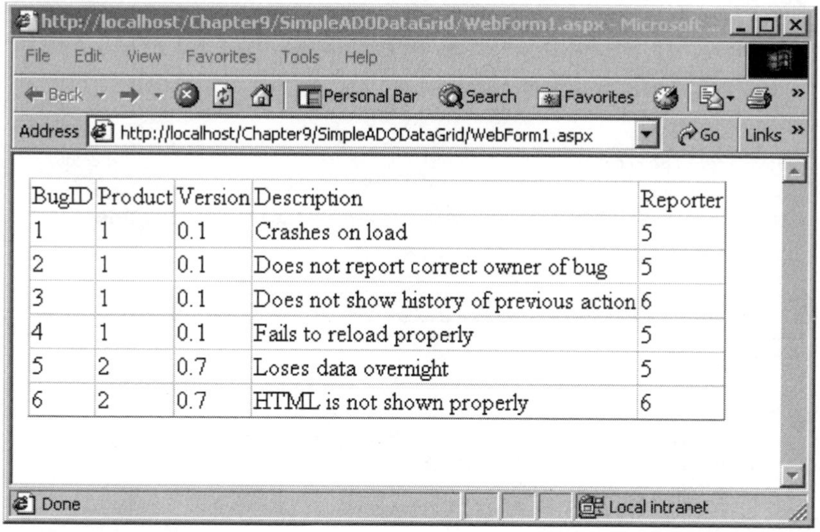

Figure 11-9. Showing the ID fields

The information you would like to show is the name of the product and the name of the person filing the report. You accomplish this by using a more sophisticated SQL select statement in the command string:

```
string commandString =
"Select b.BugID, b.Description, p.ProductDescription,
peo.FullName from Bugs b join lkProduct p on b.Product = p.ProductID
join People peo on b.Reporter = peo.PersonID ";
```

In this select statement, you are drawing fields from three tables: Bugs, Product, and People. You join the Product table to the Bugs table on the ProductID in the Bugs record, and you join the People table to the PersonID of the Reporter field in Bugs.

The results are shown in Figure 11-10.

This is better, but the headers are not what we might hope, and the grid is a bit ugly. The best way to solve these problems is with attributes for the DataGrid, as you saw in Chapter 10. Adding just a few attributes to the data grid, you can control which columns are displayed and how the headers are written, and you can provide a nicer background color for the header row. The following code does this:

```
<asp:DataGrid id="DataGrid1" runat="server" CellPadding="5"
HeaderStyle-BackColor="PapayaWhip" BorderWidth="5px"
BorderColor="#000099" AlternatingItemStyle-BackColor="LightGrey"
HeaderStyle-Font-Bold="True" AutoGenerateColumns="False">
```

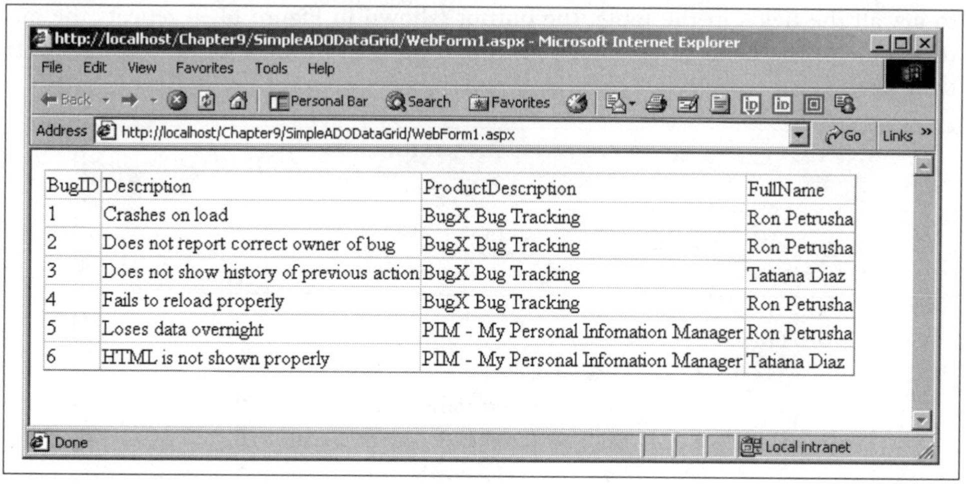

Figure 11-10. Using the join statement

```
<Columns>
    <asp:BoundColumn DataField="BugID" HeaderText="ID" />
    <asp:BoundColumn DataField="Description"
    HeaderText="Description" />
    <asp:BoundColumn DataField="ProductDescription"
    HeaderText="Product" />
    <asp:BoundColumn DataField="FullName"
    HeaderText="Reported By" />
</Columns>
</asp:DataGrid>
```

You will remember from Chapter 10 that the AutoGenerateColumns attribute tells the grid whether to pick up all the columns from the data source; by setting it to false, you tell the grid that you will specify which columns to display in the Columns attribute.

Nested within the Columns attribute are BoundColumn attributes, which delineate which field will supply the data (e.g., BugID, ProductDescription, FullName) and the header to display in the DataGrid (e.g., BugID, Product, Reported By). The result is shown in Figure 11-11.

Displaying Parent/Child Relationships

You would like to offer the user the ability to see the complete history for a given Bug. To do this, you'll add a column with a button marked "History." When the user clicks on the button, you'll display a second grid with the Bug History.

The BugHistory records act as child records to the Bug records. For each Bug there will be a set of one or more BugHistory records. For each BugHistory record there will be exactly one Bug parent record. This section will explore the first of a number of ways to display these related records. Alternative ways to display this relationship will be shown later in this chapter.

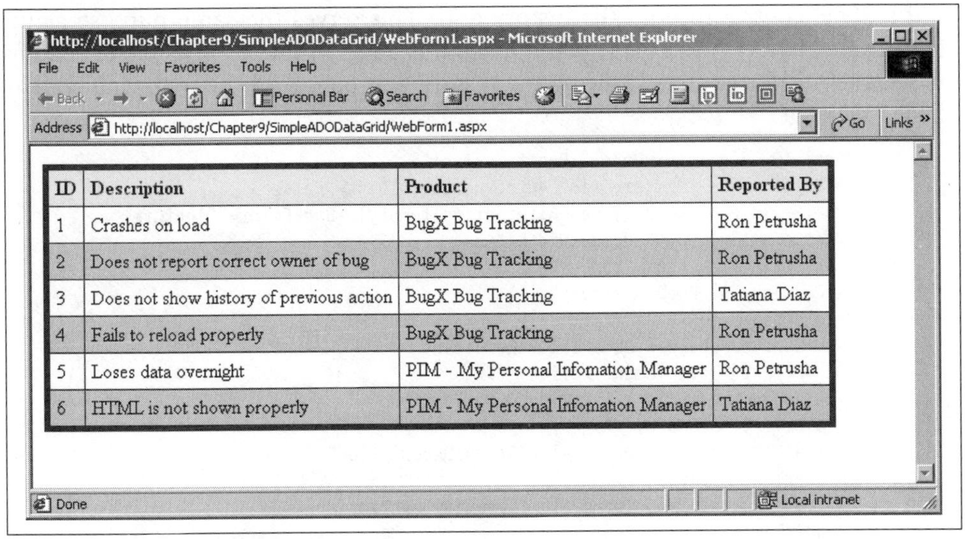

ID	Description	Product	Reported By
1	Crashes on load	BugX Bug Tracking	Ron Petrusha
2	Does not report correct owner of bug	BugX Bug Tracking	Ron Petrusha
3	Does not show history of previous action	BugX Bug Tracking	Tatiana Diaz
4	Fails to reload properly	BugX Bug Tracking	Ron Petrusha
5	Loses data overnight	PIM - My Personal Infomation Manager	Ron Petrusha
6	HTML is not shown properly	PIM - My Personal Infomation Manager	Tatiana Diaz

Figure 11-11. Using attributes to control the display

To start, add the ButtonColumn to the Data Grid and add an attribute for the OnSelectedIndexChanged event. Set the `DataKeyField` attribute to BugID; this is the primary key for the Bugs table and will serve as the foreign key for the BugHistory grid:

```
<asp:DataGrid id="DataGrid1" runat="server" DataKeyField="BugID"
CellPadding="5" HeaderStyle-BackColor="PapayaWhip" BorderWidth="5px"
BorderColor="#000099" OnItemDataBound="OnItemDataBoundEventHandler"
OnSelectedIndexChanged="OnSelectedIndexChangedHandler"
AlternatingItemStyle-BackColor="LightGrey" HeaderStyle-Font-Bold="True"
AutoGenerateColumns="False" EnableViewState="true">
   <Columns>
      <asp:ButtonColumn Text="History" CommandName="Select" />
      <asp:BoundColumn DataField="BugID" HeaderText="Bug ID" />
      <asp:BoundColumn DataField="Description"
      HeaderText="Description" />
      <asp:BoundColumn DataField="Reporter"
      HeaderText="Reported By" />
      <asp:BoundColumn DataField="Response"
      HeaderText="Most Recent Action" />
      <asp:BoundColumn DataField="Owner"
      HeaderText="Owned By" />
      <asp:BoundColumn DataField="StatusDescription"
      HeaderText="Status" />
      <asp:BoundColumn DataField="SeverityDescription"
      HeaderText="Severity" />
      <asp:BoundColumn DataField="DateStamp"
      HeaderText="LastUpdated" />
   </Columns>
</asp:DataGrid>
```

Add a Panel control to hold the history grid. This serves the same purpose as the details panel in Example 10-11; you'll make this panel visible or invisible depending on whether or not you are showing the history of a bug. Add the following code to the HTML page:

```
<asp:Panel ID="BugHistoryPanel" Runat="server">
   <asp:DataGrid id="HistoryGrid" AutoGenerateColumns="False"
   HeaderStyle-Font-Bold="True" AlternatingItemStyle-BackColor="LightGrey"
   BorderColor="#000099" BorderWidth="5px"
   HeaderStyle-BackColor="PapayaWhip"
   CellPadding="5" Runat="server">
      <Columns>
         <asp:BoundColumn DataField="Response"
      HeaderText="Most Recent Action" />
         <asp:BoundColumn DataField="Owner"
      HeaderText="Owned By" />
         <asp:BoundColumn DataField="StatusDescription"
      HeaderText="Status" />
         <asp:BoundColumn DataField="SeverityDescription"
      HeaderText="Severity" />
         <asp:BoundColumn DataField="DateStamp"
      HeaderText="LastUpdated" />
      </Columns>
   </asp:DataGrid>
</asp:Panel>
```

The supporting code-behind page is shown in Example 11-5 for C# and Example 11-6 for VB.NET. Complete analysis follows the listings.

Example 11-5. C# code-behind page

```
using System;
using System.Collections;
using System.ComponentModel;
using System.Data;
using System.Data.SqlClient;
using System.Drawing;
using System.Text;
using System.Web;
using System.Web.SessionState;
using System.Web.UI;
using System.Web.UI.WebControls;
using System.Web.UI.HtmlControls;

namespace BugHistoryDynamic
{
   /// <summary>
   /// Summary description for WebForm1.
   /// </summary>
   public class WebForm1 : System.Web.UI.Page
   {
      protected System.Web.UI.WebControls.DataGrid DataGrid1;
      protected System.Web.UI.WebControls.DataGrid HistoryGrid;
```

Example 11-5. C# code-behind page (continued)

```csharp
protected System.Web.UI.WebControls.Panel BugHistoryPanel;

public WebForm1( )
{
    Page.Init += new System.EventHandler(Page_Init);
}

// When the item is added to the bug grid,
// if the status is high write it in red
public void OnItemDataBoundEventHandler(
    Object sender, DataGridItemEventArgs e)
{
    ListItemType itemType = (ListItemType)e.Item.ItemType;
    if (itemType == ListItemType.Header ||
        itemType == ListItemType.Footer ||
        itemType == ListItemType.Separator)
        return;

    if (((DataRowView)e.Item.DataItem).
        Row.ItemArray[8].ToString( ) == "High")
    {
        TableCell severityCell =
            (TableCell) e.Item.Controls[6];
        severityCell.ForeColor = Color.FromName("Red");
    }
}

// the user has selected a row
// display the history for that bug
public void OnSelectedIndexChangedHandler(
    Object sender, EventArgs e)
{
    UpdateBugHistory( );
}

// If the user has selected a row
// display the history panel
private void UpdateBugHistory( )
{

    int index = DataGrid1.SelectedIndex;
    if (index != -1)
    {
        // get the bug id from the data grid
        int bugID =
            (int) DataGrid1.DataKeys[index];

        // Get a dataset based on that BugID
        DataSet dataSet =
            CreateBugHistoryDataSet(bugID);

        // bind to the table returned and make
```

Example 11-5. C# code-behind page (continued)

```csharp
                // the panel visible
                HistoryGrid.DataSource=dataSet.Tables[0];
                HistoryGrid.DataBind( );
                BugHistoryPanel.Visible=true;
        }
        else
        {
                // no history to display, hide the panel
                BugHistoryPanel.Visible=false;
        }
}


// The first time you load the page, populate the
// bug grid and hide the history grid
private void Page_Load(
        object sender, System.EventArgs e)
{
        if (!IsPostBack)
        {
                // hide the history panel
                UpdateBugHistory( );

                // set the data source for the
                // grid to the first table
                DataSet ds = CreateBugDataSet( );
                DataGrid1.DataSource=ds.Tables[0];
                DataGrid1.DataBind( );
        }
}

// create a dataset  for the bug history records
private DataSet CreateBugHistoryDataSet(int bugID)
{
        // connection string to connect to the Bugs Database
        string connectionString =
            "server=YourServer; uid=sa;
        pwd=YourPassword; database=ProgASPDotNetBugs";

        // Create connection object, initialize with
        // connection string. Open it.
        System.Data.SqlClient.SqlConnection connection =
            new System.Data.SqlClient.SqlConnection(connectionString);
        connection.Open( );

        // create a second command object for the bugs hisotry table
        System.Data.SqlClient.SqlCommand command =
            new System.Data.SqlClient.SqlCommand( );
        command.Connection = connection;

        StringBuilder s =
```

Example 11-5. C# code-behind page (continued)

```
            new StringBuilder("Select BugID, StatusDescription, ");
        s.Append("SeverityDescription, Response, ");
        s.Append("FullName as Owner, DateStamp ");
        s.Append("from BugHistory h ");
        s.Append("join People o on h.Owner = o.PersonID ");
        s.Append("join lkStatus s on s.statusid = h.status ");
        s.Append(
            "join lkSeverity sev on sev.SeverityID = h.severity ");
        s.Append("where BugID = " + bugID);
        command.CommandText= s.ToString( );

        // create a second data adapter and add the command
        // and map the table
        // then fill the dataset from this second adapter
        SqlDataAdapter dataAdapter = new SqlDataAdapter( );
        dataAdapter.SelectCommand = command;
        dataAdapter.TableMappings.Add("Table", "BugHistory");

        DataSet dataSet = new DataSet( );
        dataAdapter.Fill(dataSet);
        return dataSet;
    }

    // create a dataset for the bug table
    private DataSet CreateBugDataSet( )
    {

        // connection string to connect to the Bugs Database
        string connectionString =
            "server=YourServer; uid=sa;
        pwd=YourPassword; database=ProgASPDotNetBugs";

        // Create connection object, initialize with
        // connection string. Open it.
        System.Data.SqlClient.SqlConnection connection =
            new System.Data.SqlClient.SqlConnection(connectionString);
        connection.Open( );

        // Create a SqlCommand object and assign the connection
        System.Data.SqlClient.SqlCommand command =
            new System.Data.SqlClient.SqlCommand( );
        command.Connection=connection;

        // build the selection statement
        StringBuilder s =
            new StringBuilder(
            "Select b.BugID, h.BugHistoryID, b.Description,h.Response, ");
        s.Append("o.FullName as owner, ");
        s.Append("p.ProductDescription, ");
        s.Append("r.FullName as reporter, ");
```

Example 11-5. C# code-behind page (continued)

```
            s.Append("s.StatusDescription, ");
            s.Append("sev.SeverityDescription, ");
            s.Append("h.DateStamp ");
            s.Append("from  ");
            s.Append(
              "(select bugID, max(bugHistoryID) as maxHistoryID ");
            s.Append("from BugHistory group by bugID) t ");
            s.Append("join bugs b on b.bugid = t.bugid ");
            s.Append(
              "join BugHistory h on h.bugHistoryID = t.maxHistoryID ");
            s.Append("join lkProduct p on b.Product = p.ProductID  ");
            s.Append("join People r on b.Reporter = r.PersonID  ");
            s.Append("join People o on h.Owner = o.PersonID ");
            s.Append("join lkStatus s on s.statusid = h.status ");
            s.Append(
              "join lkSeverity sev on sev.SeverityID = h.severity ");

            // set the command text to the select statement
            command.CommandText=s.ToString( );

            // create a data adapter and assign the command object
            // and add the table mapping for bugs
            SqlDataAdapter dataAdapter = new SqlDataAdapter( );
            dataAdapter.SelectCommand=command;
            dataAdapter.TableMappings.Add("Table","Bugs");

            // Create the dataset  and use the data adapter to fill it
            DataSet dataSet = new DataSet( );
            dataAdapter.Fill(dataSet);
            return dataSet;
        }

        private void Page_Init(object sender, EventArgs e)
        {
            InitializeComponent( );
        }

        #region Web Form Designer generated code
        /// <summary>
        /// Required method for Designer support - do not modify
        /// the contents of this method with the code editor.
        /// </summary>
        private void InitializeComponent( )
        {
            this.Load += new System.EventHandler(this.Page_Load);

        }
        #endregion
    }
}
```

The Visual Basic .NET source code is shown in Example 11-6.

Example 11-6. VB.NET code-behind page

```
Imports System
Imports System.Web
Imports System.Web.UI
Imports System.Web.UI.WebControls
Imports System.Data

Public Class WebForm1
    Inherits System.Web.UI.Page

    Protected WithEvents DataGrid1 As _
        System.Web.UI.WebControls.DataGrid
    Protected WithEvents HistoryGrid As _
        System.Web.UI.WebControls.DataGrid
    Protected WithEvents BugHistoryPanel As _
        System.Web.UI.WebControls.Panel

#Region " Web Form Designer Generated Code "

    'This call is required by the Web Form Designer.
    <System.Diagnostics.DebuggerStepThrough()> Private Sub InitializeComponent()

    End Sub

    Private Sub Page_Init(ByVal sender As System.Object, _
                        ByVal e As System.EventArgs) _
                        Handles MyBase.Init
        'CODEGEN: This method call is required by the Web Form Designer
        'Do not modify it using the code editor.
        InitializeComponent()
    End Sub

#End Region

    Private Sub Page_Load( _
        ByVal sender As System.Object, _
        ByVal e As System.EventArgs) Handles MyBase.Load
        'Put user code to initialize the page here
        If Not IsPostBack Then
            UpdateBugHistory()
            Dim ds As DataSet = CreateBugDataSet()
            DataGrid1.DataSource = ds.Tables(0)
            DataGrid1.DataBind()
        End If

    End Sub

    Public Sub DataGrid1_ItemDataBound( _
        ByVal sender As Object, _
        ByVal e As System.Web.UI.WebControls.DataGridItemEventArgs) _
        Handles DataGrid1.ItemDataBound

        Dim myItemtype As ListItemType
```

Example 11-6. VB.NET code-behind page (continued)

```
    myItemtype = CType(e.Item.ItemType, ListItemType)
    If (myItemtype = ListItemType.Header) _
    Or (myItemtype = ListItemType.Footer) _
    Or (myItemtype = ListItemType.Separator) Then
        Return
    End If

    Dim obj As Object = _
        CType(e.Item.DataItem, DataRowView).Row.ItemArray(8)

    If CType(e.Item.DataItem, DataRowView).Row.ItemArray(8).ToString() _
        = "High" Then
        Dim severityCell As TableCell = _
            CType(e.Item.Controls(6), TableCell)
        severityCell.ForeColor = Color.FromName("Red")

    End If

End Sub

Private Function CreateBugHistoryDataSet(ByVal bugID As Integer) _
    As DataSet
    Dim connectionString As String = _
        "server=Neptune; uid=sa; pwd=oWenmEany; database=ProgASPDotNetBugs"
    Dim connection As _
        New System.Data.SqlClient.SqlConnection(connectionString)
    connection.Open()

    Dim command As New System.Data.SqlClient.SqlCommand()
    command.Connection = connection

    Dim s As New String( _
        "Select BugID, StatusDescription, severityDescription, ")
    s = s & "Response, FullName as owner, DateStamp from BugHistory h "
    s = s & "join People p on h.owner = p.personID "
    s = s & "join lkStatus s on s.statusid = h.status "
    s = s & "join lkSeverity sev on sev.severityID = h.severity "
    s = s & "where bugid = " & bugID
    command.CommandText = s

    Dim myDataAdapter As New SqlClient.SqlDataAdapter()
    myDataAdapter.SelectCommand = command
    myDataAdapter.TableMappings.Add("Table", "BugHistory")
    Dim ds As New DataSet()
    myDataAdapter.Fill(ds)
    Return ds
End Function

Private Function CreateBugDataSet() As DataSet
    Dim connectionString As String = _
        "server=yourServer; uid=sa; pwd=yourPW; database=ProgASPDotNetBugs"
    Dim connection As _
        New System.Data.SqlClient.SqlConnection(connectionString)
```

Example 11-6. VB.NET code-behind page (continued)

```
    connection.Open( )

    Dim command As New System.Data.SqlClient.SqlCommand( )
    command.Connection = connection

    Dim s As New String( _
       "Select b.bugID, h.bugHistoryID, b.description, h.response, ")
    s = s & "o.Fullname as owner, p.ProductDescription, "
    s = s & "r.FullName as reporter, "
    s = s & "s.statusDescription, sev.SeverityDescription, h.DateStamp "
    s = s & "from (select bugID, max(bugHistoryID) as maxHistoryID "
    s = s & "from BugHistory group by bugID) t "
    s = s & "join bugs b on b.bugid = t.bugID "
    s = s & "join BugHistory h on h.bugHistoryID = t.maxHistoryID "
    s = s & "join lkProduct p on b.Product = p.ProductID  "
    s = s & "join People r on b.Reporter = r.PersonID  "
    s = s & "join People o on h.Owner = o.PersonID  "
    s = s & "join lkStatus s on s.statusid = h.status  "
    s = s & "join lkSeverity sev on sev.SeverityID = h.severity  "

    command.CommandText = s

    Dim myDataAdapter As New SqlClient.SqlDataAdapter( )
    myDataAdapter.SelectCommand = command
    myDataAdapter.TableMappings.Add("Table", "Bugs")
    Dim ds As New DataSet( )
    myDataAdapter.Fill(ds)
    Return ds
End Function

Public Sub DataGrid1_SelectedIndexChanged( _
    ByVal sender As Object, _
    ByVal e As System.EventArgs) _
    Handles DataGrid1.SelectedIndexChanged
    UpdateBugHistory( )
End Sub

Private Sub UpdateBugHistory( )
    Dim index As Integer = DataGrid1.SelectedIndex
    If index <> -1 Then
       Dim bugID As Integer = _
          CType(DataGrid1.DataKeys(index), Integer)
       Dim myDataSet As DataSet = CreateBugHistoryDataSet(bugID)
       HistoryGrid.DataSource = myDataSet.Tables(0)
       HistoryGrid.DataBind( )
       BugHistoryPanel.Visible = True
    Else
       BugHistoryPanel.Visible = False
    End If
End Sub

End Class
```

The Page_Load event handler creates the dataset for the bug grid the first time the page is viewed (that is, the IsPostBack property is false).

When the user clicks on the History button, the OnSelectedIndexChangedHandler event fires. You call a private method, UpdateBugHistory, that determines if the Panel control should be shown or not.

UpdateBugHistory checks the SelectedIndex property from the DataGrid. If the value of SelectedIndex is not -1 (that is, if a selection has been made), the index is used as an offset into the DataGrid's DataKeys collection.

The dataset itself is created by the CreateBugHistoryDataSet method into which you pass the bugID as a parameter. This method formulates an SQL select statement and fills a dataset with the resulting records.

When you first display the page, only the Bug data grid is displayed, as shown in Figure 11-12.

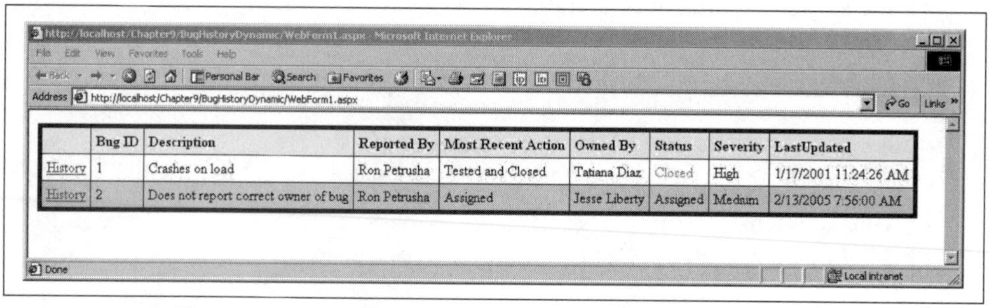

Figure 11-12. Displaying the Bug DataGrid

If the user clicks on the History button, you retrieve the index of the item clicked on and use that as an offset into the Datakeys collection to get the BugID. With the BugID, you can create a dataset of the matching history records, which is displayed in the HistoryDataGrid in the BugHistoryPanel that you now make visible, as shown in Figure 11-13.

Using a DataReader

In the previous example, the BugHistory grid was filled from a table in a dataset. While datasets are very powerful disconnected data sources, they may require more overhead than is needed in this example.

If what you want to do is to retrieve a set of records and then immediately display them, an SqlDataReader or an OleDbDataReader object may be more efficient.

DataReaders are very limited compared to datasets. They offer only a "firehose" cursor for forward-only iteration through a set of results. You can also use DataReaders to execute a simple insert, update, or delete SQL statement.

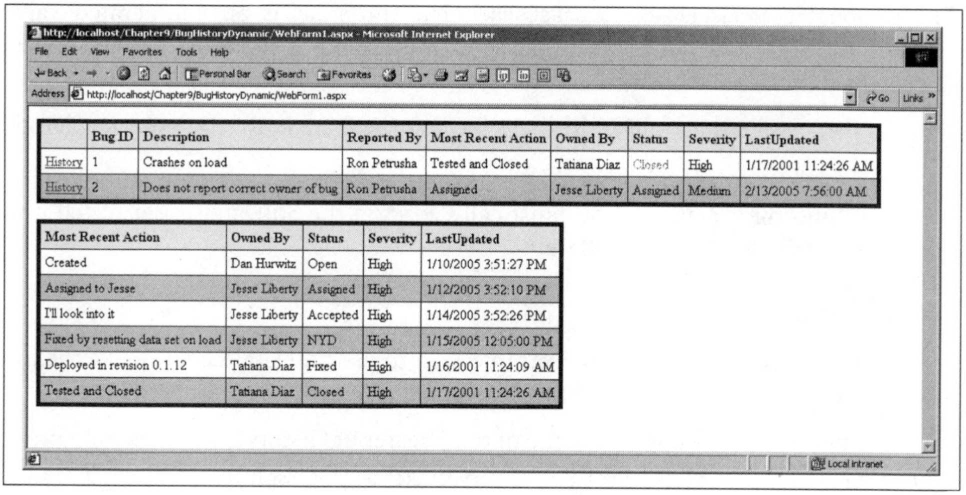

Figure 11-13. Displaying the bug history

Because datasets have greater overhead than DataReaders, you should choose a DataReader as your data source whenever possible. DataReaders are *not* disconnected, however, and so you lose the specific advantages of disconnected datasets. You will certainly need a dataset to meet any of the following requirements:

- To pass a disconnected set of data to another tier in your application or to a client application.

- To persist your results either to a file or to a Session object.

- To provide access to more than one table and to relationships among the tables.

- To bind the same data to multiple controls. Remember, a DataReader object provides forward-only access to the data; you can not reiterate through the data for a second control.

- To jump to a particular record or to go backwards through a set of data.

- To update a number of records in the back-end database using a batch operation.

When you have simpler requirements, however, the DataReader object is a great lightweight alternative to the more complicated dataset. Rewriting the previous example to use a DataReader is almost trivial. You'll modify the CreateBugHistory-DataSet method to return an SqlDataReader object rather than a dataset.

To get started, set up the connection string, SqlConnection object, and SqlCommand object exactly as you did previously. Once your Command object is established, create the DataReader. You cannot call the DataReader's constructor directly; instead you call ExecuteReader on the SqlCommand object; what you get back is an instance of SqlDataReader, as the following code fragment shows:

```
SqlDataReader reader =
    command.ExecuteReader(CommandBehavior.CloseConnection);
```

The optional CommandBehavior.CloseConnection argument is an enumerated value that tells the SqlDataReader object that when it is closed, it should close the connection to the database.

You can then assign that SqlDataReader object as the DataSource for your DataGrid:

```
HistoryGrid.DataSource=reader;
```

After you bind the DataGrid, you must call Close on the SqlDataReader to tell it to break the connection to the database:

```
HistoryGrid.DataBind( );
reader.Close( );
```

That's all there is to it. To modify Example 11-5 to use SqlDataReader, make the following three changes:

1. Modify the return value and name of the CreateBugHistoryDataSet as follows:

```
private SqlDataReader CreateBugHistoryDataReader(int bugID)
```

2. Replace the following lines from what was CreateBugHistoryDataSet:

```
SqlDataAdapter dataAdapter = new SqlDataAdapter( );
dataAdapter.SelectCommand = command;
dataAdapter.TableMappings.Add("Table", "BugHistory");

DataSet dataSet = new DataSet( );
dataAdapter.Fill(dataSet);
return dataSet;
```

with these lines:

```
SqlDataReader reader =
    command.ExecuteReader(CommandBehavior.CloseConnection);
return reader;
```

3. Modify these three lines from UpdateBugHistory:

```
DataSet dataSet =
    CreateBugHistoryDataSet(bugID);
 HistoryGrid.DataSource=dataSet.Tables[0];
 HistoryGrid.DataBind( );
```

with this replacement:

```
SqlDataReader  reader = CreateBugHistoryDataReader(bugID);
HistoryGrid.DataSource=reader;
HistoryGrid.DataBind( );
reader.Close( );
```

Recompile and the program will now use a (connected forward-only firehose) SqlDataReader rather than a (disconnected) SqlDataSet to bind the Bug History data grid.

DataView

In Example 11-5, you query the database for the history records each time you redraw the history grid. An alternative is to retrieve all of the history records once, and then to filter the results to retrieve the history records you want to display. In a larger database, this might become unwieldy, but, for example, you might fill the Bugs table with just the 50 most recent bugs, and you would then fill the history table with the history records for just those 50 bugs. In this way you can reduce the number of calls to the database, in exchange for holding many more records in memory.

To make this work, you'll assign the historyGrid's data source to a DataView object, rather than to a table. The DataView object will represent a "view" of the table, typically filtered by the particular bug of interest.

You can revise the previous example by getting all the BugHistory records at the same time that you get all the bug records. You'll put the Bug records into one table in the dataset, and the BugHistory records into a second table in the dataset.

When the page is first created, you'll create a DataView object based on the second table (BugHistory), and you'll make that view be the DataSource for the HistoryGrid:

```
DataView historyView = new DataView(ds.Tables[1]);
HistoryGrid.DataSource = historyView;
```

When the user clicks on a record you will once again get the BugID by using the selected row as an index into the DataGrid object's DataKeys collection. This time, however, you will use that bugID to filter the view you've created:

```
historyView.RowFilter = "BugID = " + bugID;
```

The RowFilter property of the DataView object allows you to filter the view for those records you want. The view will only present records which match the filter. RowFilters use the SQL syntax of a where clause. The RowFilter above equates to the clause "where BugID = 2".

Unfortunately, your class is destroyed and recreated each time the page is posted. Your historyView object will not persist, even if you were to make it an instance variable of the WebForm1 class. You could, of course, recreate the view by reissuing the query, but this would undermine the point of getting the entire set of history records in the first place.

In a production system, you might get the view from outside your application. For example, you might be interacting with a web service that provides the DataView. In this example, since you don't have such a web service, you'll stash the DataView into the session state.

 Saving your view in session state works fine as long as your server is on a single machine. Once your server grows to multiple machines, you'll probably save session state to a database, in which case it is silly to keep the DataView in session state. At that point, you might as well issue smaller queries directly to the database for each update, rather than retrieving the entire set of history records from the database into session state and then back into your program and then filtering the results.

To save the DataView in session state, you just create a "key"—a string which will be used to identify your session state variable:

```
Session["historyView"] = historyView;
```

Here the DataView object historyView is saved to session state with the string "historyView" as its key. Session variables act like properties; you can simply assign them to an object, remembering to cast to the appropriate type:

```
DataView historyView = (DataView) Session["historyView"];
```

Creating Data Relations

Because the DataSet acts as a disconnected model of the database, it must be able to represent not only the tables within the database, but the relations among the tables as well.

The DataSet captures these relationships in a DataRelationCollection that you access through the read-only Relations property. The DataRelationCollection is a collection of DataRelation objects, each of which represents a relationship between two tables.

Each DataRelation object relates a pair of DataTable objects to each other through DataColumn objects. The relationship is established by matching columns in the two tables.

The DataRelation objects retrieved through the Relations property of the DataSet provides you with meta-data: data about the relationship among the tables in the database. You can use this meta-data in a number of ways. For example, you can generate a schema for your database from the information contained in the dataset.

In the next example, you will create DataRelation objects to model two relationships within the Bugs database. The first DataRelation object you create will represent the relationship between the Bugs table and the BugHistory table through the BugID. The second relationship you will model is between the BugHistory table and the lkSeverity table through the SeverityID.

You will remember that the BugHistory table uses the BugID from the Bugs table as a foreign key. You thus need a column object for the BugID column in each of the tables:

```
System.Data.DataColumn dataColumn1;
System.Data.DataColumn dataColumn2;
dataColumn1 =
    dataSet.Tables["Bugs"].Columns["BugID"];
dataColumn2 =
    dataSet.Tables["BugHistory"].Columns["BugID"];
```

With these two columns in hand, you are ready to initialize the DataRelation object that you will use to model the relationship between the Bugs and BugHistory tables. You pass in the two data columns along with a name for the relationship, in this case BugsToHistory:

```
dataRelation = new System.Data.DataRelation(
    "BugsToHistory",
    dataColumn1,
    dataColumn2);
```

 You can of course combine the declaration and initialization of the DataRelation object:

```
System.Data.DataRelation dataRelation =
    new System.Data.DataRelation(
    "BugsToHistory",
    dataColumn1,
    dataColumn2);
```

You now add the Relation to the DataRelationCollection collection in the dataset:

```
dataSet.Relations.Add(dataRelation);
```

To create the second DataRelation, between the BugHistory and lkSeverity tables, you first create a "lkSeverity" table within the dataset:

```
StringBuilder s3 =
    new StringBuilder(
    "Select SeverityID, SeverityDescription from lkSeverity");
command3.CommandText= s3.ToString( );

SqlDataAdapter dataAdapter3 = new SqlDataAdapter( );
dataAdapter3.SelectCommand = command3;
dataAdapter3.TableMappings.Add("Table", "lkSeverity");
dataAdapter3.Fill(dataSet);
```

You are now ready to create the data relation between the History table and the Severity table:

```
dataColumn1 = dataSet.Tables["lkSeverity"].Columns["SeverityID"];
dataColumn2 = dataSet.Tables["BugHistory"].Columns["Severity"];

dataRelation =
    new System.Data.DataRelation(
    "HistoryToSeverity",
    dataColumn1,
    dataColumn2);

dataSet.Relations.Add(dataRelation);
```

In the previous example, you did not need to get the Severity value in the select statement that builds the BugHistory table. You joined on the lkSeverity table and got the SeverityDescription, but not the ID. To create the relation, however, you now do need that value. Be sure to modify the select statement:

```
StringBuilder s2 =
    new StringBuilder("Select BugID, BugHistoryID,
    StatusDescription, ");
s2.Append(
    "Severity, SeverityDescription, Response, FullName as
    Owner, DateStamp ");
s2.Append("from BugHistory h ");
s2.Append("join People o on h.Owner = o.PersonID ");
s2.Append("join lkStatus s on s.statusid = h.status ");
s2.Append(
    "join lkSeverity sev on sev.SeverityID = h.severity ");
command2.CommandText= s2.ToString( );
```

If you neglect to select the SeverityID (History.Severity) and you try to establish a relation between History.Severity and lkSeverity.SeverityID you will get an error at run time that the column is null. This can make you a bit crazy until you figure out that there is no Severity column in the BugHistory table within the dataset even though that column certainly does exist in the database.

You can now display these relations by creating a data grid and setting its data-Source to the Relations table of the dataSet. In the *.aspx* file add this code:

```
<asp:DataGrid ID="BugRelations" Runat="server"
    HeaderStyle-Font-Bold AlternatingItemStyle-BackColor="LightGrey"
    BorderColor="#000099" BorderWidth="5px"
    HeaderStyle-BackColor="PapayaWhip"
    CellPadding="5" Runat="server"/>
    <br>
```

In the Page_Load method of the code-behind file, add these two lines:

```
BugRelations.DataSource=ds.Relations;
BugRelations.DataBind( );
```

In a real product, you might create a nested grid structure in which you would show first a Bug and then all its history elements. Rather than focusing on the user interface, in this example you'll just build a string output of these relationships, printing these to an HTML page using an ASP Label control.

Figure 11-14 shows the result of displaying both the collection of DataRelation objects and a hand-built string produced by iterating through the Bugs table and the related BugHistory records.

Figure 11-14 shows three grids. The first is created from the Bugs table, as seen in previous examples. The second is created from the lkSeverity table added in this

File   Edit   View   Favorites   Tools   Help

Back ▾ ▸ ▾ ⊗ ⧉ ⌂ | 🗔 Personal Bar ⊙ Search 🖻 Favorites ⊗ | 🗗▾ 🖨 ⊠ ⧉ 🗒 🗒 ⊡ ⧉ 🗒

Address | http://localhost/Chapter9/BugHistoryDataGridRelations/WebForm1.aspx

	Bug ID	Description	Reported By	Most Recent Action	Owned By	Status	Severity	LastUpdated
History	1	Crashes on load	Ron Petrusha	Tested and Closed	Tatiana Diaz	Closed	High	1/17/2001 11:24:26 AM
History	2	Does not report correct owner of bug	Ron Petrusha	Assigned	Jesse Liberty	Assigned	Medium	2/13/2005 7:56:00 AM

SeverityID	SeverityDescription
1	Show Stopper
2	High
3	Medium
4	Low
5	Trivial

RelationName	Nested
BugsToHistory	False
HistoryToSeverity	False

BugID: 1
1: Created
2: Assigned to Jesse
3: I'll look into it
6: Fixed by resetting data set on load
7: Deployed in revision 0.1.12
8: Tested and Closed

BugID: 2
4: Created
5: Assigned

Done   Local Intranet

Figure 11-14. Showing the Bug and BugHistory relations

example. The final grid's data source is the Relations table from the dataset. It shows that you've created two relation objects: BugsToHistory and HistoryTo-Severity.

Below the three grids is the text output produced by walking through the relationships between Bugs and BugHistory. For each Bug (e.g., BugID 1) you see the BugHistory records with that same BugID (e.g, the eight bug History records for BugID 1).

> Normally, as here, the parent/child relationship between two tables is managed by the DataRelation object; the two tables are otherwise independent of one another.
>
> With XML however, parent/child relationships are represented by nesting attributes one within the other. To facilitate synchronizing with an XML document or writing out the dataset as XML (using the DataSet object's WriteXml method), the DataRelation object has a Nested property. When Nested is set to true, the child rows of the relation are nested within the parent column when written as XML or when synchronized with an XML data document.

The *.aspx* file is very similar to the previous examples, you have only to add the new grids and the label for output:

```
<asp:DataGrid ID="SeverityGrid" Runat="server"
    HeaderStyle-Font-Bold AlternatingItemStyle-BackColor="LightGrey"
    BorderColor="#000099" BorderWidth="5px" HeaderStyle-BackColor="PapayaWhip"
    CellPadding="5" Runat="server"/>
    <br>
<asp:DataGrid ID="BugRelations" Runat="server"
    HeaderStyle-Font-Bold AlternatingItemStyle-BackColor="LightGrey"
    BorderColor="#000099" BorderWidth="5px" HeaderStyle-BackColor="PapayaWhip"
    CellPadding="5" Runat="server"/>
    <br>
<asp:Label ID="showRelations" Runat="server"></asp:Label>
```

To create the label showing the relationships, you'll work your way through the Bugs table by hand, finding all the related BugHistory items for each of the Bug objects.

You iterate through the rows in the Bugs data table. For each row, you create an output string with the BugID, and then you get a collection of the child rows defined by the BugsToHistory relation:

```
DataTable tblBugs = ds.Tables["Bugs"];
foreach (DataRow currentRow in tblBugs.Rows)
{
    outputString += "BugID: " + currentRow["BugID"] + "<br/>";
    DataRow[] childRows = currentRow.GetChildRows("BugsToHistory");
```

The childRows DataRow collection contains all the child rows for the current row in the Bugs table. The childRow relationship is established by the DataRelation named BugsToHistory, which established a relationship between the BugID foreign key in BugHistory and the BugID key in Bugs.

You can now iterate through that childRows collection, printing whatever information you wish to display for each BugHistory record for the current bug:

```
foreach (DataRow historyRow in childRows)
{
    outputString += historyRow["BugHistoryID"] + ": " +
        historyRow["Response"] + "<br>";
}
```

When you've iterated through all the rows, you can assign the resulting string to the Text property of the label you've added to your *.aspx* page:

```
showRelations.Text=outputString;
```

The complete annotated source code for the code-behind page is shown in Example 11-7.

Example 11-7. Code-behind page

```
using System;
using System.Collections;
using System.ComponentModel;
```

Example 11-7. Code-behind page (continued)

```
using System.Data;
using System.Data.SqlClient;
using System.Drawing;
using System.Text;
using System.Web;
using System.Web.SessionState;
using System.Web.UI;
using System.Web.UI.WebControls;
using System.Web.UI.HtmlControls;

namespace BugHistoryDataGridRelations
{
    /// <summary>
    /// Summary description for WebForm1.
    /// </summary>
    public class WebForm1 : System.Web.UI.Page
    {
        // the Bugs Data Grid
        protected System.Web.UI.WebControls.DataGrid DataGrid1;

        // the Data Grid for the history items displayed using
        // a filtered view
        protected System.Web.UI.WebControls.DataGrid HistoryGrid;

        // the Data Grid to show the lkSeverity table
        protected System.Web.UI.WebControls.DataGrid SeverityGrid;

        // the Data Grid to show the DataRelations you've created
        protected System.Web.UI.WebControls.DataGrid BugRelations;

        // The panel to hold the history grid
        protected System.Web.UI.WebControls.Panel BugHistoryPanel;

        // The label for the hand-crafted string showing the
        // relation between a Bug and its child History records
        protected System.Web.UI.WebControls.Label showRelations;


        // unchanged from previous example
        public WebForm1( )
        {
            Page.Init += new System.EventHandler(Page_Init);
        }

        // unchanged from previous example
        public void OnItemDataBoundEventHandler(
            Object sender, DataGridItemEventArgs e)
        {
            ListItemType itemType = (ListItemType)e.Item.ItemType;
            if (itemType == ListItemType.Header ||
                itemType == ListItemType.Footer ||
                itemType == ListItemType.Separator)
```

Example 11-7. Code-behind page (continued)

```
        return;

    if (((DataRowView)e.Item.DataItem).Row.ItemArray[8].ToString( )
        == "High")
    {
        TableCell severityCell = (TableCell) e.Item.Controls[6];
        severityCell.ForeColor = Color.FromName("Red");
    }
}


// unchanged from previous example
public void OnSelectedIndexChangedHandler(
    Object sender, EventArgs e)
{
    UpdateBugHistory( );
}


// unchanged from previous example
private void UpdateBugHistory( )
{

    int index = DataGrid1.SelectedIndex;
    if (index != -1)
    {
        // get the bug id from the data grid
        int bugID =  (int) DataGrid1.DataKeys[index];
        DataView historyView = (DataView) Session["historyView"];
        historyView.RowFilter = "BugID = " + bugID;
        HistoryGrid.DataSource = historyView;
        HistoryGrid.DataBind( );
        BugHistoryPanel.Visible=true;
    }
    else
    {
        BugHistoryPanel.Visible=false;
    }
}

// build the various tables, views, dataSets  and data relations
private void Page_Load(object sender, System.EventArgs e)
{
    if (!IsPostBack)
    {
        // hide the history panel
        UpdateBugHistory( );

        // call the method which creates the tables and the relations
        DataSet ds = CreateDataSet( );

        // set the data source for the grid to the first table
        DataGrid1.DataSource=ds.Tables[0];
        DataGrid1.DataBind( );
```

Example 11-7. Code-behind page (continued)

```
        // create the DataView and bind to the History grid
        DataView historyView = new DataView(ds.Tables[1]);
        HistoryGrid.DataSource = historyView;
        Session["historyView"] = historyView;
        HistoryGrid.DataBind();

        // bind the severity grid to the
        SeverityGrid.DataSource=ds.Tables["lkSeverity"];
        SeverityGrid.DataBind();

        // bind the BugRelations grid to the Relations collection
        BugRelations.DataSource=ds.Relations;
        BugRelations.DataBind();

        // create the output string to show the relationship
        // between each bug and its related BugHistory records
        String outputString = "";
        DataTable tblBugs = ds.Tables["Bugs"];

        // for each Bug show its bugID and get all the
        // related history records
        foreach (DataRow currentRow in tblBugs.Rows)
        {
            outputString += "BugID: " + currentRow["BugID"] + "<br/>";

            // the child relationship is created by the BugsToHistory
            // data relationship created in CreateDataSet()
            DataRow[] childRows =
              currentRow.GetChildRows("BugsToHistory");

            // for each historyRow in the child collection
            // display the response (current status) field
            foreach (DataRow historyRow in childRows)
            {
                outputString += historyRow["BugHistoryID"] + ": " +
                    historyRow["Response"] + "<br>";
            }
            outputString += "<br/>";
        }

        // update the label
        showRelations.Text=outputString;
    }
}

// updated to get the lkSeverity table and to create
// two DataRelation objects - one for Bug to BugHistory
// and a second for BugHistory to lkSeverity
private DataSet CreateDataSet()
{

    // connection string to connect to the Bugs Database
```

Example 11-7. Code-behind page (continued)

```
string connectionString =
    "server=YourServer; uid=sa; pwd=YourPassword;
    database=ProgASPDotNetBugs";

// Create connection object, initialize with
// connection string and open the connection
System.Data.SqlClient.SqlConnection connection =
    new System.Data.SqlClient.SqlConnection(connectionString);
connection.Open();


// Create a SqlCommand object and assign the connection
System.Data.SqlClient.SqlCommand command =
    new System.Data.SqlClient.SqlCommand();
command.Connection=connection;

// build the selection statement
StringBuilder s = new StringBuilder(
    "Select b.BugID, h.BugHistoryID, b.Description,h.Response, ");
s.Append("o.FullName as owner, ");
s.Append("p.ProductDescription, ");
s.Append("r.FullName as reporter, ");
s.Append("s.StatusDescription, ");
s.Append("sev.SeverityDescription, ");
s.Append("h.DateStamp ");
s.Append("from  ");
s.Append(
    "(select bugID, max(bugHistoryID) as maxHistoryID ");
s.Append("from BugHistory group by bugID) t ");
s.Append("join bugs b on b.bugid = t.bugid ");
s.Append(
    "join BugHistory h on h.bugHistoryID = t.maxHistoryID ");
s.Append("join lkProduct p on b.Product = p.ProductID  ");
s.Append("join People r on b.Reporter = r.PersonID  ");
s.Append("join People o on h.Owner = o.PersonID ");
s.Append("join lkStatus s on s.statusid = h.status ");
s.Append(
    "join lkSeverity sev on sev.SeverityID = h.severity ");

// set the command text to the select statement
command.CommandText=s.ToString();

// create a data adapter and assign the command object
// and add the table mapping for bugs
SqlDataAdapter dataAdapter = new SqlDataAdapter();
dataAdapter.SelectCommand=command;
dataAdapter.TableMappings.Add("Table","Bugs");

// Create the dataset  and use the data adapter to fill it
DataSet dataSet = new DataSet();
dataAdapter.Fill(dataSet);
```

Example 11-7. Code-behind page (continued)

```
// create a second command object for the bugs hisotry table
System.Data.SqlClient.SqlCommand command2 =
    new System.Data.SqlClient.SqlCommand( );
command2.Connection = connection;

// This time be sure to add a column for Severity so that you can
// create a relation to lkSeverity
StringBuilder s2 =
    new StringBuilder(
    "Select BugID, BugHistoryID, StatusDescription, ");
s2.Append(
    "Severity, SeverityDescription, Response,
        FullName as Owner, DateStamp ");
s2.Append("from BugHistory h ");
s2.Append("join People o on h.Owner = o.PersonID ");
s2.Append("join lkStatus s on s.statusid = h.status ");
s2.Append(
    "join lkSeverity sev on sev.SeverityID = h.severity ");
command2.CommandText= s2.ToString( );

// create a second data adapter and
// add the command and map the table
// then fill the dataset  from this second adapter
SqlDataAdapter dataAdapter2 = new SqlDataAdapter( );
dataAdapter2.SelectCommand = command2;
dataAdapter2.TableMappings.Add("Table", "BugHistory");
dataAdapter2.Fill(dataSet);


// create a third command object for the lkSeverity table
System.Data.SqlClient.SqlCommand command3 =
    new System.Data.SqlClient.SqlCommand( );
command3.Connection = connection;

StringBuilder s3 =
    new StringBuilder(
    "Select SeverityID, SeverityDescription from lkSeverity");
command3.CommandText= s3.ToString( );

// create a third data adapter
// and add the command and map the table
// then fill the dataset  from this second adapter
SqlDataAdapter dataAdapter3 = new SqlDataAdapter( );
dataAdapter3.SelectCommand = command3;
dataAdapter3.TableMappings.Add("Table", "lkSeverity");
dataAdapter3.Fill(dataSet);


// declare the DataRelation and DataColumn objects
System.Data.DataRelation dataRelation;
System.Data.DataColumn dataColumn1;
System.Data.DataColumn dataColumn2;
```

Example 11-7. Code-behind page (continued)

```
            // set the dataColumns to create the relationship
            // between Bug and BugHistory on the BugID key
        dataColumn1 =
            dataSet.Tables["Bugs"].Columns["BugID"];
        dataColumn2 =
            dataSet.Tables["BugHistory"].Columns["BugID"];

        dataRelation =
            new System.Data.DataRelation(
            "BugsToHistory",
            dataColumn1,
            dataColumn2);

            // add the new DataRelation to the dataset
        dataSet.Relations.Add(dataRelation);

            // reuse the DataColumns and DataRelation objects
            // to create the relation between BugHistory and lkSeverity
        dataColumn1 = dataSet.Tables["lkSeverity"].Columns["SeverityID"];
        dataColumn2 = dataSet.Tables["BugHistory"].Columns["Severity"];

        dataRelation =
            new System.Data.DataRelation(
            "HistoryToSeverity",
            dataColumn1,
            dataColumn2);

            // add the HistoryToSeverity relationship to the dataset
        dataSet.Relations.Add(dataRelation);

        return dataSet;
    }

    // unchanged from previous example
    private void Page_Init(object sender, EventArgs e)
    {
        InitializeComponent( );
    }


    #region Web Form Designer generated code
    /// <summary>
    /// Required method for Designer support - do not modify
    /// the contents of this method with the code editor.
    /// </summary>
    private void InitializeComponent( )
    {
        this.Load += new System.EventHandler(this.Page_Load);

    }
    #endregion

  }
}
```

Creating Data Objects by Hand

In all of the examples so far, you have created the DataSet object and its DataTable and DataRow objects by selecting data from the database. There are, however, occasions when you will want to fill a dataset or a table by hand.

For example, you may want to gather data from a user and then push that data into the database. It can be convenient to add records to a table manually, and then update the database from that table.

The dataset is also an excellent transport mechanism for data. You may even want to create a dataset by hand only to pass it to another tier in your application where it will be used as a data source.

In the next example you will create a dataset and populate three tables by hand. You'll start by creating the Bugs table and specifying its data structure. You'll then fill that table with records. You'll do the same for the lkProduct table and the People table.

Once the tables are created, you'll set constraints on a number of columns, set default values, establish identity columns, and create keys. In addition, you'll establish a foreign key relationship between two tables, and you'll create a data relation tying two tables together. It sounds like more work than it really is.

Creating the DataTable by Hand

Start by creating a method named CreateDataSet. The job of this method is to create a DataSet and to populate it by hand, and then to return that resulting DataSet to the calling method, in this case Page_Load.

CreateDataSet begins by instantiating a new DataTable object, passing in the name of the table as a parameter to the constructor:

```
DataTable tblBugs = new DataTable("Bugs");
```

The table you are creating should mimic the data structure of the Bugs table in SQL Server. Figure 11-15 shows that structure.

To add a column to this DataTable object, you do not call a constructor. Instead you call the Add method of the DataTable object's Columns collection. The Add method takes two parameters, the name of the column and its data type:

```
DataColumn newColumn;
newColumn =
    tblBugs.Columns.Add("BugID", Type.GetType("System.Int32"));
```

In Visual Basic .NET, this is:

```
dim newColumn as DataColumn
newColumn = _
    tblBugs.Columns.Add("BugID", Type.GetType("System.Int32"));
```

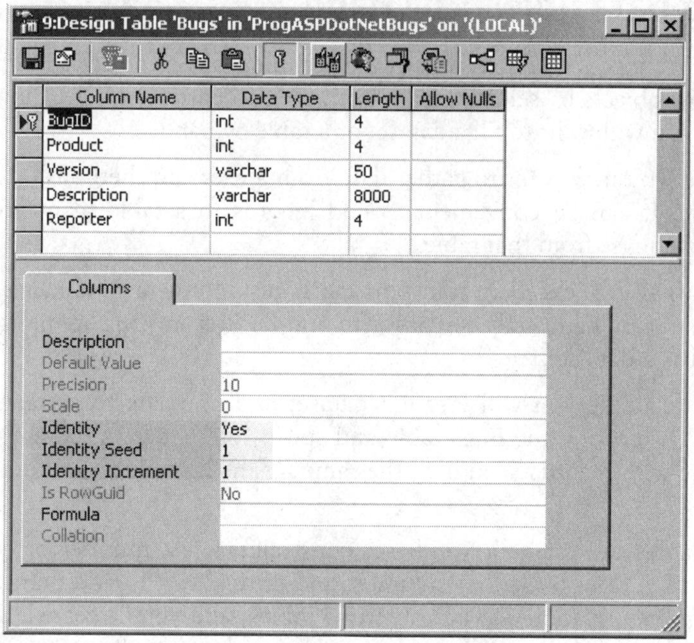
9:Design Table 'Bugs' in 'ProgASPDotNetBugs' on '(LOCAL)'
Column Name
Data Type
Length
Allow Nulls
BugID
int
4
Product
int
4
Version
varchar
50
Description
varchar
8000
Reporter
int
4
Columns
Description
Default Value
Precision
10
Scale
0
Identity
Yes
Identity Seed
1
Identity Increment
1
Is RowGuid
No
Formula
Collation

Figure 11-15. The structure of the Bugs table in SQL server

Setting column properties

The Add method creates the new column and returns a reference to it, which you may now manipulate. Since this is to be an identity column (see the highlighted area of Figure 11-16), you'll want to set its AutoIncrement property to `true`, and you'll set the AutoIncrementSeed and AutoIncrementStep properties to set the seed and step values of the identity, respectively. The following code fragment does this:

```
newColumn.AutoIncrement = true;
newColumn.AutoIncrementSeed=1;
newColumn.AutoIncrementStep=1;
```

> The AutoIncrementSeed property sets the initial value for the identity column, and the AutoIncrementStep property sets the increment for each new record. Thus, if the seed were 5 and the step were 3, the first five records would have IDs of 5, 8, 11, 14, and 17. In the case shown, where both the seed and step are 1, the first four records have IDs of 1,2,3,4.

Setting constraints

Identity columns must not be null, so you'll set the AllowDBNull property of the new column to `false`:

```
newColumn.AllowDBNull=false;
```

You can set the Unique property to `false` to ensure that each entry in this column must be unique:

```
newColumn.Unique=true;
```

This creates an unnamed constraint in the Bugs table's Constraints collection. You can, if you prefer, add a named constraint. To do so, you create an instance of the UniqueConstraint class and pass a name for it into the constructor, along with a reference to the column:

```
UniqueConstraint constraint =
    new UniqueConstraint("Unique_BugID",newColumn);
```

You then manually add that constraint to the table's `Constraints` collection:

```
tblBugs.Constraints.Add(constraint);
```

If you do add a named constraint, be sure to comment out the Unique property.

This completes the first column in the table. The second column is the Product column, as you can see in Figure 11-16. Notice that this column is of type integer, with no nulls and a default value of 1 (see the highlighted property in Figure 11-16). You create the Product column by calling the Add method of the Columns collection of the tblBugs table, this time passing in the type for an integer. You then set the AllowDBNull property as you did with the earlier column, and you set the Default-Value property to set the default value for the column. This is illustrated in the following code fragment:

```
newColumn = tblBugs.Columns.Add(
    "Product", Type.GetType("System.Int32"));
newColumn.AllowDBNull=false;
newColumn.DefaultValue = 1;
```

Looking at Figure 11-16 again, you can see that the third column is `Version`, with a type of `varChar`.

A varChar is a variable length character string. A varChar can be declared to be any length between 1 and 8000 bytes. Typically you will limit the length of the string as a form of documentation indicating the largest string you expect in the field.

You declare the column type to be `string` for a varchar, and you can set the length of the string with the MaxLength property, as shown in the following code fragment:

```
newColumn = tblBugs.Columns.Add(
    "Version", Type.GetType("System.String"));
newColumn.AllowDBNull=false;
newColumn.MaxLength=50;
newColumn.DefaultValue = "0.1";
```

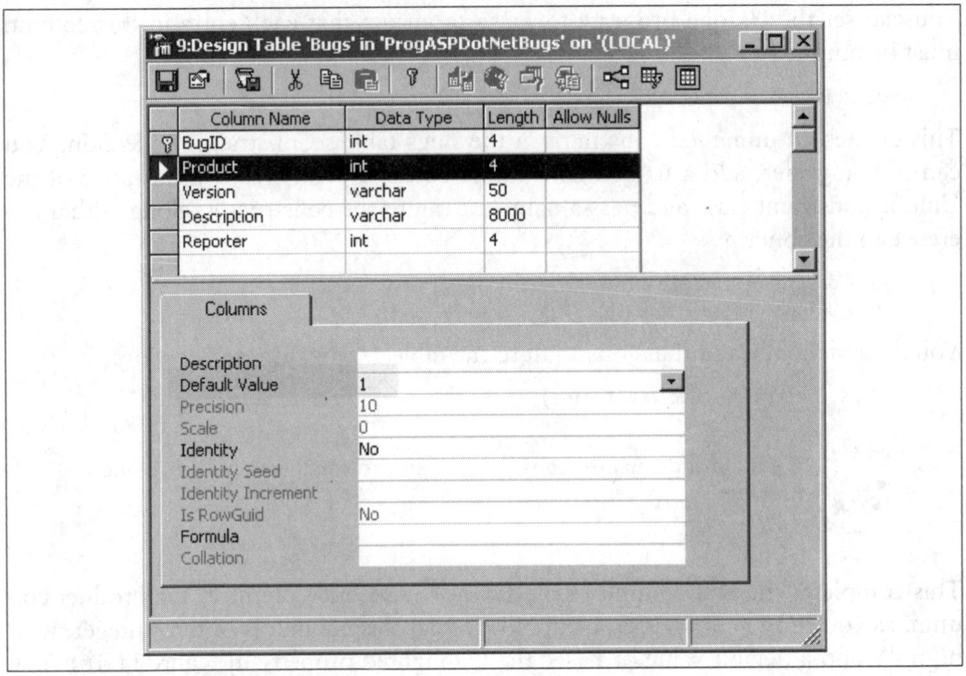

Figure 11-16. The Products column

You declare the Description and Reporter columns in a like manner:

```
newColumn = tblBugs.Columns.Add("Description", Type.GetType("System.String"));
newColumn.AllowDBNull=false;
newColumn.MaxLength=8000;
newColumn.DefaultValue = "";

newColumn = tblBugs.Columns.Add(
    "Reporter", Type.GetType("System.Int32"));
newColumn.AllowDBNull=false;
```

Adding data to the table

With all the columns declared, you're ready to add rows of data to the table. You do so by calling the DataTable object's NewRow method, which returns an empty DataRow object with the right structure:

```
newRow = tblBugs.NewRow( );
```

You can use the column name as an index into the row's collection of DataColumns, assigning the appropriate value for each column, one by one:

```
newRow["Product"] = 1;
newRow["Version"] = "0.1";
newRow["Description"] = "Crashes on load";
newRow["Reporter"] = 5;
```

The authors of the DataRows class have implemented the indexer for their class to access the contained Columns collection invisibly. Thus, when you write newRow["Product"], you actually access the Product column within the Columns collection of the DataRow object.

When the columns are complete, you add the row to the table's Rows collection by calling the Add method, passing in the row you just created:

```
tblBugs.Rows.Add(newRow);
```

You are now ready to create a new row:

```
newRow = tblBugs.NewRow( );
newRow["Product"] = 1;
newRow["Version"] = "0.1";
newRow["Description"] = "Does not report correct owner of bug";
newRow["Reporter"] = 5;
tblBugs.Rows.Add(newRow);
```

When all the rows have been created, you can create an instance of a DataSet object and add the table:

```
DataSet dataSet = new DataSet( );
dataSet.Tables.Add(tblBugs);
```

Adding additional tables to the DataSet

With the Bugs table added to the new dataset, you are ready to create a new table for lkProduct:

```
DataTable tblProduct = new DataTable("lkProduct")
```

Once again you'll define the columns and then add data. You'll then go on to add a new table for People. In theory, you could also add all the other tables from the previous example, but to keep things simpler, you'll stop with these three.

Adding rows with an array of objects

The DataRowCollection object's Add method is overloaded. In the code shown above, you created a new DataRow object, populated its columns, and added the row. You are also free to create an array of Objects, fill the array, and pass the array to the Add method. For example, rather than writing:

```
newRow = tblPeople.NewRow( );
newRow["FullName"] = "Jesse Liberty";
newRow["email"] = "jliberty@libertyassociates.com";
newRow["Phone"] = "617-555-7301";
newRow["Role"] = 1;
tblPeople.Rows.Add(newRow);
```

you can instead create an array of five objects and fill that array with the values you would have added to the columns of the row:

```
Object[] PersonArray = new Object[5];
PersonArray[0] = 1;
PersonArray[1] = "Jesse Liberty";
PersonArray[2] = "jliberty@libertyassociates.com";
PersonArray[3] = "617-555-7301";
PersonArray[4] = 1;
tblPeople.Rows.Add(PersonArray);
```

Note that in this case, you must manually add a value for the identity column, BugID. When you created the row object, the identity column value was automatically created for you with the right increment from the previous row, but since you are now just creating an array of objects, you must do this by hand.

While this technique works, it is generally not very desirable. The overloaded version of the Add method that takes a DataRow object is typesafe. Each column must match the definition of the column you've created. With an array of objects, just about anything goes; remember that in .NET, everything derives from Object and thus you can pass in any type of data to an array of objects.

Creating Primary Keys

The Bugs table uses the PersonID as a foreign key into the People table. To recreate this, you'll first need to create a primary key in the People table.

You start by declaring the PersonID column as a unique non-null identity column, just as you did earlier for the BugID column in Bugs:

```
newColumn = tblPeople.Columns.Add("PersonID", Type.GetType("System.Int32"));
newColumn.AutoIncrement = true;      // autoincrementing
newColumn.AutoIncrementSeed=1;       // starts at 1
newColumn.AutoIncrementStep=1;       // increments by 1
newColumn.AllowDBNull=false;         // nulls not allowed

// add the unique constraint
UniqueConstraint uniqueConstraint =
   new UniqueConstraint("Unique_PersonID",newColumn);
tblPeople.Constraints.Add(uniqueConstraint);
```

To create the primary key you must set the PrimaryKey property of the table. This property takes an array of DataColumn objects.

In many tables, the primary key is not a single column but rather two or more columns. For example, you might keep track of orders for a customer. A given order might be order number 17. Your database may have many orders whose order number is 17. What uniquely identifies a given order is the order number combined with the customer number. Thus, that table would use a compound key of the order number and the customer number.

The primary key for the People table is a single column: PersonID. To set the primary key, you create an array (in this case with one member), and assign to that member the column(s) you want to make the primary key:

```
columnArray = new DataColumn[1];
columnArray[0] = newColumn;
```

The newColumn object contains a reference to the PersonID column returned from calling Add. You assign the array to the PrimaryKey property of the table:

```
tblPeople.PrimaryKey=columnArray;
```

Creating Foreign Keys

The PersonID acts as a primary key in People and as a foreign key in Bugs. To create the foreign key relationship, you'll instantiate a new object of type ForeignKeyConstraint, passing in the name of the constraint ("FK_BugToPeople") as well as a reference to the two columns.

To facilitate passing references to the key fields to the ForeignKeyConstraint constructor, you'll want to squirrel away a reference to the PersonID column in People and the Reporter column in Bugs. Immediately after you create the columns, save a reference:

```
newColumn =
    tblBugs.Columns.Add("Reporter", Type.GetType("System.Int32"));
newColumn.AllowDBNull=false;
DataColumn bugReporterColumn =
    newColumn; // save for foreign key creation
```

Assuming you've saved the Reporter column in bugReporterColumn and the PersonID column from People in PersonIDColumn, you are ready to create the ForeignKeyConstraint object:

```
ForeignKeyConstraint fk =
    New ForeignKeyConstraint(
        "FK_BugToPeople",PersonIDColumn,bugReporterColumn);
```

This creates the Foreign Key Constraint named fk. Before you add it to the Bugs table, you must set two properties:

```
fk.DeleteRule=Rule.Cascade;
fk.UpdateRule=Rule.Cascade;
```

The DeleteRule determines the action that will occur when a row is deleted from the parent table. Similarly, the UpdateRule determines what will happen when a row is updated in the parent column. The potential values are enumerated by the Rule enumeration, as shown in Table 11-6.

Table 11-6. The Rule enumeration

Member name	Description
Cascade	Delete or update related rows; this is the default.
None	Take no action on related rows.
SetDefault	Set the values in the related rows to the value contained in the DefaultValue property.
SetNull	Set the related rows to null.

In the case shown, the value is set to Rule.Cascade; if a record is deleted from the parent table, all the child records will be deleted as well. You are now ready to add the foreign key constraint to the Bugs table:

```
tblBugs.Constraints.Add(fk);
```

Creating Data Relations

As you saw earlier in the chapter, you can encapsulate the relationship among tables in a DataRelation object. The code for building relationships among hand-crafted DataTables is just like the code you saw earlier when you pulled the data structure from the database itself:

```
System.Data.DataRelation dataRelation;
System.Data.DataColumn dataColumn1;
System.Data.DataColumn dataColumn2;

// set the dataColumns to create the relationship
// between Bug and BugHistory on the BugID key
dataColumn1 =
    dataSet.Tables["People"].Columns["PersonID"];
dataColumn2 =
    dataSet.Tables["Bugs"].Columns["Reporter"];

dataRelation =
    new System.Data.DataRelation(
    "BugsToReporter",
    dataColumn1,
    dataColumn2);

// add the new DataRelation to the dat
dataSet.Relations.Add(dataRelation);
```

To display this output, you'll use two DataGrids: one to show the Bugs table, and another to show the Constraints you've added to that table:

```
<body>
    <form id="Form1" method="post" runat="server">
        <asp:DataGrid id="DataGrid1" runat="server" DataKeyField="BugID"
        CellPadding="5" HeaderStyle-BackColor="PapayaWhip" BorderWidth="5px"
        BorderColor="#000099" AlternatingItemStyle-BackColor="LightGrey"
```

```
        HeaderStyle-Font-Bold AutoGenerateColumns="False"
        EnableViewState="true">
            <Columns>
                <asp:BoundColumn DataField="BugID"
                HeaderText="Bug ID" />
                <asp:BoundColumn DataField="Description"
                HeaderText="Description" />
                <asp:BoundColumn DataField="Reporter"
                HeaderText="Reported By" />
            </Columns>
        </asp:DataGrid>
        <br />
        <asp:DataGrid ID="BugConstraints" Runat="server"
          HeaderStyle-Font-Bold AlternatingItemStyle-BackColor="LightGrey"
          BorderColor="#000099" BorderWidth="5px"
          HeaderStyle-BackColor="PapayaWhip" CellPadding="5" Runat="server" />
    </form>
</body>
```

The output is shown in Figure 11-17. The complete source code for this version of the application is shown in Example 11-8.

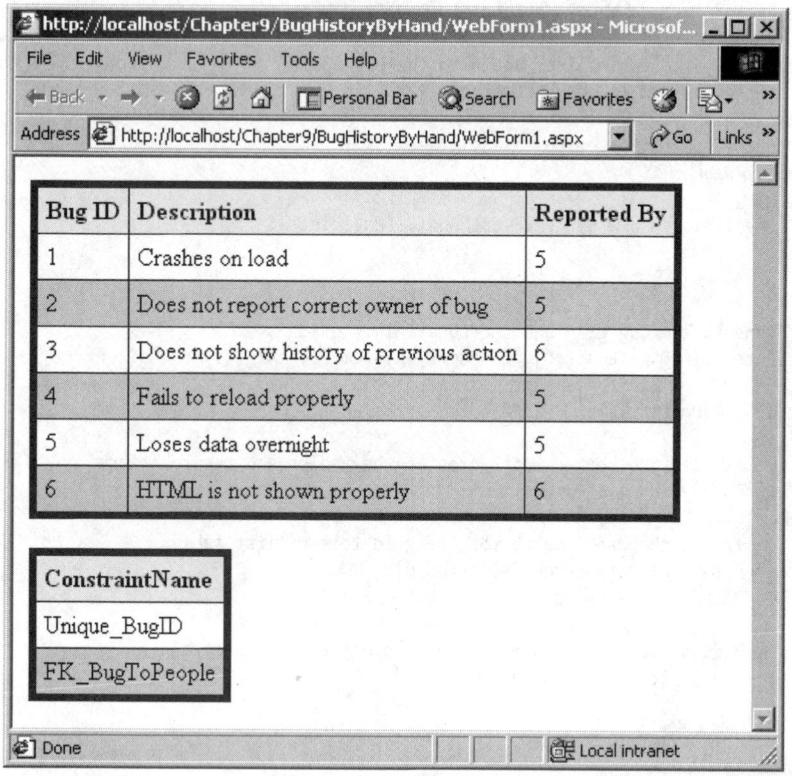

Figure 11-17. The hand-coded table

Example 11-8. Creating a DataSet by hand

```csharp
using System;
using System.Collections;
using System.ComponentModel;
using System.Data;
using System.Data.SqlClient;
using System.Drawing;
using System.Text;
using System.Web;
using System.Web.SessionState;
using System.Web.UI;
using System.Web.UI.WebControls;
using System.Web.UI.HtmlControls;

namespace BugHistoryByHand
{
    /// <summary>
    /// Summary description for WebForm1.
    /// </summary>
    public class WebForm1 : System.Web.UI.Page
    {
        // the Bugs Data Grid
        protected System.Web.UI.WebControls.DataGrid DataGrid1;

        // display the constraints added to the bug table
        protected System.Web.UI.WebControls.DataGrid BugConstraints;

        // unchanged from previous example
        public WebForm1( )
        {
            Page.Init += new System.EventHandler(Page_Init);
        }


        // bind to the bug grid and the constraints grid
        private void Page_Load(object sender, System.EventArgs e)
        {
            if (!IsPostBack)
            {
                // call the method which creates the tables and the relations
                DataSet ds = CreateDataSet( );

                // set the data source for the grid to the first table
                DataGrid1.DataSource=ds.Tables[0];
                DataGrid1.DataBind( );

                BugConstraints.DataSource = ds.Tables["Bugs"].Constraints;
                BugConstraints.DataBind( );

            }
        }

        //hand carved
        private DataSet CreateDataSet( )
```

Example 11-8. Creating a DataSet by hand (continued)

```
{
    // instantiate a new DataSet object that
    // you will fill with tables and relations
    DataSet dataSet = new DataSet();

    // make the bug table and its columns
    // mimic the attributes from the SQL database
    DataTable tblBugs = new DataTable("Bugs");

    DataColumn newColumn; // hold the new columns as you create them

    newColumn =
      tblBugs.Columns.Add(
          "BugID", Type.GetType("System.Int32"));
    newColumn.AutoIncrement = true;        // autoincrementing
    newColumn.AutoIncrementSeed=1;         // starts at 1
    newColumn.AutoIncrementStep=1;         // increments by 1
    newColumn.AllowDBNull=false;           // nulls not allowed

    // or you can provide a named constraint
    UniqueConstraint constraint =
        new UniqueConstraint("Unique_BugID",newColumn);
    tblBugs.Constraints.Add(constraint);

    // create an array of columns for the primary key
    DataColumn[] columnArray = new DataColumn[1];
    columnArray[0] = newColumn;

    // add the array to the Primary key property
    tblBugs.PrimaryKey=columnArray;

    // The Product column
    newColumn = tblBugs.Columns.Add(
        "Product", Type.GetType("System.Int32"));
    newColumn.AllowDBNull=false;
    newColumn.DefaultValue = 1;

    // save for foreign key creation
    DataColumn bugProductColumn = newColumn;

    // The Version column
    newColumn = tblBugs.Columns.Add(
      "Version", Type.GetType("System.String"));
    newColumn.AllowDBNull=false;
    newColumn.MaxLength=50;
    newColumn.DefaultValue = "0.1";

    // The Description column
    newColumn = tblBugs.Columns.Add(
      "Description", Type.GetType("System.String"));
    newColumn.AllowDBNull=false;
    newColumn.MaxLength=8000;
    newColumn.DefaultValue = "";
```

Example 11-8. Creating a DataSet by hand (continued)

```
// The Reporter column
newColumn = tblBugs.Columns.Add(
    "Reporter", Type.GetType("System.Int32"));
newColumn.AllowDBNull=false;

// save for foreign key creation
DataColumn bugReporterColumn = newColumn;

// Add rows based on the db schema you just created
DataRow newRow;          // holds the new row

newRow = tblBugs.NewRow( );
newRow["Product"] = 1;
newRow["Version"] = "0.1";
newRow["Description"] = "Crashes on load";
newRow["Reporter"] = 5;
tblBugs.Rows.Add(newRow);

newRow = tblBugs.NewRow( );
newRow["Product"] = 1;
newRow["Version"] = "0.1";
newRow["Description"] =
    "Does not report correct owner of bug";
newRow["Reporter"] = 5;
tblBugs.Rows.Add(newRow);

newRow = tblBugs.NewRow( );
newRow["Product"] = 1;
newRow["Version"] = "0.1";
newRow["Description"] =
    "Does not show history of previous action";
newRow["Reporter"] = 6;
tblBugs.Rows.Add(newRow);

newRow = tblBugs.NewRow( );
newRow["Product"] = 1;
newRow["Version"] = "0.1";
newRow["Description"] =
    "Fails to reload properly";
newRow["Reporter"] = 5;
tblBugs.Rows.Add(newRow);

newRow = tblBugs.NewRow( );
newRow["Product"] = 2;
newRow["Version"] = "0.1";
newRow["Description"] = "Loses data overnight";
newRow["Reporter"] = 5;
tblBugs.Rows.Add(newRow);

newRow = tblBugs.NewRow( );
newRow["Product"] = 2;
newRow["Version"] = "0.1";
```

Example 11-8. Creating a DataSet by hand (continued)

```
newRow["Description"] = "HTML is not shown properly";
newRow["Reporter"] = 6;
tblBugs.Rows.Add(newRow);

// add the table to the dataset
dataSet.Tables.Add(tblBugs);


// Product Table

// make the Products table and add the columns
DataTable tblProduct = new DataTable("lkProduct");
newColumn = tblProduct.Columns.Add(
    "ProductID", Type.GetType("System.Int32"));
newColumn.AutoIncrement = true;      // autoincrementing
newColumn.AutoIncrementSeed=1;       // starts at 1
newColumn.AutoIncrementStep=1;       // increments by 1
newColumn.AllowDBNull=false;         // nulls not allowed
newColumn.Unique=true;               // each value must be unique

newColumn = tblProduct.Columns.Add(
    "ProductDescription", Type.GetType("System.String"));
newColumn.AllowDBNull=false;
newColumn.MaxLength=8000;
newColumn.DefaultValue = "";

newRow = tblProduct.NewRow( );
newRow["ProductDescription"] = "BugX Bug Tracking";
tblProduct.Rows.Add(newRow);

newRow = tblProduct.NewRow( );
newRow["ProductDescription"] =
    "PIM - My Personal Information Manager";
tblProduct.Rows.Add(newRow);

// add the products table to the dataset
dataSet.Tables.Add(tblProduct);


// People


// make the People table and add the columns
DataTable tblPeople = new DataTable("People");
newColumn = tblPeople.Columns.Add(
    "PersonID", Type.GetType("System.Int32"));
newColumn.AutoIncrement = true;      // autoincrementing
newColumn.AutoIncrementSeed=1;       // starts at 1
newColumn.AutoIncrementStep=1;       // increments by 1
newColumn.AllowDBNull=false;         // nulls not allowed

UniqueConstraint uniqueConstraint =
    new UniqueConstraint(
```

Example 11-8. Creating a DataSet by hand (continued)

```
            "Unique_PersonID",newColumn);
tblPeople.Constraints.Add(uniqueConstraint);

// stash away the PersonID column for the foreign
// key constraint
DataColumn PersonIDColumn = newColumn;

columnArray = new DataColumn[1];
columnArray[0] = newColumn;
tblPeople.PrimaryKey=columnArray;


newColumn = tblPeople.Columns.Add(
  "FullName", Type.GetType("System.String"));
newColumn.AllowDBNull=false;
newColumn.MaxLength=8000;
newColumn.DefaultValue = "";

newColumn = tblPeople.Columns.Add(
  "eMail", Type.GetType("System.String"));
newColumn.AllowDBNull=false;
newColumn.MaxLength=100;
newColumn.DefaultValue = "";

newColumn = tblPeople.Columns.Add(
   "Phone", Type.GetType("System.String"));
newColumn.AllowDBNull=false;
newColumn.MaxLength=20;
newColumn.DefaultValue = "";

newColumn = tblPeople.Columns.Add(
   "Role", Type.GetType("System.Int32"));
newColumn.DefaultValue = 0;
newColumn.AllowDBNull=false;

newRow = tblPeople.NewRow( );
newRow["FullName"] = "Jesse Liberty";
newRow["email"] = "jliberty@libertyassociates.com";
newRow["Phone"] = "617-555-7301";
newRow["Role"] = 1;
tblPeople.Rows.Add(newRow);

newRow = tblPeople.NewRow( );
newRow["FullName"] = "Dan Hurwitz";
newRow["email"] = "dhurwitz@stersol.com";
newRow["Phone"] = "781-555-3375";
newRow["Role"] = 1;
tblPeople.Rows.Add(newRow);

newRow = tblPeople.NewRow( );
newRow["FullName"] = "John Galt";
newRow["email"] = "jGalt@franconia.com";
newRow["Phone"] = "617-555-9876";
```

Example 11-8. Creating a DataSet by hand (continued)

```
        newRow["Role"] = 1;
        tblPeople.Rows.Add(newRow);

        newRow = tblPeople.NewRow( );
        newRow["FullName"] = "John Osborn";
        newRow["email"] = "jOsborn@oreilly.com";
        newRow["Phone"] = "617-555-3232";
        newRow["Role"] = 3;
        tblPeople.Rows.Add(newRow);

        newRow = tblPeople.NewRow( );
        newRow["FullName"] = "Ron Petrusha";
        newRow["email"] = "ron@oreilly.com";
        newRow["Phone"] = "707-555-0515";
        newRow["Role"] = 2;
        tblPeople.Rows.Add(newRow);

        newRow = tblPeople.NewRow( );
        newRow["FullName"] = "Tatiana Diaz";
        newRow["email"] = "tatiana@oreilly.com";
        newRow["Phone"] = "617-555-1234";
        newRow["Role"] = 2;
        tblPeople.Rows.Add(newRow);

        // add the People table to the dataset
        dataSet.Tables.Add(tblPeople);

        // create the Foreign Key constraint
        // pass in the parent column from people
        // and the child column from Bugs
        ForeignKeyConstraint fk =
           new ForeignKeyConstraint(
              "FK_BugToPeople",PersonIDColumn,bugReporterColumn);
        fk.DeleteRule=Rule.Cascade;    // like father like son
        fk.UpdateRule=Rule.Cascade;
        tblBugs.Constraints.Add(fk);  // add the new constraint


        // declare the DataRelation and DataColumn objects
        System.Data.DataRelation dataRelation;
        System.Data.DataColumn dataColumn1;
        System.Data.DataColumn dataColumn2;

        // set the dataColumns to create the relationship
        // between Bug and BugHistory on the BugID key
        dataColumn1 =
           dataSet.Tables["People"].Columns["PersonID"];
        dataColumn2 =
           dataSet.Tables["Bugs"].Columns["Reporter"];

        dataRelation =
           new System.Data.DataRelation(
           "BugsToReporter",
```

Example 11-8. Creating a DataSet by hand (continued)

```
        dataColumn1,
        dataColumn2);

    // add the new DataRelation to the dataset
    dataSet.Relations.Add(dataRelation);

    return dataSet;
}

// unchanged from previous example
private void Page_Init(object sender, EventArgs e)
{
    InitializeComponent();
}

#region Web Form Designer generated code
/// <summary>
/// Required method for Designer support - do not modify
/// the contents of this method with the code editor.
/// </summary>
private void InitializeComponent()
{
    this.Load += new System.EventHandler(this.Page_Load);

}
#endregion

}
}
```

Stored Procedures

Until now, you've interacted with the database using nothing but SQL statements. Many real world applications interacting with SQL Server or other large databases will use stored procedures. Stored procedures can be compiled by the database, and thus offer better performance.

The easiest way to create a stored procedure (often referred to as a *sproc*) is to begin with a working SQL statement. If you return to Example 11-5, you will find two SQL Select statements. The first is in the CreateBugDataSet method:

```
StringBuilder s =
    new StringBuilder(
    "Select b.BugID, h.BugHistoryID, b.Description,h.Response, ");
s.Append("o.FullName as owner, ");
s.Append("p.ProductDescription, ");
s.Append("r.FullName as reporter, ");
s.Append("s.StatusDescription, ");
s.Append("sev.SeverityDescription, ");
s.Append("h.DateStamp ");
```

```
s.Append("from  ");
s.Append(
    "(select bugID, max(bugHistoryID) as maxHistoryID ");
s.Append("from BugHistory group by bugID) t ");
s.Append("join bugs b on b.bugid = t.bugid ");
s.Append(
    "join BugHistory h on h.bugHistoryID = t.maxHistoryID ");
s.Append("join lkProduct p on b.Product = p.ProductID  ");
s.Append("join People r on b.Reporter = r.PersonID  ");
s.Append("join People o on h.Owner = o.PersonID ");
s.Append("join lkStatus s on s.statusid = h.status ");
s.Append(
    "join lkSeverity sev on sev.SeverityID = h.severity ");
```

If you extract the SQL from this statement and insert it into the SQL Server Query analyzer, you can run that statement and get back the Bug records, as shown in Figure 11-18.

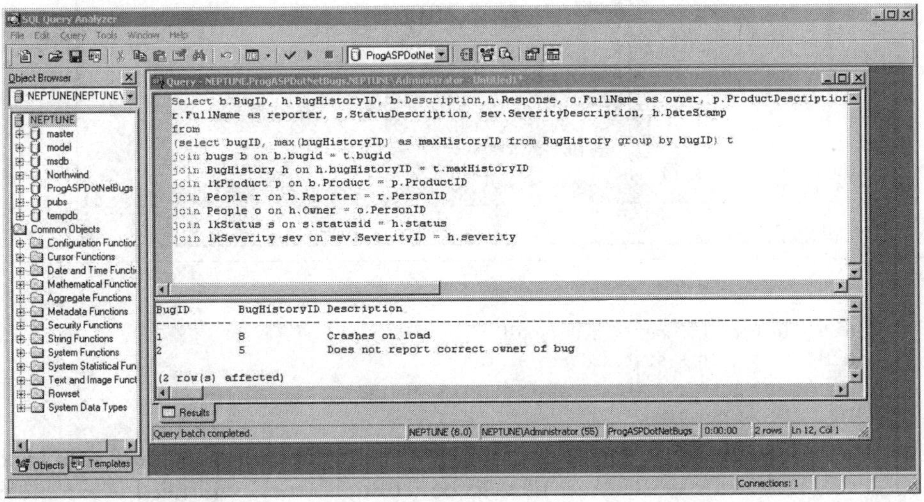

Figure 11-18. Executing the query in Query Analyzer

You are now ready to drop this into a new stored procedure, which you will name spBugs. In SQL Server the easiest way to do this is to right-click on the Stored Procedures listing in SQL Enterprise Manager, as shown in Figure 11-19.

This opens the New Stored Procedure window. Preface the select statement with the string "CREATE PROCEDURE spBugs AS" to create a new sproc named spBugs, as shown in Figure 11-20.

The second SQL select statement in Example 11-5 is slightly more complicated:

```
Select BugID, StatusDescription, SeverityDescription,
Response, FullName as Owner, DateStamp
from BugHistory h
```

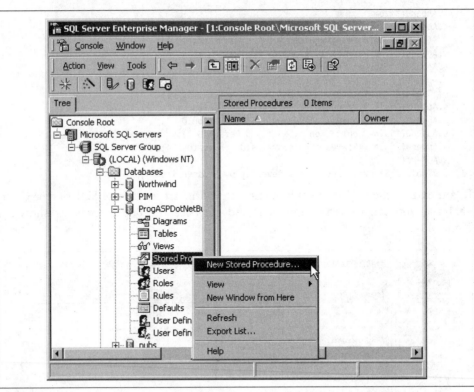

Figure 11-19. Creating a new stored procedure

```
join People o on h.Owner = o.PersonID
join lkStatus s on s.statusid = h.status
join lkSeverity sev on sev.SeverityID = h.severity
where BugID =  + bugID
```

The problem here is that each time you run this procedure, you must supply the bugID. To make this work, your new sproc (spBugHistory) will need a parameter: *@BugID*. Here's the sproc:

```
CREATE PROCEDURE spBugHistory
@BugID integer
 AS
Select BugID, StatusDescription, SeverityDescription, Response, FullName as Owner,
DateStamp
from BugHistory h
join People o on h.Owner = o.PersonID
join lkStatus s on s.statusid = h.status
join lkSeverity sev on sev.SeverityID = h.severity
where BugID = @BugID
```

You might invoke this sproc from within the Query Analyzer like this:

```
spBugID 2
```

A value of 2 would be passed in as the *@BugID*argument.

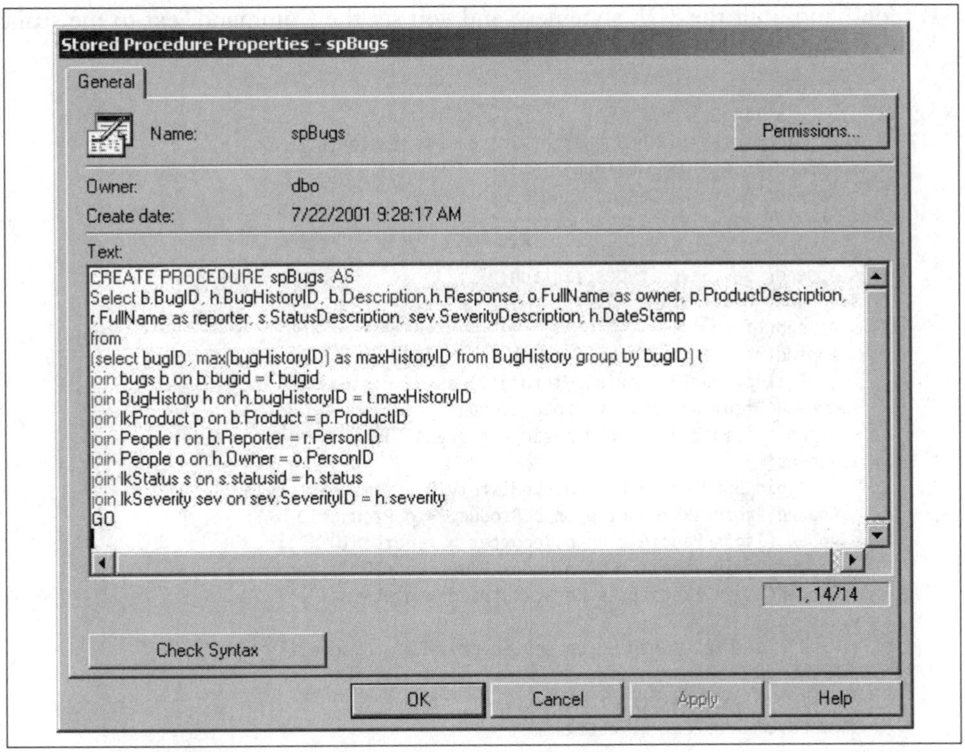

Figure 11-20. Saving the new sproc

Invoking the Stored Procedure Programmatically

To use stored procedures rather than a simple SQL select statement, you need modify only the CreateBugDataSet and CreateBugHistoryDataSet methods. CreateBugDataSet will invoke spBugs with no parameters. CreateBugHistoryDataSet will invoke spBugHistory, passing in the chosen BugID as a parameter.

Invoking a sproc with no parameters

The rewrite to CreateBugDataSet is very straightforward. You'll remember from Example 11-5 that your steps were as follows:

1. First you created the connection string:

   ```
   string connectionString =
       "server=YourServer; uid=sa;
   pwd=YourPassword; database=ProgASPDotNetBugs";
   ```

2. Then you created the new connection object and opened it:

   ```
   System.Data.SqlClient.SqlConnection connection =
       new System.Data.SqlClient.SqlConnection(connectionString);
   connection.Open();
   ```

3. You hand-built the SQL statement and you set the CommandText to the string you built:

```
StringBuilder s =
    new StringBuilder(
    "Select b.BugID, h.BugHistoryID, b.Description,h.Response, ");
s.Append("o.FullName as owner, ");
s.Append("p.ProductDescription, ");
s.Append("r.FullName as reporter, ");
s.Append("s.StatusDescription, ");
s.Append("sev.SeverityDescription, ");
s.Append("h.DateStamp ");
s.Append("from ");
s.Append(
    "(select bugID, max(bugHistoryID) as maxHistoryID ");
s.Append("from BugHistory group by bugID) t ");
s.Append("join bugs b on b.bugid = t.bugid ");
s.Append(
    "join BugHistory h on h.bugHistoryID = t.maxHistoryID ");
s.Append("join lkProduct p on b.Product = p.ProductID ");
s.Append("join People r on b.Reporter = r.PersonID ");
s.Append("join People o on h.Owner = o.PersonID ");
s.Append("join lkStatus s on s.statusid = h.status ");
s.Append(
    "join lkSeverity sev on sev.SeverityID = h.severity ");

// set the command text to the select statement
command.CommandText=s.ToString();
```

4. Finally, you created a data adapter and you set its Command object to the Command object you just built. You added the table mappings, created a dataset, filled the dataset, and returned the dataset.

The steps with a stored procedure are *identical* except for step 3. Rather than building an SQL statement, you'll instead set the command text to the name of the sproc, and you'll set the Command object's CommandType property to CommandType. StoredProcedure:

```
command.CommandText="spBugs";
command.CommandType=CommandType.StoredProcedure;
```

 When you set the CommandType property to StoredProcedure, the sproc can be run more efficiently then when you use the default value of Text.

That's it; the method is otherwise unchanged. The complete replacement for Create-BugDataSet is shown in Example 11-9.

Example 11-9. Replacement CreateBugDataSet using a stored procedure

```
private DataSet CreateBugDataSet()
{
```

```
    // connection string to connect to the Bugs Database
    string connectionString =
        "server=Neptune; uid=sa; pwd=oWenmEany; database=ProgASPDotNetBugs";

    // Create connection object, initialize with
    // connection string. Open it.
    System.Data.SqlClient.SqlConnection connection =
        new System.Data.SqlClient.SqlConnection(connectionString);
    connection.Open( );


    // Create a SqlCommand object and assign the connection
    System.Data.SqlClient.SqlCommand command =
        new System.Data.SqlClient.SqlCommand( );
    command.Connection=connection;
    command.CommandText="spBugs";
    command.CommandType=CommandType.StoredProcedure;

    // create a data adapter and assign the command object
    // and add the table mapping for bugs
    SqlDataAdapter dataAdapter = new SqlDataAdapter( );
    dataAdapter.SelectCommand=command;
    dataAdapter.TableMappings.Add("Table","Bugs");

    // Create the dataset  and use the data adapter to fill it
    DataSet dataSet = new DataSet( );
    dataAdapter.Fill(dataSet);
    return dataSet;
}
```

Invoking a Stored Procedure with Parameters

To invoke the sproc spBugHistory, you will need to pass in the BugID. There are two ways to do this. The first option is simply to invoke the sproc name and its argument in the CommandText property:

```
    command.CommandText= "spBugHistory " + bugID;
```

The second option is to create explicit Parameter objects. You'll explore each of these options in turn.

Inline arguments

To see the first option at work, modify the CreatebugHistoryDataSet method, changing only step 3 as described above for CreateDataSet. Rather than building the SQL Select statement, you'll invoke the sproc directly:

```
    command.CommandText= "spBugHistory " + bugID;
```

When the user clicks on the bug whose ID is 2, this will set the command text equal to spBugHistory 2. You would like to set the CommandType property to CommandType.StoredProcedure but you may not do so with an "in line" parameter. If you do, the compiler will look for a sproc named spBugHistory 2, and since no such sproc exists, an error will be generated. You must instead set the CommandType property to Command.CommandText, which is somewhat less efficient.

The complete replacement for CreateBugHistoryDataSet is shown in Example 11-10.

Example 11-10. Replacement CreateBugHistoryDataSet using a stored procedure

```
private DataSet CreateBugHistoryDataSet(int bugID)
{
    // connection string to connect to the Bugs Database
    string connectionString =
        "server=Neptune; uid=sa; pwd=oWenmEany; database=ProgASPDotNetBugs";

    // Create connection object, initialize with
    // connection string. Open it.
    System.Data.SqlClient.SqlConnection connection =
        new System.Data.SqlClient.SqlConnection(connectionString);
    connection.Open( );

    // create a second command object for the bugs hisotry table
    System.Data.SqlClient.SqlCommand command =
        new System.Data.SqlClient.SqlCommand( );
    command.Connection = connection;

    command.CommandText= "spBugHistory " + bugID;
    command.CommandType = CommandType.Text;

    // create a second data adapter and add the command
    // and map the table
    // then fill the dataset  from this second adapter
    SqlDataAdapter dataAdapter = new SqlDataAdapter( );
    dataAdapter.SelectCommand = command;
    dataAdapter.TableMappings.Add("Table", "BugHistory");

    DataSet dataSet = new DataSet( );
    dataAdapter.Fill(dataSet);
    return dataSet;
}
```

Invoking a sproc with explicit parameters

Implicit parameters are straightforward and easy to use. Unfortunately, if you need a return (out) parameter to get a result back, you will need to use explicit Parameter objects. Many programmers also use explicit parameters when they have a large number of parameters. In any case, explicit parameter invocation is more efficient.

The SqlCommand object and its cousin OleDbCommand both expose a Parameters collection that can contain any number of Parameter objects.

To use an explicit parameter, you add it to the Parameters collection by calling the Add method. The return value is a reference to an object of type Parameter. You may then modify that object's properties, setting its direction (e.g., Input, Output, or InputOutput) as well as its value, as the following code fragment shows:

```
System.Data.SqlClient.SqlParameter param;
param = command.Parameters.Add("@BugID",SqlDbType.Int);
param.Direction = ParameterDirection..Input;
param.Value = bugID;
```

Now that you are using an explicit Parameter object, you can modify the command text to be just the name of the stored procedure, and you may modify the Command-Type property to be the more efficient CommandType.StoredProcedure. The complete replacement for CreateBugHistoryDataSet is shown in Example 11-11.

Example 11-11. Replacement CreateBugHistoryDataSetusing explicit parameters to a stored procedure

```
private DataSet CreateBugHistoryDataSet(int bugID)
{
    // connection string to connect to the Bugs Database
    string connectionString =
        "server=Neptune; uid=sa; pwd=oWenmEany; database=ProgASPDotNetBugs";

    // Create connection object, initialize with
    // connection string. Open it.
    System.Data.SqlClient.SqlConnection connection =
        new System.Data.SqlClient.SqlConnection(connectionString);
    connection.Open( );

    // create a second command object for the bugs hisotry table
    System.Data.SqlClient.SqlCommand command =
        new System.Data.SqlClient.SqlCommand( );
    command.Connection = connection;

    command.CommandText= "spBugHistory";
    command.CommandType = CommandType.StoredProcedure;

    // declare the parameter object
    System.Data.SqlClient.SqlParameter param;

    // Add a new parameter, get back a reference to it
    param = command.Parameters.Add("@BugID",SqlDbType.Int);

    // set the parameter's direction and value
    param.Direction = ParameterDirection.Input;
    param.Value = bugID;

    // create a second data adapter and add the command
    // and map the table
    // then fill the dataset  from this second adapter
    SqlDataAdapter dataAdapter = new SqlDataAdapter( );
    dataAdapter.SelectCommand = command;
```

Example 11-11. Replacement CreateBugHistoryDataSetusing explicit parameters to a stored procedure (continued)

```
    dataAdapter.TableMappings.Add("Table", "BugHistory");

    DataSet dataSet = new DataSet( );
    dataAdapter.Fill(dataSet);
    return dataSet;
}
```

Return values from a sproc

You can imagine that your stored procedure might return the total number of history items found when you pass in a BugID. To capture this return value, you will need an output parameter. To experiment with output parameters you will add a new sproc, SpBugHistoryCount, which will take two parameters: @BugID, and a new parameter, @TotalFound. The stored procedure is written as follows:

```
CREATE PROCEDURE spBugHistoryCount
@BugID integer,
@TotalFound integer output
 AS
select @totalFound =  count(bugHistoryID)
from BugHistory where BugID = @BugID
```

Note that the second parameter is marked as an output parameter. To display the output value returned by this sproc, you'll add a new label to the Panel control in the *aspx* file:

```
<asp:Label ID="lblTotalFound" Runat="server"/>
```

Remember to declare this label in the *.cs* file so that you can refer to it programatically:

```
protected System.Web.UI.WebControls.Label lblTotalFound;
```

You now add a new method, TotalRecordsFound, which will invoke the sproc and return the value the sproc returns as a string. You'll then insert the string into the label you just created.

To start, modify UpdateBugHistory and add the following line as the last line in the existing if statement:

```
lblTotalFound.Text =
   "<b>Total History Records Found:</b> " +
   TotalRecordsFound(bugID);
```

Thus, if the user selects a bug, you'll run the sproc and display the total number of bugs found. The implementation of TotalRecordsFound is fairly straightforward:

1. Create the connection and command objects.

2. Set the command text to the name of the sproc and set the command type to StoredProcedure.

3. Set up the two parameters, remembering to set their direction.

4. Invoke the sproc.

5. Extract the values.

What is new this time, however, is that rather than using the sproc to fill a dataset or even a data adapter, you need only run the sproc and get back the output value in the Parameters collection of the command object. To make this most efficient, the command object offers a ExecuteNonQuery method. This highly efficient method simply executes the SQL statement (in this case the sproc) but does not return a dataset. You can use ExecuteNonQuery when you need to poke the database but do not need to get back records. For Update, Insert, and Delete statements, ExecuteNonQuery returns the number of rows affected; otherwise it returns -1.

To extract the value from the output parameter, you must first extract it from the Parameters collection. You may use the name of the parameter as an index into the collection:

```
param = command.Parameters["@TotalFound"];
```

The Parameter object has a Value property which is an object. You must cast that object to the appropriate type, in this case int:

```
int val = (int) param.Value;
```

The TotalRecordsFound method returns a string. You can easily turn the int into a string because int, like all objects, implements ToString:

```
string output = val.ToString( );
```

You can of course combine all these steps in your return statement:

```
return command.Parameters["@TotalFound"].Value.ToString( );
```

The complete source code for the TotalRecordsFound method is shown in Example 11-12.

Example 11-12. Retrieving an output value

```
private string TotalRecordsFound(int bugID)
{
   // connection string to connect to the Bugs Database
   string connectionString =
      "server=YourServer; uid=sa;
        pwd=YourPW; database=ProgASPDotNetBugs";

   // Create connection object, initialize with
   // connection string. Open it.
   System.Data.SqlClient.SqlConnection connection =
      new System.Data.SqlClient.SqlConnection(connectionString);
   connection.Open( );

   // create a  command object for the sproc
   System.Data.SqlClient.SqlCommand command =
```

Example 11-12. Retrieving an output value (continued)

```
    new System.Data.SqlClient.SqlCommand( );
command.Connection = connection;

command.CommandText= "spBugHistoryCount";
command.CommandType = CommandType.StoredProcedure;

// declare the parameter object
System.Data.SqlClient.SqlParameter param;

// Add a new parameter, get back a reference to it
param = command.Parameters.Add("@BugID",SqlDbType.Int);

// set the parameter's direction and value
param.Direction = ParameterDirection.Input;
param.Value = bugID;


// Add a new parameter, get back a reference to it
param = command.Parameters.Add("@TotalFound",SqlDbType.Int);

// set the parameter's direction
param.Direction = ParameterDirection.Output;

// call ExecuteNonQuery because no dataset
// will be returned
command.ExecuteNonQuery( );

// get the param from the collection
param = command.Parameters["@TotalFound"];

// extract the value
int val = (int) param.Value;

// cast to a string
string output = val.ToString( );

// return the value as a string
return output;
}
```

ADO Data Updates

Chapter 11 focused on retrieving data from the database and managing the complexity of related tables. All of the examples focused on displaying data. In many applications, however, you will also want to allow the user to *update* the data in the database.

There are two aspects to writing web applications that allow users to update data. The first aspect is providing the user with a user interface that facilitates modifying the data. The second is to provide the programmatic support for the update: how do you insert new records, or modify or delete existing records once you know what changes you want to make? This chapter focuses on this second aspect; how you write the code to update the data in the database. To simplify the examples, this chapter shows very little of the user interface. Many of the examples will use hard-coded changes; others will use a very crude and simple form for updating the data tables.

Updating data in a database is very simple if you only update a single table, but once you update related tables, things get complicated. This chapter will explore how transactions can be used to ensure the integrity of your data. In addition, if your program will be used by more than one user at a time, you will encounter issues with concurrency; is it possible for one user's changes to overwrite the changes of another user. This chapter also explores how you manage concurrency issues, and shows some of the powerful support available in the class library to simplify this difficult task.

Updating with SQL

The simplest way to update the database is to generate a SQL Insert, Update, or Delete statement, and execute it using the Command object's ExecuteNonQuery method. For example, you can insert a few records into the Bugs table, edit existing rows, and delete rows, all with the appropriate SQL statements.

To illustrate this, you'll use Visual Studio to create a simple form to display the current records in a grid. Choose whichever language you feel most comfortable using, and name the project BugHistoryHandEdits. In addition to the DataGrid control, you'll add three buttons to allow the user to add, edit, or delete a record, and you'll also add a text field for the description, as shown in Figure 12-1. Table 12-1 shows the properties that you should set for the example to work.

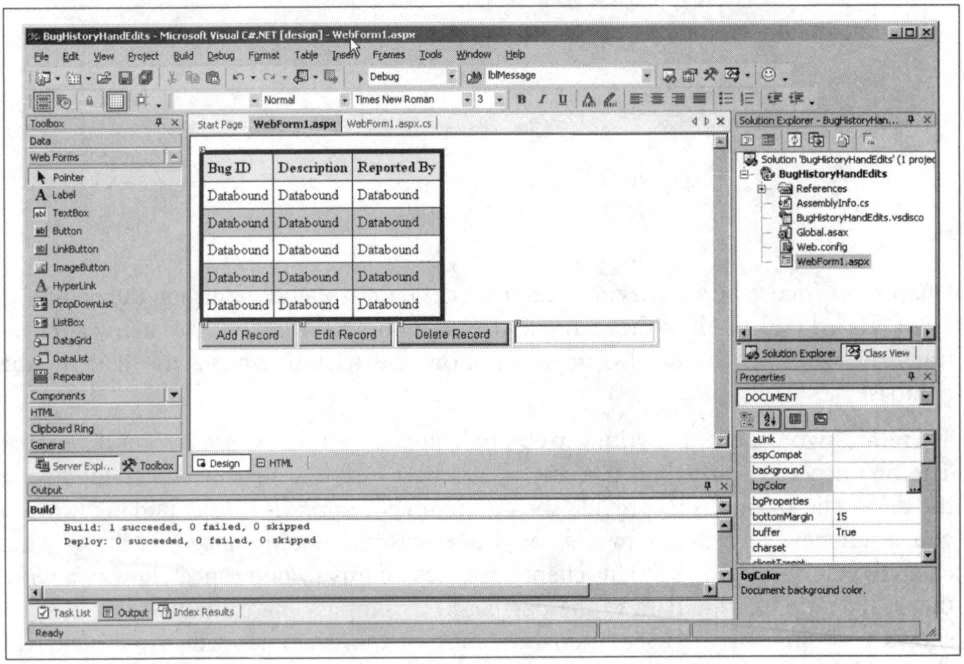

Figure 12-1. The data entry page

The data entry page in Figure 12-1 is a quick and dirty application with a crude user interface. While this may seem to have little relevance to real-world applications at first glance, the truth is that this is exactly the kind of starter program programmers often use to prove an approach or to experiment with an alternative. In a final product, the user interface will certainly be more attractive (for example, you might allow the user to click on the various fields and edit them in place), but the back-end functionality will likely be unchanged. (Manipulation of grids and the more attractive components for a user interface will be explored in detail in Chapter 13.)

Table 12-1. Non-default properties of the BugHistoryHandEdits controls

Control	Property	Value
DataGrid	AlternatingItemStyle.Backcolor	LightGray
	BorderColor	Blue
	BorderStyle	Solid

Table 12-1. Non-default properties of the BugHistoryHandEdits controls (continued)

Control	Property	Value
	BorderWidth	4px
	HeaderStyle.BackColor	BlanchedAlmond
	HeaderStyle.Font.Bold	True
Add Button	ID	btnAdd
	Text	Add Record
Edit Button	ID	btnEdit
	Text	Edit Record
Delete Button	ID	btnDelete
	Text	Delete Record
TextBox	ID	TxtDescription

Next, you'll write Click event handlers for the buttons, and in these event handlers you will interact with the database, executing the SQL statements needed to add a record, edit a record, or delete a record. To simplify the user interface even further, you'll always edit or delete the last record in the table. (In a real application, of course, the user would indicate which record to modify.) The complete C# source code is shown in Example 12-1, and the complete VB.NET source code is shown in Example 12-2. Code not automatically generated by Visual Studio .NET is shown in boldface. Note that in order to keep the example as simple as possible, the code has no error checking.

Example 12-1. C# source for the data entry page

```
using System;
using System.Collections;
using System.ComponentModel;
using System.Data;
using System.Data.SqlClient;
using System.Drawing;
using System.Text;
using System.Web;
using System.Web.SessionState;
using System.Web.UI;
using System.Web.UI.WebControls;
using System.Web.UI.HtmlControls;

namespace BugHistoryHandEdits
{
    public class WebForm1 : System.Web.UI.Page
    {
        // the three buttons
        protected System.Web.UI.WebControls.Button btnAdd;
        protected System.Web.UI.WebControls.Button btnEdit;
        protected System.Web.UI.WebControls.Button btnDelete;
```

Example 12-1. C# source for the data entry page (continued)

```csharp
// text box to get user input
protected System.Web.UI.WebControls.TextBox TxtDescription;

// the data grid to display the contents of the bug table
protected System.Web.UI.WebControls.DataGrid DataGrid1;

public WebForm1( )
{
    Page.Init += new System.EventHandler(Page_Init);
}

// when you load the page bind the data from the db
private void Page_Load(
    object sender, System.EventArgs e)
{
    BindData( );
}

// bind the grid to the DataReader produced by
// the sproc and then update the data
private void BindData( )
{
    DataGrid1.DataSource = CreateBugDataReader( );
    DataGrid1.DataBind( );
}

// return a DataReader object based on the sproc
private SqlDataReader CreateBugDataReader( )
{

    // connection string to connect to the Bugs Database
    string connectionString =
        "server=yourServer; uid=sa; pwd=yourPassword;
    database=ProgASPDotNetBugs";

    // Create connection object, initialize with
    // connection string. Open it.
    System.Data.SqlClient.SqlConnection connection =
        new System.Data.SqlClient.SqlConnection(
    connectionString);
    connection.Open( );

    // Create a SqlCommand object and assign the connection
    System.Data.SqlClient.SqlCommand command =
        new System.Data.SqlClient.SqlCommand( );
    command.Connection=connection;

    // set the stored procedure to get the bug records
    command.CommandText="spBugsNoHistory";
    command.CommandType=CommandType.StoredProcedure;

    // return the data reader
```

Example 12-1. C# source for the data entry page (continued)

```csharp
    return command.ExecuteReader(
        CommandBehavior.CloseConnection);
}

private void Page_Init(object sender, EventArgs e)
{
    InitializeComponent();
}

#region Web Form Designer generated code
/// <summary>
/// Required method for Designer support - do not modify
/// the contents of this method with the code editor.
/// </summary>
private void InitializeComponent()
{
    this.btnAdd.Click +=
        new System.EventHandler(this.btnAdd_Click);
    this.btnEdit.Click +=
        new System.EventHandler(this.btnEdit_Click);
    this.btnDelete.Click +=
        new System.EventHandler(this.btnDelete_Click);
    this.Load +=
        new System.EventHandler(this.Page_Load);

}
#endregion

// event handler for the edit button
// edit the last record based on the user's input
private void btnEdit_Click(object sender, System.EventArgs e)
{
    string cmd = @"Update bugs set description = '" +
        TxtDescription.Text +
            @"' where bugid = (select max(BugID) from bugs)";

    UpdateDB(cmd);
    BindData();
}

// delete the last record in the table
private void btnDelete_Click(object sender, System.EventArgs e)
{
    string cmd =
        @"delete from bugs where bugid =
    (select max(BugID) from bugs)";

    UpdateDB(cmd);
    BindData();
}

// add a new record to the table
```

Example 12-1. C# source for the data entry page (continued)

```csharp
    // pick up the description field from the text box
    private void btnAdd_Click(object sender, System.EventArgs e)
    {
        string cmd = @"Insert into bugs values (1,'0.1', '" +
            TxtDescription.Text + @"',1)";

        UpdateDB(cmd);
        BindData();
    }

    // common routine for all database updates
    private void UpdateDB(string cmd)
    {
        // connection string to connect to the Bugs Database
        string connectionString =
            "server=yourServer; uid=sa;
        pwd=YourPassword; database=ProgASPDotNetBugs";

        // Create connection object, initialize with
        // connection string. Open it.
        System.Data.SqlClient.SqlConnection connection =
            new System.Data.SqlClient.SqlConnection(connectionString);
        connection.Open();

        // Create a SqlCommand object and assign the connection
        System.Data.SqlClient.SqlCommand command =
            new System.Data.SqlClient.SqlCommand();
        command.Connection=connection;
        command.CommandText=cmd;

        // clear the text box
        TxtDescription.Text = "";

        // execute the sproc
        command.ExecuteNonQuery();
        return;
    }
  }
}
```

Example 12-2. VB.NET source for the data entry page

```vbnet
Imports System.Data.SqlClient

Public Class WebForm1
    Inherits System.Web.UI.Page
        Protected WithEvents DataGrid1 As System.Web.UI.WebControls.DataGrid
        Protected WithEvents btnAdd As System.Web.UI.WebControls.Button
        Protected WithEvents btnEdit As System.Web.UI.WebControls.Button
        Protected WithEvents btnDelete As System.Web.UI.WebControls.Button
        Protected WithEvents TxtDescription As System.Web.UI.WebControls.TextBox
```

Example 12-2. VB.NET source for the data entry page (continued)

```vbnet
#Region " Web Form Designer Generated Code "

    'This call is required by the Web Form Designer.
    <System.Diagnostics.DebuggerStepThrough()> _
    Private Sub InitializeComponent()

    End Sub

    Private Sub Page_Init(ByVal sender As System.Object, _
                        ByVal e As System.EventArgs) Handles MyBase.Init
        'CODEGEN: This method call is required by the Web Form Designer
        'Do not modify it using the code editor.
        InitializeComponent()
    End Sub

#End Region

    Private Sub Page_Load(ByVal sender As System.Object, _
                        ByVal e As System.EventArgs) Handles MyBase.Load
        BindData()
    End Sub

    ' bind the grid to the DataReader produced by
    ' the sproc and then update the data
    Private Sub BindData()
        DataGrid1.DataSource = CreateBugDataReader()
        DataGrid1.DataBind()
    End Sub

    ' return a DataReader object based on the sproc
    Private Function CreateBugDataReader() As SqlDataReader
        ' connection string to connect to the Bugs Database
        Dim connectionString As String = _
            "server=yourServer; uid=sa; pwd=yourPassword; " & _
            "database=ProgASPDotNetBugs"

        ' Create connection object, initialize with
        ' connection string. Open it.
        Dim connection As SqlDbConnection = New SqlDbConnection(connectionString)
        connection.Open()

        ' Create a SqlCommand object and assign the connection
        Dim command As New SqlDbCommand()
        command.Connection = connection

        ' set the stored procedure to get the bug records
        command.CommandText = "spBugsNoHistory"
        command.CommandType = CommandType.StoredProcedure

        ' return the data reader
        Return command.ExecuteReader(CommandBehavior.CloseConnection)
    End Function
```

Example 12-2. VB.NET source for the data entry page (continued)

```
' event handler for the edit button
' edit the last record based on the user's input
Private Sub btnEdit_Click(ByVal sender As Object, _
                    ByVal e As System.EventArgs) Handles btnEdit.Click
    Dim cmd As String = "Update bugs set description = '" & _
                        TxtDescription.Text & _
                        "' where bugid = (select max(BugID) from bugs)"
    UpdateDB(cmd)
    BindData()
End Sub


' delete the last record in the table
Private Sub btnDelete_Click(ByVal sender As Object, _
            ByVal e As System.EventArgs) Handles btnDelete.Click
    Dim cmd As String = _
            "delete from bugs where bugid = (select max(BugID) from bugs)"
    UpdateDB(cmd)
    BindData()
End Sub


' add a new record to the table
' pick up the description field from the text box
Private Sub btnAdd_Click(ByVal sender As Object, _
                    ByVal e As System.EventArgs) Handles btnAdd.Click
    Dim cmd As String = "Insert into bugs values (1,'0.1', '" & _
        TxtDescription.Text + "',1)"
    UpdateDB(cmd)
    BindData()
End Sub


' common routine for all database updates
Private Sub UpdateDB(ByVal cmd As String)
    ' connection string to connect to the Bugs Database
    Dim connectionString As String = _
        "server=yourServer; uid=sa; pwd=yourPassword; " & _
        "database=ProgASPDotNetBugs"

    ' Create connection object, initialize with
    ' connection string. Open it.
    Dim connection As SqlDbConnection = New SqlDbConnection(connectionString)
    connection.Open()

    ' Create a SqlCommand object and assign the connection
    Dim command As New SqlDbCommand()
    command.Connection = connection
    command.CommandText = cmd

    ' clear the text box
    TxtDescription.Text = ""
```

Example 12-2. VB.NET source for the data entry page (continued)

```
        ' execute the sproc
        command.ExecuteNonQuery( )
        Return
    End Sub

End Class
```

For each of the three event handlers for the Click event, you will want to execute the same steps:

1. Create the SQL string.
2. Create a connection object and a command object.
3. Set the command object's CommandText property to the SQL statement you've created.
4. Execute the SQL statement.
5. Rebind the data to update the display.

All three event handlers require identical steps 2 through 4, so this work is factored out into a common method, UpdateDB, to which you pass the command string you want executed. The syntax of the UpdateDB method in C# is:

```
    private void UpdateDB(string cmd)
```

and in VB.NET is:

```
    Private Sub UpdateDB(cmd As String)
```

You create your connection string and connection object as you have in previous examples. You then set the command object's CommandText property to the string passed in as a parameter and execute the query with the ExecuteNonQuery method:

```
    command.CommandText=cmd;
    command.ExecuteNonQuery( );
```

Remember that ExecuteNonQuery, as you saw in Chapter 11, is used when you do not expect to get back a result set. The return value is the number of records affected, which you pass back to the calling program.

The SQL statement for adding a record is a simple Insert statement. In this example, you'll hardwire the values for the Product, Version, and Reporter fields, but you'll pick up the text for the Description field from the text box:

```
    string cmd = @"Insert into bugs values (1,'0.1', '" +
        TxtDescription.Text + @"',1)";
```

 C# Tip: The @ symbol creates a verbatim string, allowing you to pass in single quotation marks without escaping them.

You pass this cmd string to the UpdateDB method as described previously, and then you update the label with the number of rows affected. Finally, you call BindData, which rebinds the data grid with data from the database, and updates the label to display your progress.

```
int numRowsAdded = UpdateDB(cmd);

lblMessage.Text = "Added " + numRowsAdded.ToString() + " rows.";
BindData();
```

The three event handlers are identical except for the particular SQL statement executed. The call to BindData rebinds the data grid to the data extracted from the database. BindData in turn calls CreateBugDataReader, which creates an SqlDataReader from the result set returned by the spBugsNoHistory stored procedure. This is a simple stored procedure to retrieve only the few fields from Bugs, lkProduct, and People that we care about for this example program:

```
CREATE PROCEDURE spBugsNoHistory  as
Select b.BugID, b.Description,p.ProductDescription,
r.FullName as reporter
from
bugs b
join lkProduct p on b.Product = p.ProductID
join People r on b.Reporter = r.PersonID
```

Updating Data with Transactions

A very important feature of most industrial-strength databases is support for transactions. A *transaction* is a set of database operations that must all complete or fail together. That is, either all the operations must complete successfully (commit the transaction), or all must be undone (roll back the transaction) so that the database is left in the state it was in before the transaction began.

The canonical transaction is depositing a check. If I write a check to you for $50 and you deposit it, we both expect that once the bank transaction is completed, your account will have increased by $50 and mine will have decreased by $50. Presumably the bank computer accomplishes this in two steps:

1. Reduce my account by $50.
2. Increase your account by $50.

If the system fails between steps 1 and 2 or for any reason your account cannot be increased by $50, the transaction should be rolled back; that is, it should fail as a whole (neither account should be affected).

If my account is reduced by $50 and your account is not increased, then the database has become corrupted. This should never be allowed, and it is the job of transactions to ensure either that both actions are taken or that neither is.

The remaining alternative, in which my account is not decreased but yours is increased, may be a happy outcome for you ("Bank Error In Your Favor—Collect $50"), but the bank would not be pleased.

The ACID Test

Database designers define the requirements of a transaction in the so-called "ACID" test. ACID is an acronym for **A**tomic, **C**onsistent, **I**solated, and **D**urable. Here's a brief summary of what each of these terms means:

Atomic

An atomic interaction is indivisible (i.e., it cannot be partially implemented). Every transaction must be atomic. For instance, in the previous banking example, it must not be possible to decrement my account but fail to increment yours. If the transaction fails, it must return the database to the state it would have been in without the transaction.

 All transactions, even failed ones, affect the database in trivial ways (e.g., resources are expended, performance is affected). The atomic requirement only implies that, if a transaction is rolled back, all of the tables and data will be in the state they would have been in had the transaction not been attempted at all.

Consistent

The database is presumed to be in a consistent state before the transaction begins, and the transaction must leave it in a consistent state when it completes. While the transaction is being processed, however, the database need not be in a consistent state. To continue with our example of depositing a check, the database need not be consistent during the transaction (e.g., it is okay to decrement my account before incrementing your account), but it must end in a consistent state (i.e., when the transaction completes, the books must balance).

Isolated

Transactions are not processed one at a time. Typically a database may be processing many transactions at once, switching its attention back and forth among various operations. This creates the possibility that a transaction can view and act upon data that reflects intermediate changes from another transaction that is still in progress and that therefore currently has its data in an inconsistent state. Transaction isolation is designed to prevent this problem. For a transaction to be isolated, the effects of the transaction must be exactly as if the transaction were acted on alone; there can be no effects on or dependencies on other database activities. For more information, see the sidebar, "Data Isolation."

Durable

Once a transaction is committed, the effect on the database is permanent.

Data Isolation

Creating fully-isolated transactions in a multithreaded environment is a non-trivial exercise. There are three ways isolation can be violated:

Lost update: One thread reads a record, a second thread updates the record, and then the first thread overwrites the second thread's update.

Dirty read: Thread one writes data; thread two reads what thread one wrote. Thread one then overwrites the data, thus leaving thread two with old data.

Unrepeatable read: Thread one reads data; the data is then overwritten by thread two. Thread one tries to re-read the data but it has changed.

Database experts identify four degrees of isolation:

Degree 0 is limited only to preventing the overwriting of data by any other transaction that is of degree 1 or greater.

Degree 1 isolation has no lost updates.

Degree 2 isolation has no lost updates and no dirty reads but may have unrepeatable reads.

Degree 3 isolation has no lost updates, no dirty reads, and no unrepeatable reads.

While details about transaction isolation is beyond the scope of this book, the section on multi-user updates, later in this chapter, discusses issues related to avoiding violation of isolation.

Implementing Transactions

There are two ways to implement transactions in ASP.NET. You can allow the database to manage the transaction by using transactions within your stored procedure, or you can use connection-based transactions. In the latter case, the transaction is created and enforced outside of the database. This allows you to add transaction support to databases that do not otherwise provide for it.

As Appendix B shows, the Bug database is designed so that each bug event is recorded as one record in Bugs and one or more records in BugHistory. In the next example, you will elicit information from the user about a new bug (e.g., the description, severity, etc.), and you will update both the Bugs table and the BugHistory table.

If the update to the BugHistory table fails for any reason, you want to make sure the update to the Bugs table rolls back as well. In order to ensure this, you wrap these updates in a transaction.

In this example, you will offer the user the option to have the transaction implemented either by the database or by the connection, as shown in Figure 12-2.

If the user selects DB Transaction, call a stored procedure that implements the transaction semantics. If the user selects Connection Transaction, implement the transaction yourself, using an instance of the System.Data.SqlClient.SqlTransaction class.

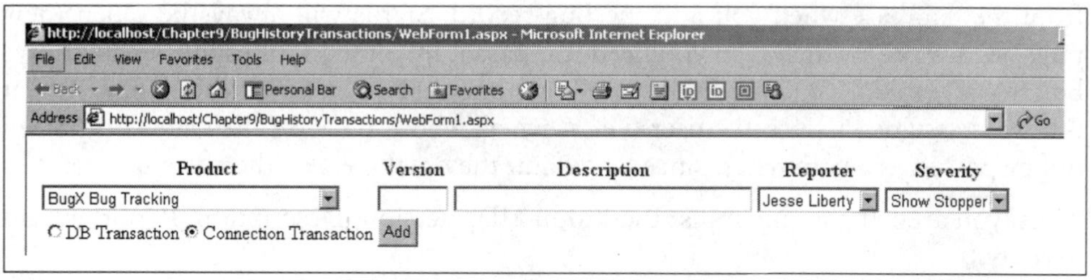

Figure 12-2. Data form for transaction-based add

Database transactions

To implement the DB Transaction option, you need a stored procedure (or *sproc*) that adds a record to the Bugs table and a record to the BugsHistory table, using SQL transaction support.

```
CREATE PROCEDURE spAddBugWithTransactions
```

To decide what parameters to provide to this sproc, you must examine the two tables you will update, as shown in Figure 12-3.

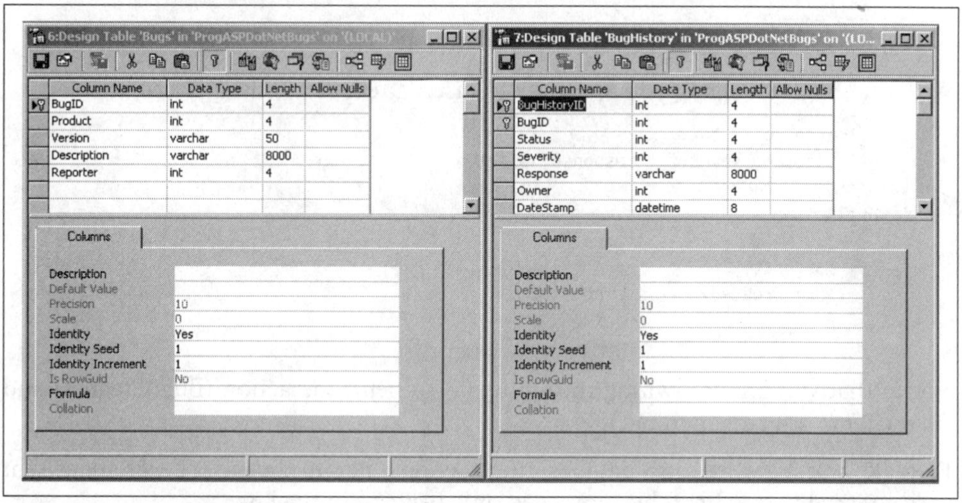

Figure 12-3. Bugs and BugHistory

There are 12 fields that must be filled in for the two tables. For Bugs, the required fields are BugID, Product, Version, Description, and Reporter. Note, however, that you don't need to provide a BugID, which is an identity column provided by the database.

For BugHistory, the obligatory fields are BugHistoryID, BugID, Status, Severity, Response, Owner, and DateStamp. BugHistoryID is another identity column and is thus provided by the database. Note that BugID must match the BugID generated by Bugs. Thus, rather than passing that into the stored procedure, you'll get it back from the database when you add the Bug record. Status will always be Open (new bugs are always open) and so you need not pass it in. Similarly, Response will always be "Bug Created." To simplify this, we'll assume that when you create a new bug, it is always assigned first to the user (i.e., Owner) whose ID is 6. The DateStamp need not be passed as a parameter, since by default the database gets the current date.

Thus, you are left passing in just the ProductID, Version, Description, Reporter, and Severity:

```
@ProductID int,
@Version varChar(50),
@Description varChar(8000),
@Reporter int,
@Severity int
```

The core of the procedure is a pair of Insert statements. First you will insert values into the Bugs table:

```
Insert into Bugs values (@ProductID, @Version, @Description, @Reporter)
```

The Bugs table has an identity column, which you can retrieve with the SQL keyword @@identity:

```
declare @bugID int
select @bugID = @@identity
```

With that bugID in hand, you are ready to insert a record into BugHistory:

```
Insert into BugHistory
(bugID, status, severity, response, owner)
values
( @bugID,
        1,              -- status
        @Severity,
        'Bug Created', -- action
        6               -- owner
)
```

Notice that you are hardwiring the status (1 = open), the action (Bug Created) and the owner (6 = a person in QA).

To make this all work with database transactions, before the Insert statement that adds a record to the first table, you need only begin with the line:

```
Begin Transaction
```

After the insert, you'll check the @@error value, which should be 0 if the Insert succeeded:

```
if @@Error <> 0 goto ErrorHandler
```

If there is an error, you'll jump to the error handler, where you'll call Rollback Transaction:

```
ErrorHandler:
rollback transaction
```

If there is no error, you continue on to the second Insert statement. If there is no error after that insert, you are ready to commit the transaction and exit the sproc:

```
if @@Error <> 0 goto ErrorHandler
commit transaction
return
```

The net effect is that either both Insert statements are acted on, or neither is. The complete sproc is shown in Example 12-3.

Example 12-3. Stored procedure spAddBugWithTransactions

```
CREATE PROCEDURE spAddBugWithTransactions
@ProductID int,
@Version varChar(50),
@Description varChar(8000),
@Reporter int,
@Severity int
 AS
Begin Transaction
declare @bugID int
Insert into Bugs values (@ProductID, @Version, @Description, @Reporter)
select @bugID = @@identity
if @@Error <> 0 goto ErrorHandler

Insert into BugHistory
(bugID, status, severity, response, owner)
values
( @bugID,
      1,                -- status
      @Severity,
      'Bug Created', -- action
      6                -- owner
)
if @@Error <> 0 goto ErrorHandler
commit transaction
return
ErrorHandler:
rollback transaction
return
GO
```

With the stored procedure in hand, you are ready to create the ASP.NET page that allows the user to choose a database transaction or a connection-based transaction.

You'll start by creating the radio button list in the *.aspx* page: To do so, drag a RadioButtonList control onto the form and then drag two RadioButton controls on top of it. Label one of the buttons DB Transaction and label the second button Connection Transaction, as shown in Figure 12-4.

○ DB Transaction ◉ Connection Transaction

Figure 12-4. The radio button list

Set the properties for the buttons as shown in the following code snippet. You can do this from the Property window or by clicking on the HTML tag and updating the HTML directly:

```
<asp:radiobuttonlist id="rbTransaction" Runat="server"
TextAlign="Right" RepeatLayout="flow"
RepeatDirection="Vertical" repeatColumns="2" CellSpacing="3">
   <asp:ListItem Text="DB Transaction" Value="0" />
   <asp:ListItem Text="Connection Transaction"
      Value="1" Selected="True" />
</asp:radiobuttonlist>
```

You also need controls for the various drop-downs and text fields (shown in the Example 12-6 later in this chapter), as well as a button.

```
<asp:button id="btnAdd" Runat="server" Text="Add"/>
```

When the user clicks the Add button, your button handler is fired. In C#, it takes the form:

```
private void btnAdd_Click(object sender, System.EventArgs e)
{
   int whichTransaction =
     Convert.ToInt32(rbTransaction.SelectedItem.Value);
   if (whichTransaction == 0)
     UpdateDBTransaction();
   else
     UpdateConnectionTransaction();
}
```

In VB.NET, the btnAdd_Click event handler appears as follows:

```
Private Sub btnAdd_Click(sender As Object, e As EventArgs) _
                    Handles btnAdd.Click
   Dim whichTransaction = _
       Convert.ToInt32(rbTransaction.SelectedItem.Value)
   If whichTransaction = 0 Then
      UpdateDBTransaction()
   Else
      UpdateConnectionTransaction
   End If
End Sub
```

The entire job of the button handler is to determine which of the two buttons is chosen and to invoke the appropriate method. If the user chooses a database transaction, you will invoke the private UpdateDBTransaction helper method, which in turn will invoke the spAddBugWithTransactions stored procedure.

You will create a connection and a command object in the normal way, setting the command object's CommandType property to `CommandType.StoredProcedure`. You will then create all of the parameters and invoke the stored procedure by calling the ExecuteNonQuery method. There is nothing new or surprising here; all the work to support the transaction is actually done in the stored procedure itself. The C# version of UpdateDBTransaction looks like this:

```
private void UpdateDBTransaction( )
{
    // connection string to connect to the Bugs Database
    string connectionString =
        "server=YourServer; uid=sa; pwd=YourPw; database=ProgASPDotNetBugs";

    // Create connection object, initialize with
    // connection string. Open it.
    System.Data.SqlClient.SqlConnection connection =
        new System.Data.SqlClient.SqlConnection(connectionString);
    connection.Open( );

    // create a second command object for the bugs hisotry table
    System.Data.SqlClient.SqlCommand command =
        new System.Data.SqlClient.SqlCommand( );
    command.Connection = connection;

    command.CommandText= "spAddBugWithTransactions";
    command.CommandType = CommandType.StoredProcedure;

    // declare the parameter object
    System.Data.SqlClient.SqlParameter param;

    // add each parameter and set its direciton and value
    param = command.Parameters.Add("@ProductID",SqlDbType.Int);
    param.Direction = ParameterDirection.Input;
    param.Value = lbProduct.SelectedItem.Value;  // from the list box

    param = command.Parameters.Add("@Version",SqlDbType.VarChar,50);
    param.Direction = ParameterDirection.Input;
    param.Value = txtVersion.Text;              // from the text box

    param = command.Parameters.Add("@Description",SqlDbType.VarChar,8000);
    param.Direction = ParameterDirection.Input;
    param.Value = txtDescription.Text;          // from the text box

    param = command.Parameters.Add("@Reporter",SqlDbType.Int);
    param.Direction = ParameterDirection.Input;
    param.Value = lbReporter.SelectedItem.Value; // from the list box

    param = command.Parameters.Add("@Severity",SqlDbType.Int);
    param.Direction = ParameterDirection.Input;
    param.Value = lbSeverity.SelectedItem.Value; // from the list box

    command.ExecuteNonQuery( ); // execute the sproc
}
```

Connection transaction

The user may choose to use a connection transaction rather than a DB transaction. If so, the method UpdateConnectionTransaction is called. With a Connection transaction there is no transaction support provided by the stored procedure, instead you add the transaction support by creating an SQLTransaction object.

For illustration purposes, you'll add to the Bugs table using a stored procedure, but one that does not provide transaction support. You'll add to the BugHistory table using a simple SQL Insert statement. You want the simple update and the stored procedure call to be wrapped inside a transaction, however, to ensure that either both succeed or neither does.

To get started, you'll write the spAddBug sproc shown in Example 12-4 to insert a record into Bugs.

Example 12-4. The spAddBug stored procedure

```
CREATE PROCEDURE spAddBug
@ProductID int,
@Version varChar(50),
@Description varChar(8000),
@Reporter int,
@BugID int output
 AS
Insert into Bugs values (@ProductID, @Version, @Description, @Reporter)
select @BugID = @@identity
```

You need only those parameters required for the Bugs table; the BugHistory table is not updated by this sproc. In addition, you must add an output parameter, *@BugID*, to return the identity of the new Bug record, so that you can pass this to the new record in BugHistory.

The body of the sproc is nothing more than an Insert statement and a statement to set the *@BugID* parameter with the new BugID retrieved from the *@@identity* value.

The job of the UpdateConnectionTransaction method, shown in the complete listing below (see Example 12-5) is to invoke both the stored procedure and the SQL Update statement, using a Connection transaction. The steps are as follows:

1. Create the connection string and the SqlConnection object.
2. Create the SqlCommand object.
3. Open the connection.
4. Instantiate a SqlTransaction object by calling the BeginTransaction method of the SqlConnection object.
5. Set the SqlCommand object's Transaction property to the SqlTransaction object you've instantiated, and set the SqlCommand object's Connection property to the SqlConnection object you've created.

6. Open a try block in which you will try to update the two tables. If an exception is thrown, you will catch the exception and roll back the transaction.

7. Set the SQL command object's CommandText property to the name of the stored procedure, and set the CommandType property to CommandType. StoredProcedure.

8. Add all the parameters, including the output parameters.

9. Invoke the Query.

10. Get back the BugID and use that to invoke a SQL statement to update the Bug-History table.

11. Commit the transaction.

Example 12-5 shows the complete source code for this example in C#. This code is very similar to the examples in Chapter 11, with the addition of UpdateDBTransaction and UpdateConnectionTransaction, which are shown in bold.

Example 12-5. Updating with transactions

```csharp
using System;
using System.Collections;
using System.ComponentModel;
using System.Data;
using System.Data.SqlClient;
using System.Drawing;
using System.Text;
using System.Web;
using System.Web.SessionState;
using System.Web.UI;
using System.Web.UI.WebControls;
using System.Web.UI.HtmlControls;

namespace BugHistoryTransactions
{
    public class WebForm1 : System.Web.UI.Page
    {
        protected System.Web.UI.WebControls.DataGrid DataGrid1;
        protected System.Web.UI.WebControls.DataGrid HistoryGrid;
        protected System.Web.UI.WebControls.Panel BugHistoryPanel;
        protected System.Web.UI.WebControls.DropDownList lbProduct;
        protected System.Web.UI.WebControls.TextBox txtVersion;
        protected System.Web.UI.WebControls.TextBox txtDescription;
        protected System.Web.UI.WebControls.DropDownList lbSeverity;
        protected System.Web.UI.WebControls.Button btnAdd;
        protected System.Web.UI.WebControls.DropDownList lbReporter;
        protected System.Web.UI.WebControls.RadioButtonList rbTransaction;

        public WebForm1( )
        {
            Page.Init += new System.EventHandler(Page_Init);
        }
```

Example 12-5. Updating with transactions (continued)

```
public void OnItemDataBoundEventHandler(
    Object sender, DataGridItemEventArgs e)
{
    ListItemType itemType = (ListItemType)e.Item.ItemType;
    if (itemType == ListItemType.Header ||
        itemType == ListItemType.Footer ||
        itemType == ListItemType.Separator)
        return;

    if (((DataRowView)e.Item.DataItem).
        Row.ItemArray[8].ToString() == "High")
    {
        TableCell severityCell =
            (TableCell) e.Item.Controls[7];
        severityCell.ForeColor = Color.FromName("Red");
    }
}

public void OnSelectedIndexChangedHandler(
    Object sender, EventArgs e)
{
    UpdateBugHistory();
}

private void UpdateBugHistory()
{

    int index = DataGrid1.SelectedIndex;
    if (index != -1)
    {
        // get the bug id from the data grid
        int bugID =
            (int) DataGrid1.DataKeys[index];

        // Get a dataset based on that BugID
        DataSet dataSet =
            CreateBugHistoryDataSet(bugID);

        // bind to the table returned and make
        // the panel visible
        HistoryGrid.DataSource=dataSet.Tables[0];
        HistoryGrid.DataBind();
        BugHistoryPanel.Visible=true;

    }
    else
    {
        // no history to display, hide the panel
        BugHistoryPanel.Visible=false;
    }
}
```

Example 12-5. Updating with transactions (continued)

```csharp
private void Page_Load(
    object sender, System.EventArgs e)
{
    if (!IsPostBack)
    {
        // hide the history panel
        UpdateBugHistory();

        // set the data source for the
        // grid to the first table
        DataSet ds = CreateBugDataSet();
        DataGrid1.DataSource=ds.Tables[0];
        DataGrid1.DataBind();

        lbProduct.DataSource=GetDataReader("lkProduct");
        lbProduct.DataBind();

        lbSeverity.DataSource = GetDataReader("lkSeverity");
        lbSeverity.DataBind();

        lbReporter.DataSource = GetDataReader("People");
        lbReporter.DataBind();

    }
}

private SqlDataReader GetDataReader(string whichTable)
{
    // connection string to connect to the Bugs Database
    string connectionString =
        "server=YourServer; uid=sa; pwd=YourPW; database=ProgASPDotNetBugs";

    // Create connection object, initialize with
    // connection string. Open it.
    System.Data.SqlClient.SqlConnection connection =
        new System.Data.SqlClient.SqlConnection(
        connectionString);

    connection.Open();

    // Create a SqlCommand object and assign the connection
    System.Data.SqlClient.SqlCommand command =
        new System.Data.SqlClient.SqlCommand();
    command.Connection=connection;

    // set the stored procedure to get the bug records
    command.CommandText="select * from " + whichTable;

    // return the data reader
    return command.ExecuteReader(
        CommandBehavior.CloseConnection);
}
```

Example 12-5. Updating with transactions (continued)

```
private DataSet CreateBugHistoryDataSet(int bugID)
{
    // connection string to connect to the Bugs Database
    string connectionString =
        "server=YourServer; uid=sa; pwd=YourPW; database=ProgASPDotNetBugs";

    // Create connection object, initialize with
    // connection string. Open it.
    System.Data.SqlClient.SqlConnection connection =
        new System.Data.SqlClient.SqlConnection(connectionString);
    connection.Open( );

    // create a second command object for the bugs hisotry table
    System.Data.SqlClient.SqlCommand command =
        new System.Data.SqlClient.SqlCommand( );
    command.Connection = connection;

    command.CommandText= "spBugHistory";
    command.CommandType = CommandType.StoredProcedure;

    // declare the parameter object
    System.Data.SqlClient.SqlParameter param;

    // Add a new parameter, get back a reference to it
    param = command.Parameters.Add("@BugID",SqlDbType.Int);

    // set the parameter's direction and value
    param.Direction = ParameterDirection.Input;
    param.Value = bugID;

    // create a second data adapter and add the command
    // and map the table
    // then fill the dataset from this second adapter
    SqlDataAdapter dataAdapter = new SqlDataAdapter( );
    dataAdapter.SelectCommand = command;
    dataAdapter.TableMappings.Add("Table", "BugHistory");

    DataSet dataSet = new DataSet( );
    dataAdapter.Fill(dataSet);

    return dataSet;
}

private DataSet CreateBugDataSet( )
{

    // connection string to connect to the Bugs Database
    string connectionString =
        "server=YourServer; uid=sa; pwd=YourPW; database=ProgASPDotNetBugs";

    // Create connection object, initialize with
```

Example 12-5. Updating with transactions (continued)

```
            // connection string. Open it.
            System.Data.SqlClient.SqlConnection connection =
                new System.Data.SqlClient.SqlConnection(connectionString);
            connection.Open( );

            // Create a SqlCommand object and assign the connection
            System.Data.SqlClient.SqlCommand command =
                new System.Data.SqlClient.SqlCommand( );
            command.Connection=connection;
            command.CommandText="spBugs";
            command.CommandType=CommandType.StoredProcedure;

            // create a data adapter and assign the command object
            // and add the table mapping for bugs
            SqlDataAdapter dataAdapter = new SqlDataAdapter( );
            dataAdapter.SelectCommand=command;
            dataAdapter.TableMappings.Add("Table","Bugs");

            // Create the dataset and use the data adapter to fill it
            DataSet dataSet = new DataSet( );
            dataAdapter.Fill(dataSet);
            return dataSet;
        }

        private void Page_Init(object sender, EventArgs e)
        {
            InitializeComponent( );
        }


        #region Web Form Designer generated code
        /// <summary>
        /// Required method for Designer support - do not modify
        /// the contents of this method with the code editor.
        /// </summary>
        private void InitializeComponent( )
        {
            this.btnAdd.Click += new System.EventHandler(this.btnAdd_Click);
            this.Load += new System.EventHandler(this.Page_Load);

        }
        #endregion

        private void UpdateConnectionTransaction( )
        {
            string connectionString =
                "server=YourServer; uid=sa; pwd=YourPW; database=ProgASPDotNetBugs";

            // Create connection object, initialize with
            // connection string. Open it.
            System.Data.SqlClient.SqlConnection connection =
                new System.Data.SqlClient.SqlConnection(connectionString);
```

Example 12-5. Updating with transactions (continued)

```
    // declare the command object for the sql statements
    System.Data.SqlClient.SqlCommand command =
        new System.Data.SqlClient.SqlCommand( );

    // declare an instance of SqlTransaction
    SqlTransaction transaction;

    // connection string to connect to the Bugs Database
    connection.Open( );

    // begin the transaction
    transaction = connection.BeginTransaction( );

    // attach the transaction to the command
    command.Transaction = transaction;

    // attach connection to the command
    command.Connection = connection;

    try
    {

        command.CommandText = "spAddBug";
        command.CommandType = CommandType.StoredProcedure;

        // declare the parameter object
        System.Data.SqlClient.SqlParameter param;

        // add each parameter and set its direciton and value
        param = command.Parameters.Add("@ProductID",SqlDbType.Int);
        param.Direction = ParameterDirection.Input;
     // from the list box
        param.Value = lbProduct.SelectedItem.Value;
        param = command.Parameters.Add(
    "@Version",SqlDbType.VarChar,50);
        param.Direction = ParameterDirection.Input;
// from the text box
        param.Value = txtVersion.Text;
        param = command.Parameters.Add(
    "@Description",SqlDbType.VarChar,8000);
        param.Direction = ParameterDirection.Input;
        // from the text box
param.Value = txtDescription.Text;
        param = command.Parameters.Add("@Reporter",SqlDbType.Int);
        param.Direction = ParameterDirection.Input;
// from the list box
        param.Value = lbReporter.SelectedItem.Value;
        param = command.Parameters.Add("@BugID",SqlDbType.Int);
        param.Direction = ParameterDirection.Output;

        command.ExecuteNonQuery( ); // execute the sproc
```

Example 12-5. Updating with transactions (continued)

```
            // retrieve the identity column
            int BugID =
            Convert.ToInt32(command.Parameters["@BugID"].Value);

            // formulate the string to update the bug history
            string strAddBugHistory = "Insert into BugHistory " +
                "(bugID, status, severity, response, owner) values (" + BugID + ",1," +
                lbSeverity.SelectedItem.Value + ", 'Bug Created', 6)";

            // set up the command object to update the bug hsitory
            command.CommandType = CommandType.Text;
            command.CommandText = strAddBugHistory;

            // execute the insert statement
            command.ExecuteNonQuery( );

            // commit the transaction
            transaction.Commit( );
        }
        catch (Exception e)
        {
            Trace.Write(e.Message);
            transaction.Rollback( );
        }
    }

    private void UpdateDBTransaction( )
    {
        // connection string to connect to the Bugs Database
        string connectionString =
            "server=YourServer; uid=sa; pwd=YourPW; database=ProgASPDotNetBugs";

        // Create connection object, initialize with
        // connection string. Open it.
        System.Data.SqlClient.SqlConnection connection =
            new System.Data.SqlClient.SqlConnection(connectionString);
        connection.Open( );

        // create a second command object for the bugs hisotry table
        System.Data.SqlClient.SqlCommand command =
            new System.Data.SqlClient.SqlCommand( );
        command.Connection = connection;

        command.CommandText= "spAddBugWithTransactions";
        command.CommandType = CommandType.StoredProcedure;

        // declare the parameter object
        System.Data.SqlClient.SqlParameter param;

        // add each parameter and set its direciton and value
        param = command.Parameters.Add("@ProductID",SqlDbType.Int);
        param.Direction = ParameterDirection.Input;
```

Example 12-5. Updating with transactions (continued)

```
        param.Value = lbProduct.SelectedItem.Value; // from the list box

        param = command.Parameters.Add("@Version",SqlDbType.VarChar,50);
        param.Direction = ParameterDirection.Input;
        param.Value = txtVersion.Text;              // from the text box

        param = command.Parameters.Add(
    "@Description",SqlDbType.VarChar,8000);
        param.Direction = ParameterDirection.Input;
    // from the text box
        param.Value = txtDescription.Text;
        param = command.Parameters.Add("@Reporter",SqlDbType.Int);
        param.Direction = ParameterDirection.Input;
        param.Value = lbReporter.SelectedItem.Value; // from the list box

        param = command.Parameters.Add("@Severity",SqlDbType.Int);
        param.Direction = ParameterDirection.Input;
        param.Value = lbSeverity.SelectedItem.Value; // from the list box

        command.ExecuteNonQuery( ); // execute the sproc
    }

    private void btnAdd_Click(object sender, System.EventArgs e)
    {
        int whichTransaction = Convert.ToInt32(rbTransaction.SelectedItem.Value);
        if (whichTransaction == 0)
            UpdateDBTransaction( );
        else
            UpdateConnectionTransaction( );
    }

    }
}
```

The complete source code for the *.aspx* file is shown in Example 12-6. Again, this is relatively unchanged from the examples in Chapter 11, with the addition of the list boxes, text boxes, and buttons necessary to gather the new Bug data.

Example 12-6. The .aspx file

```
<%@ Page language="c#" Codebehind="WebForm1.aspx.cs"
AutoEventWireup="false" Inherits="BugHistoryTransactions.WebForm1" Trace="true"%>
<!DOCTYPE HTML PUBLIC "-//W3C//DTD HTML 4.0 Transitional//EN" >
<HTML>
    <HEAD>
        <meta name="GENERATOR" content="Microsoft Visual Studio.NET 7.0">
        <meta name="CODE_LANGUAGE" content="Visual Basic 7.0">
        <meta name="vs_defaultClientScript" content="JavaScript">
        <meta name="vs_targetSchema"
        content="http://schemas.microsoft.com/intellisense/ie5">    </HEAD>
    <body>
        <form id="Form1" method="post" runat="server">
```

Example 12-6. The .aspx file (continued)

```
<table>
    <tr>
        <th>Product</th>
        <th>Version</th>
        <th>Description</th>
        <th>Reporter</th>
        <th>Severity</th>
    </tr>
    <tr>
        <td>
            <asp:dropdownlist id="lbProduct" runat="server"
            DataValueField="ProductID"
            DataTextField="ProductDescription" />
        </td>
        <td>
            <asp:textbox id="txtVersion" Runat="server" Width="60"/>
        </td>
        <td>
            <asp:textbox id="txtDescription"
             Runat="server" Width="250"/>
        </td>
        <td>
            <asp:dropdownlist id="lbReporter" Runat="server"
            DataValueField="PersonID" DataTextField="FullName"/>
        </td>
        <td>
            <asp:dropdownlist id="lbSeverity" Runat="server"
            DataValueField="SeverityID"
            DataTextField="SeverityDescription"/>
        </td>
    </tr>
    <tr>
        <td>
            <asp:radiobuttonlist id="rbTransaction" Runat="server"
            TextAlign="Right" RepeatLayout="flow"
            RepeatDirection="Vertical" repeatColumns="2"
             CellSpacing="3">
                <asp:ListItem Text="DB Transaction" Value="0" />
                <asp:ListItem Text="Connection Transaction"
                    Value="1" Selected="True" />
            </asp:radiobuttonlist>
        </td>
        <td>
            <asp:button id="btnAdd" Runat="server" Text="Add" />
        </td>
    </tr>
</table>
<br>
<asp:datagrid id="DataGrid1" runat="server" EnableViewState="true"
AutoGenerateColumns="False" HeaderStyle-Font-Bold
AlternatingItemStyle-BackColor="LightGrey"
OnSelectedIndexChanged="OnSelectedIndexChangedHandler"
```

Example 12-6. The .aspx file (continued)

```
            OnItemDataBound="OnItemDataBoundEventHandler"
            BorderColor="#000099" BorderWidth="5px"
            HeaderStyle-BackColor="PapayaWhip" CellPadding="5"
             DataKeyField="BugID">
              <Columns>
                  <asp:ButtonColumn Text="History" CommandName="Select" />
                  <asp:BoundColumn DataField="BugID" HeaderText="Bug ID" />
                  <asp:BoundColumn DataField="Description"
                   HeaderText="Description" />
                  <asp:BoundColumn DataField="Reporter"
                   HeaderText="Reported By" />
                  <asp:BoundColumn DataField="Response"
                   HeaderText="Most Recent Action" />
                  <asp:BoundColumn DataField="Owner" HeaderText="Owned By" />
                  <asp:BoundColumn DataField="StatusDescription"
                   HeaderText="Status" />
                  <asp:BoundColumn DataField="SeverityDescription"
                   HeaderText="Severity" />
                  <asp:BoundColumn DataField="DateStamp"
                   HeaderText="LastUpdated" />
              </Columns>
          </asp:datagrid>
      </form>
      <asp:panel id="BugHistoryPanel" Runat="server">
          <asp:DataGrid id="HistoryGrid" AutoGenerateColumns="False"
          HeaderStyle-Font-Bold AlternatingItemStyle-BackColor="LightGrey"
          BorderColor="#000099" BorderWidth="5px"
          HeaderStyle-BackColor="PapayaWhip" CellPadding="5" Runat="server">
              <Columns>
                  <asp:BoundColumn DataField="Response"
                   HeaderText="Most Recent Action" />
                  <asp:BoundColumn DataField="Owner" HeaderText="Owned By" />
                  <asp:BoundColumn DataField="StatusDescription"
                   HeaderText="Status" />
                  <asp:BoundColumn DataField="SeverityDescription"
                   HeaderText="Severity" />
                  <asp:BoundColumn DataField="DateStamp"
                   HeaderText="LastUpdated" />
              </Columns>
          </asp:DataGrid>
      </asp:panel>
   </body>
</HTML>
```

Updating Data Using Datasets

So far in this chapter, you have seen how to update a database and how to add transactions to ensure data integrity. All of that is fine as far as it goes, but nothing you've done so far to update the database takes advantage of the DataSet object, which you will remember is the keystone of ADO.NET.

If you are using the DataSet object to retrieve data and pass it from tier to tier within your application, you would also like to manipulate that data within the dataset and push the changes back to the database. To make this more sophisticated model of data updating work, you will need to take advantage of the advanced capabilities of the DataSet and the DataAdapter classes, and you'll need to understand how they in turn use the Command and Connection objects to mediate between the dataset and the database itself.

The Dataset and the Data Adapter

As explained in Chapter 11, the DataSet object interacts with the database through a DataAdapter object. Until now, you've created the data adapter by passing in a command string and a connection string to the DataAdapter object's constructor and then calling the Fill method. It turns out that Fill interacts with the database by creating a command object on your behalf and assigning that command object to the SelectCommand property of the DataAdapter object.

Each SqlDataAdapter object has four command properties (SelectCommand, UpdateCommand, InsertCommand, and DeleteCommand), each of which takes an object of type SqlCommand. Thus far, you've been using the Fill method to create a SelectCommand object (that is, a command object assigned to the SelectCommand property) by employing the command string parameter you've passed in to the Data-Adapter object's constructor. For example, in Example 11-2 you wrote:

```
// get records from the Bugs table
string commandString =
    "Select BugID, Description from Bugs";

// create the dataset command object
// and the DataSet object
SqlDataAdapter dataAdapter =
    new SqlDataAdapter(
    commandString, connectionString);

DataSet dataSet = new DataSet( );

// fill the dataset object
dataAdapter.Fill(dataSet,"Bugs");
```

You could just as easily have explicitly set the SelectCommand property of the Data-Adapter by writing:

```
// define the SQL Select command
string commandString = "Select BugID, Description from Bugs";

// create the data adapter; do not pass in the select statement
SqlDataAdapter dataAdapter = new SqlDataAdapter(connectionString);

// explicitly create a command object with the select statement
SqlCommand cmd = new SqlCommand(commandString);
```

```
// assign the new command object to the SelectCommand property
dataAdapter.SelectCommand = cmd;
```

To update the database with the changes you'll make to your dataset, you'll need to explicitly set the other three properties: UpdateCommand, DeleteCommand, and InsertCommand. You will fill these three properties with either SQL statements, or, more commonly, the names of stored procedures. When the data adapter is told to update the database, it will examine the changes to the dataset and call the appropriate command objects to update, delete, or insert records. Often, a single request to a dataset to update the database will cause each of these commands to be called repeatedly, once for each modified row.

Steps for Updating the Database

The steps to updating a database using a dataset are:

1. Create a dataset by retrieving data from the database and display it.

2. Persist the dataset.

3. Update the records in the dataset. This might include adding new records, deleting records, and updating existing records. You may choose to rebind the changed dataset to display widgets on your page to show the user what has changed, and optionally to give the user an opportunity to make further changes before the database is updated.

4. Create stored procedures in the database to manage the update, insert, and delete commands.

5. Create command objects to invoke the stored procedures. Add parameters to the command objects as needed.

6. Add transaction support to ensure all updates are done or none is done.

7. Call the Update method on the data adapter. The data adapter will examine the changes in the dataset and call the appropriate command objects, which will update the database on your behalf.

The example program described in the next section will walk you through each of these steps and examine their implementation and implications in some detail.

Creating and displaying a dataset

As you have done in many previous examples, you start by retrieving data from the database using a stored procedure, and displaying that data in a grid, as shown in Figure 12-5.

This data grid is created once again by calling the CreateBugDataSet method:

```
private DataSet CreateBugDataSet( )
{
```

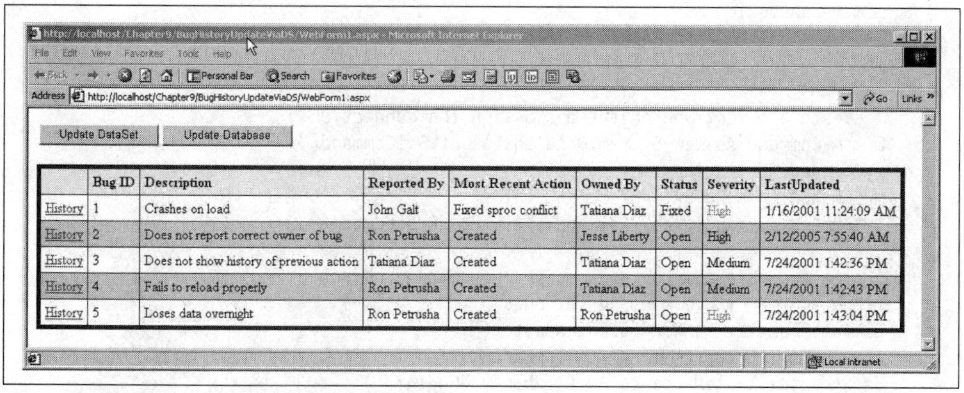

	Bug ID	Description	Reported By	Most Recent Action	Owned By	Status	Severity	LastUpdated
History	1	Crashes on load	John Galt	Fixed sproc conflict	Tatiana Diaz	Fixed	High	1/16/2001 11:24:09 AM
History	2	Does not report correct owner of bug	Ron Petrusha	Created	Jesse Liberty	Open	High	2/12/2005 7:55:40 AM
History	3	Does not show history of previous action	Tatiana Diaz	Created	Tatiana Diaz	Open	Medium	7/24/2001 1:42:36 PM
History	4	Fails to reload properly	Ron Petrusha	Created	Tatiana Diaz	Open	Medium	7/24/2001 1:42:43 PM
History	5	Loses data overnight	Ron Petrusha	Created	Ron Petrusha	Open	High	7/24/2001 1:43:04 PM

Figure 12-5. Displaying bug and bug history information

```
    // connection string to connect to the Bugs Database
    string connectionString =
       "server=YourServer; uid=sa; pwd=YourPW; database=ProgASPDotNetBugs";

    // Create connection object, initialize with
    // connection string. Open it.
    System.Data.SqlClient.SqlConnection connection =
       new System.Data.SqlClient.SqlConnection(connectionString);
    connection.Open( );

    // Create a SqlCommand object and assign the connection
    System.Data.SqlClient.SqlCommand command =
       new System.Data.SqlClient.SqlCommand( );
    command.Connection=connection;
    command.CommandText="spBugsWithIDs";
    command.CommandType=CommandType.StoredProcedure;

    // create a data adapter and assign the command object
    // and add the table mapping for bugs
    SqlDataAdapter dataAdapter = new SqlDataAdapter( );
    dataAdapter.SelectCommand=command;
    dataAdapter.TableMappings.Add("Table","BugInfo");

    // Create the dataset and use the data adapter to fill it
    DataSet dataSet = new DataSet( );
    dataAdapter.Fill(dataSet);
    return dataSet;
}
```

The VB.NET equivalent is:

```
Private Function CreateBugDataSet( ) As DataSet
   ' connection string to connect to the Bugs Database
   Dim connectionString As String = _
      "server=YourDB; uid=sa; pwd=YourPW; database=ProgASPDotNetBugs"

   ' Create connection object, initialize with
   ' connection string. Open it.
```

```
Dim myConnection As _
    New System.Data.SqlClient.SqlConnection(connectionString)
myConnection.Open()

' Create a SqlCommand object and assign the connection
Dim myCommand As New System.Data.SqlClient.SqlCommand()
myCommand.Connection = myConnection
myCommand.CommandText = "spBugsWithIDs"
myCommand.CommandType = CommandType.StoredProcedure

' create a data adapter and assign the command object
' and add the table mapping for bugs
Dim dataAdapter As New SqlDataAdapter()
dataAdapter.SelectCommand = myCommand
dataAdapter.TableMappings.Add("Table", "BugInfo")

' Create the dataset and use the data adapter to fill it
Dim myDataSet As New DataSet()
dataAdapter.Fill(myDataSet)
Return myDataSet
End Function
```

The only change to the previous example is that this time CreateBugDataSet calls a new stored procedure, spBugsWithIDs.

The source code for the spBugsWithIDs stored procedure itself is shown in Example 12-7. There are two important things to note in this stored procedure. The first is that the data displayed in the grid is once again drawn from a number of different tables. The Description field is from the Bugs table. The Response field (used to populate the Most Recent Action column on the grid) is taken from the last Bug-History record for each Bug. The Owner is drawn from the People table based on the Owner value in the latest BugHistory record (described in the sidebar "Finding the Last BugHistory").

Example 12-7. The spBugsWithIDs stored procedure

```
CREATE PROCEDURE spBugsWithIDs  AS
select b.BugID, h.BugHistoryID, b.Description, b.Version, h.Response,
o.FullName as owner, h.owner as ownerID,
b.Product as ProductID, p.ProductDescription,
b.Reporter as ReporterID, r.FullName as reporter,
h.status as statusID, s.StatusDescription,
h.severity as severityID, sev.SeverityDescription, h.DateStamp
from
(select bugID, max(bugHistoryID) as maxHistoryID from BugHistory group by bugID) t
join bugs b on b.bugid = t.bugid
join BugHistory h on h.bugHistoryID = t.maxHistoryID
join lkProduct p on b.Product = p.ProductID
join People r on b.Reporter = r.PersonID
join People o on h.Owner = o.PersonID
join lkStatus s on s.statusid = h.status
join lkSeverity sev on sev.SeverityID = h.severity
GO
```

The second important thing to note about this stored procedure is that it not only retrieves the values to be displayed, it also carefully retrieves the IDs of the fields as they appear in Bugs and BugHistory. That is, not only do you retrieve the severity description (High, Medium, Low) to display in the grid, but you also retrieve the corresponding severity ID values (5, 4, 3) as they are stored in the underlying records. This is important because in this example you will update these records, and you'll need the IDs to appear in the table you have created in the dataset. If the user indicates he wants to change the severity from High to Medium, your update will actually change the value from 5 to 4.

Once a command object that can invoke the new stored procedure is created, as shown in the previous C# code fragment, a new data adapter is created and the SelectCommand property is manually set to that command object, as shown in the following code fragment:

```
SqlDataAdapter dataAdapter = new SqlDataAdapter();
dataAdapter.SelectCommand=command;
```

You then add a new TableMapping object to the TableMappings collection to map the results of the stored procedure to a table within the BugInfo dataset named BugInfo:

```
dataAdapter.TableMappings.Add("Table","BugInfo");
```

It is critical to understand that *to the dataset* BugInfo appears as a single table, consisting of the fields and values returned by the stored procedure. The dataset, in this example, is oblivious to the underlying data structure of multiple interrelated tables.

Finally, a new dataset is created and filled using the data adapter you've crafted:

```
DataSet dataSet = new Data
dataAdapter.Fill(dataSet);
```

Persisting the dataset

Later in this example, you will modify this dataset in response to the user pressing a button. When the user presses the button, however, there is a round trip to the server, and web pages are stateless. Thus, just as you are ready to update the dataset, it is gone (poof!), disappearing in a puff of stateless smoke.

You have a number of options for dealing with this problem. First, you can recreate the dataset by reissuing the query. This is not a great solution, not least because, after you update the dataset, you'll want to write it back to the database—and you *must* hold on to the dataset at that point in order to know what changes to write. In short, you can't recreate the dataset; you need to *persist* it.

For this example, you'll persist the dataset to session state. Session state is covered in detail in Chapter 6, but writing and retrieving is dead simple. As soon as you get back the DataSet object from the CreateBugDataSet method, you save it in a session variable named BugsDataSet. In order to do this, you include the following code in the Page_Load method:

```
DataSet ds = CreateBugDataSet();
Session["BugsDataSet"] = ds;
```

The VB.NET equivalent is:

```
Dim ds As DataSet = CreateBugDataSet
Session("BugsDataSet") = ds
```

In the handler for the Update DataSet button, you'll retrieve the dataset from session state. Remember that session state stores objects, and so you will have to cast the dataset back to its correct type:

```
DataSet ds = (DataSet) Session["BugsDataSet"];
DataTable bugTable = ds.Tables["BugInfo"];
```

In VB.NET, use:

```
ds = CType(Session("BugsDataSet"), DataSet)
Dim bugTable As DataTable = ds.Tables("BugInfo")
```

Hey! Presto! You have the same dataset after your round trip. Even better, because Session objects are stored on the server, the dataset did not make the round trip.

Updating the records in the dataset

There are many ways to allow the user to indicate how he wants to modify the data. This example ignores all user interface issues (which are covered in Chapters 10 and 13) and focuses on interacting with the data. To keep things simple, you'll have only two buttons: Update DataSet and Update Database.

The event handler for the first button, Update DataSet, implements hard-coded changes to the data in the dataset and then draws a second grid showing the changes. This will have no effect on the underlying database. If you close the web page after updating and displaying these changes, the database tables will be unaffected. The second button, Update Database, writes the changes to the dataset back to the database.

The user interface is bare bones. As shown in Figure 12-5, the web page opens by displaying data from the Bugs and BugHistory tables with two rather ugly buttons above the data grid.

In a real application, the user may indicate changes to the dataset in any number of ways. You might provide buttons and links to allow the user to interact with the data directly in the data grid. Or you might provide a form for adding and changing the data. For this application, as indicated earlier, you'll just hardwire a number of changes that will mimic the changes that might be requested by a user. You provide only a single button, Update DataSet, as described in the following section.

Updating the dataset

When a user clicks on the Update DataSet button, the btnUpdateDataSet_Click event handler is called. In the previous step, you stashed the dataset away in session state; you retrieve it now, using the code:

```
DataSet ds = (DataSet) Session["BugsDataSet"];
```

which in VB.NET is:

```
Dim ds As DataSet = CType(Session("BugsDataSet"), DataSet)
```

With the dataset in hand, you can extract the table you created earlier named BugInfo.

```
DataTable bugTable = ds.Tables["BugInfo"];
```

which in VB.NET is:

```
Dim bugTable As DataTable = ds.Tables("BugInfo")
```

You are now ready to edit, insert, and delete values. The DataRow class has an Item property that returns the data stored in a specified column. Because this is implemented as the *indexer* in C#, you can access the value for a particular field in a given row by providing the row offset and the field name. For example, the following line of code will change the Response value in the first row (remember that in C# and VB.NET arrays are zero-indexed) to the value This is a test:

```
bugTable.Rows[0]["Response"] = "This is a test";
```

In VB.NET, Item is the default property of the DataRow class. Hence, the VB.NET code is similar to the C# code:

```
bugTable.Rows(0)("Response") = "This is a test"
```

You can delete a row by calling the Delete method on the row itself:

```
bugTable.Rows[1].Delete();
```

You add a new row using exactly the same syntax you saw for creating new data rows by hand in Chapter 11:

```
DataRow newRow = bugTable.NewRow( );
newRow["Description"] = "New bug test";
newRow["Response"] = "Created new bug";
newRow["Owner"] = "Jesse Liberty";
newRow["OwnerID"] = 1;
newRow["ProductID"] = 2;
newRow["ProductDescription"] = "PIM - My Personal Infomation Manager";
newRow["Version"] = "0.01";
newRow["ReporterID"] = 3;
newRow["Reporter"] = "John Galt";
newRow["StatusID"] = 1;
newRow["StatusDescription"] = "open";
newRow["SeverityID"] = 2;
newRow["SeverityDescription"] = "High";
newRow["DateStamp"] = "07-27-2005";
bugTable.Rows.Add(newRow);
```

In VB.NET, the code looks like:

```
Dim newRow As DataRow = bugTable.NewRow( )
newRow("Description") = "New bug test"
newRow("Response") = "Created new bug"
newRow("Owner") = "Jesse Liberty"
newRow("OwnerID") = 1
newRow("ProductID") = 2
newRow("ProductDescription") = "PIM - My Personal Infomation Manager"
newRow("Version") = "0.01"
newRow("ReporterID") = 3
newRow("Reporter") = "John Galt"
newRow("StatusID") = 1
newRow("StatusDescription") = "open"
newRow("SeverityID") = 2
newRow("SeverityDescription") = "High"
newRow("DateStamp") = "07-27-2005"
bugTable.Rows.Add(newRow)
```

Keep in mind that you're filling the BugInfo table in the dataset that was created by calling the spBugsWithIDs stored procedure. You must add a field for every field in the resulting set returned by that sproc.

It is up to you, as the programmer, to ensure the data integrity of the hand-created rows. For example, nothing stops you from adding a SeverityID of 4 (normally Low) with a SeverityDescription of High, except that if you do you will display a value to the user that will not correspond to the value with which you'll update the database!

Once you've made all the changes to the dataset, you will bind a second grid (DataGrid2) to the BugInfo table and make that grid visible, so that the user can see the new values, as shown in Figure 12-6.

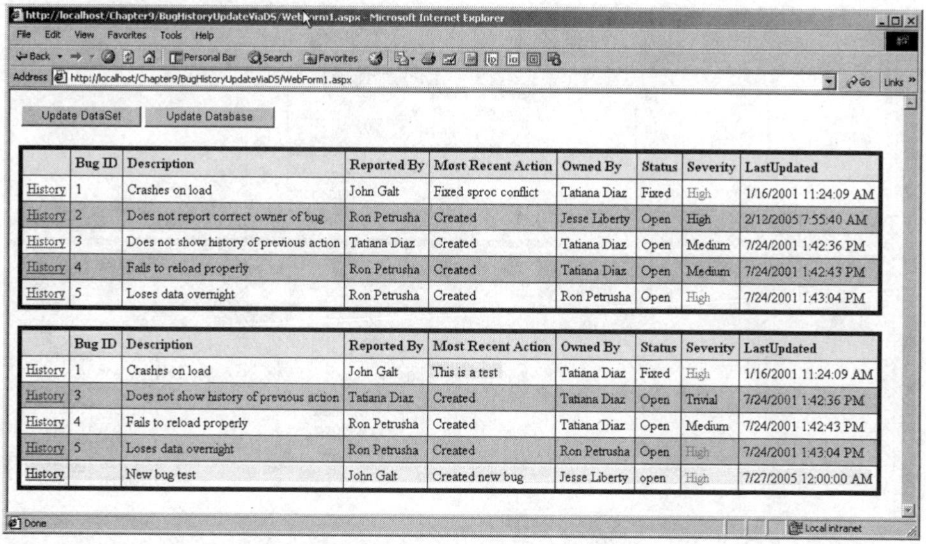

Figure 12-6. DataGrids showing change to DataSet

Notice in Figure 12-6 that the first record has been updated with a new Most Recent Action value. This new value reflects the change to the Response field:

```
bugTable.Rows[0]["Response"] = "This is a test";
```

or in VB.NET:

```
bugTable.Rows(0)("Response") = "This is a test"
```

> The Most Recent Action value is highlighted in the image of Figure 12-6 to make it easier for you to locate the change.

BugID 2, which was the second record (bugTable.Rows[1]), appears to have been deleted. In fact, it has only been marked for deletion, but the data grid is smart enough not to display records marked for deletion.

A new record has been added, as shown on the final line in the grid. Notice that there is no BugID. (Looking back at the example, you will note that you did not provide a BugID.) The BugID field is an identity column, which will be provided by the database when you write this data back to the database.

The absence of a BugID illustrates quite clearly that while you've updated the dataset, you have not yet written these changes back to the database. You can prove this to yourself by examining the tables in the database directly, as shown in Figure 12-7.

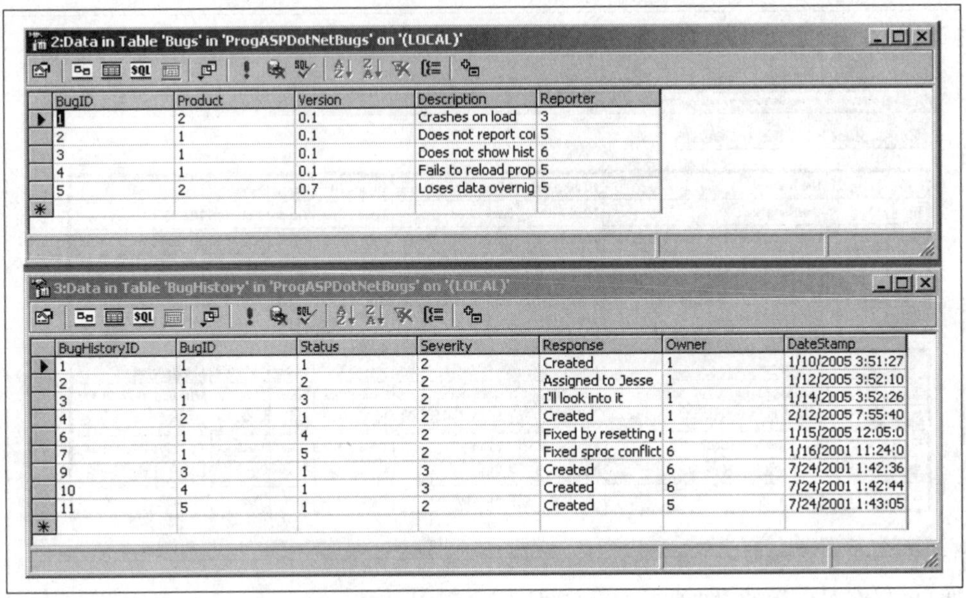

Figure 12-7. Bug and history table after dataset update, but before database update

Updating in the database

When the user clicks on the second button, Update Database, the btnUpdateDataBase_Click event handler is invoked. Your goal in this method is to update the database with the changes in the dataset.

The dataset keeps track of the changes to its data. You can update the database with all the changes just by calling the Update method on the DataAdapter, passing in a reference to the DataSet object and the name of the table you want to update.

That said, there is a bit of preparation work. For the update to work, you first need to provide command objects to the InsertCommand, UpdateCommand, and Delete-Command properties of the data adapter. We'll examine each of these preparatory steps in the following sections.

The delete command. As indicated earlier, you must begin by creating the appropriate stored procedures. Example 12-8 shows the spDeleteBugFromDataSet stored procedure for deleting bug records. If the user deletes a record from the grid, he intends to delete all record of that bug. Because of referential integrity, you must *first* remove all records from that bug within BugHistory, and then you may remove the record from the Bugs table.

Example 12-8. The stored procedure to delete bugs

```
CREATE PROCEDURE spDeleteBugFromDataSet
@bugID int,
```

Example 12-8. The stored procedure to delete bugs (continued)

```
@BugHistoryID int
as

    Delete from BugHistory where
            bugID = @BugID and BugHistoryID = @BugHistoryID
    Delete from Bugs where bugID = @BugID
GO
```

Notice that you will pass in two parameters that will be used to identify the record to delete. With this stored procedure, you are ready to create the Command object you will assign to the DataAdapters DeleteCommand property.

You begin by creating a new SqlCommand object:

```
SqlCommand deleteCmd =
    new SqlCommand("spDeleteBugFromDataSet",connection);
deleteCmd.CommandType=CommandType.StoredProcedure;
```

or in VB.NET:

```
Dim deleteCmd As New SqlCommand("spDeleteBugFromDataSet", myConnection)
deleteCmd.CommandType = CommandType.StoredProcedure
```

This SqlCommand object is just like every command object you've created to date. You will name it deleteCmd to make it easy to identify, but it is just a garden-variety SqlCommand object, just like all the others you've used so far to invoke stored procedures.

You'll add two parameters, BugID and BugHistoryID. These are input parameters, but this time rather than assigning a value to them, you must set two new properties of the Parameter object, SourceColumn and SourceVersion. The SourceColumn property identifies the column within the table in the dataset that this parameter will get its value from. That is, when you invoke the stored procedure, the parameter (*@BugID*) will draw its value from this column in the record to be deleted. The column you want, of course, is BugID:

```
param.SourceColumn="bugID";
```

The second property of the parameter is the SourceVersion, which must be set to one of the DataRowVersion enumerated values (Current, Default, Original, or Proposed).

The Default value is used only when you wish to use a default value, which does not apply to this example.

The Original value is the value the field had when the dataset was created. The original value is compared to the value in the database when the update is performed to see if the database has been changed by another process. This is covered later in the "Multiuser Updates" section.

The Current value holds the changes to the column you've made since the dataset was created. That is, as you update columns, the Current value holds the changes you've made, while the Original value has the value as you originally obtained it from the database.

In the case of the BugID, you'll tell the Param to use the Original value (though of course since you've not changed the value, you can use the Current value as well):

```
param.SourceVersion=DataRowVersion.Original;
```

You create a Parameter object for the BugHistory in exactly the same way:

```
param = deleteCmd.Parameters.Add("@BugHistoryID",SqlDbType.Int);
param.Direction = ParameterDirection.Input;
param.SourceColumn="BugHistoryID";
param.SourceVersion=DataRowVersion.Original;
```

You are now ready to assign the command object to the DeleteCommand property of the data adapter:

```
dataAdapter.DeleteCommand=deleteCmd;
```

The update command. The stored procedure for updating the database is somewhat more complicated than the procedure for deleting records. This time, you want to pass in parameters for each of the fields that may be changed. You will also pass in the BugID and BugHistory ID to uniquely identify the bug you wish to alter. The complete stored procedure is shown in Example 12-9.

Example 12-9. The stored procedure for updating a bug

```
CREATE PROCEDURE spUpdateBugFromDataSet
@ProductID int,
@Description varChar(8000),
@Response varChar(8000),
@Reporter int,
@Owner int,
@Status int,
@Severity int,
@bugID int,
@BugHistoryID int
as
Update Bugs
set
        Product = @productID,
        [Description] = @Description,
        Reporter = @Reporter
        where bugID = @BugID

Update BugHistory
Set
        bugID = @BugID,
        status = @Status,
        severity = @Severity,
        response = @Response,
        owner = @Owner
```

Example 12-9. The stored procedure for updating a bug (continued)

```
where BugHistoryID = @bugHistoryID and bugID = @bugID
GO
```

Once again you create a command object, this time to hold the Update command stored procedure:

```
SqlCommand updateCmd =
    new SqlCommand("spUpdateBugFromDataSet",connection);
updateCmd.CommandType=CommandType.StoredProcedure;
```

or in VB.NET:

```
Dim updateCmd As New SqlCommand("spUpdateBugFromDataSet", myConnection)
updateCmd.CommandType = CommandType.StoredProcedure
```

You'll add a SqlParameter object for each parameter to the stored procedure:

```
param = updateCmd.Parameters.Add("@ProductID",SqlDbType.Int);
param.Direction = ParameterDirection.Input;
param.SourceColumn="ProductID";
param.SourceVersion=DataRowVersion.Current;
```

The ProductID parameter is like the BugID parameter, except that now you use the enumerated value DataRowVersion.Current for the SourceVersion property. You will use Current for any value that may have been changed in the dataset; this instructs the data adapter to update the dataset with the value current in the dataset, rather than with the value that may reside back in the database.

When you create the parameters for the Reporter, Owner, Status, and Severity fields, you must be careful to use the ReporterID, OwnerID, StatusID, and SeverityID SourceColumns, respectively. Remember that while you are displaying the full names of the reporter and owner, and the text value of the status and severity, the records you are updating in the Bugs and BugHistory tables use the ID.

The insert command. The final command you'll need to implement is the insert command. You start, once again, by creating the necessary stored procedure, as shown in Example 12-10.

Example 12-10. The stored procedure spInsertBugFromDataSet

```
CREATE PROCEDURE spInsertBugFromDataSet
@ProductID int,
@Version varChar(50),
@Description varChar(8000),
@Response varChar(8000),
@Reporter int,
@Owner int,
@Status int,
@Severity int
as
declare @bugID int
Insert into Bugs values (@ProductID, @Version, @Description, @Reporter)
```

Example 12-10. The stored procedure spInsertBugFromDataSet (continued)

```
select @bugID = @@identity
Insert into BugHistory
(bugID, status, severity, response, owner)
values
( @bugID,
        @status,        -- status
        @Severity,
        @response,
        @owner
)
GO
```

You must remember to insert into the Bugs table before inserting into the BugHistory table because referential integrity constraints require that the BugID must exist in Bugs before it can be inserted into BugHistory.

Note that you do not pass in either the BugID nor the BugHistoryID as parameters; these are created by the database itself. The BugHistory table requires the BugID generated by adding a record to Bugs; you obtain this value from @@identity.

It is this stored procedure that will be called to insert the record you created by hand in the btnUpdateDataSet_Click event procedure. Once again, you must create a command object, this time for the InsertCommand property of the DataAdapter object:

```
param = insertCmd.Parameters.Add("@ProductID",SqlDbType.Int);
```

Once again, you create all the parameters and set their values. You then assign the command object to the DataAdapter object's InsertCommand property:

```
dataAdapter.InsertCommand=insertCmd;
```

Adding transaction support

It is possible for one or another of the updates to fail, and if they do not all fail, it can be difficult to return the database to a valid state. You will therefore add transaction support. You start, as last time, by obtaining a reference to a SqlTransaction object by calling BeginTransaction on the connection object:

```
SqlTransaction transaction;
connection.Open( );
transaction = connection.BeginTransaction( );
```

or in VB.NET:

```
Dim transaction As SqlTransaction
myConnection.Open( )
transaction = myConnection.BeginTransaction( )
```

With all three Command properties set, you can add the transaction to each command's Transaction property:

```
dataAdapter.UpdateCommand.Transaction = transaction;
dataAdapter.DeleteCommand.Transaction = transaction;
```

```
dataAdapter.InsertCommand.Transaction = transaction;
```

Calling the Update method

You are now ready to call the Update method of the SqlDataAdapter object, which you will do from within a try block. The Update method will return the number of rows that are updated, which you will use to fill in the text of a label at the bottom of the data grid. The code is as follows:

```
try
{
    int rowsUpdated = dataAdapter.Update(ds,"BugInfo");
    transaction.Commit();
    CountUpdatedRows.Visible=true;
    CountUpdatedRows.Text =
      rowsUpdated.ToString() + " rows Updated.";
}
catch
{
    transaction.Rollback();
}
```

or in VB.NET:

```
Try
    Dim rowsUpdated As Int32
    rowsUpdated = CType(dataAdapter.Update(ds, "BugInfo"), Int32)
    transaction.Commit()
    ' transaction.Rollback()
    CountUpdatedRows.Visible = True
    CountUpdatedRows.Text = rowsUpdated.ToString() + " rows Updated."

Catch
    transaction.Rollback()

End Try
```

If no exception is thrown, you commit the transactions; otherwise, you roll them back.

You can then rebind to the data grid, which will remain unchanged. The label is now visible, however, showing the number of rows that were updated, as shown in Figure 12-8. (The label is highlighted in the figure to make it easy to find.)

If you examine the Bugs and BugHistory tables, you should now see that the data has been updated, as shown in Figure 12-9.

Most of the methods in this example are unchanged from earlier listings. The important changes are in declaring the user interface elements and three methods: Page_Load, btnUpdateDataSet_Click, and btnUpdateDataBase_Click. These changes are shown in Example 12-11 (C#) and Example 12-12 (VB.NET).

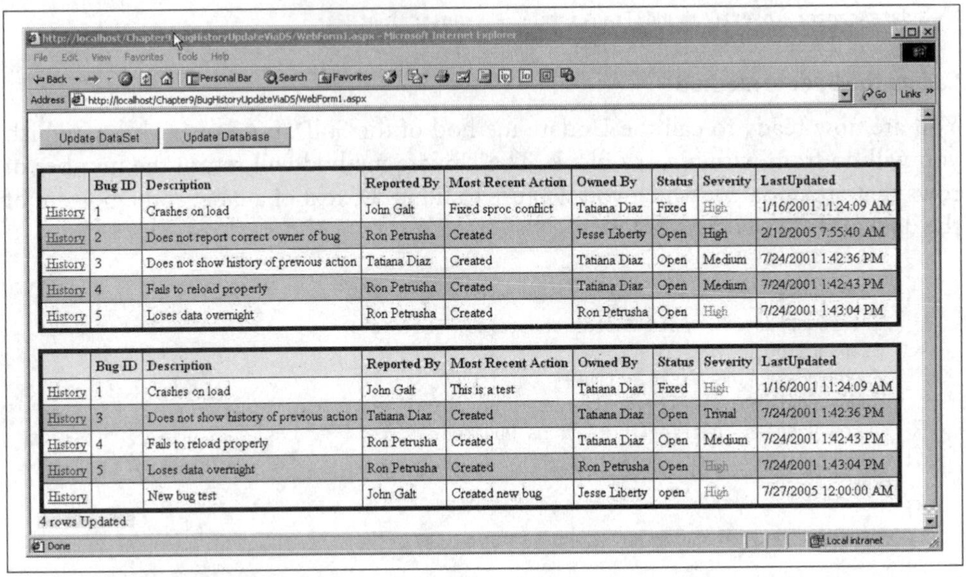

Figure 12-8. After updating the database

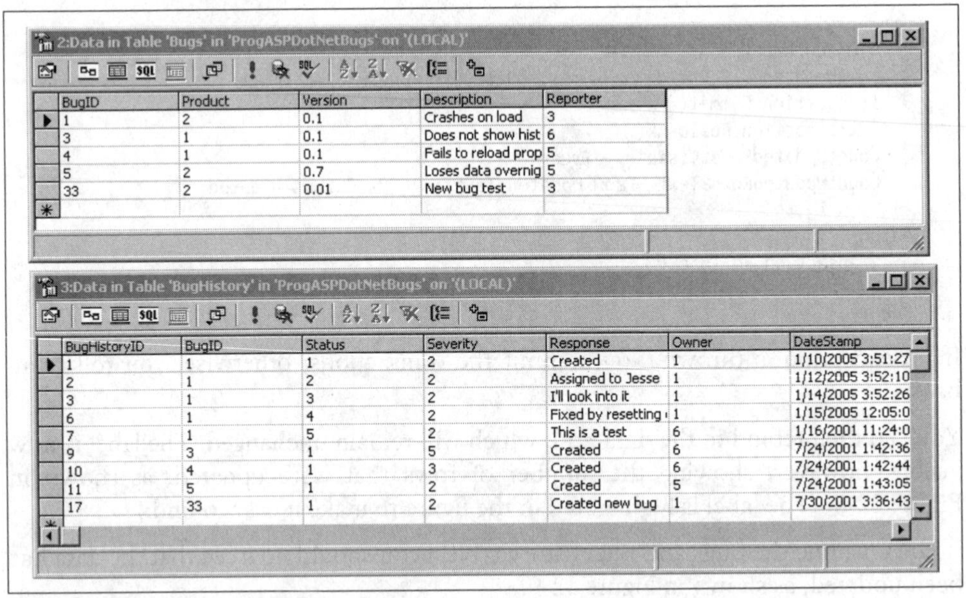

Figure 12-9. Bug and BugHistory table after database update

Example 12-11. Updating the database from a dataset

```
protected System.Web.UI.WebControls.DataGrid DataGrid1;
protected System.Web.UI.WebControls.DataGrid DataGrid2;
protected System.Web.UI.WebControls.DataGrid HistoryGrid;
protected System.Web.UI.WebControls.Panel BugHistoryPanel;
```

Example 12-11. Updating the database from a dataset (continued)

```
protected System.Web.UI.WebControls.Panel DataGrid2Panel;
protected System.Web.UI.WebControls.Button btnUpdateDataSet;
protected System.Web.UI.WebControls.Button btnUpdateDataBase;
protected System.Web.UI.WebControls.Label CountUpdatedRows;

private void Page_Load(
    object sender, System.EventArgs e)
{
    if (!IsPostBack)
    {
        // hide the history panel
        UpdateBugHistory();
        DataGrid2Panel.Visible=false;

        // set the data source for the
        // grid to the first table
        DataSet ds = CreateBugDataSet();
        Session["BugsDataSet"] = ds;
        DataGrid1.DataSource=ds.Tables[0];
        DataGrid1.DataBind();
    }
}
// respond to the request to update
 // the dataset. This would normally be
 // replaced by a complete user interface to allow
 // the user to specify what changes to make
 private void btnUpdateDataSet_Click(object sender, System.EventArgs e)
 {
    // retrieve the dataset from session state
    DataSet ds = (DataSet) Session["BugsDataSet"];

    // extract the table of Bug and BugHistory information
    DataTable bugTable = ds.Tables["BugInfo"];

    // change one field in row 0
    bugTable.Rows[0]["Response"] = "This is a test";

    // delete row 1
    bugTable.Rows[1].Delete();

    // append a new row
    DataRow newRow = bugTable.NewRow();
    newRow["Description"] = "New bug test";
    newRow["Response"] = "Created new bug";
    newRow["Owner"] = "Jesse Liberty";
    newRow["OwnerID"] = 1;
    newRow["ProductID"] = 2;
    newRow["ProductDescription"] =
        "PIM - My Personal Infomation Manager";
    newRow["Version"] = "0.01";
    newRow["ReporterID"] = 3;
    newRow["Reporter"] = "John Galt";
```

Example 12-11. Updating the database from a dataset (continued)

```
        newRow["StatusID"] = 1;
        newRow["StatusDescription"] = "open";
        newRow["SeverityID"] = 2;
        newRow["SeverityDescription"] = "High";
        newRow["DateStamp"] = "07-27-2005";
        bugTable.Rows.Add(newRow);

        // update two fields in row 2 - note we update the id
        // for writing back to the db. We are responsible
        // for ensuring that the id matches the description
        bugTable.Rows[2]["SeverityID"] = 5;
        bugTable.Rows[2]["SeverityDescription"] = "Trivial";

        // bind the DataSet to the second data grid
        // and make it visible
        DataGrid2.DataSource = ds.Tables["BugInfo"];
        DataGrid2.DataBind( );
        DataGrid2Panel.Visible=true;
        Session["BugsDataSet"] = ds;
    }

    private void btnUpdateDataBase_Click(object sender, System.EventArgs e)
    {
        DataSet ds = (DataSet) Session["BugsDataSet"];
        SqlDataAdapter dataAdapter = new SqlDataAdapter( );

        string connectionString =
            "server=YourServer; uid=sa;
                pwd=YourPassword; database=ProgASPDotNetBugs";

        // Create connection object, initialize with
        // connection string. Open it.
        System.Data.SqlClient.SqlConnection connection =
            new System.Data.SqlClient.SqlConnection(connectionString);

        SqlTransaction transaction;
        connection.Open( );
        transaction = connection.BeginTransaction( );

        // *** create the update command object
        SqlCommand updateCmd =
            new SqlCommand("spUpdateBugFromDataSet",connection);
        updateCmd.CommandType=CommandType.StoredProcedure;

        // declare the parameter object
        System.Data.SqlClient.SqlParameter param;

        // Add new parameters, get back a reference
        // set the parameters' direction and value
        param =
            updateCmd.Parameters.Add("@ProductID",SqlDbType.Int);
        param.Direction = ParameterDirection.Input;
```

Example 12-11. Updating the database from a dataset (continued)

```
param.SourceColumn="ProductID";
param.SourceVersion=DataRowVersion.Current;

param =
    updateCmd.Parameters.Add("@Description",SqlDbType.Text,8000);
param.Direction = ParameterDirection.Input;
param.SourceColumn="Description";
param.SourceVersion=DataRowVersion.Current;

param =
    updateCmd.Parameters.Add("@Response",SqlDbType.Text,8000);
param.Direction = ParameterDirection.Input;
param.SourceColumn="Response";
param.SourceVersion=DataRowVersion.Current;

param =
    updateCmd.Parameters.Add("@Reporter",SqlDbType.Int);
param.Direction = ParameterDirection.Input;
param.SourceColumn="ReporterID";
param.SourceVersion=DataRowVersion.Current;

param =
    updateCmd.Parameters.Add("@Owner",SqlDbType.Int);
param.Direction = ParameterDirection.Input;
param.SourceColumn="OwnerID";
param.SourceVersion=DataRowVersion.Current;

param =
    updateCmd.Parameters.Add("@Status",SqlDbType.Int);
param.Direction = ParameterDirection.Input;
param.SourceColumn="StatusID";
param.SourceVersion=DataRowVersion.Current;

param =
    updateCmd.Parameters.Add("@Severity",SqlDbType.Int);
param.Direction = ParameterDirection.Input;
param.SourceColumn="SeverityID";
param.SourceVersion=DataRowVersion.Current;

param =
    updateCmd.Parameters.Add("@bugID",SqlDbType.Int);
param.Direction = ParameterDirection.Input;
param.SourceColumn="bugID";
param.SourceVersion=DataRowVersion.Original; // note Original

param =
    updateCmd.Parameters.Add("@BugHistoryID",SqlDbType.Int);
param.Direction = ParameterDirection.Input;
param.SourceColumn="BugHistoryID";
param.SourceVersion=DataRowVersion.Original; // note Original

dataAdapter.UpdateCommand=updateCmd;
```

Example 12-11. Updating the database from a dataset (continued)

```
// *** the delete command
SqlCommand deleteCmd =
   new SqlCommand("spDeleteBugFromDataSet",connection);
deleteCmd.CommandType=CommandType.StoredProcedure;

param = deleteCmd.Parameters.Add("@bugID",SqlDbType.Int);
param.Direction = ParameterDirection.Input;
param.SourceColumn="bugID";
param.SourceVersion=DataRowVersion.Original;  // note Original

param = deleteCmd.Parameters.Add("@BugHistoryID",SqlDbType.Int);
param.Direction = ParameterDirection.Input;
param.SourceColumn="BugHistoryID";
param.SourceVersion=DataRowVersion.Original;  // note Original

dataAdapter.DeleteCommand=deleteCmd;

// *** insert command
SqlCommand insertCmd =
   new SqlCommand("spInsertBugFromDataSet",connection);
insertCmd.CommandType=CommandType.StoredProcedure;

// Add new parameters, get back a reference
// set the parameters' direction and value
param = insertCmd.Parameters.Add("@ProductID",SqlDbType.Int);
param.Direction = ParameterDirection.Input;
param.SourceColumn="ProductID";
param.SourceVersion=DataRowVersion.Current;

param =
   insertCmd.Parameters.Add("@Version",SqlDbType.Text,50);
param.Direction = ParameterDirection.Input;
param.SourceColumn="Version";
param.SourceVersion=DataRowVersion.Current;

param =
   insertCmd.Parameters.Add("@Description",SqlDbType.Text,8000);
param.Direction = ParameterDirection.Input;
param.SourceColumn="Description";
param.SourceVersion=DataRowVersion.Current;

param =
   insertCmd.Parameters.Add("@Response",SqlDbType.Text,8000);
param.Direction = ParameterDirection.Input;
param.SourceColumn="Response";
param.SourceVersion=DataRowVersion.Current;

param = insertCmd.Parameters.Add("@Reporter",SqlDbType.Int);
param.Direction = ParameterDirection.Input;
param.SourceColumn="ReporterID";
param.SourceVersion=DataRowVersion.Current;
```

Example 12-11. Updating the database from a dataset (continued)

```
param = insertCmd.Parameters.Add("@Owner",SqlDbType.Int);
param.Direction = ParameterDirection.Input;
param.SourceColumn="OwnerID";
param.SourceVersion=DataRowVersion.Current;

param = insertCmd.Parameters.Add("@Status",SqlDbType.Int);
param.Direction = ParameterDirection.Input;
param.SourceColumn="StatusID";
param.SourceVersion=DataRowVersion.Current;

param = insertCmd.Parameters.Add("@Severity",SqlDbType.Int);
param.Direction = ParameterDirection.Input;
param.SourceColumn="SeverityID";
param.SourceVersion=DataRowVersion.Current;

dataAdapter.InsertCommand=insertCmd;

// add transaction support for each command
dataAdapter.UpdateCommand.Transaction = transaction;
dataAdapter.DeleteCommand.Transaction = transaction;
dataAdapter.InsertCommand.Transaction = transaction;

// try to update, if all succeed commit
// otherwise roll back
try
{
    int rowsUpdated = dataAdapter.Update(ds,"BugInfo");
    transaction.Commit();
    CountUpdatedRows.Visible=true;
    CountUpdatedRows.Text = rowsUpdated.ToString() + " rows Updated.";
}
catch
{
    transaction.Rollback();
}

// rebind the grid to show the results
// grid should be unchanged
DataGrid2.DataSource = ds.Tables["BugInfo"];
DataGrid2.DataBind();
}
```

Example 12-12. Updating the database from a dataset

```
Private Sub Page_Load( _
    ByVal sender As System.Object, ByVal e As System.EventArgs) _
        Handles MyBase.Load
    If Not IsPostBack Then

        ' hide the history panel
        UpdateBugHistory()
```

Example 12-12. Updating the database from a dataset (continued)

```
        DataGrid2Panel.Visible = False

        ' set the data source for the
        ' grid to the first table
        Dim ds As DataSet = CreateBugDataSet
        Session("BugsDataSet") = ds
        DataGrid1.DataSource = ds.Tables(0)
        DataGrid1.DataBind( )
    End If
Private Sub btnUpdateDataSet_Click( _
    ByVal sender As Object, ByVal e As System.EventArgs)

    ' retrieve the dataset from session state
    Dim ds As DataSet
    ds = CType(Session("BugsDataSet"), DataSet)

    ' extract the table of Bug and BugHistory information
    Dim bugTable As DataTable = ds.Tables("BugInfo")

    ' change one field in row 0
    bugTable.Rows(0)("Response") = "This is a test"

    ' delete row 1
    bugTable.Rows(1).Delete( )

    ' append a new row
    Dim newRow As DataRow = bugTable.NewRow( )
    newRow("Description") = "New bug test"
    newRow("Response") = "Created new bug"
    newRow("Owner") = "Jesse Liberty"
    newRow("OwnerID") = 1
    newRow("ProductID") = 2
    newRow("ProductDescription") = _
        "PIM - My Personal Infomation Manager"
    newRow("Version") = "0.01"
    newRow("ReporterID") = 3
    newRow("Reporter") = "John Galt"
    newRow("StatusID") = 1
    newRow("StatusDescription") = "open"
    newRow("SeverityID") = 2
    newRow("SeverityDescription") = "High"
    newRow("DateStamp") = "07-27-2005"
    bugTable.Rows.Add(newRow)

    ' update two fields in row 2 - note we update the id
    ' for writing back to the db. We are responsible
    ' for ensuring that the id matches the description
    bugTable.Rows(2)("SeverityID") = 5
    bugTable.Rows(2)("SeverityDescription") = "Trivial"

    ' bind the dataset to the second data grid
    ' and make it visible
```

Example 12-12. Updating the database from a dataset (continued)

```
    DataGrid2.DataSource = ds.Tables("BugInfo")
    DataGrid2.DataBind( )
    DataGrid2Panel.Visible = True
    Session("BugsDataSet") = ds
End Sub
Private Sub btnUpdateDataBase_Click( _
    ByVal sender As Object, ByVal e As System.EventArgs)

    Dim ds As DataSet = CType(Session("BugsDataSet"), DataSet)
    Dim dataAdapter As New SqlDataAdapter( )

    Dim connectionString As String = _
        "server=YourDB; uid=sa; pwd=YourPW; database=ProgASPDotNetBugs"

    ' Create connection object, initialize with
    ' connection string. Open it.
    Dim myConnection As New System.Data.SqlClient.SqlConnection(connectionString)

    Dim transaction As SqlTransaction
    myConnection.Open( )
    transaction = myConnection.BeginTransaction( )

    ' *** create the update command object
    Dim updateCmd As New SqlCommand("spUpdateBugFromDataSet", myConnection)
    updateCmd.CommandType = CommandType.StoredProcedure

    ' declare the parameter object
    Dim param As System.Data.SqlClient.SqlParameter

    ' Add new parameters, get back a reference
    ' set the parameters' direction and value
    param = updateCmd.Parameters.Add("@ProductID", SqlDbType.Int)
    param.Direction = ParameterDirection.Input
    param.SourceColumn = "ProductID"
    param.SourceVersion = DataRowVersion.Current

    param = updateCmd.Parameters.Add("@Description", SqlDbType.Text, 8000)
    param.Direction = ParameterDirection.Input
    param.SourceColumn = "Description"
    param.SourceVersion = DataRowVersion.Current

    param = updateCmd.Parameters.Add("@Response", SqlDbType.Text, 8000)
    param.Direction = ParameterDirection.Input
    param.SourceColumn = "Response"
    param.SourceVersion = DataRowVersion.Current

    param = updateCmd.Parameters.Add("@Reporter", SqlDbType.Int)
    param.Direction = ParameterDirection.Input
    param.SourceColumn = "ReporterID"
    param.SourceVersion = DataRowVersion.Current

    param = updateCmd.Parameters.Add("@Owner", SqlDbType.Int)
```

Example 12-12. Updating the database from a dataset (continued)

```
param.Direction = ParameterDirection.Input
param.SourceColumn = "OwnerID"
param.SourceVersion = DataRowVersion.Current

param = updateCmd.Parameters.Add("@Status", SqlDbType.Int)
param.Direction = ParameterDirection.Input
param.SourceColumn = "StatusID"
param.SourceVersion = DataRowVersion.Current

param = updateCmd.Parameters.Add("@Severity", SqlDbType.Int)
param.Direction = ParameterDirection.Input
param.SourceColumn = "SeverityID"
param.SourceVersion = DataRowVersion.Current

param = updateCmd.Parameters.Add("@bugID", SqlDbType.Int)
param.Direction = ParameterDirection.Input
param.SourceColumn = "bugID"
param.SourceVersion = DataRowVersion.Original ' note Original

param = updateCmd.Parameters.Add("@BugHistoryID", SqlDbType.Int)
param.Direction = ParameterDirection.Input
param.SourceColumn = "BugHistoryID"
param.SourceVersion = DataRowVersion.Original ' note Original

dataAdapter.UpdateCommand = updateCmd

' *** the delete command
Dim deleteCmd As New SqlCommand("spDeleteBugFromDataSet", myConnection)
deleteCmd.CommandType = CommandType.StoredProcedure

param = deleteCmd.Parameters.Add("@bugID", SqlDbType.Int)
param.Direction = ParameterDirection.Input
param.SourceColumn = "bugID"
param.SourceVersion = DataRowVersion.Original ' note Original

param = deleteCmd.Parameters.Add("@BugHistoryID", SqlDbType.Int)
param.Direction = ParameterDirection.Input
param.SourceColumn = "BugHistoryID"
param.SourceVersion = DataRowVersion.Original ' note Original

dataAdapter.DeleteCommand = deleteCmd

' *** insert command
Dim insertCmd As New SqlCommand("spInsertBugFromDataSet", myConnection)
insertCmd.CommandType = CommandType.StoredProcedure

' Add new parameters, get back a reference
' set the parameters' direction and value
param = insertCmd.Parameters.Add("@ProductID", SqlDbType.Int)
param.Direction = ParameterDirection.Input
param.SourceColumn = "ProductID"
param.SourceVersion = DataRowVersion.Current
```

Example 12-12. Updating the database from a dataset (continued)

```
param = insertCmd.Parameters.Add("@Version", SqlDbType.Text, 50)
param.Direction = ParameterDirection.Input
param.SourceColumn = "Version"
param.SourceVersion = DataRowVersion.Current

param = insertCmd.Parameters.Add("@Description", SqlDbType.Text, 8000)
param.Direction = ParameterDirection.Input
param.SourceColumn = "Description"
param.SourceVersion = DataRowVersion.Current

param = insertCmd.Parameters.Add("@Response", SqlDbType.Text, 8000)
param.Direction = ParameterDirection.Input
param.SourceColumn = "Response"
param.SourceVersion = DataRowVersion.Current

param = insertCmd.Parameters.Add("@Reporter", SqlDbType.Int)
param.Direction = ParameterDirection.Input
param.SourceColumn = "ReporterID"
param.SourceVersion = DataRowVersion.Current

param = insertCmd.Parameters.Add("@Owner", SqlDbType.Int)
param.Direction = ParameterDirection.Input
param.SourceColumn = "OwnerID"
param.SourceVersion = DataRowVersion.Current

param = insertCmd.Parameters.Add("@Status", SqlDbType.Int)
param.Direction = ParameterDirection.Input
param.SourceColumn = "StatusID"
param.SourceVersion = DataRowVersion.Current

param = insertCmd.Parameters.Add("@Severity", SqlDbType.Int)
param.Direction = ParameterDirection.Input
param.SourceColumn = "SeverityID"
param.SourceVersion = DataRowVersion.Current

dataAdapter.InsertCommand = insertCmd

' add transaction support for each command
dataAdapter.UpdateCommand.Transaction = transaction
dataAdapter.DeleteCommand.Transaction = transaction
dataAdapter.InsertCommand.Transaction = transaction

' try to update, if all succeed commit
' otherwise roll back
Try
   Dim rowsUpdated As Int32
   rowsUpdated = CType(dataAdapter.Update(ds, "BugInfo"), Int32)
   transaction.Commit()
   ' transaction.Rollback()
   CountUpdatedRows.Visible = True
   CountUpdatedRows.Text = rowsUpdated.ToString() + " rows Updated."
```

Example 12-12. Updating the database from a dataset (continued)

```
    Catch
        transaction.Rollback( )

    End Try

    ' rebind the grid to show the results
    ' grid should be unchanged
    DataGrid2.DataSource = ds.Tables("BugInfo")
    DataGrid2.DataBind( )
End Sub
```

Multiuser Updates

In the previous section, you read data from the database into a dataset, updated the data in the dataset, and then wrote the changes back to the database. It is possible, of course, that many other people were simultaneously reading the same data into datasets of their own, editing *their* data, and writing *their* changes back to the database.

You can easily imagine that this could cause tremendous problems of data corruption. Imagine, for example, that a QA person downloads the current open bugs and begins to review the bugs with an eye towards updating some of the information. Meanwhile, across the office (or across town) a developer has read a few open bugs into a form of his own. It happens that they both are reading bug 17, which looks like this:

```
BugID 17
Reporter: John Galt
Severity: High
Status: Assigned
Owner: Jesse Liberty
```

The QA person decides to change the Severity to Medium and to reassign the bug to Dan Hurwitz. Meanwhile the developer is updating *his* dataset to change the action taken on the bug. The QA person writes back his changes, and the database now thinks the Owner is Dan and the Severity is Medium. The record now appears as follows:

```
BugID 17
Reporter: John Galt
Severity: Medium
Status: Assigned
Owner: Dan Hurwitz
```

Then the developer writes back his dataset, in which the Owner was Jesse and the Severity was High. These earlier values are written over the values updated by QA, and the QA edits are lost. The technical term for this is *bad*.

To prevent this kind of problem, you may use any of the following strategies:

1. Locking the records. When one user is working with a record, other users can read the records but they cannot update them.

2. Updating only the columns you change. In the previous example, QA would have changed only the owner and the status, while the developer would have changed only the description.

3. Previewing whether the database has changed before you make your updates. If so, notify the user.

4. Attempting the change and handling the error, if any.

The following sections explore each of these possible strategies.

Locking the Records

Many databases provide pessimistic record-locking. When a user opens a record, it is locked, and no other user may write to that record. For database efficiency, most databases also implement pessimistic page-locking; not only is the particular record locked, but a number of surrounding records are locked as well.

While record and page locking is not uncommon in some database environments, it is generally undesirable, especially in large web applications. It's possible for a record to be locked, and the user never returns to the database to unlock it. You would need to write monitoring processes that keep track of how long records have been locked, and unlock records after a time-out period.

A single query may touch many records in many tables. If you were to lock all those records for each user, it wouldn't take long before the entire database was locked. In addition, it often isn't necessary. While each user may look at dozens of records, typically each user will update only a very few. Locking is a very big, blunt weapon; what is needed in a web application is a small, delicate surgical tool.

Comparing Original Against New

To understand how to compare the dataset against the database, you must keep in mind three possible values for each of your fields:

1. The value currently in the database.

2. The value that was in the database when you first filled the dataset.

3. The value that is now in the data set because you have changed it.

The dataset provides support for this approach even though it is not an efficient way to manage data updates. This method involves creating an event handler for the RowUpdating event. The event handler examines the original value of each field and queries the database for the value currently in the database. If these values are different, then someone has changed the database since the dataset was filled, and you can take corrective action.

There are two significant problems with this approach. First, you must query the database for the current values before each update. Second, there is no guarantee you have solved the problem. It is certainly possible that someone will update a record after you've queried the database, but before you write back your changes! In any case, this approach is so inefficient, we won't bother to demonstrate it here.

Handling the Errors

Odd as it may seem at first, it turns out that the best approach to managing concurrency is to try the update and then respond to errors as they arise. For this approach to be effective, you must craft your Update statement so that it will fail if someone else has updated the records.

This approach has tremendous efficiency advantages. In the vast majority of cases, your update will succeed, and you will not have bothered with extra reads of the database. If your update succeeds, there is no lag between checking the data and the update, so there is no chance of someone sneaking in another write. Finally, if your update fails, you know why, and you can take corrective action.

For this approach to work, your stored procedure for updates must fail if the data has changed in the database since the time you retrieved the dataset. Since the dataset can tell you the original values that it received from the database, you need pass only those values back into the stored procedure as parameters, and then add them to the Where clause in your Update statement, as shown in Example 12-13.

Example 12-13. Modified update stored procedure

```
CREATE PROCEDURE spUpdateBugFromDataSetWithConcurrency
@ProductID int,
@OldProductID int,
@Description varChar(8000),
@OldDescription varChar(8000),
@Response varChar(8000),
@OldResponse varChar(8000),
@Reporter int,
@OldReporter int,
@Owner int,
@OldOwner int,
@Status int,
@OldStatus int,
@Severity int,
@OldSeverity int,
@bugID int,
@BugHistoryID int
```

Example 12-13. Modified update stored procedure (continued)

```
as
        Update Bugs
        set
        Product = @productID,
        [Description] = @Description,
        Reporter = @Reporter
        where bugID = @BugID and Product = @OldProductID
                and [Description] = @OldDescription and Reporter = @OldReporter

if @@RowCount > 0
begin

        Update BugHistory
        Set
        bugID = @BugID,
        status = @Status,
        severity = @Severity,
        response = @Response,
        owner = @Owner
        where BugHistoryID = @bugHistoryID and bugID = @bugID
        and status = @oldStatus and severity = @OldSeverity
        and response = @oldResponse and owner = @OldOwner

end
GO
```

When you update the record, the original values will now be checked against the values in the database. If they have changed, no records will match, and you will not update any records. After you attempt to update the Bugs Table, you check the @@RowCount to see if any rows were successfully added. If so, you can add to the BugHistory table:

```
if @@RowCount > 0
begin

Update BugHistory
```

The result of this test of @@RowCount is that if no records are added to the Bugs table, then no records will be added to the BugHistory table. You can test for how many rows were added altogether in the RowUpdated event handler. If no row was updated, you can assume that it was because the original row was changed and take appropriate corrective action.

> The careful reader will note that it is possible that the update to Bugs will work, but the update to BugHistory will fail, and the program will return 1 record updated. For simplicity this example does not handle that permutation. A well-crafted Update statement could catch this problem, but at the cost of making the code somewhat more difficult to understand.

You will of course need to modify the btnUpdateDataBase_Click method to create the new parameters you need. Notice that you have pairs of parameters, such as:

```
@ProductID int,
@OldProductID int,
@Description varChar(8000),
@OldDescription varChar(8000)
```

Both the ProductID and the OldProductID will be drawn from the same field in the dataset: ProductID. In the former case, you will use the Current version of that field; in the latter case, you'll use the Original version:

```
param =
    updateCmd.Parameters.Add("@ProductID",SqlDbType.Int);
param.Direction = ParameterDirection.Input;
param.SourceColumn="ProductID";
param.SourceVersion=DataRowVersion.Current;

// pass in the original value for the where statement
param =
updateCmd.Parameters.Add("@OldProductID",SqlDbType.Int);
param.Direction = ParameterDirection.Input;
param.SourceColumn="ProductID";
param.SourceVersion=DataRowVersion.Original;

param =
    updateCmd.Parameters.Add("@Description",SqlDbType.Text,8000);
param.Direction = ParameterDirection.Input;
param.SourceColumn="Description";
param.SourceVersion=DataRowVersion.Current;

param =
    updateCmd.Parameters.Add("@OldDescription",SqlDbType.Text,8000);
param.Direction = ParameterDirection.Input;
param.SourceColumn="Description";
param.SourceVersion=DataRowVersion.Original;
```

Other than setting the new parameters for the Update command, the only other change to btnUpdateDataBase_Click comes just before you call Update on the data adapter. You will add an event handler for the RowUpdated event:

```
dataAdapter.RowUpdated +=
    new SqlRowUpdatedEventHandler(OnRowUpdate);
```

The RowUpdate event is called each time a row is updated and offers you an opportunity to examine the row that was updated. In the event handler, you will get the statement type, which will be one of the StatementTypeEnumeration values: Delete, Insert, Select, or Update. You can turn the enumerated value into a string by calling the static GetName method on the System.Enum class, passing in the type and the value:

```
string s =
    System.Enum.GetName(
        e.StatementType.GetType( ),e.StatementType);
```

Use the type to inform the user of the success or failure of updating (or inserting or deleting) each row. You can now examine the number of rows affected by the update:

```
if (e.RecordsAffected < 1)
```

Each update action affects zero or more rows. It is of course possible that a single update will affect two or more rows. You saw that in the update stored procedure, which updates a row in Bugs and also a row in BugsHistory. If this procedure succeeds, e.RecordsAffected will be 2 (one record each in Bugs and BugHistory). You have crafted the update procedure so that if the update fails, no rows are affected, and you can catch the error:

```
if (e.RecordsAffected < 1)
{
    Trace.Write(s + "Error updating BugID: " +
        e.Row["BugID",DataRowVersion.Original].ToString( ));
```

Or in VB.NET:

```
If e.RecordsAffected < 1 Then
    ' write to the trace log
    Trace.Warn(s & "Error updating BugID: " & _
        e.Row("BugID", DataRowVersion.Original))
```

In this example, you are handling the error by writing a statement to the trace output. You could, in a real-world application, determine which row update had the problem and display that row (perhaps along with the current contents of the database) to the user for resolution.

One of the properties of the SqlRowUpdatedEventArgs object passed into your RowUpdated event handler is the Status property. This will be one of the UpdateStatus enumerated values: Continue, ErrorsOccurred, SkipAllRemainingRows, or SkipCurrentRow. If an error was found (e.g., the update failed), this value will be set to ErrorsOccurred, and if you do not change it, an exception will be thrown. Since you have now handled the error (by displaying it to the user or in whatever way you've chosen), you will want to change the value to SkipCurrentRow, which will allow the update command to continue, skipping over the row whose update failed:

```
e.Status = UpdateStatus.SkipCurrentRow;
```

To test whether the update will be protected against concurrency issues, you will hand-update one field in one record before attempting the automated update. To do so, just before you begin the transaction, in btnUpdateDataBase_Click, you will create a new connection, open it, and execute a SQL statement to update the Bugs table; you will also set the Product value to 1 where the BugID equals 1:

```
System.Data.SqlClient.SqlConnection connection2 =
    new System.Data.SqlClient.SqlConnection(connectionString);
connection2.Open( );
string cmd = "Update Bugs set Product = 1 where BugID = 1";
SqlCommand cmd1 = new SqlCommand(cmd,connection2);
cmd1.ExecuteNonQuery( );
```

Or in VB.NET:

```
Dim myConnection2 As _
    New System.Data.SqlClient.SqlConnection(connectionString)
myConnection2.Open( )
Dim cmd As String = _
    "Update Bugs set Product = 1 where BugID = 1"
Dim cmd1 As New SqlCommand(cmd, myConnection2)
cmd1.ExecuteNonQuery( )
```

The sequence of events is now:

1. Fill the dataset from the database and display it in a grid and stash it in a session variable.

2. When the user clicks Update DataSet, retrieve the dataset from the session variable, modify the dataset, and display the changes.

3. When the user clicks Update Database, hand-modify one record in the database, then tell the dataset to update the database. The record you modified (for BugID =1) should make the update from the dataset for that bug fail.

4. Catch the failure by noting that for one record, RecordsAffected is zero and handle the error.

5. Report on the remaining updates, deletes, and inserts. (They should all work fine.)

The source code is once again mostly unchanged. The only affected methods are btnUpdateDataBase_Click and the new method, OnRowUpdate. These are annotated and shown in full in Example 12-14 for C# and in Example 12-15 for VB.NET.

 One change must be made to the btnUpdateDataSet_Click method for this test to be meaningful. The field you update in BugID1 should be a field in Bugs rather than in BugHistory. In previous examples, you wrote:

```
bugTable.Rows[0]["Response"] =
"This is a test";
```

In this example, you will modify this to:

```
bugTable.Rows[0]["ReporterID"] = "1";
```

Example 12-14. Support for concurrency (C#)

```
private void btnUpdateDataBase_Click(
    object sender, System.EventArgs e)
{

    //retrieve the dataset from session variable
    DataSet ds = (DataSet) Session["BugsDataSet"];

    // create a new data adapter
    SqlDataAdapter dataAdapter = new SqlDataAdapter( );
```

Example 12-14. Support for concurrency (C#) (continued)

```
// set up the connection string
string connectionString =
   "server=YourServer; uid=sa;
          pwd=YourPassword; database=ProgASPDotNetBugs";

// Create connection object, initialize with
// connection string. Open it.
System.Data.SqlClient.SqlConnection connection =
   new System.Data.SqlClient.SqlConnection(connectionString);

// mimic another user writing to your data after
// you have retrieved the data from the database
System.Data.SqlClient.SqlConnection connection2 =
   new System.Data.SqlClient.SqlConnection(connectionString);
connection2.Open( );
string cmd = "Update Bugs set Product = 1 where BugID = 1";
SqlCommand cmd1 = new SqlCommand(cmd,connection2);
cmd1.ExecuteNonQuery( );

// create the transaction
SqlTransaction transaction;
connection.Open( );
transaction = connection.BeginTransaction( );

// *** create the update command object
SqlCommand updateCmd =
   new SqlCommand("spUpdateBugFromDataSetWithConcurrency",connection);
updateCmd.CommandType=CommandType.StoredProcedure;

// declare the parameter object
System.Data.SqlClient.SqlParameter param;

// Add new parameters, get back a reference
// set the parameters' direction and value
param =
   updateCmd.Parameters.Add("@ProductID",SqlDbType.Int);
param.Direction = ParameterDirection.Input;
param.SourceColumn="ProductID";
param.SourceVersion=DataRowVersion.Current;

// pass in the original value for the where statement
param =
updateCmd.Parameters.Add("@OldProductID",SqlDbType.Int);
param.Direction = ParameterDirection.Input;
param.SourceColumn="ProductID";
param.SourceVersion=DataRowVersion.Original;

param =
   updateCmd.Parameters.Add("@Description",SqlDbType.Text,8000);
param.Direction = ParameterDirection.Input;
param.SourceColumn="Description";
```

Example 12-14. Support for concurrency (C#) (continued)

```csharp
    param.SourceVersion=DataRowVersion.Current;

    param =
        updateCmd.Parameters.Add("@OldDescription",SqlDbType.Text,8000);
    param.Direction = ParameterDirection.Input;
    param.SourceColumn="Description";
    param.SourceVersion=DataRowVersion.Original;

    param =
        updateCmd.Parameters.Add("@Response",SqlDbType.Text,8000);
    param.Direction = ParameterDirection.Input;
    param.SourceColumn="Response";
    param.SourceVersion=DataRowVersion.Current;

    param =
        updateCmd.Parameters.Add("@OldResponse",SqlDbType.Text,8000);
    param.Direction = ParameterDirection.Input;
    param.SourceColumn="Response";
    param.SourceVersion=DataRowVersion.Original;

    param =
        updateCmd.Parameters.Add("@Reporter",SqlDbType.Int);
    param.Direction = ParameterDirection.Input;
    param.SourceColumn="ReporterID";
    param.SourceVersion=DataRowVersion.Current;

    param =
        updateCmd.Parameters.Add("@OldReporter",SqlDbType.Int);
    param.Direction = ParameterDirection.Input;
    param.SourceColumn="ReporterID";
    param.SourceVersion=DataRowVersion.Original;

    param =
        updateCmd.Parameters.Add("@Owner",SqlDbType.Int);
    param.Direction = ParameterDirection.Input;
    param.SourceColumn="OwnerID";
    param.SourceVersion=DataRowVersion.Current;

    param =
        updateCmd.Parameters.Add("@OldOwner",SqlDbType.Int);
    param.Direction = ParameterDirection.Input;
    param.SourceColumn="OwnerID";
    param.SourceVersion=DataRowVersion.Original;

    param =
        updateCmd.Parameters.Add("@Status",SqlDbType.Int);
    param.Direction = ParameterDirection.Input;
    param.SourceColumn="StatusID";
    param.SourceVersion=DataRowVersion.Current;
```

Example 12-14. Support for concurrency (C#) (continued)

```csharp
param =
    updateCmd.Parameters.Add("@OldStatus",SqlDbType.Int);
param.Direction = ParameterDirection.Input;
param.SourceColumn="StatusID";
param.SourceVersion=DataRowVersion.Original;

param =
    updateCmd.Parameters.Add("@Severity",SqlDbType.Int);
param.Direction = ParameterDirection.Input;
param.SourceColumn="SeverityID";
param.SourceVersion=DataRowVersion.Current;

param =
    updateCmd.Parameters.Add("@OldSeverity",SqlDbType.Int);
param.Direction = ParameterDirection.Input;
param.SourceColumn="SeverityID";
param.SourceVersion=DataRowVersion.Original;

param =
    updateCmd.Parameters.Add("@bugID",SqlDbType.Int);
param.Direction = ParameterDirection.Input;
param.SourceColumn="bugID";
param.SourceVersion=DataRowVersion.Original; // note Original

param =
    updateCmd.Parameters.Add("@BugHistoryID",SqlDbType.Int);
param.Direction = ParameterDirection.Input;
param.SourceColumn="BugHistoryID";
param.SourceVersion=DataRowVersion.Original; // note Original

dataAdapter.UpdateCommand=updateCmd;

// *** the delete command
SqlCommand deleteCmd =
    new SqlCommand("spDeleteBugFromDataSet",connection);
deleteCmd.CommandType=CommandType.StoredProcedure;

param = deleteCmd.Parameters.Add("@bugID",SqlDbType.Int);
param.Direction = ParameterDirection.Input;
param.SourceColumn="bugID";
param.SourceVersion=DataRowVersion.Original;  // note Original

param = deleteCmd.Parameters.Add("@BugHistoryID",SqlDbType.Int);
param.Direction = ParameterDirection.Input;
param.SourceColumn="BugHistoryID";
param.SourceVersion=DataRowVersion.Original;  // note Original

dataAdapter.DeleteCommand=deleteCmd;

// *** insert command
SqlCommand insertCmd =
    new SqlCommand("spInsertBugFromDataSet",connection);
```

Example 12-14. Support for concurrency (C#) (continued)

```csharp
insertCmd.CommandType=CommandType.StoredProcedure;

// Add new parameters, get back a reference
// set the parameters' direction and value
param = insertCmd.Parameters.Add("@ProductID",SqlDbType.Int);
param.Direction = ParameterDirection.Input;
param.SourceColumn="ProductID";
param.SourceVersion=DataRowVersion.Current;

param =
    insertCmd.Parameters.Add("@Version",SqlDbType.Text,50);
param.Direction = ParameterDirection.Input;
param.SourceColumn="Version";
param.SourceVersion=DataRowVersion.Current;

param =
    insertCmd.Parameters.Add("@Description",SqlDbType.Text,8000);
param.Direction = ParameterDirection.Input;
param.SourceColumn="Description";
param.SourceVersion=DataRowVersion.Current;

param =
    insertCmd.Parameters.Add("@Response",SqlDbType.Text,8000);
param.Direction = ParameterDirection.Input;
param.SourceColumn="Response";
param.SourceVersion=DataRowVersion.Current;

param = insertCmd.Parameters.Add("@Reporter",SqlDbType.Int);
param.Direction = ParameterDirection.Input;
param.SourceColumn="ReporterID";
param.SourceVersion=DataRowVersion.Current;

param = insertCmd.Parameters.Add("@Owner",SqlDbType.Int);
param.Direction = ParameterDirection.Input;
param.SourceColumn="OwnerID";
param.SourceVersion=DataRowVersion.Current;

param = insertCmd.Parameters.Add("@Status",SqlDbType.Int);
param.Direction = ParameterDirection.Input;
param.SourceColumn="StatusID";
param.SourceVersion=DataRowVersion.Current;

param = insertCmd.Parameters.Add("@Severity",SqlDbType.Int);
param.Direction = ParameterDirection.Input;
param.SourceColumn="SeverityID";
param.SourceVersion=DataRowVersion.Current;

dataAdapter.InsertCommand=insertCmd;

// add transaction support for each command
dataAdapter.UpdateCommand.Transaction = transaction;
```

Example 12-14. Support for concurrency (C#) (continued)

```csharp
      dataAdapter.DeleteCommand.Transaction = transaction;
      dataAdapter.InsertCommand.Transaction = transaction;

      // try to update, if all succeed commit
      // otherwise roll back
      try
      {
         dataAdapter.RowUpdated += new SqlRowUpdatedEventHandler(OnRowUpdate);
         int rowsUpdated = dataAdapter.Update(ds,"BugInfo");
         transaction.Commit( );
         CountUpdatedRows.Visible=true;
         CountUpdatedRows.Text = rowsUpdated.ToString( ) + " rows Updated.";
      }
      catch
      {
         transaction.Rollback( );
      }

      // rebind the grid to show the results
      // grid should be unchanged
      DataGrid2.DataSource = ds.Tables["BugInfo"];
      DataGrid2.DataBind( );
}

// handle the Row Updated event
public void OnRowUpdate(object sender, SqlRowUpdatedEventArgs e)
{
   // get the type of update (update, insert, delete)
   // as a string
   string s = "Attempted " +
      System.Enum.GetName(
         e.StatementType.GetType( ),e.StatementType) + ". ";

   // if the update failed
   if (e.RecordsAffected < 1)
   {
      // write to the trace log
      Trace.Warn(
         s + "Error updating BugID: " +
         e.Row["BugID",DataRowVersion.Original].ToString( ));

      // skip over this row, continue with the next
      e.Status = UpdateStatus.SkipCurrentRow;
   }
   else // the update succeeded
   {
      // write a success message to the trace log
      Trace.Write(s + " Row updated, BugID: " +
         e.Row["BugID",DataRowVersion.Original].ToString( ));
   }
}
```

Example 12-15. Support for concurrency (VB.NET)

```vbnet
Private Sub btnUpdateDataBase_Click( _
    ByVal sender As Object, ByVal e As System.EventArgs)

    Dim ds As DataSet = CType(Session("BugsDataSet"), DataSet)
    Dim dataAdapter As New SqlDataAdapter( )

    Dim connectionString As String = _
        "server=YourDB; uid=sa; pwd=YourPW; database=ProgASPDotNetBugs"

    ' Create connection object, initialize with
    ' connection string. Open it.
    Dim myConnection As _
     New System.Data.SqlClient.SqlConnection(connectionString)
    Dim myConnection2 As _
     New System.Data.SqlClient.SqlConnection(connectionString)

    Dim transaction As SqlTransaction
    myConnection.Open( )
    myConnection2.Open( )

    Dim cmd As String = "Update Bugs set Product = 1 where BugID = 1"
    Dim cmd1 As New SqlCommand(cmd, myConnection2)
    cmd1.ExecuteNonQuery( )

    transaction = myConnection.BeginTransaction( )

    ' *** create the update command object
    Dim updateCmd As _
     New SqlCommand("spUpdateBugFromDataSetWithConcurrency", myConnection)
    updateCmd.CommandType = CommandType.StoredProcedure

    ' declare the parameter object
    Dim param As System.Data.SqlClient.SqlParameter

    ' Add new parameters, get back a reference
    ' set the parameters' direction and value
    param = updateCmd.Parameters.Add("@ProductID", SqlDbType.Int)
    param.Direction = ParameterDirection.Input
    param.SourceColumn = "ProductID"
    param.SourceVersion = DataRowVersion.Current

    param = updateCmd.Parameters.Add("@OldProductID", SqlDbType.Int)
    param.Direction = ParameterDirection.Input
    param.SourceColumn = "ProductID"
    param.SourceVersion = DataRowVersion.Original

    param = updateCmd.Parameters.Add("@Description", SqlDbType.Text, 8000)
    param.Direction = ParameterDirection.Input
    param.SourceColumn = "Description"
    param.SourceVersion = DataRowVersion.Current

    param = updateCmd.Parameters.Add( _
```

Example 12-15. Support for concurrency (VB.NET) (continued)

```
    "@OldDescription", SqlDbType.Text, 8000)
param.Direction = ParameterDirection.Input
param.SourceColumn = "Description"
param.SourceVersion = DataRowVersion.Original

param = updateCmd.Parameters.Add("@Response", SqlDbType.Text, 8000)
param.Direction = ParameterDirection.Input
param.SourceColumn = "Response"
param.SourceVersion = DataRowVersion.Current

param = updateCmd.Parameters.Add("@OldResponse", SqlDbType.Text, 8000)
param.Direction = ParameterDirection.Input
param.SourceColumn = "Response"
param.SourceVersion = DataRowVersion.Original

param = updateCmd.Parameters.Add("@Reporter", SqlDbType.Int)
param.Direction = ParameterDirection.Input
param.SourceColumn = "ReporterID"
param.SourceVersion = DataRowVersion.Current

param = updateCmd.Parameters.Add("@OldReporter", SqlDbType.Int)
param.Direction = ParameterDirection.Input
param.SourceColumn = "ReporterID"
param.SourceVersion = DataRowVersion.Original

param = updateCmd.Parameters.Add("@Owner", SqlDbType.Int)
param.Direction = ParameterDirection.Input
param.SourceColumn = "OwnerID"
param.SourceVersion = DataRowVersion.Current

param = updateCmd.Parameters.Add("@OldOwner", SqlDbType.Int)
param.Direction = ParameterDirection.Input
param.SourceColumn = "OwnerID"
param.SourceVersion = DataRowVersion.Original

param = updateCmd.Parameters.Add("@Status", SqlDbType.Int)
param.Direction = ParameterDirection.Input
param.SourceColumn = "StatusID"
param.SourceVersion = DataRowVersion.Current

param = updateCmd.Parameters.Add("@OldStatus", SqlDbType.Int)
param.Direction = ParameterDirection.Input
param.SourceColumn = "StatusID"
param.SourceVersion = DataRowVersion.Original

param = updateCmd.Parameters.Add("@Severity", SqlDbType.Int)
param.Direction = ParameterDirection.Input
param.SourceColumn = "SeverityID"
param.SourceVersion = DataRowVersion.Current

param = updateCmd.Parameters.Add("@OldSeverity", SqlDbType.Int)
param.Direction = ParameterDirection.Input
```

Example 12-15. Support for concurrency (VB.NET) (continued)

```
param.SourceColumn = "SeverityID"
param.SourceVersion = DataRowVersion.Original

param = updateCmd.Parameters.Add("@bugID", SqlDbType.Int)
param.Direction = ParameterDirection.Input
param.SourceColumn = "bugID"
param.SourceVersion = DataRowVersion.Original ' note Original

param = updateCmd.Parameters.Add("@BugHistoryID", SqlDbType.Int)
param.Direction = ParameterDirection.Input
param.SourceColumn = "BugHistoryID"
param.SourceVersion = DataRowVersion.Original ' note Original

dataAdapter.UpdateCommand = updateCmd

' *** the delete command
Dim deleteCmd As New SqlCommand("spDeleteBugFromDataSet", myConnection)
deleteCmd.CommandType = CommandType.StoredProcedure

param = deleteCmd.Parameters.Add("@bugID", SqlDbType.Int)
param.Direction = ParameterDirection.Input
param.SourceColumn = "bugID"
param.SourceVersion = DataRowVersion.Original ' note Original

param = deleteCmd.Parameters.Add("@BugHistoryID", SqlDbType.Int)
param.Direction = ParameterDirection.Input
param.SourceColumn = "BugHistoryID"
param.SourceVersion = DataRowVersion.Original ' note Original

dataAdapter.DeleteCommand = deleteCmd

' *** insert command
Dim insertCmd As New SqlCommand("spInsertBugFromDataSet", myConnection)
insertCmd.CommandType = CommandType.StoredProcedure

' Add new parameters, get back a reference
' set the parameters' direction and value
param = insertCmd.Parameters.Add("@ProductID", SqlDbType.Int)
param.Direction = ParameterDirection.Input
param.SourceColumn = "ProductID"
param.SourceVersion = DataRowVersion.Current

param = insertCmd.Parameters.Add("@Version", SqlDbType.Text, 50)
param.Direction = ParameterDirection.Input
param.SourceColumn = "Version"
param.SourceVersion = DataRowVersion.Current

param = insertCmd.Parameters.Add("@Description", SqlDbType.Text, 8000)
param.Direction = ParameterDirection.Input
param.SourceColumn = "Description"
param.SourceVersion = DataRowVersion.Current
```

Example 12-15. Support for concurrency (VB.NET) (continued)

```
    param = insertCmd.Parameters.Add("@Response", SqlDbType.Text, 8000)
    param.Direction = ParameterDirection.Input
    param.SourceColumn = "Response"
    param.SourceVersion = DataRowVersion.Current

    param = insertCmd.Parameters.Add("@Reporter", SqlDbType.Int)
    param.Direction = ParameterDirection.Input
    param.SourceColumn = "ReporterID"
    param.SourceVersion = DataRowVersion.Current

    param = insertCmd.Parameters.Add("@Owner", SqlDbType.Int)
    param.Direction = ParameterDirection.Input
    param.SourceColumn = "OwnerID"
    param.SourceVersion = DataRowVersion.Current

    param = insertCmd.Parameters.Add("@Status", SqlDbType.Int)
    param.Direction = ParameterDirection.Input
    param.SourceColumn = "StatusID"
    param.SourceVersion = DataRowVersion.Current

    param = insertCmd.Parameters.Add("@Severity", SqlDbType.Int)
    param.Direction = ParameterDirection.Input
    param.SourceColumn = "SeverityID"
    param.SourceVersion = DataRowVersion.Current

    dataAdapter.InsertCommand = insertCmd

    ' add transaction support for each command
    dataAdapter.UpdateCommand.Transaction = transaction
    dataAdapter.DeleteCommand.Transaction = transaction
    dataAdapter.InsertCommand.Transaction = transaction

    ' try to update, if all succeed commit
    ' otherwise roll back
    Try
        Dim rowsUpdated As Int32
        rowsUpdated = CType(dataAdapter.Update(ds, "BugInfo"), Int32)
        transaction.Commit( )
        ' transaction.Rollback( )
        CountUpdatedRows.Visible = True
        CountUpdatedRows.Text = rowsUpdated.ToString( ) + " rows Updated."

    Catch
        transaction.Rollback( )

    End Try

    ' rebind the grid to show the results
    ' grid should be unchanged
    DataGrid2.DataSource = ds.Tables("BugInfo")
    DataGrid2.DataBind( )
End Sub
```

Example 12-15. Support for concurrency (VB.NET) (continued)

```
Public Sub OnRowUpdate( _
    ByVal sender As Object, ByVal e As SqlRowUpdatedEventArgs)
    ' get the type of update (update, insert, delete)
    ' as a string
    Dim s As String = _
        "Attempted " & _
        System.Enum.GetName(e.StatementType.GetType(), e.StatementType) & _
        ". "

    ' if the update failed
    If (e.RecordsAffected < 1) Then
        ' write to the trace log
        Trace.Warn(s & "Error updating BugID: " & _
            e.Row("BugID", DataRowVersion.Original))
        ' skip over this row, continue with the next
        e.Status = UpdateStatus.SkipCurrentRow
    Else ' the update succeeded
        ' write a success message to the trace log
        Trace.Write(s & " Row updated, BugID: " & _
            e.Row("BugID", DataRowVersion.Original))
    End If
End Sub
```

Command Builder

In the previous section, you painstakingly created the update, insert, and delete commands. You first created stored procedures, and then you created command objects for each procedure, passing in the necessary parameters. ASP.NET will do a lot of this work for you, if the update, insert, and delete commands are simple enough.

ASP.NET provides a Command Builder (SqlCommandBuilder and OleDbCommandBuilder) to generate the necessary delete, update, and insert commands without your writing stored procedures. To take advantage of these objects, the following conditions must be met:

- The rows in the table you are generating must have come from a single table in the database.
- The table must have a primary key or a field with values guaranteed to be unique.
- The unique value column must be returned by the query used to fill the dataset (the select command).
- The name of the table must not have spaces, periods, quotation marks, or other special characters.

To see how using the command builder classes simplifies the task when these conditions are met, you'll modify the program to build the dataset only from the Bugs table. Your user interface will be much simpler because you'll use a very simple Select statement, Select * from Bugs.

Strip down the *.aspx* page, and do not use custom columns; allow the data grid to get its value right from its source table. Discard the BugHistory data grid, since you won't be using it for this example. The complete *.aspx* page is shown in Example 12-16.

Example 12-16. The simpler .aspx file

```
<%@ Page language="c#" Codebehind="WebForm1.aspx.cs" AutoEventWireup="false"
Inherits="BugHistoryUpdateAutoGenerated.WebForm1" trace="true" %>
<!DOCTYPE HTML PUBLIC "-//W3C//DTD HTML 4.0 Transitional//EN" >
<HTML>
  <HEAD>
<meta content="Microsoft Visual Studio 7.0" name=GENERATOR>
<meta content=C# name=CODE_LANGUAGE>
<meta content="JavaScript (ECMAScript)" name=vs_defaultClientScript>
<meta content=http://schemas.microsoft.com/intellisense/ie5 name=vs_targetSchema>
  </HEAD>
<body>
<form id=Form1 method=post runat="server">
   <table>
      <tr>
         <td><asp:Button ID="btnUpdateDataSet"
             Text="Update DataSet" Runat="server" /></td>
         <td><asp:Button ID="btnUpdateDataBase"
             Text="Update Database" Runat="server" /></td>
      </tr>
   </table>
   <br>
   <asp:datagrid id="DataGrid1" runat="server" EnableViewState="true"
   HeaderStyle-Font-Bold AlternatingItemStyle-BackColor="LightGrey"
   BorderColor="#000099"
   BorderWidth="5px" HeaderStyle-BackColor="PapayaWhip"
      CellPadding="5" DataKeyField="BugID">
   </asp:datagrid></FORM>
   <asp:Panel ID="DataGrid2Panel" Runat="server" >
      <asp:datagrid id="DataGrid2" runat="server"
             DataKeyField="BugID" CellPadding="5"
      HeaderStyle-BackColor="PapayaWhip"
             BorderWidth="5px" BorderColor="#000099"
      AlternatingItemStyle-BackColor="LightGrey" HeaderStyle-Font-Bold
      EnableViewState="true">
      </asp:datagrid>
      <asp:Label id="CountUpdatedRows"
             Runat="server" visible="False"></asp:Label>
   </asp:Panel>
   </body>
</HTML>
```

You must toss out all the code that deals with the BugHistory table in the code-behind page. Notice that the event handling has been removed from the data grid as well. To keep things simple, you'll just display the Bugs table, modify it, and then update the database.

You must modify btnUpdateDataSet_Click so that you are updating and adding fields only in Bugs:

```
DataRow newRow = bugTable.NewRow( );
newRow["Product"] = 2;
newRow["Version"] = "0.01";
newRow["Description"] = "New bug test";
newRow["Reporter"] = 3;
bugTable.Rows.Add(newRow);
```

The important change is in btnUpdateDataBase_Click, which is now far simpler. You simply retrieve the dataset and set up the connection object, exactly as you did earlier in Example 12-11:

```
DataSet ds = (DataSet) Session["BugsDataSet"];
string connectionString =
    "server=YourServer; uid=sa;
            pwd=YourPassword; database=ProgASPDotNetBugs";

System.Data.SqlClient.SqlConnection connection =
    new System.Data.SqlClient.SqlConnection(connectionString);

connection.Open( );
```

You then create a data adapter and a SqlCommandBuilder:

```
SqlDataAdapter dataAdapter =
    new SqlDataAdapter("select * from Bugs", connection);
SqlCommandBuilder bldr = new SqlCommandBuilder(dataAdapter);
```

You use the Command Builder to build the DeleteCommand, UpdateCommand, and InsertCommand objects required by the data adapter, which you previously built by hand:

```
dataAdapter.DeleteCommand = bldr.GetDeleteCommand( );
dataAdapter.UpdateCommand = bldr.GetUpdateCommand( );
dataAdapter.InsertCommand = bldr.GetInsertCommand( );
```

That's it! You are ready to enlist the commands in the transaction:

```
SqlTransaction transaction;
transaction = connection.BeginTransaction( );

dataAdapter.DeleteCommand.Transaction = transaction;
dataAdapter.UpdateCommand.Transaction = transaction;
dataAdapter.InsertCommand.Transaction = transaction;
```

With that done, you are ready to call Update on the dataAdapter, just as you did previously:

```
int rowsUpdated = dataAdapter.Update(ds,"Bugs");
```

The CommandBuilder object has created the necessary commands on your behalf. You can see what these are by adding `Trace` statements to the btnUpdateDataBase_ Click method:

```
Trace.Write(dataAdapter.InsertCommand.CommandText);
Trace.Write(dataAdapter.UpdateCommand.CommandText);
Trace.Write(dataAdapter.DeleteCommand.CommandText);
```

This will display the parameterized commands in the Trace window, as shown in Figure 12-10.

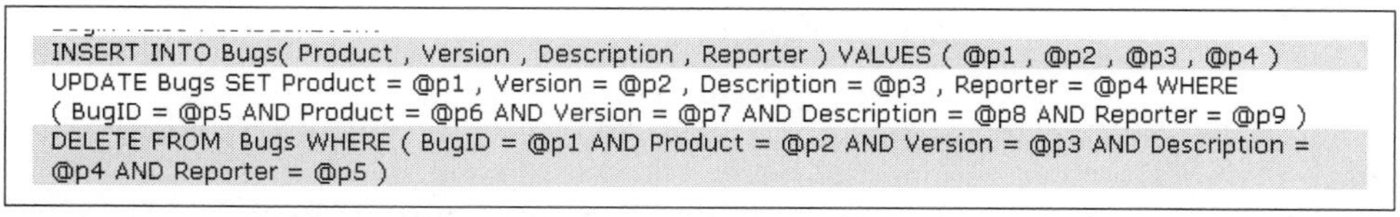

```
INSERT INTO Bugs( Product , Version , Description , Reporter ) VALUES ( @p1 , @p2 , @p3 , @p4 )
UPDATE Bugs SET Product = @p1 , Version = @p2 , Description = @p3 , Reporter = @p4 WHERE
( BugID = @p5 AND Product = @p6 AND Version = @p7 AND Description = @p8 AND Reporter = @p9 )
DELETE FROM  Bugs WHERE ( BugID = @p1 AND Product = @p2 AND Version = @p3 AND Description =
@p4 AND Reporter = @p5 )
```

Figure 12-10. Trace statements showing generated commands

Pay particular attention to the Update command; you can see that the Where clause is built exactly as you built it by hand in the earlier section.

To save space, the complete program is not reproduced here, but it is available for download from my web site. See the Preface for details.

CHAPTER 13

List-Bound Controls, Part II

In Chapter 10, you saw that there are three list-bound controls: Repeater, DataList, and DataGrid. Chapter 10 explained the similarities among these controls and focused on the DataGrid control, which it bound to an ArrayList of Bug objects. In Chapters 11 and 12, you saw how to extract data from a database and bind a Data-View or a DataTable object to a DataGrid control.

Now that you've seen how to extract data from the database and bind it to a control, we will now return to the list-bound controls, since they are most often used for displaying data from the database. In this chapter you will see how templates are used to manage the presentation of the Repeater and the DataList controls. You'll also see how to update data using in-place editing with the DataList and the Data-Grid controls.

Binding to the DataList and Repeater Controls

Chapter 10 showed the differences among the entirely "lookless" Repeater control and the somewhat more robust DataList control, as well as the DataGrid control that we have already examined in some detail. The table is reproduced here for your convenience as Table 13-1.

Table 13-1. Comparison of the Repeater, DataList, and DataGrid controls

Feature	Repeater	DataList	DataGrid
Table layout	No	No	Yes
Flow layout	Yes	Yes	No
Column layout	No	Yes	No
Style properties	No	Yes	Yes
Templates	Yes	Yes	Columns/ optional
Select/ Edit/Delete	No	Yes	Yes

Feature	Repeater	DataList	DataGrid
Sort	No	No	Yes
Paging	No	No	Yes

You can see that the repeater and the data list do not automatically provide a table layout. In fact, you can use either control to display data horizontally or vertically, and the DataList control can provide automatic support for columns.

The key difference between the DataList and Repeater controls, on the one hand, and the DataGrid control, on the other, is that the first two use *templates* to determine their look and feel.

The Repeater Control

The Repeater class provides a great many properties and exposes a number of useful events. The most important of these are summarized in Table 13-2.

Table 13-2. Properties and events of the Repeater control

Property or event name	Description
AlternatingItemTemplate property	Gets or sets the alternating item template
Controls property	Gets the ControlCollection object containing all the child controls
DataMember property	Gets or sets the specific table in the DataSource to bind to the control
DataSource property	Gets or sets the data source
FooterTemplate property	Gets or sets the footer template
HeaderTemplate property	Gets or sets the header template
ItemCommand event	Fired when a button is clicked
ItemCreated event	Fired when an item is created
ItemDataBound event	Fired after an item is databound but before it is rendered
Items property	Gets a collection of repeater item objects
PreRender event	Fired when the control is about to render its containing Page object
SeparatorTemplate property	Gets or sets the separator template

The Repeater control is often referred to as *lookless* to indicate that the control has no intrinsic appearance. You control the look and feel of the Repeater control through templates.

There are templates to control the appearance of the header, the footer, each item, alternating items, and the separator between items, as shown in Table 13-3.

Table 13-3. Templates supported by the Repeater control

Template	Description
AlternatingItemTemplate	Used exactly as you would the item template; however, the alternating item is rendered for every other row in the control
FooterTemplate	Elements to render after all items and other templates have been rendered
HeaderTemplate	Elements to render before any other templates are rendered
ItemTemplate	Elements rendered once for each row in the data source
SeparatorTemplate	Elements to render between each row in the data source

To see how these templates work together, you will create a simple web page with a repeater that will display data from the various tables in the ProgASPDotNetBugs database, as shown in Figure 13-1. The complete *.aspx* page is shown in Example 13-1.

Example 13-1. The .aspx file

```
<%@ Page language="c#" Codebehind="WebForm1.aspx.cs"
AutoEventWireup="false" Inherits="RepeaterControl.WebForm1" %>

<!DOCTYPE HTML PUBLIC "-//W3C//DTD HTML 4.0 Transitional//EN" >
<HTML>
  <HEAD>
      <meta name="GENERATOR" Content="Microsoft Visual Studio 7.0">
      <meta name="CODE_LANGUAGE" Content="C#">
      <meta name="vs_defaultClientScript"
            content="JavaScript (ECMAScript)">
      <meta name="vs_targetSchema"
            content="http://schemas.microsoft.com/intellisense/ie5">
      <style>
         .header
         {
            FONT-FAMILY: Verdana, Ariel, Helvetica, sans-serif;
            FONT-SIZE: 22pt;
            FONT-WEIGHT bold;
            MARGIN-BOTTOM 2pt
         }
         .item
         {
            FONT-FAMILY: Verdana, Ariel, Helvetica, sans-serif;
            FONT-SIZE: 10pt;
            FONT-WEIGHT: normal;
            MARGIN-BOTTOM 2pt
         }

      </style>

  </HEAD>
  <body>
```

Example 13-1. The .aspx file (continued)

```
    <form id="Form1" method="post" runat="server">

        <asp:Repeater ID="Repeater1" Runat="server">
            <HeaderTemplate>
                <div class="header">
                   Bugs<hr>
                </div>
            </HeaderTemplate>

            <ItemTemplate>
                <div class ="item">
                <b>Bug: </b>
<%# Convert.ToString(
    DataBinder.Eval(Container.DataItem, "BugID")) %> <br />
                <b>Description: </b>
<%# Convert.ToString(
    DataBinder.Eval(Container.DataItem,"Description")) %> <br />
                <b>Product: </b>
<%# Convert.ToString(
    DataBinder.Eval(Container.DataItem,"ProductDescription")) %><br />
                <b>Reported by: </b> </b>
<%# Convert.ToString(
    DataBinder.Eval(Container.DataItem,"FullName")) %>
                </div>
            </ItemTemplate>

            <SeparatorTemplate>
                <br/><hr> <br/>
            </SeparatorTemplate>

            <FooterTemplate>
                    <hr>
                    Report additional bugs to
                    <a href=mailto:jliberty@libertyassociates.com>
                    Jesse Liberty</a>
            </FooterTemplate>

        </asp:Repeater>
    </form>
  </body>
</HTML>
```

To create this web page, you add a DataRepeater control to your form, which produces the following HTML source:

```
    <form id="Form1" method="post" runat="server">
    <asp:Repeater ID="Repeater1" Runat="server">
    </asp:Repeater>
```

Within the Repeater control, you add `HeaderTemplate`, `ItemTemplate`, `SeparatorTemplate`, and `FooterTemplate` tags.

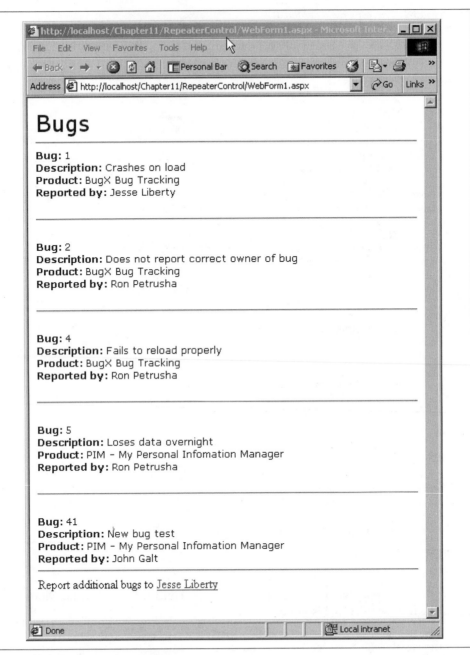

Figure 13-1. Repeater using templates

The HeaderTemplate

The HeaderTemplate is rendered once. You use it to write the title in the appropriate font. Its HTML source is:

```
<HeaderTemplate>
   <div class="header">
     Bugs<hr>
   </div>
</HeaderTemplate>
```

The div element uses a class element from the following style sheet that you add to the Head section of the page:

```
<style>
   .header
   {
      FONT-FAMILY: Verdana, Ariel, Helvetica, sans-serif;
      FONT-SIZE: 22pt;
      FONT-WEIGHT bold;
      MARGIN-BOTTOM 2pt
   }
   .item
   {
      FONT-FAMILY: Verdana, Ariel, Helvetica, sans-serif;
      FONT-SIZE: 10pt;
      FONT-WEIGHT: normal;
      MARGIN-BOTTOM 2pt
   }
</style>
```

The SeparatorTemplate

The item template is the only tricky one, so let's concentrate on that last. After each item you want the browser to draw a rule with white space above and below. You accomplish that in the SeparatorTemplate, which in the case of our example consists of the following:

```
<SeparatorTemplate>
     <br/><hr> <br/>
</SeparatorTemplate>
```

The FooterTemplate

Finally, after all the elements are rendered, you'll draw a final rule and add the mailto link in the footer. Notice that the SeparatorTemplate will not be called after the final element, and so if you want a final hard rule, you must draw it yourself in the FooterTemplate. The HTML source for this example's <FooterTemplate> is:

```
<FooterTemplate>
     <hr>
     Report additional bugs to
```

```
        <a href=mailto:jliberty@libertyassociates.com>
      Jesse Liberty</a>
  </FooterTemplate>
```

The ItemTemplate

The item template dictates how each item will be rendered. The content of the
<ItemTemplate> tag is as follows:

```
<ItemTemplate>
  <div class ="item">
  <b>Bug: </b>
    <%# Convert.ToString(DataBinder.Eval(Container.DataItem,
        "BugID")) %> <br />
  <b>Description: </b>
    <%# Convert.ToString(DataBinder.Eval(Container.DataItem,
        "Description")) %> <br />
  <b>Product: </b>
    <%# Convert.ToString(DataBinder.Eval(Container.DataItem,
        "ProductDescription")) %><br />
  <b>Reported by: </b> </b>
    <%# Convert.ToString(DataBinder.Eval(Container.DataItem,
      "FullName")) %>
  </div>
</ItemTemplate>
```

You use a <div> element here just as you did in the header. You can use normal
HTML elements such as <b> to control the display of text and other elements. The
only tricky part is how you display the contents of the data item you've bound to the
row. To render the bugID you start by displaying the word Bug in bold:

```
<b>Bug: </b>
```

You then display the actual BugID by calling the static Eval method on the Data-
Binder object. You pass in the DataItem you obtain from the Container. The Container is the Repeater control itself, and the DataItem is the item you are rendering
(in this case, a DataRow object from a data set). The result of the Eval must be converted to a String for display purposes, which is handled by the following line of
code:

```
<%# Convert.ToString(DataBinder.Eval(Container.DataItem, "BugID")) %>
```

If you prefer, you can call ToString on the object returned by Eval, as follows:

```
<%# DataBinder.Eval(Container.DataItem, "BugID").ToString( ) %>
```

The Code-Behind File

The supporting code for this example is very simple. All the work is done in the
Page_Load event, where you obtain the data set based on a Select statement, and
bind it to the Repeater. The Page_Load event procedure is shown in C# in
Example 13-2 and in VB.NET in Example 13-3.

Example 13-2. The Page_Load method in C#

```csharp
private void Page_Load(object sender, System.EventArgs e)
{
    // connect to the Bugs database
    string connectionString =
        "server=YourServer; uid=sa;
            pwd=YourPassword; database=ProgASPDotNetBugs";

    // get records from the Bugs table
    string commandString =
        "Select b.BugID, b.Description, p.ProductDescription,
            peo.FullName from Bugs b ";
    commandString += "join lkProduct p on b.Product = p.ProductID ";
    commandString += "join People peo on b.Reporter = peo.PersonID ";
    // create the data set command object
    // and the DataSet
    SqlDataAdapter dataAdapter =
        new SqlDataAdapter(
        commandString, connectionString);

    DataSet dataSet = new DataSet();

    // fill the data set object
    dataAdapter.Fill(dataSet,"Bugs");

    // Get the one table from the DataSet
    DataTable dataTable = dataSet.Tables[0];

    Repeater1.DataSource = dataTable;
    Repeater1.DataBind();
}
```

Example 13-3. The Page_Load method in VB.NET

```vbnet
Private Sub Page_Load( ByVal sender As System.Object, _
        ByVal e As System.EventArgs) Handles MyBase.Load

    ' connect to the Bugs database
    Dim connectionString As String = _
        "server=YourServer; uid=sa; " & _
        "pwd=YourPassword; database=ProgASPDotNetBugs"

    ' get records from the Bugs table
    Dim commandString As String = _
        "Select b.BugID, b.Description, p.ProductDescription, " & _
        "peo.FullName from Bugs b " & _
        "join lkProduct p on b.Product = p.ProductID " & _
        "join People peo on b.Reporter = peo.PersonID "

    ' create the data set command object and the data set
    Dim dataAdapter As New SqlDataAdapter( commandString, connectionString)

    Dim dataSet As New DataSet()
```

Example 13-3. The Page_Load method in VB.NET (continued)

```
' fill the data set object
dataAdapter.Fill(dataSet, "Bugs")

' Get the one table from the DataSet
Dim dataTable As DataTable = dataSet.Tables(0)

Repeater1.DataSource = dataTable
Repeater1.DataBind( )
```

End Sub

The DataList Control

The DataList control is very similar to the Repeater control. In fact, you can render exactly the same output using exactly the same controls, changing only the Repeater to a DataList control. If you examine Table 13-1, however, you will see that the DataList control provides support for column and flow layout. To see how this works, you'll add radio buttons to offer the user the choice of vertical vs. horizontal flow, and one vs. two columns, as shown in Figure 13-2.

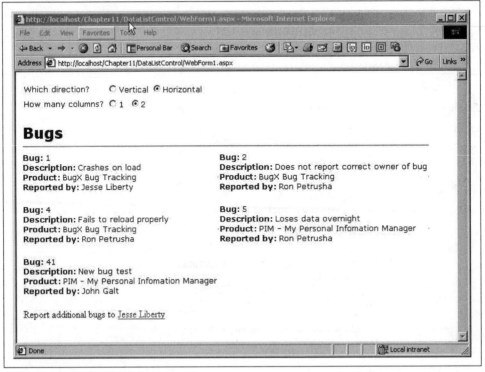

Figure 13-2. DataList with flow control

To create this page, you will modify the previous *.aspx* page and change the Repeater to a DataList, changing its name from Repeater1 to DataList1:

```
<asp:DataList ID="DataList1" Runat="server">
```

You'll also need to modify the end tag by changing:

```
</asp:Repeater>
```

to:

```
</asp:DataList>
```

The template for the DataList is identical; no changes are needed at all! You will want to add RadioButtons, however, to allow the user to specify the direction the items will flow, and number of columns:

```
<table>
  <tr>
    <td class="item">Which direction?</td>
    <td class="item" colspan="2">
       <asp:RadioButton ID="Vertical"
       GroupName="Direction" Runat="server"
       AutoPostBack="True" Checked="True" />Vertical</td>
    <td class="item" colspan="2">
       <asp:RadioButton ID="Horizontal" GroupName="Direction"
       Runat="server" AutoPostBack="True"  />Horizontal</td>
  </tr>
  <tr>
    <td class="item">How many columns?</td>
    <td class="item">
       <asp:RadioButton ID="Col1" GroupName="NumCols"
       Runat="server" AutoPostBack="True"  Checked="True"/>1</td>
    <td class="item">
       <asp:RadioButton ID="Col2" GroupName="NumCols"
       Runat="server" AutoPostBack="True" />2</td>
  </tr>
</table>
```

That's it. No other changes are needed in the *.aspx* file. The code-behind page is almost identical as well. You will, of course, change the declaration for the DataList:

```
protected System.Web.UI.WebControls.DataList DataList1;
```

The VB.NET declaration is identical except for the final semicolon.

While you are at it, you'll add declarations for the four radio buttons as well.

```
protected System.Web.UI.WebControls.RadioButton Vertical;
protected System.Web.UI.WebControls.RadioButton Horizontal;
protected System.Web.UI.WebControls.RadioButton Col1;
protected System.Web.UI.WebControls.RadioButton Col2;
```

Once again, the VB.NET version of these statements is identical, except for the final semicolon.

The Page_Load event is slightly different. In the Repeater example, there was no need to check for a postback because the page was drawn only once. This time, you will check for a postback and load the data set only if IsPostBack is false. If IsPost-Back is true, however, you will check the status of the Radio Buttons, and you'll set the RepeatDirection and the RepeatColumns properties of the DataList control accordingly. In C#, this is done as follows:

```
DataList1.RepeatDirection =
    Vertical.Checked ?
        RepeatDirection.Vertical : RepeatDirection.Horizontal;

DataList1.RepeatColumns =
    Col1.Checked ? 1 : 2;
```

The ? operator in C# is evaluated as follows: if the condition (Vertical. Checked) evaluates to true, then return the first argument (RepeatDirection.Vertical); otherwise, return the second argument (RepeatDirection.Horizontal). The returned result is then assigned to the RepeatDirection property of the DataList1 control.

Similarly, the second invocation evaluates whether Col1.Checked is true, and if so assigns 1 to RepeatColumns; otherwise, 2 is assigned.

In VB.NET, this is handled by the following code:

```
DataList1.RepeatDirection = IIf(Vertical.Checked, _
    RepeatDirection.Vertical, RepeatDirection.Horizontal)

DataList1.RepeatColumns = IIF(Col1.Checked, 1, 2)
```

The complete Page_Load method for the DataList control example is shown in C# in Example 13-4 and and in VB.NET in Example 13-5.

Example 13-4. C# version of Page_Load for the DataList control example

```
private void Page_Load(object sender, System.EventArgs e)
{

    if (!Page.IsPostBack)
    {
        // connect to the Bugs database
        string connectionString =
            "server=YourServer; uid=sa;
             pwd=YourPasword; database=ProgASPDotNetBugs";

        // get records from the Bugs table
        string commandString =
            "Select b.BugID, b.Description, p.ProductDescription, ";
        commandString += "peo.FullName from Bugs b ";
        commandString += "join lkProduct p on b.Product = p.ProductID ";
        commandString += "join People peo on b.Reporter = peo.PersonID ";
```

Example 13-4. C# version of Page_Load for the DataList control example (continued)

```
      // create the data set command object
      // and the DataSet
      SqlDataAdapter dataAdapter =
          new SqlDataAdapter(
          commandString, connectionString);

      DataSet dataSet = new DataSet( );

      // fill the data set object
      dataAdapter.Fill(dataSet,"Bugs");

      // Get the one table from the DataSet
      DataTable dataTable = dataSet.Tables[0];

      DataList1.DataSource = dataTable;
      DataList1.DataBind( );
  }
  else
  {
      // set the Repeat direction based on the value
      // in the radio buttons
      DataList1.RepeatDirection =
          Vertical.Checked ?
            RepeatDirection.Vertical :
                RepeatDirection.Horizontal;

      // set the number of columns based on the value
      // in the radio buttons
      DataList1.RepeatColumns =
          Col1.Checked ? 1 : 2;
  }
}
```

Example 13-5. VB.NET version of Page_Load for the DataList control example

```
Private Sub Page_Load(ByVal sender As System.Object, _
                      ByVal e As System.EventArgs) Handles MyBase.Load
   If Not Page.IsPostBack Then
      ' connect to the Bugs database
      Dim connectionString As String = "server=YourServer; uid=sa; " & _
             "pwd=YourPasword; database=ProgASPDotNetBugs"

      ' get records from the Bugs table
      Dim commandString As String = _
          "Select b.BugID, b.Description, p.ProductDescription, " & _
          "peo.FullName from Bugs b " & _
          "join lkProduct p on b.Product = p.ProductID " & _
          "join People peo on b.Reporter = peo.PersonID "

      ' create the data set command object and the data set
      Dim dataAdapter As New SqlDataAdapter(commandString, connectionString)
```

```
    Dim dataSet As New DataSet( )

    ' fill the data set object
    dataAdapter.Fill(dataSet, "Bugs")

    ' Get the one table from the DataSet
    Dim dataTable As DataTable = dataSet.Tables(0)

    DataList1.DataSource = dataTable
    DataList1.DataBind( )
  Else
    ' set the Repeat direction based on the value
    ' in the radio buttons
    DataList1.RepeatDirection = IIf(Vertical.Checked, _
            RepeatDirection.Vertical, RepeatDirection.Horizontal)
    ' set the number of columns based on the value
    ' in the radio buttons
    DataList1.RepeatColumns = IIf(Col1.Checked, 1, 2)
  End If
End Sub
```

In-Place Editing

You now finally have all the necessary ingredients to create a web page with in-place editing:

- Mastery of the DataGrid and DataList controls, which support in-place editing
- Mastery of retrieving data from and writing data back to the database
- Mastery of templates for creating the editable columns

In the next example, you will create a grid with an Edit column. When the user clicks on the edit link, the selected row will be redrawn for editing, as shown in Figure 13-3. The user is free to change any or all fields and then to click the Save link to have the changes written back to the database, or Cancel to cancel the changes and return to non-edit mode.

Notice that the Product and Reported By fields are drop-down lists. These are populated from the lkProduct and People tables, respectively. What must be written back to the Bugs table, however, is the ID rather than the text for each of these values. The complete *.aspx* page for the project is shown in Example 13-6; the complete code-behind page is shown in C# in Example 13-7 and in VB.NET in Example 13-8. Analysis follows.

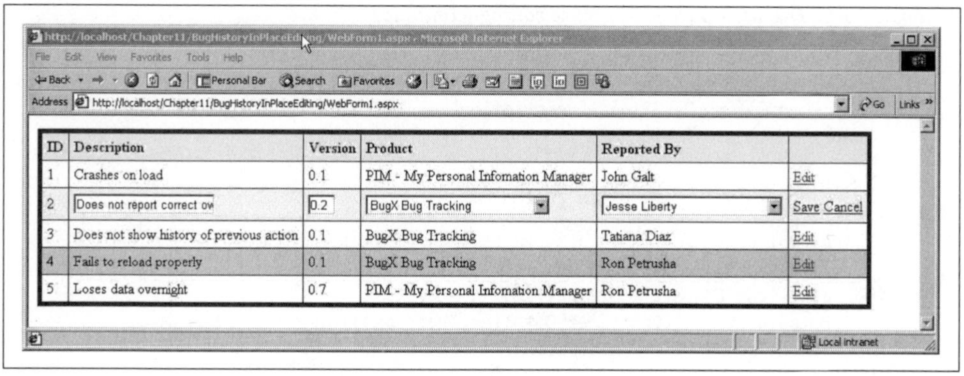

Figure 13-3. Editing in place

Example 13-6. The .aspx page for in-place editing

```
<%@ Page language="c#"
Codebehind="WebForm1.aspx.cs"
AutoEventWireup="false"
Inherits="BugHistoryInPlaceEditing.WebForm1"
trace="false"%>

<!DOCTYPE HTML PUBLIC "-//W3C//DTD HTML 4.0 Transitional//EN" >
<HTML>
<HEAD>
    <meta name="GENERATOR" Content="Microsoft Visual Studio 7.0">
    <meta name="CODE_LANGUAGE" Content="C#">
    <meta name="vs_defaultClientScript"
    content="JavaScript (ECMAScript)">
    <meta name="vs_targetSchema"
    content="http://schemas.microsoft.com/intellisense/ie5">
</HEAD>
<body>
   <form id="Form1" method="post" runat="server">
    <asp:DataGrid
    id="DataGrid1"
    runat="server"
    AutoGenerateColumns="False"
    CellPadding="5"
    HeaderStyle-BackColor="PapayaWhip"
    BorderWidth="5px"
    BorderColor="#000099"
    AlternatingItemStyle-BackColor="LightGrey"
    HeaderStyle-Font-Bold
    EditItemStyle-BackColor="Yellow"
    EditItemStyle-ForeColor="Black"
    DataKeyField ="BugID"
    OnEditCommand="OnEdit"
    OnCancelCommand="OnCancel"
    OnUpdateCommand="OnUpdate">
        <Columns>
```

Example 13-6. The .aspx page for in-place editing (continued)

```
<asp:BoundColumn DataField="BugID"
HeaderText="ID" ReadOnly="True" />
<asp:BoundColumn DataField="Description"
HeaderText="Description" />

<asp:TemplateColumn HeaderText="Version">

<ItemTemplate>
    <asp:Label
    Text='<%# Convert.ToString(
    DataBinder.Eval(Container.DataItem,"Version")) %>'
    Runat="server" ID="lblVersion"/>
</ItemTemplate>

<EditItemTemplate>
    <asp:TextBox
    Runat="server"
    ID="txtVersion"
    Text = '<%# Convert.ToString(
    DataBinder.Eval(Container.DataItem,"Version")) %>'
    Width="30"
    />
</EditItemTemplate>

</asp:TemplateColumn>

<asp:TemplateColumn HeaderText="Product">

<ItemTemplate>
    <asp:Label
    Text='<%# Convert.ToString(
    DataBinder.Eval(
    Container.DataItem,"ProductDescription")) %>'
    Runat="server" ID="lblProduct"/>
</ItemTemplate>

<EditItemTemplate>
    <asp:DropDownList
    Runat="server"
    ID="editProduct"
    DataSource='<%# GetValues("lkProduct") %>'
    DataTextField ="ProductDescription"
    DataValueField ="ProductID"
    Width ="200" />
</EditItemTemplate>

</asp:TemplateColumn>

<asp:TemplateColumn HeaderText="Reported By">

<ItemTemplate>
    <asp:Label
```

Example 13-6. The .aspx page for in-place editing (continued)

```
        Text='<%# Convert.ToString(
        DataBinder.Eval(Container.DataItem,"FullName")) %>'
        ID="lblReported"
        Runat="server"/>
    </ItemTemplate>

    <EditItemTemplate>
        <asp:DropDownList
        Runat="server"
        ID="editReporter"
        DataSource='<%# GetValues("People") %>'
        DataTextField ="FullName"
        DataValueField ="PersonID"
        Width ="200" />
    </EditItemTemplate>

    </asp:TemplateColumn>

    <asp:EditCommandColumn
    EditText="Edit"
    CancelText="Cancel"
    UpdateText="Save" />

    </Columns>
    </asp:DataGrid>
    </form>
</body>
</HTML>
```

> Some of the indentation was removed and some lines were broken up to enable printing the listing in this book.

Example 13-7. The C# code-behind page for in-place editing

```
using System;
using System.Collections;
using System.ComponentModel;
using System.Data;
using System.Data.SqlClient;
using System.Drawing;
using System.Web;
using System.Web.SessionState;
using System.Web.UI;
using System.Web.UI.WebControls;
using System.Web.UI.HtmlControls;

namespace BugHistoryInPlaceEditing
{
    public class WebForm1 : System.Web.UI.Page
    {
```

Example 13-7. The C# code-behind page for in-place editing (continued)

```csharp
   protected System.Web.UI.WebControls.Repeater Repeater1;
   protected System.Web.UI.WebControls.DataList DataList1;
   protected System.Web.UI.WebControls.DataGrid DataGrid1;
   protected System.Web.UI.WebControls.ListBox lbReportedby;
   public System.Data.SqlClient.SqlDataReader personReader;

   public WebForm1( )
   {
      Page.Init += new System.EventHandler(Page_Init);
   }

   private void Page_Load(object sender, System.EventArgs e)
   {
      if (! Page.IsPostBack)
      {
         BindGrid( );
      }
   }

   // extract the bug records and bind to the datagrid
   private void BindGrid( )
   {
      // connect to the Bugs database
      string connectionString =
         "server=YourServer; uid=sa;
         pwd=YourPassword; database=ProgASPDotNetBugs";

      System.Data.SqlClient.SqlConnection connection =
         new System.Data.SqlClient.SqlConnection(connectionString);
      connection.Open( );

      // get records from the Bugs table
      string commandString =
         "Select b.BugID, b.Version, b.Description, ";
      commandString += "p.ProductDescription, ";
      commandString += "peo.FullName from Bugs b ";
      commandString += "join lkProduct p on b.Product = p.ProductID ";
      commandString += "join People peo on b.Reporter = peo.PersonID ";


      System.Data.SqlClient.SqlCommand command =
         new System.Data.SqlClient.SqlCommand( );
      command.CommandText = commandString;
      command.Connection = connection;

      // Create the Reader adn bind it to the datagrid
      SqlDataReader reader =
         command.ExecuteReader(CommandBehavior.CloseConnection);
      DataGrid1.DataSource=reader;
      DataGrid1.DataBind( );
   }
```

Example 13-7. The C# code-behind page for in-place editing (continued)

```csharp
// Given the name of a table, return a DataReader for
// all values from that table
public System.Data.SqlClient.SqlDataReader
   GetValues(string tableName)
{
   // connect to the Bugs database
   string connectionString =
      "server=YourServer; uid=sa;
      pwd=YourPassword; database=ProgASPDotNetBugs";

      // create and open the connection object
   System.Data.SqlClient.SqlConnection connection =
      new System.Data.SqlClient.SqlConnection(connectionString);
   connection.Open( );

   // get records from the Bugs table
   string commandString = "Select * from " + tableName;

   // create the command object and set its
   // command string and connection
   System.Data.SqlClient.SqlCommand command =
      new System.Data.SqlClient.SqlCommand( );
   command.CommandText = commandString;
   command.Connection = connection;

   // create the DataReader and return it
   return command.ExecuteReader(CommandBehavior.CloseConnection);

}

// Handle the Edit event - set the EditItemIndex of the
// selected row
public void OnEdit(Object source, DataGridCommandEventArgs e)
{
   DataGrid1.EditItemIndex = e.Item.ItemIndex;
   BindGrid( );
}

// Handle the cancel event - set the EditItemIndex to -1
public void OnCancel(Object source, DataGridCommandEventArgs e)
{
   DataGrid1.EditItemIndex = -1;
   BindGrid( );
}

// Handle the Update event
// Extract the new values
// Update the database and rebind the datagrid
public void OnUpdate(Object source, DataGridCommandEventArgs e)
{

   string PersonID =
```

Example 13-7. The C# code-behind page for in-place editing (continued)

```
            ((DropDownList)(e.Item.FindControl("editReporter"))).
                SelectedItem.Value;

        string newDescription =
            ((TextBox) e.Item.Cells[1].Controls[0]).Text;

        string ProductID =
            ((DropDownList)(e.Item.FindControl("editProduct"))).
                SelectedItem.Value;

        string newVersion =
            ((TextBox)(e.Item.FindControl("txtVersion"))).Text;

        // form the update statement
        string cmd = "Update Bugs set Product = " + ProductID +
            ", Version = '" + newVersion +
            "', Description = '" + newDescription +
            " ', Reporter = " + PersonID +
            " where BugID = " + DataGrid1.DataKeys[e.Item.ItemIndex];

        // connect to the Bugs database
        string connectionString =
            "server=YourServer; uid=sa;
            pwd=YourPassword; database=ProgASPDotNetBugs";

        System.Data.SqlClient.SqlConnection connection =
            new System.Data.SqlClient.SqlConnection(connectionString);
        connection.Open( );

        // call the update and rebind the datagrid
        System.Data.SqlClient.SqlCommand command =
            new System.Data.SqlClient.SqlCommand( );
        command.CommandText = cmd;
        command.Connection = connection;
        command.ExecuteNonQuery( );

        DataGrid1.EditItemIndex = -1;
        BindGrid( );
    }

    private void Page_Init(object sender, EventArgs e)
    {
        InitializeComponent( );
    }

    #region Web Form Designer generated code

    private void InitializeComponent( )
    {
        this.Load += new System.EventHandler(this.Page_Load);
```

Example 13-7. The C# code-behind page for in-place editing (continued)

```
        }
            #endregion
    }

}
```

Example 13-8. The VB.NET code-behind page for in-place editing

```
Imports System.Data.SqlClient

Public Class WebForm1
    Inherits System.Web.UI.Page

    Protected WithEvents repeater1 As System.Web.UI.WebControls.Repeater
    Protected WithEvents DataList1 As System.Web.UI.WebControls.DataList
    Protected WithEvents DataGrid1 As System.Web.UI.WebControls.DataGrid
    Protected WithEvents lbReportedby As System.Web.UI.WebControls.ListBox
    Public personReader As System.Data.SqlClient.SqlDataReader

#Region " Web Form Designer Generated Code "

    'This call is required by the Web Form Designer.
    <System.Diagnostics.DebuggerStepThrough()> Private Sub InitializeComponent()

    End Sub

    Private Sub Page_Init(ByVal sender As System.Object, _
                        ByVal e As System.EventArgs) Handles MyBase.Init
        'CODEGEN: This method call is required by the Web Form Designer
        'Do not modify it using the code editor.
        InitializeComponent()
    End Sub

#End Region

    Private Sub Page_Load(ByVal sender As System.Object, _
                        ByVal e As System.EventArgs) Handles MyBase.Load
        If Not Page.IsPostBack Then
            BindGrid()
        End If
    End Sub

    ' extract the bug records and bind to the datagrid
    Private Sub BindGrid()
        ' connect to the Bugs database
        Dim connectionString As String = _
            "server=YourServer; uid=sa; pwd=YourPassword; " & _
            "database=ProgASPDotNetBugs"

        Dim connection As New SqlConnection(connectionString)
        connection.Open()
```

```
            ' get records from the Bugs table
            Dim commandString As String = _
                "Select b.BugID, b.Version, b.Description, " & _
                "p.ProductDescription, peo.FullName from Bugs b " & _
                "join lkProduct p on b.Product = p.ProductID " & _
                "join People peo on b.Reporter = peo.PersonID "

            Dim command As New SqlCommand( )

            command.CommandText = commandString
            command.Connection = connection

            ' Create the Reader and bind it to the datagrid
            Dim reader As SqlDataReader = _
                command.ExecuteReader(CommandBehavior.CloseConnection)
            DataGrid1.DataSource = reader
            DataGrid1.DataBind( )
    End Sub

    ' Given the name of a table, return a DataReader for
    ' all values from that table
    Public Function GetValues(tableName As String) As SqlDataReader
            ' connect to the Bugs database
            Dim connectionString As String = _
                "server=YourServer; uid=sa; " & _
                "pwd=YourPassword; database=ProgASPDotNetBugs"

            ' create and open the connection object
            Dim connection As New SqlConnection(connectionString)
            connection.Open( )

            ' get records from the Bugs table
            Dim commandString As String = "Select * from " & tableName

            ' create the command object and set its
            ' command string and connection
            Dim command As New SqlCommand

            command.CommandText = commandString
            command.Connection = connection

            ' create the DataReader and return it
            Return command.ExecuteReader(CommandBehavior.CloseConnection)
    End Function

    ' Handle the Edit event - set the EditItemIndex of the
    ' selected row
    Public Sub OnEdit(ByVal source As Object, ByVal e As DataGridCommandEventArgs)
            DataGrid1.EditItemIndex = e.Item.ItemIndex
```

```
      BindGrid( )
   End Sub

   ' Handle the cancel event - set the EditItemIndex to -1
   Public Sub OnCancel(ByVal source As Object, ByVal e As DataGridCommandEventArgs)
      DataGrid1.EditItemIndex = -1
      BindGrid( )
   End Sub

   ' Handle the Update event
   ' Extract the new values
   ' Update the database and rebind the datagrid
   Public Sub OnUpdate(ByVal source As Object, ByVal e As DataGridCommandEventArgs)
      Dim PersonID As String = CType(e.Item.FindControl( _
                  "editReporter"), DropDownList).SelectedItem.Value

      Dim newDescription As String = CType(e.Item.Cells(1).Controls(0), _
                                 TextBox).Text

      Dim ProductID As String = CType(e.Item.FindControl( _
                  "editProduct"), DropDownList).SelectedItem.Value

      Dim newVersion As String = CType(e.Item.FindControl( _
                  "txtVersion"), TextBox).Text

      ' form the update statement
      Dim cmd As String = "Update Bugs set Product = " & ProductID & _
         ", Version = '" & newVersion & _
         "', Description = '" & newDescription & _
         " ', Reporter = " & PersonID & _
         " where BugID = " & DataGrid1.DataKeys(e.Item.ItemIndex)

      ' connect to the Bugs database
      Dim connectionString As String = _
         "server=YourServer; uid=sa; pwd=YourPassword; " & _
         "database=ProgASPDotNetBugs"

      Dim connection As New SqlConnection(connectionString)
      connection.Open( )

      ' call the update and rebind the datagrid
      Dim command As New SqlCommand( )
      command.CommandText = cmd
      command.Connection = connection
      command.ExecuteNonQuery( )

      DataGrid1.EditItemIndex = -1
      BindGrid( )
   End Sub

End Class
```

Creating the EditTemplate Columns

To get started with this exercise, you'll create an *.aspx* page with just a single Data-Grid control:

```
<asp:DataGrid
id="DataGrid1"
runat="server"
AutoGenerateColumns="False"
CellPadding="5"
HeaderStyle-BackColor="PapayaWhip"
BorderWidth="5px"
BorderColor="#000099"
AlternatingItemStyle-BackColor="LightGrey"
HeaderStyle-Font-Bold
EditItemStyle-BackColor="Yellow"
EditItemStyle-ForeColor="Black"
DataKeyField ="BugID"
OnEditCommand="OnEdit"
OnCancelCommand="OnCancel"
OnUpdateCommand="OnUpdate">
```

Once again, you will set AutoGenerateColumns to false. As you have in the past, you must set DataKeyField to BugID so that the data grid can keep track of the primary key for each record on your behalf. You'll see how this comes in handy when we're ready to update the database with the edits you'll make.

There are three new attributes: OnEditCommand, OnCancelCommand, and OnUpdateCommand. These are used to wire up the event handlers for the Edit, Cancel, and Update events, which are fired in response to clicking on the Edit, Cancel, and Update links, respectively.

You create these links by adding an EditCommandColumn tag to your data grid:

```
<asp:EditCommandColumn
EditText="Edit"
CancelText="Cancel"
UpdateText="Save" />
```

The EditText is displayed when not in edit mode. Clicking on that link redraws the data grid in edit mode and displays the links with the text set in CancelText and UpdateText.

All that is left is to add the columns for each field you'll display in the data grid. You have a few choices. For straightforward text, you can use a normal BoundColumn tag:

```
<asp:BoundColumn DataField="Description" HeaderText="Description" />
```

For columns that you do not want to be edited, you can add the ReadOnly attribute:

```
<asp:BoundColumn DataField="BugID" HeaderText="ID" ReadOnly="True" />
```

For some columns, you will want to take control of how the item is displayed in normal and in edit mode. For example, the Version string is quite small, and you might want to control the size of the text box used when editing the data. To accomplish this, you will add a TemplateColumn tag. Within the TemplateColumn tag, you will add an ItemTemplate to control the display in normal mode, and an EditItemTemplate to control the display in edit mode:

```
<asp:TemplateColumn HeaderText="Version">
  <ItemTemplate>
    <asp:Label
    Text='<%#
Convert.ToString(DataBinder.Eval(Container.DataItem,"Version")) %>'
    Runat="server" ID="lblVersion"/>
  </ItemTemplate>
  <EditItemTemplate>
    <asp:TextBox
    Runat="server"
    ID="txtVersion"
    Text = '<%#
Convert.ToString(DataBinder.Eval(Container.DataItem,"Version")) %>'
    Width="30"
      />
  </EditItemTemplate>
</asp:TemplateColumn>
```

This is very similar to the way you created template columns in the previous section, except that in this example, you add the new EditItemTemplate. In this code shown here you display a text box when you enter edit mode. The text box is initialized with the current value of the Version field.

For the Product and Reporter fields, you want to provide a drop-down with the legal values for each field. To facilitate this, you'll create a code-behind method, GetValues, which takes the name of a table and returns a DataReader object filled with the values in that table:

```
public System.Data.SqlClient.SqlDataReader GetValues(string tableName)
{
    // connect to the Bugs database
    string connectionString =
        "server=YourServer; uid=sa;
         pwd=YourPassword; database=ProgASPDotNetBugs";

    // create and open the connection object
    System.Data.SqlClient.SqlConnection connection =
       new System.Data.SqlClient.SqlConnection(connectionString);
    connection.Open( );

    // get records from the Bugs table
    string commandString = "Select * from " + tableName;

    // create the command object and set its
    // command string and connection
    System.Data.SqlClient.SqlCommand command =
        new System.Data.SqlClient.SqlCommand( );
    command.CommandText = commandString;
```

```
    command.Connection = connection;

    // create the DataReader and return it
    return command.ExecuteReader(CommandBehavior.CloseConnection);
}
```

There is nothing surprising about this method. What is new is that you will assign this method to the Product EditItemTemplate declaratively. You will also set the DataTextField to determine what value will be displayed in the dropdown, and you'll set the DataValueField to determine the value held in the list box for each selection:

```
<asp:TemplateColumn HeaderText="Product">

    <ItemTemplate>
      <asp:Label
      Text='<%#
Convert.ToString(DataBinder.Eval(Container.DataItem,"ProductDescription"))
      %>'
      Runat="server" ID="lblProduct"/>
    </ItemTemplate>

    <EditItemTemplate>
      <asp:DropDownList
      Runat="server"
      ID="editProduct"
      DataSource='<%# GetValues("lkProduct") %>'
      DataTextField ="ProductDescription"
      DataValueField ="ProductID"
      Width ="200" />
    </EditItemTemplate>

</asp:TemplateColumn>
```

When not in edit mode, the ItemTemplate is used to display the asp:Label with the current value taken from the ProductDescription field returned by the Sql query used to fill the data grid. When in edit mode, however, the asp:ListBox is populated by binding to the DataReader returned by GetValues, and the Text and Value fields are bound based on the attributes shown.

The Reported By column is built in exactly the same way. Once again, you call GetValues, except that this time you pass in the name of the People table. You bind the DataTextField to the FullName field and the DataValueField to the PersonID field:

```
<asp:TemplateColumn HeaderText="Reported By">

    <ItemTemplate>
      <asp:Label Text='<%#
Convert.ToString(DataBinder.Eval(Container.DataItem,"FullName")) %>'
      ID="lblReported" Runat="server"/>
    </ItemTemplate>
```

```
<EditItemTemplate>
   <asp:DropDownList
   Runat="server"
   ID="editReporter"
   DataSource='<%# GetValues("People") %>'
   DataTextField ="FullName"
   DataValueField ="PersonID"
   Width ="200" />
</EditItemTemplate>

</asp:TemplateColumn>
```

Implementing the Edit Cycle

With the *.aspx* file in hand and the GetValues method working, you are able to display the items and enter edit mode. All that remains is to write the event handlers.

The data grid is drawn in normal or edit mode based on the value of the EditItemIndex property of the DataGrid control. Setting this zero-based property to a value other than -1 enables editing controls for that item.

Implementing the OnEditCommand event handler

When the user clicks the Edit link on an item, the OnEditCommand event handler is called. At this point, you have an opportunity to intercept the event and redirect editing in any way you want. You could, for example, check permissions to see if the user is allowed to edit the item and cancel editing if it should not be permitted. The simplest and most common thing to do, however, is simply to set the DataGrid control's EditItemIndex property to the ItemIndex property of the data grid item that was selected, and rebind the data grid, as shown in the following event handler:

```
public void OnEdit(Object source, DataGridCommandEventArgs e)
{
   DataGrid1.EditItemIndex = e.Item.ItemIndex;
   BindGrid();
}
```

The BindGrid method is the same method you called originally to populate the data grid:

```
private void BindGrid()
{
   // connect to the Bugs database
   string connectionString =
      "server=YourServer; uid=sa;
        pwd=YourPassword; database=ProgASPDotNetBugs";

   System.Data.SqlClient.SqlConnection connection =
      new System.Data.SqlClient.SqlConnection(connectionString);
   connection.Open();

   // get records from the Bugs table
```

```
string commandString =
    "Select b.BugID, b.Version, b.Description, p.ProductDescription,";
commandString += "peo.FullName from Bugs b ";
commandString += "join lkProduct p on b.Product = p.ProductID ";
commandString += "join People peo on b.Reporter = peo.PersonID ";

System.Data.SqlClient.SqlCommand command =
    new System.Data.SqlClient.SqlCommand( );
command.CommandText = commandString;
command.Connection = connection;

SqlDataReader reader =
    command.ExecuteReader(CommandBehavior.CloseConnection);

DataGrid1.DataSource=reader;
DataGrid1.DataBind( );
}
```

By rebinding the data grid with the EditItemIndex property set to the selected item (the row in the data grid), that row will be displayed in edit mode.

Implementing the OnCancelCommand event handler

If the user clicks Cancel, you can reset the EditItemIndex property to -1 and rebind the data grid:

```
public void OnCancel(Object source, DataGridCommandEventArgs e)
{
    DataGrid1.EditItemIndex = -1;
    BindGrid( );
}
```

The data grid will be redrawn in normal mode.

Implementing the OnUpdateCommand event handler

The OnUpdateCommand event handler is where all the real action is. Here you want to extract the new values from each of your widgets and then update the database accordingly.

There are two approaches to extracting the data. If you've used a bound control, as you have in this example with the Version value, you can access the control directly through the Item property of the DataGridCommandEventArgs parameter.

The Item property is of type DataGridItem. Every DataGridItem object has a Cells collection that it inherits from the TableRow class. You can offset into that collection to extract the Controls collection from the appropriate cell. The first control in that collection will be the text box. The Controls collection returns an object of type Control, so you must cast it to TextBox. Once cast to TextBox, you can access the Text property, which is a string:

```
string newDescription =
   ((TextBox) e.Item.Cells[1].Controls[0]).Text;
```

In VB.NET, this is done with a call to the *CType* function:

```
Dim newDescription As String = CType(e.Item.Cells(1).Controls(0), _
                                 TextBox).Text
```

The alternative method for extracting the data in your edit controls is to use the FindControl method of the Item. You pass in the name of the control and get back an object of type Control, which again you will cast:

```
string newVersion =
   ((TextBox)(e.Item.FindControl("txtVersion"))).Text;
```

In VB.NET, this would be done using:

```
Dim newVersion As String = CType(e.Item.FindControl("txtVersion"), TextBox).Text
```

When extracting the value from the drop-down listboxes, you will need to cast the Control object to a DropDownList object and then access the SelectedItem property, which returns a ListItem object. You can then access the Text property on that List-Item object to get the text displayed in the selected list item, or, in this case, you can access the Value property. The code to do this in C# is:

```
string PersonID =
   ((DropDownList)(e.Item.FindControl("editReporter"))).
       SelectedItem.Value;

string ProductID =
   ((DropDownList)(e.Item.FindControl("editProduct"))).
       SelectedItem.Value;
```

The relationship between the Text and the Value properties of the list-box and the values displayed and retrieved is established declaratively in the template with the DataTextField and DataValueField attributes, respectively.

In VB.NET, the code is:

```
Dim PersonID As String = CType(e.Item.FindControl("editReporter"), _
                         DropDownList).SelectedItem.Value

Dim ProductID As String = CType(e.Item.FindControl("editProduct"), _
                          DropDownList).SelectedItem.Value
```

With the values retrieved from the controls, you are ready to formulate an Update statement and update the database:

```
string cmd = "Update Bugs set Product = " + ProductID +
   ", Version = '" + newVersion +
   "', Description = '" + newDescription +
   " ', Reporter = " + PersonID +
   " where BugID = " + DataGrid1.DataKeys[e.Item.ItemIndex];
```

Notice that the Where clause includes the BugID from the current record. You obtain this by indexing the selected item index into the data grid's DataKeys collection. This, finally, is why you set the DataKeyField attribute on the data grid.

To invoke this SQL command you create the connection string and the connection object and use both to set the properties of a SqlCommand object on which you invoke the ExecuteNonQuery method:

```
// connect to the Bugs database
string connectionString =
    "server=YourServerYourServer; uid=sa; pwd=YourPWYourPW;
database=ProgASPDotNetBugs";

System.Data.SqlClient.SqlConnection connection =
    new System.Data.SqlClient.SqlConnection(connectionString);
connection.Open( );

System.Data.SqlClient.SqlCommand command =
    new System.Data.SqlClient.SqlCommand( );
command.CommandText = cmd;
command.Connection = connection;
command.ExecuteNonQuery( );
```

All that remains is to return to non-edit mode and rebind the data grid with the new values from the newly updated database:

```
DataGrid1.EditItemIndex = -1;
BindGrid( );
```

DataList Editing

The DataList control also provides extensive support for in-place editing. In the next example, you'll modify the data list you built earlier to display Bugs, but this time you'll add in-place editing.

The same control over look and feel that the data list provides through templates can be extended to the look and feel of the editing process. In the next example, you'll create a data list with two columns of data. Each record will include an Edit button to put your grid into edit mode for that record, as shown in Figure 13-4.

When the user presses the Edit button the EditItemTemplate tag will dictate the exact look and feel of the editing user interface, as shown in Figure 13-5.

To accomplish this, you'll create an *aspx* file with a single data list. You'll add attributes to set the edit, cancel, and update commands, and this time you'll also add an attribute for the delete command. The DataList tag appears as follows:

```
<asp:DataList
id ="DataList1"
runat="server"
CellPadding="5"
HeaderStyle-BackColor="PapayaWhip"
```

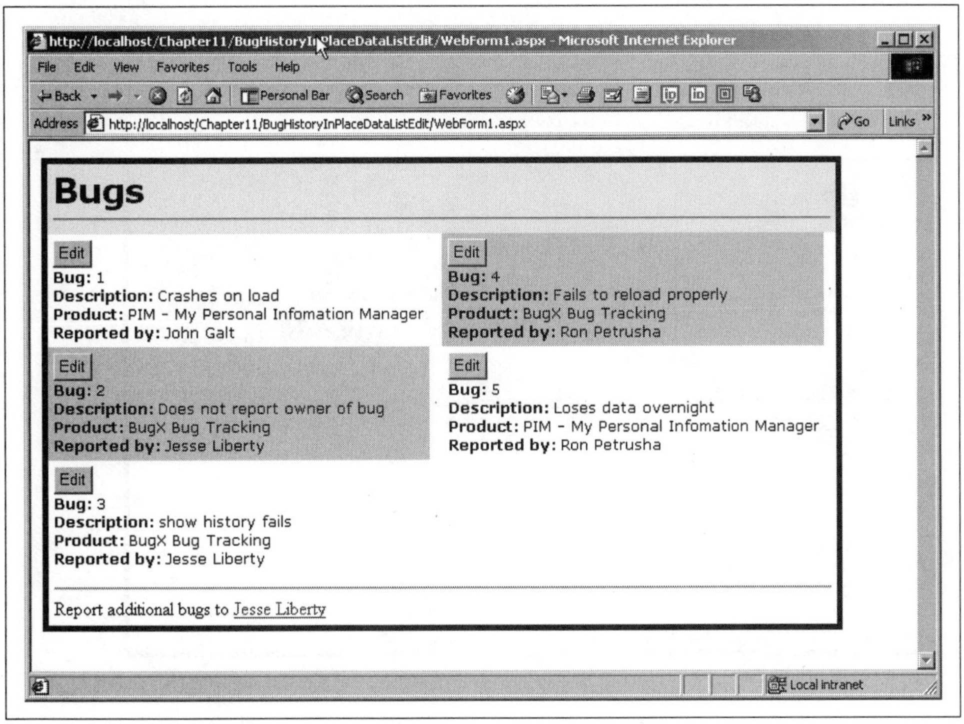

Figure 13-4. The DataList with Edit buttons

```
BorderWidth="5px"
BorderColor="#000099"
AlternatingItemStyle-BackColor="LightGrey"
HeaderStyle-Font-Bold
EditItemStyle-BackColor="Yellow"
EditItemStyle-ForeColor="Black"
RepeatColumns="2"
RepeatDirection="Vertical"
DataKeyField ="BugID"
OnEditCommand="OnEdit"
OnDeleteCommand="OnDelete"
OnCancelCommand="OnCancel"
OnUpdateCommand="OnUpdate">
```

Within the DataList definition, you'll add templates for the header, items, edititems, separator, and footer.

The Header, Separator, and Footer are unchanged from the previous example. The ItemTemplate is also unchanged, except for the addition of a Button object before the `<div>` that holds the other elements:

```
<ItemTemplate>
<asp:Button CommandName="Edit" Text="Edit" Runat="server" />
    <div class ="item">
<b>Bug: </b>
```

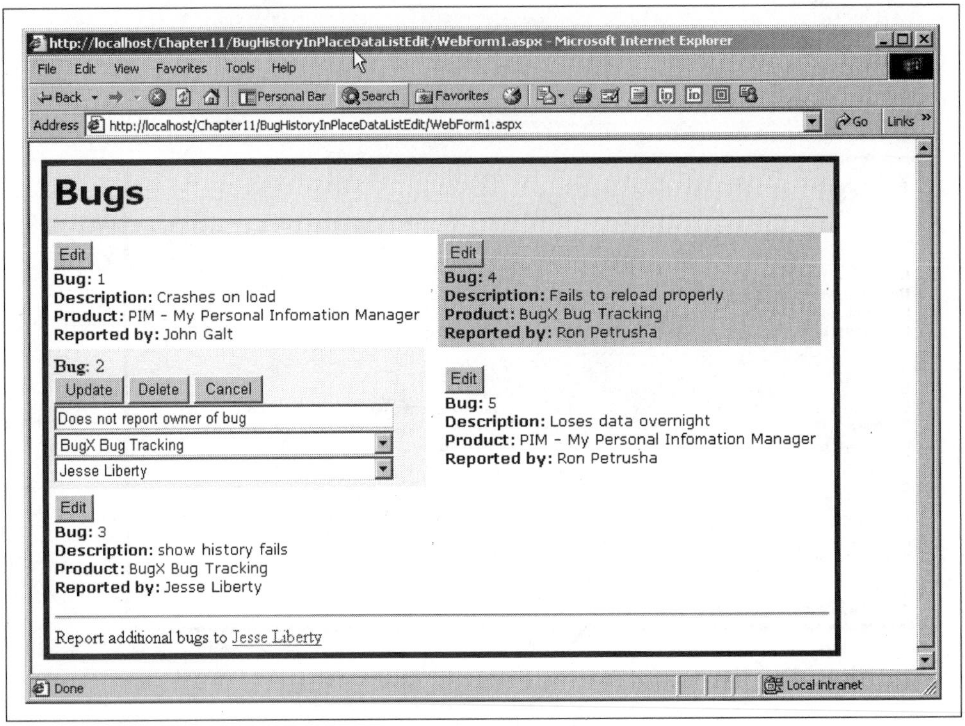

Figure 13-5. The DataList in edit mode

```
<%# Convert.ToString(
    DataBinder.Eval(Container.DataItem, "BugID")) %> <br />
<b>Description: </b>
  <%# Convert.ToString(
      DataBinder.Eval(Container.DataItem,"Description")) %> <br />
<b>Product: </b>
  <%# Convert.ToString(
      DataBinder.Eval(Container.DataItem,"ProductDescription")) %><br />
<b>Reported by: </b> </b>
  <%# Convert.ToString(
      DataBinder.Eval(Container.DataItem,"FullName")) %>
  </div>
</ItemTemplate>
```

So far, not much change from the previous data list. The one new element will be the EditItemTemplate tag which, no surprise, will be used to draw the data list item when it is in edit mode.

You begin with the EditItemTemplate element. You will then add text to show the BugID. For example:

```
<EditItemTemplate>
<b>Bug: </b>
<%# Convert.ToString(
    DataBinder.Eval(Container.DataItem, "BugID")) %> <br />
```

With the BugID displayed, you want to place the three Buttons:

```
<asp:Button CommandName ="Update" Text="Update"
Runat="server" ID="btnUpdate" />

<asp:Button CommandName ="Delete" Text="Delete"
Runat="server" ID="btnDelete"/>

<asp:Button CommandName ="Cancel" Text="Cancel"
Runat="server" ID="btnCancel"/>
```

After the buttons, you'll add a break so that the edit boxes are each on their own line. The attributes for the TextBox and DropDownLists are obtained directly from the previous example, as is the supporting GetValues method:

```
            <br>

<asp:TextBox
            Runat="server"
            ID="txtDescription"
            Text = '<%# Convert.ToString(
            DataBinder.Eval(Container.DataItem,"Description")) %>'
            Width="300"
            />
   <br>
   <asp:DropDownList
            Runat="server"
            ID="editProduct"
            DataSource='<%# GetValues("lkProduct") %>'
            DataTextField ="ProductDescription"
            DataValueField ="ProductID"
            Width ="300" />
<br>
<asp:DropDownList
            Runat="server"
            ID="editReporter"
            DataSource='<%# GetValues("People") %>'
            DataTextField ="FullName"
            DataValueField ="PersonID"
            Width ="300" />

<br>
            </EditItemTemplate>
```

All that is left is to implement the event handlers. The Cancel and Edit events are nearly identical to the previous example:

```
public void OnEdit(Object source, DataListCommandEventArgs e)
{
   DataList1.EditItemIndex = e.Item.ItemIndex;
   BindGrid( );
}

public void OnCancel(Object source, DataListCommandEventArgs e)
{
```

```
        DataList1.EditItemIndex = -1;
        BindGrid( );
    }
```
Note: the VB.NET code is identical except for the semicolons.

The only change is to the type of the second argument, now set to DataListCommandEventArgs.

Both the Update and the Delete event handlers will need to invoke a SQL statement, so you'll factor out the common code into a helper routine, ExecuteQuery:

```
private int ExecuteQuery(string sqlCmd)
{
    // connect to the Bugs database
        string connectionString =
    "server=YourServer; uid=sa;
        pwd=YourPassword; database=ProgASPDotNetBugs";

    System.Data.SqlClient.SqlConnection connection =
        new System.Data.SqlClient.SqlConnection(connectionString);
    connection.Open( );

    // call the update and rebind the datagrid
    System.Data.SqlClient.SqlCommand command =
        new System.Data.SqlClient.SqlCommand( );
    command.CommandText = sqlCmd;
    command.Connection = connection;
    return command.ExecuteNonQuery( );
}
```

In VB.NET, the code is:

```
Private Function ExecuteQuery(ByVal sqlCmd As String) As Integer
    ' connect to the Bugs database
    Dim connectionString As String = "server=YourServer uid=sa " & _
        "pwd=YourPassword database=ProgASPDotNetBugs"

    Dim myConnection As New System.Data.SqlClient.SqlConnection(connectionString)
    myConnection.Open( )

    ' call the update and rebind the datagrid
    Dim myCommand As New System.Data.SqlClient.SqlCommand( )
    myCommand.CommandText = sqlCmd
    myCommand.Connection = myConnection
    Return myCommand.ExecuteNonQuery( )
End Function
```

The Update statement is also very similar to that used in the previous example:

```
public void OnUpdate(Object source, DataListCommandEventArgs e)
{

    string PersonID =
        ((DropDownList)(e.Item.FindControl("editReporter"))).
```

```
        SelectedItem.Value;

    string newDescription =
        ((TextBox)(e.Item.FindControl("txtDescription"))).Text;

    string ProductID =
        ((DropDownList)(e.Item.FindControl("editProduct"))).
        SelectedItem.Value;

    // form the update statement
    string cmd = "Update Bugs set Product = " + ProductID +
        ", Description = '" + newDescription +
        " ', Reporter = " + PersonID +
        " where BugID = " + DataList1.DataKeys[e.Item.ItemIndex];

    ExecuteQuery(cmd);
    DataList1.EditItemIndex = -1;
    BindGrid( );

}
```

In VB.NET, the code is:

```
Public Sub OnUpdate( _
    ByVal source As Object, ByVal e As DataListCommandEventArgs)
    Dim PersonID As String = CType(e.Item.FindControl( _
                "editReporter"), DropDownList).SelectedItem.Value

    Dim newDescription As String = _
        CType(e.Item.FindControl("txtDescription"), _
                            TextBox).Text

    Dim ProductID As String = CType(e.Item.FindControl( _
                "editProduct"), DropDownList).SelectedItem.Value

    Dim newVersion As String = CType(e.Item.FindControl( _
                "txtVersion"), TextBox).Text

    ' form the update statement
    Dim cmd As String = "Update Bugs set Product = " & ProductID & _
        ", Version = '" & newVersion & _
        "', Description = '" & newDescription & _
        " ', Reporter = " & PersonID & _
        " where BugID = " & DataList1.DataKeys(e.Item.ItemIndex)

    ExecuteQuery(cmd)
    DataList1.EditItemIndex = -1
    BindGrid( )
End Sub
```

Notice that once again you use the DataKeys collection (this time of the DataList control) to retrieve the BugID. This depends on your setting the DataKeyField attribute of the DataList.

Finally, you add a delete command event handler that forms the SQL statement to delete the current record:

```
public void OnDelete(Object source, DataListCommandEventArgs e)
{

    string cmd = "Delete from Bugs where BugID = " +
        DataList1.DataKeys[e.Item.ItemIndex];
    int rowsDeleted = ExecuteQuery(cmd);

    DataList1.EditItemIndex = -1;
    BindGrid( );
}
```

In VB.NET, the code is:

```
Public Sub OnDelete( _
    ByVal source As Object, ByVal e As DataListCommandEventArgs)
    Dim cmd As String = "Delete from Bugs where BugID = " & _
            DataList1.DataKeys(e.Item.ItemIndex)
    DataList1.EditItemIndex = -1
    BindGrid( )
End Sub
```

The complete C# listing is shown in Example 13-9 and the VB.NET code in Example 13-10.

Example 13-9. Using the DataList to edit in place (C#)

```
using System;
using System.Collections;
using System.ComponentModel;
using System.Data;
using System.Data.SqlClient;
using System.Drawing;
using System.Web;
using System.Web.SessionState;
using System.Web.UI;
using System.Web.UI.WebControls;
using System.Web.UI.HtmlControls;

namespace BugHistoryInPlaceDataListEdit
{
    public class WebForm1 : System.Web.UI.Page
    {
        protected System.Web.UI.WebControls.DataList DataList1;
        protected System.Web.UI.WebControls.ListBox lbReportedby;
        public System.Data.SqlClient.SqlDataReader personReader;

        public WebForm1( )
        {
            Page.Init += new System.EventHandler(Page_Init);
        }

        private void Page_Load(object sender, System.EventArgs e)
        {
```

Example 13-9. Using the DataList to edit in place (C#) (continued)

```csharp
        if (! Page.IsPostBack)
        {
            BindGrid( );
        }
    }


    // extract the bug records and bind to the datagrid
    private void BindGrid( )
    {
        // connect to the Bugs database
        string connectionString =
            "server=YourServer; uid=sa; pwd=YourPW; database=ProgASPDotNetBugs";

        System.Data.SqlClient.SqlConnection connection =
            new System.Data.SqlClient.SqlConnection(connectionString);
        connection.Open( );

        // get records from the Bugs table
        string commandString =
            "Select b.BugID, b.Version, b.Description, ";
        commandString += "p.ProductDescription, peo.FullName from Bugs b ";
        commandString += "join lkProduct p on b.Product = p.ProductID ";
        commandString += "join People peo on b.Reporter = peo.PersonID ";


        System.Data.SqlClient.SqlCommand command =
            new System.Data.SqlClient.SqlCommand( );
        command.CommandText = commandString;
        command.Connection = connection;

        // Create the Reader adn bind it to the datagrid
        SqlDataReader reader =
            command.ExecuteReader(CommandBehavior.CloseConnection);
        DataList1.DataSource=reader;
        DataList1.DataBind( );
    }

    // Given the name of a table, return a DataReader for
    // all values from that table
    public System.Data.SqlClient.SqlDataReader GetValues(string tableName)
    {
        // connect to the Bugs database
        string connectionString =
            "server=YourServer; uid=sa; pwd=YourPW; database=ProgASPDotNetBugs";

        // create and open the connection object
        System.Data.SqlClient.SqlConnection connection =
            new System.Data.SqlClient.SqlConnection(connectionString);
        connection.Open( );

        // get records from the Bugs table
        string commandString = "Select * from " + tableName;
```

Example 13-9. Using the DataList to edit in place (C#) (continued)

```
        // create the command object and set its
        // command string and connection
        System.Data.SqlClient.SqlCommand command =
            new System.Data.SqlClient.SqlCommand( );
        command.CommandText = commandString;
        command.Connection = connection;

        // create the DataReader and return it
        return command.ExecuteReader(CommandBehavior.CloseConnection);

    }

    // Handle the Edit event - set the EditItemIndex of the
    // selected row
    public void OnEdit(Object source, DataListCommandEventArgs e)
    {
        DataList1.EditItemIndex = e.Item.ItemIndex;
        BindGrid( );
    }

    private int ExecuteQuery(string sqlCmd)
    {
        // connect to the Bugs database
        string connectionString =
            "server=YourServer; uid=sa; pwd=YourPW; database=ProgASPDotNetBugs";

        System.Data.SqlClient.SqlConnection connection =
            new System.Data.SqlClient.SqlConnection(connectionString);
        connection.Open( );

        // call the update and rebind the datagrid
        System.Data.SqlClient.SqlCommand command =
            new System.Data.SqlClient.SqlCommand( );
        command.CommandText = sqlCmd;
        command.Connection = connection;
        return command.ExecuteNonQuery( );
    }

    public void OnDelete(Object source, DataListCommandEventArgs e)
    {

        string cmd = "Delete from Bugs where BugID = " +
            DataList1.DataKeys[e.Item.ItemIndex];
        int rowsDeleted = ExecuteQuery(cmd);

        DataList1.EditItemIndex = -1;
        BindGrid( );
    }

    // Handle the cancel event - set the EditItemIndex to -1
    public void OnCancel(Object source, DataListCommandEventArgs e)
    {
```

Example 13-9. Using the DataList to edit in place (C#) (continued)

```
        DataList1.EditItemIndex = -1;
        BindGrid( );

    }

    // Handle the Update event
    // Extract the new values
    // Update the database and rebind the datagrid
    public void OnUpdate(Object source, DataListCommandEventArgs e)
    {

        string PersonID =
            ((DropDownList)(e.Item.FindControl("editReporter"))).
            SelectedItem.Value;

        string newDescription =
            ((TextBox)(e.Item.FindControl("txtDescription"))).Text;

        string ProductID =
            ((DropDownList)(e.Item.FindControl("editProduct"))).
            SelectedItem.Value;

        // form the update statement
        string cmd = "Update Bugs set Product = " + ProductID +
            ", Description = '" + newDescription +
            " ', Reporter = " + PersonID +
            " where BugID = " + DataList1.DataKeys[e.Item.ItemIndex];

        ExecuteQuery(cmd);
        DataList1.EditItemIndex = -1;
        BindGrid( );

    }

    private void Page_Init(object sender, EventArgs e)
    {
        //
        // CODEGEN: This call is required by the ASP.NET Web Form Designer.
        //
        InitializeComponent( );
    }

      #region Web Form Designer generated code
    /// <summary>
    /// Required method for Designer support - do not modify
    /// the contents of this method with the code editor.
    /// </summary>
    private void InitializeComponent( )
    {
        this.Load += new System.EventHandler(this.Page_Load);

    }
```

Example 13-9. Using the DataList to edit in place (C#) (continued)

```
        #endregion
    }
}
```

Example 13-10. Using the DataList to edit in place (VB.NET)

```vbnet
Imports System.Data.SqlClient

Public Class WebForm1
    Inherits System.Web.UI.Page

    Protected WithEvents DataList1 As System.Web.UI.WebControls.DataList
    Protected WithEvents lbReportedby As System.Web.UI.WebControls.ListBox
    Public personReader As System.Data.SqlClient.SqlDataReader

#Region " Web Form Designer Generated Code "

    'This call is required by the Web Form Designer.
    <System.Diagnostics.DebuggerStepThrough()> Private Sub InitializeComponent()

    End Sub

    Private Sub Page_Init(ByVal sender As System.Object, ByVal e As System.EventArgs) _
Handles MyBase.Init
        'CODEGEN: This method call is required by the Web Form Designer
        'Do not modify it using the code editor.
        InitializeComponent()
    End Sub

#End Region

    Private Sub Page_Load(ByVal sender As System.Object, _
                          ByVal e As System.EventArgs) Handles MyBase.Load
        If Not Page.IsPostBack Then
            BindGrid()
        End If
    End Sub

    ' extract the bug records and bind to the datagrid
    Private Sub BindGrid()
        ' connect to the Bugs database
        Dim connectionString As String = _
            "server=YourServer; uid=sa; pwd=YourPW; " & _
            "database=ProgASPDotNetBugs"

        Dim connection As New SqlConnection(connectionString)
        connection.Open()

        ' get records from the Bugs table
        Dim commandString As String = _
            "Select b.BugID, b.Version, b.Description, " & _
            "p.ProductDescription, peo.FullName from Bugs b " & _
            "join lkProduct p on b.Product = p.ProductID " & _
```

Example 13-10. Using the DataList to edit in place (VB.NET) (continued)

```
            "join People peo on b.Reporter = peo.PersonID "

    Dim command As New SqlCommand( )

    command.CommandText = commandString
    command.Connection = connection

    ' Create the Reader and bind it to the datagrid
    Dim reader As SqlDataReader = _
        command.ExecuteReader(CommandBehavior.CloseConnection)
    DataList1.DataSource = reader
    DataList1.DataBind( )
End Sub

' Given the name of a table, return a DataReader for
' all values from that table
Public Function GetValues(ByVal tableName As String) As SqlDataReader
    ' connect to the Bugs database
    Dim connectionString As String = _
        "server=YourServer; uid=sa; " & _
        "pwd=YourPassword; database=ProgASPDotNetBugs"

    ' create and open the connection object
    Dim connection As New SqlConnection(connectionString)
    connection.Open( )

    ' get records from the Bugs table
    Dim commandString As String = "Select * from " & tableName

    ' create the command object and set its
    ' command string and connection
    Dim command As New SqlCommand( )

    command.CommandText = commandString
    command.Connection = connection

    ' create the DataReader and return it
    Return command.ExecuteReader(CommandBehavior.CloseConnection)
End Function

' Handle the Edit event - set the EditItemIndex of the
' selected row
Public Sub OnEdit(ByVal source As Object, ByVal e As DataListCommandEventArgs)
    DataList1.EditItemIndex = e.Item.ItemIndex
    BindGrid( )
End Sub

' Handle the cancel event - set the EditItemIndex to -1
Public Sub OnCancel(ByVal source As Object, ByVal e As DataListCommandEventArgs)
    DataList1.EditItemIndex = -1
    BindGrid( )
End Sub
```

Example 13-10. Using the DataList to edit in place (VB.NET) (continued)

```vb.net
' Handle the delete event
Public Sub OnDelete(ByVal source As Object, ByVal e As DataListCommandEventArgs)
    Dim cmd As String = "Delete from Bugs where BugID = " & _
            DataList1.DataKeys(e.Item.ItemIndex)
    DataList1.EditItemIndex = -1
    BindGrid( )
End Sub

' Handle the Update event
' Extract the new values
' Update the database and rebind the datagrid
Public Sub OnUpdate(ByVal source As Object, ByVal e As DataListCommandEventArgs)
    Dim PersonID As String = CType(e.Item.FindControl( _
                "editReporter"), DropDownList).SelectedItem.Value

    Dim newDescription As String = CType(e.Item.FindControl("txtDescription"), _
                            TextBox).Text

    Dim ProductID As String = CType(e.Item.FindControl( _
                "editProduct"), DropDownList).SelectedItem.Value

    Dim newVersion As String = CType(e.Item.FindControl( _
                "txtVersion"), TextBox).Text

    ' form the update statement
    Dim cmd As String = "Update Bugs set Product = " & ProductID & _
        ", Version = '" & newVersion & _
        "', Description = '" & newDescription & _
        " ', Reporter = " & PersonID & _
        " where BugID = " & DataList1.DataKeys(e.Item.ItemIndex)

    ExecuteQuery(cmd)
    DataList1.EditItemIndex = -1
    BindGrid( )
End Sub
Private Function ExecuteQuery(ByVal sqlCmd As String) As Int32
    ' connect to the Bugs database
    Dim connectionString As String = _
        "server=YourServer uid=sa pwd=YourPassword database=ProgASPDotNetBugs"

    Dim myConnection As New System.Data.SqlClient.SqlConnection(connectionString)
    myConnection.Open( )

    ' call the update and rebind the datagrid
    Dim myCommand As New System.Data.SqlClient.SqlCommand( )
    myCommand.CommandText = sqlCmd
    myCommand.Connection = myConnection
    Return myCommand.ExecuteNonQuery( )
End Function

End Class
```

Custom and User Controls

Chapter 4 includes a chart of the five types of controls supported in ASP.NET: HTML controls, HTML server controls, web server controls, validation controls, and controls created by the developer. This chapter will discuss this last type of control, known as custom controls, and a subset of them called user controls.

Custom controls are compiled controls that act, from the client's perspective, much like web (ASP) controls. Custom controls can be created in one of three ways:

- By deriving a new custom control from an existing control (e.g., deriving your own specialized text box from asp:textbox). This is known as a *derived custom control*.

- By composing a new custom control out of two or more existing controls. This is known as a *composite custom control*.

- By deriving from the base control class, thus creating a new custom control from scratch. This is known as a *full custom control*.

Of course, all three of these methods, and the three control types that correspond to them, are variations on the same theme. We'll consider these custom controls later in this chapter. The simplest category of custom controls is a subset called *user controls*. Microsoft distinguishes user controls as a special case because they are quite different from other types of custom controls. In short, *user controls* are segments of ASP.NET pages that can be reused from within other pages. This is similar to "include files" familiar to ASP developers. However, user controls are far more powerful. User controls support properties and events, and thus provide reusable functionality as well as reusable HTML.

User Controls

User controls allow you to save a part of an existing ASP.NET page and reuse it in many other ASP.NET pages. A user control is almost identical to a normal *.aspx* page, with two differences: the user control has the *.ascx* extension rather than *.aspx*, and it may not have <HTML>, <Body>, or <Form> tags.

The simplest user control is one that displays HTML only. A classic example of a simple user control is an HTML page that displays a copyright notice. Example 14-1 shows the complete listing for *copyright.ascx*.

Example 14-1. copyright.ascx

```
<%@ Control %>
<hr>
<table>
   <tr>
      <td align="center">Copyright 2005 Liberty Associates, Inc.</td>
   </tr>
   <tr>
      <td align="center">Support at http://www.LibertyAssociates.com</td>
   </tr>
</table>
```

To see this at work, you'll modify Example 8-1, adding just two lines. At the top of the *.aspx* file, you'll add the registration of your new user control:

```
<%@Register tagprefix="OReilly" Tagname="copyright" src="copyright.ascx" %>
```

This registers the control with the page and establishes both the prefix (OReilly) and the TagName (copyright). In the page you are modifying, there are any number of ASP elements such as <asp:ListItem>. The letters asp before the colon are the tag prefix that identifies this tag as being a web control, and the token ListItem is the TagName.

Your user controls will have a tag prefix as well (in this case, Oreilly), in addition to a specific tag name (in this case, copyright). Interestingly, there is nothing in the *.ascx* file itself that identifies the tag prefix.

The modified *.aspx* code is shown in Example 14-2. The output from this page is shown in Figure 14-1.

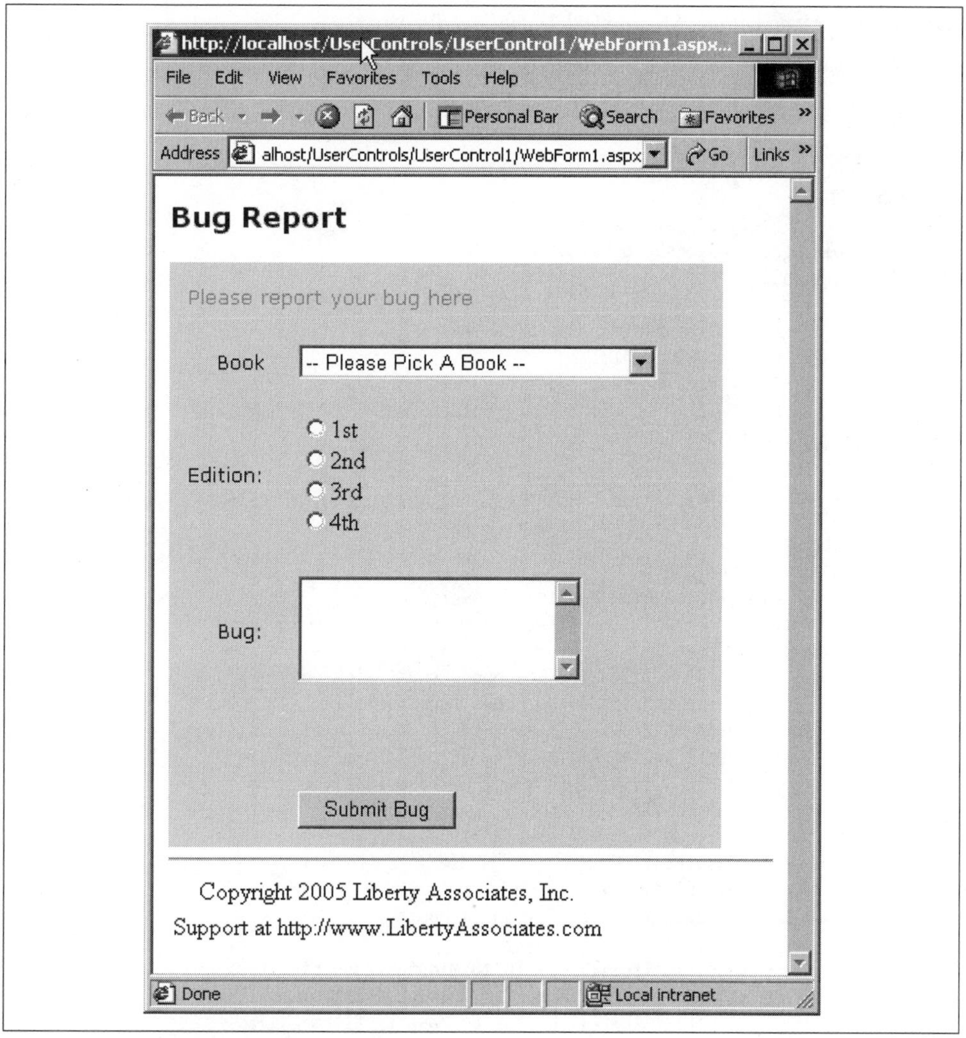

Figure 14-1. The copyright user control

Example 14-2. Modification of Example 8-1

```
<%@ Page language="c#" Codebehind="WebForm1.aspx.cs"
AutoEventWireup="false" Inherits="Validation04.WebForm1" %>

<%@Register tagprefix="OReilly" Tagname="copyright" src="copyright.ascx" %>

<HTML>
  <HEAD>

<!-- Demonstrate simple required field validation -->
    <meta name=vs_targetSchema content="Internet Explorer 5.0">
    <meta name="GENERATOR" Content="Microsoft Visual Studio 7.0">
```

Example 14-2. Modification of Example 8-1 (continued)

```
        <meta name="CODE_LANGUAGE" Content="C#">
</HEAD>
 <body>
    <h3>
        <font face="Verdana">Bug Report</font>
    </h3>
    <form runat="server" ID="frmBugs">
        <table bgcolor=gainsboro cellpadding=10>
            <tr valign="top">
                <td colspan=3>
                    <!-- Display error messages -->
                    <asp:Label ID="lblMsg"
                    Text="Please report your bug here"
                    ForeColor="red" Font-Name="Verdana"
                    Font-Size="10" runat=server />
                    <br>
                </td>
            </tr>
            <tr>
                <td align=right>
                    <font face=Verdana size=2>Book</font>
                </td>
                <td>
                <!-- Drop down list with the books (must pick one) -->
                    <ASP:DropDownList id=ddlBooks runat=server>
                        <asp:ListItem>-- Please Pick A Book --</asp:ListItem>
                        <asp:ListItem>Programming ASP.NET</asp:ListItem>
                        <asp:ListItem>Programming C#</asp:ListItem>
                        <asp:ListItem>
                            Teach Yourself C++ In 21 Days
                        </asp:ListItem>
                        <asp:ListItem>
                            Teach Yourself C++ In 24 Hours
                        </asp:ListItem>
                        <asp:ListItem>TY C++ In 10 Minutes</asp:ListItem>
                        <asp:ListItem>TY More C++ In 21 Days</asp:ListItem>
                        <asp:ListItem>C++ Unleashed</asp:ListItem>
                        <asp:ListItem>C++ From Scratch</asp:ListItem>
                        <asp:ListItem>XML From Scratch</asp:ListItem>
                        <asp:ListItem>Web Classes FS</asp:ListItem>
                        <asp:ListItem>Beg. OO Analysis & Design</asp:ListItem>
                        <asp:ListItem>Clouds To Code</asp:ListItem>
                        <asp:ListItem>
                            CIG Career Computer Programming
                        </asp:ListItem>
                    </ASP:DropDownList>
                </td>
                <!-- Validator for the drop down -->
                <td align=middle rowspan=1>
                    <asp:RequiredFieldValidator
                    id="reqFieldBooks"
                    ControlToValidate="ddlBooks"
```

Example 14-2. Modification of Example 8-1 (continued)

```
                Display="Static"
                InitialValue="-- Please Pick A Book --"
                Width="100%" runat=server>
                    Please choose a book
                </asp:RequiredFieldValidator>
            </td>
        </tr>
        <tr>
            <td align=right>
            <!-- Radio buttons for the edition -->
                <font face=Verdana size=2>Edition:</font>
            </td>
            <td>
                <ASP:RadioButtonList id=rblEdition
                RepeatLayout="Flow" runat=server>
                    <asp:ListItem>1st</asp:ListItem>
                    <asp:ListItem>2nd</asp:ListItem>
                    <asp:ListItem>3rd</asp:ListItem>
                    <asp:ListItem>4th</asp:ListItem>
                </ASP:RadioButtonList>
            </td>
            <!-- Validator for editions -->
            <td align=middle rowspan=1>
                <asp:RequiredFieldValidator
                id="reqFieldEdition"
                ControlToValidate="rblEdition"
                Display="Static"
                InitialValue=""
                Width="100%" runat=server>
                    Please pick an edition
                </asp:RequiredFieldValidator>
            </td>
        </tr>
        <tr>
            <td align=right style="HEIGHT: 97px">
                <font face=Verdana size=2>Bug:</font>
            </td>
            <!-- Multi-line text for the bug entry -->
            <td style="HEIGHT: 97px">
                <ASP:TextBox id=txtBug runat=server width="183px"
                textmode="MultiLine" height="68px"/>
            </td>
            <!-- Validator for the text box-->
            <td style="HEIGHT: 97px">
                <asp:RequiredFieldValidator
                id="reqFieldBug"
                ControlToValidate="txtBug"
                Display="Static"
                Width="100%" runat=server>
                    Please provide bug details
                </asp:RequiredFieldValidator>
```

Example 14-2. Modification of Example 8-1 (continued)

```
                </td>
            </tr>
            <tr>
                <td>
                </td>
                <td>
                    <ASP:Button id=btnSubmit
                    text="Submit Bug" runat=server />
                </td>
                <td>
                </td>
            </tr>
        </table>
    </form>
<OReilly:copyright runat="server" />
    </body>
</HTML>
```

In Figure 14-1 the horizontal rule at the bottom of the page, and the copyright notice below it, comes from the *.ascx* user control you've created. This control can be reused in many pages. If you update the copyright, you will make that update only in the one *.ascx* file, and it will be displayed appropriately in all the pages that use that control.

In the next example, you will recreate the book drop-down list itself, this time as a user control. The process of converting part of an existing HTML page into a user control is very simple; you just extract the code that creates the drop-down list into its own HTML file and name that file with the *.ascx* extension.

Visual Studio .NET provides support for creating user controls. Right-click on the project and choose Add → Add New Item. One of the choices is New User Control. This choice opens a new form. The HTML at the top of the form includes the Control directive, which sets the language attributes, etc.

Rename the new item *BookList.ascx* and copy in the code for creating the book list, as shown in Example 14-3.

Example 14-3. The BookList user control

```
<!-- Drop down list with the books (must pick one) -->
    <ASP:DropDownList id=ddlBooks runat=server>
        <asp:ListItem>-- Please Pick A Book --</asp:ListItem>
        <asp:ListItem>Programming ASP.NET</asp:ListItem>
        <asp:ListItem>Programming C#</asp:ListItem>
        <asp:ListItem>
            Teach Yourself C++ In 21 Days
        </asp:ListItem>
        <asp:ListItem>
            Teach Yourself C++ In 24 Hours
```

Example 14-3. The BookList user control (continued)

```
        </asp:ListItem>
        <asp:ListItem>TY C++ In 10 Minutes</asp:ListItem>
        <asp:ListItem>TY More C++ In 21 Days</asp:ListItem>
        <asp:ListItem>C++ Unleashed</asp:ListItem>
        <asp:ListItem>C++ From Scratch</asp:ListItem>
        <asp:ListItem>XML From Scratch</asp:ListItem>
        <asp:ListItem>Web Classes FS</asp:ListItem>
        <asp:ListItem>Beg. OO Analysis & Design</asp:ListItem>
        <asp:ListItem>Clouds To Code</asp:ListItem>
        <asp:ListItem>
            CIG Career Computer Programming
        </asp:ListItem>
    </ASP:DropDownList>
```

 In Example 14-3, you'll strip out the validator code, to keep the focus on working with the user control. The validator can be used with the user control exactly as it was with the ASP control.

To make this work in your page, you'll add a new `Register` statement:

```
<%@Register tagprefix="OReilly" Tagname="bookList" src="bookList.ascx" %>
```

In the body of the page, you'll add the new user control, exactly where you cut the original code:

```
<OReilly:bookList runat="server" ID="Booklist"/>
```

Adding Code

So far, all you've put into the user control is straight HTML. This is simple, but also somewhat limited. There is no reason to so severely limit the user control. In the next example, you'll add support for filling the list box with books from a database. To do so, you'll need to add a table to the ProgASPNetBugs database, as shown in Figure 14-2.

You'll also need to populate this table with the values shown in Figure 14-3, or simply download the entire database with data already provided.

You are ready to fill the list box dynamically, using data binding. Strip out all the code that fills the list box by hand. This reduces Example 14-3 to two lines:

```
<ASP:DropDownList id=ddlBooks runat=server>
</ASP:DropDownList>
```

The key to making this work is now in the `Control` tag:

```
<%@ Control Language="c#" AutoEventWireup="false"
Codebehind="BookList.ascx.cs"
Inherits="UserControl1.WebUserControl1"%>
```

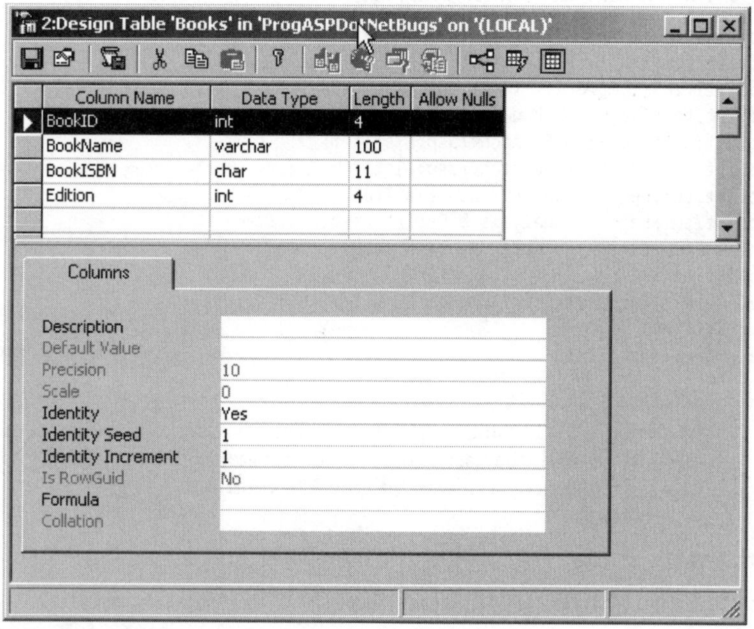

Figure 14-2. Design of the Books table

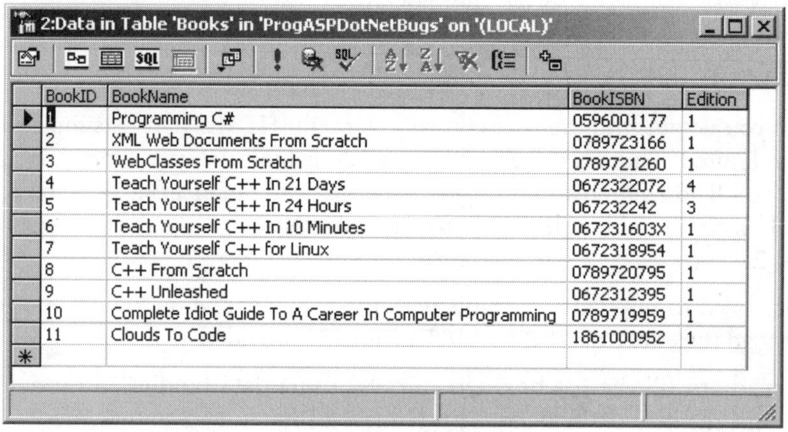

Figure 14-3. Contents of the Books table

The Codebehind attribute points to the code-behind page. In that page, you'll add code to the Page_Load method to bind the list box to the appropriate table in the database. That code is shown in Example 14-4 for C# and Example 14-5 for VB.NET.

Example 14-4. C# Page_Load from the code-behind page for the user control

```csharp
private void Page_Load(object sender, System.EventArgs e)
{
    if (!IsPostBack)
    {
        string connectionString =
            "server= " + ServerName +
            "; uid=sa;pwd=" +
            Password + "; database= " + DB;

        // get records from the Bugs table
        string commandString =
            "Select BookName from Books";

        // create the data set command object
        // and the DataSet
        SqlDataAdapter dataAdapter =
            new SqlDataAdapter(
            commandString, connectionString);

        DataSet dataSet = new DataSet();

        // fill the data set object
        dataAdapter.Fill(dataSet,"Bugs");

        // Get the one table from the DataSet
        DataTable dataTable = dataSet.Tables[0];

        ddlBooks.DataSource = dataTable.DefaultView;
        ddlBooks.DataTextField = "BookName";
        ddlBooks.DataBind();
    }
}
```

Example 14-5. VB.NET Page_Load from the code-behind page for the user control

```vbnet
Private Sub Page_Load(ByVal sender As System.Object, _
                    ByVal e As System.EventArgs) Handles MyBase.Load
    If Not IsPostBack Then
        Dim connectionString As String = _
                "server= " & ServerName &
                "; uid=sa;pwd=" +
                Password + "; database= " + DB;

            ' get records from the Bugs table
            Dim commandString As String = _
                "Select BookName from Books"

            ' create the data set command object
            ' and the DataSet
             Dim dataAdapter as SqlDataAdapter = _
               new SqlDataAdapter( _
```

```
            commandString, connectionString);

        Dim dataSet As DataSet = New DataSet()

        ' fill the data set object
        dataAdapter.Fill(dataSet, "Books")

        ' Get the one table from the DataSet
        Dim dataTable As DataTable = dataSet.Tables(0)

        ddlBooks.DataSource = dataTable.DefaultView
        ddlBooks.DataTextField = "BookName"
        ddlBooks.DataBind()
    End If
End Sub
```

The host page does not change at all. The updated user control now works as intended, loading the list of books from the database, as shown in Figure 14-4.

@Control Properties

There can be only one @Control directive for each user control. This attribute is used by the ASP.NET page parser and compiler to set attributes for your user control. Possible values are shown in Table 14-1.

Table 14-1. Values for @Control properties

Attribute	Description	Possible values
AutoEventWireup	true (the default) indicates the page automatically posts back to the server. If false, the developer must fire the server event manually.	true or false; default is true.
ClassName	The class name for the page.	Any valid class name.
CompilerOptions	Passed to compiler.	Any valid compiler string indicating options.
Debug	Whether to compile with debug symbols.	true or false; default is false.
Description	Text description of the page.	Any valid text.
EnableViewState	Is view state maintained for the user control?	true or false; default is true.
Explicit	Should page be compiled with VB.NET option explicit	true or false; default is false.
Inherits	Defines a code-behind class.	Any class derived from UserControl.
Language	The language used for inline rendering and server-side script blocks.	Any .NET-supported language.
Strict	Page should be compiled using VB.NET Strict option?	true or false; default is false.
Src	Name of the source file for the code-behind.	Any valid filename.
WarningLevel	Compiler warning level at which compilation will abort.	0–4.

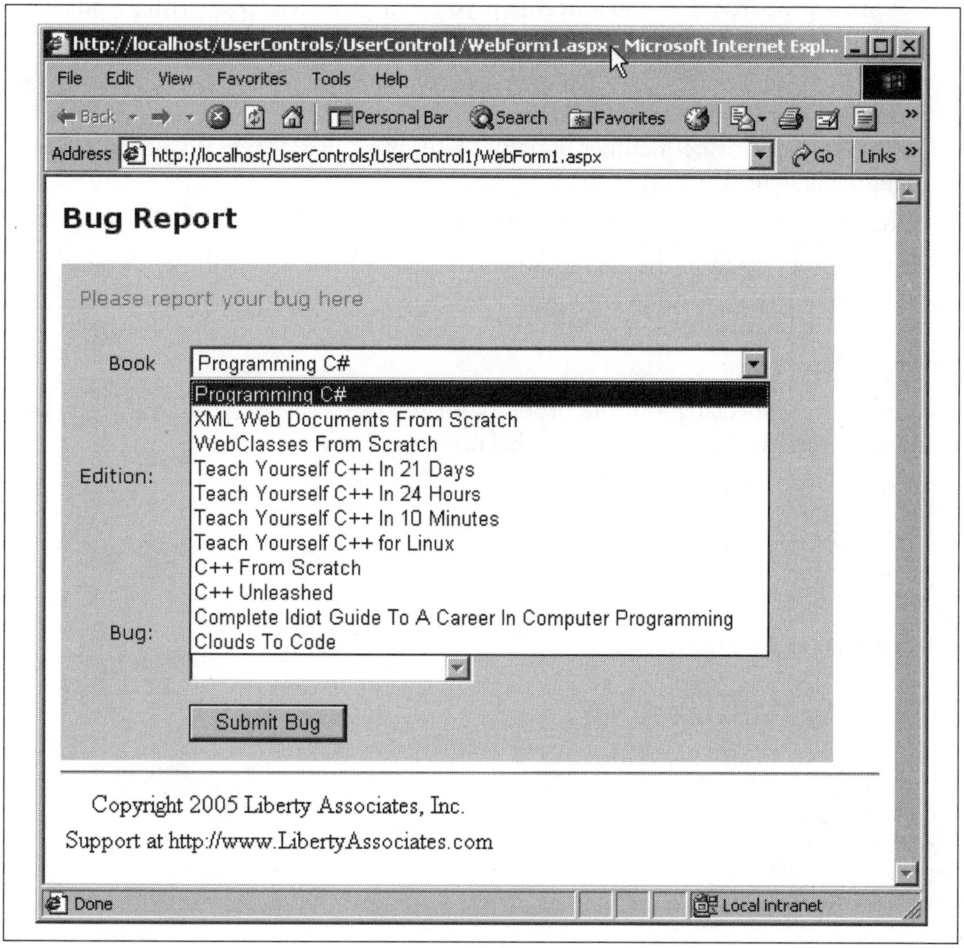

> http://localhost/UserControls/UserControl1/WebForm1.aspx - Microsoft Internet Expl...
>
> File   Edit   View   Favorites   Tools   Help
>
> ← Back → ⊗ ⬚ ⌂ | ⬚ Personal Bar   ⬚ Search   ⬚ Favorites   ⬚   ⬚ ⬚ ⬚ ⬚   »
>
> Address ⬚ http://localhost/UserControls/UserControl1/WebForm1.aspx   ▼ ⬚ Go Links »

Bug Report

Please report your bug here

Book | Programming C# ▼ |

> Programming C#
> XML Web Documents From Scratch
> WebClasses From Scratch
> Teach Yourself C++ In 21 Days
> Teach Yourself C++ In 24 Hours
> Teach Yourself C++ In 10 Minutes
> Teach Yourself C++ for Linux
> C++ From Scratch
> C++ Unleashed
> Complete Idiot Guide To A Career In Computer Programming
> Clouds To Code

Edition:

Bug: ▼

    Submit Bug

Copyright 2005 Liberty Associates, Inc.

Support at http://www.LibertyAssociates.com

⬚ Done   ⬚ Local intranet

Figure 14-4. Loading the book list from the database in a user control

> The src attribute is not used in Visual Studio .NET. VS.NET uses pre-compiled code-behind classes with the Inherits attribute.

Adding Properties

You can make your user control far more powerful by adding properties. Properties allow your client (in this case WebForm1) to interact with your control, setting attributes either declaratively (when the user control is added to the form) or programmatically (while the program is running).

You can, for example, give your book list control properties for the server name, the password, and the database to which you will connect. You do this in four steps:

1. Create a property. You must decide if you will provide a read-write, read-only, or write-only property. For this example, you'll provide read-write properties.

2. Provide an underlying value for the property. You can do this by computing the property, retrieving it from a database or, as you'll do here, storing the underlying value in a private member variable. You must also decide if you'll provide a default value for your properties.

3. Integrate the underlying values into the body of the code.

4. Set the property from the client, either declaratively (as an attribute) or programmatically.

Creating a property

There is nothing special about the property for the user control; you create it as you would any property for a class. In C#, this takes the form:

```csharp
public string ServerName
{
   get
   {
      return serverName;
   }
   set
   {
      serverName = value;
   }
}
public string Password
{
      get { return password; } set { password = value; }
}

public string DB
{
   get { return db; } set { db = value; }
}
```

In VB.NET, the code is:

```vb
Public Property ServerName As String
   Get
       Return sServerName
   End Get
   Set
       sServerName = Value
   End Set
End Property

Public Property Password As String
   Get
       Return sPassword
   End Get
   Set
```

```
        sPassword = Value
    End Set
End Property

Public Property DB As String
    Get
        Return sDB
    End Get
    Set
        sDB = Value
    End Set
End Property
```

Note that you can take advantage of C#'s case-sensitivity to differentiate the property name (such as ServerName) from the private variable representing the underlying property value (such as serverName). However, because VB.NET is case-insensitive, you must use a property name (such as ServerName) that is clearly distinctive from the private variable holding the underlying property value (such as sServerName).

When coding in C#, we tend to prefer the more extended property declaration style, as shown with ServerName. However, in this book we often use the terser form to save space, as shown for Password and DB.

Providing an underlying value for the property

You certainly can compute the value of a property, or look up the value in a database. In this example, however, you'll simply create member variables to hold the underlying value. In C#, the code is:

```
private string serverName;
private string password;
private string db = "ProgASPDotNetBugs";
```

In VB.NET, it's:

```
Private sServerName, sPassword As String
Private sDB As String = "ProgASPDotNegBugs"
```

Acting in the role of control designer, you have decided to provide a default value for the db property (the name of the database), but you have *not* provided a default value for the name of the server or the sa (system administrator) password. This is appropriate; you can safely assume the database is ProgASPDotNetBugs, but you can't possibly know in advance what database server will be used, or what the sa password is.

Integrating the property into your code

Having declared the properties, you must now modify the connection string to use the properties, rather than the hard-coded values. In C#, the code is:

```
string connectionString =
    "server= " + serverName +
```

```
        "; uid=sa;pwd=" +
        password + "; database= " + db;
```

and in VB.NET, it's:

```
Dim connectionString As String = _
    "server= " & sServerName & _
    "; uid=sa;pwd=" & _
    sPassword & "; database= " & sDB
```

Here you concatenate hard-coded string values ("server=") with the member variables that will be set through the properties. You could, as an alternative, just use the properties' Get accessors, rather than using the underlying values:

```
string connectionString =
    "server= " + ServerName +
    "; uid=sa;pwd=" +
    Password + "; database= " + DB;
```

While using the underlying value is trivially more efficient, using the property has the advantage of allowing you to change the implementation of the property without breaking this code.

Setting the property from the client

In the client you *must* now provide values for the two required attributes, ServerName and Password, and you *may* provide a value for the DB property. For example, you might write:

```
<OReilly:bookList runat="server" ID="Booklist"
DB="ProgASPDotNetBugs" Password="yourPassWord"
ServerName="YourServer"
```

Notice that in the preceding code, you have provided a value for the DB property. This code will continue to work if you leave out this attribute, but adding it makes the code self-documenting.

Handling Events

Event handling with user controls can be a bit confusing. Within a user control (e.g., bookList), you may have other controls (e.g., a list box). If those internal controls fire events, you'll need to handle them within the user control itself. The page the user control is placed in will never see those events.

That said, a user control itself can raise events. You may raise an event in response to events raised by internal controls, in response to user actions or system activity, or for any reason you choose.

Handling events in C#

You declare new events for the user control just as you would for any class. Example 14-6 shows the complete code listing for *BookList.ascx.cs*.

Example 14-6. BookList.ascx.cs

```
namespace UserControl2A1
{
   using System;
   using System.Data;
   using System.Data.SqlClient;
   using System.Drawing;
   using System.Web;
   using System.Web.UI.WebControls;
   using System.Web.UI.HtmlControls;

   public abstract class BookList : System.Web.UI.UserControl
   {
      protected System.Web.UI.WebControls.DropDownList ddlBooks;
      private string serverName;
      private string password = "oWenmEany";
      private string db = "ProgASPDotNetBugs";

      public delegate void
         ListChangedHandler(object sender, EventArgs e);
      public event ListChangedHandler ListChanged;

      protected virtual void OnListChanged(EventArgs e)
      {
         if (ListChanged != null)
            ListChanged(this, e);
      }

      public string ServerName
      {
         get
         {
            return serverName;
         }
         set
         {
            serverName = value;
         }
      }
      public string Password
      {
         get { return password; }
         set { password = value; }
      }

      public string DB
      {
         get { return db; }
         set { db = value; }
      }

      public BookList()
      {
```

Example 14-6. BookList.ascx.cs (continued)

```
      this.Init += new System.EventHandler(Page_Init);
   }

   private void Page_Load(object sender, System.EventArgs e)
   {
      if (!IsPostBack)
      {
         string connectionString =
            "server= " + ServerName +
            "; uid=sa;pwd=" +
            Password + "; database= " + DB;

         // get records from the Bugs table
         string commandString =
            "Select BookName from Books";

         // create the data set command object
         // and the DataSet
         SqlDataAdapter dataAdapter =
            new SqlDataAdapter(
            commandString, connectionString);

         DataSet dataSet = new DataSet( );

         // fill the data set object
         dataAdapter.Fill(dataSet,"Bugs");

         // Get the one table from the DataSet
         DataTable dataTable = dataSet.Tables[0];

         ddlBooks.DataSource = dataTable.DefaultView;
         ddlBooks.DataTextField = "BookName";
         ddlBooks.DataBind( );
      }

   }

   private void Page_Init(object sender, EventArgs e)
   {
      InitializeComponent( );
   }

     #region Web Form Designer generated code
   ///         Required method for Designer support - do not modify
   ///         the contents of this method with the code editor.
   /// </summary>
   private void InitializeComponent( )
   {
      this.ddlBooks.SelectedIndexChanged +=
         new System.EventHandler(this.OnSelectedIndexChanged);
      this.Load += new System.EventHandler(this.Page_Load);
```

Example 14-6. BookList.ascx.cs (continued)

```
    }
      #endregion

    public class BookListArgs : EventArgs
    {
       public string bookSelected;
    }

    private void OnSelectedIndexChanged(
       object sender, System.EventArgs e)
    {
       OnListChanged(e);
    }
  }
}
```

You start by declaring a delegate that describes the event procedure:

```
    public delegate void ListChangedHandler(object sender, EventArgs e);
```

You then declare the event itself:

```
    public event ListChangedHandler ListChanged;
```

You *must* create a method that begins with the letters "On" followed by the name of the event, as follows:

```
    protected virtual void OnListChanged(EventArgs e)
    {
    }
```

This method typically checks that the event has one or more handlers registered, and if so, it raises the event, as the following code shows:

```
    protected virtual void OnListChanged(EventArgs e)
    {
       if (ListChanged != null)
          ListChanged(this, e);
    }
```

You are now ready to test the event. For this example, go back to the list box within the book list user control and add an event handler for the selected item being changed:

```
    private void OnSelectedIndexChanged (object sender, System.EventArgs e)
    {
       OnListChanged(e);
    }
```

When the item is changed, you call the OnListChanged method, which in turn fires the ListChanged event. More about this shortly.

Your web page can add an event handler for its BookList element. The declaration in the *.aspx* page is unchanged:

```
<td><OREILLY:BOOKLIST id=Booklist runat="server"
    ServerName="yourServer" Password="yourPW"
    DB="ProgASPDotNetBugs"></OReilly:bookList></TD></TR>
```

The code-behind changes, however. To register the event, you'll need an instance of a booklist object:

```
protected UserControl3.BookList Booklist;
```

You now have only to register the event handler. Within the `InitializeComponent` method of *WebForm1.aspx.cs*, add this code:

```
this.Booklist.ListChanged +=
new UserControl3.BookList.ListChangedHandler(this.Booklist_ListChanged);
```

The event handler Booklist_ListChanged is thus wired to the ListChanged event of the booklist. When the user chooses a book, the internal list box fires a postback event, the OnSelectedIndexChanged event fires within the *.ascx* page, and the OnSelectedIndexChanged event handler within the user control responds.

When the ListChanged event is fired, it is caught in the containing page's BookList_ListChanged method, and the label is updated:

```
public void Booklist_ListChanged(object sender, System.EventArgs e)
{
    lblMsg.Text = "The list changed!!";
}
```

To the user, it appears just as it should; the list box within the user control appears just to be another control with which the user can interact, as shown in Figure 14-5.

Handling events in VB.NET

Defining a custom event, trapping the DropDownList control's SelectedIndexChanged event, raising a custom event, and handling it within the *.aspx* page are very easy and require fewer lines of code in VB.NET than in C#. Within the class definition of the BookList control, you simply declare the event and its signature, as follows:

```
Public Event ListChanged(ByVal sender As Object, ByVal e As EventArgs)
```

Since Visual Studio automatically declares the DropDownList control in the code-behind file using the `WithEvents` keyword, the control's events are automatically trapped by VB.NET, and any event handler, if one is present, is executed. Hence, you simply need to define the following event handler, which raises the custom ListChanged event:

```
Private Sub ddlBooks_SelectedIndexChanged(ByVal sender As Object, _
        ByVal e As System.EventArgs) _
        Handles ddlBooks.SelectedIndexChanged
    RaiseEvent ListChanged(sender, e)
End Sub
```

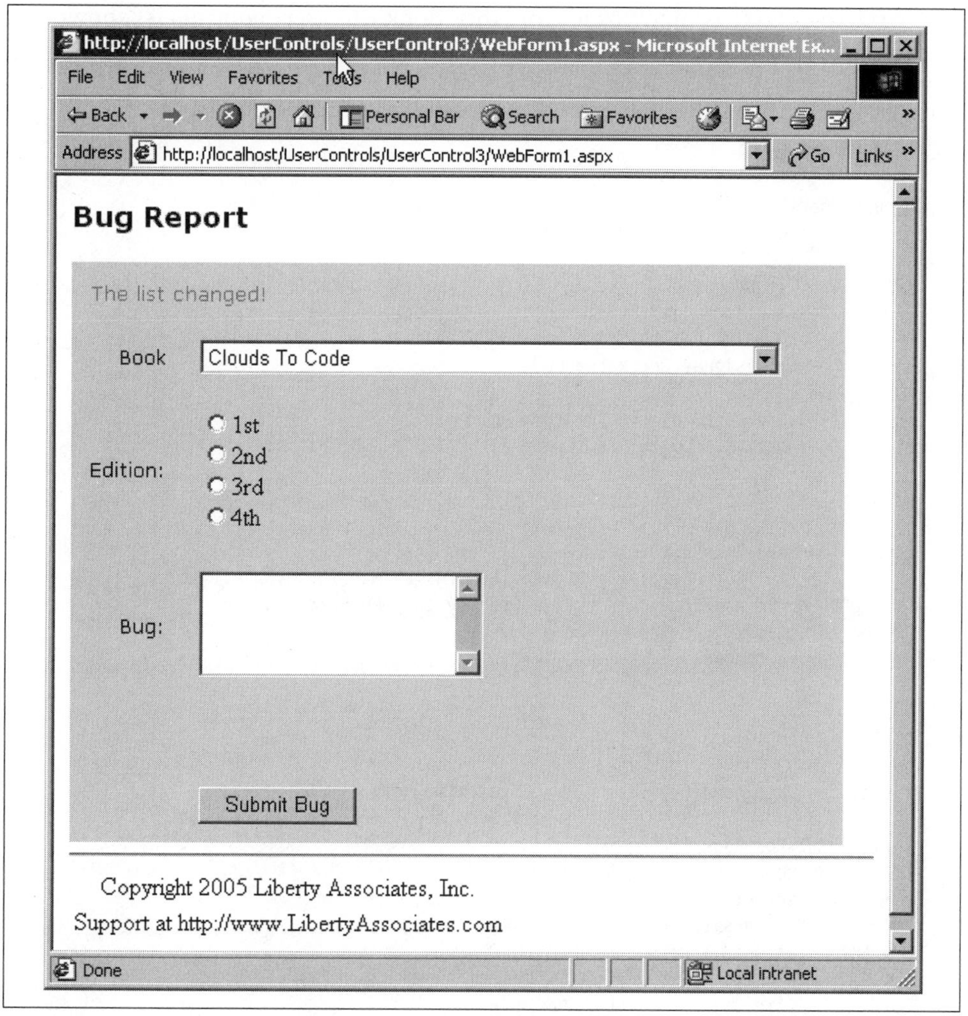

Figure 14-5. The List event fired

That's all the code that's required in the user control's code-behind file. In the ASP.NET application, you have to declare the instance of the Booklist class using the WithEvents keyword:

```
Protected WithEvents Booklist1 As UserControl1VB.Booklist
```

The final step is to provide the event handler, as follows:

```
Private Sub Booklist1_ListChanged(ByVal sender As System.Object, _
                          ByVal e As System.EventArgs) _
                          Handles Booklist1.ListChanged
    lblMsg.Text = "The list changed!!"
End Sub
```

The complete code-behind page for the Booklist user control is shown in Example 14-7.

Example 14-7. The VB.NET version of the Booklist user control's code-behind file

```
Imports System.Data.OleDb

Public MustInherit Class Booklist
    Inherits System.Web.UI.UserControl

        Protected WithEvents ddlBooks As System.Web.UI.WebControls.DropDownList
        Public Event ListChanged(ByVal sender As Object, ByVal e As EventArgs)

#Region " Web Form Designer Generated Code "

    'This call is required by the Web Form Designer.
    <System.Diagnostics.DebuggerStepThrough()> Private Sub InitializeComponent()

    End Sub

    Private Sub Page_Init(ByVal sender As System.Object, _
                          ByVal e As System.EventArgs) Handles MyBase.Init
        'CODEGEN: This method call is required by the Web Form Designer
        'Do not modify it using the code editor.
        InitializeComponent()
    End Sub

#End Region

    Private Sub Page_Load(ByVal sender As System.Object, _
                          ByVal e As System.EventArgs) Handles MyBase.Load
        If Not IsPostBack Then
            Dim connectionString As String = _
                "server= " & ServerName &
                "; uid=sa;pwd=" &
                Password & "; database= " & DB

            ' get records from the Bugs table
            Dim commandString As String = _
                "Select BookName from Books"

            ' create the data set command object
            ' and the DataSet
            Dim dataAdapter as SqlDataAdapter = _
                new SqlDataAdapter( _
                commandString, connectionString);

            Dim dataSet As DataSet = New DataSet()

            ' fill the data set object
            dataAdapter.Fill(dataSet, "Books")

            ' Get the one table from the DataSet
```

```
        Dim dataTable As DataTable = dataSet.Tables(0)

        ddlBooks.DataSource = dataTable.DefaultView
        ddlBooks.DataTextField = "BookName"
        ddlBooks.DataBind( )
    End If

  End Sub

  Private Sub ddlBooks_SelectedIndexChanged(ByVal sender As Object,_
                          ByVal e As System.EventArgs) _
                          Handles ddlBooks.SelectedIndexChanged
    RaiseEvent ListChanged(sender, e)
  End Sub

End Class
```

Custom event arguments

It would be even more useful if the control could tell the page what book was chosen. The idiom for doing so is to provide a *custom* event argument type derived from System.EventArgs. To accomplish this, you'll add a class declaration nested within the Booklist class. In C#, this takes the form:

```
public class BookListArgs : EventArgs
{
    public string bookSelected;
}
```

In VB.NET:

```
Public Class BookListArgs
    Inherits EventArgs

    Public bookSelected As String

End Class
```

You can now declare the event to use this new type of Event argument. In C#, you do this by modifying the delegate statement:

```
public delegate void ListChangedHandler(object sender, BookListArgs e);
```

In VB.NET, you modify the Event statement:

```
Public Event ListChanged(ByVal sender As Object, ByVal e As BookListArgs)
```

In C#, the event handler for the list box change event is now updated to get the selected item's text and add that to the BookListArgs object's bookSelected property:

```
private void OnSelectedIndexChanged(
    object sender, System.EventArgs e)
{
```

```
        BookListArgs bookListArgs =
            new BookListArgs();
        bookListArgs.bookSelected =
            ddlBooks.SelectedItem.ToString();
        OnListChanged(bookListArgs);
    }
```

Remember to update `OnListChanged` to take the new type of event argument:

```
protected virtual void OnListChanged(BookListArgs e)
{
    if (ListChanged != null)
        ListChanged(this, e);
}
```

In VB.NET, you just have to modify the handler for the DropDownList control's SelectedIndexChanged event:

```
Private Sub ddlBooks_SelectedIndexChanged(ByVal sender As Object, _
                    ByVal e As System.EventArgs) _
                        Handles ddlBooks.SelectedIndexChanged

    Dim bla As New BookListArgs()
    bla.bookSelected = ddlBooks.SelectedItem.ToString()
    RaiseEvent ListChanged(sender, bla)

End Sub
```

All of the changes noted so far are within the *BookList.ascx* file. The only change in the page is to the event handler itself. In C#, the code is:

```
public void Booklist_ListChanged(object sender, UserControl3.BookList.BookListArgs e)
{
    lblMsg.Text = "Selected: " + e.bookSelected;
}
```

In VB.NET, it's:

```
Private Sub Booklist1_ListChanged(ByVal sender As System.Object, _
        ByVal e As UserControl1VB.Booklist.BookListArgs) _
        Handles Booklist1.ListChanged
    lblMsg.Text = "Selected: " & e.bookSelected
End Sub
```

When you view the web page, it is now able to display the text of the selection, even though the selection event occurs within the user control, as shown in Figure 14-6.

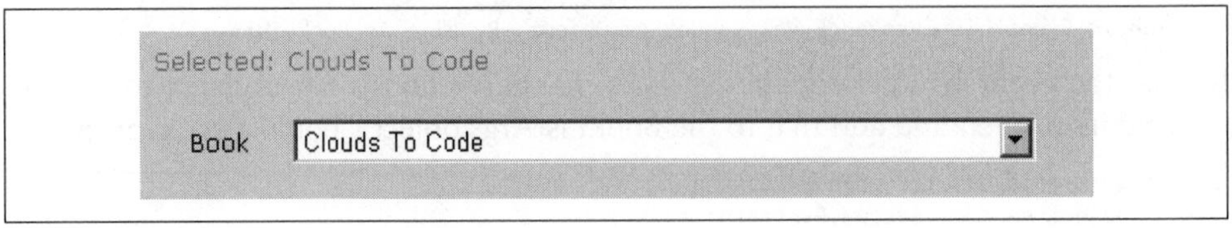

Figure 14-6. Passing text from the list box within the user control to the page

Custom Controls

In addition to creating user controls, which are essentially reusable small web pages, you can also create your own compiled custom controls. There are three ways to create custom controls:

- Create a derived custom control by deriving from an existing control.
- Create a composite control by grouping existing controls together into a new compiled control.
- Create a full custom control by deriving from System.Web.UI.WebControls. WebControl.

Composite controls are most similar to user controls. The key difference is that composite controls are compiled into a DLL and used as you would any server control.

To get started, you'll create a Web Control Library in which you'll create the various custom controls for this chapter. Open Visual Studio .NET and choose New Project. In the New Project Window, select either Visual C# Projects or Visual Basic Projects and create a Web Control Library called CustomControls, as shown in Figure 14-7.

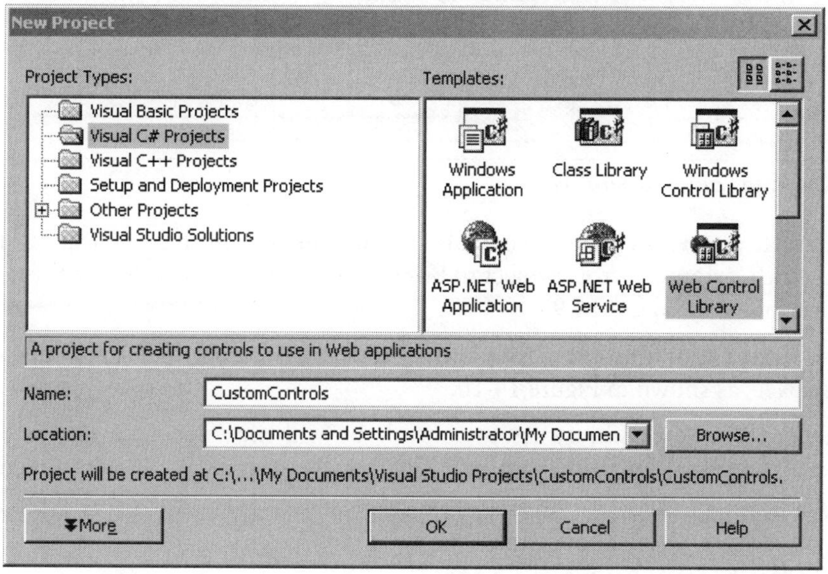

Figure 14-7. Custom control New Project window

You'll notice that Visual Studio has created a complete custom control named WebCustomControl1. Before examining this control, create a Web Application to test it. From the File menu choose New Project (Ctrl-Shift-N) and create a project named CustomControlWebPage in the same directory. Be sure to choose the "Add to Solution" radio button, as shown in Figure 14-8.

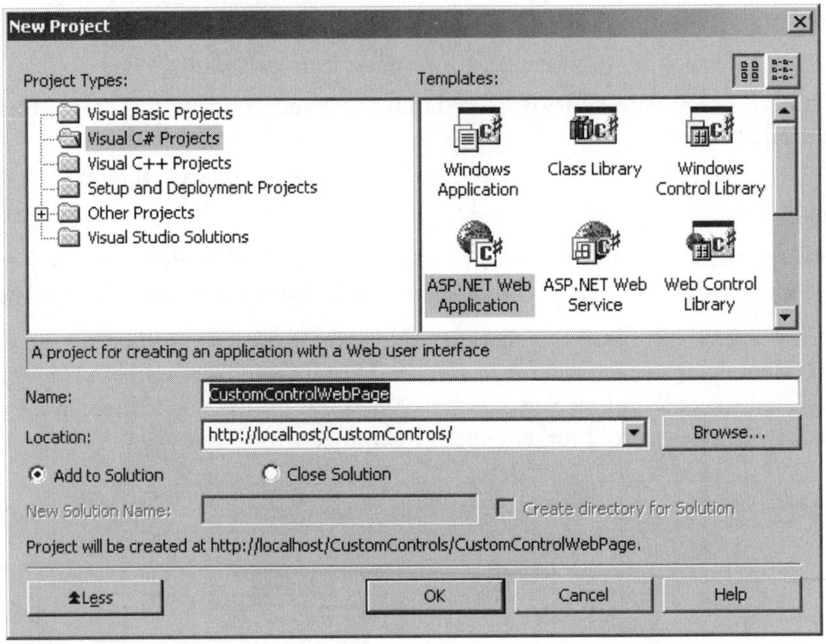

Figure 14-8. Add custom control web page

You'll create a series of custom controls and test them from this application. Right-click on the CustomControls project to bring up the context menu, and choose Properties, as shown in Figure 14-9.

Choose the configuration properties and set the output path to the same directory as the test page, as shown in Figure 14-10.

Normally, when you build a custom control you will copy the *.DLL* file to the \bin directory of the page that will test it. By setting the output to the \bin directory of your test page you will save that step and thus be able to test the control quickly.

The Default (Full) Custom Control

Visual Studio .NET has provided a custom control named WebCustomControl1, as we saw. This is a full custom control, derived from System.Web.UI.WebControls. WebControl. Even before you fully understand how this code works, you can test it

Figure 14-9. Choosing project properties

in the test page you created. Open *WebForm1.aspx* and add a statement to register the new control:

```
<%@Register TagPrefix="OReilly"
Namespace="CustomControls"
Assembly="CustomControls" %>
```

This registers the custom control with the web page, similar to how you registered the user control in Example 14-2. Once again you use the @Register tag and provide a tag prefix (OReilly). Rather than providing a Tagname and src, however, you provide a Namespace and Assembly, which uniquely identify the control and the DLL that the page must use.

You now add the control to the page. The two attributes you must set are the Runat attribute, which is needed for all server-side controls, and the Text attribute, which dictates how the control is displayed at runtime. The tag should appear as follows:

```
<OReilly:WebCustomControl1 Runat="Server" Text="Hello World!" Id="WC1" />
```

When you view this page, the text you passed in is displayed, as shown in Figure 14-11.

Example 14-8 shows the C# version of the complete custom control provided by Visual Studio .NET, while Example 14-9 shows the VB.NET version.

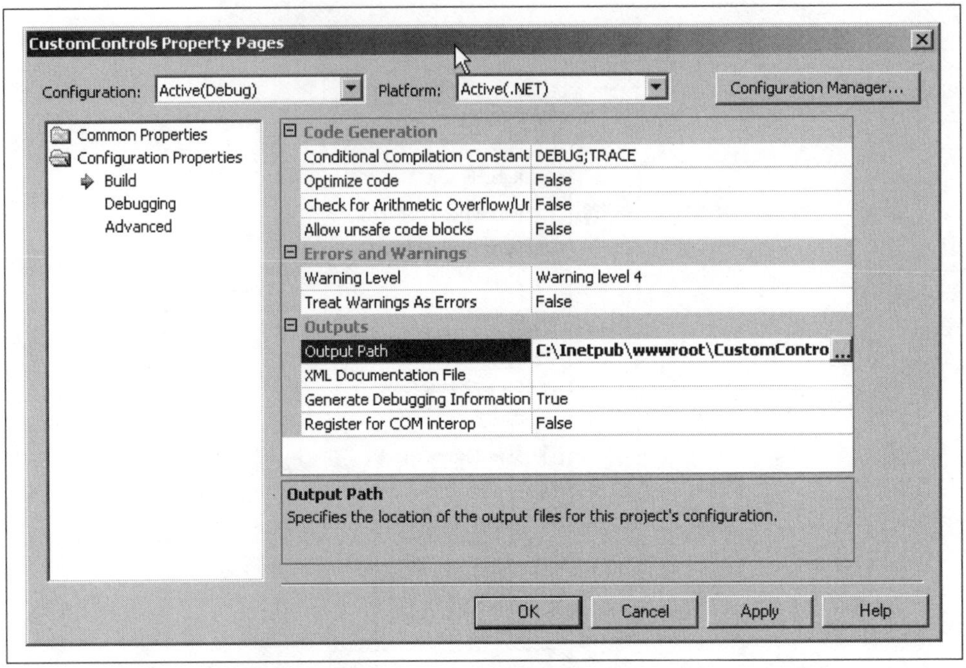

Figure 14-10. Setting the output path

Figure 14-11. Viewing the default custom control

Example 14-8. VS.NET default custom control (C#)

```csharp
using System;
using System.Web.UI;
using System.Web.UI.WebControls;
using System.ComponentModel;

namespace CustomControls
{
    [DefaultProperty("Text"),
        ToolboxData("<{0}:WebCustomControl1
            runat=server></{0}:WebCustomControl1>")]
    public class WebCustomControl1 : System.Web.UI.WebControls.WebControl
```

Example 14-8. VS.NET default custom control (C#) (continued)

```csharp
{
    private string text;

    [Bindable(true),
        Category("Appearance"),
        DefaultValue("")]
    public string Text
    {
        get
        {
            return text;
        }

        set
        {
            text = value;
        }
    }

    protected override void Render(HtmlTextWriter output)
    {
        output.Write(Text);
    }
  }
}
```

Example 14-9. VB.NET default custom control

```vbnet
Imports System.ComponentModel
Imports System.Web.UI

<DefaultProperty("Text"), ToolboxData("<{0}:WebCustomControl1 runat=server></{0}:
WebCustomControl1>")> Public Class WebCustomControl1
    Inherits System.Web.UI.WebControls.WebControl

    Dim text As String

    <Bindable(True), Category("Appearance"), DefaultValue("")> Property [Text]() As String
        Get
            Return text
        End Get

        Set(ByVal Value As String)
            text = Value
        End Set
    End Property

    Protected Overrides Sub Render(ByVal output As System.Web.UI.HtmlTextWriter)
        output.Write([Text])
    End Sub

End Class
```

This control contains a single property, Text, backed by a private string variable, text.

Note that there are attributes provided both for the property and for the class. These attributes are used by Visual Studio .NET and are not required when creating custom controls. The most common attributes for custom controls are shown in Table 14-2.

Table 14-2. Common attributes for custom controls

Attribute	Description
Bindable	Boolean. `true` indicates that VS .NET will display this control in the databindings dialog box.
Browsable	Boolean. Is the property displayed in the designer?
Category	Determines in which category this control will be displayed when the Properties dialog is sorted by category.
DefaultValue	The default value.
Description	The text you provide is displayed in the description box in the Properties panel.

Properties

Custom controls can expose properties just as any other class can. You access these properties either programmatically (e.g., in code-behind) or declaratively, by setting attributes of the custom control, as you did in the text page, and as shown here:

```
<OReilly:WebCustomControl1 Runat="Server" Text="Hello World!" />
```

The Text property of the control is accessed through the Text attribute in the web page.

In the case of the Text property and the Text attribute, the mapping between the attribute and the underlying property is straightforward because both are strings. ASP.NET will provide intelligent conversion of other types, however. For example, if the underlying type is an integer or a long, the attribute will be converted to the appropriate value type. If the value is an enumeration, ASP.NET matches the string value against the evaluation name and sets the correct enumeration value. If the value is a Boolean, ASP.NET matches the string value against the Boolean value; that is, it will match the string "True" to the Boolean value true.

The Render method

The key method of the custom control is Render. This method is declared in the base class, and must be overridden in your derived class if you wish to take control of rendering to the page. In Examples 14-8 and 14-9, the Render method uses the HtmlTextWriter object passed in as a parameter to write the string held in the Text property.

The HtmlTextWriter class derives from TextWriter and provides rich formatting capabilities. HtmlTextWriter will ensure that the elements produced are well-formed, and it will manage the attributes, including style attributes. Thus, if you want to set the text to red, you can add a color attribute, passing in an enumerated color object that you've translated to HTML, as shown here:

```
output.AddStyleAttribute("color", ColorTranslator.ToHtml(Color.Red));
```

You can set the text to be within header (<h2>) tags with the HtmlTextWriter's RenderBeginTag and RenderEndTag methods:

```
output.RenderBeginTag("h2");
output.Write(Text);
output.RenderEndTag( );
```

The result is that when the text is output, the correct tags are created, as shown in Figure 14-12. (The source output that illustrates the HTML rendered by the Html-TextWriter is circled and highlighted.)

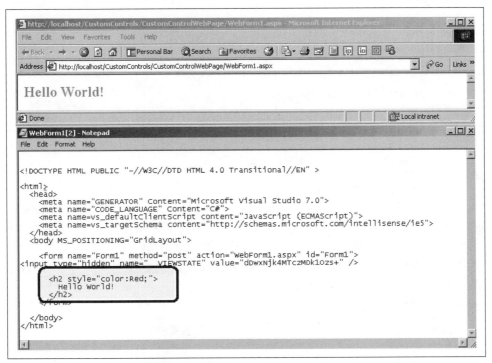

Figure 14-12. The output and its source

Maintaining state

In the next example, you'll add a button to increase the size of the text. To accomplish this, you'll eschew the rendering support of the HtmlTextWriter, instead writing the text yourself, using a new Size property (to set the size of the output text). The C# code for the Render method should appear as follows:

```
protected override void Render(HtmlTextWriter output)
{
```

```
    output.Write("<font size = " + Size + ">" + Text + "</font>");
}
```

While the VB.NET code should appear as:

```
Protected Overrides Sub Render(ByVal output As _
                             System.Web.UI.HtmlTextWriter)
    output.Write("<font size = " & Size & ">" & [Text] & "</font>")
End Sub
```

The Size property must maintain its state through the postback fired by pressing the button. This is as simple as writing to and reading from the ViewState collection maintained by the page (see Chapter 6), as shown in the C# property definition of the Size property:

```
public int Size
{
    get { return Convert.ToInt32((string) ViewState["Size"]);  }
    set { ViewState["Size"] = value.ToString(); }
}
```

In VB.NET, the Size property is defined as follows:

```
Public Property Size() As Integer
    Get
        Return Convert.ToInt32(ViewState("Size"))
    End Get
    Set(ByVal Value As Integer)
        ViewState("Size") = Value.ToString()
    End Set
End Property
```

The property Get method retrieves the value from ViewState, casts it to a string in the case of C#, and then converts that string to its integer equivalent. The property Set method stashes a string representing the size into ViewState.

To ensure that a valid value is in ViewState to start with, you'll also add a constructor to this control. In C#, the constructor is:

```
public WebCustomControl1()
{
    ViewState["Size"] = "1";
}
```

In VB.NET, it is:

```
Public Sub New()
    ViewState("Size") = "1"
End Sub
```

The constructor initializes the value held in ViewState to 1. Each press of the button will update the Size property. To make this work, you'll add a button declaration in the test page:

```
<asp:Button
    Runat="server"
```

```
        Text="Increase Size"
        OnClick="Button1_Click"
        id="Button1" />
```

The important changes here are that you've added an ID attribute (Button1) and defined an event handler for the button. You will also need to create an event handler in the code-behind page.

Be sure to add a reference to the CustomControls DLL file to the web page. That will allow Intellisense to see your object, and you'll be able to declare the control in the code-behind page. In C#, this takes the form:

```
public class WebForm1 : System.Web.UI.Page
{
    protected System.Web.UI.WebControls.Button Button1;
    protected CustomControls.WebCustomControl1 WC1;
```

In VB.NET, it takes the form:

```
Public Class WebForm1
    Inherits System.Web.UI.Page

    Protected WithEvents Button1 As System.Web.UI.WebControls.Button
    Protected WC1 As VBCustomControls.WebCustomControl1
```

You can then use that declaration to set the Size property in the event handler in C# for the button click:

```
public void Button1_Click(object sender, System.EventArgs e)
{
    WC1.Size += 1;
}
```

The VB.NET code is nearly identical:

```
Public Sub Button1_Click(ByVal sender As Object, _
                ByVal e As System.EventArgs) Handles Button1.Click
    WC1.Size += 1
End Sub
```

Example 14-10 is the complete *.aspx* page for testing, Example 14-11 is the complete C# code-behind page (with the Visual Studio .NET generated code removed to save space), and Example 14-12 is the complete C# source for the custom control. Example 14-13 is the complete VB.NET code-behind page (again, with the Visual Studio .NET-generated code removed to save space), and Example 14-14 provides the complete VB.NET source for the custom control.

Example 14-10. WebForm1.aspx

```
<%@ Page language="c#"
Codebehind="WebForm1.aspx.cs"
AutoEventWireup="false"
Inherits="CustomControlWebPage.WebForm1" %>

<%@ Register TagPrefix="OReilly"
```

Example 14-10. WebForm1.aspx (continued)

```
Namespace="CustomControls"
Assembly="CustomControls" %>

<!DOCTYPE HTML PUBLIC "-//W3C//DTD HTML 4.0 Transitional//EN" >

<HTML>
  <HEAD>

  </HEAD>
<body MS_POSITIONING="GridLayout">
<form id=Form1 method=post runat="server">

      <asp:Button Runat="server"
      Text="Increase Size"
      OnClick="Button1_Click"
      id="Button1" />

      <OReilly:WebCustomControl1
      Runat="Server"
      Text="Hello World!"
      id="WC1" />

</FORM>
  </body>
</HTML>
```

Example 14-11. WebForm1.aspx.cs

```
using System;
using System.Collections;
using System.ComponentModel;
using System.Data;
using System.Drawing;
using System.Web;
using System.Web.SessionState;
using System.Web.UI;
using System.Web.UI.WebControls;
using System.Web.UI.HtmlControls;

namespace CustomControlWebPage
{
    public class WebForm1 : System.Web.UI.Page
    {
        protected System.Web.UI.WebControls.Button Button1;
        protected CustomControls.WebCustomControl1 WC1;

        public WebForm1( )
        {
            Page.Init += new System.EventHandler(Page_Init);
        }

        // ASP.NET generated code elided from listing
```

Example 14-11. WebForm1.aspx.cs (continued)

```
    private void InitializeComponent( )
    {
       this.Button1.Click += new System.EventHandler(this.Button1_Click);
       this.Load += new System.EventHandler(this.Page_Load);
    }

    public void Button1_Click(object sender, System.EventArgs e)
    {
       WC1.Size += 1;
    }
  }
}
```

Example 14-12. WebCustomControl1.cs

```
using System;
using System.Web.UI;
using System.Web.UI.WebControls;
using System.ComponentModel;

namespace CustomControls
{
   [DefaultProperty("Text"),
      ToolboxData("<{0}:WebCustomControl1
      runat=server></{0}:WebCustomControl1>")]
   public class WebCustomControl1 : System.Web.UI.WebControls.WebControl
   {
      private string text;

      // constructor initializes the value in ViewState
      public WebCustomControl1( )
      {
         ViewState["Size"] = "1";
      }

      // Created by VS.NET
      [Bindable(true),
         Category("Appearance"),
         DefaultValue("")]
      public string Text
      {
         get {   return text; }
         set{   text = value; }
      }

      // Your custom attribute to hold the Size in ViewState
      public int Size
      {
         get { return Convert.ToInt32((string) ViewState["Size"]);  }
         set { ViewState["Size"] = value.ToString( ); }
      }
```

Example 14-12. WebCustomControl1.cs (continued)

```
    // Render method hand renders the size
    protected override void Render(HtmlTextWriter output)
    {
       output.Write("<font size = " + Size + ">" +
               Text + "</font>");
    }
  }
}
```

Example 14-13. WebForm1.aspx.vb

```
Imports CustomControls.WebCustomControl1

Public Class WebForm1
    Inherits System.Web.UI.Page

    Protected WithEvents Button1 As System.Web.UI.WebControls.Button
    Protected WC1 As VBCustomControls.WebCustomControl1

    Public Sub Button1_Click(ByVal sender As Object, _
                             ByVal e As System.EventArgs) _
                             Handles Button1.Click
      WC1.Size += 1
    End Sub
End Class
```

Example 14-14. WebCustomControl1.vb

```
Imports System.ComponentModel
Imports System.Web.UI
Imports System.Drawing

<DefaultProperty("Text"), ToolboxData("<{0}:WebCustomControl1 _
runat=server></{0}:WebCustomControl1>")> _
Public Class WebCustomControl1
   Inherits System.Web.UI.WebControls.WebControl

   Dim _text As String

   Public Sub WebCustomControl1()
      ViewState("Size") = "1"
   End Sub

    <Bindable(True), Category("Appearance"), DefaultValue("")> _
    Property [Text]() As String
       Get
          Return _text
       End Get

       Set(ByVal Value As String)
          _text = Value
       End Set
```

Example 14-14. WebCustomControl1.vb (continued)

```
    End Property

    Protected Overrides Sub Render( _
                        ByVal output As System.Web.UI.HtmlTextWriter)
        output.Write("<font size = " & Size & ">" & [Text] & "</font>")
    End Sub

    Public Property Size() As Integer
        Get
            Return Convert.ToInt32(ViewState("Size"))
        End Get
        Set(ByVal Value As Integer)
            ViewState("Size") = Value.ToString()
        End Set
    End Property

End Class
```

To illustrate the effect of clicking the button, in Figure 14-13 I created two instances of the program, and in the second instance I pressed the button three times.

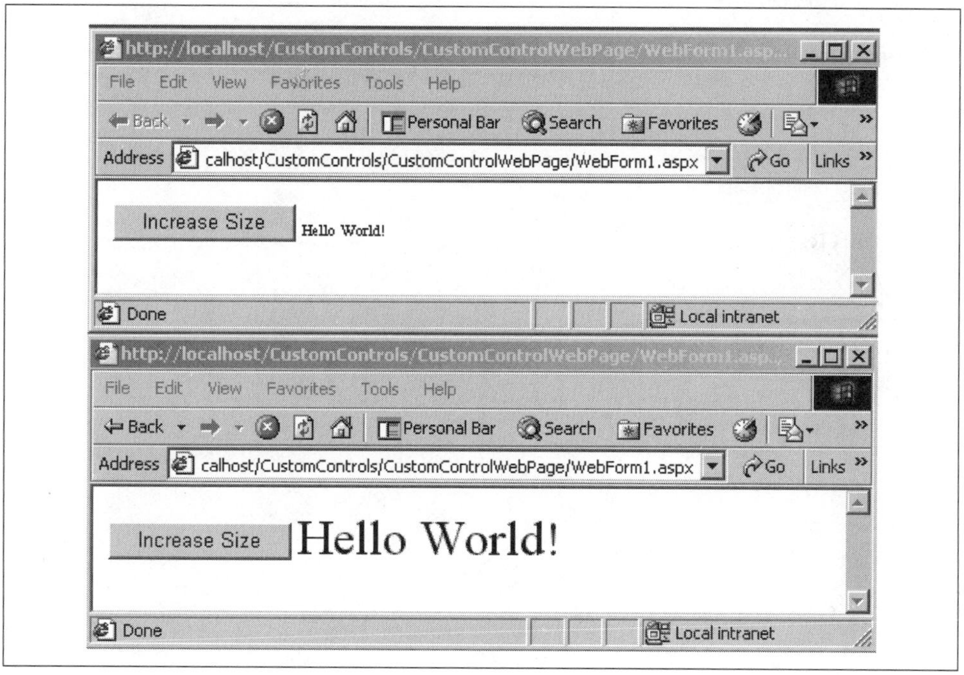

Figure 14-13. Maintaining state

Each time the button is clicked, the state variable Size is incremented; when the page is drawn, the state variable is retrieved and used to set the size of the text.

Creating Derived Controls

There are times when it is not necessary to create your own control from scratch. You may simply want to extend the behavior of an existing control type. You can derive from an existing control just as you might derive from any class.

Imagine, for example, that you would like a button to maintain a count of the number of times it has been clicked. Such a button might be useful in any number of applications, but unfortunately the web Button control does not provide this functionality.

To overcome this limitation of the button class, you'll derive a new custom control from System.Web.UI.WebControls.Button, as shown in Example 14-15 (for C#) and Example 14-16 (for VB.NET).

Example 14-15. CountedButton implementation in C#

```
using System;
using System.Web.UI;
using System.Web.UI.WebControls;
using System.ComponentModel;

namespace CustomControls
{
    // custom control derives from button
    public class CountedButton : System.Web.UI.WebControls.Button
    {

        // constructor initializes view state value
        public CountedButton( )
        {
            this.Text = "Click me";
            ViewState["Count"] = 0;
        }

        // count as property maintained in view state
        public int Count
        {
            get
            {
                return (int) ViewState["Count"];
            }

            set
            {
                ViewState["Count"] = value;
            }
        }

        // override the OnClick to increment the count,
        // update the button text and then invoke the base method
        protected override void OnClick(EventArgs e)
        {
            ViewState["Count"] =  ((int)ViewState["Count"]) + 1;
```

Example 14-15. CountedButton implementation in C# (continued)

```
        this.Text = ViewState["Count"] + " clicks";
        base.OnClick(e);
    }
  }
}
```

Example 14-16. CountedButton implementation in VB.NET

```
Imports System.ComponentModel
Imports System.Web.UI
Imports System.Web.UI.WebControls

' custom control derives from button
Public Class CountedButton
   Inherits System.Web.UI.WebControls.Button

   ' constructor initializes view state value
   Public Sub New( )
      Me.Text = "Click me"
      ViewState("Count") = 0
   End Sub

   ' count as property maintained in view state
   Public Property Count( ) As Integer
      Get
          Return CInt(ViewState("Count"))
      End Get
      Set(ByVal Value As Integer)
          ViewState("Count") = Value
      End Set
   End Property

   ' override the OnClick to increment the count,
   ' update the button text and then invoke the base method
   Protected Overrides Sub OnClick(ByVal e As EventArgs)
      ViewState("Count") = CInt(ViewState("Count")) + 1
      Me.Text = ViewState("Count") & " clicks"
      MyBase.OnClick(e)
   End Sub
End Class
```

You begin by deriving your new class from the existing Button type:

```
public class CountedButton : System.Web.UI.WebControls.Button
```

The VB.NET equivalent is:

```
Public Class CountedButton
   Inherits System.Web.UI.WebControls.Button
```

The work of this class is to maintain its state: how many times the button has been clicked. You provide a public property, Count, which is backed not by a private member variable but rather by a value stored in view state. This is necessary because the button will post the page, and the state would otherwise be lost. The Count property is defined as follows in C#:

```csharp
public int Count
{
   get
   {
      return (int) ViewState["Count"];
   }

   set
   {
      ViewState["Count"] = value;
   }
}
```

and it is defined as follows in VB.NET:

```vb
Public Property Count() As Integer
   Get
      Return CInt(ViewState("Count"))
   End Get
   Set(ByVal Value As Integer)
      ViewState("Count") = Value
   End Set
End Property
```

To retrieve the value "Count" from view state, you use the string Count as an offset into the ViewState collection. What is returned is an object that you cast to an int in C# or an Integer in VB.NET.

To ensure that the property will return a valid value, you initialize the Count property in the constructor, where you also set the initial text for the button. The constructor in C# is:

```csharp
public CountedButton()
{
   this.Text = "Click me";
   ViewState["Count"] = 0;
}
```

and in VB.NET it appears as follows:

```vb
Public Sub New()
   Me.Text = "Click me"
   ViewState("Count") = 0
End Sub
```

Because CountedButton derives from Button, it is easy to override the behavior of a Click event. In this case, when the user clicks the button, you will increment the Count value held in view state and update the text on the button to reflect the new count. You will then call the base class' OnClick method to carry on with the normal processing of the Click event. The C# event handler is as follows:

```
protected override void OnClick(EventArgs e)
{
    ViewState["Count"] =  ((int)ViewState["Count"]) + 1;
    this.Text = ViewState["Count"] + " clicks";
    base.OnClick(e);
}
```

While the source code for the VB.NET Click event handler is:

```
Protected Overrides Sub OnClick(ByVal e As EventArgs)
    ViewState("Count") = CInt(ViewState("Count")) + 1
    Me.Text = ViewState("Count") & " clicks"
    MyBase.OnClick(e)
End Sub
```

You add this control to the *.aspx* form just as you would your composite control:

```
<OReilly:CountedButton Runat="Server" id="CB1" />
```

You do not need to add an additional Register statement because this control, like the custom control, is in the CustomControls namespace and the CustomControls assembly.

When you click the button four times, the button reflects the current count of clicks, as shown in Figure 14-14.

Figure 14-14. Counted button

Creating Composite Controls

The third way to create a custom control is to combine two or more existing controls. In the next example, you will act as a contract programmer, and I will act as the client. I'd like you to build a slightly more complex control that I might use to keep track of the number of inquiries I receive about my books.

As your potential client, I might ask you to write a control that lets me put in one or more books, and each time I click on a book the control will keep track of the number of clicks for that book, as shown in Figure 14-15.

The *.aspx* file for this program is shown in Example 14-17. Its C# and VB versions are identical, except for the @ Page directive.

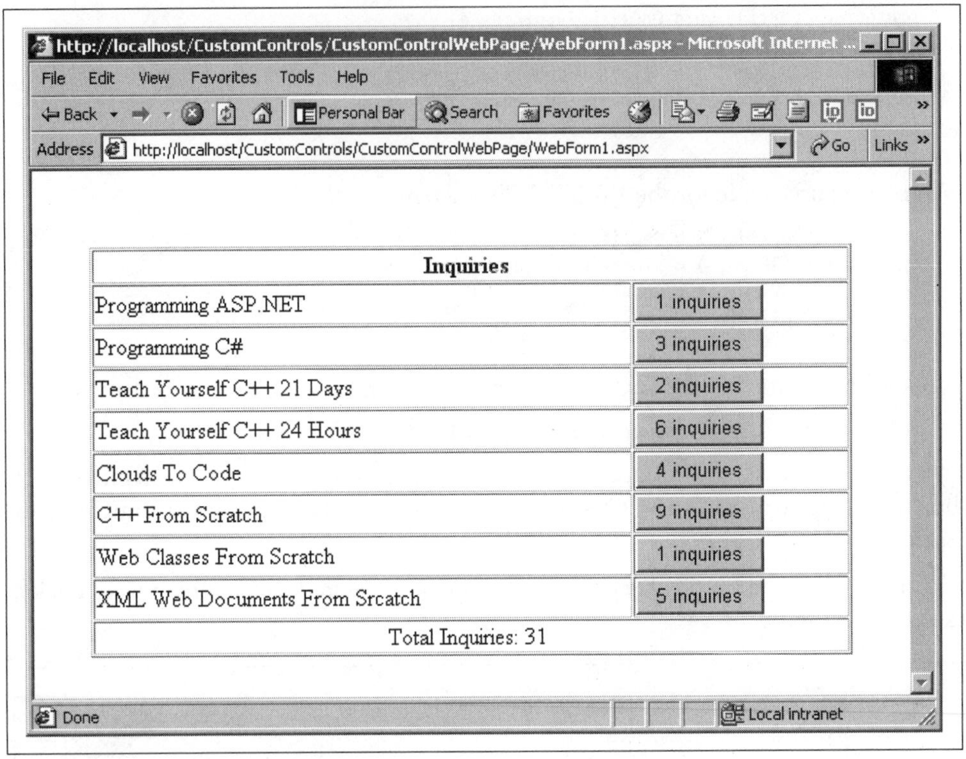

Figure 14-15. Composite control

Example 14-17. The .aspx file for the composite control

```
<%@ Page language="c#"
Codebehind="WebForm1.aspx.cs"
AutoEventWireup="false"
Inherits="CustomControlWebPage.WebForm1" %>

<%@ Register TagPrefix="OReilly" Namespace="CustomControls" Assembly="CustomControls" %>

<!DOCTYPE HTML PUBLIC "-//W3C//DTD HTML 4.0 Transitional//EN" >
<HTML>
  <HEAD>
<meta content="Microsoft Visual Studio 7.0" name=GENERATOR>
<meta content=C# name=CODE_LANGUAGE>
<meta content="JavaScript (ECMAScript)" name=vs_defaultClientScript>
<meta content=http://schemas.microsoft.com/intellisense/ie5 name=vs_targetSchema>
  </HEAD>
<body MS_POSITIONING="GridLayout">
<form id=Form1 method=post runat="server">

     <OReilly:BookInquiryList
     Runat="Server"
     id="bookInquiry1">
```

Example 14-17. The .aspx file for the composite control (continued)

```
        <OReilly:BookCounter
        Runat="server"
        BookName="Programming ASP.NET"
        ID="Bookcounter1"/>

        <OReilly:BookCounter
        Runat="server"
        BookName="Programming C#"
        ID="Bookcounter2" />

        <OReilly:BookCounter
        Runat="server"
        BookName="Teach Yourself C++ 21 Days"
        ID="BookCounter3" />

        <OReilly:BookCounter
        Runat="server"
        BookName="Teach Yourself C++ 24 Hours"
        ID="Bookcounter4" />

        <OReilly:BookCounter
        Runat="server"
        BookName="Clouds To Code"
        ID="Bookcounter5" />

        <OReilly:BookCounter
        Runat="server"
        BookName="C++ From Scratch"
        ID="Bookcounter6" />

        <OReilly:BookCounter
        Runat="server"
        BookName="Web Classes From Scratch"
        ID="Bookcounter7" />

        <OReilly:BookCounter
        Runat="server"
        BookName="XML Web Documents From Srcatch"
        ID="Bookcounter8" />

    </OReilly:BookInquiryList>

</FORM>
  </body>
</HTML>
```

The key thing to note in this code is that the BookInquiryList component contains a number of BookCounter elements. There is one BookCounter element for each book I wish to track in the control. The control is quite flexible. I can track one, eight (as shown here), or any arbitrary number of books. Each BookCounter element has a BookName attribute that is used to display the name of the book being tracked.

You can see from Figure 14-15 that each book is tracked using a CountedButton custom control, but you do not see a declaration of the CountedButton in the *.aspx* file. The CountedButton control is entirely encapsulated within the BookCounter custom control.

The entire architecture therefore is as follows:

1. The BookInquiry composite control derives from WebControl and implements INamingContainer, as described shortly.

2. The BookInquiry control has a Controls property that it inherits from the Control class (through WebControl) and that returns a collection of child controls.

3. Within this Controls collection is an arbitrary number of BookCounter controls.

4. BookCounter is itself a composite control that derives from WebControl and that also implements INamingContainer.

   a. Each instance of BookContainer has two properties, BookName and Count.

   b. The Name property is backed by view state and is initialized through the BookName BookName in the *.aspx* file

   c. The Count property delegates to a private CountedButton object, which is instantiated in BookContainer.CreateChildControls( ).

The BookInquiry object has only two purposes: it acts as a container for the Book-Counter objects, and it is responsible for rendering itself and ensuring that its contained BookCounter objects render themselves on demand.

The best way to see how all this works is to work your way through the code from the inside out. The most contained object is the CountedButton.

Modifying the CountedButton derived control

CountedButton needs only minor modification, as shown in Example 14-18 for C# and Example 14-19 for VB.NET.

Example 14-18. The modified CountedButton.cs file

```
using System;
using System.Web.UI;
using System.Web.UI.WebControls;
using System.ComponentModel;

namespace CustomControls
{
    // custom control derives from button
    public class CountedButton : System.Web.UI.WebControls.Button
    {

        private string displayString;

        // default constructor
        public CountedButton( )
```

Example 14-18. The modified CountedButton.cs file (continued)

```csharp
        {
            displayString = "clicks";
            InitValues( );
        }

        // overloaded, takes string to display (e.g., 5 books)
        public CountedButton(string displayString)
        {
            this.displayString = displayString;
            InitValues( );
        }

        // called by constructors
        private void InitValues( )
        {
            if (ViewState["Count"] == null)
                ViewState["Count"] = 0;
            this.Text = "Click me";
        }

        // count as property maintained in view state
        public int Count
        {
            get
            {
                // initialized in constructor
                // can not be null
                return (int) ViewState["Count"];
            }

            set
            {
                ViewState["Count"] = value;
            }
        }

        // override the OnClick to increment the count,
        // update the button text and then invoke the base method
        protected override void OnClick(EventArgs e)
        {
            ViewState["Count"] = ((int)ViewState["Count"]) + 1;
            this.Text = ViewState["Count"] + " " + displayString;
            base.OnClick(e);
        }
    }
}
```

Example 14-19. The modified CountedButton.vb file

```vb
Imports System.ComponentModel
Imports System.Web.UI
Imports System.Web.UI.WebControls
```

Example 14-19. The modified CountedButton.vb file (continued)

```vb
' custom control derives from button
Public Class CountedButton
    Inherits System.Web.UI.WebControls.Button

    Private displayString As String

    ' constructor initializes view state value
    Public Sub New()
        displayString = "clicks"
        Init()
    End Sub

   ' overloaded, takes string to display (e.g., 5 books)
    Public Sub New(ByVal displayString As String)
        Me.displayString = displayString
        Init()
    End Sub

    ' called by constructors
    Private Shadows Sub Init()
        If ViewState("Count") = Is Nothing Then
            ViewState("Count") = 0
            Me.Text = "Click me"
        End If
    End Sub

    ' count as property maintained in view state
    Public Property Count() As Integer
        Get
            Return CInt(ViewState("Count"))
        End Get
        Set(ByVal Value As Integer)
            ViewState("Count") = Value
        End Set
    End Property

    ' override the OnClick to increment the count,
    ' update the button text and then invoke the base method
    Protected Overrides Sub OnClick(ByVal e As EventArgs)
        ViewState("Count") = CInt(ViewState("Count")) + 1
        Me.Text = CStr(ViewState("Count")) & " " & displayString
        MyBase.OnClick(e)
    End Sub
End Class
```

Because you want the button to be able to display the string 5 Inquiries rather than 5 clicks, you must change the line within the OnClick method that sets the button's text:

```
this.Text = ViewState["Count"] + " " + displayString;
```

The VB.NET equivalent is:

```
Me.Text = ViewState("Count") & " " & displayString
```

Rather than hard-wiring the string, you'll use a private member variable, display-String, to store a value passed in to the constructor:

```
private string displayString;
```

In VB.NET, you'd use:

```
Private displayString As String
```

You must set this string in the constructor. To protect client code that already uses the default constructor (with no parameters), you'll overload the constructor, adding a version that takes a string:

```
public CountedButton(string displayString)
{
    this.displayString = displayString;
    Init();
}
```

In VB.NET, the code is:

```
Public Sub New(ByVal displayString As String)
    Me.displayString = displayString
    Initialize()
End Sub
```

You can now modify the default constructor to set the displayString member variable to a reasonable default value. In C#, the code is:

```
public CountedButton()
{
    displayString = "clicks";
    InitValues();
}
```

In VB.NET, use:

```
Public Sub New()
    displayString = "clicks"
    Init()
End Sub
```

The code common to both constructors has been factored out to the private helper method Init, which ensures that the Count property is initialized to zero and sets the initial text for the button:

```
private void Init()
{
    if (ViewState["Count"] == null)
        ViewState["Count"] = 0;
    this.Text = "Click me";
}
```

In VB.NET, the same thing is accomplished using:

```
Private Shadows Sub Init( )
    If ViewState("Count") = Nothing Then
        ViewState("Count") = 0
        Me.Text = "Click me"
    End If
End Sub
```

With these changes, the CountedButton is ready to be used in the first composite control, BookCounter.

Creating the BookCounter composite control

The BookCounter composite control is responsible for keeping track of and displaying the number of inquiries about an individual book. Its complete source code is shown in C# in Example 14-20 and in VB.NET in Example 14-21.

Example 14-20. BookCounter.cs

```
using System;
using System.Web.UI;
using System.Web.UI.WebControls;
using System.ComponentModel;

namespace CustomControls
{
    public class BookCounter :
        System.Web.UI.WebControls.WebControl,
        INamingContainer
    {

        // intialize the counted button member
        CountedButton btn = new CountedButton("inquiries");

        public string BookName
        {
            get
            {
                return (string) ViewState["BookName"];
            }

            set
            {
                ViewState["BookName"] = value;
            }
        }

        public int Count
        {
            get
            {
                return btn.Count;
```

Example 14-20. BookCounter.cs (continued)

```
        }
        set
        {
            btn.Count = value;
        }
    }

    public void Reset( )
    {
        btn.Count = 0;
    }

    protected override void CreateChildControls( )
    {
        Controls.Add(btn);
    }
    }
}
```

Example 14-21. BookCounter.vb

```vb
Imports System
Imports System.Web.UI
Imports System.Web.UI.WebControls
Imports System.ComponentModel

Public Class BookCounter
    Inherits System.Web.UI.WebControls.WebControl
    Implements INamingContainer

    ' intialize the counted button member
    Public btn As CountedButton = New CountedButton("inquiries")

    Public Property BookName( ) As String
        Get
            Return CStr(ViewState("BookName"))
        End Get
        Set(ByVal Value As String)
            ViewState("BookName") = Value
        End Set
    End Property

    Public Property Count( ) As Integer
        Get
            Return btn.Count
        End Get
        Set(ByVal Value As Integer)
            btn.Count = Value
        End Set
    End Property

    Public Sub Reset( )
```

Example 14-21. BookCounter.vb (continued)

```
        btn.Count = 0
    End Sub

    Protected Overrides Sub CreateChildControls()
        Controls.Add(btn)
    End Sub

End Class
```

INamingContainer. The first thing to note about the BookCounter class is that it implements the INamingContainer interface. This is a "marker" interface that has no methods. The purpose of this interface is to identify a container control that creates a new ID namespace, guaranteeing that all child controls have IDs that are unique to the application.

Containing CountedButton. The BookCounter class contains an instance of Counted-Button:

```
    CountedButton btn = new CountedButton("inquiries");
```

or:

```
    Public btn As CountedButton = New CountedButton("inquiries")
```

The btn member is instantiated in the CreateChildControls method inherited from System.Control:

```
    protected override void CreateChildControls()
    {
        Controls.Add(btn);
    }
```

The VB.NET equivalent is:

```
    Protected Overrides Sub CreateChildControls()
        Controls.Add(btn)
    End Sub
```

CreateChildControls is called in preparation for rendering and offers the Book-Counter class the opportunity to add the btn object as a contained control.

There is no need for BookCounter to override the Render method; the only thing it must render is the CountedButton, which can render itself. The default behavior of Render is to render all the child controls, so you need not do anything special to make this work.

BookCounter also has two properties: BookName and Count. BookName is a string to be displayed in the control and is managed through ViewState. Its C# source code is:

```
    public string BookName
    {
        get
        {
```

```
        return (string) ViewState["BookName"];
    }

    set
    {
        ViewState["BookName"] = value;
    }
}
```

Its VB.NET source code is:

```
Public Property BookName( ) As String
    Get
        Return CStr(ViewState("BookName"))
    End Get
    Set(ByVal Value As String)
        ViewState("BookName") = Value
    End Set
End Property
```

Count is the count of inquires about this particular book; responsibility for keeping track of this value is delegated to the CountedButton. In C#, the code is:

```
public int Count
{
    get
    {
        return btn.Count;
    }
    set
    {
        btn.Count = value;
    }
}
```

and in VB.NET, it's:

```
Public Property Count( ) As Integer
    Get
        Return btn.Count
    End Get
    Set(ByVal Value As Integer)
        btn.Count = Value
    End Set
End Property
```

There is no need to place the value in ViewState, since the button itself is responsible for its own data.

Creating the BookInquiryList composite control

Each of the BookCounter objects is contained within the Controls collection of the BookInquiryList. This control has no properties or state. Its only method is Render, as shown in C# in Example 14-22 and in VB.NET in Example 14-23.

Example 14-22. BookInquiryList source in C#

```csharp
[ControlBuilderAttribute(typeof(BookCounterBuilder)),ParseChildren(false)]
public class BookInquiryList : System.Web.UI.WebControls.WebControl, INamingContainer
{

    protected override void Render(HtmlTextWriter output)
    {
        int totalInquiries = 0;
        BookCounter current;

        // Write the header
        output.Write("<Table border='1' width='90%' cellpadding='1'" +
            "cellspacing='1' align = 'center' >");
        output.Write("<TR><TD colspan = '2' align='center'>");
        output.Write("<B> Inquiries </B></TD></TR>");

        // if you have no contained controls, write the default msg.
        if (Controls.Count == 0)
        {
            output.Write("<TR><TD colspan = '2'> align='center'");
            output.Write("<B> No books listed </B></TD></TR>");
        }
        // otherwise render each of the contained controls
        else
        {
            // iterate over the controls colelction and
            // display the book name for each
            // then tell each contained control to render itself
            for (int i = 0; i < Controls.Count; i++)
            {
                current = (BookCounter) Controls[i];
                totalInquiries += current.Count;
                output.Write("<TR><TD align='left'>" +
                    current.BookName + "</TD>");
                output.RenderBeginTag("TD");
                current.RenderControl(output);
                output.RenderEndTag();   // end td
                output.Write("</tr>");
            }
            output.Write("<TR><TD colspan='2' align='center'> " +
                " Total Inquiries: " +
                totalInquiries + "</TD></TR>");
        }
        output.Write("</TABLE>");
    }
}
```

Example 14-23. BookInquiryList source in VB.NET

```vbnet
Imports System.ComponentModel
Imports System.Web.UI
```

Example 14-23. BookInquiryList source in VB.NET (continued)

```vbnet
<ControlBuilder(GetType(BookCounterBuilder)), ParseChildren(False)> _
Public Class BookInquiryList
    Inherits System.Web.UI.WebControls.WebControl
    Implements INamingContainer

    Protected Overrides Sub Render(ByVal output As HtmlTextWriter)

        Dim totalInquiries As Integer = 0

        ' Write the header
        output.Write("<Table border='1' width='90%' cellpadding='1'" & _
            "cellspacing='1' align = 'center' >")
        output.Write("<TR><TD colspan = '2' align='center'>")
        output.Write("<B> Inquiries </B></TD></TR>")

        ' if you have no contained controls, write the default msg.
        If Controls.Count = 0 Then
            output.Write("<TR><TD colspan = '2'> align='center'")
            output.Write("<B> No books listed </B></TD></TR>")
            ' otherwise render each of the contained controls
        Else
            ' iterate over the controls colelction and
            ' display the book name for each
            ' then tell each contained control to render itself
            Dim current As BookCounter

            For Each current In Controls
                totalInquiries += current.Count
                output.Write("<TR><TD align='left'>" & _
                    current.BookName + "</TD>")
                output.RenderBeginTag("TD")
                current.RenderControl(output)
                output.RenderEndTag()              ' end td
                output.Write("</tr>")
            Next
            Dim strTotalInquiries As String
            strTotalInquiries = totalInquiries.ToString
            output.Write("<TR><TD colspan='2' align='center'> " & _
                " Total Inquiries: " & _
                CStr(strTotalInquiries) & "</TD></TR>")
        End If
        output.Write("</TABLE>")
    End Sub

End Class

Friend Class BookCounterBuilder
    Inherits ControlBuilder

    Public Overrides Function GetChildControlType( _
        ByVal tagName As String, ByVal attributes As IDictionary) As Type
        If tagName = "BookCounter" Then
```

Example 14-23. BookInquiryList source in VB.NET (continued)

```
        Dim x As BookCounter
        Return x.GetType
    Else
        Return Nothing
    End If
End Function

Public Overrides Sub AppendLiteralString(ByVal s As String)
End Sub

End Class
```

ControlBuilder and ParseChildren attributes. The BookCounter class must be associated with the BookInquiryClass so ASP.NET can translate the elements in the *.aspx* page into the appropriate code. This is accomplished using the `ControlBuilder` attribute:

```
[ControlBuilderAttribute(typeof(BookCounterBuilder)),ParseChildren(false)]
```

The argument to the `ControlBuilderAttribute` is a Type object that you obtain by passing in BookCounterBuilder, a class you will define to return the type of the BookCounter class given a tag named BookCounter. The code for the BookCounter-Builder is shown in C# in Example 14-24 and in VB.NET in Example 14-25.

Example 14-24. C# version of BookCounterBuilder

```
internal class BookCounterBuilder : ControlBuilder
{
    public override Type GetChildControlType(
        string tagName, IDictionary attributes)
    {
        if (tagName == "BookCounter")
            return typeof(BookCounter);
        else
            return null;
    }

    public override void AppendLiteralString(string s)
    {
    }
}
```

Example 14-25. VB.NET version of BookCounterBuilder

```
Friend Class BookCounterBuilder
    Inherits ControlBuilder

    Public Overrides Function GetChildControlType(_
        ByVal tagName As String, ByVal attributes As Idictionary) As Type
        If tagName = "BookCounter" Then
            Dim x As BookCounter
            Return x.GetType
```

Example 14-25. VB.NET version of BookCounterBuilder (continued)

```
      Else
         Return Nothing
      End If
   End Function

   Public Overrides Sub AppendLiteralString(ByVal s As String)
   End Sub
```

```
End Class
```

ASP.NET will use this BookCounterBuilder, which derives from ControlBuilder, to determine the type of the object indicated by the BookCounter tag. Through this association, each of the BookCounter objects will be instantiated and added to the Controls collection of the BookInquiryClass.

The second attribute, ParseChildren, must be set to false to tell ASP.NET that you have handled the children attributes and no further parsing is required. A value of false indicates that the nested child attributes are not properties of the outer object, but rather are child controls.

Render. The only method of the BookInquiryClass is the override of Render. The purpose of Render is to draw the table shown earlier in Figure 14-15, using the data managed by each of the BookCounter child controls.

The BookInquiryClass provides a count of the total number of inquiries, as shown in Figure 14-16.

The code tallies inquiries by initializing an integer variable, totalInquiries, to zero and then iterating over each control in turn, asking the control for its Count property. The statement is the same in C# and VB.NET, except for the closing semicolon in C#:

```
   totalInquiries += current.Count;
```

The Count property of the control delegates to the CountedButton's count property, as you can see if you step through this code in a debugger, as illustrated in Figure 14-17.

Rendering the output. That same loop renders each of the child controls by iterating over each of the controls. In C#, this is done using:

```
   for (int i = 0; i < Controls.Count; i++)
   {
      current = (BookCounter) Controls[i];
      totalInquiries += current.Count;
      output.Write("<TR><TD align='left'>" +
         current.BookName + "</TD>");
      output.RenderBeginTag("TD");
```

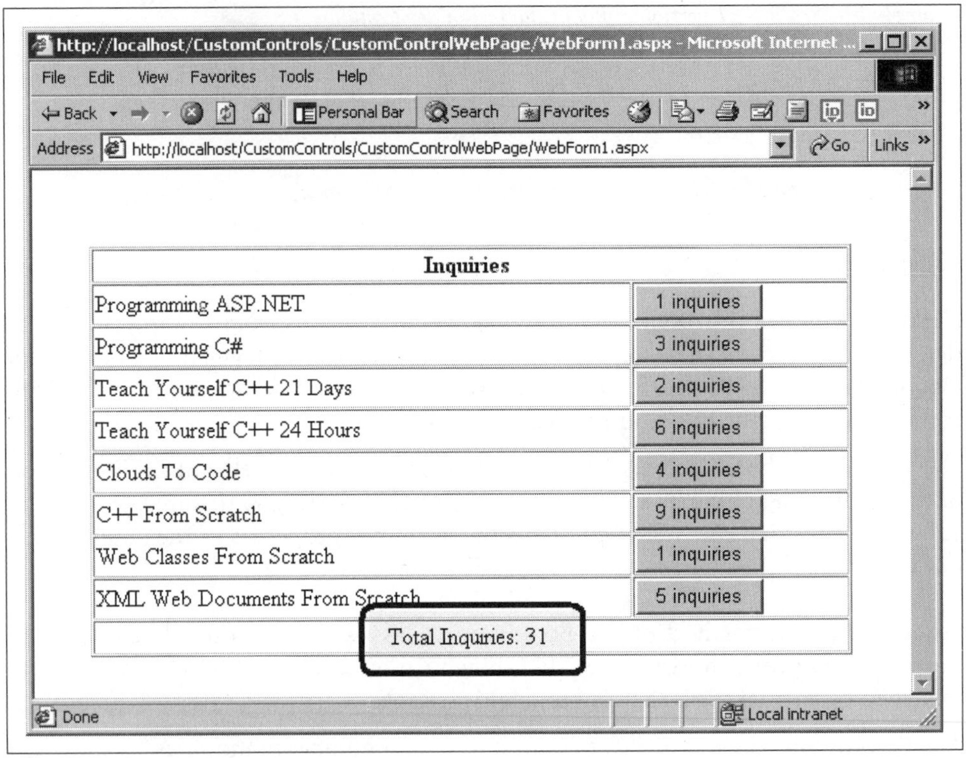

Figure 14-16. Total inquiries displayed

```
        current.RenderControl(output);
        output.RenderEndTag( );   // end td
        output.Write("</tr>");
    }
```

In VB.NET, the code is:

```
For Each current in Controls
    totalInquiries += current.Count
    output.Write("<TR><TD align='left'>" & _
        current.BookName + "</TD>")
    output.RenderBeginTag("TD")
    current.RenderControl(output)
    output.RenderEndTag( )                ' end td
    output.Write("</tr>")
Next
```

The local BookCounter object, current, is assigned to each object in the Controls collection in succession:

```
for (int i = 0; i < Controls.Count; i++)
{
    current = (BookCounter) Controls[i];
```

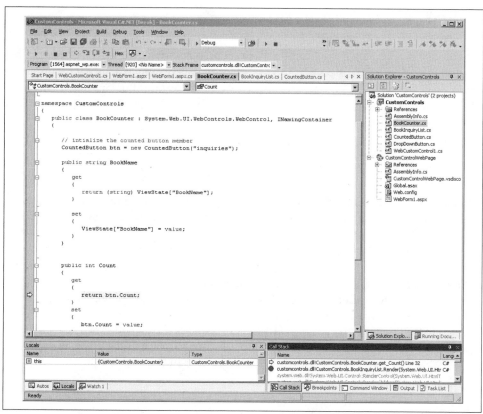

Figure 14-17. Stepping into BookCounter.Count

With that object, you are able to get the Count, as described previously:

```
totalInquiries += current.Count;
```

and then you proceed to render the object. The HtmlTextWriter is used first to create a row and to display the name of the book, using the BookName property of the current BookCounter object:

```
output.Write("<TR><TD align='left'>" +
    current.BookName + "</TD>");
```

You then render a TD tag, and within that tag you tell the BookCounter object to render itself. Finally, you render an ending TD tag using RenderEndTag, and an ending row tag using the Write method of the HTMLTextWriter:

```
output.RenderBeginTag("TD");
 current.RenderControl(output);
 output.RenderEndTag( );  // end td
 output.Write("</tr>");
```

When you tell the contained control to render itself:

```
current.RenderControl(output);
```

the Render method of BookCounter is called. Since you have not overridden this method, the Render method of the base class is called, which tells each contained object to render itself. The only contained object is CountedButton. Since you have not overridden Render in CountedButton, the base Render method in Button is called, and the button is rendered.

Assignment of Responsibilities

This simple example of a composite control is interesting because the various responsibilities are spread among the participating objects. The BookInquiryList object assumes all responsibility for laying out the control, creating the table, and deciding what will be rendered where. However, it delegates responsibility for rendering the button object to the individual contained controls.

Similarly, the BookInquiryList is responsible for the total number of inquiries—because that information transcends what any individual BookCounter object might know. However, the responsibility for the count held by each BookCounter is delegated to the BookCounter itself. As far as the BookInquiryList is concerned, it gets that information directly from the BookCounter's Count property. It turns out, however, that BookCounter in turn delegates that responsibility to the CountedButton.

Rendering the summary. Once all of the child controls have been rendered, the BookInquiryList creates a new row to display the total inquiries:

```
output.Write("<TR><TD colspan='2' align='center'> " +
   " Total Inquiries: " +
   totalInquiries + "</TD></TR>");
```

Web Services Overview

The World Wide Web has opened up distributed computing on a large scale. However, normal web pages only allow interaction between the client browser and the web server hosting the web page. The goal of web services is to create web-based applications that interact with other applications with no user interface. If you're a web page developer, having such web services available can greatly increase your productivity. Imagine, for instance, you are creating a web site for a stock brokerage firm. Rather than having to integrate your back-end database with all the various databases of the different stock exchanges, your application can simply communicate with their web services, exchanging data in XML format.

Web services are very similar to web pages. The principal difference is that a web page is intended for viewing by a person, while a web service is used strictly for one program to interact with another and has no user interface.

Web services are entirely independent of the operating system or programming language used on either the server or the client side. Unlike previous technologies for distributed computing, such as DCOM, web services make it unnecessary for either end of the connection to be running the same operating system or to be programmed in the same language. For example, the server code might be written in VB.NET on Windows 2000 while the client is C++ running on a Unix machine, or vice versa. In other words, while previous technologies required that the client and server be tightly coupled, web services permit the client and server to be loosely coupled.

All that is necessary is that both server and client support the industry standard protocols HTTP, SOAP, and XML. HTTP is the protocol used by the Web. SOAP (Simple Object Access Protocol) is a lightweight, object-oriented protocol based on XML, which in turn is a cross-platform standard for formatting and organizing information.

This chapter provides a high-level view of what web services are and how they work. It describes, briefly, the standard protocols that make web services possible, as well as introducing how web services are created and consumed.

Chapter 16 covers in detail what is actually involved in creating web services. Through the development of a simple stock ticker, it demonstrates how to create a web service using either a text editor or Visual Studio .NET. It also shows you how to create a discovery file and how to deploy the web service.

Chapter 17 looks at web services from the other side of the fence, i.e., from the consumer's point of view. This chapter builds on the stock ticker web service created in Chapter 16 to create a client web application that consumes, or uses, the stock ticker web service. Again, we demonstrate doing this using both a text editor and Visual Studio .NET.

How Web Services Work

Web services allow an object on the server to expose program logic to clients over the Internet. Clients call exposed methods on the web service using standard Internet protocols. In short, a web service is merely a function or method call over the Internet.

The web services infrastructure has several defining characteristics:

- Both the web service server and the client application are connected to the Internet and are able to communicate with any other device connected to the Internet.

- The data format with which the two ends of the connection communicate conforms to the same open standard. This standard is usually the SOAP protocol. SOAP messages consist of self-describing, text-based XML documents. It is also possible to communicate via HTTP-GET or HTTP–POST requests.

- The systems at the two ends of the connection are loosely coupled. In other words, web services do not care what operating system, object model, or programming language is used on either end of the connection, as long as both the web service and the consuming application are able to send and receive messages that conform to the proper protocol standard.

The logic behind the web services process is shown schematically in Figure 15-1.

In Figure 15-1 at position 1, a web service consumer (i.e., a program that uses a particular web service, sometimes called the consuming program) makes a call to the web service (position 2). The consumer thinks it is talking directly to the web service over the Internet. This is only an illusion.

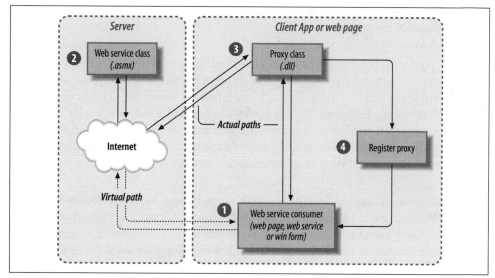

Figure 15-1. What goes on behind a web service

The actual call is being made to a proxy class (position 3) which is local to the consumer. The proxy handles all the complex infrastructure of sending the request over the Internet to the server machine, as well as getting results back and presenting them to the consumer.

All of this is made possible because the proxy was previously registered with the consuming application (position 4). This is done by the developer of the consuming application.

This chapter, along with the next two chapters, will explain in detail all of the concepts outlined in Figure 15-1.

In addition to creating and consuming the web service, there are other aspects to consider. These include:

Protocol

> The web service must communicate with the client, and vice versa, in a manner that both sides will understand.

Directories

> Web services will be developed by literally thousands or tens of thousands of companies. Directories will be created to list these services and make them available to developers. For directories to be useful, however, there must be conventions for discovery and description.

> *Discovery*

>> Potential clients will need to locate, or *discover*, documents that describe the web service. Thus, the service will often provide discovery documents— XML

files that contain information allowing potential clients to find other files that describe the web service.

Description

Once a web service has been identified, either through discovery or other means, it must make available a document that describes the protocols it supports and the programmatic interface to its usage. The Web Services Description Language (WSDL) is used to describe the web service and all of its exposed methods with their parameters. In short, the description indicates what methods the web service exposes, what parameters those methods require, and what data the methods return.

Security

Many servers connected to the Internet are set up to be very conscious of security, with firewalls and other means of blocking all traffic except that which is deemed not harmful. Web services must live within these security constraints. Web services must not be portals for malicious people or software to enter your network.

Also, it is often necessary to restrict access to specific clients. For example, suppose you are developing a stock ticker for a brokerage firm. You might want to restrict access to the web service to paying clients, excluding anyone who has not paid a usage fee.

Security for both web pages and web services is covered in detail in Chapter 19.

State

Like web pages, web services use HTTP, which is a stateless protocol. And as with web pages, the .NET Framework provides tools to preserve state, if the application requires this.

Developing a Web Service

The process of developing a web service is nearly identical to developing a web page:

- All the source files comprising both web pages and services are flat text files. They can be created and edited in any text editor, then compiled using a command-line tool from a command prompt.

- Both web pages and services can be created in Visual Studio .NET.

- Both web pages and web services can use code-behind. Code-behind is generally considered a technique intended to separate visual content from programmatic content in web pages. As such, its use in web services is less imperative, since a web service does not have any visual content. However, since Visual Studio .NET uses code-behind for every web project, whether visual or not, it gets used for web services as well. In fact, when using Visual Studio .NET to create web services, just as with web pages, code-behind is used by default. (For a full discussion of code-behind, see Chapter 6.)

- Both web pages and web services make full use of the CLR and the .NET Framework.

However, while a web page is defined by its *.aspx* file, a web service is defined by its *.asmx* file.

Creating web services will be covered in detail in Chapter 16. For now, think of a web service as a web page without any user interface or visual components in which some (but not necessarily all) of the methods or functions in the web service class are exposed to outside requests as *web methods*. Web services allow method calls over the Internet.

Once the *.asmx* page is complete, the web service class must be compiled into a dynamic link library (*.dll*) file, the form in which it is made available to requests. You can compile either from a command prompt or through Visual Studio .NET. Both techniques have advantages and disadvantages; Chapter 16 will demonstrate both.

You can easily test the *.asmx* file by entering its URL into any browser, as shown in Figure 15-2. This test shows a list of usable links to each of the web methods exposed by the web service. It also displays useful information and links pertaining to its deployment, including code samples in both VB.NET and C#.

Creating the Proxy

Before a client application can use a web service, a proxy must be created. A *proxy* is a substitute, a stand-in, for the actual code you want to call. It is responsible for *marshalling*—or managing—the call across machine boundaries. Requests to the web service *dll* on the server must conform to the proper protocol and format, usually SOAP and/or HTTP. You could write all the code to serialize and send the proper data to the web service yourself, but that would be a lot of work. The proxy does it all for you.

The proxy is registered with the client application. Then the client application makes method calls *as though it were calling a local dll*. The proxy does all the work of taking your calls, wrapping them in the proper format, and sending them as a SOAP request to the server. When the server returns the SOAP package to the client, the proxy decodes everything and presents it to the client application as though it were returning from local calls. This process is shown schematically in Figure 15-3.

To make this work, a developer must create the proxy and register it with the client application under development. This registration consists of a list of the exposed web methods and their signatures. The owner of the web service can add new web methods or update existing ones without changing their signature, and the existing proxy will not break.

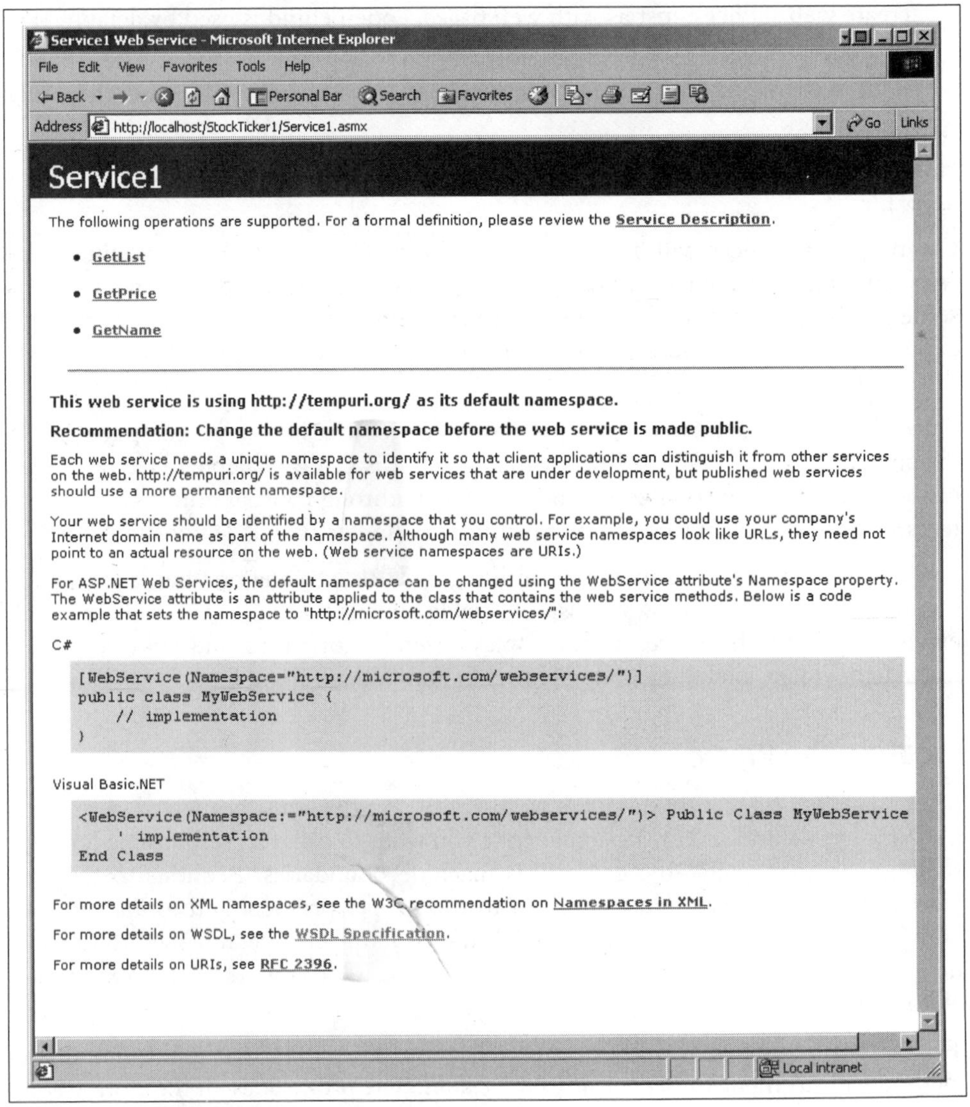
Service1 Web Service - Microsoft Internet Explorer
File Edit View Favorites Tools Help
Back Personal Bar Search Favorites
Address http://localhost/StockTicker1/Service1.asmx
Go Links
Service1
The following operations are supported. For a formal definition, please review the Service Description.
GetList
GetPrice
GetName
This web service is using http://tempuri.org/ as its default namespace.
Recommendation: Change the default namespace before the web service is made public.
Each web service needs a unique namespace to identify it so that client applications can distinguish it from other services on the web. http://tempuri.org/ is available for web services that are under development, but published web services should use a more permanent namespace.
Your web service should be identified by a namespace that you control. For example, you could use your company's Internet domain name as part of the namespace. Although many web service namespaces look like URLs, they need not point to an actual resource on the web. (Web service namespaces are URIs.)
For ASP.NET Web Services, the default namespace can be changed using the WebService attribute's Namespace property. The WebService attribute is an attribute applied to the class that contains the web service methods. Below is a code example that sets the namespace to "http://microsoft.com/webservices/":
C#
[WebService(Namespace="http://microsoft.com/webservices/")]
public class MyWebService {
// implementation
}
Visual Basic.NET
<WebService(Namespace:="http://microsoft.com/webservices/")> Public Class MyWebService
' implementation
End Class
For more details on XML namespaces, see the W3C recommendation on Namespaces in XML.
For more details on WSDL, see the WSDL Specification.
For more details on URIs, see RFC 2396.
Local intranet

Figure 15-2. Testing the .asmx file in a browser

Creating the Consumer

The consumer of a web service can be a desktop application, a web page, or another web service. All that is required is that the consumer be able to send and receive SOAP or HTTP packages.

If you develop your client using Visual Studio .NET, you need only register the proxy DLL with the application. If you are working from a command prompt, simply make a reference to the proxy DLL when you compile the application.

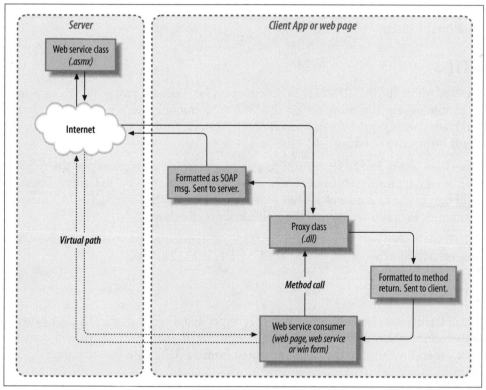

Figure 15-3. Web service proxy operation

If the consuming application is a web page or another web service, then the proxy DLL will be located on the server that hosts the consuming web page or service. If the consumer application is a desktop application, then the proxy DLL will be located on the desktop machine. In any case, once the proxy DLL is created and registered with the consuming application, then all that application has to do to use a web service is make a method or function call against that DLL, as though it were a call against a local DLL. Creating an application that consumes a web service will be covered in detail in Chapter 17.

Protocols and Standards

Various protocols are mentioned throughout this chapter, as well as in Chapters 16 and 17. While going into detail about the various protocols is beyond the scope of this book and also not necessary for an understanding of how web services work, some understanding is useful.

A *protocol* is a set of rules that describe the transmission and receipt of data between two or more computing devices. For example, TCP/IP (Transmission

Control Protocol/Internet Protocol) governs the low-level transport of packets of data on the Internet.

HTTP

Layered on top of TCP/IP is HTTP (the HyperText Transfer Protocol), which is used to enable servers and browsers on the Web to communicate. It is primarily used to establish connections between servers and browsers and to transmit HTML to the client browser.

The client sends an HTTP request to the server, which then processes the request. The server typically returns HTML pages to be rendered by the client browser, although in the case of web services, the server may instead return a SOAP message containing the returned data of the web service method call.

HTTP requests pass name/value pairs from the requesting browser to a server. The request can be either of two types: HTTP-GET, or HTTP-POST.

HTTP-GET

In GET requests, the name/value pairs are appended directly to the URL. The data is uuencoded (which guarantees that only legal ASCII characters are passed over the wire), then appended to the URL, separated from the URL by a question mark.

For example, in the following URL:

```
http://localhost/StockTicker1/Service1.asmx/GetName?StockSymbol=msft
```

the question mark indicates that this is an HTTP-GET request, the name of the variable passed to the GetName method is StockSymbol, and the value is msft.

GET requests are suitable when all the data that needs to be passed can be handled by name/value pairs, there are few fields to pass, and the length of the fields is relatively short. GET requests are also suitable when security is not an issue. This last point arises because the URL is sent over the wire and is included in server logs as plain text. As such they can be easily captured by a network sniffer or an unscrupulous person.

The .NET Framework provides a class, HttpGetClientProtocol (shown in Figure 15-4), for using the HTTP-GET protocol in your clients.

HTTP-POST

In POST requests, the name/value pairs are also uuencoded, but instead of being appended to the URL, they are sent as part of the request message.

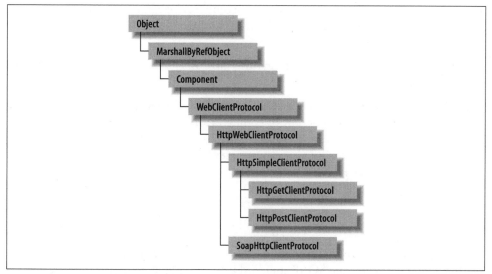

Figure 15-4. WebClientProtocol hierarchy

POST requests are suitable for large numbers of fields or when lengthy parameters need to be passed. Also, if security is an issue, a POST request is safer than a GET request, since the HTTP request can be encrypted.

As with GET requests, with POST requests only name/value pairs can be passed. This precludes passing complex data types, such as classes, structs, or datasets.

The .NET Framework provides a class, HttpPostClientProtocol (see Figure 15-4), for using the HTTP-POST protocol in your clients.

XML

XML (eXtensible Markup Language) is an open standard promulgated by the World Wide Web Consortium (W3C) as a means of describing data (for more information visit *www.w3c.org*). At the time of this writing, the current version of the XML protocol is Version 1.0.

XML is similar to HTML. In fact, both XML and HTML are derived from SGML (Standard Generalized Markup Language). Like HTML documents, XML documents are plain text documents containing tags. However, while HTML uses predefined tags that specify how the HTML document will display in a browser, XML allows tags to be defined by the document developer, so that virtually any data can be conveyed.

XML documents are text files that are human readable. However, they are typically not meant to actually be read by humans, except developers doing programming and debugging. Since tags are used to define every field in an XML document, the files are generally much larger than the same data in a proprietary binary database file.

However, that is rarely an issue, since it is computer programs, not people, reading the document, and the difference in transmission time over the Internet is usually negligible at today's speeds.

An XML *schema* is a file used to define the tags. In the schema, both the tag name and content type are specified.

One significant difference between HTML and XML is that while most HTML readers (i.e., web browsers) are tolerant of coding errors, XML readers generally are not. XML must be *well-formed*. (For a complete discussion of well-formed XML code, see Chapter 4.) For example, while browsers generally do not care if tags are upper- or lowercase, in XML they must be lowercase or an error will be generated.

SOAP

When you combine XML with HTTP, the result is SOAP (Simple Object Access Protocol). SOAP is a simple, lightweight protocol for the exchange of information over the Internet. Like XML, the SOAP standard is promulgated by the W3C.

SOAP uses XML syntax to format its content. It is, by design, as simple as possible and provides a minimum of functionality. Therefore, it is very modular and flexible. Since SOAP messages consist of XML, which is plain text, they can easily pass through firewalls, unlike many proprietary, binary formats. At the time of this writing, the latest SOAP version is 1.2. The SOAP protocol was originally developed by Compaq, HP, IBM, Lotus, Microsoft, and others.

SOAP is not limited to name/value pairs as HTTP-GET and HTTP-POST are. Instead, SOAP can also be used to send more complex objects, including datasets, classes, and other objects.

One drawback to using SOAP to pass requests back and forth to web services is that SOAP messages tend to be very verbose, due to the nature of XML. Therefore, if bandwidth or transmission performance is an issue, you may be better off using either HTTP-GET or HTTP-POST.

The .NET Framework provides a class, SoapHttpClientProtocol (see Figure 15-4), for using the SOAP protocol in your clients.

.NET Support for Protocols

The .NET Framework provides a number of classes for interacting with the HTTP protocol. Figure 15-4 shows a hierarchy of classes for the SOAP, HTTP-GET and HTTP-POST client protocols, all deriving from WebClientProtocol and HttpWebClientProtocol.

CHAPTER 16

Creating Web Services

The previous chapter provided an overview of web services, which are basically web applications with no user interface. Web services allow an application to make method calls against another application over the Internet as though it were calling a local *dll*.

There are two broad aspects to web service development: creating the web service and consuming the web service. This chapter covers the creation of web services. Chapter 17 covers the creation of web service client applications, also known as consumers.

Although a web service has no user interface and no visual component, the architecture and files used to create a web service are very similar to those used to create a web page, which are described in detail in Chapters 2 through 6. Some of these similarities include:

- Full implementation of the .NET Framework and Common Language Runtime (CLR), including the object-oriented architecture and all the base class libraries, as well as features such as caching, state, and data access

- Nearly identical file and code structures

- All source code files in plain text, which can be created in any text editor

- Full support by Visual Studio .NET, with all its productivity features, including IntelliSense, code completion, and integrated debugging

- Configurable on a global or application-wide basis using plain text configuration files

That said, web pages and web services are conceptually very different. A web page entails an interface designed for interaction with a person sitting at a web browser. A web service, on the other hand, consists only of methods, some of which are available for remote calls by client applications.

A web service can be coded inline, in a single file with an extension of *.asmx*. Alternatively, the application logic of the web service can be segregated into a code-behind file, which is the default behavior of Visual Studio .NET. While code-behind is generally preferred, especially for large projects, both methods will be demonstrated in this chapter.

 The rationale for code-behind is that it provides a clean separation between the presentation and programmatic portions of an application. While this is extremely useful in the development of web pages, it is not really relevant to web services. However, since code-behind is the default coding technique for Visual Studio .NET (which offers so many productivity enhancements), code-behind becomes the *de facto* preferred technique. In addition, code-behind confers a performance advantage over inline code because the code-behind class must be precompiled for web services, while the *.asmx* file is compiled into a class the first time it is run.

Whether using an inline or code-behind architecture, the *.asmx* file is the target entered into the browser for testing or referenced by the utilities that create the proxy *dll*. (Recall from Chapter 15 that the client application actually makes calls to a proxy *dll*. Creation of this proxy *dll* will be described in detail in the next chapter.)

As a first step in understanding how web services work, we will create a simple web service, called StockTicker, using any favorite text editor. In subsequent sections of this chapter, we will create the same web service using Visual Studio .NET.

A Simple StockTicker

The StockTicker web service will expose two web methods:

GetName
> Expects a stock symbol as an argument and returns a string containing the name of the stock

GetPrice
> Expects a stock symbol as an argument and returns a number containing the current price of the stock

If this web service were an actual production program, the data returned would be fetched from a live database. In order not to confuse web service issues with data access issues, for this example the data will be stored in a two-dimensional array of strings. For a complete discussion of accessing a database, please see Chapters 11 and 12.

A single file will be created. The VB.NET version will be called *vbStockTicker.asmx* and is shown in Example 16-1. The C# version will be called *csStockTicker.asmx* and is shown in Example 16-2.

The *.asmx* file contains the entire web service inline. It defines a namespace called ProgAspNet, and creates a class called csStockTicker for the C# version, or vbStockTicker for the VB.NET version. The class instantiates and fills an array to contain the stock data, then creates the two WebMethods that comprise the public aspects of the web service.

If you're familiar with web page code, you may notice in glancing over Examples 16-1 and 16-2 that the code for a web service is virtually identical to the code in a code-behind page for an equivalent web page. There are some differences, however, which are highlighted in the code examples and are discussed in the sections following the examples.

Example 16-1. StockTicker web service in VB.NET, vbStockTicker.asmx

```
<%@ WebService Language="VB" Class="ProgAspNet.vbStockTicker" %>

Option Strict On
Option Explicit On
Imports System
Imports System.Web.Services

namespace ProgAspNet

    public class vbStockTicker
        inherits System.Web.Services.WebService
            '  Construct and fill an array of stock symbols and prices.
            '  Note: the stock prices are as of 7/4/01.
        dim stocks as string(,) = _
        { _
            {"MSFT","Microsoft","70.47"}, _
            {"DELL","Dell Computers","26.91"}, _
            {"HWP","Hewlett Packard","28.40"}, _
            {"YHOO","Yahoo!","19.81"}, _
            {"GE","General Electric","49.51"}, _
            {"IBM","International Business Machine","112.98"}, _
            {"GM","General Motors","64.72"}, _
            {"F","Ford Motor Company","25.05"} _
        }

        dim i as integer

        <WebMethod>public function GetPrice(StockSymbol as string) as Double
        '  Given a stock symbol, return the price.
            '  Iterate through the array, looking for the symbol.
            for i = 0 to stocks.GetLength(0) - 1
                '  Do a case-insensitive string compare.
                if (String.Compare(StockSymbol, stocks(i,0), true) = 0) then
                    return Convert.ToDouble(stocks(i,2))
                end if
            next

            return 0
        End Function
```

Example 16-1. StockTicker web service in VB.NET, vbStockTicker.asmx (continued)

```
    <WebMethod>public function GetName(StockSymbol as string) as string
    ' Given a stock symbol, return the name.
        ' Iterate through the array, looking for the symbol.
        for i = 0 to stocks.GetLength(0) - 1
            ' Do a case-insensitive string compare.
            if (String.Compare(StockSymbol, stocks(i,0), true) = 0) then
                return stocks(i,1)
            end if
        next


        return "Symbol not found."
    End Function
    End Class
End namespace
```

Example 16-2. StockTicker web service in C#, csStockTicker.asmx

```
<%@ WebService Language="C#" Class="ProgAspNet.csStockTicker" %>

using System;
using System.Web.Services;

namespace ProgAspNet
{
    public class csStockTicker : System.Web.Services.WebService
    {
        //  Construct and fill an array of stock symbols and prices.
        //  Note: the stock prices are as of 7/4/01.
        string[,] stocks =
        {
            {"MSFT","Microsoft","70.47"},
            {"DELL","Dell Computers","26.91"},
            {"HWP","Hewlett Packard","28.40"},
            {"YHOO","Yahoo!","19.81"},
            {"GE","General Electric","49.51"},
            {"IBM","International Business Machine","112.98"},
            {"GM","General Motors","64.72"},
            {"F","Ford Motor Company","25.05"}
        };

        [WebMethod]
        public double GetPrice(string StockSymbol)
        //  Given a stock symbol, return the price.
        {
            //  Iterate through the array, looking for the symbol.
            for (int i = 0; i < stocks.GetLength(0); i++)
            {
                //  Do a case-insensitive string compare.
                if (String.Compare(StockSymbol, stocks[i,0], true) == 0)
                    return Convert.ToDouble(stocks[i,2]);
            }
            return 0;
```

```
    }

    [WebMethod]
    public string GetName(string StockSymbol)
    //  Given a stock symbol, return the name.
    {
        //  Iterate through the array, looking for the symbol.
        for (int i = 0; i < stocks.GetLength(0); i++)
        {
            //  Do a case-insensitive string compare.
            if (String.Compare(StockSymbol, stocks[i,0], true) == 0)
                return stocks[i,1];
        }
        return "Symbol not found.";
    }
  }
}
```

The WebService Directive

The first difference between a web service and a web page is seen in the first line of Examples 16-1 and 16-2. A normal *.aspx* file will have a Page directive as its first line, but a web service has a WebService directive, as reproduced here in VB.NET:

```
<%@ WebService Language="VB" Class="ProgAspNet.vbStockTicker" %>
```

and here in C#:

```
<%@ WebService Language="C#" Class="ProgAspNet.csStockTicker" %>
```

The WebService directive is required of all web services. Like all directives, it has the syntax:

```
<%@ DirectiveName Attribute="value" %>
```

where there can be multiple attribute/value pairs. The order of the attribute/value pairs does not matter.

The Language attribute

The WebService directive's Language attribute specifies the language used in the web service. Legal values include C#, VB, and JS for C#, VB.NET, and JScript.NET, respectively. The value is not case-sensitive.

The Language attribute is not required. If it is missing, the default value is C#.

The Class attribute

The WebService directive's Class attribute specifies the name of the class implementing the web service. The Class attribute is required. The class specified can reside in the *.asmx* file or in a separate file, a technique referred to as *code-behind*.

If the implementing class resides in a separate file, then that file must be compiled and the resulting *dll* placed in the *bin* subdirectory under the directory where the *.asmx* file resides. This will be demonstrated shortly.

Notice that in the code listings in Examples 16-1 and 16-2, a namespace, ProgAsp-Net, has been defined. In order to specify the implementing class contained in this namespace fully, the namespace is prepended to the class name in the WebService directive.

 Strictly speaking, the namespace containing the WebService class does not need to be prepended to the inherited class name, since the System.Web.Services namespace is referenced with the Imports keyword in VB.NET and the using keyword in C#. The longer syntax is used to clarify the relationships.

Deriving from the WebService Class

In the StockTicker web service in Examples 16-1 and 16-2, the StockTicker class (the vbStockTicker class for VB.NET and the csStockTicker class for C#) inherits from the WebService class.

Deriving from the WebService class is optional, but it offers several advantages. The principal one is that you gain access to several common ASP.NET objects, including:

Application and Session
> These objects allow the application to take advantage of state management. For a complete discussion of state management, see Chapter 6. State as it pertains specifically to web services will be covered in more detail later in this chapter.

User
> This object is useful for authenticating the caller of a web service. For a complete discussion of security, see Chapter 19.

Context
> This object provides access to all HTTP-specific information about the caller's request contained in the HttpContext class.

Application State via HttpContext

Web services have access to the Application object, as do all ASP.NET resources, via the HttpContext object.

So, for example, you could modify Examples 16-1 and 16-2 to add the web methods shown in Example 16-3 (for VB.NET) and Example 16-4 (for C#) to set and retrieve a value in application state.

Example 16-3. Code modification to vbStockTicker.asmx adding application state

```
<WebMethod>public sub SetStockExchange(Exchange as string)
    Application("exchange") = Exchange
end sub
<WebMethod>public function GetStockExchange( ) as string
    return Application("exchange").ToString( )
end function
```

Example 16-4. Code modification to csStockTicker.asmx adding application state

```
 [WebMethod]
public void SetStockExchange(string Exchange)
{
    Application["exchange"] = Exchange;
}

[WebMethod]
public string GetStockExchange( )
{
    return Application["exchange"].ToString( );
}
```

You could accomplish the same thing without inheriting from System.Web.Services. WebService by using the HttpContext object, as demonstrated in Examples 16-5 and 16-6.

Example 16-5. Code modification to vbStockTicker.asmx adding application state without inheriting WebService

```
Option Strict On
Option Explicit On
Imports System
Imports System.Web
Imports System.Web.Services

namespace ProgAspNet

    public class vbStockTicker
.
.
.
        <WebMethod>public sub SetStockExchange(Exchange as string)
            dim app as HttpApplicationState
            app = HttpContext.Current.Application
            app("exchange") = Exchange
        end sub

        <WebMethod>public function GetStockExchange( ) as string
            dim app as HttpApplicationState
            app = HttpContext.Current.Application
            return app("exchange").ToString( )
        end function
```

Example 16-6. Code modification to csStockTicker.asmx adding application state without inheriting WebService

```
using System;
using System.Web;
using System.Web.Services;

namespace ProgAspNet
{
   public class csStockTicker
.
.
.

      [WebMethod]
      public void SetStockExchange(string Exchange)
      {
         HttpApplicationState app;
         app = HttpContext.Current.Application;
         app["exchange"] = Exchange;
      }

      [WebMethod]
      public string GetStockExchange( )
      {
         HttpApplicationState app;
         app = HttpContext.Current.Application;
         return app["exchange"].ToString( );
      }
```

Notice that in Examples 16-5 and 16-6, a reference to System.Web has been added at the top of the listing. Also, the web service class, vbStockTicker or csStockTicker, no longer inherits from the class WebService. Finally, an HttpApplicationState object is declared in order to access the application state.

The main reason you might not want to inherit from WebService is to overcome the limitation imposed by the .NET Framework that a class can only inherit from one other class. It would be very inconvenient to have to inherit from WebService if you also needed to inherit from another class.

The WebMethod Attribute

As explained previously, a web service is defined by a WebService class. It is not necessary for the WebService class to expose all of its methods to consumers of the web service. Each method you do want to expose must:

- Be declared as public.
- Have the WebMethod attribute placed before the method declaration. (The WebMethod attribute comes from the WebMethodAttribute class, which is contained in the System.Web.Services namespace.)

As you saw in Examples 16-1 and 16-2, the syntax for defining a web method is slightly different, depending on the language. In VB.NET, it looks like this:

```
<WebMethod>public function GetName(StockSymbol as string) as string
```

and in C# it looks like this:

```
[WebMethod]
public string GetName(string StockSymbol)
```

WebMethod properties

The WebMethod attribute has properties that are used to configure the behavior of the specific web method. The syntax, again, is language-dependent.

In VB.NET, the syntax is:

```
<WebMethod(PropertyName:=value)> _
public function GetName(StockSymbol as string) as string
```

and in C# the syntax is:

```
[WebMethod(PropertyName=value)]
public string GetName(string StockSymbol)
```

PropertyName is a valid property accepted by the WebMethod attribute (these are described below), and *value* is the value to be assigned to that property. Note the colon (:) in VB.NET (which is standard VB.NET syntax for named arguments), as well as the use of the line continuation character if the combination of the Web-Method property and method/function call stretches to more than one line.

Regardless of the language, if there are multiple WebMethod properties, separate each property/value pair with a comma within a single set of parentheses. So, for example, in VB.NET:

```
<WebMethod(BufferResponse:=False, Description:="Sample description")>
```

or in C#:

```
[WebMethod(BufferResponse=false, Description="Sample description")]
```

The following sections describe the valid WebMethod properties.

The BufferResponse property. By default, ASP.NET buffers the entire response to a request before sending it from the server to the client. Under most circumstances, this is the optimal behavior. However, if the response is very lengthy, you might want to disable this buffering by setting the WebMethod attribute's BufferResponse property to false. If set to false, the response will be returned to the client in 16KB chunks. The default value is true.

For VB.NET, the syntax for BufferResponse is:

```
<WebMethod(BufferResponse:=False)>
```

and for C#:

```
[WebMethod(BufferResponse=false)]
```

The CacheDuration property. Web services, like web pages, can cache the results returned to clients, as is described fully in Chapter 18. If a client makes a request that is identical to a request made recently by another client, then the server will return the response stored in the cache. This can result in a huge performance gain, especially if servicing the request is an expensive operation, such as querying a database or performing a lengthy computation.

It should be emphasized that in order for the cached results to be used, the new request must be identical to the previous request. If the web method has parameters, the parameter values must be identical. So, for example, if the GetPrice web method of the StockTicker web service is called with a value of msft passed in as the stock symbol, that result will be cached separately from a request with a value of dell passed in. If the web method has multiple parameters, all the parameter values must be the same as the previous request for the cached results from that request to be returned.

The CacheDuration property defines how many seconds after the initial request the cached page is sent in response to subsequent requests. Once this period has expired, a new page is sent. CacheDuration is set to 30 seconds as follows for VB.NET:

```
<WebMethod(CacheDuration:=30)>
```

and for C#:

```
[WebMethod(CacheDuration=30)]
```

The default value for CacheDuration is zero, which disables caching of results.

If the web method is returning data that does not change much—say a query against a database that is updated once hourly—then the cache duration can be set to a suitably long value, say 1800 (e.g., 30 minutes). You could even set the cache duration in this case to 3600 (60 minutes) if the process of updating the database also forces the cache to refresh by making a call to the WebMethod after the database is updated.

On the other hand, if the data returned is very dynamic, then you would want to set the cache duration to a very short time, or to disable it altogether. Also, if the web method does not have a relatively finite range of possible parameters, then caching may not be appropriate.

The Description property. The WebMethod attribute's Description property allows you to attach a descriptive string to a web method. This description will appear on the web service help page when you test the web service in a browser.

Also, the WebMethod description will be made available to the consumer of the web service, as will be seen in Chapter 17. When a representation of the web service is encoded into the SOAP message that is sent out to potential consumers, the WebMethod Description property is included.

The syntax for Description is as follows for VB.NET:

```
<WebMethod(Description:="Returns the stock price for the input stock symbol.")>
```

and for C#:

```
[WebMethod(Description="Returns the stock price for the input stock symbol.")]
```

The EnableSession property. The WebMethod attribute's EnableSession property, if set to true, enables session state for the web method. The default value is false. (For a general discussion of session state, see Chapter 6.)

If the EnableSession property is set to true and the web service inherits from the WebService class (see earlier sections for a description of inheriting from the WebService class), the session state collection can be accessed with the WebService.Session property. If the web service does not inherit from the WebService class, then the session state collection can be accessed directly from HttpContext.Current.Session.

As an example, the code in Examples 16-7 and 16-8 adds a per-session hit counter to the ongoing StockTicker web service example.

Example 16-7. HitCounter WebMethod in VB.NET

```
<WebMethod(Description:="Number of hits per session.", EnableSession:=true)> _
public function HitCounter() as integer
    if Session("HitCounter") is Nothing then
        Session("HitCounter") = 1
    else
        Session("HitCounter") = CInt(Session("HitCounter")) + 1
    end if

    return CInt(Session("HitCounter"))
end function
```

Example 16-8. HitCounter WebMethod in C#

```
 [WebMethod(Description="Number of hits per session.", EnableSession=true)]
public int HitCounter()
{
    if (Session["HitCounter"] == null)
    {
        Session["HitCounter"] = 1;
    }
    else
    {
        Session["HitCounter"] = ((int) Session["HitCounter"]) + 1;
    }

    return ((int) Session["HitCounter"]);
}
```

Enabling session state adds additional overhead to the application. By leaving session state disabled, performance may be improved.

In Examples 16-7 and 16-8, it would probably be more efficient to use a member variable to maintain the hit counter, rather than session state, since the examples as written entail two reads of the session state and one write, while a member variable would entail only one read and one write. However, session state is often useful as a global variable that can exceed the scope of a member variable.

Session state is implemented via HTTP cookies, so if the transport mechanism is something other than HTTP, say SMTP, then the session state functionality will not be available.

The MessageName property. It is possible to have more than one method or function in your web service class with the same name. They are differentiated by their *signature*— the quantity, data type, and order of their parameters. Each unique signature can be called independently. This is called method *overloading*, and can cause some confusion.

The WebMethod attribute's MessageName property eliminates confusion caused by overloaded methods. It allows you to assign a unique alias to a method signature. When this method is referred to in SOAP messages, the MessageName will be used, and not the method name.

Consider Examples 16-9 and 16-10. In both examples, two methods are added to the StockTicker web service, both named GetValue. They differ in that one accepts only a single string parameter, while the other takes both a string and an integer.

Example 16-9. GetValue WebMethods in VB.NET

```
' WebMethod generates an error
<WebMethod(Description:="Returns the value of the users holdings " & _
                " in a specified stock symbol.")> _
public Function GetValue(StockSymbol as string) as double
    '  Put code here to get the username of the current user, fetch both
    '  the current price of the specified StockSymbol and number of shares
    '  held by the current user, multiply the two together, and return the
    '  result.
    return 0
end Function


' WebMethod generates an error
<WebMethod(Description:="This method returns the value of a " & _
            "specified number of shares in a specified stock symbol.")> _
public Function GetValue(StockSymbol as string, NumShares as integer) as double
    '  Put code here to get the current price of the specified StockSymbol,
    '   multiply it times NumShares, and return the result.
    return 0
end function
```

Example 16-10. GetValue WebMethods in C#

```
// WebMethod generates an error
[WebMethod(Description="T Returns the value of the users holdings " +
                    " in a specified stock symbol.")]
public double GetValue(string StockSymbol)
{
    /* Put code here to get the username of the current user, fetch both
        the current price of the specified StockSymbol and number of shares
```

Example 16-10. GetValue WebMethods in C# (continued)

```
        held by the current user, multiply the two together, and return the
        result.
    */
    return 0;
}


// WebMethod generates an error
[WebMethod(Description="This method returns the value of a " +
            "specified number of shares in a specified stock symbol.")]
public double GetValue(string StockSymbol, int NumShares)
{
    /*  Put code here to get the current price of the specified
        StockSymbol, multiply it times NumShares, and return the result.
    */
    return 0;
}
```

If you attempt to test either of these in a browser, it will return an error similar to that shown in Figure 16-1.

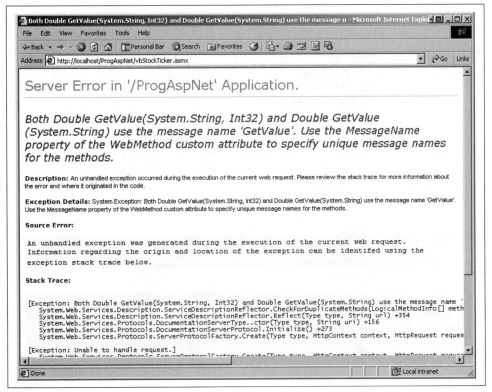

Figure 16-1. Conflicting WebMethod names

If you modify the code in Examples 16-9 and 16-10 by adding the MessageName property, highlighted in Examples 16-11 and 16-12, then everything compiles nicely.

Example 16-11. GetValue WebMethods with MessageName in VB.NET

```
<WebMethod(Description:="Returns the value of the users holdings " & _
            "in a specified stock symbol.", _
        MessageName:="GetValuePortfolio")> _
public Function GetValue(StockSymbol as string) as double
    ' Put code here to get the username of the current user, fetch
    ' both the current price of the specified StockSymbol and number
    ' of shares held by the current user, multiply the two together,
    ' and return the result.
    return 0
end Function


<WebMethod(Description:="Returns the value of a specified number " & _
            "of shares in a specified stock symbol.", _
        MessageName:="GetValueStock")> _
public Function GetValue(StockSymbol as string, NumShares as integer) as double
    ' Put code here to get the current price of the specified StockSymbol,
    '  multiply it times NumShares, and return the result.
    return 0
end function
```

Example 16-12. GetValue WebMethods with MessageName in C#

```
[WebMethod(Description="Returns the value of the users holdings " +
            "in a specified stock symbol.",
        MessageName="GetValuePortfolio")]
public double GetValue(string StockSymbol)
{
    /*  Put code here to get the username of the current user, fetch
        both the current price of the specified StockSymbol and number
        of shares held by the current user, multiply the two together,
        and return the result.
    */  return 0;
}

[WebMethod(Description="Returns the value of a specified " +
                "number of shares in a specified stock symbol.",
        MessageName="GetValueStock")]
public double GetValue(string StockSymbol, int NumShares)
{
    /*  Put code here to get the current price of the specified
        StockSymbol, multiply it times NumShares, and return the
        result.
    */
    return 0;
}
```

Now consumers of the web service will call GetValuePortfolio or GetValueStock rather than GetValue.

To see the impact of this change, examine the WSDL, which is the description of the web service used by clients of the web service. You can look at the WSDL by entering the URL for the *.asmx* file in a browser, followed by ?WSDL. If you do that for Examples 16-11 or 16-12, then search for the first occurrence of GetValuePortfolio, you will see something like Figure 16-2.

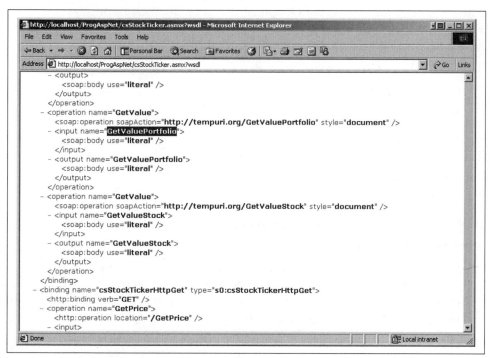

Figure 16-2. MessageName WSDL

You can see that the section defined by the tag:

```
<operation name="GetValue">
```

is present twice. However, in the first instance, the method name used within the operation section of the document is GetValuePortfolio, and in the second instance it is GetValueStock.

The TransactionOption Property. ASP.NET web methods can participate in transactions (see Chapter 12 for more details on transactions), but only if the transaction originates in that web method. In other words, the web method can only participate as the *root object* in a transaction. This means that a consuming application cannot call a web method as part of a transaction and have that web method participate in the transaction. However, if the web method starts its own transaction, which then fails, the calling transaction will also fail.

The WebMethod attribute's TransactionOption property specifies whether or not a web method should start a transaction. There are five legal values of the property, all contained in the TransactionOption enumeration. However, due to the fact that a web method transaction must be the root object, there are only two different behaviors: either a new transaction is started or it is not.

These values in the TransactionOption enumeration are used throughout the .NET Framework. However, in the case of web services, the first three values produce the same behavior, and the last two values produce the same behavior.

The three values of TransactionOption that do not start a new transaction are:

- Disabled (the default)
- NotSupported
- Supported

The two values that do start a new transaction are:

- Required
- RequiresNew

In order to use transactions in a web service, you must take several additional steps:

1. Add a reference to *System.EnterpriseServices.dll*.

   In Visual Studio .NET, this is done through the Solution Explorer or the Project/ Add Reference... menu item. If using the Solution Explorer, right-click on References and select Add References.... In either case, you get the dialog box shown in Figure 16-3. Click on the desired component in the list, and then click OK.

    When coding outside of Visual Studio .NET, you must add an Assembly directive pointing to System.EnterpriseServices:

   ```
   <%@ assembly name="System.EnterpriseServices" %>
   ```

2. Add the System.EnterpriseServices namespace to the web service. This is done with the Imports statement in VB.NET and the using statement in C#. In VB. NET, this would be:

   ```
   Imports System.EnterpriseServices
   ```
   and in C#:

   ```
   using System.EnterpriseServices;
   ```

3. Add a TransactionOption property with a value of RequiresNew to the WebMethod attribute. (The value of Required will have the same effect.)

   The syntax for TransactionOption is as follows for VB.NET:

   ```
   <WebMethod(TransactionOption:=TransactionOption.RequiresNew)>
   ```
   and for C#:

   ```
   [WebMethod(Description=TransactionOption.RequiresNew)]
   ```

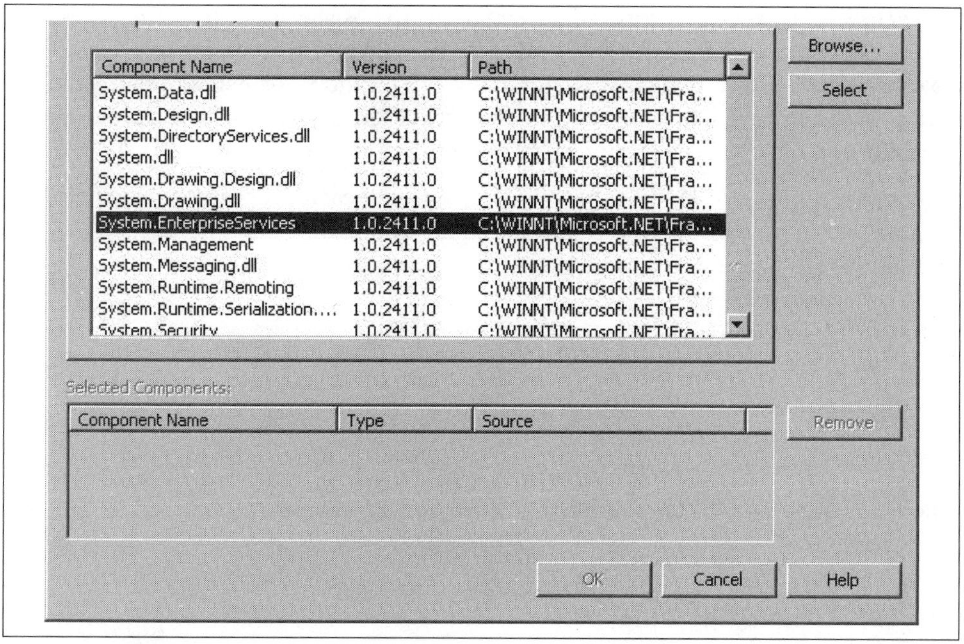

Figure 16-3. Adding a reference to a project in Visual Studio .NET

If there are no exceptions thrown by the web method, then the transaction will automatically commit unless the SetAbort method is explicitly called. If any exceptions are thrown, the transaction will automatically abort.

The WebService Attribute

The WebService attribute (not to be confused with the WebMethod attribute or the WebService directive) allows additional information to be added to a web service. The WebService attribute is optional.

The syntax for a WebService attribute is dependent on the language used. For VB. NET, it is:

```
<WebService(PropertyName:=value)>public class vbStockTicker( )
```

or:

```
<WebService(PropertyName:=value)> _
public class vbStockTicker( )
```

and for C# it is:

```
[WebService(PropertyName=value)]
public class csStockTicker( )
```

PropertyName is a valid property accepted by the WebService attribute (these are described below), and *value* is the value to be assigned to that property. Note the colon (:) in VB. NET (which is standard VB.NET syntax for named arguments), as well as the use of the line continuation character if the combination of the WebService attribute and the class declaration stretches to more than one line.

If there are multiple WebService properties, separate each property/value pair with a comma within a single set of parenthesis. So for example, in VB. NET:

```
<WebService (Description:="A stock ticker using VB.NET.", _
        Name:="StockTicker", _
        Namespace:="www.LibertyAssociates.com")> _
```

or in C#:

```
[WebService (Description="A stock ticker using C#.",
        Name="StockTicker",
        Namespace="www.LibertyAssociates.com")]
```

There are three possible properties for a WebService attribute, described in the next three sections.

The Description property

The WebService attribute's Description property assigns a descriptive message to the web service. As with the WebMethod attribute's Description property, the WebService description will be displayed in the web service help page when the page is tested in a browser, and also made available in the SOAP message to any potential consumers of the web service.

The Name property

The name of a web service is displayed at the top of a web service help page when the page is tested in a browser. It is also made available to any potential consumers of the service.

By default, the name of a web service is the name of the class implementing the web service. The WebService attribute's Name property allows the name to be changed. If you glance back at the syntax given in the section "The WebService Attribute," you'll notice that the two language implementations of the stock ticker web service have different class names, but the code specifies that both will now be seen as Stock-Ticker.

The Namespace property

Each web service has an XML namespace associated with it. An XML namespace allows you to create names in an XML document that are uniquely identified by a

Uniform Resource Identifier (URI). The web service is described using a WSDL document, which is defined in XML. It is important that each WebService attribute has a unique XML namespace associated with it to prevent name conflicts.

The default URI of a web service is *http://tempuri.org/*. Typically, you will define a new namespace using a unique name, such as a firm's web site. Although the XML namespace often looks like a web site, it does not need to be a valid URL.

In the syntax given in "The WebService Attribute," notice that the Namespace property is set to the web site, *www.LibertyAssociates.com*.

Data Types

ASP.NET web services can use any CLR-supported primitive data type as either a parameter or a return value. Table 16-1 summarizes the valid types.

Table 16-1. CLR-supported primitive data types

VB.NET	C#	Description
Byte	byte	1-byte unsigned integer
Short	short	2-byte signed integer
Integer	int	4-byte signed integer
Long	long	8-byte signed integer
Single	float	4-byte floating point
Double	double	8-byte floating point
Decimal	decimal	16-byte floating point
Boolean	bool	True/False
Char	char	Single Unicode character
String	string	Sequence of Unicode characters
DateTime	DateTime	Represents dates and times
Object	object	Any type

In addition to the primitive data types, you can also use arrays and ArrayLists of the primitive types. Since data is passed between a web service and its clients using XML, whatever is used as either a parameter or return value must be represented in an XML schema, or XSD.

The examples shown so far in this chapter have used simple primitive types, such as strings and numbers, as parameters and return values. You could also use an array of simple types, as in the code shown here in C#:

```
[WebMethod]
public string[] GetArray()
{
```

```
        string[] TestArray = {"a","b","c"};
        return TestArray;
    }
```

The main limitation of using arrays, of course, is that you must know the number of elements at design time. If the number of elements is dynamic, then an ArrayList is called for. If an ArrayList is used in the web service, it is converted to an object array when the web service description is created. The client proxy will return an array of objects, which will then have to be converted to an array of strings.

The ArrayList is contained within the System.Collections namespace. To use an Array-List, you must include the proper reference, with the Imports keyword in VB.NET, as in the following:

```
    Imports System.Collections
```

or the using keyword in C#:

```
    using System.Collections;
```

The code in Examples 16-13 and 16-14 contains a web method called GetList. It takes a string as a parameter. This match string is then compared with all the firm names in the data store (the array defined at the top of the web service class shown in Examples 16-1 and 16-2), and the web service returns all the firm names that contain the match string anywhere within the firm name.

Example 16-13. GetList WebMethod in VB.NET

```
<WebMethod(Description:="Returns all the stock symbols whose firm " & _
            "name matches the input string as *str*.")> _
public function GetList(MatchString as string) as ArrayList
    dim a as ArrayList = new ArrayList()

    ' Iterate through the array, looking for matching firm names.
    for i = 0 to stocks.GetLength(0) - 1
        ' Search is case sensitive.
        if stocks(i,1).ToUpper().IndexOf(MatchString.ToUpper()) >= 0 then
            a.Add(stocks(i,1))
        end if
    next
    a.Sort()
    return a
end function
```

Example 16-14. GetList WebMethod in C#

```
 [WebMethod(Description="Returns all the stock symbols whose firm " +
            "matches the input string as *str*.")]
public ArrayList GetList(string MatchString)
{
    ArrayList a = new ArrayList();
```

Example 16-14. GetList WebMethod in C# (continued)

```
   // Iterate through the array, looking for matching firm names.
   for (int i = 0; i < stocks.GetLength(0); i++)
   {
      // Search is case sensitive.
      if ( stocks[i,1].ToUpper().IndexOf(MatchString.ToUpper()) >= 0)
         a.Add(stocks[i,1]);
   }
   a.Sort();
   return a;
}
```

The web method in Examples 16-13 and 16-14 first instantiates a new ArrayList, then iterates through the store of firms. This time the web method uses the IndexOf method of the String class. This IndexOf method does a case-sensitive search in a string, looking for the match string. If it finds a match, it returns the index of the first occurrence. If it does not find a match, it returns -1. In order to implement a case-insensitive search, the code first converts both the MatchString and the firm name to uppercase.

If the IndexOf method finds a match, the web method adds the firm name to the ArrayList. The firm name is contained in the second field of the array record, i.e., the field with index 1 (remember that array indices are zero-based). After completing the search, the web method then sorts the ArrayList before returning it to the client.

In order to test this, enter the following URL into a browser. For VB.NET, use:

```
http://localhost/ProgAspNet/vbStockTicker.asmx
```

and for C# use:

```
http://localhost/ProgAspNet/csStockTicker.asmx
```

In either case, you will get a page with each of the web methods as a link, similar to the page shown in Figure 15-2 in Chapter 15. Clicking on GetList will bring up a page for testing the method. If you enter "or", as shown in Figure 16-4, you will see the results that would be returned to a client, shown in Figure 16-5. Notice that in the test output, Ford comes before General Motors, even though their order is reversed in the input data. That is a result of sorting the ArrayList prior to return.

Web services can also use user-defined classes and structs as either parameters or return types. The rules to remember are:

- All the class variables must be primitive data types or arrays of primitive data types.
- All the class variables must be public.

To demonstrate the use of classes with web services, add the class definitions shown in Examples 16-15 and 16-16 to the Stock Ticker being built in this chapter.

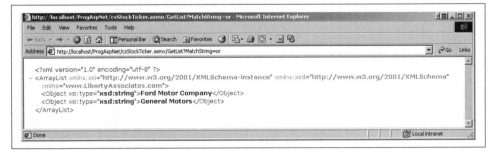

Figure 16-4. GetList test page

Figure 16-5. GetList test results

Example 16-15. Class Definitions in VB.NET

```
public class Stock
    public StockSymbol as string
    public StockName as string
    public Price as double
```

Example 16-15. Class Definitions in VB.NET (continued)

```
    public History(2) as StockHistory
end class

public class StockHistory
    public TradeDate as DateTime
    public Price as double
end class
```

Example 16-16. Class Definitions in C#

```
public class Stock
{
    public string StockSymbol;
    public string StockName;
    public double Price;
    public StockHistory[] History =
        new StockHistory[2];
}

public class StockHistory
{
    public DateTime TradeDate;
    public double Price;
}
```

The first class definition, Stock, is comprised of two strings, a double, and an array of type StockHistory. The StockHistory class consists of a date, called the TradeDate, and the stock price on that date.

> In a real-world application, you would never design a stock ticker like this. Instead of the Stock class having an array with a fixed number of stock history records, you would probably want to use a collection. You would also store the data in a database, rather than filling an array. That way, the number of history records returned by the web method would be dependent upon the number of records returned from the database query. In the example here, the data is hard-coded in an array in order to focus on the topic of using classes with web services.

The web method shown in Examples 16-17 and 16-18 uses the Stock class to return stock history data for the stock symbol passed in to it.

Example 16-17. GetHistory WebMethod in VB.NET

```
<WebMethod(Description:="Returns stock history for " & _
            "the stock symbol specified.")> _
public function GetHistory(StockSymbol as string) as Stock
    dim stock as new Stock

    ' Iterate through the array, looking for the symbol.
```

Example 16-17. GetHistory WebMethod in VB.NET (continued)

```
    for i = 0 to stocks.GetLength(0) - 1
        ' Do a case-insensitive string compare.
        if (String.Compare(StockSymbol, stocks(i,0), true) = 0) then
            stock.StockSymbol = StockSymbol
            stock.StockName = stocks(i,1)
            stock.Price = Convert.ToDouble(stocks(i,2))

            ' Populate the StockHistory data.
            stock.History(0) = new StockHistory()
            stock.History(0).TradeDate = Convert.ToDateTime("5/1/2001")
            stock.History(0).Price = Convert.ToDouble(23.25)

            stock.History(1) = new StockHistory()
            stock.History(1).TradeDate = Convert.ToDateTime("6/1/2001")
            stock.History(1).Price = Convert.ToDouble(28.75)

            return stock
        end if
    next
    stock.StockSymbol = StockSymbol
    stock.StockName = "Stock not found."
    return stock
end function
```

Example 16-18. GetHistory WebMethod in C#

```
[WebMethod(Description="Returns stock history for " +
           "the stock symbol specified.")]
public Stock GetHistory(string StockSymbol)
{
    Stock stock = new Stock();

    // Iterate through the array, looking for the symbol.
    for (int i = 0; i < stocks.GetLength(0); i++)
    {
        // Do a case-insensitive string compare.
        if (String.Compare(StockSymbol, stocks[i,0], true) == 0)
        {
            stock.StockSymbol = StockSymbol;
            stock.StockName = stocks[i,1];
            stock.Price = Convert.ToDouble(stocks[i,2]);

            // Populate the StockHistory data.
            stock.History[0] = new StockHistory();
            stock.History[0].TradeDate = Convert.ToDateTime("5/1/2001");
            stock.History[0].Price = Convert.ToDouble(23.25);

            stock.History[1] = new StockHistory();
            stock.History[1].TradeDate = Convert.ToDateTime("6/1/2001");
            stock.History[1].Price = Convert.ToDouble(28.75);

            return stock;
```

Example 16-18. GetHistory WebMethod in C# (continued)

```
        }
    }
    stock.StockSymbol = StockSymbol;
    stock.StockName = "Stock not found.";
    return stock;
}
```

In Examples 16-17 and 16-18, notice that each class is instantiated before it can be used. Iterating over the array of stocks finds the data to return. The class variables are populated from the array, and then the class itself is returned. If the stock symbol is not found, a message is placed in a convenient field of the stock class and that is returned.

Since a web service can return any data that can be encoded in an XML file, it can also return a DataSet, since that is represented internally as XML by ADO.NET. A DataSet is the only type of ADO.NET data store that can be returned by a web service.

As an exercise, we will modify an example shown previously in Chapter 11 to return a DataSet from the Bugs database used in that chapter.

 Although this sample web method does not really conform to the ongoing Stock Ticker example, we will use it for convenience.

Add the namespaces shown in Examples 16-19 and 16-20 to the Stock Ticker example.

Example 16-19. Namespace references for DataSet in VB.NET

```
Imports System.Data
Imports System.Data.SqlClient
```

Example 16-20. Namespace references for DataSet in C#

```
using System.Data;
using System.Data.SqlClient;
```

Now add the web method shown in Examples 16-21 (VB.NET) and 16-22 (C#). This web method, called GetDataSet, takes no parameters and returns a DataSet object consisting of all the BugIDs and Descriptions from the Bugs database.

Example 16-21. GetDataSet in VB.NET

```
<WebMethod(Description:="Returns a data set from the Bugs database.")> _
public function GetDataset() as DataSet
    dim connectionString as string
    dim commandString as string
```

Example 16-21. GetDataSet in VB.NET (continued)

```
    dim dataAdapter as SqlDataAdapter
    dim dataSet as new DataSet( )

    ' connect to the Bugs database
    connectionString = "YourServer; uid=sa;
       pwd=YourPassword; database= ProgASPDotNetBugs "

    ' get records from the Bugs table
    commandString = "Select BugID, Description from Bugs"

    ' create the data set command object and the DataSet
    dataAdapter = new SqlDataAdapter(commandString, connectionString)

    ' fill the data set object
    dataAdapter.Fill(dataSet,"Bugs")

    return dataSet
end function
```

Example 16-22. GetDataSet in C#

```
[WebMethod(Description="Returns a data set from the Bugs database.")]
public DataSet GetDataset( )
{
    // connect to the Bugs database
    string connectionString = "server=YourServer; uid=sa;
       pwd= YourPassword; database= ProgASPDotNetBugs ";

    // get records from the Bugs table
    string commandString = "Select BugID, Description from Bugs";

    // create the data set command object and the DataSet
    SqlDataAdapter dataAdapter = new SqlDataAdapter(commandString, connectionString);

    DataSet dataSet = new DataSet( );

    // fill the data set object
    dataAdapter.Fill(dataSet,"Bugs");

    return dataSet;
}
```

The code is copied nearly verbatim from the Page_Load method in the code in Example 11-2 and Example 11-3 and was described fully in that chapter. The important thing to note here is that a DataSet object is created from a query, then returned by the web method to the consuming client.

Examples 16-23 and 16-24 show the completed source code for the example web service that we've developed in this chapter up to this point. The code is included here to show how all the snippets of code presented so far fit together.

Example 16-23. vbStockTicker.asmx in VB.NET

```vbnet
<%@ WebService Language="VB" Class="ProgAspNet.vbStockTicker" %>

Option Strict On
Option Explicit On
Imports System
Imports System.Web.Services
Imports System.Collections
Imports System.Data
Imports System.Data.SqlClient

namespace ProgAspNet

   <WebService (Description:="A stock ticker using VB.NET.", _
          Name:="StockTicker", _
          Namespace:="www.LibertyAssociates.com")> _
   public class vbStockTicker
       inherits System.Web.Services.WebService

        ' Construct and fill an array of stock symbols and prices.
        ' Note: the stock prices are as of 7/4/01.
      dim stocks as string(,) = _
      { _
         {"MSFT","Microsoft","70.47"}, _
         {"DELL","Dell Computers","26.91"}, _
         {"HWP","Hewlett Packard","28.40"}, _
         {"YHOO","Yahoo!","19.81"}, _
         {"GE","General Electric","49.51"}, _
         {"IBM","International Business Machine","112.98"}, _
         {"GM","General Motors","64.72"}, _
         {"F","Ford Motor Company","25.05"} _
      }

      dim i as integer

      public class Stock
         public StockSymbol as string
         public StockName as string
         public Price as double
         public History(2) as StockHistory
      end class

      public class StockHistory
         public TradeDate as DateTime
         public Price as double
      end class

      <WebMethod(Description:="Returns stock history for " & _
               "the stock symbol specified.")> _
      public function GetHistory(StockSymbol as string) as Stock
         dim stock as new Stock

         ' Iterate through the array, looking for the symbol.
```

Example 16-23. vbStockTicker.asmx in VB.NET (continued)

```vb
     for i = 0 to stocks.GetLength(0) - 1
        ' Do a case-insensitive string compare.
        if (String.Compare(StockSymbol, stocks(i,0), true) = 0) then
           stock.StockSymbol = StockSymbol
           stock.StockName = stocks(i,1)
           stock.Price = Convert.ToDouble(stocks(i,2))

           ' Populate the StockHistory data.
           stock.History(0) = new StockHistory( )
           stock.History(0).TradeDate = Convert.ToDateTime("5/1/2001")
           stock.History(0).Price = Convert.ToDouble(23.25)

           stock.History(1) = new StockHistory( )
           stock.History(1).TradeDate = Convert.ToDateTime("6/1/2001")
           stock.History(1).Price = Convert.ToDouble(28.75)

           return stock
        end if
     next
     stock.StockSymbol = StockSymbol
     stock.StockName = "Stock not found."
     return stock
  end function

  <WebMethod(Description:="Returns all the stock symbols whose " & _
                "firm name matches the input string as *str*.")> _
  public function GetList(MatchString as string) as ArrayList
     dim a as ArrayList = new ArrayList( )

     ' Iterate through the array, looking for matching firm names.
     for i = 0 to stocks.GetLength(0) - 1
        ' Search is case sensitive.
        if stocks(i,1).ToUpper().IndexOf(MatchString.ToUpper( )) _
                         >= 0 then
              a.Add(stocks(i,1))
        end if
     next
      a.Sort( )
      return a
  end function

  <WebMethod(Description:="Returns the stock price for the " & _
                "input stock symbol.", _
         CacheDuration:=20)> _
  public function GetPrice(StockSymbol as string) as Double
  ' Given a stock symbol, return the price.
     ' Iterate through the array, looking for the symbol.
     for i = 0 to stocks.GetLength(0) - 1
        ' Do a case-insensitive string compare.
        if (String.Compare(StockSymbol, stocks(i,0), true) = 0) then
           return Convert.ToDouble(stocks(i,2))
        end if
```

Example 16-23. vbStockTicker.asmx in VB.NET (continued)

```
        next

        return 0
End Function

<WebMethod(Description:="Returns the firm name for the input " & _
                "stock symbol.", _
        CacheDuration:=86400)> _
public function GetName(StockSymbol as string) as string
'   Given a stock symbol, return the name.
        ' Iterate through the array, looking for the symbol.
        for i = 0 to stocks.GetLength(0) - 1
           ' Do a case-insensitive string compare.
           if (String.Compare(StockSymbol, stocks(i,0), true) = 0) then
              return stocks(i,1)
           end if
        next

        return "Symbol not found."
End Function

<WebMethod(Description:="Sets the stock exchange for the " & _
                    "application.")> _
public sub SetStockExchange(Exchange as string)
        Application("exchange") = Exchange
end sub

<WebMethod(Description:="Gets the stock exchange for the " & _
                    "application. It must previously be set.")> _
public function GetStockExchange() as string
        return Application("exchange").ToString()
end function

<WebMethod(Description:="Number of hits per session.", _
        EnableSession:=true)> _
public function HitCounter() as integer
        if Session("HitCounter") is Nothing then
           Session("HitCounter") = 1
        else
           Session("HitCounter") = CInt(Session("HitCounter")) + 1
        end if

        return CInt(Session("HitCounter"))
end function

<WebMethod(Description:="Returns the value of the users " & _
                "holdings in a specified stock symbol.", _
                MessageName:="GetValuePortfolio")> _
public Function GetValue(StockSymbol as string) as double
        ' Put code here to get the username of the current user, fetch
        ' both the current price of the specified StockSymbol and number
        ' of shares held by the current user, multiply the two together,
```

Example 16-23. vbStockTicker.asmx in VB.NET (continued)

```
        '   and return the result.
        return 0
     end Function

     <WebMethod(Description:="Returns the value of a specified " & _
                    "number of shares in a specified stock symbol.", _
                    MessageName:="GetValueStock")> _
     public Function GetValue(StockSymbol as string, _
                    NumShares as integer) as double
        '  Put code here to get the current price of the specified
        '  StockSymbol,   multiply it times NumShares, and return
        '  the result.
        return 0
     end function

     <WebMethod(Description:="Returns a data set from the Bugs " & _
                    "database.")> _
     public function GetDataset() as DataSet
        dim connectionString as string
        dim commandString as string
        dim dataAdapter as SqlDataAdapter
        dim dataSet as new DataSet()

        ' connect to the Bugs database
        connectionString = "server=Ath13; uid=sa; pwd=stersol; " & _
                    "database=Bugs"

        ' get records from the Bugs table
        commandString = "Select BugID, Description from Bugs"

        ' create the data set command object and the DataSet
        dataAdapter = new SqlDataAdapter(commandString, connectionString)

        ' fill the data set object
        dataAdapter.Fill(dataSet,"Bugs")

        return dataSet
     end function

  End Class
End namespace
```

Example 16-24. csStockTicker.asmx in C#

```
<%@ WebService Language="C#" Class="ProgAspNet.csStockTicker" %>

using System;
using System.Web.Services;
using System.Collections;
using System.Data;
using System.Data.SqlClient;
```

Example 16-24. csStockTicker.asmx in C# (continued)

```csharp
namespace ProgAspNet
{
   [WebService (Description="A stock ticker using C#.",
            Name="StockTicker",
            Namespace="www.LibertyAssociates.com")]
   public class csStockTicker : System.Web.Services.WebService
     {
        // Construct and fill an array of stock symbols and prices.
        // Note: the stock prices are as of 7/4/01.
      string[,] stocks =
      {
         {"MSFT","Microsoft","70.47"},
         {"DELL","Dell Computers","26.91"},
         {"HWP","Hewlett Packard","28.40"},
         {"YHOO","Yahoo!","19.81"},
         {"GE","General Electric","49.51"},
         {"IBM","International Business Machine","112.98"},
         {"GM","General Motors","64.72"},
         {"F","Ford Motor Company","25.05"}
      };

      public class Stock
      {
         public string StockSymbol;
         public string StockName;
         public double Price;
         public StockHistory[] History =
               new StockHistory[2];
      }

      public class StockHistory
      {
         public DateTime TradeDate;
         public double Price;
      }

      [WebMethod(Description="Returns stock history for " +
                  "the stock symbol specified.")]
      public Stock GetHistory(string StockSymbol)
      {
         Stock stock = new Stock();

         // Iterate through the array, looking for the symbol.
         for (int i = 0; i < stocks.GetLength(0); i++)
         {
            // Do a case-insensitive string compare.
            if (String.Compare(StockSymbol, stocks[i,0], true) == 0)
            {
               stock.StockSymbol = StockSymbol;
               stock.StockName = stocks[i,1];
               stock.Price = Convert.ToDouble(stocks[i,2]);

               // Populate the StockHistory data.
```

Example 16-24. csStockTicker.asmx in C# (continued)

```csharp
            stock.History[0] = new StockHistory( );
            stock.History[0].TradeDate =
                Convert.ToDateTime("5/1/2001");
            stock.History[0].Price = Convert.ToDouble(23.25);

            stock.History[1] = new StockHistory( );
            stock.History[1].TradeDate =
                Convert.ToDateTime("6/1/2001");
            stock.History[1].Price = Convert.ToDouble(28.75);

            return stock;
        }
    }
    stock.StockSymbol = StockSymbol;
    stock.StockName = "Stock not found.";
    return stock;
}

[WebMethod(Description="Returns all the stock symbols whose firm " +
                "name matches the input string as *str*.")]
public ArrayList GetList(string MatchString)
{
    ArrayList a = new ArrayList( );

    //  Iterate through the array, looking for matching firm names.
    for (int i = 0; i < stocks.GetLength(0); i++)
    {
        //  Search is case sensitive.
        if ( stocks[i,1].ToUpper().IndexOf(MatchString.ToUpper( )) >= 0)
            a.Add(stocks[i,1]);
    }
    a.Sort( );
    return a;
}

[WebMethod(Description="Returns the stock price for the input " +
                "stock symbol.",
        CacheDuration=20)]
public double GetPrice(string StockSymbol)
//  Given a stock symbol, return the price.
{
    //  Iterate through the array, looking for the symbol.
    for (int i = 0; i < stocks.GetLength(0); i++)
    {
        //  Do a case-insensitive string compare.
        if (String.Compare(StockSymbol, stocks[i,0], true) == 0)
            return Convert.ToDouble(stocks[i,2]);
    }
    return 0;
}

[WebMethod(Description="Returns the firm name for the input " +
                    "stock symbol.",
```

Example 16-24. csStockTicker.asmx in C# (continued)

```
            CacheDuration=86400)]
    public string GetName(string StockSymbol)
    //  Given a stock symbol, return the name.
    {
        //  Iterate through the array, looking for the symbol.
        for (int i = 0; i < stocks.GetLength(0); i++)
        {
            //  Do a case-insensitive string compare.
            if (String.Compare(StockSymbol, stocks[i,0], true) == 0)
                return stocks[i,1];
        }
        return "Symbol not found.";
    }


    [WebMethod(Description="Sets the stock exchange for the " +
                        "application.")]
    public void SetStockExchange(string Exchange)
    {
        Application["exchange"] = Exchange;
    }


    [WebMethod(Description="Gets the stock exchange for the " +
                "application. It must previously be set.")]
    public string GetStockExchange()
    {
        return Application["exchange"].ToString();
    }


    [WebMethod(Description="Number of hits per session.",
                EnableSession=true)]
    public int HitCounter()
    {
        if (Session["HitCounter"] == null)
        {
            Session["HitCounter"] = 1;
        }
        else
        {
            Session["HitCounter"] = ((int) Session["HitCounter"]) + 1;
        }

        return ((int) Session["HitCounter"]);
    }


    [WebMethod(Description="Returns the value of the users holdings " +
                        "in a specified stock symbol.",
                MessageName="GetValuePortfolio")]
    public double GetValue(string StockSymbol)
    {
        /*  Put code here to get the username of the current user, fetch
            both the current price of the specified StockSymbol and number
            of shares held by the current user, multiply the two together,
            and return the result.
```

Example 16-24. csStockTicker.asmx in C# (continued)

```csharp
    */
    return 0;
}

[WebMethod(Description="Returns the value of a specified " +
                "number of shares in a specified stock symbol.",
        MessageName="GetValueStock")]
public double GetValue(string StockSymbol, int NumShares)
{
    /*  Put code here to get the current price of the specified
        StockSymbol, multiply it times NumShares, and return the
        result.
    */
    return 0;
}

[WebMethod(Description="Returns a data set from the Bugs " +
                "database.")]
public DataSet GetDataset( )
{
    // connect to the Bugs database
    string connectionString = "server=Ath13; uid=sa; pwd=stersol; " +
                "database=Bugs";

    // get records from the Bugs table
    string commandString = "Select BugID, Description from Bugs";

    // create the data set command object and the DataSet
    SqlDataAdapter dataAdapter = new SqlDataAdapter(commandString,
                    connectionString);

    DataSet dataSet = new DataSet( );

    // fill the data set object
    dataAdapter.Fill(dataSet,"Bugs");

    return dataSet;
}
}
}
```

Using Code-Behind

When you are creating web pages, code-behind allows you to separate application logic from design or user interface (UI) elements.

Code-behind is the default code model of Visual Studio .NET. In fact, it is very inconvenient to use Visual Studio .NET to write any ASP.NET application without using code-behind.

Since web services have no design or UI component, the case for using code-behind is not quite so compelling. However, there is a performance benefit to code-behind. As we will discuss, the class implementing the code-behind must be compiled into a *dll* ahead of time and made available to the web service. By contrast, the WebService class contained in the *.asmx* file, similar to the page class in the *.aspx* file, is compiled on the fly by the .NET Framework the first time the class is called. That compiled version is then cached on the server for subsequent requests. For a complete discussion of caching and performance, see Chapter18. For now, suffice it to say that the first time a web service or web page is called, there will be a delay for inline code while the class is compiled, while a code-behind implementation will never experience that delay.

It is very easy to convert the Stock Ticker web service created so far in this chapter from an inline code model to a code-behind model. In this section, you will first do code-behind in a text editor, then in Visual Studio .NET.

Using a text editor

In a text editor, create a new file called *vbStockTickerCodeBehind.asmx* for the VB.NET version, and *csStockTickerCodeBehind.asmx* for the C# version. Each file will consist of a single line of code, as shown in Examples 16-25 and 16-26.

Example 16-25. vbStockTickerCodeBehind.asmx

```
<%@ WebService Language="vb" Class="ProgAspNet.vbStockTicker" %>
```

Example 16-26. csStockTickerCodeBehind.asmx

```
<%@ WebService Language="c#" Class="ProgAspNet.csStockTicker" %>
```

This WebService directive uses the same attributes for code-behind as a normal web page, as described in Chapter 6. The Language attribute specifies the language, either VB, C#, or JS for VB.NET, C#, or JScript, respectively.

The Class attribute specifies the name of the code-behind class that implements the web service. In the code in Examples 16-25 and 16-26, the class specified is ProgAsp-Net.vbStockTicker or ProgAspNet.csStockTicker, depending on the language used. These are the fully qualified web service class names used in the examples in this chapter. The class names themselves have prepended to them the namespace ProgAspNet, from Examples 16-1 and 16-2.

Herein lies a significant difference between using code-behind and using inline code. With code-behind, the code-behind class must be compiled prior to calling the *.asmx* file (or *.aspx* file for normal web pages; it works the same for both web pages and web services). The compiled *dll* then must be placed in a *bin* subdirectory directly beneath the directory containing the *.asmx* (or *.aspx*) file. This is shown schematically in Figure 16-6, using the names for the C# implementation.

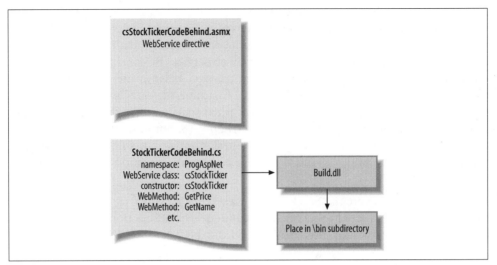

Figure 16-6. Using code-behind

In order to create the code-behind file, follow these steps:

1. Save the inline *.asmx* file being developed throughout this chapter as either *StockTickerCodeBehind.vb* or *StockTickerCodeBehind.cs*, depending on the language.

2. Open this new code-behind file in an editor and delete the first line in the file, the WebService directive.

3. Save the new code-behind file.

The code-behind file can then be compiled into a *dll*. This is done using a language-specific command from the command prompt.

In order for this (or any other .NET) command line to work, the path must be set to include the executable being called. To do this manually would not be trivial. Instead, there is an item in the Start menu:

```
Programs\Microsoft Visual Studio .NET\Visual Studio .NET
Tools\Visual Studio .NET Command Prompt
```

that opens a command prompt window (what used to be known as a DOS prompt, for you old-timers) with the proper path set.

First change the current directory of the command window to be the directory containing the code-behind file. The command to do this is something like:

```
cd projects\programming asp.net
```

The generic syntax for the compiler is:

```
compilerExe [parameters] inputFile.ext
```

where *compilerExe* is either vbc for VB.NET or csc for C#. This is followed by one or more parameters, which is then followed by the name of the source code file being compiled.

For VB.NET, use the following single-line command to compile the DLL:

```
vbc /out:bin\vbStockTickerCodeBehind.dll /t:library /r:system.dll,system.web.
dll,system.web.services.dll,
system.data.dll,system.XML.dll StockTickerCodebehind.vb
```

and for C# use this single-line command:

```
csc /out:bin\csStockTickerCodeBehind.dll /t:library /r:system.dll,system.web.
dll,system.web.services.dll StockTickerCodebehind.cs
```

The command-line compilers have a large number of parameters available to them, three of which are used here. In order to see the complete list of parameters available, enter the following command at the command prompt:

```
compilerExe /?
```

Table 16-2 lists the parameters used in the preceding command lines.

Table 16-2. Parameters used in commands to compile the dll

Parameter	Short form	Description
/out:<filename>		Output filename. If not specified, then the output filename is derived from the first source file.
/target:library	/t:library	Build a library file. Alternative values for target are exe, winexe, and module.
/reference:<file list>	/r:	Reference the specified assembly files. If more than one file, either include multiple reference parameters or separate filenames with commas within a single reference parameter. Be certain not to include any spaces between filenames.

Notice there is a correlation between the namespaces referenced in the source code and the files referenced in the compile command. Table 16-3 shows the correspondence.

Table 16-3. Correspondence of source code and compiler references

Source code reference	Compiler reference	Description
System	*system.dll*	Supplies fundamental classes and base classes.
-	*system.web.dll*	Supplies classes and interfaces to enable client/server communications. Not necessary in source code because it is referenced automatically by the ASP.NET runtime.
System.Web.Services	*system.web.services.dll*	Classes that enable web services.
System.Collections	-	Provides classes and interfaces used by various collections, including Arrays and ArrayLists. Not necessary in the compiler reference because it is included in *mscorlib.dll*, which is referenced by default.

Once the *dll* is created and located in the proper *bin* subdirectory (which the previous command lines do for you), then the *.asmx* file can be tested in a browser or called by a client, just like any other *.asmx* file.

Using Visual Studio .NET

Visual Studio .NET offers the programmer several advantages over a plain text editor, in addition to automating the creation of code-behind. Among them are color coding of the source code, integrated debugging, IntelliSense, integrated compiling, and full integration with the development environment. Use of the Visual Studio .NET IDE is covered in detail in Chapter 6.

Open Visual Studio .NET to create a web service using code-behind. Click on the New Project button to start a new project. You will be presented with the dialog box shown in Figure 16-7.

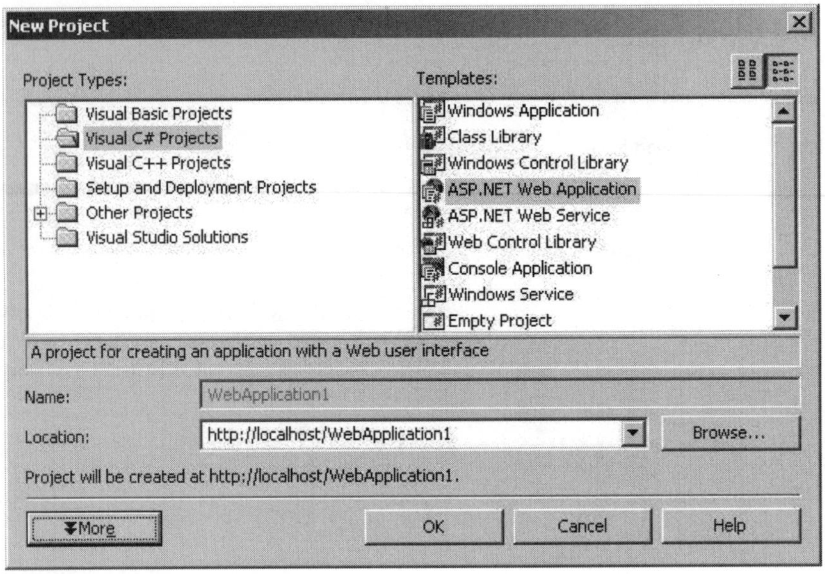

Figure 16-7. New Project dialog box

You can select a Project Type of the language of your choice. This example will use VB.NET.

Select the ASP.NET web service template.

The default name for the project will be WebService1. Change that to StockTickerVB, as shown in Figure 16-7. When you click the OK button, Visual Studio .NET will cook for few a moments, and then it will open in design mode.

Be careful if using any non-alpha characters in the project name. I originally named this project StockTicker-VB. Visual Studio .NET seemed to accept this, but on moving through the process, the hyphen was converted to an underscore under some circumstances and the project would not compile and run properly.

Pay particular attention to the Solution Explorer, located in the upper right quadrant of the screen by default, and shown in Figure 16-8.

Figure 16-8. Default Solution Explorer

The Solution Explorer shows most, but not all, of the files that comprise the project. In a desktop .NET application (i.e., not an ASP.NET project), all of the files in a project would be located in a subdirectory, named the same as the project name, located under the default project directory. One of these files has an extension of *.sln*. The *.sln* file tells Visual Studio .NET what files to include in the project. An associated file has an extension of *.suo*.

The default project location can be set by selecting Tools → Options... → Environment → Projects and Solutions and changing the directory in the edit box.

When creating an ASP.NET project, either a web page or a web service, the project directory is still created under the default projects directory. That directory still contains the *.sln* and *.suo* files. If these files are missing, then Visual Studio .NET cannot open the project. However, all the other files comprising the project are contained in the virtual root directory of the application, which is a subdirectory with the project name created under the physical directory corresponding to localhost. On most machines the physical directory corresponding to localhost is *c:\inetpub\wwwroot*.

There are other files Visual Studio .NET does not display by default. You can force the Solution Explorer to show all files by clicking on the Show All Files icon in the

Solution Explorer tool bar. (It is the second icon from the right, just below the word "StockTicker" in Figure 16-8.) Clicking on this icon and expanding all the nodes results in the Solution Explorer shown in Figure 16-9.

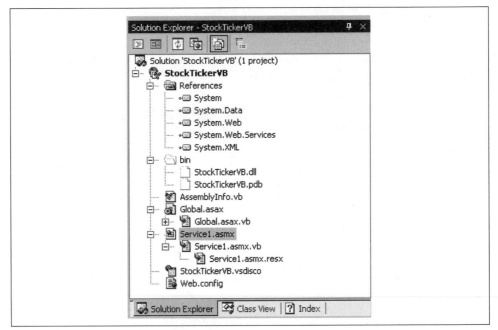

Figure 16-9. Expanded Solution Explorer

Under *References*, you can see all the namespaces that are referenced by default. Under *bin*, you can see any files contained in that subdirectory. (The IDE automatically put the *dll* and *pdb* files there on startup.)

The rest of the entries in the Solution Explorer are files contained in the virtual root directory of the application. For this application, that virtual root directory will typically be:

```
c:\InetPub\wwwroot\StockTickerVB
```

AssemblyInfo.vb contains versioning information and will be covered in more detail in Chapter 20.

The *global.asax* file contains global configuration information for the entire application. It was covered in Chapter 6, and will be covered further in Chapter 20. Notice that it is now apparent that the *global.asax* file uses code-behind, with the actual Global class contained in the code-behind file (*global.asax.vb* for VB.NET projects, *global.asax.cs* for C# projects).

The *.resx* files are resource files created by the IDE which contain localization information.

The *Service1* files contain the actual web service code. They will be covered shortly.

The *StockTickerVB.vsdisco* is a discovery file, used by the consumer of the web service. Discovery will be covered in Chapter 17.

Web.config is another configuration file, which was covered in Chapter 6 and will be covered further in Chapter 20.

This leaves the *Service1* files. Click on either the *Service1.asmx* or the *Service1.asmx. vb* files in the Solution Explorer. Nothing appears in the design window. This is because Visual Studio .NET displays design objects by default, and web services do not use any. They are all code.

In order to see the contents of *Service1.asmx*, right-click on the file in the Solution Explorer, select Open With..., and select Source Code (Text) Editor from the list of choices. Looking at *Service1.asmx*, you will see that the file has a single line of code, shown in Example 16-27.

Example 16-27. Service1.asmx in Visual Studio .NET

```
<%@ WebService Language="vb" Codebehind="Service1.asmx.vb" Class="StockTickerVB.Service1"
%>
```

Compare this to the WebService directives in Examples 16-1 and 16-2. The Codebehind attribute is used by Visual Studio .NET to know where to find the code-behind file. The Class attribute points to the default code-behind class defined in the code-behind file.

You can view any of the other files in the Solution Explorer by right-clicking on the file and selecting either Open or View Code, as appropriate. Once a code window is open in the design window, you can switch back and forth among the various files by clicking on the correct tab at the top of the design window.

Click on the *Service1.asmx* file, right-click, and select View Code from the context-sensitive menu. The contents of the code-behind file, *Service1.asmx.vb*, are displayed. Notice that there is already code in place, as shown in Figure 16-10.

In addition to all the other infrastructure Visual Studio puts into the project, it includes the minimum necessary code to implement a code-behind web service file. The Imports statement necessary to allow the web service class, Service1, to derive from the WebService base class is added, and that class is defined, at least in skeleton form.

The class definition is followed by a collapsed region, indicated by the plus symbol along the left margin, which contains boilerplate code inserted by and necessary to the IDE.

Next comes some commented code demonstrating a very simple web method. You can delete the commented sample code.

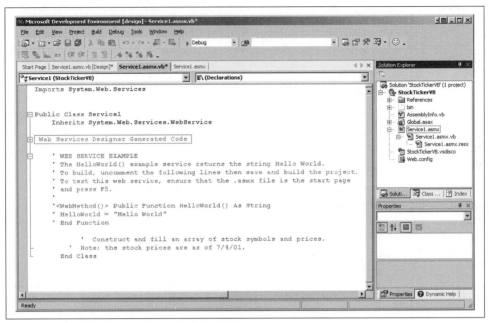

Figure 16-10. Boilerplate code in code-behind file

Even though you have not yet added any custom code to this project, you can prove to yourself that this is indeed a valid web service by clicking on the Start icon, or pressing F5, to compile and run the web service. After the code-behind class is compiled and automatically placed in the *\bin* directory, a browser will open with the familiar web service test page. However, since there are not yet any web methods defined, there will be nothing to test.

Now cut and paste the code from the code-behind file created earlier in this chapter into the code-behind file in Visual Studio .NET, *Service1.asmx.vb*. Be careful not to duplicate the line importing System.Web.Services. Also, be sure to put the Option lines at the very beginning of the file and the namespace opening line before the Service1 class definition with the end namespace line at the very end of the file.

The beginning of the code-behind file now looks like Figure 16-11.

Notice that the WebService attribute's Description property has been slightly edited to clearly identify this as coming from Visual Studio .NET, although the Name property remains unchanged as "StockTicker."

Before this will run correctly, the web service file, *Service1.asmx*, must be edited slightly to take into account the addition of the namespace to the code-behind file. Switch to that file and edit the Class attribute value by including the ProgAspNet namespace as part of the class name. The contents of the modified *Service1.asmx* should now look like Example 16-28.

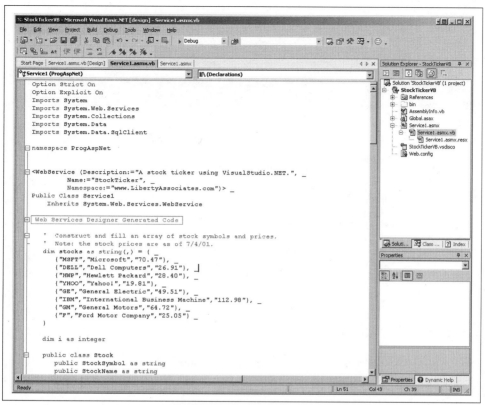

Figure 16-11. Beginning of code-behind file

Example 16-28. Modified Service1.asmx in Visual Studio .NET

```
<%@ WebService Language="vb" Codebehind="Service1.asmx.vb" Class="StockTickerVB.
ProgAspNet.Service1" %>
```

Now run test the web service by clicking on the Run icon or pressing F5. You should get a browser window looking something like Figure 16-12.

Notice that the name of the web service reflects the name property specified in the WebService attribute's Name property. Also, the new WebService attribute's Description property is displayed in the test. Everything else is exactly the same as the web service created in a text editor.

Creating a Discovery File

Once you have created a web service, there must be some way for the developers who will develop the consuming applications to find out about the methods exposed by the web service. This process is called *discovery*.

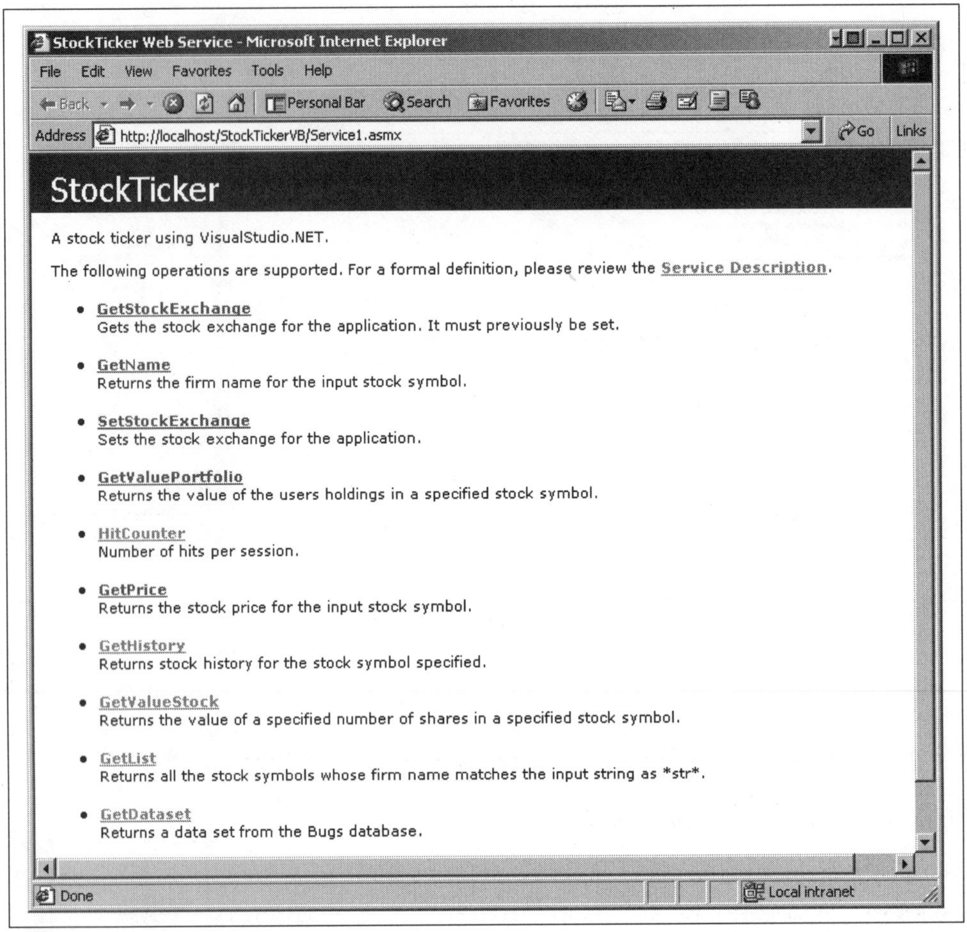

Figure 16-12. Visual Studio .NET code-behind test

The description of the web service is contained in a service description document, an XML document written in a format called WSDL (Web Service Description Language). You have already seen the WSDL document for our example web service in this chapter, in Figure 16-2. There are two ways to generate a WSDL file.

The first is to enter the URL of the web service *.asmx* file in a browser to generate the web service test page, as shown in several of the figures in this chapter, including Figures 16-4 and 16-12. Near the top of the test page will be a link to a Service Description. Clicking on that link will bring up the WSDL document.

Alternatively, enter the URL for a web service *.asmx* file in a browser with ?WSDL appended to the end of the URL. For example, entering the following URL in a browser would display the WSDL for the web service *csStickTicker.asmx*:

```
http://localhost/ProgAspNet/csStockTicker.asmx?WSDL
```

In order to ease the chore of generating a WSDL document for the developer creating the consuming application, you can create a *.disco* file. This is an XML file located in the same virtual directory as the *.asmx* file. The developer creating the consuming application can then use the *.disco* file, as will be demonstrated shortly.

Example 16-29 shows a *.disco* file for the web service in the above URL.

Example 16-29. csStockTicker.disco, a discovery file for StockTicker web service

```
<?xml version="1.0" ?>
<disco:discovery
    xmlns:disco="http://schemas.xmlsoap.org/disco"
    xmlns:scl="http://schemas.xmlsoap.org/disco/scl">
    <scl:contractRef ref="http://localhost/ProgAspNet/csStockTicker.asmx?WSDL"/>
</disco:discovery>
```

The first line in Example 16-29 specifies the file as XML and the version. The rest of the file is contained within a pair of disco:discovery tags. This tag points to the links a client should follow if it wants to find out about the web service. The next two lines specify XML namespace aliases, which refer to URLs that define the disco and scl tags.

The scl:contractRef tag specifies where the service description can be found. Notice that it is the same URL mentioned above for manually generating the WSDL. It is not always the case that the URL of the *.disco* file and URL of the *.asmx* file it references point to the same location.

The *.disco* file can also reference another *.disco* file by including a line similar to:

```
<disco:discoveryRef ref="SomeFolder/default.disco" />
```

where *default.disco* is another *.disco* file in a subdirectory below the current directory, called *SomeFolder*.

Although you can create the *.disco* file manually, it is far easier to use the *disco.exe* command-line utility. In order to do this, open a command prompt window (remember to use the Visual Studio .NET Command Prompt from the Start Menu in order to get the correct path). Then enter a command similar to the following:

```
disco /out:<output directory name> http://localhost/ProgAspNet/csStockTicker.asmx
```

As an alternative to using the out switch to specify the output directory, change the directory to the directory you want the output to be located in before executing the command and run the disco utility from that directory. The output will go to the current directory.

The disco utility executed in the above command line will put three files (summarized in Table 16-4) in the output directory.

Table 16-4. Files output by the disco utility

Filename	Description
csStockTicker.disco	Discovery document you are trying to create
csStockTicker.WSDL	This is the exact same WSDL for the web service generated by entering the *.asmx* file in a browser with "?wsdl"? appended to the URL
results.discomap	Alternative discovery document

At this stage of the process, the *.disco* file is the main output you are interested in. The other two files may be used by a developer creating a consuming application, as will be described in the next chapter.

For a complete listing of all the parameters available to the disco utility, enter the following command line:

```
disco /?
```

Deployment

Deploying web services is very similar to deploying web pages. The *.asmx* file must be located in a virtual directory exposed by IIS so that it is accessible to a browser on the Internet. If you have a *.disco* file for the web service (described in the previous section), then this file should also be in the application virtual directory. This allows the web service to be discovered and also allows proxies to be created by consuming applications. Both of these concepts will be described in the next chapter.

Also, just as with web pages, if there is a code-behind class that implements the web service, the assembly file (i.e., the *dll*) must be located in the *\bin* directory immediately beneath the virtual directory containing the *.asmx* file.

If the application requires a *web.config* file (described fully in Chapter 20), then this file too should be copied to the application virtual directory.

Figure 16-13 shows a typical directory structure on a production web server for a web service called csStockTicker.

Referring to Figure 16-13, if a virtual directory was defined on the web server called StockTicker, which was mapped to the directory called csStockTicker, then the URL for referring to the *.asmx* file would be:

```
http://YourDomain.com/StockTicker/csStockTicker.asmx
```

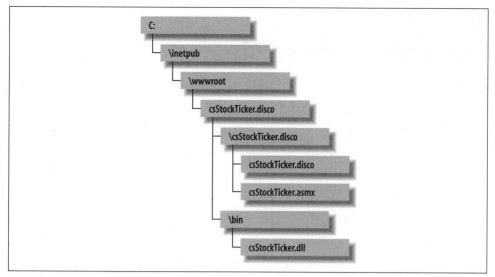

Figure 16-13. Typical deployment directory structure

CHAPTER 17

Consuming Web Services

While Chapter 15 gave an overview of web services and Chapter 16 described in detail how to create a web service, this chapter will explain how to create a web service client application or web service consumer. The consuming application can be a web page, another web service, or a desktop application.

Once a web service is created and made available to consumers on the Internet, it is up to the developer creating the client application to find the web service, create the client proxy, and incorporate the proxy into the client. The client can then make method calls against the remote web service as though it were making local calls. In fact, the client application *is* making local method calls against the proxy—it just behaves as if it is making calls directly to the web service over the Internet.

Discovery

Discovery is the process of finding out what web services are available, what methods and properties are exposed by a specific web service, what parameters those methods and properties expect to receive, and what data type the web method returns. All of this information is contained in the WSDL (Web Services Description Language) document, introduced in the preceding chapter.

Discovery is an optional process. If the consuming developer knows the URL of the web service file (*.asmx*) itself, then there is no need to do discovery. However, it will often be the case that the consuming developer will not know the location of the web service file or the WSDL document. In these instances, ASP.NET provides a discovery command-line utility called *disco.exe* that provides the consuming developer with the information necessary to create the client.

You have already seen in Chapter 16 how the disco utility allows the developer who created the web service to generate a *.disco* file. Now the consuming developer can use the same utility to aid in creation of the client.

There are two equivalent ways of using the disco utility to generate the WSDL file. If you know the URL of the web service file, you can use that as input, as shown in the following command line:

```
disco http://WebSrvcDomain.com/csStockTicker.asmx?WSDL
```

If you don't know the URL of the *.asmx* file but do know the URL of the *.disco* file, you can use that file as input to disco, as in:

```
disco http://WebSrvcDomain.com/csStockTicker.disco
```

In either case, a WSDL file will be generated in the output directory.

To force the output directory to be somewhere other than the current directory, use the /out: parameter, or /o: for short, as in:

```
disco /out:<output directory name>
      http://WebSrvcDomain.com/csStockTicker.disco
```

The disco utility executed in the above command line will put three files, summarized in Table 17-1, in the output directory.

Table 17-1. Files output by the disco utility

Filename	Description
csStockTicker.disco	Discovery document you are trying to create
csStockTicker.WSDL	The exact same WSDL for the Web Service generated by entering the *.asmx* file in a browser with "?wsdl? appended to the URL
results.discomap	Alternative discovery document

For a complete listing of all the parameters available to the disco utility, enter the following command line:

```
disco /?
```

In addition to outputting a *.disco* file and a WSDL file, the disco utility will also create a *.discomap* file, which can be used as input to the WSDL utility, described later in this chapter.

Creating the Proxy

As described in Chapter 15 and shown schematically in Figure 15-1, a web service is consumed by a client application by use of a *proxy*. A proxy is a substitute, or local stand-in, for the web service. Once the proxy is created and registered with the consuming application, then method calls can be made against the web service. In actuality, those method calls will be made against the local proxy. It will seem to the consuming application that the web service is local to the application.

UDDI

UDDI (Universal Description, Discovery, and Integration) is a registry that allows businesses to locate web services exposed on the Internet. For complete information about UDDI, visit *www.UDDI.org*. UDDI is a joint project of IBM, Microsoft, and Ariba and will eventually be turned over to a standards organization, such as the W3C (*www.w3c.org*).

UDDI will have two main components:

- A web-based registry for locating web services. Any business can publish information about the web services it is making available. This registry can be searched either through a web page interface or programmatically via web services.
- Standard XML Schema for business descriptions. The data contained in the UDDI Registry is contained in XML documents with standardized fields used to describe a business.

At the time of this writing, the UDDI specification is still under development. However, it is reasonable to expect that in time, UDDI will become a universal "phone book" for finding and consuming web services.

There are two ways to generate the proxy. The first way, described in the next section, is to generate the source code for the proxy class manually and compile that into the proxy DLL. The advantages to this method are:

- You do not need to use Visual Studio .NET.
- The command-line approach offers more flexibility and features over Visual Studio .NET.

The alternative method is to allow Visual Studio .NET to create the proxy and register it with the consuming application in a single step. The advantage to this method is that it is much less work. Using Visual Studio .NET will be demonstrated shortly.

Manually Generating the Proxy Class Source Code

To create the proxy, use another command-line utility called *wsdl.exe*. This utility takes a WSDL file as input. The WSDL file can either be stored locally, having been previously created using the disco command-line utility, or it can be generated on the fly from the web service file itself. The following two command lines will yield the same result, assuming that the local WSDL file came from the remote *.asmx* file:

```
wsdl csStockTicker.WSDL
wsdl http://localhost/ProgAspNet/csStockTicker.asmx?wsdl
```

Alternatively, the WSDL utility can take a *.discomap* file, described earlier in the "Discovery" section, created by the disco utility as input.

The output from the WSDL utility is a source code file containing the proxy class, which can then be compiled into a library, or *dll*, file. The default language for this output source is C#. To change the language of the output file, use the `/language:` parameter, or `/l:` for short. Valid values for the language parameter are `CS`, `VB`, or `JS`, for C#, VB.NET, and JScript.NET, respectively. So to force the output to be VB.NET, you would use a command line similar to:

```
wsdl /l:VB http://localhost/ProgAspNet/vbStockTicker.asmx?wsdl
```

By default, the first component of the output filename is based on the input file as follows. If the `WebService` attribute in the *.asmx* file has a Name property, then the output file will have that name. If not, the output name will have the name of the web service class. Note that every output filename also has an extension corresponding to the language.

For example, suppose that the file *vbStockTicker.asmx* has the following `WebService` attribute and class definition:

```
<WebService (Description:="A stock ticker using VB.NET.", _
        Name:="StockTicker", _
        Namespace:="www.LibertyAssociates.com")> _
public class vbStockTicker
    inherits System.Web.Services.WebService
```

If the WSDL utility is run against the WSDL file generated from this *.asmx* file with the language set to VB, then the output filename would be *StockTicker.vb*. However, if the Name property is removed from the *.asmx* source file, then the output name will be *vbStockTicker.vb*. By default the output file will be in the current directory of the command prompt.

You can specify both the output filename and location by using the `/out:` parameter, or `/o:` for short. For example, the following command line will force the output file to have the name *Test.vb* and be located in the *bin* directory below the current directory:

```
wsdl /l:VB /o:bin\test.vb
        http://localhost/ProgAspNet/vbStockTicker.asmx?WSDL
```

Table 17-2 shows some of the other switches available to the WSDL utility.

Table 17-2. WSDL utility switches

Parameter	Description
`/nologo`	Suppress the Microsoft banner.
`/namespace:<namespace>`	Specify the namespace for the generated proxy. The default is the global namespace.
`/protocol:<protocol>`	Specify the protocol to implement. Valid values are `HttpGet`, `HttpPost`, or `SOAP`. The default is `SOAP`.

`/username:<username>`
`/password:<password>`
`/domain:<domain>`
	Credentials to use when connecting to a server that requires authentication.

For a complete list of parameters for *wsdl.exe*, enter the following from the command line:

```
wsdl /?
```

Proxy Class Details

Compare the beginning of the original web service source file, *csStockTicker.asmx*, reproduced in Example 17-1, with the beginning of the generated source code for the proxy class, *StockTicker.cs*, shown in Example 17-2.

Example 17-1. Beginning of csStockTicker.asmx

```
<%@ WebService Language="C#" Class="ProgAspNet.csStockTicker" %>

using System;
using System.Web.Services;
using System.Collections;
using System.Data;
using System.Data.SqlClient;

namespace ProgAspNet
{
   [WebService (Description="A stock ticker using C#.",
           Name="StockTicker",
           Namespace="www.LibertyAssociates.com")]
   public class csStockTicker : System.Web.Services.WebService
       {
       // Construct and fill an array of stock symbols and prices.
       // Note: the stock prices are as of 7/4/01.
      string[,] stocks =
      {
          {"MSFT","Microsoft","70.47"},
          {"DELL","Dell Computers","26.91"},
          {"HWP","Hewlett Packard","28.40"},
          {"YHOO","Yahoo!","19.81"},
          {"GE","General Electric","49.51"},
          {"IBM","International Business Machine","112.98"},
          {"GM","General Motors","64.72"},
          {"F","Ford Motor Company","25.05"}
      };

      public class Stock
      {
          public string StockSymbol;
          public string StockName;
          public double Price;
          public StockHistory[] History =
                new StockHistory[2];
      }

      public class StockHistory
      {
```

Example 17-1. Beginning of csStockTicker.asmx (continued)

```
      public DateTime TradeDate;
      public double Price;
   }

   [WebMethod(Description="Returns stock history for " +
               "the stock symbol specified.")]
   public Stock GetHistory(string StockSymbol)
   {
      Stock stock = new Stock( );

      //  Iterate through the array, looking for the symbol.
      for (int i = 0; i < stocks.GetLength(0); i++)
      {
         //  Do a case-insensitive string compare.
         if (String.Compare(StockSymbol, stocks[i,0], true) == 0)
         {
            stock.StockSymbol = StockSymbol;
            stock.StockName = stocks[i,1];
            stock.Price = Convert.ToDouble(stocks[i,2]);

            //  Populate the StockHistory data.
            stock.History[0] = new StockHistory( );
            stock.History[0].TradeDate =
               Convert.ToDateTime("5/1/2001");
            stock.History[0].Price = Convert.ToDouble(23.25);

            stock.History[1] = new StockHistory( );
            stock.History[1].TradeDate =
            Convert.ToDateTime("6/1/2001");
            stock.History[1].Price = Convert.ToDouble(28.75);

            return stock;
         }
      }
      stock.StockSymbol = StockSymbol;
      stock.StockName = "Stock not found.";
      return stock;
   }
```

Example 17-2. Beginning of Proxy class source code file StockTicker.cs

```
//------------------------------------------------------------------------------
// <autogenerated>
//     This code was generated by a tool.
//     Runtime Version: 1.0.2914.16
//
//     Changes to this file may cause incorrect behavior and will be lost if
//     the code is regenerated.
// </autogenerated>
//------------------------------------------------------------------------------

//
```

Example 17-2. Beginning of Proxy class source code file StockTicker.cs (continued)

```
// This source code was auto-generated by wsdl, Version=1.0.2914.16.
//
using System.Diagnostics;
using System.Xml.Serialization;
using System;
using System.Web.Services.Protocols;
using System.Web.Services;


[System.Web.Services.WebServiceBindingAttribute(Name="StockTickerSoap", Namespace="www.
LibertyAssociates.com")]
public class StockTicker : System.Web.Services.Protocols.SoapHttpClientProtocol {

    [System.Diagnostics.DebuggerStepThroughAttribute()]
    public StockTicker() {
        this.Url = "http://localhost/ProgAspNet/csStockTicker.asmx";
    }

    [System.Diagnostics.DebuggerStepThroughAttribute()]
    [System.Web.Services.Protocols.SoapDocumentMethodAttribute(
        "www.LibertyAssociates.com/GetHistorys",
        RequestNamespace="www.LibertyAssociates.com",
        ResponseNamespace="www.LibertyAssociates.com",
        Use=System.Web.Services.Description.SoapBindingUse.Literal,
        ParameterStyle=System.Web.Services.Protocols.
            SoapParameterStyle.Wrapped)]
    public Stock GetHistory(string StockSymbol) {
        object[] results = this.Invoke("GetHistory", new object[] {
                StockSymbol});
        return ((Stock)(results[0]));
    }

    [System.Diagnostics.DebuggerStepThroughAttribute()]
    public System.IAsyncResult BeginGetHistory(string StockSymbol,
            System.AsyncCallback callback, object asyncState) {
        return this.BeginInvoke("GetHistory", new object[] {
                StockSymbol}, callback, asyncState);
    }

    [System.Diagnostics.DebuggerStepThroughAttribute()]
    public Stock EndGetHistory(System.IAsyncResult asyncResult) {
        object[] results = this.EndInvoke(asyncResult);
        return ((Stock)(results[0]));
    }
```

There is no need to understand fully all the nuances of the proxy class source code
file. But there are several points worth noting:

- The namespaces referenced with the using statements at the beginning of Examples 17-1 and 17-2 are not the same. This is because the proxy class is not actually using System.Data. It is merely taking the call to the method that will

ultimately use System.Data, wrapping it in the proper protocol (SOAP in this case), and passing it over the Internet to the web service. Therefore, the only namespaces actually needed by the proxy class are those necessary for interacting with a web service, serializing the data into an XML data stream, and sending and receiving those XML packages.

- The StockTicker class inherits from SoapHttpClientProtocol rather than from WebService. This inherited class provides the methods for the proxy to talk to the web service using the SOAP protocol.

- Immediately following the StockTicker class declaration in the generated proxy is a *constructor*, which is a public method with the same name as the class. In the constructor, the URL of the web service is specified.

 A constructor is the method in a class that is invoked when the class is first instantiated. The constructor is used to initialize the class and put it into a valid state. If a class does not have a constructor, the CLR will create one by default.

- While the original *.asmx* file has the Stock and StockHistory classes, followed by the GetHistory method, the proxy class goes directly to GetHistory. Again, the proxy does not need the first two classes, since the proxy only substitutes for method calls.

- While the original *.asmx* file has the public method GetHistory, the proxy class has that method plus two additional, related public methods, BeginGetHistory and EndGetHistory. In fact, you will notice that every web method in the original *.asmx* file has the same method in the proxy class, plus two others, one for Begin... and another for End.... These additional methods are used to implement *asynchronous* processing.

Normal method calls are *synchronous*. In other words, the calling application halts all further processing until the called method returns. If this takes a long time, either because of a slow or intermittent Internet connection (not that that ever happens, of course) or because the method is inherently time-consuming (e.g., a lengthy database query), then the application will appear to hang, waiting.

On the other hand, if the method call is made asynchronously, then the Begin method call is sent out, and processing can continue. When the results come back, the corresponding End method call receives the results. Asynchronous method calls will be demonstrated later in this chapter.

Compiling the Proxy Class

The output of the WSDL utility is a class source code file for the proxy. This source code then needs to be compiled with the appropriate command-line compiler.

For VB.NET, use the following single command line to compile the proxy:

```
vbc /out:bin\vbStockTickerProxy.dll /t:library
    /r:system.dll,system.web.dll,system.web.services.dll,
        system.xml.dll,system.data.dll StockTicker.vb
```

and for C# use the following single command line:

```
csc /out:bin\csStockTickerProxy.dll /t:library
    /r:system.dll,system.web.dll,system.web.services.dll
    StockTicker.cs
```

You will notice that although the VB.NET and C# versions of the StockTicker proxy being compiled are functionally identical, with the exact same set of referenced namespaces (using the Imports statement in VB.NET and the using statement in C#) as can be seen by referring back to Examples 16-23 and 16-24 in Chapter 16, the command-line compile commands are different for the two languages, in that the VB.NET version has two additional namespaces referenced.

This is one of those mysterious, undocumented differences between VB.NET and C#. It turns out that there is a configuration file located in the .NET Framework program directory, called *csc.rsp*, which contains the list of default references for the C# compiler. There is no comparable configuration file or default list for VB.NET. Presumably the list of default references are hard-coded somewhere.

Automating the Process with a Batch File

Creating the proxy file requires several steps, all performed at a command prompt. Further, several of those steps involve a fair amount of typing of parameters, with lots of places to make mistakes. Finally, when all is done, you probably need to move or copy the resulting *dll* file to a different directory.

This entire process can be automated somewhat by creating a *batch file*. Batch files are text files that contain one or more command-line operations. The batch file, which has an extension of *.bat*, can then be executed from the command line, and all the operations within the file are executed one after the other, just as though they were manually entered at the command line.

Back in the days of DOS, batch files were used extensively. It is possible to make them fairly sophisticated, with replaceable parameters, conditional processing, and other programmatic niceties. For our purposes, a simple batch file will do.

Example 17-3 shows the contents of a batch file that changes to the correct current directory, runs the WSDL utility, compiles the resulting source code, then copies the resulting *dll* from one *bin* directory to another.

Example 17-3. csStockTickerProxy.bat

```
e:
cd \projects\Programming ASP.NET
```

Example 17-3. csStockTickerProxy.bat (continued)

```
rem   Generate the proxy class source file
wsdl /l:CS http://localhost/ProgAspNet/csStockTicker.asmx?wsdl

rem  Compile the proxy class source file
csc /out:bin\csStockTickerProxy.dll /t:library
    /r:system.dll,system.web.dll,system.web.services.dll
    StockTicker.cs

rem  Copy the dll
copy bin\csStockTickerProxy.dll
     c:\inetpub\wwwroot\csWebServiceConsumer1\bin
```

The first line in the batch file makes drive E the current drive. The next line changes the current directory. Blank lines are ignored. Lines beginning with rem are comments and are also ignored, although the contents are displayed on the screen as the file is processed. After the WSDL utility is run and the resulting file is compiled, it is copied. This last command is equivalent to:

```
copy e:\projects\Programming ASP.NET\bin\csStockTickerProxy.dll
     c:\inetpub\wwwroot\csWebServiceConsumer1\bin
```

Be careful of inadvertent line breaks. A line break in a batch file is the equivalent of hitting the Enter key on the keyboard.

Creating the Consuming Application

Once the proxy DLL is created and placed in the *bin* subdirectory, then it is a simple matter to create the consuming application. All that is necessary is to add the necessary reference to that DLL in the consuming application. This will be demonstrated for a web page created in a text editor and also for a web page created in Visual Studio .NET.

As long as the signatures and return types of the exposed web service methods do not change, the proxy will continue to work. The *signature* of a web method is the name of the method and its parameter list.

The web service can have additional web methods added without breaking the proxy, although the new web methods will not be visible to the consuming application until the proxy source code is regenerated and recompiled. Likewise, existing web methods can have their underlying code modified, but as long as their signature does not change, the proxy will still work fine.

Using a Text Editor

To create a web page that will consume a web service, create a normal ASP.NET web page. Then create a *bin* subdirectory immediately below the directory containing the

.aspx file. Put the compiled proxy *dll* in the *bin* directory. Then in the source code of the web page, instantiate the proxy class. This is either done in the script block of the *.aspx* file, if it is coded inline, or just inside the class definition, if it uses a code-behind class.

Examples 17-4 and 17-5 show a consuming web page, coded inline, using VB.NET and C#, respectively. Example 17-4 shows the complete *.aspx* file, while Example 17-5 shows only the script block (since the HTML is identical for both the C# and the VB.NET versions). The resulting web page is shown in Figure 17-1.

Example 17-4. vbStockTickerConsumer.aspx

```
<%@ Page Language="VB" %>
<script runat="server">

    dim proxy = new StockTicker( )

    sub txtFirmNameStockSymbol_TextChanged(ByVal Sender as Object, _
                              ByVal e as EventArgs)
       lblFirmName.Text = proxy.GetName(txtFirmNameStockSymbol.Text)
    end sub

    sub txtPriceStockSymbol_TextChanged(ByVal Sender as Object, _
                                ByVal e as EventArgs)
       lblStockPrice.Text = "$ " & _
            Convert.ToString(proxy.GetPrice(txtPriceStockSymbol.Text))
    end sub

    sub btnStockExchangeSet_Click(ByVal Sender as Object, _
                          ByVal e as EventArgs)
       proxy.SetStockExchange(txtStockExchange.Text)
    end sub

    sub btnStockExchangeGet_Click(ByVal Sender as Object, _
                          ByVal e as EventArgs)
       txtStockExchange.Text = proxy.GetStockExchange( )
    end sub

    sub btnGetHistory_Click(ByVal Sender as Object, _
                        ByVal e as EventArgs)
       dim theStock as Stock = _
            proxy.GetHistory(txtHistoryStockSymbol.Text)
       dim StockName as string = theStock.StockName
       dim StockPrice as double = theStock.Price

       dim TradeDate1 as DateTime = theStock.History(0).TradeDate
       dim Price1 as double = theStock.History(0).Price

       dim TradeDate2 as DateTime = theStock.History(1).TradeDate
       dim Price2 as double = theStock.History(1).Price

       ' Display the results.
```

Example 17-4. vbStockTickerConsumer.aspx (continued)

```
        pnlHistory.Visible = true
        lblHistoryStockName.Text = StockName
        lblHistoryStockPrice.Text = "$ " + Convert.ToString(StockPrice)
        lblHistoryDate1.Text =TradeDate1.ToString("d")
        lblHistoryPrice1.Text = "$ " + Convert.ToString(Price1)
        lblHistoryDate2.Text = TradeDate2.ToString("d")
        lblHistoryPrice2.Text = "$ " + Convert.ToString(Price2)
    end sub
</script>

<html>
    <body>
    <form runat="server">

        <h1>StockTicker Web Service Consumer</h1>

        <br/>

        Firm Name:   
        <asp:textBox
            id="txtFirmNameStockSymbol"
            OnTextChanged="txtFirmNameStockSymbol_TextChanged"
            size="40"
            text="Enter stock symbol."
            AutoPostBack="true"
            runat="server" />
           
        <asp:label id="lblFirmName" text="" runat="server"/>

        <br/>

        Stock Price:   
        <asp:textBox
            id="txtPriceStockSymbol"
         OnTextChanged="txtPriceStockSymbol_TextChanged"
            size="40"
            text="Enter stock symbol."
         AutoPostBack="true"
            runat="server" />
           
        <asp:label id="lblStockPrice" text="" runat="server"/>

        <br/>

        StockExchange:   
        <asp:textBox
            id="txtStockExchange"
            size="40"
            text=""
         AutoPostBack="false"
            runat="server" />
```

Example 17-4. vbStockTickerConsumer.aspx (continued)

```
           
        <asp:button
            id="btnStockExchangeSet"
            text="Set"
            onClick="btnStockExchangeSet_Click"
            runat="server" />
           
        <asp:button
            id="btnStockExchangeGet"
            text="Get"
            onClick="btnStockExchangeGet_Click"
            runat="server" />

        <br/>

        Stock History:   
        <asp:textBox
            id="txtHistoryStockSymbol"
            size="40"
            text=""
            runat="server" />

           
        <asp:button
            id="btnGetHistory"
            text="Get History"
            onClick="btnGetHistory_Click"
            runat="server" />

    <br/>

    <asp:Panel
        id="pnlHistory"
        visible="false"
        runat="Server" >

            <br/>
                  Stock Name:   
            <asp:label id="lblHistoryStockName" text="" runat="server"/>

            <br/>
                  
            Stock Price:   
            <asp:label id="lblHistoryStockPrice" text="" runat="server"/>

            <br/>
                  
             Transaction 1:   
            <asp:label id="lblHistoryDate1" text="" runat="server"/>
                  
            <asp:label id="lblHistoryPrice1" text="" runat="server"/>
```

Example 17-4. vbStockTickerConsumer.aspx (continued)

```
        <br/>
              
        Transaction 2:   
        <asp:label id="lblHistoryDate2" text="" runat="server"/>
              
        <asp:label id="lblHistoryPrice2" text="" runat="server"/>
   </asp:Panel>

   </form>
   </body>
</html>
```

Example 17-5. Script block from csStockTickerConsumer.aspx

```
<%@ Page Language="C#" %>
<script runat="server">

    StockTicker proxy = new StockTicker( );

    void txtFirmNameStockSymbol_TextChanged(Object Source, EventArgs E)
    {
        lblFirmName.Text = proxy.GetName(txtFirmNameStockSymbol.Text);
    }

    void txtPriceStockSymbol_TextChanged(Object Source, EventArgs E)
    {
        lblStockPrice.Text = "$ " +
            Convert.ToString(proxy.GetPrice(txtPriceStockSymbol.Text));
    }

    void btnStockExchangeSet_Click(Object Source, EventArgs E)
    {
        proxy.SetStockExchange(txtStockExchange.Text);
    }

    void btnStockExchangeGet_Click(Object Source, EventArgs E)
    {
        txtStockExchange.Text = proxy.GetStockExchange( );
    }

    void btnGetHistory_Click(Object Source, EventArgs E)
    {
        Stock theStock = proxy.GetHistory(txtHistoryStockSymbol.Text);
        string StockName = theStock.StockName;
        double StockPrice = theStock.Price;

        DateTime TradeDate1 = theStock.History[0].TradeDate;
        double Price1 = theStock.History[0].Price;

        DateTime TradeDate2 = theStock.History[1].TradeDate;
        double Price2 = theStock.History[1].Price;
```

Example 17-5. Script block from csStockTickerConsumer.aspx (continued)

```
    // Display the results.
    pnlHistory.Visible = true;
    lblHistoryStockName.Text = StockName;
    lblHistoryStockPrice.Text = "$ " + Convert.ToString(StockPrice);
    lblHistoryDate1.Text =TradeDate1.ToString("d");
    lblHistoryPrice1.Text = "$ " + Convert.ToString(Price1);
    lblHistoryDate2.Text = TradeDate2.ToString("d");
    lblHistoryPrice2.Text = "$ " + Convert.ToString(Price2);
  }

</script>
```

In Examples 17-4 and 17-5, the first line of code inside the script block instantiates the web service proxy class that was recently compiled and placed in the *bin* directory. By instantiating the proxy here, the proxy variable can be used in any of the code that consumes the web service.

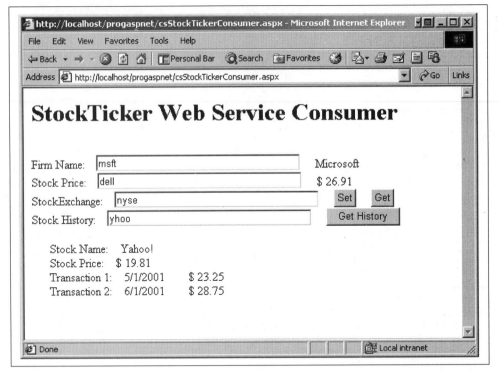

Figure 17-1. Web service consumer web page

The HTML portion of Examples 17-4 and 17-5 provides only the minimum user input necessary to allow demonstration of the principles. There are four textboxes, with the following names: txtFirmNameStockSymbol, txtPriceStockSymbol, txtStockExchange, and txtHistoryStockSymbol. The first two have their AutoPostBack property set to true. Therefore, as soon as the value in those text boxes changes, it will fire the onTextChanged event, which will cause the designated event handler to execute. Each event handler makes a call to the relevant proxy method and displays the returned value in a label next to the text box.

The txtStockExchange text box does not do anything when the value in the text box changes. However, it has two buttons associated with it. The Set button sets an application variable with the contents of the txtStockExchange text box, while the Get button fills the txtStockExchange text box with the contents of the application variable.

The txtHistoryStockSymbol text box also does not do anything when the value in the text box changes. It has the btnGetHistory button associated with it. When that button is clicked, the btnGetHistory_Click event handler is called. This method demonstrates how to retrieve class member variables from within the web service class.

In order to retrieve the Stock member variables, you must first instantiate the Stock class. Looking back at Examples 16-17 and 16-18 in Chapter 16, you will recall that the GetHistory web method returns an object of type Stock. The Stock object is instantiated here in the event handler with the following line of code in VB.NET:

```
dim theStock as Stock = proxy.GetHistory(txtHistoryStockSymbol.Text)
```

while in C# it is done with this line of code:

```
Stock theStock = proxy.GetHistory(txtHistoryStockSymbol.Text);
```

Once the class is instantiated, it is a simple matter to assign its member variables to local variables in the event handler using dot notation. In VB.NET:

```
dim StockName as string = theStock.StockName
```

and in C#:

```
string StockName = theStock.StockName;
```

Accessing the array variables contained in the StockHistory class contained within the Stock class is similar. In VB.NET:

```
dim TradeDate1 as DateTime = theStock.History(0).TradeDate
```

and in C#:

```
DateTime TradeDate1 = theStock.History[0].TradeDate;
```

Recall that array indices are zero-based.

 To repeat a point made in Chapter 16 when the web service example was first created, a real-world application would not store this type of history data in an array, nor would it display the history data in fixed variables as shown here. More likely, you would have the data in a collection or a dataset and display the data in some sort of data-bound control, as described in Chapter 9.

To display the history, several labels contained within an ASP panel control are used. The panel is used to control the labels' visibility. When the page is originally designed, the panel has its visibility property set to false. When it is time to display the results in the button event handler, the panel then has its visibility property set to true, which also makes all the labels contained within the panel visible.

The important point to understand here is that calls to the web service are made instead to the proxy, as though the web service were a local DLL or component. When your code makes a method call to the proxy DLL, it has no idea that the call is being satisfied over the Internet by a web service. The proxy hides all the complex *stuff* required to package the method call up as a SOAP message, send it out over the wire using the proper protocol (typically HTTP), receive the SOAP message response, and return that back to your calling program as though the Internet was never involved.

Using Visual Studio .NET

In order to make the same web page in Visual Studio .NET, open the program and start a new project. For this demonstration, choose the Visual Basic Project type, using the ASP.NET Web Application template. Name the project vbWebServiceConsumer, as shown in Figure 17-2.

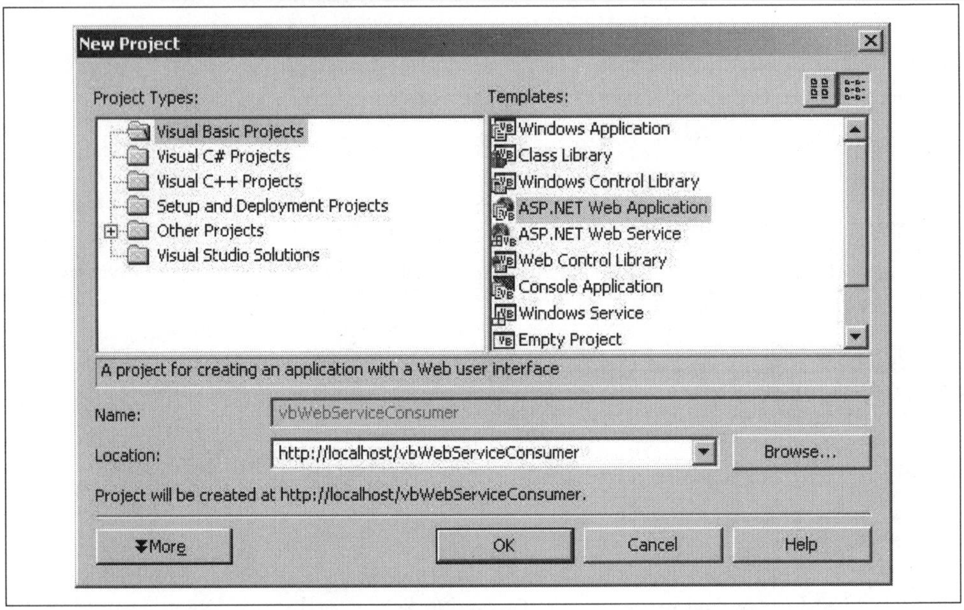

Figure 17-2. New project for web service consumer

When the new project opens, change the pageLayout property of the document from GridLayout to FlowLayout. This changes the page layout from absolute positioning of the HTML elements to a layout more like a word processor, where positioning is achieved with spaces and line breaks.

Working on the *WebForm1.aspx* design screen, place controls and lay out the page so that it looks similar to that shown in Figure 17-3.

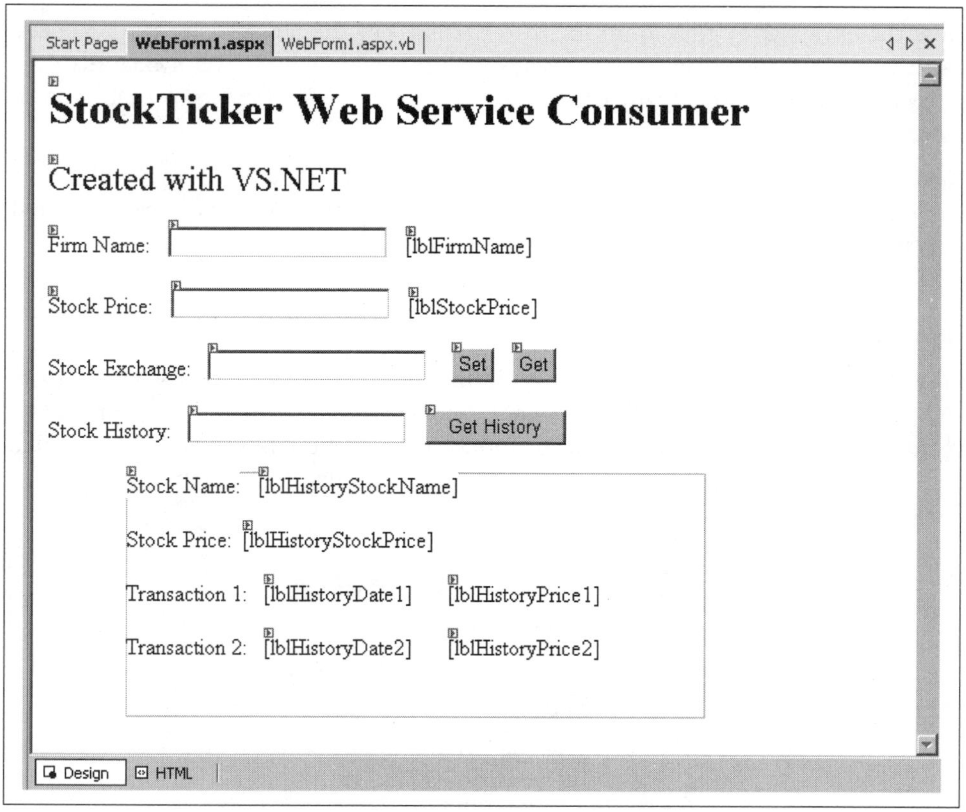

Figure 17-3. Page layout for web service consumer

Name the text boxes, the labels to the right of the text boxes and in the panel, the panel itself, and the buttons the same as in Examples 17-4 and 17-5, for consistency and to clarify the analysis. Be sure to clear the Text values from lblFirmName, lblStockPrice, and the labels in the panel, and set the AutoPostBack property of the first two text boxes (txtFirmNameStockSymbol and txtPriceStockSymbol) to True. Also, set the Visible property of pnlHistory to False.

Add event handlers for the first two text boxes and the buttons. To add an event handler, simply double-click on the control. This will automatically bring you to the code-behind page and insert a subroutine with the default name and declaration. Enter in the lines of code for each event handler from the code in Examples 17-4 and 17-5.

When you do this, you will notice that Visual Studio .NET underlines *proxy* in each line. This flags those terms as compile errors waiting to happen. To solve that, enter the line of code at the top of the code-behind class that instantiates the proxy. To repeat a line of code already placed in Examples 17-4 and 17-5, this will look like:

```
dim proxy = new StockTicker( )
```

Now the error flag is gone from the proxy terms, but the StockTicker class name is flagged as a compile error. This is because the proxy class is not yet available to the project. If you have not already created and compiled the VB.NET proxy DLL, do so now.

Next comes the magic. Using the Solution Explorer, add a Reference to the DLL you just created. Right-click on References in the Solution Explorer. You are presented with two choices:

- Add Reference...
- Add Web Reference...

In this example select the first choice, Add Reference.... Click on the Browse button and browse to the location of the proxy DLL, which here is called *vbStockTickerProxy.dll*. When you are done, the Solution Explorer will look like Figure 17-4. Once the reference is added, the error flag will disappear from the StockTicker class name.

Figure 17-4. Adding reference to web service consumer

The project can now be run by pressing F5, clicking the Start icon, or selecting Start under the Debug menu.

If you would rather let Visual Studio .NET create and compile the proxy, then select Add Web Reference... after right-clicking on References in Solution Explorer. You will be presented with the dialog box shown in Figure 17-5.

 The Add Web Reference... option also allows you to add a reference from a web service found in a UDDI directory. UDDI is described earlier in the chapter.

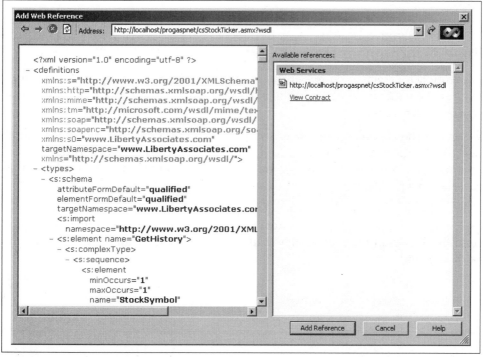

Figure 17-5. Adding web reference to web service consumer

Enter a URL pointing to the web service *.asmx* file with ?WSDL appended to the end. For this example, the URL entered is:

```
http://localhost/progaspnet/csStockTicker.asmx?WSDL
```

The resulting WSDL will be displayed in the left side of the dialog box. The right side will show the available web service and the Add Reference button will become enabled. Click on the Add Reference button. Visual Studio .NET will automatically create the proxy DLL and register it with the project.

Add (or modify, if you have already added the equivalent line above) the following line to the code-behind file. In VB.NET, add:

```
dim proxy = new localhost.StockTicker()
```

and in C# add:

```
localhost.StockTicker proxy = new localhost.StockTicker( );
```

Also, modify the line instantiating the Stock object in the btnGetHistory event handler. In VB.NET, it should look like:

```
dim theStock as localhost.Stock =
    proxy.GetHistory(txtHistoryStockSymbol.Text
```

and in C# it should look like:

```
localhost.Stock theStock = proxy.GetHistory(txtHistoryStockSymbol.Text);
```

Using Asynchronous Method Calls

As mentioned previously in this chapter in the section on "Creating the Proxy," web services allow the developer to call any of the exposed web methods either synchronously or asynchronously.

When a method is called synchronously, which is the "normal" way of doing method calls, the program execution waits for the method to return. As long as the method does not take too long to process and there is not too much network delay, this pause is not a problem.

Figure 17-6 shows synchronous processing. Methods are called on the server via the proxy. The calling program is not aware that a proxy is intervening in the process. A call goes out and when the results come back, the calling program continues processing.

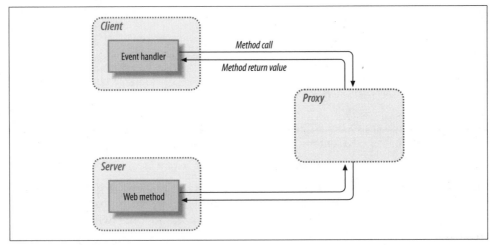

Figure 17-6. Synchronous method calls

However, in situations where the method is time-consuming to process—for example, a lengthy database operation or extensive computation—or where the network delay is significant, then this delay can be an unacceptable performance hit. In the case of web services, where all the method calls entail a round trip over the Internet, long network delays are common. Broadband Internet connections can help, but performance will still suffer.

One solution is to use asynchronous processing. In this model, a web service method is called, with instructions to notify the client when the result is ready. The client can go about its business, not waiting for the method to return. When the asynchronous method completes, a callback method is called. The client then retrieves the data from the server. Asynchronous processing is shown schematically in Figure 17-7.

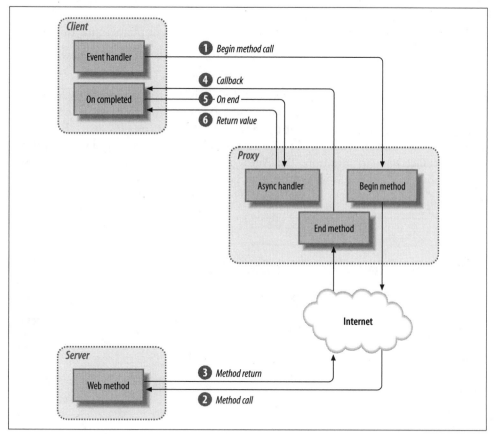

Figure 17-7. Asynchronous method calls

As with the synchronous method call, the client is not aware that the proxy is intercepting the method call and passing it along to the server. The client event handler calls the Begin... method on the web service (actually on the proxy) passing in a delegate for the callback method (step 1 in Figure 17-7). The client then goes on to do other work.

The proxy calls the web method on behalf of the client (step 2). When the server has completed the method, it returns the result to the proxy (step 3). The proxy calls the client's callback method and passes in an object implementing IAsyncResult (step 4).

The client passes that IAsyncResult back to the proxy's End... method (step 5). The End... method then returns the data to the client (step 6).

The client does not have to poll the server; it is notified by the callback when the method completes.

The callback method is a *delegate*. A delegate is a reference type that encapsulates a method with a specific signature and return type. The async Begin... and End... methods define a delegate for the callback mechanism you implement in your client.

To illustrate the use of delegates and asynchronous proxy calls, create a new C# web application project named csWebServiceConsumerAsync in Visual Studio .NET.

The page layout should look like Figure 17-8. It is nearly identical to the layout shown in Figure 17-3, including the panel used to control the visibility of the labels it contains. The only difference is that there is no field or buttons for Stock Exchange, the Get History button from Figure 17-3 is now labeled Get Data, and the button ID is now btnGetData. In addition, the AutoPostBack property of the txtFirmName-StockSymbol and txtPriceStockSymbol text boxes should be set to false rather than true.

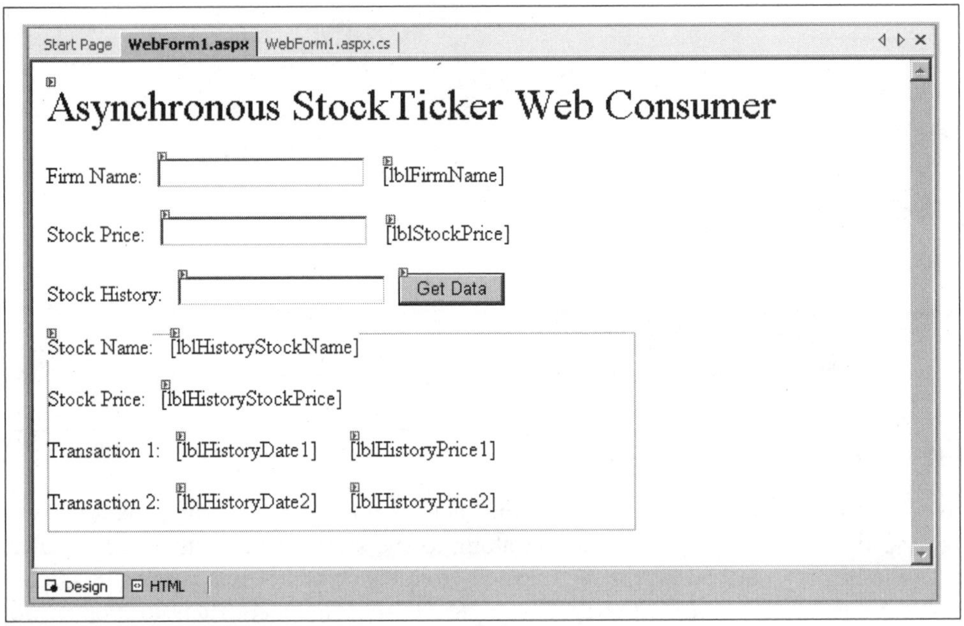

Figure 17-8. Asynchronous web page layout

The web page will accept stock symbols in each of the text fields. When the Get Data button is clicked, all the processing for each field will be done asynchronously. If this were a real-world application where each field would typically be hitting a different web service on different servers, this asynchronous processing would prevent one slow connection from holding up the works. All three web service calls will essentially be occurring simultaneously.

Before entering the asynchronous code, you will make the page work synchronously to see how it works. To the end user, the synchronous and asynchronous implementations will look identical, except the latter should be somewhat faster (although that will not be noticeable in this example, where all of the web method calls are actually going to localhost).

Add the single event handler to the Get Data button by double-clicking on the button. This will bring you to the btnGetData_Click event handler in the code-behind page. Enter the code in Example 17-6 to the event handler.

Example 17-6. Synchronous event handler

```
lblFirmName.Text = proxy.GetName(txtFirmNameStockSymbol.Text);
lblStockPrice.Text = "$ " +
    Convert.ToString(proxy.GetPrice(txtPriceStockSymbol.Text));

Stock theStock = proxy.GetHistory(txtHistoryStockSymbol.Text);
string StockName = theStock.StockName;
double StockPrice = theStock.Price;

DateTime TradeDate1 = theStock.History[0].TradeDate;
double Price1 = theStock.History[0].Price;

DateTime TradeDate2 = theStock.History[1].TradeDate;
double Price2 = theStock.History[1].Price;

// Display the results.
pnlHistory.Visible = true;
lblHistoryStockName.Text = StockName;
lblHistoryStockPrice.Text = "$ " + Convert.ToString(StockPrice);
lblHistoryDate1.Text =TradeDate1.ToString("d");
lblHistoryPrice1.Text = "$ " + Convert.ToString(Price1);
lblHistoryDate2.Text = TradeDate2.ToString("d");
lblHistoryPrice2.Text = "$ " + Convert.ToString(Price2);
```

This code is identical to that in Example 17-5, except it is condensed into a single event handler rather than spread over three different event handlers.

Run the web application, fill in the stock symbols, and press the Get Data button; the resulting web page will look something like Figure 17-9.

Before adding the code to convert this web page from synchronous processing to asynchronous processing, examine the proxy class source code shown in

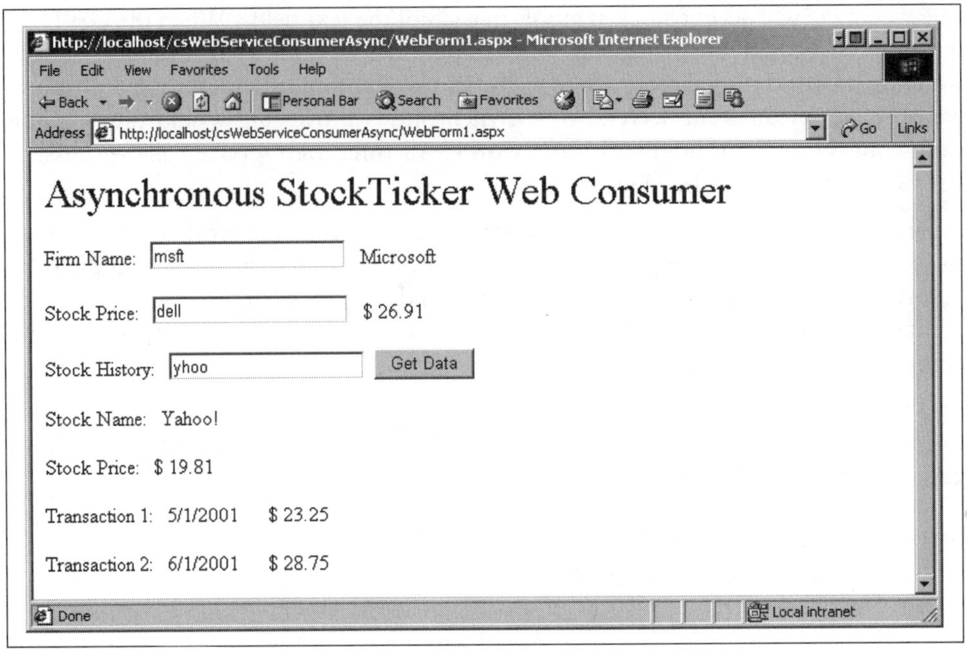

Figure 17-9. Synchronous test result

Example 17-2. That segment of the source code shows the proxy method calls available for the GetHistory method. There are three of them:

GetHistory
> This is the synchronous method. It takes a single parameter, the StockSymbol string.

BeginGetHistory
> This method starts the asynchronous processing. It takes three parameters: the StockSymbol string, the delegate callback method of type AsyncCallback, and an object called asyncState.

EndGetHistory
> This method takes a single parameter, asyncResult, which is of type IAsyncResult.

Each of the methods exposed in the web service has equivalent Begin... and End... methods to enable asynchronous processing.

The code in Example 17-7 shows the complete code listing for the code-behind page demonstrating asynchronous event handling for a web service consumer. The lines of code relevant to converting the event handling from synchronous to asynchronous are highlighted.

Example 17-7. Asynchronous event handler

```csharp
using System;
using System.Collections;
using System.ComponentModel;
using System.Data;
using System.Drawing;
using System.Threading;
using System.Web;
using System.Web.SessionState;
using System.Web.UI;
using System.Web.UI.WebControls;
using System.Web.UI.HtmlControls;

namespace csWebServiceConsumerAsync
{
    /// <summary>
    /// Summary description for WebForm1.
    /// </summary>
    public class WebForm1 : System.Web.UI.Page
    {
        protected System.Web.UI.WebControls.Label Label1;
        protected System.Web.UI.WebControls.TextBox txtFirmNameStockSymbol;
        protected System.Web.UI.WebControls.Label lblFirmName;
        protected System.Web.UI.WebControls.TextBox txtPriceStockSymbol;
        protected System.Web.UI.WebControls.Label lblStockPrice;
        protected System.Web.UI.WebControls.TextBox txtHistoryStockSymbol;
        protected System.Web.UI.WebControls.Panel pnlHistory;
        protected System.Web.UI.WebControls.Label Label2;
        protected System.Web.UI.WebControls.Label lblHistoryStockName;
        protected System.Web.UI.WebControls.Label lblHistoryStockPrice;
        protected System.Web.UI.WebControls.Label lblHistoryDate1;
        protected System.Web.UI.WebControls.Label lblHistoryPrice1;
        protected System.Web.UI.WebControls.Label lblHistoryDate2;
        protected System.Web.UI.WebControls.Label lblHistoryPrice2;
        protected System.Web.UI.WebControls.Button btnGetData;

        int flags;

        StockTicker proxy = new StockTicker( );

        //  Create delegates.
        private AsyncCallback myCallBackFirmNameStockSymbol;
        private AsyncCallback myCallBackPriceStockSymbol;
        private AsyncCallback myCallBackHistory;

        public WebForm1( )
        {
            Page.Init += new System.EventHandler(Page_Init);

            // assign the call back
            myCallBackFirmNameStockSymbol = new
                        AsyncCallback(this.onCompletedGetName);
            myCallBackPriceStockSymbol = new
                        AsyncCallback(this.onCompletedGetPrice);
```

Example 17-7. Asynchronous event handler (continued)

```
        myCallBackHistory = new
                       AsyncCallback(this.onCompletedGetHistory);
    }

    private void Page_Load(object sender, System.EventArgs e)
    {
        // Put user code to initialize the page here
    }

    private void Page_Init(object sender, EventArgs e)
    {
        //
        // CODEGEN: This call is required by the Web Form Designer.
        //
        InitializeComponent( );
    }

    #region Web Form Designer generated code
    /// <summary>
    /// Required method for Designer support - do not modify
    /// the contents of this method with the code editor.
    /// </summary>
    private void InitializeComponent( )
    {
        this.btnGetData.Click += new
                        System.EventHandler(this.btnGetData_Click);
        this.Load += new System.EventHandler(this.Page_Load);
    }
    #endregion

    private void btnGetData_Click(object sender, System.EventArgs e)
    {
        flags = 0;
        // lblFirmName.Text = proxy.GetName(txtFirmNameStockSymbol.Text);
        proxy.BeginGetName(txtFirmNameStockSymbol.Text,
                        myCallBackFirmNameStockSymbol,
                        0);

        // lblStockPrice.Text = "$ " +
              Convert.ToString(proxy.GetPrice(txtPriceStockSymbol.Text));
        proxy.BeginGetPrice(txtPriceStockSymbol.Text,
                        myCallBackPriceStockSymbol,
                        0);

        // Stock theStock = proxy.GetHistory(txtHistoryStockSymbol.Text);
        proxy.BeginGetHistory(txtHistoryStockSymbol.Text,
                        myCallBackHistory,
                        0);

        while (flags < 3)
        {
            Thread.Sleep(100);
        }
```

Example 17-7. Asynchronous event handler (continued)

```
    }

    private void onCompletedGetName(IAsyncResult asyncResult)
    {
        string s = proxy.EndGetName(asyncResult);
        lblFirmName.Text = s;
        flags++;
    }

    private void onCompletedGetPrice(IAsyncResult asyncResult)
    {
        lblStockPrice.Text = "$ " +
                        Convert.ToString(proxy.EndGetPrice(asyncResult));
        flags++;
    }

    private void onCompletedGetHistory(IAsyncResult asyncResult)
    {
        Stock theStock = proxy.EndGetHistory(asyncResult);
        string StockName = theStock.StockName;
        double StockPrice = theStock.Price;

        DateTime TradeDate1 = theStock.History[0].TradeDate;
        double Price1 = theStock.History[0].Price;

        DateTime TradeDate2 = theStock.History[1].TradeDate;
        double Price2 = theStock.History[1].Price;

        // Display the results.
        pnlHistory.Visible = true;
        lblHistoryStockName.Text = StockName;
        lblHistoryStockPrice.Text = "$ " + Convert.ToString(StockPrice);
        lblHistoryDate1.Text =TradeDate1.ToString("d");
        lblHistoryPrice1.Text = "$ " + Convert.ToString(Price1);
        lblHistoryDate2.Text = TradeDate2.ToString("d");
        lblHistoryPrice2.Text = "$ " + Convert.ToString(Price2);
        flags++;
    }
  }
}
```

The first step is to declare the delegates. Add the following lines of code to the code-behind page inside the WebForm1 class:

```
private AsyncCallback myCallBackFirmNameStockSymbol;
private AsyncCallback myCallBackPriceStockSymbol;
private AsyncCallback myCallBackHistory;
```

These lines declare the delegates as private members of the class. Note that the delegates are of type AsyncCallback. This is the same type as the second parameter required by the Begin... methods.

An AsyncCallback delegate is declared in the System namespace as follows:

```
public delegate void AsyncCallback (IAsyncResult ar);
```

Thus this delegate can be associated with any method that returns void and takes the IAsyncResult interface as a parameter.

You will create three methods in your client to act as callback methods: onCompletedGetName, onCompletedGetPrice, and onCompletedGetHistory. You encapsulate these methods within their delegates in the constructor, as follows:

```
myCallBackFirmNameStockSymbol = new
               AsyncCallback(this.onCompletedGetName);
myCallBackPriceStockSymbol = new AsyncCallback(this.onCompletedGetPrice);
myCallBackHistory = new AsyncCallback(this.onCompletedGetHistory);
```

You will see how to implement the three callback methods shortly.

The next step is to call all the Begin... methods to start the asynchronous processing. Replace each of the lines of code in btnGetData_Click that calls one of the proxy methods with its equivalent Begin... method. (For now, just comment out the original lines of code and keep them for reference.) The first parameter for each Begin... method is the same as the parameter for the original synchronous method. The second parameter is the delegate created above. The third parameter is an object for maintaining state, if necessary. For this example, use zero. The btnGetData_Click event procedure should appear as follows:

```
private void btnGetData_Click(object sender, System.EventArgs e)
{
    flags = 0;
    // lblFirmName.Text = proxy.GetName(txtFirmNameStockSymbol.Text);
    proxy.BeginGetName(txtFirmNameStockSymbol.Text,
                       myCallBackFirmNameStockSymbol,
                       0);

    // lblStockPrice.Text = "$ " +
    //     Convert.ToString(proxy.GetPrice(txtPriceStockSymbol.Text));
    proxy.BeginGetPrice(txtPriceStockSymbol.Text,
                        myCallBackPriceStockSymbol,
                        0);

    // Stock theStock = proxy.GetHistory(txtHistoryStockSymbol.Text);
    proxy.BeginGetHistory(txtHistoryStockSymbol.Text,
                          myCallBackHistory,
                          0);

    while (flags < 3)
    {
        Thread.Sleep(100);
    }
}
```

The flags variable and the while loop will be explained shortly.

Create the three callback methods, and move the code from the current btnGetData_ Click to the appropriate method. Call the new methods onCompletedGetName, onCompletedGetPrice, and onCompletedGetHistory. The contents of these methods is shown in Example 17-7.

In each of the callback methods, the End.. method associated with the appropriate web method in the proxy is called in order to construct the label Text properties to be set for display in the web page. In onCompletedGetName, a string is set to the return value from the proxy.EndGetName method. This string is then assigned to the label Text property. onCompletedGetPrice uses a similar technique, using a single line of code to replace the two lines in onCompletedGetName. onCompletedGetHistory is similar, except that it instantiates a Stock object with the return value from proxy.EndGetHistory. As you will recall from Example 17-1, a Stock object contains a stock symbol, stock name, price, and an array of StockHistory objects.

The last thing to explain is the flags variable, which is a counter. Notice that this variable is declared as a member variable.

```
int flags;
```

Each one of the callback methods increments the flags counter:

```
flags++;
```

Within the button click event handler, btnGetData_Click, the flags counter is reset to zero. Then every callback method increments the counter. The while loop prevents the button click event from completing until all three callback method methods have completed.

```
while (flags < 3)
{
   Thread.Sleep(100);
}
```

When the web page is run, the three Begin... methods are called. As each returns results, the onCompleted... methods call the appropriate End method and increment the counter.

When the counter reaches 3, the web page redraws. The end result looks indistinguishable from that shown in Figure 17-9.

 Asynchronous consumption of web services can be very useful under the correct circumstances but may not scale well. This is because each asynchronous method call spawns a new thread. So Example 17-7 would spawn three additional threads in addition to the main thread. This would be fine for a low volume web site, but the performance penalty could overwhelm a large, busy web site.

CHAPTER 18

Caching and Performance

There are several ways to achieve higher performance and better scalability in ASP.NET. One way is through the use of caching. *Caching* is a technique whereby frequently requested data is stored in a quickly accessible location, so that the next time the same data is requested, it can be quickly fetched from the cache location rather than regenerated by the application.

This can result in a significant performance boost, especially for dynamically generated content such as ASP.NET web pages and components, and in cases where the data underlying the response is expensive to gather, such as database queries.

Most web browsers cache pages received so that if the same page is requested again, it does not have to be sent over the Internet, but rather is retrieved directly from the local hard drive. Most operating systems also employ caching of some sort to store frequently requested data in memory, rather than require additional hard drive reads.

The only caching this chapter will be concerned with is server-side caching performed by the .NET Framework.

In some respects, caching is similar to the storage of state objects. (See Chapter 6 for a complete discussion of state in ASP.NET.) In both cases, data is saved for use across multiple requests, and in the case of application state, across multiple sessions. However, there the similarity ends. With state objects, the developer explicitly saves a particular piece of data in a particular place, intending to be able to retrieve that data at any time later in the session or in other sessions. The data stored in state objects will last as long as the session or application, and will not be lost until the developer specifies it is to be removed or replaced. In short, the developer can count on the data in a state object being available.

In contrast, cached data is non-deterministic. You cannot assume that any piece of data you are looking for will be in the cache. As will be shown later in this chapter, whenever your program attempts to retrieve data from the cache, it must test to see if the data is there, and make provisions to retrieve the data elsewhere if it is not present in the cache. The data may be missing because its lifetime expired, because the application needed to free memory for other purposes, or simply because the cache was never populated.

Types of Caching

There are several different types of caching present in ASP.NET. Some are automatic and require no intervention on the part of the developer, while others require explicit coding.

Class Caching

When a web page or web service (*.aspx* or *.asmx* file, respectively) contains all its code inline, then that code is compiled into a page class the first time the page or service is run. This causes some delay, but that compiled class file is then cached on the server and is called directly every subsequent time the page (or service) is referenced. This is done automatically—there is no user or developer interaction required for this to happen.

The CLR watches for source code changes. If the source code changes, the CLR knows to recompile the next time the page or service is called.

 If code-behind is used, the page or web service class is already pre-compiled, either manually by the developer or automatically by Visual Studio .NET.

Configuration Caching

Application-wide configuration information is contained in the configuration files. The specifics of configuration will be covered in detail in Chapter 20. For now, the relevant point is that when the application is started, i.e., the first time a page or service is called from the application virtual root directory, all the configuration information must be loaded. This can take some time, especially if the configuration files are extensive. Configuration caching allows the application to store the configuration information in memory, thus saving time when the information is subsequently needed.

Output Caching

Output caching is the caching of pages or portions of pages that are output to the client. This is one of the main performance enhancing techniques available to the developer. Since the page does not have to be recreated from scratch each time a request is made for it, the web site throughput, measured in requests per second, can be significantly increased.

Cached pages or portions of pages are stored on the server's hard drive. Subsequent requests for the same page or portion of page are fulfilled directly from the hard drive, rather than recreated by the page's program logic. Since hard drive space is usually not at a premium, output caching scales well.

Output caching will be covered in the next section of this chapter.

Object Caching

Object caching is the caching of objects on the page, such as data bound controls. In contrast to output caching, object caching stores the cached data in server memory. Since server memory is a limited resource, object caching must be used more carefully than output caching to avoid scaling problems.

Object caching will be covered in detail later in this chapter.

Output Caching

Output caching is the caching of pages or portions of pages that are output to the client. This does not happen automatically—the developer must enable output caching using either the OutputCache page directive or the HttpCachePolicy class. Both methods will be described.

Output caching can be applied to an entire page or a portion of the page. In order to cache only a portion of a page, the caching is applied to a user control contained within the page. This too will be described later in this section.

The OutputCache Page Directive

The OutputCache page directive, like all page directives, goes at the top of the page file. (For a complete description of page directives, see Chapter 6.) A typical example of an OutputCache page directive looks something like the following:

```
<%@ OutputCache Duration="60" VaryByParam="*" %>
```

The full syntax is:

```
<%@ OutputCache Duration="number of seconds"
VaryByParam="parameter list" Location="location"
VaryByControl="control list" VaryByCustom="custom output" VaryByHeader=
    "header list" %>
```

Only the first two parameters, Duration and VaryByParam, are required

The VaryBy... parameters allow different versions of the cached page to be stored, with each version satisfying the combination of conditions being varied.

The various parameters are described in the following sections.

Duration

The Duration parameter specifies the number of seconds that the page or user control is cached. Items placed in the output cache are only valid for this specified time period. When the time limit is reached, then the cache is said to be *expired*. The next request for the cached page or user control after the cache is expired causes the page or user control to be regenerated, and the cache is refilled with the fresh copy.

An example will clarify this. Examples 18-1 and 18-2 show the VB.NET and C# versions, respectively, of a very simple web page with output caching implemented. Each time the page is loaded, it will display the time in a Label control. The HTML is omitted from Example 18-2, since it is identical to that in 18-1. Running the page in a browser gives the result shown in Figure 18-1.

Example 18-1. Simple output caching in VB.NET, vbOutputCache-01.aspx

```
<%@ Page Language="VB" %>
<%@ OutputCache Duration="10" VaryByParam="*" %>

<script runat="server">
    sub Page_Load(ByVal Sender as Object, _
                  ByVal e as EventArgs)
        lblMsg.Text = "This page was loaded at " & _
                      DateTime.Now.ToString("T")
    end sub
</script>

<html>
    <body>
    <form runat="server">

        <h1>Output Caching</h1>

        <asp:Label
            id="lblMsg"
            runat="server"/>

    </form>
    </body>
</html>
```

Example 18-2. Simple output caching in C#, csOutputCache-01.aspx

```
<%@ Page Language="C#" %>
<%@ OutputCache Duration="10" VaryByParam="*" %>

<script runat="server">
    void Page_Load(Object Source, EventArgs E)
    {
        lblMsg.Text = "This page was loaded at " +
                      DateTime.Now.ToString("T");
    }
</script>
```

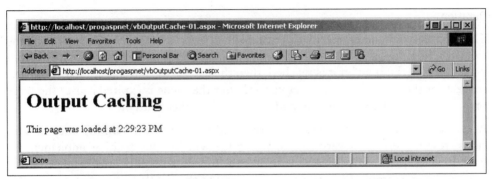

Figure 18-1. Results of simple caching demo

In Examples 18-1 and 18-2, the only thing necessary to implement output caching is the second line in the listing, the OutputCache page directive. It specifies a Duration of 10 seconds. (The other parameter, VaryByParam, will be explained in the next section.) This means that if the same page is requested from the server within 10 seconds of the original request, the subsequent request will be served out of the cache, rather than being regenerated by ASP.NET.

This is easy to verify. Run the page and note the time. Then quickly refresh the page in the browser. If you refresh within 10 seconds of originally running the page, the displayed time will not have changed. You can refresh the page as many times as you wish, but the displayed time will not change until 10 seconds have passed.

VaryByParam

The VaryByParam parameter allows you to cache different versions of the page depending on which parameters are submitted to the server when the page is requested. These parameters are contained in a semicolon-separated list of strings.

In the case of a GET request, the strings in the parameter list represent query string values contained in the URL. In the case of a POST request, the strings represent variables sent as part of the form.

There are two special values for the VaryByParam parameter:

Value	Description
none	Don't vary by parameter—i.e., save only a single version of the page in the cache and return that version no matter what query string values or form variables are passed in as part of the request.
*	Save a separate version of the page in cache for each unique combination of query string values or form variables. The order of the query string values or form variables have no effect on the caching. However, the parameter values are case sensitive: state=ma is different from state=MA.

To see the effects of the VaryByParam parameter, modify the previous example. Add two labels for displaying parameters passed in as a query string as part of the URL in a GET request. Also, change the `Duration` parameter to 60 seconds to give you more time to explore the effects. The resulting *.aspx* page is shown in Example 18-3 (for VB.NET) and 18-4 (for C#). (The HTML is omitted from Example 18-4 since it is identical to that in 18-3.)

Example 18-3. Output caching using the VaryByParam parameter in VB.NET, vbOutputCache-02. aspx

```
<%@ Page Language="VB" %>
<%@ OutputCache Duration="60" VaryByParam="*" %>

<script runat="server">
   sub Page_Load(ByVal Sender as Object, _
              ByVal e as EventArgs)
      lblMsg.Text = "This page was loaded at " & _
                    DateTime.Now.ToString("T")
      lblUserName.Text = Request.Params("username")
      lblState.Text = Request.Params("state")
   end sub
</script>

<html>
   <body>
   <form runat="server">

      <h1>Output Caching</h1>

      <asp:Label
         id="lblMsg"
         runat="server"/>

      <br/>
      <br/>

      UserName:   
      <asp:Label
         id="lblUserName"
         runat="server"/>

      <br/>

      State:   
      <asp:Label
         id="lblState"
         runat="server"/>

   </form>
   </body>
</html>
```

Example 18-4. Output caching using the VaryByParam in parameter in C#, csOutputCache-02.
aspx

```
<%@ Page Language="C#" %>
<%@ OutputCache Duration="60" VaryByParam="*" %>

<script runat="server">
   void Page_Load(Object Source, EventArgs E)
   {
       lblMsg.Text = "This page was loaded at " +
                      DateTime.Now.ToString("T");
       lblUserName.Text = Request.Params["username"];
       lblState.Text = Request.Params["state"];

   }
</script>
```

To test Examples 18-3 and 18-4, enter the following URL in a browser:

> http://localhost/progaspnet/vbOutputCache-02.aspx?username=Dan&state=MA

This will give the result shown in Figure 18-2.

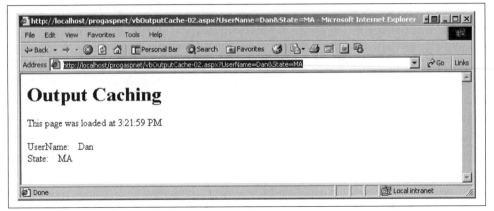

Figure 18-2. Results of caching in VaryByParam demo

Now enter the same URL but with different parameters, say username=Jesse and state=NY, as in:

> http://localhost/progaspnet/vbOutputCache-02.aspx?username=Jesse&state=NY

This will give a different time in the resulting page. Now go back and enter the original URL with username=Dan and state=MA. You will see the original time shown in Figure 18-2, assuming 60 seconds have not passed since you first entered the URL.

Suppose the above example was part of an application where the username was needed for login purposes and the state was used to query a database to return information about publicly traded firms in that state. In that case, it would make no sense to cache based on the username, but it would make a lot of sense to cache based on the state parameter.

To accomplish this, set VaryByParam equal to the parameter(s) you wish to cache by. So, for example, to cache only by state, use the following OutputCache directive:

```
<%@ OutputCache Duration="60" VaryByParam="state" %>
```

If you need to cache by the unique combination of two parameters, say state and city, use a directive similar to:

```
<%@ OutputCache Duration="60" VaryByParam="state;city" %>
```

Location

The Location parameter specifies the hard drive where the cached data is stored. The permissible values for this parameter are contained in the OutputCacheLocation enumeration (see Table 18-1).

Table 18-1. Location parameter values

Parameter value	Description
Client	The cache is located on the same machine as the client browser. Useful if the page requires authentication.
Downstream	The cache is located on a server downstream from the web server. This might be a proxy server.
Server	The cache is located on the web server processing the request.
None	Output caching is disabled.
Any	The output cache can be located either on the client, on a downstream server, or on the web server. This is the default value.

The Location parameter is not supported when output caching user controls.

VaryByControl

The VaryByControl parameter is used when caching user controls, which will be described in "Fragment Caching: Caching Part of a Page" later in this chapter. This parameter is not supported in OutputCache directives in web pages (*.aspx* files).

The values for this parameter consist of a semicolon-separated list of strings. Each string represents a fully qualified property name on a user control.

VaryByCustom

The VaryByCustom parameter allows the cache to be varied by browser if the value of the parameter is set to browser. In this case, the cache is varied by browser name and major version. In other words, there will be separate cached versions of the page for IE 4, IE 5, Netscape 6, or any other browser type or version used to access the page.

VaryByHeader

The VaryByHeader parameter allows the cache to by varied by HTTP header. The value of the parameter consists of a semicolon-separated list of HTTP headers. This parameter is not supported in OutputCache directives in user controls.

Fragment Caching: Caching Part of a Page

All of the examples shown so far have cached the entire page. Sometimes all you want to cache is part of the page. In order to do this, wrap that portion of the page you wish to cache in a user control and cache just the user control. This is known as *fragment caching*. (For a complete discussion of user controls, see Chapter 14.)

For example, suppose you develop a stock portfolio analysis page, where the top portion of the page displays the contents of the user's stock portfolio, and the bottom portion contains a data grid showing historical data about one specific stock. There would be little benefit in caching the top portion of the page, since it will be different for every user. However, it is likely that in a heavily used web site, many people will be requesting historical information about the same stock, so there would be benefit to caching the bottom portion of the page. This is especially true since generating the historical data requires a relatively expensive database query. In this case, you can wrap the data grid in a user control and cache just that.

To demonstrate fragment caching, create the very simple user control shown in Example 18-5 using VB.NET and in Example 18-6 using C#.

Example 18-5. Simple user control in VB.NET, vbUserControl.ascx

```
<%@ Control Language="VB" %>
<%@ OutputCache Duration="10" VaryByParam="*" %>

<script runat="server">
   sub Page_Load(ByVal Sender as Object, _
               ByVal e as EventArgs)
      lblMsg.Text = "This User Control was loaded at " & _
                    DateTime.Now.ToString("T")
   end sub
</script>

<hr/>
<h1>User Control</h1>

<asp:Label
   id="lblMsg"
   runat="server"/>

<hr/>
```

Example 18-6. Simple user control in C#, csUserControl.ascx

```
<%@ Control Language="C#" %>
<%@ OutputCache Duration="10" VaryByParam="*" %>

<script runat="server">
   void Page_Load(Object Source, EventArgs E)
   {
      lblMsg.Text = "This User Control was loaded at " +
```

Example 18-6. Simple user control in C#, csUserControl.ascx (continued)

```
                    DateTime.Now.ToString("T");
   }
</script>

<hr/>
<h1>User Control</h1>

<asp:Label
   id="lblMsg"
   runat="server"/>

<hr/>
```

This user control does nothing more than display the time it was loaded. The visible portion of the control is surrounded by horizontal rules (<hr/>) to distinguish it when it is used in a web page. Notice that the OutputCache directive specifies a Duration of 10 seconds.

Now create a web page to use this user control, as shown in Examples 18-7 and 18-8, in VB.NET and C#, respectively.

Example 18-7. Fragment caching demo in VB.NET, vbOutputCache-UserControl.aspx

```
<%@ Page Language="vb" %>
<%@ Register TagPrefix="SampleUserControl" TagName="LoadTime"
        Src="vbUserControl.ascx" %>

<script runat="server">
   sub Page_Load(ByVal Sender as Object, _
              ByVal e as EventArgs)
      lblMsg.Text = "This page was loaded at " & _
                     DateTime.Now.ToString("T")
   end sub
</script>

<html>
   <body>
   <form runat="server">

      <h1>Fragment Caching</h1>

      <asp:Label
         id="lblMsg"
         runat="server"/>

      <br/>

      <SampleUserControl:LoadTime
         runat="server"/>

   </form>
```

Example 18-7. Fragment caching demo in VB.NET, vbOutputCache-UserControl.aspx (continued)

```
  </body>
</html>
```

Example 18-8. Fragment caching demo in C#, csOutputCache-UserControl.aspx

```
<%@ Page Language="C#" %>
<%@ Register TagPrefix="SampleUserControl" TagName="LoadTime"
        Src="csUserControl.ascx" %>

<script runat="server">
   void Page_Load(Object Source, EventArgs E)
   {
      lblMsg.Text = "This page was loaded at " +
                      DateTime.Now.ToString("T");
   }
</script>

<html>
   <body>
   <form runat="server">

      <h1>Fragment Caching</h1>

      <asp:Label
          id="lblMsg"
          runat="server"/>

      <br/>

      <SampleUserControl:LoadTime
          runat="server"/>

   </form>
   </body>
</html>
```

Notice that the web page that uses the user control does not have any caching implemented; there is no OutputCache directive.

When you run the web page from Examples 18-7 or 18-8 in a browser, you will initially see something like Figure 18-3.

The time displayed for both the user control and the containing page are the same. However, if you refresh the view, you will notice that the time the page was loaded will be the current time, while the time the user control was loaded is static until the 10-second cache duration has expired.

One caveat to keep in mind when caching user controls is that it is not possible to programmatically manipulate the user control being cached. This is because a user control in cache is only generated dynamically the first time it is requested. After

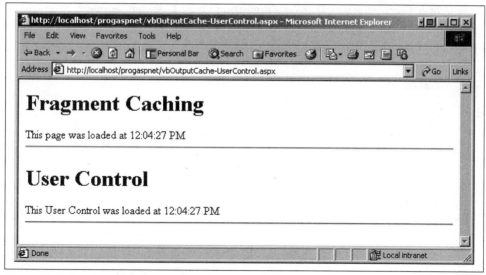

Figure 18-3. Results of fragment caching demo

that, the object is not available for the code to interact with. If you need to manipulate the contents of the user control programmatically, the code to do so must be contained within the user control.

To demonstrate this, modify the code in Example 18-5 to add a property called User-Name to the sample user control. The new user control is shown (in VB.NET only) in Example 18-9.

Example 18-9. User control with UserName property in VB.NET, vbUserControl-02.
ascx

```
<%@ Control Language="VB" %>
<%@ OutputCache Duration="10" VaryByParam="*" %>

<script runat="server">
   sub Page_Load(ByVal Sender as Object, _
                 ByVal e as EventArgs)
      lblMsg.Text = "This User Control was loaded at " & _
                    DateTime.Now.ToString("T")
   end sub

   public property UserName() as string
      get
         return lblUserName.Text
      end get

      set
         lblUserName.Text = value
      end set
   end property
```

Example 18-9. User control with UserName property in VB.NET, vbUserControl-02. ascx (continued)

```
</script>

<hr/>
<h1>User Control</h1>

<asp:Label
    id="lblMsg"
    runat="server"/>

<br/>

<asp:Label
    id="lblUserName"
    Text="Dan"
    runat="server"/>

<hr/>
```

In Example 18-9, a property named UserName was added to the code, with both a Get and a Set method. Also, a label was added to display the UserName. For now, this label is hard-coded to Dan.

Now modify the code in Example 18-7 to call this modified user control. The code for this modified page is shown in Example 18-10 (in VB.NET only).

Example 18-10. Fragment caching demo with a property in VB.NET, vbOutputCache-UserControl-02.aspx

```
<%@ Page Language="vb" %>
<%@ Register TagPrefix="SampleUserControl" TagName="LoadTime"
            Src="vbUserControl-02.ascx" %>

<script runat="server">
   sub Page_Load(ByVal Sender as Object, _
            ByVal e as EventArgs)
      lblMsg.Text = "This page was loaded at " & _
                    DateTime.Now.ToString("T")

      lblUserControlText.Text = MyUserControl.UserName
   end sub

   sub btn_OnClick(ByVal Sender as Object, _
            ByVal e as EventArgs)
      MyUserControl.UserName = "Jesse"
   end sub
</script>

<html>
   <body>
```

```
    <form runat="server">

        <h1>Fragment Caching</h1>

        <asp:Label
            id="lblMsg"
            runat="server"/>

        <br/>

        <SampleUserControl:LoadTime
          ID="MyUserControl"
          runat="server"/>

        <br/>

        <asp:Label
            id="lblUserControlText"
            runat="server"/>

        <br/>

        <asp:Button
            id="btn"
          Text="Change Name to Jesse"
            OnClick="btn_OnClick"
            runat="server"/>

    </form>
  </body>
</html>
```

The code in Example 18-10 adds the highlighted code to populate the lblUserControlText label with the initial value of the lblUserName control contained in the user control. This works fine when the page is first called, giving the result shown in Figure 18-4.

It even works as expected if you click the button to change the name to Jesse. This is because the button causes the form to be posted to the server, so everything is regenerated and the request for the user control is not being satisfied from the cache. However, as soon as you refresh the page and ASP.NET attempts to satisfy the request for the user control from the cache, an error occurs.

The only way around this is to move all the code that accesses the user control property into the user control itself, as shown in Example 18-11 for the user control. The calling page then reverts back to the same page shown in Examples 18-7 and 18-8. (Be certain to change the name of the Src parameter in the Register directive in Example 18-7 or 18-8 to point to the correct user control.)

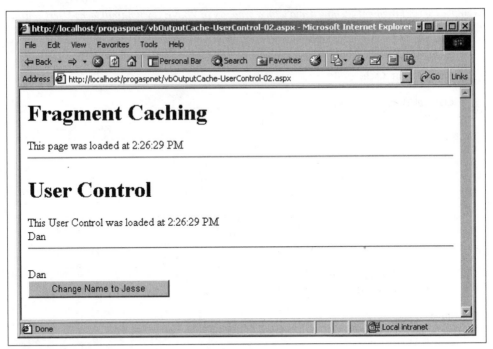

Figure 18-4. Results of fragment caching with property

Example 18-11. User control setting UserName property in VB.NET, vbUserControl-03.
ascx

```vb
<%@ Control Language="VB" %>
<%@ OutputCache Duration="10" VaryByParam="*" %>

<script runat="server">
   sub Page_Load(ByVal Sender as Object, _
              ByVal e as EventArgs)
      lblMsg.Text = "This User Control was loaded at " & _
                    DateTime.Now.ToString("T")
   end sub

   public property UserName() as string
      get
         return lblUserName.Text
      end get

      set
         lblUserName.Text = value
      end set
   end property

   sub btn_OnClick(ByVal Sender as Object, _
              ByVal e as EventArgs)
      lblUserName.Text = "Jesse"
   end sub
```

Example 18-11. User control setting UserName property in VB.NET, vbUserControl-03. ascx (continued)

```
</script>

<hr/>
<h1>User Control</h1>

<asp:Label
    id="lblMsg"
    runat="server"/>

<br/>

<asp:Label
    id="lblUserName"
    Text="Dan"
    runat="server"/>

<br/>

<asp:Button
 id="btn"
 Text="Change Name to Jesse"
 OnClick="btn_OnClick"
 runat="server"/>

<hr/>
```

While this restriction on programmatically modifying user controls that are in the cache might seem significant, as a practical matter it should not be. The entire point of putting user controls in the cache is that they will not change while cached. If that is not the case, then they are probably not a good candidate for caching.

Object Caching

All the examples in this chapter so far have cached pages or parts of pages wrapped in user controls. But ASP.NET allows you much more caching flexibility. You can use *object caching* to place any object in the cache. The object can be of almost any type: a data type, a web control, a class, a data set, etc.

Unlike output caching, which stores its data on a hard drive somewhere, the object cache is stored in server memory. As such, it is a limited resource and the careful developer will husband that resource carefully. That said, it is an easy way to buy significant performance benefits when used wisely.

Suppose you are developing a retail shopping catalogue web application. Many of the page requests contain queries against the same database to return a relatively static price list and descriptive data. Instead of your control requerying the database each time the data is requested, the data set is cached, so that subsequent requests for the data will be satisfied from high speed cache rather than the slow and expensive regeneration of the data. You might want to set the cache to expire every minute, hourly, or daily, depending on the needs of the application and the frequency with which the data is likely to change.

Object caching is implemented by the Cache class. One instance of this class is created automatically per application domain when the application starts. The class remains valid for the life of the application. The Cache class uses syntax very similar to that of session and application state. Objects are stored in Cache as key/value pairs in a Hashtable object. The object being stored is the value, and the key is a descriptive string.

To clarify object caching, look at the code shown in Example 18-12. The web page in this listing will display a data grid containing data from the Bugs database. It will initially query data from the Bugs database, then store it in cache for subsequent requests. Example 18-12 contains the VB.NET source, while Example 18-13 shows the C# source. Example 18-13 omits the HTML, since it is identical to the VB.NET version shown in Example 18-12.

Example 18-12. Object caching a data set in VB.NET, vbObjCache-01.aspx

```
<%@ Page Language="vb" %>
<%@ Import namespace="System.Data" %>
<%@ Import namespace="System.Data.SqlClient" %>

<script runat="server">

    sub Page_Load(ByVal Sender as Object, _
                ByVal e as EventArgs)
        if not IsPostBack then
           CreateDataGrid( )
        end if
    end sub

    sub btn_OnClick(ByVal Sender as Object, _
                ByVal e as EventArgs)
        Cache.Remove("DataGridDataSet")
        CreateDataGrid( )
    end sub

    sub CreateDataGrid( )
        dim dsGrid as DataSet

        dsGrid = CType(Cache("DataGridDataSet"), DataSet)

        if dsGrid is Nothing then
           dsGrid = GetDataSet( )
           Cache("DataGridDataSet") = dsGrid
           lbl.Text = "Data from database."
        else
           lbl.Text = "Data from cache."
```

```vb
        end if

        dg.DataSource=dsGrid.Tables(0)
        dg.DataBind( )
    end sub

    public function GetDataSet( ) as DataSet
        ' connect to the Bugs database
        dim connectionString as string = "server=MyServer; uid=sa; " & _
                        "pwd=dan; database=Bugs"

        ' get records from the Bugs table
        dim commandString as string = "Select BugID, Description from Bugs"

        ' create the data set command object and the DataSet
        dim da as SqlDataAdapter = new SqlDataAdapter(commandString, _
                        connectionString)

        dim dsData as DataSet = new DataSet( )

        ' fill the data set object
        da.Fill(dsData,"Bugs")

        return dsData
    end function

</script>

<html>
    <body>
    <form runat="server">

        <h1>Object Caching</h1>

        <asp:Label
            id="lbl"
             runat="server"/>

        <br/>
        <br/>

            <asp:DataGrid
              id="dg"
               runat="server"/>

        <br/>

        <asp:Button
            id="btn"
            Text="Clear Cache"
            OnClick="btn_OnClick"
            runat="server"/>
```

Example 18-12. Object caching a data set in VB.NET, vbObjCache-01.aspx (continued)

```
   </form>
  </body>
</html>
```

Example 18-13. Object Caching a DataSet in C#, csObjCache-01.aspx

```
<%@ Page Language="C#" %>
<%@ Import namespace="System.Data" %>
<%@ Import namespace="System.Data.SqlClient" %>

<script runat="server">
   void Page_Load(Object Source, EventArgs E)
   {
      if (! IsPostBack)
      {
         CreateDataGrid( );
      }
   }

   void btn_OnClick(Object Source, EventArgs E)
   {
      Cache.Remove("DataGridDataSet");
      CreateDataGrid( );
   }

   public void CreateDataGrid( )
   {
      DataSet dsGrid;

      dsGrid = (DataSet)Cache["DataGridDataSet"];

      if (dsGrid == null)
      {
         dsGrid = GetDataSet( );
         Cache["DataGridDataSet"] = dsGrid;
         lbl.Text = "Data from database.";
      }
      else
      {
         lbl.Text = "Data from cache.";
      }

      dg.DataSource=dsGrid.Tables[0];
      dg.DataBind( );
   }

   public DataSet GetDataSet( )
   {
      // connect to the Bugs database
      string connectionString = "server=MyServer; uid=sa; pwd=dan; " +
                    "database=Bugs";
```

```
    // get records from the Bugs table
    string commandString = "Select BugID, Description from Bugs";

    // create the data set command object and the DataSet
    SqlDataAdapter dataAdapter = new SqlDataAdapter(commandString,
                        connectionString);

    DataSet dsData = new DataSet( );

    // fill the data set object
      dataAdapter.Fill(dsData,"Bugs");

    return dsData;
  }
</script>
```

The heart of Examples 18-12 and 18-13 involves data access. For a complete discussion of data access in ASP.NET, see Chapters 11 and 12. For now, notice that the directives at the top of the code listing include two Import directives in order to make the classes and methods from the System.Data and System.Data.SqlClient namespaces available to the code.

While looking at the page directives, also notice that there is no OutputCache directive, since this example does not use output caching.

A method named CreateDataGrid is called every time the data grid needs to be created. Notice that it is called in the Page_Load method the first time the page is loaded, but not on postback.

Looking at the CreateDataGrid method, a DataSet object is instantiated to contain the data that will be bound and displayed by the data grid. In VB.NET:

```
dim dsGrid as DataSet
```

and in C#:

```
DataSet dsGrid;
```

The Cache object with the key DataGridDataSet is then retrieved and assigned to the dsGrid DataSetobject. In VB.NET:

```
dsGrid = CType(Cache("DataGridDataSet"), DataSet)
```

and in C#:

```
dsGrid = (DataSet)Cache["DataGridDataSet"];
```

As with the Session and Application objects seen in Chapter 6, whatever is retrieved from the Cache object must be explicitly *cast*, or converted, to the correct data type, here DataSet. For this purpose, C# uses an explicit cast, while VB.NET uses the *CType* function.

The dsGrid data set is then tested to see if it actually exists. Although the DataSet object has been instantiated, it is only a placeholder until it actually contains data. If the Cache object with the key `DataGridDataSet` has not yet been created or has expired, then dsGrid still has no data in it. In VB.NET, this is done using:

```
if dsGrid is Nothing then
```

and in C#, it's:

```
if (dsGrid == null)
```

If the DataSet object does already contain data, meaning the Cache had been previously filled and was not expired, then the Label control's Text property is set accordingly to convey this to you on the web page. Otherwise, the GetDataSet method is called, the cache is filled with the data set returned by GetDataSet, and the Label control's Text property is set accordingly. In VB.NET, the code is:

```
dsGrid = GetDataSet( )
Cache("DataGridDataSet") = dsGrid
lbl.Text = "Data from database."
```

and in C#, it's:

```
dsGrid = GetDataSet( );
Cache["DataGridDataSet"] = dsGrid;
lbl.Text = "Data from database.";
```

In either case, once the data set is filled, the DataSource property of the DataGrid control on the web page is set to be the data set, and the DataGrid control is data bound. In VB.NET, the code is:

```
dg.DataSource=dsGrid.Tables(0)
dg.DataBind( )
```

and in C#, it's:

```
dg.DataSource=dsGrid.Tables[0];
dg.DataBind( );
```

The result of running the code in Examples 18-12 and 18-13 is shown in Figure 18-5.

The first time the web page is run, the label just above the DataGrid control will indicate that the data is coming directly from the database. Every subsequent time the form is requested, the label will change to say "Data from cache."

There is no way for the cache in this example to expire (i.e., to go away). As you will see shortly, there are several ways to force a cache to expire. In this example, however, even opening a new browser instance on a different machine will cause the data to come from the cache unless the application on the server is restarted. That is because the cache is available to the entire application, just as the Application object is.

In this example, a button, called btn, is added to the form to empty the cache and refill it. The event handler for this button calls the Cache.Remove method. This

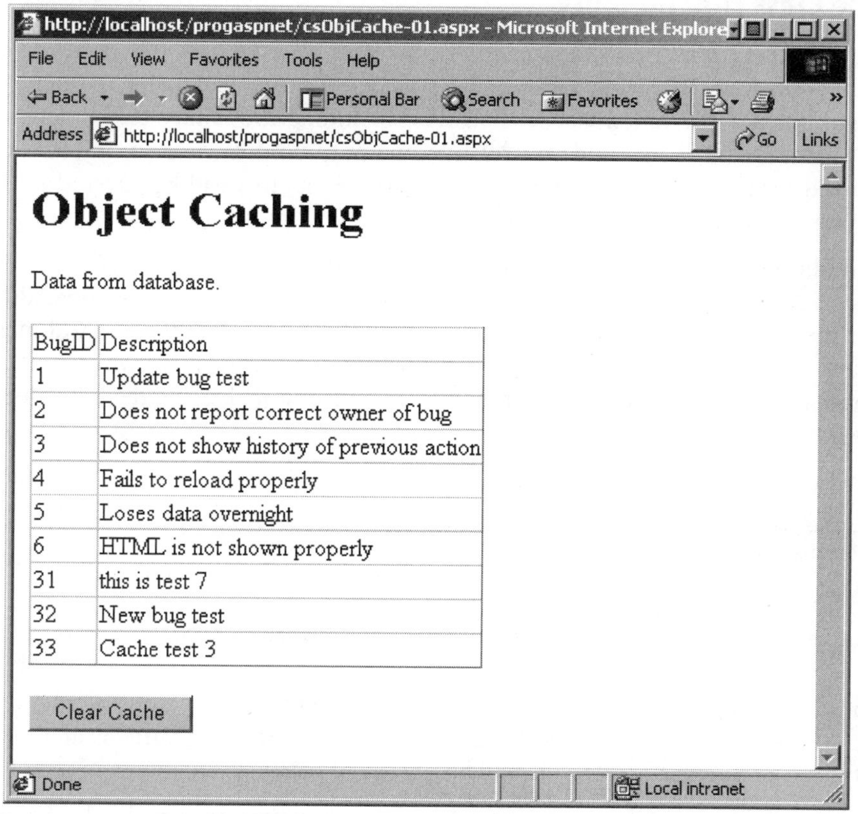

Figure 18-5. Results of object caching

method removes the cache record specified by the key named as the parameter to the method. In VB.NET, the code is:

```
Cache.Remove("DataGridDataSet")
```

and in C#, it's:

```
Cache.Remove("DataGridDataSet");
```

In Examples 18-12 and 18-13, the button event handler then refills the cache by calling the CreateDataGrid method. As an exercise in observing different behavior, comment out the line that calls CreateDataGrid in the btn_OnClick event procedure and observe the different behavior when you repost the page after clicking the Clear Cache button. When the line calling the CreateDataGrid method is *not* commented out, then the next time a browser is opened after the Clear Cache button is clicked, the data will still come from the cache. But if the line *is* commented out, the next browser instance will get the data directly from the database.

Cache Class Functionality

Examples 18-12 and 18-13 demonstrate how to add values to and retrieve values from the Object cache using a dictionary syntax of key/value pairs. The Cache class exposes much more functionality than this, including the ability to set dependencies, manage expirations, and control how memory used by cached objects can be recovered for more critical operations. All of these features will be covered in detail in the next sections.

This additional functionality is exposed through a different syntax for adding objects to the cache that uses the Add and Insert methods of the Cache class. The Add and Insert methods are very similar in effect. The only difference is that the Add method requires parameters for controlling all the exposed functionality, while the Insert method allows you to make some of the parameters optional, using default values for those parameters.

The syntax for the Add method in VB.NET is:

```
Cache.Add(KeyName, KeyValue, Dependencies, AbsoluteExpiration, _
SlidingExpiration, Priority, CacheItemRemovedCallback)
```

and for C#, it's:

```
Cache.Add(KeyName, KeyValue, Dependencies, AbsoluteExpiration, SlidingExpiration,
Priority, CacheItemRemovedCallback);
```

In these syntaxes, *KeyName* is a string with the name of the key in the Cache dictionary, and *KeyValue* is the value to be inserted into the Cache. *KeyValue* is an object of any type. All the other parameters will be described below.

While the Add method requires that all the parameters be provided, the Insert method is overloaded to allow several of the parameters to be optional.

 An object may *overload* its methods, which means it may declare two or more methods with the same name. The compiler differentiates among these methods based on the number and type of parameters provided.

The syntax for the overloaded Insert methods in VB.NET is described in this list. For C#, the syntax is identical except that there is a terminating semicolon for each statement:

- To insert a key/value pair with default values for all the other parameters:

  ```
  Cache.Insert(KeyName, KeyValue)
  ```
- To insert a key/value pair with dependencies and with default values for the other parameters:

  ```
  Cache.Insert(KeyName, KeyValue, Dependencies)
  ```

- To insert a key/value pair with dependencies and expiration policies and with default values for the other parameters:

```
Cache.Insert(KeyName, KeyValue, Dependencies, AbsoluteExpiration,
SlidingExpiration)
```

- To insert a key/value pair with dependencies, expiration policies, and priority policy, and a delegate to notify the application when the inserted item is removed from the cache:

```
Cache.Insert(KeyName, KeyValue, Dependencies, AbsoluteExpiration,
SlidingExpiration, Priority, CacheItemRemovedCallback)
```

To see this syntax in action, replace a single line from Example 18-12 or 18-13. Find the line in the CreateDataGrid method that looks like this in VB.NET:

```
Cache("DataGridDataSet") = dsGrid
```

or like this in C#:

```
Cache["DataGridDataSet"] = dsGrid;
```

Replace it with the following line in VB.NET:

```
Cache.Insert("DataGridDataSet", dsGrid)
```

or in C#:

```
Cache.Insert("DataGridDataSet", dsGrid);
```

On running the modified page in a browser, you will see no difference from the prior version.

By using the Insert method rather than the Add method, you are only required to provide the key and value, just as with the dictionary syntax.

There is much more you can do with these methods.

Dependencies

One very useful feature exposed by the Cache class is dependencies. A *dependency* is a relationship between a cached item and either a point in time or an external object. If the designated point in time is reached or if the external object changes, then the cached item will be automatically expired and removed from the cache.

The external object controlling the dependency can be a file, a directory, an array of files or directories, another item stored in the cache (represented by its key), or an array of items stored in the cache. The designated point in time can be either an absolute time or a relative time. In the following sections, we'll examine each of these dependencies and how they can be used to control the contents of the cache programmatically.

File change dependency

With a file change dependency, a cached item will become expired and be removed from the cache if a specified file has changed. This feature is typically used when a cached data set is derived from an XML file. You do not want the application to get the data set from the cache if the underlying XML file has changed.

To generate the XML file:

1. Use Start/Programs/Microsoft SQL Server\Configure SQL XML Support in IIS.

2. Set a virtual directory—BugsDB

3. Use the following URL in a browser:

   ```
   http://localhost/bugsdb?sql=select+*+from+bugs+for+xml+auto&root=ROOT
   ```

Example 18-14 shows the contents of an XML file that contains all the records from the Bugs table in the Bugs database. The code in Example 18-14 can be modified to demonstrate a file change dependency. Since the data set will be coming from XML rather than SQL Server, replace the Import directive pointing to System.Data.SqlClient with a directive pointing to System.Xml.

Example 18-14. Bugs.xml

```xml
<?xml version="1.0" encoding="utf-8" ?>
<ROOT>
    <bugs BugID="1" Product="2" Version="0.1" Description="Update bug test" Reporter="3" />
    <bugs BugID="2" Product="1" Version="0.1" Description="Does not report correct owner of
bug" Reporter="5" />
    <bugs BugID="3" Product="1" Version="0.1" Description="Does not show history of previous
action" Reporter="6" />
    <bugs BugID="4" Product="1" Version="0.1" Description="Fails to reload properly"
Reporter="5" />
    <bugs BugID="5" Product="2" Version="0.7" Description="Loses data overnight"
Reporter="5" />
    <bugs BugID="6" Product="2" Version="0.7" Description="HTML is not shown properly"
Reporter="6" />
    <bugs BugID="31" Product="1" Version="0.3" Description="this is test 7" Reporter="1" />
    <bugs BugID="32" Product="2" Version="0.1" Description="New bug test" Reporter="3" />
    <bugs BugID="33" Product="2" Version="0.1" Description="Cache test 3" Reporter="3" />
    <bugs BugID="34" Product="2" Version="0.1" Description="Object cache test 1"
Reporter="3" />
    <bugs BugID="35" Product="2" Version="0.1" Description="Obj Cache test 2" Reporter="4" /
>
</ROOT>
```

Next, modify the CreateDataGrid and GetDataSet methods as shown in Example 18-15 for VB.NET and Example 18-16 for C#, where the highlighted lines of code are different from the code in Example 18-12 and 18-13.

Example 18-15. Cache file dependency in VB.NET, vbObjCache-02.aspx

```
sub CreateDataGrid( )
   dim dsGrid as DataSet
   dsGrid = CType(Cache("DataGridDataSet"), DataSet)

   if dsGrid is Nothing then
      dsGrid = GetDataSet( )
      dim fileDepends as new CacheDependency(Server.MapPath("Bugs.xml"))
      Cache.Insert("DataGridDataSet", dsGrid, fileDepends)
      lbl.Text = "Data from XML file."
   else
      lbl.Text = "Data from cache."
   end if

   dg.DataSource=dsGrid.Tables(0)
   dg.DataBind( )
end sub

public function GetDataSet( ) as DataSet
   dim dsData as new DataSet( )
   dim doc as new XmlDataDocument( )
   doc.DataSet.ReadXml(Server.MapPath("Bugs.xml"))
   dsData = doc.DataSet
   return dsData
end function
```

Example 18-16. Cache file dependency in C#, csObjCache-02.aspx

```
public void CreateDataGrid( )
{
   DataSet dsGrid;
   dsGrid = (DataSet)Cache["DataGridDataSet"];

   if (dsGrid == null)
   {
      dsGrid = GetDataSet( );
      CacheDependency fileDepends = new
               CacheDependency(Server.MapPath("Bugs.xml"));
      Cache.Insert("DataGridDataSet", dsGrid, fileDepends);
      lbl.Text = "Data from XML file.";
   }
   else
   {
      lbl.Text = "Data from cache.";
   }

   dg.DataSource=dsGrid.Tables[0];
   dg.DataBind( );
}

public DataSet GetDataSet( )
```

```
{
    DataSet dsData = new DataSet( );
    XmlDataDocument doc = new XmlDataDocument( );
    doc.DataSet.ReadXml(Server.MapPath("Bugs.xml"));
    dsData = doc.DataSet;
    return dsData;
}
```

The goal of the GetDataSet method is still to return a data set. However, the source of the data for the data set is now the XML file called *Bugs.xml*. Since ASP.NET stores data sets internally as XML, it is very easy to move back and forth between XML and data sets. The XML object equivalent to a data set is the XmlDataDocument. An XmlDataDocument object named doc is instantiated. This XmlDataDocument object is filled using the ReadXml method. The MapPath method maps a virtual path of a file on the server to a physical path.

The DataSet object is obtained from the DataSet property of the XmlDataDocument object, then returned to the calling method.

In the CreateDataGrid method, only three lines have changed from Examples 18-12 and 18-13. A CacheDependency object is defined against the source XML file. Again, MapPath is used to map the virtual path to a physical path.

The dictionary syntax used in Examples 18-12 and 18-13 to add the item to the cache is changed to use the Insert method of the Cache class. Using the Insert method allows you to specify a dependency in addition to the key name and value.

The text string assigned to the label has been updated to reflect the fact that the data is now coming from an XML file rather than a database.

Test this page by running the code from Example 18-15 or 18-16 in a browser. You will get something similar to Figure 18-6.

If you repost the page by highlighting the URL and pressing Enter, the label at the top of the page will indicate that the data is coming from the cache.

Now open the *Bugs.xml* file in a text editor and make a change to one of the values in one of the records. Remember to save the XML file. When you repost the page in the browser, instead of the data still coming from the cache, it will once again be coming from the XML file.

As soon as the XML source file was changed, the cached data set was expired and removed from the cache. The next time the page requested the data set from the server, it had to retrieve it fresh from the XML file.

If you wish to condition the cache dependency on an array of files or directories, the syntax for the CacheDependency constructor in Examples 18-15 and 18-16 would take an array of file paths or directories rather than a single filename. So, for example, the single line of code in Examples 18-15 and 18-16 that defines the

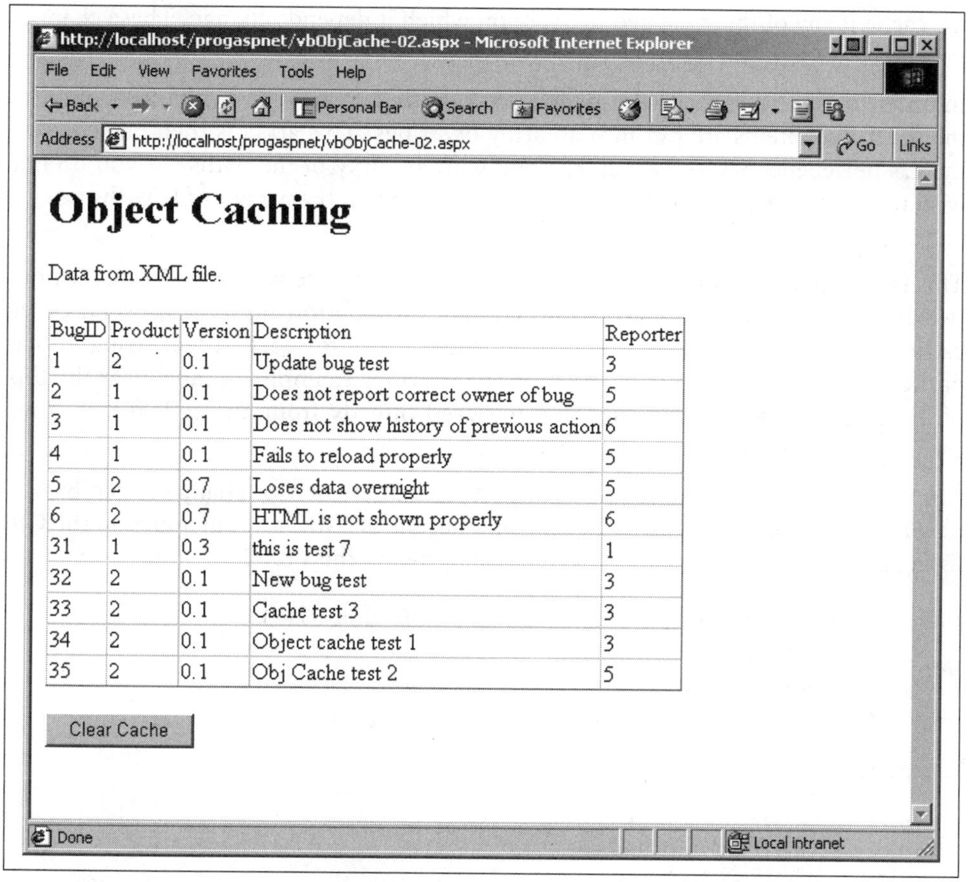

Figure 18-6. Object caching from XML file

CacheDependency object would be preceded by code defining a string array with one or more files or paths, and the CacheDependency constructor itself would take the array as a parameter. In VB.NET, it would look something like:

```
dim  fileDependsArray as string() = {Server.MapPath("Bugs.xml"), _
                            Server.MapPath("People.xml")}
dim fileDepends as new CacheDependency(fileDependsArray)
```

and in C#:

```
string[] fileDependsArray = {Server.MapPath("Bugs.xml"),
                        Server.MapPath("People.xml")};
CacheDependency fileDepends = new CacheDependency(fileDependsArray);
```

Cached item dependency

A cached item can be dependent on other items in the cache. If a cached item is dependent on one or more other cached items, it will be expired and removed from the cache if any of those cached items upon which it depends change. These changes include either removal from the cache or a change in value.

In order to make a cached item dependent on other cached items, the keys of all of the controlling items are put into an array of strings. This array is then passed in to the CacheDependency constructor, along with an array of file paths. (If you do not wish to define a dependency on any files or paths, then the array of file paths can be Nothing in VB.NET or null in C#.)

This is demonstrated in Examples 18-17 and 18-18. In the web page in this listing, two buttons have been added to the UI. The first button initializes several other cached items. The second button changes the value of the cached text string in one of the controlling cached items. As with the previous examples, a label near the top of the page indicates if the data was retrieved directly from an XML file or from cache. The Clear Cache button is unchanged.

The lines of code in Examples 18-17 and 18-18 that are new or changed from Examples 18-15 and 18-16 are highlighted. Note that the HTML is not included in the C# listing in Example 18-18, since it is identical to that in the VB.NET listing.

Example 18-17. Cache item dependency in VB.NET, vbObjCache-03.aspx

```
<%@ Page Language="vb" %>
<%@ Import namespace="System.Data" %>
<%@ Import namespace="System.Xml" %>

<script runat="server">

   sub Page_Load(ByVal Sender as Object, _
             ByVal e as EventArgs)
      if not IsPostBack then
         CreateDataGrid( )
      end if
   end sub

   sub btnClear_OnClick(ByVal Sender as Object, _
                        ByVal e as EventArgs)
      Cache.Remove("DataGridDataSet")
      CreateDataGrid( )
   end sub

   sub btnInit_OnClick(ByVal Sender as Object, _
                   ByVal e as EventArgs)
      '  Initialize caches to depend on.
      Cache("Depend0") = "This is the first dependency."
      Cache("Depend1") = "This is the 2nd dependency."
      Cache("Depend2") = "This is the 3rd dependency."
   end sub

   sub btnKey0_OnClick(ByVal Sender as Object, _
                       ByVal e as EventArgs)
```

```
      Cache("Depend0") = "This is a changed first dependency."
   end sub

sub CreateDataGrid( )
   dim dsGrid as DataSet
   dsGrid = CType(Cache("DataGridDataSet"), DataSet)

   if dsGrid is Nothing then
      dsGrid = GetDataSet( )

      dim  fileDependsArray as string( ) = {Server.MapPath("Bugs.xml")}
      dim cacheDependsArray as string( ) = _
                        {"Depend0","Depend1", "Depend2"}

      dim cacheDepends as new CacheDependency( _
                        fileDependsArray, cacheDependsArray)
      Cache.Insert("DataGridDataSet", dsGrid, cacheDepends)

      lbl.Text = "Data from XML file."
   else
      lbl.Text = "Data from cache."
   end if

   dg.DataSource=dsGrid.Tables(0)
   dg.DataBind( )
end sub

public function GetDataSet( ) as DataSet
   dim dsData as new DataSet( )
   dim doc as new XmlDataDocument( )
   doc.DataSet.ReadXml(Server.MapPath("Bugs.xml"))
   dsData = doc.DataSet
   return dsData
end function
</script>

<html>
   <body>
   <form runat="server">

      <h1>Object Caching</h1>
      <h2>Cache Item Dependency</h2>

       <asp:Label
           id="lbl"
            runat="server"/>

      <br/>
      <br/>

         <asp:DataGrid
```

Example 18-17. Cache item dependency in VB.NET, vbObjCache-03.aspx (continued)

```
            id="dg"
             runat="server"/>

      <br/>

      <asp:Button
         id="btnClear"
         Text="Clear Cache"
         OnClick="btnClear_OnClick"
         runat="server"/>

      <br/>
      <br/>

      <asp:Button
         id="btnInit"
         Text="Initialize Keys"
         OnClick="btnInit_OnClick"
         runat="server"/>

      <asp:Button
         id="btnKey0"
         Text="Change Key 0"
         OnClick="btnKey0_OnClick"
         runat="server"/>

   </form>
  </body>
</html>
```

Example 18-18. Cache item dependency in C#, csObjCache-03.aspx

```
<%@ Page Language="C#" %>
<%@ Import namespace="System.Data" %>
<%@ Import namespace="System.Xml" %>

<script runat="server">
   void Page_Load(Object Source, EventArgs E)
   {
      if (! IsPostBack)
      {
         CreateDataGrid();
      }
   }

   void btnClear_OnClick(Object Source, EventArgs E)
   {
      Cache.Remove("DataGridDataSet");
      CreateDataGrid();
   }
```

```csharp
    void btnInit_OnClick(Object Source, EventArgs E)
    {
        //  Initialize caches to depend on.
        Cache["Depend0"] = "This is the first dependency.";
        Cache["Depend1"] = "This is the 2nd dependency.";
        Cache["Depend2"] = "This is the 3rd dependency.";
    }

    void btnKey0_OnClick(Object Source, EventArgs E)
    {
        Cache["Depend0"] = "This is a changed first dependency.";
    }

    public void CreateDataGrid()
    {
        DataSet dsGrid;
        dsGrid = (DataSet)Cache["DataGridDataSet"];

        if (dsGrid == null)
        {
            dsGrid = GetDataSet();

            string[] fileDependsArray = {Server.MapPath("Bugs.xml")};
            string[] cacheDependsArray = {"Depend0","Depend1", "Depend2"};

            CacheDependency cacheDepends = new CacheDependency
                            (fileDependsArray, cacheDependsArray);
            Cache.Insert("DataGridDataSet", dsGrid, cacheDepends);

            lbl.Text = "Data from XML file.";
        }
        else
        {
            lbl.Text = "Data from cache.";
        }

        dg.DataSource=dsGrid.Tables[0];
        dg.DataBind();
    }

    public DataSet GetDataSet()
    {
        DataSet dsData = new DataSet();
        XmlDataDocument doc = new XmlDataDocument();
        doc.DataSet.ReadXml(Server.MapPath("Bugs.xml"));
        dsData = doc.DataSet;
        return dsData;
    }
</script>
```

In the btnInit_OnClick event handler, the controlling cache items are created. The values of the cached items are not important for this example, except as something to change when the Change Key 0 button is clicked, as is done in the event handler for that button, btnKey0_OnClick.

The real action here occurs in the CreateDataGrid method. Two string arrays are defined, one to hold the file to depend upon, and one to hold the keys of the other cached items to depend upon.

The file dependency is exactly as described in the preceding section. If you do not wish to implement any file or directory dependency here, then use Nothing or null for VB.NET or C#, respectively. For example, in VB.NET, the code would be:

```
dim cacheDepends as new CacheDependency(Nothing, cacheDependsArray)
```

and in C#, it would be:

```
CacheDependency cacheDepends = new CacheDependency(null,
                                          cacheDependsArray);
```

Running the code in Examples 18-17 or 18-18 brings up the page shown in Figure 18-7. Initially, the label above the data grid will show that the data is from the XML file. Re-entering the URL will cause the data to come from the Cache. Clicking any of the buttons or changing the contents of *Bugs.xml* will cause the cached data set to expire and the data to be retrieved fresh from the XML file the next time the page is posted. Although this example does not explicitly demonstrate what would happen if one of the controlling cached items was removed from the Cache, that too would cause the dependent cached item to expire.

Time dependency

Items in the Cache can be given a dependency based on time. This is done with two parameters in either the Add or Insert methods of the Cache object.

The two parameters that control time dependency are *AbsoluteExpiration* and *SlidingExpiration*. Both parameters are required in the Add method and are optional in the Insert method through method overloading.

To insert a key/value pair into the Cache with file or cached item dependencies and time-based dependencies, use the following syntax (the same in both VB.NET and C#, except for the closing semicolon):

```
Cache.Insert(KeyName, KeyValue, Dependencies, AbsoluteExpiration, SlidingExpiration)
```

If you don't want any file or cached item dependencies, then the *Dependencies* parameter should be Nothing in VB.NET or null in C#. If this syntax is used, default values will be used for the scavenging and callback parameters (described in the next sections).

The *AbsoluteExpiration* parameter is of type DateTime. It defines a lifetime for the cached item. The time provided can be an absolute time, such as August 21, 2001 at

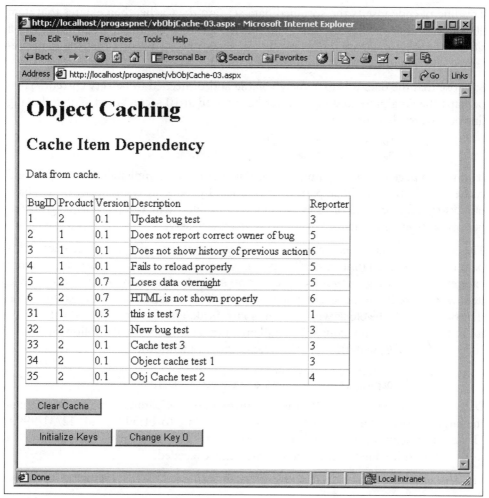

Figure 18-7. Cached item dependency

1:23:45 P.M. The code to implement that type of absolute expiration would look something like the following (in C#):

```
DateTime expDate = new DateTime(2001,8,21,13,23,45);
Cache.Insert("DataGridDataSet", dsGrid, null, expDate, TimeSpan.Zero);
```

Obviously, this is not very flexible. Of greater utility is an absolute expiration based on the current time, say 30 minutes from now. The syntax for that expiration would be (again in C#—VB.NET is identical except for the trailing semicolon and possibly a line continuation character):

```
Cache.Insert("DataGridDataSet", dsGrid, null,
        DateTime.Now.AddMinutes(30), TimeSpan.Zero);
```

This line of code inserts the specified data set into the Cache, then expires that item 30 minutes after it was inserted. This scenario would be useful when accessing a slowly changing database where it was only necessary to be sure that the data presented was no more than 30 minutes old.

Suppose that the data was extremely volatile and/or needed to be very current. Then perhaps the data presented must never be more than 10 seconds old. The following line of code implements that scenario:

```
Cache.Insert("DataGridDataSet", dsGrid, null,
        DateTime.Now.AddSeconds(10), TimeSpan.Zero);
```

If your web page is receiving hundreds of hits per minute, implementing a 10-second cache would provide a huge performance boost by reducing the number of database queries by a factor of 20 or more. Even a one-second cache can provide a significant performance enhancement to heavily trafficked web servers.

The other time-based parameter is *SlidingExpiration*, of type TimeSpan. This parameter specifies a time interval between when an item is last accessed and when it expires. If the sliding expiration is set for 30 seconds, for example, then the cached item will expire if the cache is not accessed within 30 seconds. If it is accessed within that time period, the clock will be reset, so to speak, and the cached item will persist for at least another 30 seconds. To implement this scenario, use the following line of code (again in C#, with the VB.NET version nearly identical):

```
Cache.Insert("DataGridDataSet", dsGrid, null,
        DateTime.MaxValue, TimeSpan.FromSeconds(30));
```

DateTime.MaxValue is used for the *AbsoluteExpiration* parameter. This constant is the largest possible value of DateTime, corresponding to 11:59:59 PM, 12/31/9999. (That's a millennium problem we can live with.) This guarantees that the cached item won't expire due to the absolute time being exceeded.

SlidingExpiration can be disabled by setting its value to CacheNoSlidingExpiration.

Scavenging

One of the features of object caching is *scavenging*, where ASP.NET automatically removes seldom used items from the Cache object if server memory becomes scarce. This frees up memory to handle a higher volume of page requests.

Scavenging is controlled through the Priority parameter of the Add and Insert methods of the Cache class. This parameter is required of the Add method and optional for the Insert method through method overloading.

The Priority parameter indicates the cost of the cached item relative to the other items stored in the cache. This parameter is used by the cache when it evicts objects in order to free up system memory when the web server runs low on memory. Cached items with a lower priority are evicted before items with a higher priority.

The legal values of the `Priority` parameter are contained in the `CacheItemPriority` enumeration, shown in Table 18-2 in descending order of priority.

Table 18-2. Members of the CacheItemPriority enumeration

Priority value	Description
NotRemovable	Items with this priority will not be evicted
High	Items with this priority level are the least likely to be evicted
AboveNormal	Items with this priority level are less likely to be evicted than items assigned Normal priority
Default	This is equivalent to Normal
Normal	The default value
BelowNormal	Items with this priority level are more likely to be evicted than items assigned Normal priority
Low	Items with this priority level are the most likely to be evicted

To implement scavenging, use the following line of code in VB.NET:

```
Cache.Insert("DataGridDataSet", dsGrid, null,
        DateTime.MaxValue, TimeSpan.Zero
        CacheItemPriority.High,
        Nothing)
```

and in C#:

```
Cache.Insert("DataGridDataSet", dsGrid, null,
        DateTime.MaxValue, TimeSpan.Zero
        CacheItemPriority.High,
        null);
```

The final parameter in the above lines of code pertain to callback support, which will be covered in the next section.

Since these Insert method calls use all seven parameters, you could also use the Add method with the same parameters.

Callback Support

It may be useful to be informed when an item is removed from the cache for any reason. Perhaps you will want to reinsert the item into the cache, or perhaps you will want to know if you need to install more memory in your web server. Such notification is implemented using the `CacheItemRemovedCallback` parameter of the Add or Insert methods. This parameter specifies a *callback method* to be run when the cached item is removed.

In the example web page shown in Examples 18-19 (VB.NET) and 18-20 (C#), support is added for a callback when the cached item is expired or removed from the cache. This callback method, RemovedCallback, makes a log entry in a text file in the root of drive C. The log entry has a timestamp and the reason for the removal.

The lines in Examples 18-19 and 18-20 that are changed or new from the previous example are highlighted.

Example 18-19. Cache callbacks in VB.NET, vbObjCache-04.aspx

```
<%@ Page Language="vb" %>
<%@ Import namespace="System.Data" %>
<%@ Import namespace="System.Xml" %>

<script runat="server">

   private shared onRemove as CacheItemRemovedCallback = Nothing

   sub Page_Load(ByVal Sender as Object, _
              ByVal e as EventArgs)
      if not IsPostBack then
         CreateDataGrid( )
      end if
   end sub

   sub btnClear_OnClick(ByVal Sender as Object, _
                        ByVal e as EventArgs)
      Cache.Remove("DataGridDataSet")
      CreateDataGrid( )
   end sub

   sub btnInit_OnClick(ByVal Sender as Object, _
                   ByVal e as EventArgs)
      '  Initialize caches to depend on.
      Cache("Depend0") = "This is the first dependency."
      Cache("Depend1") = "This is the 2nd dependency."
      Cache("Depend2") = "This is the 3rd dependency."
   end sub

   sub btnKey0_OnClick(ByVal Sender as Object, _
                      ByVal e as EventArgs)
      Cache("Depend0") = "This is a changed first dependency."
   end sub

   sub CreateDataGrid( )
      dim dsGrid as DataSet
      dsGrid = CType(Cache("DataGridDataSet"), DataSet)

      onRemove = new CacheItemRemovedCallback( _
                         AddressOf Me.RemovedCallback)

      if dsGrid is Nothing then
         dsGrid = GetDataSet( )

         dim  fileDependsArray as string( ) = _
                  {Server.MapPath("Bugs.xml")}
         dim cacheDependsArray as string( ) = _
                     {"Depend0","Depend1", "Depend2"}
```

Example 18-19. Cache callbacks in VB.NET, vbObjCache-04.aspx (continued)

```
        dim cacheDepends as new CacheDependency( _
                           fileDependsArray, cacheDependsArray)
        Cache.Insert("DataGridDataSet", dsGrid, cacheDepends, _
                    DateTime.Now.AddSeconds(10), _
                    TimeSpan.Zero, _
                    CacheItemPriority.Default, _
                    onRemove)

        lbl.Text = "Data from XML file."
     else
        lbl.Text = "Data from cache."
     end if

     dg.DataSource=dsGrid.Tables(0)
     dg.DataBind( )
  end sub

  public sub RemovedCallback(k As String, _
                             v As Object, _
                             r As CacheItemRemovedReason)
     Call WriteFile("Cache removed for following reason: " & _
                    r.ToString( ))
  end sub

  public sub WriteFile(strText as string)
     dim writer as System.IO.StreamWriter = new System.IO.StreamWriter( _
                    "C:\\test.txt",true)
     dim str as string
    str = DateTime.Now.ToString( ) & "   " & strText
     writer.WriteLine(str)
     writer.Close( )
  end sub

  public function GetDataSet( ) as DataSet
     dim dsData as new DataSet( )
     dim doc as new XmlDataDocument( )
     doc.DataSet.ReadXml(Server.MapPath("Bugs.xml"))
     dsData = doc.DataSet
     return dsData
  end function

</script>

<html>
   <body>
   <form runat="server">

     <h1>Object Caching</h1>
     <h2>Cache Callbacks</h2>

      <asp:Label
```

Example 18-19. Cache callbacks in VB.NET, vbObjCache-04.aspx (continued)

```
            id="lbl"
            runat="server"/>

    <br/>
    <br/>

        <asp:DataGrid
            id="dg"
            runat="server"/>

    <br/>

    <asp:Button
        id="btnClear"
        Text="Clear Cache"
        OnClick="btnClear_OnClick"
        runat="server"/>

    <br/>
    <br/>

    <asp:Button
        id="btnInit"
        Text="Initialize Keys"
        OnClick="btnInit_OnClick"
        runat="server"/>

    <asp:Button
        id="btnKey0"
        Text="Change Key 0"
        OnClick="btnKey0_OnClick"
        runat="server"/>

    </form>
    </body>
</html>
```

Example 18-20. Cache callbacks in C#, csObjCache-04.aspx

```
<%@ Page Language="C#" %>
<%@ Import namespace="System.Data" %>
<%@ Import namespace="System.Xml" %>

<script runat="server">

    private static CacheItemRemovedCallback onRemove = null;

    void Page_Load(Object Source, EventArgs E)
    {
        if (! IsPostBack)
        {
            CreateDataGrid();
```

Example 18-20. Cache callbacks in C#, csObjCache-04.aspx (continued)

```
      }
}

void btnClear_OnClick(Object Source, EventArgs E)
{
   Cache.Remove("DataGridDataSet");
   CreateDataGrid( );
}

void btnInit_OnClick(Object Source, EventArgs E)
{
   // Initialize caches to depend on.
   Cache["Depend0"] = "This is the first dependency.";
   Cache["Depend1"] = "This is the 2nd dependency.";
   Cache["Depend2"] = "This is the 3rd dependency.";
}

void btnKey0_OnClick(Object Source, EventArgs E)
{
   Cache["Depend0"] = "This is a changed first dependency.";
}

public void CreateDataGrid( )
{
   DataSet dsGrid;
   dsGrid = (DataSet)Cache["DataGridDataSet"];

   onRemove = new CacheItemRemovedCallback(this.RemovedCallback);

   if (dsGrid == null)
   {
      dsGrid = GetDataSet( );

      string[] fileDependsArray = {Server.MapPath("Bugs.xml")};
      string[] cacheDependsArray = {"Depend0","Depend1", "Depend2"};

      CacheDependency cacheDepends = new CacheDependency(
                  fileDependsArray, cacheDependsArray);
      Cache.Insert("DataGridDataSet", dsGrid, cacheDepends,
                  DateTime.Now.AddSeconds(10),
                  TimeSpan.Zero,
                  CacheItemPriority.Default,
                  onRemove);

      lbl.Text = "Data from XML file.";
   }
   else
   {
      lbl.Text = "Data from cache.";
   }

   dg.DataSource=dsGrid.Tables[0];
```

Example 18-20. Cache callbacks in C#, csObjCache-04.aspx (continued)

```
      dg.DataBind( );
  }

  public void RemovedCallback(String k,
                             Object v,
                             CacheItemRemovedReason r)
  {
     WriteFile("Cache removed for following reason: " + r.ToString( ));
  }

  void WriteFile(string strText)
  {
     System.IO.StreamWriter writer = new System.IO.StreamWriter(
                                       @"C:\test.txt",true);
     string str;
    str = DateTime.Now.ToString( ) + "   " + strText;
     writer.WriteLine(str);
     writer.Close( );
  }

  public DataSet GetDataSet( )
  {
     DataSet dsData = new DataSet( );
     XmlDataDocument doc = new XmlDataDocument( );
     doc.DataSet.ReadXml(Server.MapPath("Bugs.xml"));
     dsData = doc.DataSet;
     return dsData;
  }
</script>
```

Looking at the lines of code that call the Insert method, you can see that one more parameter has been added, *onRemove*. This is the callback.

The callback method is encapsulated within a *delegate*. A delegate is a reference type that encapsulates a method with a specific signature and return type. The callback method is of the same type and must have the same signature as the CacheItemRemovedCallback delegate. The callback method is declared as a private member of the Page class. In VB.NET, the line of code is:

```
    private shared onRemove as CacheItemRemovedCallback = Nothing
```

and in C# it's:

```
    private static CacheItemRemovedCallback onRemove = null;
```

Further down, in the CreateDataGrid method, the callback delegate is instantiated, passing in a reference to the appropriate method. In VB.NET, the code is:

```
    onRemove = new CacheItemRemovedCallback( _
                    AddressOf Me.RemovedCallback)
```

and in C#, it's:

```
    onRemove = new CacheItemRemovedCallback(this.RemovedCallback);
```

This instantiation associates the onRemove delegate with the RemovedCallback method. Notice the use of the AddressOf keyword in VB.NET to create a reference to the method, which is not necessary in C#.

The RemovedCallBack method, reproduced here in both VB.NET:

```
public sub RemovedCallback(k As String, _
                           v As Object, _
                           r As CacheItemRemovedReason)
    Call WriteFile("Cache removed for following reason: " & _
                   r.ToString())
end sub
```

and C#:

```
public void RemovedCallback(String k,
                            Object v,
                            CacheItemRemovedReason r)
{
    WriteFile("Cache removed for following reason: " + r.ToString());
}
```

has the required signature, which consists of three parameters:

- A string containing the key of the cached item
- An object that is the cached item
- A member of the CacheItemRemovedReason enumeration

This last parameter, CacheItemRemovedReason, provides the reason that the cached item was removed from the cache. It can have one of the values shown in Table 18-3.

Table 18-3. Members of the CacheItemRemovedReason enumeration

Reason	Description
DependencyChanged	A file or item key dependency has changed.
Expired	The cached item has expired.
Removed	The cached item has been explicitly removed by the Remove method, or replaced by another item with the same key.
Underused	The cached item was removed to free up system memory.

In this example, the only thing the RemovedCallback method does is call WriteFile to make a log entry. It does this by instantiating a StreamWriter on the log file. In VB.NET, the code is:

```
dim writer as System.IO.StreamWriter = new System.IO.StreamWriter( _
                   "C:\\test.txt",true)
```

and in C#, it's:

```
System.IO.StreamWriter writer = new System.IO.StreamWriter(
                               @"C:\test.txt",true);
```

The second parameter for the StreamWriter class, the Boolean, specifies to append to the file if it exists, and to create the file if it doesn't exist. If `false`, it would have overwritten the file if it existed.

The WriteLine method is then used to write the string to be logged to the log file.

The HttpCachePolicy Class

Just as the `OutputCache` page directive provides a high-level API for implementing caching, a low-level API is available through the HttpCachePolicy class. This class is contained within the System.Web namespace. It uses HTTP headers to control the caching. The HttpCachePolicy class mirrors the functionality provided by the page directive. It also provides additional low-level control, comparable to the type of control provided for object caching.

To use the HttpCachePolicy class to control output caching, do not include an `OutputCache` directive in the page file. Instead, use the Response.Cache syntax, as shown in the highlighted lines in Examples 18-21 (for VB.NET) or 18-22 (for C#). (Example 18-22 includes only the script block, since the HTML is identical to that in Example 18-21. Note that these examples are similar to Examples 18-3 and 18-4.)

Example 18-21. Output caching using HttpCachePolicy Class in VB.NET, vbOutputCache-03. aspx

```
<%@ Page Language="VB" %>

<script runat="server">
    sub Page_Load(ByVal Sender as Object, _
                 ByVal e as EventArgs)
        Response.Cache.SetExpires(DateTime.Now.AddSeconds(10))
        Response.Cache.SetCacheability(HttpCacheability.Public)

        lblMsg.Text = "This page was loaded at " & _
                     DateTime.Now.ToString("T")
        lblUserName.Text = Request.Params("username")
        lblState.Text = Request.Params("state")
    end sub
</script>

<html>
    <body>
    <form runat="server">

        <h1>Output Caching</h1>

        <asp:Label
            id="lblMsg"
            runat="server"/>

        <br/>
```

```
    <br/>

    UserName:   
    <asp:Label
        id="lblUserName"
        runat="server"/>

    <br/>

    State:   
    <asp:Label
        id="lblState"
        runat="server"/>

 </form>
 </body>
</html>
```

Example 18-22. Output Caching Using HttpCachePolicy Class in C#, csOutputCache-03.aspx

```
<%@ Page Language="C#" %>

<script runat="server">
   void Page_Load(Object Source, EventArgs E)
   {
      Response.Cache.SetExpires(DateTime.Now.AddSeconds(10));
      Response.Cache.SetCacheability(HttpCacheability.Public);

      lblMsg.Text = "This page was loaded at " +
                    DateTime.Now.ToString("T");
      lblUserName.Text = Request.Params["username"];
      lblState.Text = Request.Params["state"];

   }
</script>
```

The first highlighted line in Examples 18-21 and 18-22 sets the cache duration to 10 seconds. It is equivalent to a Duration parameter in an OutputCache page directive.

The second line corresponds to the Location parameter in the OutputCache directive. Table 18-4 compares the SetCacheability values, which are members of the HttpCacheability enumeration, with the Location values.

Table 18-4. SetCacheability versus Location

Location value	SetCacheability values	SetCacheability description
Client	Private	Default value. Response is cacheable on the client. Useful if page requires authentication.
Downstream	Public	Also uses SetNoServerCaching method to disallow caching on the web server.

Table 18-4. SetCacheability versus Location (continued)

Location value	SetCacheability values	SetCacheability description
Server	Server	Response is cached on the web server.
None	NoCache	Disables caching.
Any	Public	Response is cacheable by clients and shared (proxy) caches.

There are many other HttpCachePolicy methods and properties available. Some of the more common ones include:

SetMaxAge
> Another method, in addition to SetExpires, to set an expiration. Accepts a TimeSpan value. The following line of code would set the expiration time to 45 seconds:
>
> ```
> Response.Cache.SetMaxAge(new TimeSpan(0,0,45))
> ```

SetNoServerCaching
> Disables all further server caching. For example:
>
> ```
> Response.Cache.SetNoServerCaching( )
> ```

SetSlidingExpiration
> A method to enable sliding expiration. Takes a Boolean parameter. If true, enables sliding expiration. Sliding expiration forces the clock to start over, so to speak, every time the cache is accessed. So if SetMaxAge (described above) is set to 30 seconds, every time the cache is accessed, the 30-second clock is reset to zero. As long as the cache is accessed at least every 30 seconds, it will never expire. The following statement, for example, enables sliding expiration of the cache:
>
> ```
> Response.Cache.SetSlidingExpiration(true)
> ```

VaryByParams
> This property is the equivalent of the VaryByParam parameter in the OutputCache directive (note the slight difference in spelling). It forces a separate cache for each unique combination of parameters passed to the server in the page request.
>
> To duplicate the VaryByParam parameter in the following OutputCache directive:
>
> ```
> <%@ OutputCache Duration="60" VaryByParam="state;city" %>
> ```
>
> you would use the following lines of code:
>
> ```
> Response.Cache.VaryByParams.Item("state")=true
> Response.Cache.VaryByParams.Item("city")=true
> ```

Performance

Performance is often a vitally important issue in computer applications, especially in web applications receiving a large number of requests. One obvious way to improve performance is to buy faster hardware with more memory. But you can also tune your code to enhance performance in many ways, some of them significant. We'll begin by examining some of the areas specific to ASP.NET which offer the greatest performance improvements and then examine some of the general .NET topics related to improving performance.

 Several Microsofties involved with actually writing the .NET Framework used the word *performant* to mean that something is delivering higher performance. I can't find the word in any dictionary, but it seems like a good word to me.

ASP.NET-Specific Issues

Correctly using the following features of ASP.NET offers the greatest performance improvements when an ASP.NET application is running.

Session state

Session state is a wonderful thing, but not all applications or pages require it. For any that do not, disable it.

Session state can be disabled for an entire application by setting the EnableSessionState attribute in the Page directive to false, as in:

```
<%@ Page Language="VB" EnableSessionState="false"%>
```

If a page will not be creating or modifying session variables but still needs to access them, set the session state to read-only:

```
<%@ Page Language="VB" EnableSessionState="ReadOnly"%>
```

By default, web services do not have session state enabled. They only have access to session state if the EnableSession property of the WebMethod attribute is set to true. In VB.NET this looks like:

```
<WebMethod(EnableSession:=true)>
```

and in C#:

```
[WebMethod(EnableSession=true)]
```

Session state can be disabled for an entire application by editing the sessionState section of the application's *web.config* file:

```
<sessionState  mode="off" />
```

Session state can be stored in one of three ways:

- In-process
- Out-of-process, as a Windows service
- Out-of-process, in a SQL Server database

Each has advantages and disadvantages. Storing session state in-process is by far the most performant. The out-of-process stores are necessary in web farm or web garden scenarios (see the upcoming section "Web gardening and web farming,") or if the data must not be lost if a server or process is stopped and restarted.

For a complete discussion of session state, see Chapter 6.

View state

Automatic view state management is another great feature of ASP.NET server controls that enables the controls to correctly show property values after a round trip with no work on the part of the developer. However, there is a performance penalty. This information is passed back and forth via a hidden field, which consumes bandwidth and takes time to process. To see the amount of data used in view state, enable tracing and look at the Viewstate column of the Control Hierarchy table.

By default, view state is enabled for all server controls. To disable view state for a server control, set the EnableViewState attribute to false, as in the following example:

```
<asp:TextBox
    id="txtBookName"
    text="Enter book name."
    toolTip="Enter book name here."
    EnableViewState="false"
    runat="server" />
```

You can also disable view state for an entire page by setting the EnableViewState attribute of the Page directive to false, as in:

```
<%@ Page Language="C#"  EnableViewState="false" %>
```

Caching

Use output and data caching whenever possible. This is especially valuable for database queries that either return relatively static data or have a limited range of query parameters. Effective use of caching can have a profound effect on the performance of a web site.

Server controls

Server controls are very convenient and offer many advantages. In Visual Studio .NET, they are practically the default type of control. However, they have a certain amount of overhead and are sometimes not the optimal type of control to use.

In general, if you do not need to programmatically manipulate a control, do not use a server control. Use a classic HTML control instead. For example, if placing a simple label on a page, there is no need to use a server control unless you need to read or change the value of the label's Text property.

If you need to substitute values into HTML sent to the client browser, you can achieve the desired result without using a server control, instead using data binding or a simple rendering. For example, the following VB.NET example shows three ways of displaying a hyperlink in a browser:

```
<script language="VB" runat="server">

    Public strLink As String = "www.anysite.com"
    Sub Page_Load(sender As Object, e As EventArgs)
        '..retrieve data for strLink here
        '  Call the DataBind method for the page.
        DataBind( )
    End Sub

</script>

<%--the server control is not necessary...--%>
<a href='<%# strLink %>' runat="server">
The Name of the Link</a>

<br><br>

<%-- use DataBinding to substitute literals instead...--%>
<a href='<%# strLink %>' > The Name of the Link</a>

<br><br>

<%-- or a simple rendering expression...--%>
<a href='<%= strLink %>' > The Name of the Link</a>
```

Web gardening and web farming

Adding multiple processors to a computer is called *web gardening*. The .NET Framework takes advantage of this by distributing work to several processes, one per CPU.

For truly high-traffic sites, multiple web server machines can work together to serve the same application. This is referred to as a *web farm*.

At the least, locating the web server on one machine and the database server on another will buy a large degree of stability and performance.

Round trips

Round trips to the server are very expensive. In low bandwidth situations, they are slow for the client, and in high-volume applications, they bog down the server and inhibit scaling. You should design your applications to minimize round trips.

The only truly essential round trips to the server are those that read or write data. Most validation and data manipulations can occur on the client browser. ASP.NET server controls do this automatically for validation with uplevel browsers (i.e., IE 4 and IE 5, or any browser that supports ECMAScript).

When developing custom server controls, having the controls render client-side code for uplevel browsers will substantially reduce the number of round trips.

Another way to minimize round trips is to use the IsPostBack property in the Page_Load method. Often, you will want the page to perform some process the first time the page loads, but not on subsequent postbacks. For example, the following code in VB.NET:

```
sub Page_Load(ByVal Sender as Object, _
            ByVal e as EventArgs)
    if not IsPostBack then
        ' Do the expensive operations only the
        ' first time the page is loaded.
    end if
end sub
```

and in C#:

```
void Page_Load(Object sender, EventArgs e)
{
    if (! IsPostBack)
    {
        //  Do the expensive operations only the
        //  first time the page is loaded.
    }
}
```

shows how to make code execution conditional on the IsPostBack property. For a complete discussion of the IsPostBack property, see Chapter 3.

General .NET Issues

Many of the performance enhancements that affect an ASP.NET application are general ones that apply to any .NET application. This section lists some of the major .NET-related areas to consider when developing your ASP.NET applications.

String concatenation

Strings are immutable in the .NET Framework. This means that methods and operators that appear to change the string are actually returning a modified copy of the string. This has huge performance implications. When doing a lot of string manipulation, it is much better to use the StringBuilder class.

Consider the code shown in Example 18-23 (in C# only). It measures the time to create a string from 10,000 substrings in two different ways. The first time, a simple string concatenation is used, and the second time the StringBuilder class is used. If you want to see the resulting string, uncomment the two commented lines in the code.

Example 18-23. String concatenation benchmark in C#, csStringConcat.aspx

```
<%@ Page Language="C#" %>

<script runat="server">
```

Example 18-23. String concatenation benchmark in C#, csStringConcat.aspx (continued)

```csharp
    void Page_Load(Object Source, EventArgs E)
    {
        int intLimit = 10000;
        DateTime startTime;
        DateTime endTime;
        TimeSpan elapsedTime;
        string strSub;
        string strWhole = "";

        //  Do string concat first
        startTime = DateTime.Now;
        for (int i=0; i < intLimit; i++)
        {
            strSub = i.ToString();
            strWhole = strWhole + " " + strSub;
        }
        endTime = DateTime.Now;
        elapsedTime = endTime - startTime;
        lblConcat.Text = elapsedTime.ToString();
//      lblConcatString.Text = strWhole;

        //  Do stringBuilder next
        startTime = DateTime.Now;
        StringBuilder sb = new StringBuilder();
        for (int i=0; i < intLimit; i++)
        {
            strSub = i.ToString();
            sb.Append(" ");
            sb.Append(strSub);
        }
        endTime = DateTime.Now;
        elapsedTime = endTime - startTime;
        lblBuild.Text = elapsedTime.ToString();
//      lblBuildString.Text = sb.ToString();
    }

</script>

<html>
    <body>
    <form runat="server">

        <h1>String Concatenation Benchmark</h1>

        Concatenation:  
        <asp:Label
            id="lblConcat"
            runat="server"/>

        <br/>

        <asp:Label
```

Example 18-23. String concatenation benchmark in C#, csStringConcat.aspx (continued)

```
            id="lblConcatString"
            runat="server"/>

        <br/>
        <br/>

        StringBuilder:  
        <asp:Label
            id="lblBuild"
            runat="server"/>

        <br/>

        <asp:Label
            id="lblBuildString"
            runat="server"/>

    </form>
  </body>
</html>
```

When this page is run, you should see something like Figure 18-8. The difference between the two techniques is fairly dramatic: the StringBuilder's Append method is nearly 200 times faster than string concatenation.

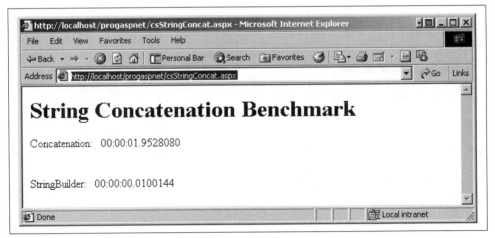

Figure 18-8. String concatenation benchmark results

Minimize exceptions

It is possible to use try...catch blocks to control program flow. However, this coding technique is a serious impediment to performance. You will do much better if you first test whether some condition will cause a failure, and if so, code around it.

For example, rather than dividing two integers inside a try...catch block and catching any Divide By Zero exceptions thrown, it is much better to first test whether the divisor is zero, and if it is, not do the operation.

Use early binding

.NET languages allow both early and late binding. Early binding occurs when all objects are declared and the object type known at compile time. Late binding occurs when the object type is not determined until runtime, at which point the CLR figures out, as best it can, what object type it is dealing with.

Early binding is much faster than late binding, although the latter can be very convenient to the developer. In VB.NET, it is perfectly legal to not declare your variables before they are used, to declare them but not assign a data type (in which case they will be of type Object), or to explicitly declare them as type Object. All these cases constitute late binding. Including an Option Explicit On statement in your code (analogous to the Option Explicit statement in VB6) helps impose discipline by requiring that all variables be declared before they are used, although you do not have to declare the type. This line should appear before any other lines of code except for page directives; for example:

```
<%@ WebService Language="VB" Class="ProgAspNet.vbStockTicker" %>
Option Explicit On
```

Alternatively, you can include an Explicit attribute for the page directive, as in:

```
<%@ Page Language="VB" Explicit="true" %>
```

There is also an Option Strict available, which, if enabled, prevents data conversions from happening implicitly if there is any possibility of lost data due to type incompatibility. This imposes type-safe behavior on the code, but does not eliminate late binding. As with Explicit, Option Strict can be either a line of code at the beginning of a module:

```
<%@ WebService Language="VB" Class="ProgAspNet.vbStockTicker" %>
Option Explicit On
Option Strict On
```

or a page directive:

```
<%@ Page Language="VB" Explicit="true" Strict="true" %>
```

Jscript.NET also supports early binding, although there are no compiler directives to enforce its use. C# supports early binding by default; you achieve late binding in C# using reflection.

Use managed code

Managed 'code is more performant than unmanaged code. It may be worthwhile porting heavily used COM components to managed code.

Disable debug mode

When you deploy your application, remember to disable Debug mode. For a complete discussion of deployment issues, refer to Chapter 20.

Database Access Issues

Almost all applications involve some form of database access, and accessing data from a database is necessarily an expensive operation. Data access can be made more efficient, however, by focusing on several areas.

Stored procedures

When interacting with a database, using stored procedures is always much faster than the same operation passed in as a command string. This is because stored procedures are compiled and optimized by the database engine. Use stored procedures whenever possible.

Use DataReader class

There are two main ways to get data from a database: from a DataReader object or a DataSet object. The DataReader classes, either `SqlDataReader` or `OleDbDataReader`, is a much faster way of accessing data if all you need is a forward-only data stream.

Use SQL classes rather than OleDB classes

Some database engines have managed classes specifically designed for interacting with that database. It is much better to use the database-specific classes rather than the generic OleDB classes. So, for example, it is faster to use a `SqlDataReader` rather than a `OleDbDataReader`.

Benchmarking and Profiling

Benchmarking is the process of conducting reproducible performance tests to see how fast an application is running. It may involve coding the same task two different ways and seeing which one runs faster. The web page shown previously in Example 18-23, which tested the relative speed of string concatenation techniques, is an example of a simple benchmarking program. Obviously, benchmarking programs will often be much more complex than that example. They should be designed to emulate your environment as closely as possible.

Profiling is the gathering of performance information about an application. There are several ways to profile an application. Two that are part of the .NET Framework are:

- Windows NT, Windows 2000, and Windows XP System Performance Monitor
- The .NET performance counters API

The System Monitor can be used to watch a huge variety of system parameters, both .NET-specific and otherwise, in real time. You can open the System Monitor by going to *Start\Settings\Control Panel\Administrative Tools\Performance*, or by opening a Command Prompt and entering perfmon. When the System Monitor opens, click on the Add icon on the toolbar to select and add any number of performance counters. The available counters cover the processor, memory, hard disk, SQL Server, .NET, and ASP.NET.

The performance counter's API includes several classes. The PerformanceCounter component in the System.Disagnostics namespace can be used for both reading existing performance counters and for creating and writing to custom counters.

CHAPTER 19

Security

Back in the good old days—before the Internet—when personal computers were mostly standalone or, at most, connected to an office LAN, security was not such a big deal. Until viruses were invented and became a real threat, security for most PCs meant screen-saver passwords and a lock on the office door.

All that has changed. Today's computers are interconnected in myriad ways, on local networks and over the Internet. The pipes of data that connect your machine to the rest of the world are double-edged swords: tremendously beneficial, but at the same time potentially harmful, opening your machine to outsiders. Some of those outsiders are malicious or just plain unwelcome. In any case, it is the job of security to let the good stuff in and keep the bad stuff out.

As part of the .NET Framework, ASP.NET has a very robust security infrastructure. ASP.NET is designed to work with Microsoft Internet Information Server (IIS), Windows NT/2000/XP, and the NTFS file system. Consequently, there is tight integration with the security provided inherently in those environments. If you can be certain that all your clients will be using Windows and Internet Explorer, there are features you can take advantage of to make your job as software developer that much easier. Alternatively, you can implement your own security system completely independent of Windows or NTFS.

The fundamental role of security in ASP.NET is to selectively restrict access to portions of a web site. It does this through the following methods:

Authentication
> Verifying that a client is who he says he is.

Authorization
> Determining whether the client has permission to access the resource he is requesting.

Impersonation
> ASP.NET assumes the role of the user gaining access, limiting system access to that which is allowed to the user.

Delegation

A more powerful form of impersonation that allows remote resources to be accessed by the web server while it is impersonating the client.

The decision to allow or deny access is made based on Windows NT/2000/XP and NTFS security features in conjunction with IIS, or by verifying credentials against a security database. The security database may be a traditional relational database, or it may be an XML file, or it may be housed in the web site configuration files.

As with much of ASP.NET, security is configurable and extensible using the configuration files discussed in detail in Chapter 20.

Security in ASP.NET is a two-layered process, as shown in Figure 19-1. All web requests are first handled by IIS. This gives IIS security a chance to accept or reject the request. If the request is accepted by IIS, it is then passed to ASP.NET, where it is again subjected to a security decision, and either accepted or rejected. The security systems of IIS and ASP.NET are completely independent of each other. They can be used either independently or in coordination, as will be described later in this chapter.

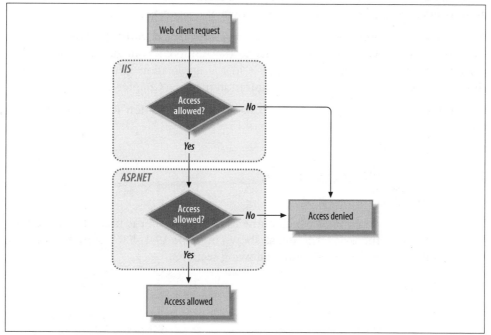

Figure 19-1. Security overview

Authentication

Authentication is the first of three fundamental functions necessary to secure a web application. (The other two functions are authorization and impersonation, as described shortly.) *Authentication* is the process of ensuring that clients are who they claim to be. Authentication is accomplished using *credentials*, or some form of identification. The requesting client presents the credentials to IIS and the ASP.NET application, usually in the form of a username and password.

The credentials are then validated against some authority. Depending on how authentication is configured, that authority might be Windows NT/2000/XP security or it might be a store of names, passwords, and rights, maintained in a configuration file such as *web.config*, a relational database such as SQL Server, or an XML file.

Authentication is not required. If no authentication is performed, then the client is an *anonymous* user. By default, all web sites allow anonymous access. However, if you need to restrict access to any part of the web site, authentication is a necessary step.

If the system cannot identify a user based on the credentials presented, and if anonymous users are disallowed, then access is denied. If the system can identify the user, than that user is considered an authenticated identity and allowed to proceed on to authorization. Sometimes the identity is known as a *principal*.

Authentication is provided through code modules called *authentication providers*. Authentication providers are enabled using the ASP.NET configuration files, either *machine.config* or the copy of *web.config* in the application virtual root directory. (For a complete description of the configuration files, see Chapter 20.)

A typical entry in a configuration file to enable authentication would look like the following:

```
<configuration>
    <system.web>
        <authentication mode="Forms" />
    </system.web>
</configuration>
```

The mode attribute determines which authentication provider is used. There are four possible values for the mode attribute, as shown in Table 19-1. Each of these authentication modes will be described in the following sections.

Table 19-1. Values of the Authentication key's mode attribute

Mode value	Description
Windows	Windows authentication will be used in conjunction with IIS. This is the default.
Forms	Unauthenticated requests are redirected to an HTML form, which gathers credentials from the user and submits them to the application for authentication.
Passport	Centralized commercial authentication service offered by Microsoft to web site developers, providing single logon across web sites.
None	No authentication will be performed. Enables anonymous access.

Anonymous Access

Anonymous access occurs when a web application does not need to know the identity of users. In this case, credentials are not requested by IIS and authentication is not performed. Allowing anonymous access is the default configuration for web sites.

In order to configure IIS to disallow anonymous authentication, use either the Computer Management console or the Internet Services console. Click on the Start button, then Settings → Control Panel, then Administrative Tools. Now you have a choice of two ways to get to the same place. Click on either Internet Services Manager or Computer Management.

From either, you get the Microsoft Management Console (MMC), which is used throughout Windows for displaying and controlling many system functions. In the left pane is a hierarchical tree structure showing resources relevant to the aspect(s) of the computer being managed. The right pane contains the child nodes of the currently selected node on the left.

From Computer Management, select "Services and Applications" in the left-hand pane, then drill down to Internet Information Services, then Default Web Site. From Internet Services Manager go directly to Internet Information Services, then Default Web Site. At this point, you can right-click on Default Web Site to set the properties for the entire server (i.e., all the web applications on the server), or you can drill down further to the application virtual directory to set the properties for a specific application. In either case, right-clicking will present a menu, from which you select Properties. Select the Directory Security tab. This tab is shown in Figure 19-2.

The Directory Security tab has sections for enabling server certificates and imposing restrictions based on IP address and domain name. (This latter section will be available only for Windows NT 4 and Windows 2000 Server, and Windows .NET Server when it ships, but will be grayed out for Windows 2000 Professional and Windows XP Professional.)

Click on the Edit button in the "Anonymous access and authentication control" section. You will get the dialog box shown in Figure 19-3.

If the "Anonymous access" checkbox is checked, then any request will be accepted by IIS without credentials being requested by IIS and with no authentication performed. This is the default configuration for web sites. (This assumes that the IP address or domain name is not restricted in the Directory Security tab shown in Figure 19-2.)

In addition to checking the "Anonymous access" checkbox in the Authentication Methods dialog box (which configures IIS), you must also configure ASP.NET by including the following section in the appropriate *web.config* configuration file:

```
<configuration>
  <system.web>
    <authentication mode="None" />
  </system.web>
</configuration>
```

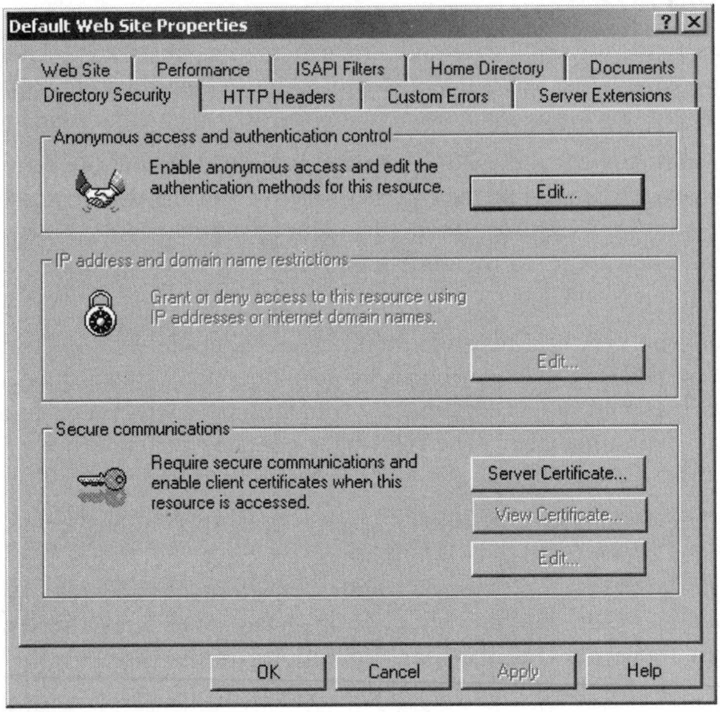

Figure 19-2. Directory Security tab

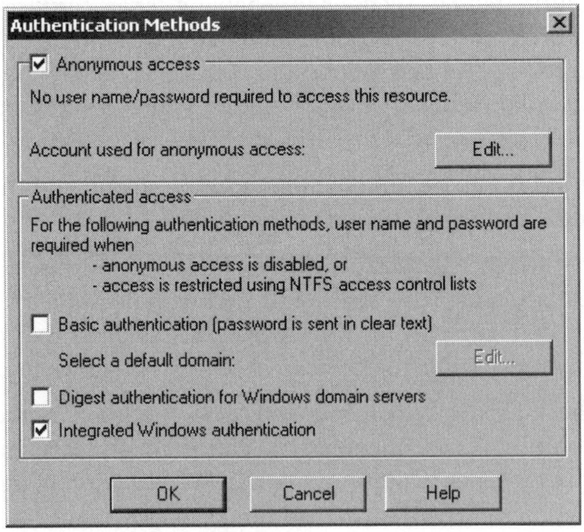

Figure 19-3. Authentication Methods dialog box

Since all requests made to IIS must have credentials, anonymous requests are assigned to a standard user account. This account defaults to IUSR_MachineName, where MachineName is the name of the web server. You can change the account assigned to anonymous access by clicking on the Edit button in that section. The IUSR_MachineName account is a built-in account, created when IIS is installed on the machine. It has a very limited set of permissions—just enough to allow access to the web site.

Anonymous access is appropriate if your application has no need to know the username or password of the person or application calling on the application, and if the information or service contained in the application is considered public. It is also possible to personalize a site without requiring login through the use of cookies. This would be useful where the content on the site is public, but you want to preserve user preferences or previous selections.

Of all the security configurations available to a web site, anonymous access provides the best performance, although it is also the least secure.

Windows Authentication

Windows authentication offers the developer a way to leverage the security built into the Windows NT/2000/XP platform and the NTFS file system. It takes advantage of the security built into IIS. Using Windows authentication, a high level of security can be built into an ASP.NET application with little or no code being written by the developer. The trade-off is that Windows authentication only works if the client is using a Windows platform and already has a user account on the web server or in the Windows domain to which the web server belongs.

In order to configure IIS for Windows authentication, follow the steps above for configuring IIS for anonymous access, shown in Figures 19-2 and 19-3. Uncheck the "Anonymous access" checkbox. Check one or more of the checkboxes under "Authenticated access."

If more than one type of authentication access is checked, then ASP.NET will first attempt to use Integrated Windows authentication, if it is checked. If that fails, it will then attempt Digest authentication, if that is checked. Finally, if all else fails, it will use Basic authentication.

In order to configure ASP.NET to use Windows authentication, ASP.NET must be configured by including the following section in the appropriate *web.config* configuration file:

```
<configuration>
  <system.web>
    <authentication mode="Windows" />
  </system.web>
</configuration>
```

There are three types of Windows authentication: basic, digest, and integrated Windows authentication. These are described in the following sections.

Role-based security

Windows NT/2000/XP provides *role-based security*. In this security scheme, *roles*, also known as *groups*, are defined. A role defines the range of actions and access that is permitted to users assigned to the role. Users are assigned to one or more roles, or groups. For example, if a user is a member of the Administrator role, then that person will have complete access to the computer and all its resources. If a user is a member only of the Guest group, then he will have very few permissions.

In Windows NT, users and groups are contained in the domain database. In Windows 2000 and Windows XP, they are maintained in the Active Directory.

Groups and users are assigned by going to Control Panel, clicking on Administrative Tools, then clicking on Computer Management. You will see the MMC console shown in Figure 19-4.

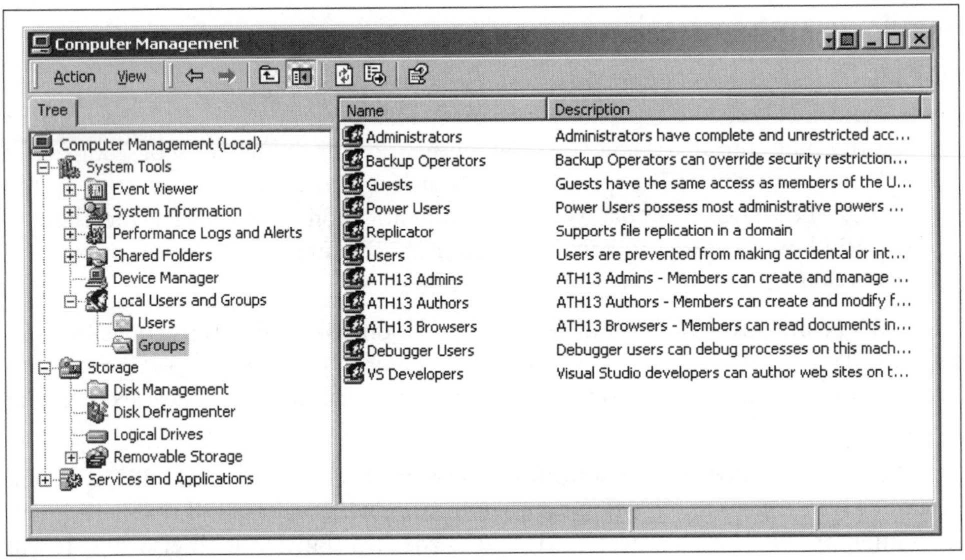

Figure 19-4. Groups in the Computer Management console

All of the groups shown in Figure 19-4 were installed by default. All are standard built-in groups, except for the three beginning with the name ATH13, which is the name of the server from which the screen shot was taken, and Debugger Users and VS Developers, which were installed by Visual Studio.NET.

Windows users log in to the operating system, providing a username and password. These constitute their *credentials*. At login time, those credentials are authenticated by the operating system. Once their credentials are verified, they will have certain permissions assigned, depending on which role(s) they have been assigned to. As you will see shortly, these credentials and roles are used by ASP.NET if the web application makes use of Windows authentication.

When a client requests an ASP.NET page or web service, all the requests are handled by IIS. If Windows authentication is the currently configured authentication scheme, then IIS hands off the authentication chores to the Windows NT, Windows 2000, Windows XP operating system. The user is authenticated based on the credentials that were presented when they first logged into their Windows system. These credentials are verified against the Windows user accounts either contained on the web server or on the domain controller that handles the web server.

Basic authentication

Basic authentication is the simplest and least secure type of Windows authentication. In this type of authentication, a standard Windows-supplied dialog box is presented to the user for entry of credentials, consisting of a username and password. These credentials are then compared against valid user accounts—either on the domain server or on the local machine. If the credentials compare, then the user is authenticated and access to the requested resource is provided.

The reason that basic authentication is the least secure method of authentication is that the username and password are sent to the server encoded as a Base64 string. However, they are not encrypted. The username and password are available to your application code in clear text. A skilled person using a network sniffer can easily intercept and extract the username and password. Therefore, basic authentication is best suited for those applications where a high level of security is not a requirement, or no other authentication method will work.

It is possible to use basic authentication in conjunction with Secure Sockets Layer (SSL) to achieve a high level of security. This encrypts the information passed over the network and prevents the password from being deciphered, although the performance hit from SSL is significant.

In order to set the authentication method to Basic, refer back to Figure 19-3. Uncheck "Anonymous access," "Digest authentication," and "Integrated Windows authentication." if any of them are checked. Then check "basic authentication." That is all that is necessary to implement basic authentication in IIS. To configure ASP.NET, include the following section in the relevant *web.config* configuration file:

```
<configuration>
  <system.web>
    <authentication mode="Windows" />
  </system.web>
</configuration>
```

By default, the local domain of the web server is active and is used for basic authentication. If you wish to authenticate against a different domain, click the Edit button and select a different default domain.

Basic authentication works across proxy servers and through firewalls. It is supported by most browsers. Basic authentication allows for delegation from one computer to another, but only for a single hop—i.e., only to one other computer. If you need to access resources beyond the first hop, you will need to log on locally to each of the other computers in the call chain. This is possible, since the username and password are available to your application in clear text.

Digest authentication

Digest authentication is very similar to basic authentication, except that the credentials are encrypted prior to being sent over the network to the server. It is a fairly secure method of authentication, although not as secure as basic authentication used with SSL, Windows integrated authentication, or certificate authentication. Like basic authentication, digest works through firewalls and proxy servers. Digest authentication does not support delegation, i.e., impersonated requests to remote machines.

Digest authentication works only with Internet Explorer 5.x and higher and .NET web services. It also requires that the web server is running on Windows 2000 or XP (or Windows .NET Server when it ships) and that all users have Windows accounts stored in an Active Directory. Due to these requirements, digest authentication is generally limited to intranet applications.

When the user requests a resource that requires digest authentication, the browser presents the same credentials dialog box as with basic authentication. The username and password are combined with a server-specified string value and encrypted to a hash value. This hash value is sent over the network. Since the server knows the string used to create the hash, it is able to decrypt the hash and extract the username and password. These are compared with the user accounts to determine if the user is authenticated, and if so, if the user has permission to access the requested resource.

In order to set the authentication method to Digest, refer back to Figure 19-3. Uncheck "Anonymous access," "Basic authentication," and "Integrated Windows authentication," if any of them are checked. Then check "Digest authentication." Note that the Digest authentication checkbox will not be available if the machine is not connected to a domain.

In addition, to configure ASP.NET you must include the following section in the relevant *web.config* configuration file:

```
<configuration>
  <system.web>
    <authentication mode="Windows" />
  </system.web>
</configuration>
```

In order for a user to be able to use digest authentication, the user account must be set to store the password using reversible encryption. To do this, go to the management console for Active Directory Users and Computers. Open the domain you want to administer and double-click on the user name that you want to use digest authentication. On the Account Options tab, select "Store password using reversible encryption."

Integrated Windows authentication

Integrated Windows authentication uses the current user's credentials presented at the time they logged into Windows. A dialog box is never presented to the user to gather credentials unless the Windows logon credentials are not adequate for a requested resource.

Integrated Windows authentication comprises two different types of authentication: NTLM (NT Lan Manager) challenge/response, and Kerberos. NTLM is the protocol used in Windows NT, Windows 2000 work groups, and environments with mixed NT and 2000 domains. If the environment is a pure Windows 2000 or Windows XP Active Directory domain, then NTLM is automatically disabled and the authentication protocol switches to Kerberos.

 Kerberos is named after the three-headed, dragon-tailed dog (Cerberus) who guarded the entrance to Hades in Greek mythology.

Integrated Windows authentication works particularly well in intranet environments, where all the users will already have Windows domain accounts and presumably all users will be using IE 3.01 or later. It is very secure, since the encrypted password is not sent over the network. Note that Integrated Windows authentication does not work through a proxy server. NTLM does not support delegation, although Kerberos does.

Integrated Windows authentication does not require any login dialog boxes. Not only is this more convenient for the user, but it is well suited to automated applications, such as those using web services.

In order to set the authentication method to Integrated Windows authentication, refer back to Figure 19-3. Uncheck "Anonymous access," "Basic authentication," and "Digest authentication," if any of them are checked. Then check "Integrated Windows authentication."

In addition, to configure ASP.NET you must include the following section in the relevant *web.config* configuration file:

```
<configuration>
  <system.web>
```

```
        <authentication mode="Windows" />
      </system.web>
    </configuration>
```

Kerberos is faster than NTLM, although neither is as fast as basic authentication or well-designed custom authentication methods. If you are anticipating a large number of concurrent users or are delegating security to back-end servers (e.g., SQL Server), then scalability may become an issue with Integrated Windows Authentication.

Passport Authentication

Passport is a centralized authentication service provided by Microsoft. It offers a single logon for all web sites that have registered with the Passport service, accepted the license agreement, paid the requisite fee, and installed the Passport SDK.

When a client makes a request to a Passport protected site, the server detects that the request does not contain a valid Passport ticket as part of the query string. The client is redirected to the Passport Logon Service along with encrypted parameters about the original request. The Passport Logon Service presents the client with a logon form, which the user fills out and posts back to the logon server using the Secure Sockets Layer (SSL) protocol. If the logon server authenticates the user, the request is redirected back to the original site, this time with the authentication ticket encrypted in the query string. When the original site receives this new request, it detects the authentication ticket and authenticates the request.

Subsequent requests to the same site are authenticated using the same authentication ticket. There are also provisions for expiring the authentication ticket and using the same ticket at other sites.

For sites that have implemented Passport and installed the Passport SDK, the PassportAuthenticationModule provides a wrapper around the SDK for ASP.NET applications.

Passport uses Triple-DES encryption to encrypt and decrypt the authentication key when passed as part of the query string. When a site registers with the Passport service, it is given a site-specific key that is used for this encryption and decryption.

It is not possible to use delegation if using Passport authentication.

In order to use Passport authentication, ASP.NET must be configured by including the following section in the relevant *web.config* configuration file:

```
<configuration>
  <system.web>
    <authentication mode="Passport" />
  </system.web>
</configuration>
```

Forms Authentication

Integrated Windows authentication offers many advantages to the developer who is deploying to an environment where all the clients are known to have user accounts in the requisite Windows domain or Active Directory and are also known to be using a recent version of Internet Explorer. However, in many web applications, one or both of these conditions will not be true. In these cases, forms authentication allows the developer to collect credentials from the client and authenticate them.

In *forms authentication*, a custom login form is presented to the unauthenticated user to gather credentials. This form does not necessarily authenticate the user itself, but rather submits the credentials, via form post, to application code that performs the authentication. The application code generally authenticates by comparing the credentials submitted with usernames and passwords contained in a data store of some sort. This data store can be a *web.config* configuration file, a relational database, an XML file, or even the Windows domain database or Active Directory.

The credentials submitted by the login form are sent unencrypted over the network, and so are vulnerable to interception by a skilled and malicious user of a network sniffer. A forms authentication scheme can be made fully secure by sending the credentials and all subsequent authenticated requests using the SSL protocol.

Once the client is authenticated, the server returns a small piece of data, called a *cookie*, back to the client. This authentication cookie is then passed from the client to the server on each subsequent request, which tells the server that this client has already been authenticated. If a request is made without a valid authentication cookie, then the user is automatically redirected to the login form, where credentials are once again gathered and authenticated.

Login form

To demonstrate forms authentication, you must first create a login form. At a minimum, this form must provide a means for the user to enter his username and password. It must also either provide the code to perform the authentication or call application code to do likewise.

Examples 19-1 and 19-2 show the code for a simple login form using VB.NET and C#, respectively. Example 19-2 shows only the script block for the login form in C#, since the HTML portion is identical to that in Example 19-1.

Example 19-1. Simple login form in VB.NET, vbLoginForm-01.aspx

```
<%@ Page Language="vb" %>
<script runat="server">
   sub btn_Click(ByVal Sender as Object, _
                 ByVal e as EventArgs)
      if (txtUserName.Text = "Dan" and txtPassword.Text = "password") then
         lblMessage.Text = "Authenticated: <br>" & txtUserName.Text & _
```

Example 19-1. Simple login form in VB.NET, vbLoginForm-01.aspx (continued)

```
                    "<br>" & txtPassword.Text
        FormsAuthentication.RedirectFromLoginPage(txtUserName.Text, _
                                        false)
      else
          lblMessage.Text = "Not Authenticated:<br>" & txtUserName.Text & _
                        "<br>" & txtPassword.Text
      end if
   end sub
</script>

<html>
<body>
   <h1>Login Form</h1>
   Please enter your credentials:
   <br>

   <form runat="server">
      Username:  
      <asp:Textbox
          id="txtUserName"
          runat="server" />
      <br>

      Password:  
      <asp:Textbox
          id="txtPassword"
          TextMode="password"
          runat="server" />
      <br>
      <br>

      <asp:Button
          id="btn"
          Text="Authenticate"
          OnClick="btn_Click"
          runat="server" />
      <br>
      <br>

      <asp:Label
          id="lblMessage"
          runat="server" />
   </form>
</body>
</html>
```

Example 19-2. Simple login form in C#, csLoginForm-01.aspx

```
<%@ Page Language="C#" %>
<script runat="server">
   void btn_Click(Object Source, EventArgs E)
   {
```

Example 19-2. Simple login form in C#, csLoginForm-01.aspx (continued)

```
        if (txtUserName.Text=="Dan" && txtPassword.Text=="password")
        {
            lblMessage.Text = "Authenticated: <br>" + txtUserName.Text +
                            "<br>" + txtPassword.Text;
            FormsAuthentication.RedirectFromLoginPage(txtUserName.Text,
                                            false);
        }
        else
        {
            lblMessage.Text = "Not Authenticated: <br>" + txtUserName.Text +
                            "<br>" + txtPassword.Text;
        }
    }
</script>
```

When the login page from Examples 19-1 or 19-2 is run in a browser and incorrect credentials are entered, you get the results shown in Figure 19-5.

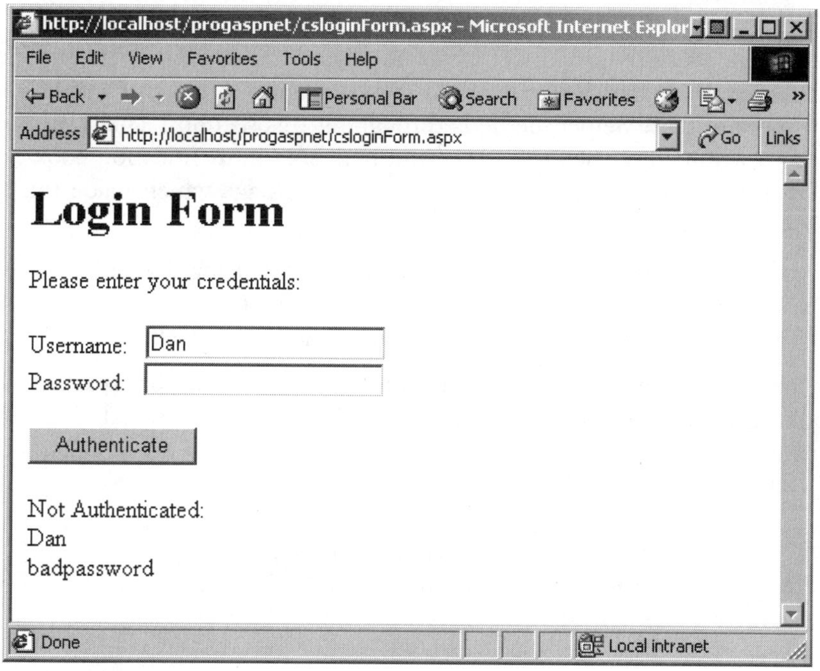

Figure 19-5. Login form

The HTML portion of the login form has an Authenticate button and two textboxes, one for the username and one for the password. Note that the password textbox has its TextMode attribute set to password, so that any characters entered will be displayed as asterisks. The HTML also includes a label for displaying the results of the authentication to the user.

When the Authenticate button is clicked, the btn_Click event handler is called. In this simple login scenario, a single username and password are hard-coded into the code. (Later in this chapter, you will see how to implement more flexible stores of usernames and passwords.) A simple if statement tests to see whether the username and password match. In VB.NET, this is done using:

```
if (txtUserName.Text = "Dan" and txtPassword.Text = "password") then
```

In C#, the code is:

```
if (txtUserName.Text=="Dan" && txtPassword.Text=="password")
```

Depending on the results of the test, the appropriate message is displayed in the label, along with the username and password (in clear text) entered in the textboxes.

The interesting action occurs in the highlighted line of code in Examples 19-1 and 19-2, reproduced here (in VB.NET, without the line continuation character):

```
FormsAuthentication.RedirectFromLoginPage(txtUserName.Text, false);
```

FormsAuthentication is a helper class in the System.Web.Security namespace that provides static or shared helper methods for managing forms authentication. (You will see more of these helper methods throughout this section.) The static Redirect-FromLoginPage method first generates and places an authentication cookie on the client, then redirects the client browser back to the page which made the original request.

The first parameter in RedirectFromLoginPage is a text string that contains the username associated with the cookie. It is not necessary for this username to be an account name; it is used only for identification of the cookie itself.

The second parameter in RedirectFromLoginPage is a Boolean that specifies whether the cookie is persistent or not. A *persistent cookie* is one that is saved across browser sessions. If a persistent cookie is set, the user will not have to log in again on subsequent visits.

 The RedirectFromLoginPage method also has an overloaded form that takes a third parameter, which specifies a path for the cookie. Use this form if you need to specify where the cookie will be saved.

Obviously, hard-coding usernames and passwords into if statements in your code is a fairly limited authentication scheme. It would be much more useful if you could do some sort of lookup in a relational database, such as SQL Server, or in an XML data store. This could be accomplished with code based on that shown in Example 19-3 (in C#).

Example 19-3. Authenticating users from an external store

```
if (CheckCredentials(txtUserName.Text, txtPassword.Text) )
{
    // Do stuff if authenticated
}
else
{
    // Do stuff if not authenticated
}

private bool CheckCredentials(string username, string password)
{
    // Do a database or XML lookup to see if the username and
    // password are valid.
...// If valid, then return true, otherwise return false.
}
```

In Example 19-3, a private method is created called CheckCredentials, which returns a Boolean. This method accesses an external store of usernames and passwords. This external store could be a relational database, an XML file, or even the Windows domain database or Active Directory. The point is that this method will do the actual work of authenticating the credentials passed in. If the credentials check out OK, the method returns true. If the credentials do not pass muster, the method returns false.

Configuring IIS

In order to implement forms authentication, IIS must be properly configured. This is done in the Authentication Methods dialog box shown in Figure 19-3. Depending upon whether you right-clicked on the default web site in the management console or in a specific virtual directory, the Authentication Methods dialog box will apply either to the entire server or to a specific web application.

Referring to Figure 19-3, uncheck all three checkboxes under "Authenticated access." That will disable integrated windows authentication.

Check the checkbox for "Anonymous access." That will tell IIS to allow any request to pass through IIS and be handled by ASP.NET. Your login form will pick it up from there, once all the pieces are in place.

Configuring ASP.NET

The final piece to setting up forms authentication is to properly configure ASP.NET. This is done using the appropriate instance of the *web.config* configuration file.

Remember that the effect of the configuration files in ASP.NET is hierarchical, in that a specific instance of *web.config* applies to its own directory and all subdirectories below it. If a subdirectory contains its own instance of *web.config*, any settings it contains will override its parent's settings and will apply to its directory and all its child subdirectories. (For a complete discussion of ASP.NET configuration files, see Chapter 20.)

To configure an entire web application, place the configuration settings in the instance of *web.config* in the application virtual root directory.

To configure ASP.NET to use forms authentication, edit the instance of *web.config* in the application virtual root directory to contain the code shown in Example 19-4.

Example 19-4. web.config entry for forms authentication

```
<configuration>
   <system.web>
      <authentication mode = "Forms">
         <forms name="ProgAspNetCookie" loginUrl="csLoginForm.aspx" />
      </authentication>

      <authorization>
         <deny users="?" />
      </authorization>
   </system.web>
</configuration>
```

In the <authentication> section, the mode is set to Forms. This tells ASP.NET to use forms authentication.

Within that section is a <forms> tag. This contains the name of the authentication cookie to be placed on the client machine. In this example, the name of the cookie will be ProgAspNetCookie. If no name is provided, the default name is .ASPXAUTH.

The next attribute within the <forms> tag is loginUrl. (Note the casing of loginUrl. Remember that *web.config* files are case sensitive.) This contains the URL of the login form to be redirected to if an unauthenticated request is received by IIS.

The <forms> tag has three other attributes, which are as follows:

protection
> Specifies whether the application should use data validation, data encryption, neither, or both to protect the cookie when it is passed between the server and the client. The default value is All, which specifies both. None specifies neither, Encryption specifies encryption only (using Triple-DES), and Validation specifies validation only.
>
> Using a value of None is the weakest form of security a forms authentication scheme can have. It is not recommended, except for sites that do not have stringent security requirements, such as personalization. It is, however, the least resource-intensive way to implement personalization, and will scale better than the other methods.

timeout
> Specifies the integer number of minutes before the authentication cookie expires. The default is 30. Whenever a new request is received for the cookie, the clock is reset. If a cookie is persistent, it never expires.

path

Specifies the path for cookies issued by the application. The default value is a backslash (/). Note that most browsers are case sensitive and will not return a cookie if there is a path/case mismatch.

The <authorization> section shown in Example 19-4 will be described in detail later in this chapter. For now, it is sufficient to know that it denies authorization to all anonymous users (i.e., all users who have not been authenticated).

Authenticating against web.config

The sample shown in Examples 19-1 and 19-2 authenticate against a username and password hard-coded into the application code. Example 19-3 shows how to authenticate against an external data store. A third option is to authenticate against names stored in *web.config*. This is done by adding a <credentials> section within the <forms> section of *web.config*.

A typical <credentials> section is shown highlighted in Example 19-5.

Example 19-5. web.config entry for <credentials> section

```
<authentication mode = "Forms">
   <forms name="ProgAspNetCookie" loginUrl="csLoginForm.aspx" >
      <credentials passwordFormat="Clear">
         <user name="Tom"   password="mot" />
         <user name="Dick"  password="kcid" />
         <user name="Harry" password="yrrah" />
      </credentials >
   </forms>
</authentication>

<authorization>
   <deny users="?" />
</authorization>
```

Other than the lines highlighted in Example 19-5, this listing is identical to that in Example 19-4. (The <authorization> section will be described later in this chapter.)

The <credentials> tag has a single attribute, passwordFormat. This specifies the *hash*, or encryption, format for storing passwords. The legal values are Clear, MD5, and SHA1. The latter two are well-known encryption algorithms that are supported by most browsers.

 In order to use the MD5 or SHA1 hash formats, the password strings actually entered into the *web.config* file must be hashed in the appropriate format. To get the string containing the hashed password, use the HashPasswordForStoringInConfigFile method of the FormsAuthentication class.

Within the <credentials> section, there are multiple <user> tags. Each specifies a username and associated password.

In order to fully implement authentication against *web.config*, you will need to modify the login form shown in Examples 19-1 and 19-2, as shown in Examples 19-6 and 19-7 for VB.NET and C#, respectively. Only the script blocks are shown in either language, since the HTML is unchanged. The highlighted lines are changed from Examples 19-1 and 19-2.

Example 19-6. Login form authenticating against web.config in VB.NET, vbLoginForm-02.aspx

```
<%@ Page Language="vb" %>
<script runat="server">
   sub btn_Click(ByVal Sender as Object, _
                 ByVal e as EventArgs)
      if FormsAuthentication.Authenticate(txtUserName.Text, _
                                 txtPassword.Text) then
         FormsAuthentication.RedirectFromLoginPage(txtUserName.Text, _
                                    false)
      else
         lblMessage.Text = "Not Authenticated:<br>" & txtUserName.Text & _
                        "<br>" & txtPassword.Text
      end if
   end sub
</script>
```

Example 19-7. Login form authenticating against web.config in C#, csLoginForm-02.aspx

```
<%@ Page Language="C#" %>
<script runat="server">
   void btn_Click(Object Source, EventArgs E)
   {
      if (FormsAuthentication.Authenticate(txtUserName.Text,
                                 txtPassword.Text))
      {
         FormsAuthentication.RedirectFromLoginPage(txtUserName.Text,
                                 false);
      }
      else
      {
         lblMessage.Text = "Not Authenticated: <br>" + txtUserName.Text +
                        "<br>" + txtPassword.Text;
      }
   }
</script>
```

The login form shown in Example 19-6 and 19-7 uses the Authenticate method of the FormsAuthentication class. This static or shared method takes two parameters: username and password. These credentials are compared against the users listed in the <credentials> section of *web.config*. If the credentials authenticate, then the Authenticate method returns true; otherwise, it returns false.

Notice that the lines of code from Example 19-1 and Example 19-2 that display a message on successful authentication have been removed from Example 19-6 and Example 19-7, since they will never actually be seen. If the request is authenticated, the user will immediately be redirected back to the originating form. That message was useful primarily when originally developing the login form.

Authenticating with redirect to a specified page

All the forms authentication samples shown so far have used the RedirectFromLoginPage method of the FormsAuthentication class. This method creates the authentication cookie, then redirects the client back to the page that made the original unauthenticated request.

It is also possible to create the authentication cookie without an automatic redirection back to the originating page. This would be useful if you wanted to control where the client is redirected to.

To accomplish this, use the static SetAuthCookie method of the FormsAuthentication class. This method creates an authentication cookie and attaches it to the outgoing response. However, there is no automatic redirect. Instead, your code must perform the redirect explicitly.

Consider the script block shown for VB.NET and C# in Example 19-8 and Example 19-9, respectively. It is identical to the code in Example 19-6 and Example 19-7 except for the highlighted lines of code.

Example 19-8. Login form using SetAuthCookie in VB.NET

```
<%@ Page Language="vb" %>
<script runat="server">
    sub btn_Click(ByVal Sender as Object, _
                  ByVal e as EventArgs)
       if FormsAuthentication.Authenticate(txtUserName.Text, _
                                 txtPassword.Text) then
          FormsAuthentication.SetAuthCookie(txtUserName.Text, _
                                  false)
          Response.redirect("default.aspx")
       else
          lblMessage.Text = "Not Authenticated:<br>" & txtUserName.Text & _
                       "<br>" & txtPassword.Text
       end if
    end sub
</script>
```

Example 19-9. Login form using SetAuthCookie in C#

```
<%@ Page Language="c#" %>
<script runat="server">
    void btn_Click(Object Source, EventArgs E)
    {
       if (FormsAuthentication.Authenticate(txtUserName.Text,
```

Example 19-9. Login form using SetAuthCookie in C# (continued)

```
                                        txtPassword.Text))
    {
        FormsAuthentication.SetAuthCookie(txtUserName.Text,
                                false);
        Response.Redirect("default.aspx");
    }
    else
    {
        lblMessage.Text = "Not Authenticated: <br>" + txtUserName.Text +
                        "<br>" + txtPassword.Text;
    }
  }
}
</script>
```

In Example 19-8 and Example 19-9, the SetAuthCookie method creates the authentication cookie for the client, using the same parameters as the RedirectFromLoginPage method. The first parameter is the username of the client, and the second parameter is a Boolean that specifies whether the cookie is persistent.

Rather than redirecting the client back to the originating page, the code in Example 19-8 and Example 19-9 redirects the client to the specified page, here called *default.aspx*.

In this example, the redirect page is hard-wired. It is easy to imagine modifying the CheckCredentials method described in Example 19-3 so that, in addition to authenticating the credentials, the method also sets a member variable containing a category to which the user belongs. Then your code could redirect to whichever page was appropriate for each category.

If you want your code to do the redirect, as in Example 19-8 and Example 19-9, but you want to redirect to the original requesting page, similar to the functionality provided by RedirectFromLoginPage, then you can use the static GetRedirectUrl method of the FormsAuthentication class. This method returns a string containing the originating URL. It takes the same parameters as RedirectFromLoginPage, and sets the authentication cookie similarly. You could replace the highlighted lines of code in Example 19-8 with the following code to redirect back to the originating page:

```
dim strUrl as string
strUrl = FormsAuthentication.GetRedirectUrl(txtUserName.Text, _
                                false)

Response.redirect(strUrl)
```

Getting the authentication cookie

Sometimes it is useful to get the authentication cookie but not immediately send it back to the client. This would be the case if you wanted to add information to the cookie or modify the information it already contains. The static GetAuthCookie method of the FormsAuthentication class serves this purpose.

Consider the code in Example 19-10 for VB.NET and Example 19-11 for C#, which modify the code shown in Examples 19-8 and 19-9, respectively. It creates the authentication cookie, modifies it, then does the redirect.

Example 19-10. Login form using GetAuthCookie in VB.NET, vbLoginForm-03.aspx

```
<%@ Page Language="vb" %>
<script runat="server">
   sub btn_Click(ByVal Sender as Object, _
                 ByVal e as EventArgs)
      if FormsAuthentication.Authenticate(txtUserName.Text, _
                                   txtPassword.Text) then

         dim myCookie as HttpCookie
         myCookie = FormsAuthentication.GetAuthCookie(txtUserName.Text, _
                                           false)
         myCookie.Expires = DateTime.Now.AddHours(24)
         Response.Cookies.Add(myCookie)

         Response.redirect("default.aspx")
      else
         lblMessage.Text = "Not Authenticated:<br>" & txtUserName.Text & _
                        "<br>" & txtPassword.Text
      end if
   end sub
</script>
```

Example 19-11. Login form using GetAuthCookie in C#, csLoginForm-03.aspx

```
<%@ Page Language="c#" %>
<script runat="server">
   void btn_Click(Object Source, EventArgs E)
   {
      if (FormsAuthentication.Authenticate(txtUserName.Text,
                                   txtPassword.Text))
      {
         HttpCookie myCookie =
            FormsAuthentication.GetAuthCookie(txtUserName.Text,
                                     false);
         myCookie.Expires = DateTime.Now.AddHours(24);
         Response.Cookies.Add(myCookie);
         Response.Redirect("Default.aspx");
      }
      else
      {
         lblMessage.Text = "Not Authenticated: <br>" + txtUserName.Text +
                        "<br>" + txtPassword.Text;
      }
   }
</script>
```

In Examples 19-10 and 19-11, if the credentials are authenticated, a cookie variable, myCookie, is instantiated. The GetAuthCookie method is called, which returns an object of type HttpCookie. This is assigned to myCookie. The Expires property of the cookie is modified to add 24 hours to the expiration date and time. Finally, the cookie myCookie is added to the Cookies collection of the HTTP Response object. If this last step is not performed, then the cookie will not be set on the client's computer and the request will not be authenticated. Once the cookie is set, the redirect can occur, as before.

Logging out

If a cookie is not persistent, it will expire when its expiration period ends. If it is persistent, it will never expire. It is possible to force an authentication cookie to expire immediately by calling the static SignOut method of the FormsAuthentication class.

The code in Example 19-12 shows a simple page that contains only a button that removes the authentication cookie, effectively logging the user out of the application. The code here is in VB.NET; the C# code within the <script> tag is very similar:

Example 19-12. Logout form in VB.NET, vbLogout.aspx

```
<%@ Page Language="vb" %>
<script runat="server">
   sub btn_Click(ByVal Sender as Object, _
                 ByVal e as EventArgs)
      FormsAuthentication.SignOut( )
   end sub
</script>

<html>
<body>
   <h1>Logout Form</h1>
   <br>

   <form runat="server">

      <asp:Button
         id="btn"
         Text="Log Out"
         OnClick="btn_Click"
         runat="server" />

   </form>
</body>
</html>
```

The page coded in Example 19-12 consists of a single button, labeled "Log Out." Clicking on this button calls the SignOut method. You can verify that this works by calling any page in the virtual directory in your browser, logging in, then calling any other page to verify that you do not need to log in with subsequent pages once you are logged in. Then call *vbLogoutForm.aspx* in your browser and click the Log Out button. Now call one of the other pages again. You will be redirected to the login form, since there is no longer a valid authentication cookie on your client machine.

Certificate Authentication

Certificates are digital keys that are installed on a computer. Certificates can be installed on either the server or the client. Certificates are generally issued by third parties, which manage the logistics of issuing and maintaining the certificates and guarantee their validity. When a request is made to a server using certificate authentication, the client certificate is passed to the server as credentials, and the server certificate is passed back to the client to verify the identity of the server. Mutual authentication can take place.

Certificate authentication is seamless: it does not present any login dialog boxes or forms, and there is no need for the client to programmatically provide the username or password. The server and the client authenticate each other automatically, with no user interaction. This not only makes it much easier for the client, but it is also ideal for automated scenarios, such as those using web services.

Certificate authentication is very secure. The data contained in the certificate is encrypted using public key encryption technology. While it is beyond the scope of this book to discuss cryptography details and the merits of public key encryption, suffice it to say that it is a widely used and very safe means of passing encrypted data over the Internet.

 You can create your own certificates conforming to the X.509 standard for authentication and encryption for testing purposes. This is done using *MakeCert.exe*, a command-line certificate creation tool included with the .NET Framework. For a complete description of *MakeCert.exe*, including all the command-line arguments, see the SDK documentation that comes with .NET.

Client certificates can be mapped to user accounts in either a Windows domain or Active Directory. This mapping can be either *one-to-one*, where a certificate is mapped to a single user, or *many-to-one*, where a single certificate is mapped to many users. With a many-to-one mapping, a single certificate can be assigned to a company, and all the users from within that company can authenticate using the same certificate.

There is a cost associated with issuing, installing, and managing certificates. There is typically a fee paid to the third party issuer of the certificates. There is also the cost of the effort by the developers and/or system administrators to implement certificate authorization on both the server and all client machines. Client certificates must be physically deployed on each client machine. This deployment can be performed over the web or via installation software on CD, but it must be performed for each client. This limits deployment of certificate authentication to closed systems, such as intranets or B2B relationships.

Authorization

Once a requesting client has been authenticated, the server must then determine whether this user is allowed to access the resources it is requesting. This process is known as *authorization*. You have already seen an example of authorization in Example 19-4 and Example 19-5, in the <authorization> sections in *web.config*. The details of authorization will now be explained. There are two ways of authorizing users: file authorization and URL authorization.

File Authorization

Any Windows operating system that supports NTFS (this includes Windows NT, Windows 2000, and Windows XP) uses a security system based on Access Control Lists (ACLs). ACLs control access to any specific file or directory based on the requesting user's membership in a Windows Domain or Active Directory and the group(s) to which that user belongs. You have seen users and groups in Figure 19-4.

 You will only be able to use file authorization if the hard drive(s) containing the resources are formatted using NTFS.

If all the legitimate users of a web application are known to have Windows user accounts, then you can use file authorization to authorize a user's access to a resource. Each user is assigned to an appropriate group and that group is given the necessary permissions, using the Computer Management console, to use the application.

 For further information on the minimum file access rights required by a web application, see the Microsoft Knowledge Base Article Q187506, "List of NTFS Permissions Required for IIS Site to Work."

You can examine the ACL for any file or directory in Windows by right-clicking on the object in Windows Explorer, selecting the Properties menu item, then going to the Security tab. You will see something similar to Figure 19-6.

In Figure 19-6, the single-headed icon represents a user and the two-headed icons represent groups. Each of the users and groups listed in the Name box can have a different set of permissions. These permissions available for each file or folder, shown in Figure 19-6, are easily set by checking and unchecking the checkboxes to allow or deny the permission.

When a request is received and authenticated by IIS, there is one of two possibilities: either it is authenticated as a known user, or it is treated as an anonymous user. If the request is from a known user, then of course the username is known. If the request comes from an anonymous user, then it is assigned to the standard user account IUSR_ *MachineName*, where the name of the server machine is substituted for *MachineName*.

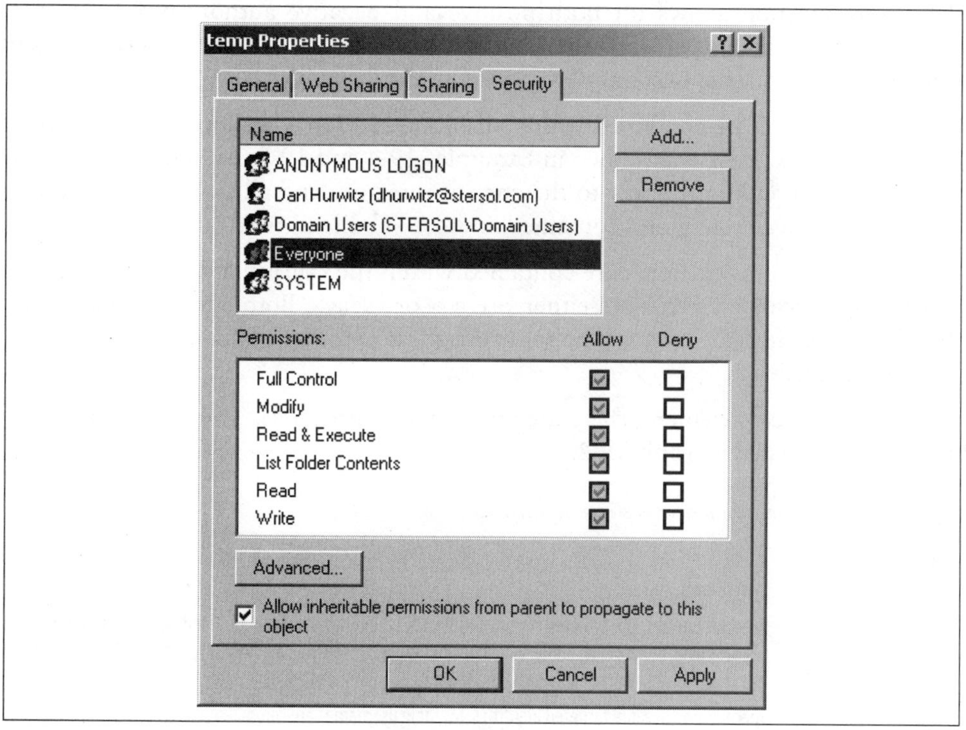

Figure 19-6. ACL for a directory

This is relevant because it is the username that ultimately determines which resources are available to a user. This depends on the impersonation mode currently set. (Impersonation will be described shortly.) If impersonation is enabled, the application will run with the permissions assigned to the user. If impersonation is not enabled, the application will run with the permissions of the built-in System user account.

There are two liabilities to file authorization:

- All the users of the web application must have a Windows user account.
- Managing ACLs for a large, complex web site can become a logistical nightmare.

URL Authorization

It is also possible to authorize users against either a list or rules, both contained in a configuration file. This is known as *URL authorization*.

> This nomenclature is very confusing. The Microsoft SDK documentation states that URL authorization "maps users and roles to pieces of the URI namespace." However, when actually implementing URL authorization, neither URIs nor URLs are used.

URL authorization allows for both positive and negative authorizations. In other words, authorizations can be either allowed or denied. In addition, authorizations can be based on usernames, on roles, or on the HTTP verb.

Access conditions are contained within an <authorization> section in the *web.config* file. A simple example was shown in Examples 19-4 and 19-5. As with all configuration files, the conditions apply to the current directory and all subdirectories unless overridden by *web.config* files contained in those subdirectories.

One or more access elements are contained within the <authorization> section. The permissible access elements are either <allow> or <deny>. Both access elements may be present in the same <authorization> section, in which case the first match found will take precedence.

Within each access element, there are one or more attributes. There are three possible attributes, listed in Table 19-2.

Table 19-2. Authorization access element attributes

Access element attribute	Description
Roles	Specifies one or more targeted roles. Multiple roles are comma-separated. The default WindowsPrincipal class uses Windows NT/2000/XP groups to determine role membership. Typical built-in roles therefore include Administrators, Guests, and Users.
Users	Specifies one or more targeted identities. Multiple usernames are comma-separated. There are two special identities: * (asterisk) specifies everyone (i.e., all identities), and ? (question mark) refers to all unauthenticated identities (i.e., anonymous users).
Verbs	Specifies HTTP verbs to which action applies. Legal values are GET, HEAD, or POST.

Either the Roles or Users attribute must be present. Both are allowed simultaneously, but both are not required. The Verbs attribute is optional.

Consider the following <authorization> section:

```
<authorization>
    <allow users="Dan, Jesse, stersol\Jennifer" roles="Administrators" />
    <deny users="Bill" />
    <deny users="?" />
</authorization>
```

This example will allow local domain users Dan and Jesse, as well as Jennifer, who is a member of the stersol domain. All members of the Administrators group will also be allowed access. Bill will be denied access, and all anonymous users will also be denied access.

Consider the next sample <authorization> section:

```
<authorization>
    <allow verb="GET" users="*" />
    <allow verb="POST" users="Dan, Jesse" />
    <deny verb="POST" users="*" />
</authorization>
```

In this example, all users will be allowed if the request is a GET request. Dan and Jesse are allowed to make POST requests, but all other users making post requests will be denied access. This type of scenario might be useful because GET requests are typically used for simple requests with few parameters, such as may be sent by a link on a web page, while POST requests are typically sent by forms, with much more robust access.

As with all configuration file settings, the system merges all the access rules from all the configuration files contained in the hierarchy of directories and subdirectories of the application. It then checks the rules for each request, starting at the head of the list and moving down the list until the first match is found. If a match is found and the access element is <deny>, then a 401 error will be returned.

The default <authorization> section contained in *machine.config* contains the following line, which allows all identities:

```
<allow users="*" />
```

Therefore, if there are no <authorization> sections in any of the *web.config* files, all users will be granted access to the application. Likewise, if no matches are found, the user will be granted access.

If you want a subdirectory of the application virtual root directory to have different access rules than its parent directory, you have two choices. One possibility is to include a *web.config* file in the desired subdirectory. However, any rules it contains will also apply to its subdirectories, and so on. This may cause logistical problems similar to ACLs.

An alternative way to apply different access rules to a specific subdirectory is to use the <location> tag in the *web.config* file. Consider the *web.config* file shown in Example 19-13.

Example 19-13. <location> tag in web.config

```
<?xml version="1.0" encoding="utf-8" ?>
<configuration>
   <system.web>
      <authentication mode = "Forms">
         <forms name="ProgAspNetCookie" loginUrl="vbLoginForm.aspx" >
            <credentials passwordFormat="Clear">
               <user name="Tom"   password="mot" />
               <user name="Dick"  password="kcid" />
               <user name="Harry" password="yrrah" />
            </credentials >
         </forms>
      </authentication>

      <authorization>
         <deny users="?" />
      </authorization>
   </system.web>
```

Example 19-13. <location> tag in web.config (continued)

```
<location path="pages/public.aspx" >
   <system.web>
      <authorization>
         <allow users="*" />
      </authorization>
   </system.web>
</location>

<location path="pages" >
   <system.web>
      <authorization>
         <allow users="Dan, Jesse " roles="Administrators" />
      </authorization>
   </system.web>
</location>

</configuration>
```

The *web.config* file shown in Example 19-13 specifies that the application will use forms authentication. Tom, Dick, and Harry will be authenticated, and all other users will be denied access, *except* that the file called *public.aspx* contained in the *pages* subdirectory of the application root will allow all users to access it. In addition, Dan, Jesse, and all members of the Administrators group will have access to the *pages* subdirectory.

Impersonation

Every process running on a Windows NT/2000 server (or Windows.NET Server, when it ships) has a username associated with it. The username, in conjunction with ACLs (described earlier in the "Authorization" section), determines what resources the process will have access to.

By default, ASP.NET processes run with a username of SYSTEM. This gives these processes full access to all resources. If there is a security breach, then a malicious user may also be able to run processes with full access to all resources.

To guard against this and provide another layer of security, ASP.NET supports *impersonation*. Using impersonation, the ASP.NET process assumes, and executes with, the identity of the client making the request. For example, if user Dan requests a web page, and this web page requests access to a resource on the server, then when ASP.NET requests that resource, it will be as though Dan made the request, not SYSTEM. The permissions assigned to Dan in the ACLs will govern the request.

Impersonation is not enabled by default, since it consumes additional server resources. Impersonation is enabled with an <identity> section in a configuration file. The default <identity> section in *machine.config* looks like the following:

```
<identity impersonate="false" />
```

To enable impersonation for an application, add a similar line to the *web.config* file in the application virtual root directory, changing the `impersonate` attribute value to true.

If impersonation is enabled and the request is from an authenticated user, then the ASP.NET process will run as though it were the authenticated user. If the request if from an anonymous user, the process will run as though it were IUSR_*MachineName*, where *MachineName* is the name of the web server.

It is also possible to configure ASP.NET to always impersonate using a specific identity. The following <identity> section configures ASP.NET to always run as Dan with a password of pwd:

```
<identity impersonate="true" name="Dan" password="pwd" />
```

If the username is part of a different domain from the web server, the domain name can be part of the username, as in Stersol\Dan.

If the application resides on a UNC (Universal Naming Convention) share, then the ASP.NET process will execute as the IIS UNC token whether impersonation is enabled or disabled. The only exception is that if impersonation is enabled with a specific username, then that username will be used for the UNC share, and access to the share will be dependent on that username's access rights.

Application Identity

As stated earlier, the default identity for ASP.NET is SYSTEM. This is controlled by the <processModel> section in the *machine.config* configuration file. The default <processModel> section looks like the following:

```
<processModel
    enable="true"
    timeout="Infinite"
    idleTimeout="Infinite"
    shutdownTimeout="0:00:05"
    requestLimit="Infinite"
    requestQueueLimit="5000"
    restartQueueLimit="10"
    memoryLimit="60"
    webGarden="false"
    cpuMask="0xffffffff"
    userName="SYSTEM"
    password="AutoGenerate"
    logLevel="Errors"
    clientConnectedCheck="0:00:05"
    comAuthenticationLevel="Connect"
    comImpersonationLevel="Impersonate"
/>
```

The relevant attributes here are userName and password. There are two special values for userName: SYSTEM and MACHINE. The default is SYSTEM. In either case the value for password needs to be AutoGenerate, which forces the system to create its own password. As described above, when ASP.NET assumes the username SYSTEM, it has full access to all resources.

In some cases, it may be desirable to change userName to MACHINE, which will then cause the process to run using a special account, installed automatically when ASP.NET is installed, which begins with the prefix ASPNET. This account is a member of the Guests group, and so has far fewer privileges.

You can also set userName and password to a specific domain or Active Directory user account, which will then become the default user for all ASP.NET processes. If you do this, the user account specified must have the following rights:

- Read/write access to *%installroot%\ASP.NET\Temporary ASP.NET Files*. Typically this is a subdirectory of *c:\Program Files*. Subdirectories here are used for dynamically compiled output.
- Read/write access to the *%temp%* directory. This is used by the compilers during dynamic compilation.
- Read access to the application directory.
- Read access to the *%installroot%* hierarchy of directories to allow access to system assemblies.

CHAPTER 20

Controlling, Configuring, and Deploying Applications

ASP.NET offers many improvements over classic ASP. The topics to be covered in this chapter highlight several of the major improvements in controlling, configuring, and deploying ASP.NET applications.

ASP.NET provides easy control of the entire application through the *global.asax* file. This text file allows you to create event handlers for a wide variety of events exposed by both the application as a whole and by individual sessions. You can also include methods and server-side include files which will apply globally to the entire application.

Configuration of web applications is handled using configuration files: *machine. config* and *web.config*. These XML files provide a flexible and hierarchical configuration scheme. Configuration settings can apply to every application on the web server, to specific applications, or to specific subdirectories within an application.

Since all of the configuration and control for ASP.NET applications is done with text files, either XML or some other variant of plain text, it is very easy to maintain and update a web application remotely. It is no longer necessary to be physically present at a web server to reconfigure the application through IIS.

Perhaps the single greatest improvement that .NET has made over previous generations of development environments is in the area of deployment:

- DLLs only have to be located in a specific directory to be visible to an application.
- There is no registration of objects, either in the Registry or elsewhere, required for an application to utilize the contents of a DLL. Installation does not require any registering of components with *regsrvr32* or any other utility, though some globally available components will be placed in the Global Assembly Cache.
- XCOPY installations are here.
- There are no versioning issues with conflicting DLLs.

All of this will be described fully in this chapter. In the meantime, shout it from the rooftops: *No more DLL hell!*

What Is an Application?

The term *application* has been used throughout this book. Everyone knows intuitively, more or less, what an application is. Here is a precise working definition for a web application: An application consists of all of the web pages, files, code, objects, executables, images, and other resources located in an Internet Information Server (IIS) virtual directory (described shortly) or a subdirectory of that virtual directory.

The application will start the first time any page or web service is requested from the web server. It will run until any of a number of events cause it to shut down. These events include:

- Editing *global.asax*, a server-side include file for *global.asax*, or a *web.config* file
- Restarting IIS
- Restarting the machine

If a page is requested and the application is not running, the application will automatically restart.

Unlike traditional EXE applications, web applications do not have a fixed starting point. A user can drop in through any number of paths or entry points. Web applications should be designed accordingly.

For example, a virtual directory may contain three web pages: *default.aspx*, *login.aspx*, and *bugs.aspx*. If you enter the following text at a browser:

```
http://localhost
```

you will go to *default.aspx*, which may send you to *login.aspx*. On the other hand, registered users may enter:

```
http://localhost/login.aspx
```

to go directly to the login page. In any event, once logged in, they can go to *bugs.aspx*. If someone tries going directly to *bugs.aspx* without logging in, your code must send them to *login.aspx* to log in first.

Classic ASP and new ASP.NET applications can coexist side-by-side on the same server. In fact, they can coexist in the same application directory. However, configuration, application, and session objects cannot be shared between them. They are totally distinct and independent.

Virtual Directories

Virtual directories in IIS are central to web applications. A *virtual directory* is any directory on the server, or accessible to the server, that has been designated as such in IIS. Virtual directories are isomorphic with applications; that is, each virtual directory is a separate application, and each application must have a single virtual root directory. When a new project is created in Visual Studio .NET, the application virtual directory is created automatically. When a new application is created using a text editor, you the developer must create the virtual directory using IIS, as described below.

Virtual directories are accessible to requests from browsers coming in over the Internet. The URL is the name of the domain name, followed by the virtual directory. For example, if an application with a starting web page called `MyPage.aspx` was using a virtual directory called `ProgAspNet`, and the domain name of the hosting web server was `SomeDomainName.com`, the URL to access that application would be:

```
www.SomeDomainName.com/ProgAspNet/MyPage.aspx
```

To create, look at, or modify virtual directories in IIS, click on the Start button, then Settings → Control Panel, then Administrative Tools. Now you have a choice of two approaches: click on either Internet Services Manager or Computer Management.

From either, you get the Microsoft Management Console (MMC), which is used throughout Windows for displaying and controlling many system functions. In the left pane is a hierarchical tree structure showing resources relevant to the aspect(s) of the computer being managed. The right pane contains the child nodes of the currently selected node on the left.

Looking at Computer Management, the tree on the left has top-level nodes for System Tools, Storage, and Services and Applications. Drilling down through Services and Applications, then Internet Information Services, to the default Web Site, the MMC window should look something like that shown in Figure 20-1.

Internet Services Manager is identical to Computer Management except that the tree on the left starts with Internet Information Services.

Drilling further down, click on Default Web Site. The contents of the default web site will be visible, as shown in Figure 20-2. The default web site, by default, is the physical directory *c:\inetpub\wwwroot*. When IIS is installed on a machine, it creates this directory, along with several subdirectories (beginning with the underscore character). If you go to a browser and enter the URL:

```
http://localhost
```

you will see the contents of the default web site. If your web server is accessible over the Internet through a domain name, a remote user at a browser who entered that domain name as a URL, say for example:

```
www.SomeDomainName.com
```

would see the same thing.

You will not actually see anything in the browser unless one of the following conditions is true:

- A suitably named file (*default.htm*, *default.asp*, *default.aspx*, or *iisstart.asp*) containing a default web page exists in the physical directory.

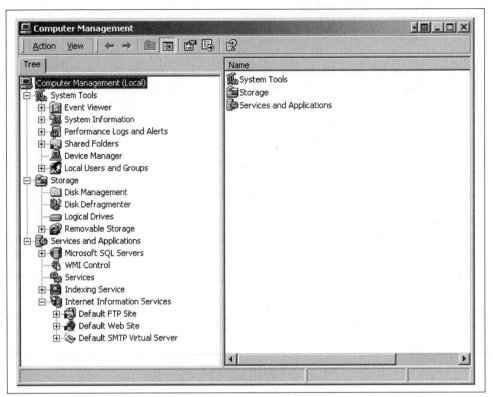

Figure 20-1. Computer Management console

- Directory Browsing is enabled by right clicking on Default Web Site, going to the Home Directory tab in the Default Web Site Properties dialog box, and checking the Directory browsing checkbox.

 Note that enabling Directory Browsing can be a serious gap in security, so it is generally not something to do on a production site unless there is a good reason.

Compare the contents of the default web site in Figure 20-2 with the actual contents of *c:\inetpub\wwwroot* shown in Figure 20-3. You can see that all the files and directories actually in the physical directory are also in the default web site in Figure 20-2. These physical directories, such as *images* and *_private*, are normal directories with standard Explorer-style directory icons.

Other directories in the default web site shown in Figure 20-2, such as *_vti_bin* and *Scripts*, have a directory icon with a small globe on the lower-right corner. These are *virtual directories*, created either by IIS or by a developer.

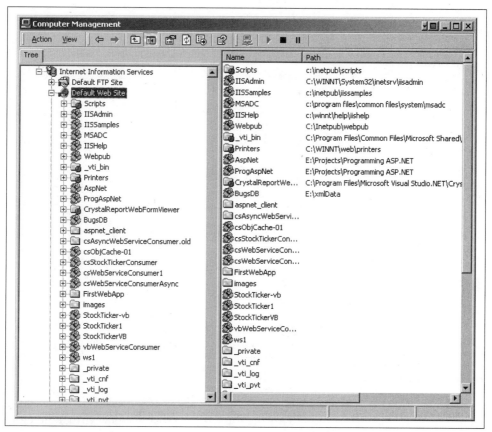

Figure 20-2. Virtual directories

Finally, some of the directories in the default web site shown in Figure 20-2 have an icon that looks like a cardboard box with a green thing inside (it's a package, get it?). These are *web application directories*. They can be either physical directories or virtual directories. The virtual directories created by developers are also application directories by default. This can be changed by right-clicking on the directory in question in the left pane, selecting Properties, then clicking either the Create Application Settings button to make it an application directory, or the Remove Application Settings button to convert the directory to a plain vanilla virtual directory.

When a new web application or web service is created in Visual Studio .NET, it automatically creates a physical directory under *c:\inetpub\wwwroot* with the same name as the application or web service. This new physical directory is also both a virtual directory and an application directory.

You can make a new virtual directory outside Visual Studio .NET using the Computer Management window shown in Figure 20-2 (or the equivalent Internet Services

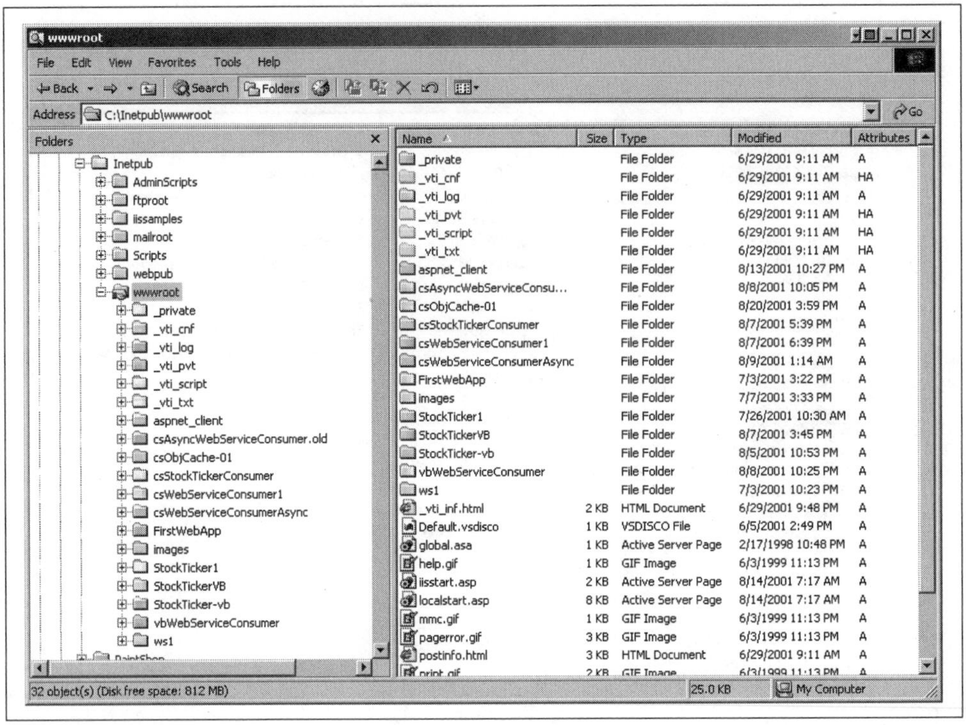

Figure 20-3. c:\inetpub\wwwroot

Manager window) by right clicking on Default Web Site in the left pane, selecting New... → Virtual Directory, and following the wizard. Once the new virtual directory is created, you can right-click on it and select Properties to modify its properties.

Back in Chapter 2, you created a virtual directory called *ProgAspNet*. This was mapped to the physical directory *c:\myProjects*. In order to access this virtual directory, enter one of the following URLs from a browser, depending on whether you are on a local machine or accessing the application over the Internet:

```
http://localhost/ProgAspNet
www.SomeDomainName.com/ProgAspNet
```

Application Domains

Each application is run in its own *application domain*, which is created by the runtime server. Each application domain is isolated from every other application domain. If one application crashes or otherwise compromises its own stability, it cannot affect any other domains. This greatly enhances security and stability.

Since each application is independent from any other application, this also means that each application has its own independent configuration and control structures.

Assemblies and the \bin Directory

All the files that comprise a .NET application are gathered into an *assembly*. Assemblies are the basic units of .NET programming. They appear to the user as a single dynamic link library (DLL) or executable (EXE) file. DLLs contain classes and methods, which are linked into an application at runtime as they are needed. Assemblies also contain versioning information so that multiple versions of the same code can run side-by-side with no conflicts.

Assemblies must be physically located somewhere; these locations are called the *assembly cache*. There are two general types of assembly cache: global and application. In order to for a class or method to be visible to an ASP.NET application, the DLL containing the class or method must be located in the assembly cache, either global or application.

The Global Assembly Cache (GAC) is used to store modules that need to be available to all the applications on a server. It is typically located at *c:\winnt\assembly*. The Global Assembly Cache will be discussed in the section "Deploying the Application" later in this chapter.

The application assembly cache contains compiled methods and classes specific to the application. Each application directory has a special \bin subdirectory to contain the application assembly cache. All that is necessary to "register" your DLL with an application is to copy it to the \bin directory. Any class or method in any DLL in the \bin directory is automatically visible to all web pages and services in the application (i.e., in the directory that is the parent directory of the \bin directory).

> If there are multiple versions of identically named classes or methods within the assembly cache, an error will occur. This is where namespaces can be useful in resolving ambiguities on otherwise identically named methods or classes.

Controlling the Application

Now that an application has been defined, you will see how applications can be controlled globally. There are two ways of doing this: using the HttpApplication object and using the *global.asax* file.

HttpApplication Object

Just as a web page instantiates the Page class, when an application runs, it instantiates an object from the HttpApplication class. This object has methods, properties, and events that are available to all the objects within the application. It provides several objects that allow you to interact with the HTTP request. These include:

- The Application object for using application state

- The Request object for getting access to the incoming request
- The Response object for sending an HttpResponse back to the client
- The Session object for access to session state

ASP.NET maintains a pool of HttpApplication instances during the lifetime of each application. Every time a page is requested from the server, an HttpApplication instance is assigned to it. This instance manages the request from start to end. Once the request is completed, that instance is freed up for reuse.

You can program against the HttpApplication object by using a file called *global.asax*, described in the next section.

global.asax

Any code contained in the *global.asax* file becomes part of the application in which it is located There can be only a single *global.asax* file per application, located in the virtual root directory of the application. However, this file is optional. If there is no *global.asax* file, then the application will run using default behavior for all the events exposed by the HttpApplication class.

 Classic ASP had a file with similar format and structure, called *global. asa*. In fact, if you copy all the code from a working copy of *global.asa* into *global.asax*, the application should run fine.

When the application runs, the contents of *global.asax* are compiled into a class that derives from the HttpApplication class. Thus, all the methods, classes, and objects of the HttpApplication class are available to your application.

The CLR monitors *global.asax* for changes. If it detects a change in the file, the application is automatically stopped and restarted. This starts a new application domain. Any requests that are currently being handled by the old application domain are allowed to complete, but any new requests are handled by the new application domain. When the last request on the old application domain is finished, that application domain is removed. This effectively *reboots* the web application without any users being aware of the fact.

In order to prevent application users from being able to see the code underlying the application, ASP.NET is configured by default to prevent users from seeing the contents of *global.asax*. If someone enters the following URL in a browser:

```
http://localhost/progaspnet/Global.asax
```

they will receive a 403 (forbidden) error message or an error message similar to the following:

```
This type of page is not served.
```

web.config files, described shortly, have behaviors similar to *global. asax*. If changed, the application will automatically restart. And it is not possible to view the files in a browser.

The *global.asax* file looks and is structured very similarly to a page file (*.aspx*). It can have one or more sections, which will be described in detail shortly. The sections are:

- Directives
- Script blocks
- Server-side includes
- Object declarations

Just as web pages and web services can use code-behind, the *global.asax* file can also use code-behind. In fact, similar to web pages and web services, the default behavior of Visual Studio .NET is to use the code-behind technique with *global.asax*. It creates a default *global.asax* file in the application root. The Application directive in that *global.asax* file, which is analogous to the Page directive in the page file and will be described fully in the next section of this chapter, then has an Inherits property that points to the code-behind class created in *global.asax.vb* or *global.asax.cs*, depending on your language.

A sample *global.asax* file is shown in Example 20-1 in VB.NET and in Example 20-2 in C#.

Example 20-1. Sample global.asax in VB.NET

```
<%@ Application  Language="VB"%>
<script runat="server">

   protected sub Application_Start(ByVal Sender as Object, _
                               ByVal e as EventArgs)
      Application("strDSN") = _
                 "SERVER=Zeus;DATABASE=Pubs;UID=sa;PWD=secret;"

      dim Books() as string = {"SciFi","Novels", "Computers", _
                 "History", "Religion"}
      Application("arBooks") = Books

      WriteFile("Application Starting")
   end sub

   protected sub Application_End(ByVal Sender as Object, _
                              ByVal e as EventArgs)
      WriteFile("Application Ending")
   end sub

   sub WriteFile(strText as string)
      dim writer as System.IO.StreamWriter = _
                 new System.IO.StreamWriter("C:\\test.txt",true)
```

Example 20-1. Sample global.asax in VB.NET (continued)

```
      dim str as string
      str = DateTime.Now.ToString( ) & "   " & strText
      writer.WriteLine(str)
      writer.Close( )
   end sub
</script>
```

Example 20-2. Sample global.asax in C#

```
<%@ Application  Language="C#"%>
<script runat="server">

   protected void Application_Start(Object sender, EventArgs e)
   {
      Application["strDSN"] =
                  "SERVER=Zeus;DATABASE=Pubs;UID=sa;PWD=secret;";

      string[] Books = {"SciFi","Novels", "Computers",
                  "History", "Religion"};
      Application["arBooks"] = Books;

      WriteFile("Application Starting");
   }

   protected void Application_End(Object sender, EventArgs e)
   {
      WriteFile("Application Ending");
   }

   void WriteFile(string strText)
   {
      System.IO.StreamWriter writer =
                  new System.IO.StreamWriter(@"C:\test.txt",true);
      string str;
      str = DateTime.Now.ToString( ) + "   " + strText;
      writer.WriteLine(str);
      writer.Close( );
   }
</script>
```

Directives

As with web page and web service files, the *global.asax* file begins with zero, one, or more application directives. These are used to specify settings to be used by the application compilers when they process the ASP.NET files. Just like page directives, application directives use a dictionary structure that accepts one or more attribute/value pairs. There are three supported directives: Application, Import, and Assembly.

Application. The Application directive specifies application-specific attributes used by the compiler. A sample Application directive might look something like this:

```
<%@ Application  Language="VB" Inherits="WebServiceConsumer.Global"
            Description="A sample application" %>
```

The Language attribute can have any of the standard language values: VB, C#, or JS for VB.NET, C#, or JScript .NET, respectively. (Any third-party language that supports the .NET platform can also be used.) The default is C#. The language specified here applies only to the language used in the *global.asax* file, not to any of the other code files in the application. It is perfectly legal to use C# in the *global.asax* file and VB.NET in the *.aspx* file, or vice versa, for example.

The Inherits attribute specifies the name of a class to inherit from. When Visual Studio .NET creates a *global.asax* file, it uses this attribute to specify the name of the class created in the code-behind file.

The Description attribute will accept a text description of the application, which is then ignored by the parser and compiler.

The CodeBehind attribute is used only by Visual Studio .NET to keep track of the file that contains the code-behind.

The ClassName attribute is used to assign a name to the class generated by the code in the *global.asax* file. This class name can then be used for identifying global static variables and instance methods, as will be shown later.

Import. The Import directive takes a single attribute, a namespace. The specified namespace is explicitly imported into the application, making all its classes and interfaces available. The imported namespace can either be part of the .NET Framework or a custom namespace.

A typical Import directive might look like:

```
<%@ Import Namespace="System.Data" %>
```

There can be only a single Namespace attribute. If you need to import multiple namespaces, use multiple Import directives.

The following namespaces are automatically imported into all web applications and so do not need an Import directive:

```
System
System.Collections
System.Collections.Specialized
System.Configuration
Sytem.IO
System.Text
System.Text.RegularExpressions
System.Web
System.Web.Caching
System.Web.Security
System.Web.SessionState
System.Web.UI
System.Web.UI.HtmlControls
System.Web.UI.WebControls
```

Assembly. The Assembly directive links an assembly to the current application during compilation. This makes all the assembly's classes and interfaces available to the application.

Using the Assembly directive enables both early binding and late binding, since the assembly can be referenced at compile time, then loaded into the application domain at runtime.

Assemblies that are physically located in the application assembly cache (i.e., the *\bin* directory) are automatically linked to the application. Therefore, any assembly located in the *\bin* directory does not need to be linked with an Assembly directive.

There are two possible attributes for the Assembly directive: Name and Src. Name is a string with the name of the assembly to link to the application. It should not include a path. Src is the path to a source file that will be dynamically compiled and linked.

Each Assembly directive can have only a single attribute. If you need to link to multiple assemblies, use multiple Assembly directives.

Assembly directives will look something like:

```
<%@ Assembly Name="SomeAssembly" %>
<%@ Assembly Src="SomeSourceFile.cs" %>
```

Script blocks

The typical *global.asax* file will contain the bulk of its code in a script block. In Examples 20-1 and 20-2, this would include all the code contained between the script tags:

```
<script runat="server">
.
.
.
</script>
```

If using code-behind, the code contained within the code-behind class in the code-behind file is equivalent to putting the code in a script block, although code in the code-behind file itself is not enclosed by script tags.

The code contained within the script block can consist of event handlers, methods, or static variables. All of these are described in the sections below. In Examples 20-1 and 20-2, the script block contains two event handlers, Application_Start and Application_End, plus a public method, WriteFile.

Events. Just as web pages and the controls that they contain expose events that can be handled by the CLR, the application and sessions running under the application also expose events. These events can be handled by event handlers contained in the *global.asax* file. For example, the Application_Start event is fired when the application starts, and the Application_End event is fired when the application ends.

Some of the application events fire every time a page is requested, while others, such as Application_Start or Application_Error, only fire under certain conditions.

The Application_Start event is fired when the application starts and the Application_End event is fired when the application ends. The sample *global.asax* file shown in Examples 20-1 and 20-2 demonstrates event handlers for these two events. The Application_Start event in Examples 20-1 and 20-2 sets two Application properties: a string called strDSN and an array of strings called arBooks. The event handler then calls a method, WriteFile, which is also contained within the *global.asax* file. This method writes a line to a log file with a message that the application is starting.

The WriteFile method is a very simple logging method. It opens a StreamWriter object on a text file, hard-coded to be *c:\test.txt*. It adds a line to the file containing a timestamp and whatever text string is passed in to the method. The Boolean parameter true in the StreamWriter method call specifies that if the file already exists, the line will be appended to the file. If the file does not exist, it is created.

The Application_End event handler simply makes another call to WriteFile to make a log entry that the application has ended.

To see the results of these two event handlers, make some meaningless edit to *global.asax* and save the file. This will force the application to end. Then request any URL in the virtual directory that contains the *global.asax* file. For this example, use one of the web pages from a previous chapter—it doesn't really matter which one—or even a very simple web page of your own creation. Example 20-3 shows an excerpt from the resulting log file.

Example 20-3. Excerpt from Test.txt

```
8/26/2001 5:46:23 PM   Application Starting
8/26/2001 6:13:35 PM   Application Ending
8/27/2001 10:17:39 PM  Application Starting
8/27/2001 10:18:23 PM  Application Ending
8/27/2001 10:18:36 PM  Application Starting
```

Just as there are Start and End events for the Application, there are Start and End events for each session, Session_Start and Session_End. This allows you to have code that will run every time every session within the application starts and ends.

By putting an event handler in *global.asax* for every possible application event, as shown in Example 20-4 for VB.NET and Example 20-5 for C#, it is easy to see the cycle of application events as the page request is received, processed, and rendered.

The following are all the events fired with every page request, in the order in which they are fired:

Application_BeginRequest
Raised for every request handled by ASP.NET. Code in this event handler is executed before the web page or service processes the request.

Application_AuthenticateRequest

Raised prior to authentication of the request. (As was covered in Chapter 19, authentication is the process whereby a user is verified as being who they say they are.) Code in this event handler allows custom security routines to be implemented.

Application_AuthorizeRequest

Raised prior to authorization of the request. (Authorization is the process of determining if the requesting user has permission to access a resource as discussed in Chapter 19.) Code in this event handler allows custom security routines to be implemented.

Application_ResolveRequestCache

Raised before ASP.NET determines whether the output should be generated fresh or fulfilled from cache. Code in this event handler is executed in either case.

Application_AcquireRequestState

Raised prior to acquiring the session state.

Application_PreRequestHandlerExecute

Raised just prior to the request being passed to the handler that is servicing the request. After the event is raised, the page is processed by the HTTP handler processing the request.

Application_PostRequestHandlerExecute

Raised when the HTTP handler is finished with the page request. At this point, the Response object now has the data to send back to the client.

Application_ReleaseRequestState

Raised when the session state is released and updated.

Application_UpdateRequestCache

Raised when the output cache is updated, if the output is to be cached.

Application_EndRequest

Raised when the request is finished.

Application_PreSendRequestHeaders

Raised prior to sending the HTTP headers to the client. If response buffering is enabled, meaning that none of the data will be sent until all the data is ready (the default condition), this event will always follow Application_EndRequest. If response buffering is disabled, then this event will be raised whenever the data is sent back to the client. Response buffering is controlled by an attribute to a Page directive or, in the case of web services, a WebMethod attribute.

Application_PreSendRequestContent

Raised prior to sending the HTTP content to the client. As with Application_PreSendRequestHeaders, the order in which the event is raised depends on whether or not response buffering is enabled.

The following are the application events that fire only under certain conditions:

Application_Start
> Raised whenever the application is started. An application is started the first time any page is requested from an application virtual directory and the application is not already running.

Application_End
> Raised whenever an application ends. An application ends whenever one of the configuration files (*global.asax*, *global.asax.cs*, *global.asax.vb*, *web.config*, or a server-side include file) is modified, or the server is crashed or restarted. Cleanup code, such as closing database connections, is normally executed in this event handler.

Session_Start
> Raised for every session that starts. This is a good place to place code that is session-specific.

Session_End
> Raised for every session that ends. This provides an opportunity to save any data stored in session state.

Application_Disposed
> Raised when the CLR removes the application from memory.

Application_Error
> Raised whenever an unhandled error occurs anywhere in the application. This provides an excellent opportunity to implement generic application-wide error handling.

You can handle specific error conditions where necessary in your code, using try..catch blocks. You can also trap for errors at the page level using the ErrorPage attribute of the Page directive. Any errors handled in these ways will not trigger the Application_Error event.

Example 20-4. global.asax event demonstration in VB.NET

```
<%@ Application  Language="VB" %>

<script runat="server">

    protected sub Application_Start(ByVal Sender as Object, _
                                  ByVal e as EventArgs)
        WriteFile("Application Starting")
    end sub

    protected sub Application_End(ByVal Sender as Object, _
                               ByVal e as EventArgs)
        WriteFile("Application Ending")
    end sub

    protected sub Session_Start(ByVal Sender as Object, _
```

Example 20-4. global.asax event demonstration in VB.NET (continued)

```
                              ByVal e as EventArgs)
    Response.Write("Session_Start" + "<br/>")
end sub

protected sub Session_End(ByVal Sender as Object, _
                          ByVal e as EventArgs)
    Response.Write("Session_End" + "<br/>")
end sub

protected sub Application_Disposed(ByVal Sender as Object, _
                                   ByVal e as EventArgs)
    Response.Write("Application_Disposed" + "<br/>")
end sub

protected sub Application_Error(ByVal Sender as Object, _
                                ByVal e as EventArgs)
    dim strError as string
    strError = Server.GetLastError().ToString( )

    Context.ClearError( )

    Response.Write("Application_Error" + "<br/>")
    Response.Write("Error Msg: " & strError + "<br/>")
end sub

protected sub Application_BeginRequest(ByVal Sender as Object, _
                                       ByVal e as EventArgs)
    Response.Write("Application_BeginRequest" + "<br/>")
end sub

protected sub Application_EndRequest(ByVal Sender as Object, _
                                     ByVal e as EventArgs)
    Response.Write("Application_EndRequest" + "<br/>")
end sub

protected sub Application_AcquireRequestState(ByVal Sender as Object, _
                                              ByVal e as EventArgs)
    Response.Write("Application_AcquireRequestState" + "<br/>")
end sub

protected sub Application_AuthenticateRequest(ByVal Sender as Object, _
                                              ByVal e as EventArgs)
    Response.Write("Application_AuthenticateRequest" + "<br/>")
end sub

protected sub Application_AuthorizeRequest(ByVal Sender as Object, _
                                           ByVal e as EventArgs)
    Response.Write("Application_AuthorizeRequest" + "<br/>")
end sub

protected sub Application_PostRequestHandlerExecute(ByVal Sender as Object, _
                                                    ByVal e as EventArgs)
```

Example 20-4. global.asax event demonstration in VB.NET (continued)

```
      Response.Write("Application_PostRequestHandlerExecute" + "<br/>")
   end sub

   protected sub Application_PreRequestHandlerExecute(ByVal Sender as Object, _
                                 ByVal e as EventArgs)
      Response.Write("Application_PreRequestHandlerExecute" + "<br/>")
   end sub

   protected sub Application_PreSendRequestContent(ByVal Sender as Object, _
                                 ByVal e as EventArgs)
      Response.Write("Application_PreSendRequestContent" + "<br/>")
   end sub

   protected sub Application_PreSendRequestHeaders(ByVal Sender as Object, _
                                 ByVal e as EventArgs)
      Response.Write("Application_PreSendRequestHeaders" + "<br/>")
   end sub

   protected sub Application_ReleaseRequestState(ByVal Sender as Object, _
                                 ByVal e as EventArgs)
      Response.Write("Application_ReleaseRequestState" + "<br/>")
   end sub

   protected sub Application_ResolveRequestCache(ByVal Sender as Object, _
                                 ByVal e as EventArgs)
      Response.Write("Application_ResolveRequestCache" + "<br/>")
   end sub

   protected sub Application_UpdateRequestCache(ByVal Sender as Object, _
                                 ByVal e as EventArgs)
      Response.Write("Application_UpdateRequestCache" + "<br/>")
   end sub

   sub WriteFile(strText as string)
      dim writer as System.IO.StreamWriter = _
         new System.IO.StreamWriter("C:\\test.txt",true)
      dim str as string
      str = DateTime.Now.ToString( ) & "   " & strText
      writer.WriteLine(str)
      writer.Close( )
   end sub

</script>
```

Example 20-5. global.asax event demonstration in C#

```
<%@ Application  Language="C#" %>

<script runat="server">

   protected void Application_Start(Object sender, EventArgs e)
   {
```

Example 20-5. global.asax event demonstration in C# (continued)

```csharp
      WriteFile("Application Starting");
   }

   protected void Application_End(Object sender, EventArgs e)
   {
      WriteFile("Application Ending");
   }

   protected void Session_Start(Object sender, EventArgs e)
   {
      Response.Write("Session_Start" + "<br/>");
   }

   protected void Session_End(Object sender, EventArgs e)
   {
      Response.Write("Session_End" + "<br/>");
   }

   protected void Application_Disposed(Object sender, EventArgs e)
   {
      Response.Write("Application_Disposed" + "<br/>");
   }

   protected void Application_Error(Object sender, EventArgs e)
   {
      string strError;
      strError = Server.GetLastError().ToString();

      Context.ClearError();

      Response.Write("Application_Error" + "<br/>");
      Response.Write("Error Msg: " + strError + "<br/>");
   }

   protected void Application_BeginRequest(Object sender, EventArgs e)
   {
      Response.Write("Application_BeginRequest" + "<br/>");
   }

   protected void Application_EndRequest(Object sender, EventArgs e)
   {
      Response.Write("Application_EndRequest" + "<br/>");
   }

   protected void Application_AcquireRequestState(Object sender, EventArgs e)
   {
      Response.Write("Application_AcquireRequestState" + "<br/>");
   }

   protected void Application_AuthenticateRequest(Object sender, EventArgs e)
   {
      Response.Write("Application_AuthenticateRequest" + "<br/>");
```

Example 20-5. global.asax event demonstration in C# (continued)

```csharp
    }

    protected void Application_AuthorizeRequest(Object sender, EventArgs e)
    {
        Response.Write("Application_AuthorizeRequest" + "<br/>");
    }

    protected void Application_PostRequestHandlerExecute(Object sender, EventArgs e)
    {
        Response.Write("Application_PostRequestHandlerExecute" + "<br/>");
    }

    protected void Application_PreRequestHandlerExecute(Object sender, EventArgs e)
    {
        Response.Write("Application_PreRequestHandlerExecute" + "<br/>");
    }

    protected void Application_PreSendRequestContent(Object sender, EventArgs e)
    {
        Response.Write("Application_PreSendRequestContent" + "<br/>");
    }

    protected void Application_PreSendRequestHeaders(Object sender, EventArgs e)
    {
        Response.Write("Application_PreSendRequestHeaders" + "<br/>");
    }

    protected void Application_ReleaseRequestState(Object sender, EventArgs e)
    {
        Response.Write("Application_ReleaseRequestState" + "<br/>");
    }

    protected void Application_ResolveRequestCache(Object sender, EventArgs e)
    {
        Response.Write("Application_ResolveRequestCache" + "<br/>");
    }

    protected void Application_UpdateRequestCache(Object sender, EventArgs e)
    {
        Response.Write("Application_UpdateRequestCache" + "<br/>");
    }

    void WriteFile(string strText)
    {
        System.IO.StreamWriter writer =
            new System.IO.StreamWriter(@"C:\test.txt",true);
        string str;
        str = DateTime.Now.ToString( ) + "   " + strText;
        writer.WriteLine(str);
        writer.Close( );
    }
</script>
```

In order to test this new version of *global.asax*, create the simple web page shown in Example 20-6 for VB.NET or Example 20-7 for C#. In the C# version of the code listing in Example 20-7, only the script block is shown, since the HTML is identical to the VB.NET version. When this web page is run, you will typically see something similar to the screen shot shown in Figure 20-4.

Example 20-6. Web page demonstrating application events in VB.NET, vbGlobalEvents-01.aspx

```
<%@ Page Language="VB" %>

<script runat="server">

    sub btnEndSession_Click(ByVal Sender as Object, _
                         ByVal e as EventArgs)
       Session.Abandon()
    end sub</script>

<html>
    <body>
    <form runat="server">

       <h1>Global Events</h1>

       <asp:Button
          id="btnEndSession"
          Text="End Session"
          OnClick="btnEndSession_Click"
          runat="server"/>

    </form>
    </body>
</html>
```

Example 20-7. Web page demonstrating application events in C#, csGlobalEvents-01.aspx

```
<%@ Page Language="C#" %>

<script runat="server">

    void btnEndSession_Click(Object Source, EventArgs E)
    {
       Session.Abandon();
    }
</script>
```

In Figure 20-4, you see that a series of application events have fired. About midway through the page, the *.aspx* file itself is finally rendered, followed by another series of application events.

Notice that the first time the page is displayed, the Session_Start event is fired, but on subsequent displays, the Session_Start event may not be fired. This is because the request is part of the same session. Clicking on the End Session button causes the

---

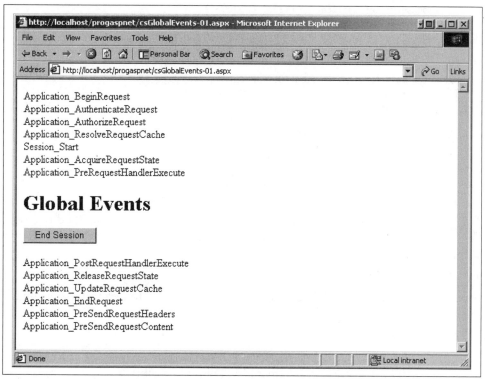

Figure 20-4. Viewing global events

Session.Abandon method to be called, which ends the current session. The next time the page is submitted to the server, the Session_Start event will again be fired.

Most of the Application event handlers in Examples 20-4 and 20-5 contain a Response.Write method to indicate that the method has been called. However, the Application_Start and Application_End methods call the WriteFile method instead. If you try using Response.Write in these event handlers, they will not display on the web page because the session in which the page is to be rendered is not running. However, by examining the log file, *c:\test.txt*, you will see entries that indicate when the application starts and ends.

The sample *global.asax* file shown in Examples 20-4 and 20-5 demonstrates one way of using the Application_Error event. That code is reproduced here for reference. In VB.NET, it is:

```
protected sub Application_Error(ByVal Sender as Object, _
                                ByVal e as EventArgs)
    dim strError as string
    strError = Server.GetLastError().ToString()

    Context.ClearError()
```

```
        Response.Write("Application_Error" + "<br/>")
        Response.Write("Error Msg: " & strError + "<br/>")
    end sub
```

and in C#, it is:

```
    protected void Application_Error(Object sender, EventArgs e)
    {
        string strError;
        strError = Server.GetLastError().ToString();

        Context.ClearError();

        Response.Write("Application_Error" + "<br/>");
        Response.Write("Error Msg: " + strError + "<br/>");
    }
```

This event handler uses the HttpServerUtility object's GetLastError method to report the last error that occurred. That error is converted to a string and assigned to a string variable:

```
    strError = Server.GetLastError().ToString()
```

Next the HttpContext object's ClearError method is called to clear all the errors for the current HTTP request:

```
    Context.ClearError()
```

If the errors are not cleared, then the error will still display on the client browser and the subsequent Response.Write statements will never be visible.

Finally the Response.Write statements display a message and the current error to the client browser.

An alternative technique for reporting an error to the user would display a custom error handling page. To do this, replace the Response.Write lines in the Application_ Error event handler with the following line of code in C#:

```
    Response.Redirect("CustomErrorPage.aspx?Msg=" +
                    Server.UrlEncode(strError));
```

and in VB.NET:

```
    Response.Redirect("CustomErrorPage.aspx?Msg=" & _
                    Server.UrlEncode(strError))
```

This line of code uses the HttpServerUtility object's UrlEncode method to pass the error message as a query string parameter to the custom error page coded in *CustomErrorPage.aspx. CustomErrorPage.aspx* would have a label control, called lblMessage, and the following code in its Page_Load method (in C#):

```
    void Page_Load(Object Source, EventArgs E)
    {
        lblMessage.Text = Request.QueryString(Msg);
    }
```

Global static variables and instance methods

It was noted previously that the code contained in the *global.asax* file is compiled into a class derived from HttpApplication and becomes part of the application. You can assign a name to this compiled class by using the ClassName attribute of the Application directive. In VB.NET, the Application directive then looks something like the following:

```
<%@ Application  Language="VB" ClassName="ProgAspNet"%>
```

and in C# it might look like:

```
<%@ Application  Language="C#" ClassName="ProgAspNet"%>
```

Once a name has been assigned to the class, it can be referred to throughout the application, making available global static variables and instance methods.

Static member variables are those variables that do not require that the class containing the variable be instantiated. Static member variables are defined using the Shared keyword in VB.NET, and with the static keyword in C#.

Public methods can also be defined using either the VB.NET Shared keyword or the C# static keyword, in which case they do not require that the class of which the method is a member be instantiated in order to invoke the method. For example, given the following Application directive in *global.asax*:

```
<%@ Application  Language="C#" ClassName="ProgAspNet"%>
```

a method named SomeMethod defined in *global.asax* can be invoked anywhere in the application with the following line of code:

```
ProgASPNet.SomeMethod( );
```

Methods can also be instance methods; that is, they can be called from an object instance. For example, given the following Application directive in *global.asax*:

```
<%@ Application  Language="VB" ClassName="ProgAspNet"%>
```

the following code invokes the method:

```
Dim oProg As New ProgAspNet
oProg.SomeMethod( )
```

To see how global static variables and instance methods defined in *global.asax* can be made available throughout an ASP.NET application, make the following modifications to the *global.asax* files in either Examples 20-4 or 20-5:

1. In order to assign a name to the class compiled from *global.asax*, modify the Application directive by adding the ClassName attribute. In VB.NET, the Application directive will then look like:

    ```
    <%@ Application  Language="VB" ClassName="ProgAspNet"%>
    ```

    and in C# it will look like:

    ```
    <%@ Application  Language="C#" ClassName="ProgAspNet"%>
    ```

2. Define and initialize a static variable named successRate by adding one of the following lines of code to the script block in the *global.asax* file. In VB.NET, it will look like:

```
public shared successRate as integer = 50
```

and in C#, it will look like:

```
public static int successRate = 50;
```

3. Add the public keyword to the WriteFile method declaration in order to make that method globally available. The C# method declaration will then look like:

```
public void WriteFile(string strText)
```

and the VB method declaration will look like:

```
Public Sub WriteFile(strText as string)
```

To demonstrate the use of global static variables and global instance methods, access the sample web page shown in Example 20-8 (for VB.NET) or Example 20-9 (for C#). The pages are similar to those shown in Examples 20-6 and 20-7, respectively, with the code changes highlighted. In the C# version of the code listing in Example 20-9, only the script block is shown, since the HTML is identical to the VB.NET version.

Example 20-8. Global static variable and instance method demonstration web page in VB.NET, vbGlobalEvents-02.aspx

```
<%@ Page Language="VB" %>

<script runat="server">
   sub Page_Load(ByVal Sender as Object, _
                 ByVal e as EventArgs)
      lblGlobalStatic.Text = ProgAspNet.successRate.ToString( ) + " %"

      dim p as new ProgAspNet

      p.WriteFile("Now in Page_Load of web page.")
   end sub

   sub btnEndSession_Click(ByVal Sender as Object, _
                           ByVal e as EventArgs)
      Session.Abandon( )
   end sub</script>

<html>
   <body>
   <form runat="server">

      <h1>Global Events</h1>

      Global Static Variable:  
      <asp:Label
         id="lblGlobalStatic"
         runat="server"/>
```

```
    <br/>

    <asp:Button
        id="btnEndSession"
        Text="End Session"
        OnClick="btnEndSession_Click"
        runat="server"/>

   </form>
  </body>
</html>
```

Example 20-9. Global static variable and instance method demonstration web page in C#, csGlobalEvents-02.aspx

```
<%@ Page Language="C#" %>

<script runat="server">

   void Page_Load(Object Source, EventArgs E)
   {
      lblGlobalStatic.Text = ProgAspNet.successRate.ToString() + " %";

      ProgAspNet p = new ProgAspNet();

      p.WriteFile("Now in Page_Load of web page.");
   }

   void btnEndSession_Click(Object Source, EventArgs E)
   {
      Session.Abandon();
   }
</script>
```

Once the class name has been assigned and a static variable is declared in *global. asax*, referencing the static variable is as simple as prepending the class name to the variable name using dot notation, as in:

```
    lblGlobalStatic.Text = ProgAspNet.successRate.ToString() + " %";
```

The ToString method must be called to convert the variable to a string so that it can be concatenated with a string literal and assigned to the Text property of the label.

Calling the instance method is slightly more involved, since the class must first be instantiated. In VB.NET the following line of code instantiates the class:

```
    dim p as new ProgAspNet
```

while in C# that is accomplished with the following line:

```
    ProgAspNet p = new ProgAspNet();
```

Once the class has been instantiated, the WriteFile method is called using dot notation. In VB.NET, the line is:

```
p.WriteFile("Now in Page_Load of web page.")
```

and in C#, it's:

```
p.WriteFile("Now in Page_Load of web page.");
```

Server-side includes

External source code files can be included in the application using *server-side includes*. The code contained within an include file is added to *global.asax* before it is compiled. The language used in the include file must match the language used in the *global.asax* file, although that may be different from the language(s) used within the application.

The syntax for a server-side include is identical for both VB.NET and C#:

```
<!--#Include PathType="fileName" -->
```

In this syntax, PathType can have one of two values, shown in Table 20-1.

Table 20-1. PathType attributes

Type of path	Description
File	*fileName* is a string containing a relative path from the directory containing the *global.asax* file.
Virtual	*fileName* is a string containing a full virtual path from a virtual directory in your web site.

Looking at the sample *global.asax* listed in Examples 20-1 or 20-2, add the following line as the second line in the file:

```
<!--#Include File="IncludeFile.vb" -->
```

or:

```
<!--#Include File="IncludeFile.cs" -->
```

depending on your language. Create a new text file, called either *IncludeFile.vb* or *IncludeFile.cs*, and store it in the same directory that contains *global.asax*. This file requires a pair of script tags, just like the *global.asax* file itself.

Move a copy of the WriteFile method from *global.asax* to the include file. Finally, comment out (or delete) the WriteFile method from *global.asax*. The include file should look like Examples 20-10 or 20-11, depending on the language.

Example 20-10. Include file for global.asax in VB.NET

```
<script runat="server" >

    sub WriteFile(strText as string)
        dim writer as System.IO.StreamWriter = _
                    new System.IO.StreamWriter("C:\\test.txt",true)
        dim str as string
```

Example 20-10. Include file for global.asax in VB.NET (continued)

```
    str = DateTime.Now.ToString( ) & "   " & strText
    writer.WriteLine(str)
    writer.Close( )
  end sub

</script>
```

Example 20-11. Include file for global.asax in C#

```
<script runat="server">

  void WriteFile(string strText)
  {
    System.IO.StreamWriter writer =
              new System.IO.StreamWriter(@"C:\test.txt",true);
    string str;
    str = DateTime.Now.ToString( ) + "   " + strText;
    writer.WriteLine(str);
    writer.Close( );
  }

</script>
```

If you run any of your web pages, there should be no difference in behavior, because all you did was move the code for a method from one file to another.

Just as the CLR watches for changes in *global.asax* and restarts the application if any occur, it also watches for changes in any include files. If an include file changes, then the application restarts for that as well.

Include files are very useful for including the same standard code into multiple applications. This common code could include such things as methods for database access, writing log entries, error handling routines, logins, or any number of infrastructure-type pieces that are part of every application.

Object declarations

One additional way to include code in the *global.asax* file is as declarative object tags. These static objects are declared as either Application objects or Session objects. They are then available for the duration of either the application or each session.

Here is a code snippet showing how an object might be declared in the *global.asax* file. This snippet would be located *outside* the script block in the file:

```
<object id="strDSN"
    class="System.String"
    scope="Application"
    runat="server"/>
```

The object in this snippet can be referred to in the application by the value of the id attribute, which in this example is strDSN.

The class attribute specifies the type of this object. In this case, it is a string object. The class attribute implies that the object is derived from a .NET assembly. Alternatively, you can use either a progid or classid instead of the class attribute to instantiate a COM object rather than a .NET object. Each object declaration can have only one of either class, progid, or classid.

In this snippet, the scope attribute specifies that this will be an Application object. The other legal value for this attribute is Session.

Objects declared in this way are not actually created upon declaration. They are created the first time they are referenced in the application. To reference the static object shown in the code snippet above in your code, refer to:

```
Application("strDSN")
```

It is also possible to store application or session information elsewhere, such as in the *web.config* file, which will be described in the next section.

Configuring the Application

ASP.NET provides a very powerful and flexible means of configuring applications. This configuration is accomplished using text-based XML configuration files. The server-wide configuration file is called *machine.config*, described in the upcoming section "Hierarchical Configuration." This is supplemented by a number of application-specific configuration files, all called *web.config*, located in the application virtual root directory and subdirectories.

This configuration scheme offers the following features:

- The XML files that control the configuration can be edited with any standard text editor or XML parser. It is not necessary to use the IIS control panel, as was the case with classic ASP.

- Since the configuration is accomplished with text files, it is easy to administer remotely. Files can be created or edited remotely, then copied into place via FTP or remote network access by anyone with suitable security clearance. There is no need for a person to be physically present at the server machine hosting the application in order to perform configuration chores, as is the case with classic ASP.

- The system is hierarchical. Each application inherits a baseline configuration from *machine.config*, located on the server. The *web.config* files then apply successive configuration attributes and parameters as the application directory tree structure is traversed. This will be explained in detail in the section "Hierarchical Configuration."

- A corollary of the hierarchical nature of the system is that each application can have its own independent configuration. It is not necessary for all applications to share a server-wide configuration, as with classic ASP.

- The system is *extensible*. The baseline system provides configurability to a large number of standard program areas. In addition, you can add custom parameters, attributes, and section handlers, as required by your application. This too will be explained in detail below.

- It is possible to modify the configuration of a running application without stopping and restarting either the application or the server. The changes automatically and immediately apply themselves to any new client requests. Any clients online at the time the changes are made will not be aware that changes are being made, other than perhaps a slight delay for the first request made after the change is put in place.

- The configuration settings for each unique URL are computed at application runtime, using all the hierarchical *web.config* files. These configuration settings are then cached so that requests to each URL can retrieve the configuration settings in a performant manner. ASP.NET automatically detects if any configuration files anywhere in the hierarchy are modified, and recomputes and recaches the configuration settings accordingly.

- Configuration files are hidden from browser access. If a browser directly requests a configuration file in a URL, an HTTP access error 403 (forbidden) will be returned. This is the same behavior seen if the *global.asax* file is requested directly by a browser.

Hierarchical Configuration

The configuration system is hierarchical, just as a directory tree structure is hierarchical. The file at the very top of the hierarchy is a file called *machine.config*. This file is contained in the subdirectory:

```
c:\winnt\Microsoft.NET\Framework\version number\CONFIG
```

where *version number* will be replaced with the version of the .NET runtime installed on your machine, such as v1.0.2914.

All the other configuration files are called *web.config*. These files are optional: if there are none anywhere in an application virtual directory or its subdirectories, then the configuration settings contained in *machine.config* will apply to your application without any modifications.

Each directory and subdirectory contained in the application can have at most a single *web.config* file. The configuration settings contained in a specific instance of *web.config* apply to the directory in which it is contained and to all its child directories. If a specific instance of *web.config* contains a setting that is in conflict with a setting higher up in the configuration hierarchy (i.e., in a parent directory or *machine.config*), then the lower-level setting will override and apply to its own directory and all child subdirectories below it (unless, of course, any of those child subdirectories have their own copies of *web.config*, which will further override the settings).

So for example, consider the directory structure shown in Figure 20-5. The virtual root of the web site is called *MyWebSite*, corresponding to the physical directory *c:\ inetpub\wwwroot\MyWebSite*. Underneath the virtual root are two child subdirectories, each of which has additional child subdirectories. The URL for this web site would be *www.MyWebSite.com* (assuming that the domain name *MyWebSite.com* was registered to the IP address assigned to the server).

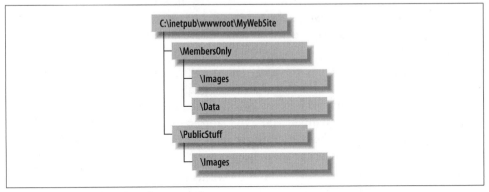

Figure 20-5. Hierarchical configuration

If there were no *web.config* files in any of these directories, then all the configuration would come directly from *machine.config*. If there is a version of *web.config* in the directory *MyWebSite*, then any settings it contains would apply to the entire application (but only to that application), including all the subdirectories beneath it. If there were another version of *web.config* in the *MembersOnly* directory, then its configuration settings would apply to the *MembersOnly* directory and its subdirectories, but not to *PublicStuff*. If any of the settings in *web.config* in *MembersOnly* conflicted with those in *MyWebSite*, then the settings in *MembersOnly* would override those in *MyWebSite*.

It is important to note that the hierarchical nature of the configuration files is based on application virtual directories first, and then physical directories. Refer again to Figure 20-5. The only virtual directory defined so far for that application is *MyWebSite*. However, suppose another virtual directory, *MyPublicWebSite*, were defined, corresponding to *c:\inetpub\wwwroot\MyWebSite\PublicStuff*. The URL for this application would be *www.MyPublicWebSite.com*. This application would inherit the configuration settings from *machine.config*, but not from *c:\inetpub\ wwwroot\MyWebSite\web.config*. Although *c:\inetpub\wwwroot\MyWebSite* is the physical parent directory of *c:\inetpub\wwwroot\MyWebSite\PublicStuff*, it is not the virtual parent. In fact, *c:\inetpub\wwwroot\MyWebSite\PublicStuff* is a virtual root and does not have a parent. Configuration settings inherit from virtual parents, not physical parents.

Format

The configuration files, *machine.config* and *web.config*, are XML files. As such they must be well formed. (For a description of well formed XML, see the sidebar "Well-Formed HTML" in Chapter 4.) Specifically, these files consist of a nested hierarchy of XML tags. All opening tags must have the corresponding closing tag or be self-closing (with a trailing / character just inside the closing angle bracket). The tag pairs must not be interleaved with other tag pairs. Subtags may be nested inside tag pairs. Both tags and subtags may have attributes and attribute values. All of these elements are case-sensitive.

Typically, tag and attribute names consist of one or more words run together. Tag and attribute names are camel-cased. Attribute values are *usually* Pascal-cased.

 Camel-casing means that all the characters are lowercase, including the first character, except the first character of each run-on word after the first. Examples of camel-casing are `appSettings`, `configSections`, `section`, and `sessionState`.

Pascal-casing is the same as camel-casing except that the first character of the name is also upper case. Examples of Pascal-casing are `SortByTime`, `InProc`, and `StateServer`.

The word *usually* is used because there are exceptions:

- `true` and `false` are always lowercase.
- Literal strings do not adhere to either camel- or Pascal-casing. For example, a database connection string may be specified as: `SERVER=Zeus;DATABASE=Pubs;UID=sa;PWD=secret;`
- If the value is the name of another tag in a configuration file, then it will be camel-cased.

The first line in the configuration file declares the file to be an XML file, with attributes specifying the version of the XML specification to which the file adheres and the character encoding used. Here is a typical XML declaration line:

```
<?xml version="1.0" encoding="UTF-8" ?>
```

The character encoding specified here is UTF-8, which is a superset of ASCII. The character encoding parameter may be omitted if, and only if, the XML document is written in either UTF-8 or UTF-32. Therefore, if the XML file is written in pure ASCII, the encoding parameter may be omitted, although including the attribute contributes to self-documentation.

The next line in the configuration files is the opening `<configuration>` tag:

```
<configuration>
```

The entire contents of the configuration file, except the initial XML declaration, is contained between the opening <configuration> tag and the closing </configuration> tag.

Comments can be contained within the file using the standard XML (and HTML) format:

```
<!-- Your comments here -->
```

Within the <configuration> tags are two broad categories of entries. They are, in the order in which they appear in the configuration files:

- Configuration section handler declarations
- Configuration sections

Configuration Section Handler Declarations

The handler declarations are contained between an opening <configSections> tag and a closing </configSections> tag. Each handler declaration specifies the name of a configuration section, contained elsewhere in the file, that provides specific configuration data. Each declaration also contains the name of the .NET class that will process the configuration data in that section.

> This terminology is very confusing. The first part of the file is enclosed in <configSections> tags, but contains only a list of the configuration sections and their handlers, not the configuration sections themselves. And as you will see shortly, the configuration sections are each contained within tags, but there is no grouping tag to contain all the separate configuration sections, analogous to <configSections>.

The *machine.config* file contains, in the default installation, many configuration section handler declarations that cover the areas subject to configuration by default. (Since this is an extensible system, you can also create your own. A typical entry containing a handler declaration is shown in Example 20-12.

> In the original *machine.config* file, the contents of Example 20-12 were all contained in a single line.

Example 20-12. Typical configuration section handler declaration

```
<section name="compilation"
         type="System.Web.UI.CompilationConfigurationHandler,
               System.Web,
               Version=1.0.2411.0,
               Culture=neutral,
               PublicKeyToken=b03f5f7f11d50a3a" />
```

Despite appearances to the contrary, the <section> tag has only two attributes: name and type. The name is compilation. This implies that somewhere else in the configuration file is a configuration section called compilation. This configuration section will contain the configuration settings, which are name/value pairs, to be used by the application(s). It will be described in detail shortly.

The type attribute has a lengthy parameter enclosed in quotation marks. This parameter contains:

- The class that will handle the named configuration section
- The assembly file (DLL) that contains that class
- Version and culture information to coordinate with the assembly file
- A public key token used to verify that the DLL being called is secure

Each handler need only be declared once, either in the base level *machine.config* file or in a *web.config* file further down the configuration hierarchy. The configuration section it refers to can then be specified as often as desired in other configuration files.

Example 20-13 shows a truncated version of the default *machine.config*.

Only a small subset of the actual entries in *machine.config* are included in Example 20-13. Also, the type attribute of each entry has been edited to remove all but the class, and lines have been broken to enhance the readability.

Example 20-13. Truncated machine.config file

```xml
<?xml version="1.0" encoding="UTF-8" ?>
<configuration>
  <configSections>
    <section name="runtime"
             type="System.Configuration.IgnoreSectionHandler" />
    <section name="mscorlib"
             type="System.Configuration.IgnoreSectionHandler" />
    <section name="startup"
             type="System.Configuration.IgnoreSectionHandler" />

    <section name="appSettings"
             type="System.Configuration.NameValueSectionHandler " />

    <sectionGroup name="system.net">
      <section name="defaultProxy"
               type="System.Net.Configuration.DefaultProxyHandler " />
    </sectionGroup>

    <sectionGroup name="system.web">
      <section name="compilation"
               type="System.Web.UI.CompilationConfigurationHandler " />
      <section name="pages"
               type="System.Web.UI.PagesConfigurationHandler " />
    </sectionGroup>
```

Example 20-13. Truncated machine.config file (continued)

```
  </configSections>

  <appSettings>
    <!-- use this section to add application specific configuration
       example: <add key="XML File Name" value="myXmlFileName.xml" /> -->
  </appSettings>

  <system.net>
    <defaultProxy>
       <proxy
           usesystemdefault="true"
        />
    </defaultProxy>
    <webRequestModules>
      <add prefix="http"
         type="System.Net.HttpRequestCreator"
      />
      <add prefix="https"
         type="System.Net.HttpRequestCreator"
      />
      <add prefix="file"
         type="System.Net.FileWebRequestCreator"
      />
    </webRequestModules>
  </system.net>

  <system.web>
    <compilation debug="false" explicit="true" defaultLanguage="vb">
      <compilers>
        <compiler language="c#;cs;csharp" extension=".cs"
                 type="Microsoft.CSharp.CSharpCodeProvider " />
        <compiler language="vb;visualbasic;vbscript" extension=".vb"
                 type="Microsoft.VisualBasic.VBCodeProvider " />
        <compiler language="js;jscript;javascript" extension=".js"
                 type="Microsoft.JScript.JScriptCodeProvider " />
      </compilers>

      <assemblies>
        <add assembly="mscorlib"/>
        <add assembly="System "/>
        <add assembly="System.Web "/>
        <add assembly="System.Data "/>
        <add assembly="System.Web.Services "/>
        <add assembly="System.Xml "/>
        <add assembly="System.Drawing "/>
        <add assembly="*"/>
      </assemblies>
    </compilation>
    <pages buffer="true" enableSessionState="true" enableViewState="true"
           enableViewStateMac="false" autoEventWireup="true" />
  </system.web>
</configuration>
```

The first three declarations in *machine.config* are runtime, mscorlib, and startup. They are special because they are the only declarations that do not have corresponding configuration sections in the file.

In Example 20-13, you can also see that many of the handler declarations are contained within <sectionGroup> tags. The name attribute of these tags corresponds to the namespace that contains the handlers. This groups together all the configuration sections that are handled out of the same namespace.

Configuration Sections

The configuration sections contain the actual configuration data. They each are contained within a pair of tags corresponding to the name of the section specified in the configuration section handler declaration. Alternatively, a single self-closing tag can be used. For example, the following two configuration sections are equivalent:

```
<globalization requestEncoding="utf-8" responseEncoding="utf-8" />
```

and:

```
<globalization
     requestEncoding="utf-8"
     responseEncoding="utf-8"
</globalization>
```

Configuration sections contain name/value pairs that hold the configuration data. They may also contain subsections.

machine.config contains one configuration section for each handler declaration. If the handler declaration was contained within a <sectionGroup> tag, then its corresponding configuration section will be contained within a tag containing the name of the <sectionGroup>. This can be seen in Example 20-13 for both system.net and system.web.

The sections that follow provide a description of each of the configuration sections contained in the default *machine.config*. There are other configuration sections that are beyond the scope of this book, including system.diagnostics, system.runtime.remoting, and system.windows.forms.

appSettings

appSettings allows you to easily store application-wide name/value pairs for read-only access. It is similar in function to application objects in the *global.asax* file.

The handler declaration for appSettings, shown in Example 20-13 and reproduced here:

```
<section name="appSettings"
        type="System.Configuration.NameValueSectionHandler " />
```

indicates that the NameValueSectionHandler class is used to handle appSettings. This class provides name/value pair configuration handling for a specific configuration section.

As seen in Example 20-13, the appSettings section in the default *machine.config* file contains only a comment. More typically, you would add an appSettings section to one or more *web.config* files.

Example 20-14 shows a *web.config* file with an appSettings section added to provide two application-wide values. Note that the appSettings section is not contained within any higher-level tag other than <configuration>.

Example 20-14. appSettings configuration section

```
<?xml version="1.0" encoding="utf-8" ?>
<configuration>
   <appSettings>
      <add key="appDSN"
           value=" SERVER=Zeus;DATABASE=Pubs;UID=sa;PWD=secret;" />
      <add key="appTitle" value="Programming ASP.NET" />
   </appSettings>
</configuration>
```

These values can be accessed anywhere in the application to which this configuration is applicable (i.e., its current directory and any child directories in which the value is not overridden by another *web.config* file). Examples 20-15 and 20-16 show a script block from an *.aspx* file to illustrate how this is done in both VB.NET and C#, respectively. The C# version of the code in Example 20-16 shows only the script block, since the HTML is identical to the VB.NET version in Example 20-15.

Example 20-15. Reading appSettings values in VB.NET

```
<%@ Page Language="vb" %>

<script runat="server">
   sub Page_Load(ByVal Sender as Object, _
            ByVal e as EventArgs)
      if not IsPostBack then
         dim strDSN as string
         strDSN = ConfigurationSettings.AppSettings("appDSN")
         '  use the DSN to connect to the database here
         lblDSN.Text = strDSN

         lblTitle.Text = ConfigurationSettings.AppSettings("appTitle")
      end if
   end sub
</script>

<html>
   <body>
   <form runat="server">
      <h1>Configuration</h1>
```

Example 20-15. Reading appSettings values in VB.NET (continued)

```
      Application DSN:
      <asp:Label
         id="lblDSN"
         runat="server"/>
      <br/>
      Application Title:
      <asp:Label
         id="lblTitle"
         runat="server"/>
   </form>
   </body>
</html>
```

Example 20-16. Reading appSettings values in C#

```
<%@ Page Language="cs" %>

<script runat="server">
   void Page_Load(Object Source, EventArgs E)
   {
      if (!IsPostBack)
      {
         string strDSN;
         strDSN = ConfigurationSettings.AppSettings["appDSN"];
         //  use the DSN to connect to the database here

         lblDSN.Text = strDSN ;

         lblTitle.Text = ConfigurationSettings.AppSettings["appTitle"];
      }
   }

</script>
```

Configuration settings are read by an application using the AppSettings property of the ConfigurationSettings class. This class provides methods and properties for reading configuration settings in an application's configuration files. It is part of the System.Configuration namespace, which is automatically imported into every ASP.NET application.

The AppSettings property of the ConfigurationSettings class is of type NameValue-Collection. It takes a key as a parameter and returns the value associated with that key.

system.net

The system.net configuration section contains subsections that deal with the .NET runtime. These subsections include authenticationModules, defaultProxy, connectionManagement, and webRequestModules. These subsections are not normally used by developers and are outside the scope of this book.

system.web

The system.web configuration section contains subsections that configure ASP.NET. Each of these subsections will be described briefly in the following sections.

browserCaps. This subsection contains information about the capabilities of all the web browsers and operating systems your clients are likely to use. This information includes such items as the name of the browser; its major and minor version numbers; whether it supports frames, tables, cookies, cascading style sheets, VBScript, JavaScript, Java applets; and so on.

The version of <browserCaps> contained in the default *machine.config* file performs fairly extensive testing of the client browser to determine both the browser capabilities and the client platform.

As new browser versions come on the market, you can update the information contained in this section by visiting *www.cyscape.com/browsercaps/*.

clientTarget. Closely related to <browserCaps>, the <clientTarget> subsection provides ASP.NET with aliases for the browsers. For example, it provides the aliases shown in Table 20-2.

Table 20-2. Browser aliases

Alias	Browser characteristics
ie5	Internet Explorer 5.5
ie4	Internet Explorer 4.0
uplevel	Internet Explorer 4.0 and higher
downlevel	All others

compilation. This subsection allows you to configure the compilation behavior in ASP.NET. For example, you can change the default language and enable or disable debugging. If the default language is VB.NET, you can also set the explicit attribute to true, which is the equivalent of including the Option Explicit On statement in your page or web service.

The default <compilation> tag in *machine.config* looks like this:

```
<compilation debug="false" explicit="true" defaultLanguage="vb">
```

In a VB.NET project created in Visual Studio .NET, the default <compilation> tag in the *web.config* file for the application looks like this:

```
<compilation defaultLanguage="vb" debug="true" />
```

and for a C# project in Visual Studio .NET, it looks like this:

```
<compilation defaultLanguage="c#" debug="true" />
```

Notice that the debug attribute in either *web.config* file overrides the value set in *machine.config*.

In addition to setting the language and debug mode, this subsection includes two other subsections: <compilers> and <assemblies>. The former subsection specifies what language names map with what file extensions. It also specifies the class containing the code provider and version information. The latter subsection specifies which assembly files are to be included when the project is compiled.

pages. This subsection specifies whether page options, such as buffering, session state, and view state, are enabled for the pages under the control of the configuration file. The default <pages> tag in the default *machine.config* file looks like:

```
<pages buffer="true"
       enableSessionState="true"
       enableViewState="true"
       enableViewStateMac="false"
       autoEventWireup="true" />
```

The autoEventWireup attribute is specific to Visual Studio .NET. If set to true, then Visual Studio .NET can automatically hook up event handlers on controls when the control is double clicked in design mode. If set to false, then you must manually hook up the event handlers.

customErrors. This subsection allows you to control what the user sees when there is an error. Example 20-17 shows a typical <customErrors> configuration section that demonstrates the available features.

Example 20-17. <customErrors> configuration section

```
<customErrors defaultRedirect="StdError.htm" mode="RemoteOnly" >
   <error statusCode="404" redirect="err404.htm" />
   <error statusCode="407" redirect="err407.htm" />
</customErrors >
```

When custom errors are enabled, if an error occurs, the web page specified in defaultRedirect is presented to the client rather than the standard ASP.NET error page.

The mode attribute specifies how custom errors are enabled. There are three possible values for this mode, which are shown in Table 20-3.

Table 20-3. Values for the mode attribute of the <customErrors> tag

Value	Description
On	Custom errors are enabled.
Off	Custom errors are disabled.
RemoteOnly	Custom errors are shown only to remote clients, not to local clients. This setting allows developers to see the full error message provided by ASP.NET while still showing end users the error page you wish them to see.

You can add multiple <error> tags to present specific error pages for specific errors.

In Example 20-17, error 404 will result in *err404.htm* being presented to the client, error 407 will result in *err407.htm*, and all other errors will result in *StdError.htm* being presented. In any case, the developer working on the local machine will see none of these custom error pages, but rather will see the standard error page put up by ASP.NET.

httpRuntime. This subsection configures the ASP.NET HTTP runtime settings. There are several attributes available in this section; they are shown in Table 20-4.

Table 20-4. Attributes of the httpRuntime subsection

Attribute	Description
useFullyQualified-RedirectUrl	Specifies if client-side redirects are fully qualified, which is necessary for some mobile controls. Legal values are `true`, for fully qualified URLs, and `false`, for relative URLs.
executionTimeout	Maximum number of seconds a request is allowed to execute before being shut down by ASP. NET.
maxRequestLength	Maximum file size for upload, in bytes. This can help prevent denial of service attacks by preventing clients from posting large files.
minFreeThreads	Minimum number of free threads for execution of new requests. These threads are available for requests that require additional threads.
minLocalRequestFree-Threads	Minimum number of free threads available for requests to localhost.
appRequestQueueLimit	Maximum number of requests queued waiting for a free thread. If incoming request rejected, then "503 Server too busy" error will be returned.

The <httpRuntime> tag in the default *machine.config* file looks like:

```
<httpRuntime
    executionTimeout="90"
    maxRequestLength="4096"
    useFullyQualifiedRedirectUrl="false"
    minFreeThreads="8"
    minLocalRequestFreeThreads="4"
    appRequestQueueLimit="10"
/>
```

globalization. This subsection is used to configure the globalization settings for an application. The attributes shown in Table 20-5 are supported.

Table 20-5. Attributes of the globalization subsection

Attribute	Description
requestEncoding	Specifies the encoding assumed for incoming requests. If not specified in any configuration file, defaults to computer's Regional Options locale setting.
responseEncoding	Specifies the encoding of responses. If not specified in any configuration file, defaults to computer's Regional Options locale setting.

Table 20-5. Attributes of the globalization subsection (continued)

Attribute	Description
fileEncoding	Specifies the default encoding for parsing *.aspx*, *.asmx*, and *.asax* files.
culture	Specifies the default culture for incoming requests.
uiCulture	Specifies the default culture for locale-dependent resource searches.

The <globalization> tag in the default *machine.config* file looks like:

```
<globalization
        requestEncoding="utf-8"
        responseEncoding="utf-8"
/>
```

httpHandlers. This subsection maps incoming requests to a class that implements either the IHttpHandler or IHttpHandlerFactory interfaces. There is a fairly extensive mapping in the default *machine.config* file, which maps standard file types to a specific class (e.g., all *.aspx* requests are mapped to the PageHandlerFactory class).

The <httpHandlers> tag has several subtags:

<add>

Specifies the mapping. A typical <add> subtag looks like:

```
<add verb="*"
     path="*.vb"
     type="System.Web.HttpForbiddenHandler"/>
```

The verb attribute can either contain a comma separated list of HTTP verbs, such as GET, PUT, or POST, or the wildcard character (*). The path attribute can contain either a single URL path or a wildcard string. The type attribute is a class name. ASP.NET first searches for the specified class in the \bin directory, then in the global assembly cache. (See the section "Deploying the Application" later in this chapter for a description of the global assembly cache.)

<remove>

Removes a previously added mapping. It has the same syntax as the <add> subtag, except that there is no type attribute.

<clear>

Clears all currently configured or inherited mappings. It has no attributes.

httpModules. This subsection configures the HTTP modules within an application. Each <add> subtag within the subsection assigns a class to a module. The default *machine.config* file includes the modules and their classes shown in Table 20-6.

Table 20-6. Modules and classes defined in the httpModules subsection

Module	Class
OutputCache	System.Web.Caching.OutputCacheModule
Session	System.Web.SessionState.SessionStateModule
WindowsAuthentication	System.Web.Security.WindowsAuthenticationModule
FormsAuthentication	System.Web.Security.FormsAuthenticationModule
PassportAuthentication	System.Web.Security.PassportAuthenticationModule
UrlAuthorization	System.Web.Security.UrlAuthorizationModule
FileAuthorization	System.Web.Security.FileAuthorizationModule

processModel. This tag configures the process model settings on an IIS web server. The <processModel> tag in the default *machine.config* file looks like this:

```
<processModel
    enable="true"
    timeout="Infinite"
    idleTimeout="Infinite"
    shutdownTimeout="0:00:05"
    requestLimit="Infinite"
    requestQueueLimit="5000"
    restartQueueLimit="10"
    memoryLimit="60"
    webGarden="false"
    cpuMask="0xffffffff"
    userName="machine"
    password="AutoGenerate"
    logLevel="Errors"
    clientConnectedCheck="0:00:05"
    comAuthenticationLevel="Connect"
    comImpersonationLevel="Impersonate"
/>
```

For a detailed description of each of these attributes, consult the SDK documentation.

sessionState. The <sessionState> tag configures session state. Session state is covered fully in Chapter 6. This tag supports the attributes shown in Table 20-7.

Table 20-7. Attributes of the <sessionState> tag

Attribute	Description
mode	Specifies where the session state is stored. It has four legal values. Off disables session state. Inproc, the default value, stores session state on the local server. StateServer stores session state on a remote server. SqlServer stores session state in a SQL Server database. One of the latter two values are required when running a web farm.
cookieless	Specifies whether cookieless sessions should be used. A value of true indicates that cookieless sessions should be used, in which case the session information will be munged as part of the URL. A value of false, the default, indicates that cookies will be used to maintain session state.

Table 20-7. Attributes of the <sessionState> tag (continued)

Attribute	Description
timeout	The number of minutes a session is idle before it is abandoned. The default is 20.
stateConnection-String	Specifies the connection string to the server where session is to be stored if mode is set to StateServer.
sqlConnection-String	Specifies the connection string to the SQL Server where session is to be stored if mode is set to SqlServer.

The default <sessionState> tag in *machine.config* is shown here:

```
<sessionState
    mode="InProc"
    stateConnectionString="tcpip=127.0.0.1:42424"
    stateNetworkTimeout="10"
    sqlConnectionString="data source=127.0.0.1;user id=sa;password="
    cookieless="false"
    timeout="20"
/>
```

trace. The <trace> tag configures the ASP.NET trace service. Tracing is described fully in Chapter 7. The <trace> tag supports the attributes shown in Table 20-8.

Table 20-8. Attributes of the <trace> tag

Attribute	Description
enabled	Enables or disables tracing. Legal values are true or false. The default is false.
requestLimit	The number of trace requests to store on the server.
pageOutput	true specifies that trace output is appended to each page. false, the default, specifies that trace output is accessible only through the trace utility.
traceMode	Specifies the sort order of the trace display. SortByTime, the default value, specifies that trace information is sorted in the order processed. SortByCategory specifies that trace information is displayed alphabetically by user-defined category.
localOnly	true, the default, specifies that the trace viewer is available only on the host web server. false specifies that the trace viewer is available remotely.

The default <trace> tag in *machine.config* is shown here:

```
<trace
    enabled="false"
    localOnly="true"
    pageOutput="false"
    requestLimit="10"
    traceMode="SortByTime"
/>
```

webControls. The <webControls> tag specifies the location of the script that is generated to be run client-side. It supports a single attribute, clientScriptsLocation.

The default `<webControls>` tag in *machine.config* is shown here:

```
<webControls
    clientScriptsLocation="/aspnet_client/{0}/{1}/"
/>
```

webServices. The `<webServices>` tag configures web services.

The default `<webServices>` tag in *machine.config* is shown here:

```
webServices>
    <protocols>
      <add name="HttpSoap"/>
      <add name="HttpPost"/>
      <add name="HttpGet"/>
      <add name="Documentation"/>
    </protocols>
    <soapExtensionTypes>
    </soapExtensionTypes>
    <soapExtensionReflectorTypes>
    </soapExtensionReflectorTypes>
    <soapExtensionImporterTypes>
    </soapExtensionImporterTypes>
    <wsdlHelpGenerator href="DefaultWsdlHelpGenerator.aspx" />
    <serviceDescriptionFormatExtensionTypes>
    </serviceDescriptionFormatExtensionTypes>
/webServices>
```

Security Settings

Many aspects of ASP.NET security are configurable, using the *machine.config* and *web.config* files. For a complete discussion of the security concepts configured here, please see Chapter 19.

There are several configuration sections controlling security. They are described in the following sections.

identity. The `<identity>` tag controls the identity of the application at runtime. Specifically, it enables and disables impersonation, and if impersonation is enabled, it allows you to specify the userName and password to use.

The `<identity>` tag supports three attributes shown in Table 20-9.

Table 20-9. Attributes of the <identity> tag

Attribute	Description
impersonate	Set to true to enable impersonation or false to disable impersonation.
userName	If impersonation is enabled, specifies the username to use.
password	If impersonation is enabled, specifies the password to use.

The <identity> tag in the default *machine.config* file looks like this:

```
<identity impersonate="false" userName="" password=""/>
```

authentication. The <authentication> tag controls authentication in ASP.NET applications. As is described fully in Chapter 19, authentication is the process whereby ASP.NET security verifies that a client making a request is who they say they are.

The <authentication> tag has one attribute, mode, which specifies the default authentication mode for the application. There are four legal values for mode, which are shown in Table 20-10.

Table 20-10. Values of the <authentication> tag's mode attribute

Mode value	Description
Windows	Sets the default authentication mode to Windows. Using this mode allows IIS to perform authentication.
Forms	Sets the default authentication mode to Forms. Using this mode, your application controls authentication through a login form created as part of the application.
Passport	Sets the default authentication mode to Passport. Passport is a centralized authentication service offered by Microsoft.
None	No authentication will be performed. This means that only anonymous users will access the site or the application will provide its own authentication.

The <authentication> tag also has two subtags. They are <forms> and <passport>.

The <forms> tag has five attributes, listed in Table 20-11.

Table 20-11. Attributes of the <forms> tag

Attribute	Description
name	Specifies the name of the HTTP cookie used for authentication. The default name is .ASPXAUTH.
loginUrl	Specifies the URL to which the request is redirected if there is no valid authentication.
protection	Four legal values. All, the default and recommended value, specifies that the application use both data validation and encryption to protect the authentication cookie. None specifies that the cookies will be neither validated nor encrypted, but will be available for personalization. Encryption specifies that the authentication cookie is encrypted but not validated. Validation specifies that the authentication cookie is validated, i.e., it is verified as not having been altered in transit between the client and the server.
timeout	The integer number of minutes after the last request that the cookie expires. Does not apply to persistent cookies. Default value is 30.
path	Specifies the path for cookies. Default value is / (backslash). Note that most browsers are case-sensitive and will not return a cookie if there is a path/case mismatch.

The <forms> tag also has one subtag, <credentials>. This subtag allows you to specify the type of password encryption used and also to define name/password pairs within the <user> subtag.

The `<credentials>` tag has a single attribute, `passwordFormat`. This attribute has three legal values, which are shown in Table 20-12.

Table 20-12. Values of the <credentials> tag's passwordFormat attribute

passwordFormat values	Description
Clear	Passwords are not encrypted.
MD5	Passwords are encrypted using the MD5 hash algorithm.
SHA1	Passwords are encrypted using the SHA1 hash algorithm.

The `<credentials>` tag enables you to specify user/password pairs using the `<user>` subtag. The `<user>` subtag has two attributes: `name` and `password`. Their values are the username and password, respectively.

The `<passport>` subtag of the `<authentication>` tag has a single attribute, `redirectUrl`. The value of this attribute is the URL to redirect to if the page requires authentication and the user has not signed on with Passport.

The `<authentication>` tag in the default *machine.config* file looks like this:

```
<authentication mode="Windows">
    <forms name=".ASPXAUTH"
            loginUrl="login.aspx"
            protection="All"
            timeout="30"
            path="/" >
        <credentials passwordFormat="SHA1">
                <!-- <user name="UserName" password="password"/> -->
        </credentials>
    </forms>
    <passport redirectUrl="internal" />
</authentication>
```

authorization. The `<authorization>` tag controls authorization in ASP.NET applications. Authorization is how ASP.NET security controls access to URL resources.

The `<authorization>` tag supports two subtags, `<allow>` and `<deny>`. Both subtags have the same set of three attributes, which are shown in Table 20-13. Those attributes are used to define access rules that are iterated at runtime. Access for a particular user is allowed or denied based on the first rule found that fits that user.

Table 20-13. Attributes of the <allow> and <deny> subtags

Attribute	Description
users	Comma-separated list of users either allowed or denied access. Question mark (?) allows anonymous users. Asterisk (*) allows all users.
roles	Comma-separated list of roles that are allowed or denied access.
verbs	Comma-separated list of HTTP verbs that are allowed or denied access. Registered verbs are GET, HEAD, POST, and DEBUG.

The default <authorization> tag in *machine.config* is shown here. It allows all users.

```
<authorization>
    <allow users="*" />
</authorization>
```

machineKey. The <machineKey> tag configures keys used for encryption and decryption of authentication cookies. This section can be declared at the server level in *machine.config* or in *web.config* files at the site or application root level. The <machineKey> tag supports three attributes, which are shown in Table 20-14.

Table 20-14. Attributes of the <machineKey> tag

Attribute	Description
validationKey	Specifies the key used for validation. Supports two types of values: AutoGenerate, the default value, specifies that ASP.NET will generate a random key. Alternatively, a value can be manually set to allow operation across a web farm. This value must be between 40 and 128 hexadecimal characters long (between 20 and 64 bytes).
decryptionKey	Specifies the key used for decrypting the cookie. Uses the same values as the validationKey.
validation	Specifies the type of encryption used for data validation. There are three legal values: SHA1 specifies SHA1 encryption, MD5 specifies MD5 encryption, and 3DES specifies Triple-DES encryption.

The default authorization in *machine.config* is shown here:

```
<machineKey validationKey="AutoGenerate"
            decryptionKey="AutoGenerate"
            validation="SHA1"/>
```

securityPolicy. The <securityPolicy> tag maps named security levels to policy files. This section can be declared at the server level in *machine.config* or in *web.config* files at the site or application root level.

The <securityPolicy> tag supports one subtag, <trustLevel>. This subtag is used to specify one security level name and an associated policy level. There is a separate <trustLevel> tag for each named security level.

The <trustLevel> tag supports the two attributes shown in Table 20-15.

Table 20-15. Attributes of the <trustLevel> tag

Attribute	Description
name	Defines a name to associate with the specified level of trust. Legal values are Full, High, Low, and None. If set to None, indicates file mapping for the Full security level.
policyFile	Specifies the policy level, relative to the directory containing *machine.config*, associated with the specified level of trust.

The default <securityPolicy> in *machine.config* is shown here:

```
securityPolicy>
    <trustLevel name="Full" policyFile="internal" />
```

```
        <trustLevel name="High" policyFile="web_hightrust.config" />
        <trustLevel name="Low"  policyFile="web_lowtrust.config" />
        <trustLevel name="None" policyFile="web_notrust.config" />
    /securityPolicy>
```

trust. The <trust> tag configures the code access security permissions for an application. This section can be declared at the server level in *machine.config* or in *web.config* files at the site or application root level.

The <trust> tag supports the two attributes shown in Table 20-16.

Table 20-16. Attributes of the <trust> tag

Attribute	Description
level	Specifies the security level under which the application will be run. Legal values are Full, High, Low, and None. **Required.**
originalUrl	Specifies an application's URL of origin. Optional.

The default <trust> in *machine.config* is shown here:

```
    <trust level="Full" originUrl="" />
```

location

The location section is used to apply configuration settings to specific resources. The <location> tag has a single attribute, path. The path attribute specifies a file or child directory (relative to the location of the current *web.config* file) to which specific configuration settings apply.

Suppose you had an application with custom error pages specified in the *web.config* file in the application virtual root directory. These custom error pages would apply to the entire application, including all child directories. Suppose further that there are two subdirectories under the virtual root directory, called *sub1* and *sub2*. *sub1* is to have the application-wide custom error handling, but *sub2* is to have its own specific error handling.

You could put another copy of *web.config* in *sub2* to override the custom error handling, but an alternative would be to use the <location> tag. You would add the following lines to the *web.config* file in the virtual root of the application:

```
    <location path="sub2">
        <system.web>
            <customErrors defaultRedirect="Sub2Error.htm" mode="RemoteOnly" >
                <error statusCode="404" redirect="err404-sub2.htm" />
                <error statusCode="407" redirect="err407-sub2.htm" />
            </customErrors >
        </system.web>
    </location>
```

Notice that the <system.web> tag must be reproduced within the location section.

The configuration settings contained in a location section will apply to the directory specified in the path attribute and also to any child directories of that directory, unless they are further overridden either by another *web.config* file or another location section.

If you want to apply specific configuration settings to a single file, that too can be done using a location section. Suppose the application root had a web page that requires special error handling. The following location section will accomplish that.

```
<location path="SpecialPage.aspx">
    <system.web>
        <customErrors defaultRedirect="SpecialError.htm"
                      mode="RemoteOnly" >
            <error statusCode="404" redirect="err404-spcl.htm" />
        </customErrors >
    </system.web>
</location>
```

Custom Configuration

In addition to all the predefined configuration sections, you can also add your own custom configuration sections. There are two different types of custom configuration sections you might wish to add:

- Sections that provide access to a collection of name/value pairs, similar to appSettings
- Sections that return any type of object

Both will be demonstrated here.

Name/value pairs

Back in Example 20-14, you added an <appSettings> key to store the database DSN string. Suppose you wanted to store DSNs for multiple databases, say one called Test (for testing purposes) and one called Content (to hold the production content). A custom configuration section returning a name/value pair would be one way to handle this situation.

The finished version of lines of code inserted into *web.config* is shown in Example 20-18. There are several steps to adding a custom configuration section that returns a name/value pair:

1. Determine which specific configuration file to add the custom section to. This will determine the scope, or visibility, of the custom section.

   Adding the section to *machine.config* will make it available to every application on that machine. Adding it to a *web.config* file in the virtual root directory of an application will make the section visible to that entire application, but to no other applications. Adding it to a *web.config* file in an application subdirectory will make it visible only to that subdirectory and its child subdirectories.

2. Declare the section handler by adding a line to the `<configSections>` section of the designated configuration file. This tells ASP.NET to expect a configuration section with the specified name, and also which class and assembly file to use to process the section.

   Add the highlighted lines between the `<configSections>` tags in Example 20-18 to the designated configuration file. If the file you are editing does not already have a pair of `<configSections>` tags, then you will need to add those as well.

3. Add the custom section itself to the configuration file. This consists of the highlighted lines in Example 20-18 between the `<altDB>` tags. This custom configuration section contains two entries, one named Test and the other named Content, each with its own value attribute.

Example 20-18. Custom sections in web.config

```
<configSections>
   <section name="altDB"
            type="System.Configuration.NameValueSectionHandler, System" />
</configSections>

<altDB>
   <add key="Test"
        value=" SERVER=Zeus;DATABASE=Test;UID=sa;PWD=secret;" />
   <add key="Content"
        value=" SERVER=Zeus;DATABASE=Content;UID=sa;PWD=secret;" />
</altDB>
```

Note that the type in the `<section>` tag is exactly the same as that provided for appSettings in the *machine.config* file. It specifies the NameValueSectionHandler class in the *System.dll* assembly file.

To read the contents of this custom configuration section, you again use a method from the ConfigurationSettings class, this time the GetConfig method. The code for a sample web page for doing this is shown in Example 20-19 in VB.NET and in Example 20-20 in C#. The C# version of the code in Example 20-20 shows only the script block, since the HTML is identical to the VB.NET version in Example 20-19.

Example 20-19. Reading custom configuration values in VB.NET, vbConfig-02.aspx

```
<%@ Page Language="vb" %>

<script runat="server">
   sub Page_Load(ByVal Sender as Object, _
                 ByVal e as EventArgs)
      if not IsPostBack then
         dim strTest as string
```

```
        dim strContent as string

        strTest = ConfigurationSettings.GetConfig("altDB")("Test")
        lblTest.Text = strTest

      lblContent.Text = _
              ConfigurationSettings.GetConfig("altDB")("Content")
      end if
   end sub
</script>

<html>
   <body>
   <form runat="server">

      <h1>Configuration</h1>

      <b>Test Database DSN:   </b>
      <asp:Label
         id="lblTest"
         runat="server"/>

      </br>
      <b>Content Database DSN:   </b>
      <asp:Label
         id="lblContent"
         runat="server"/>

   </form>
   </body>
</html>
```

Example 20-20. Reading custom configuration values in C#, csConfig-02.aspx

```
<%@ Page Language="cs" %>

<script runat="server">
   void Page_Load(Object Source, EventArgs E)
   {
      if (!IsPostBack)
      {
         string strTest;
         string strContent;

         strTest = ((NameValueCollection)
                 ConfigurationSettings.GetConfig("altDB"))["Test"];
         lblTest.Text = strTest;

         lblContent.Text = ((NameValueCollection)
                 ConfigurationSettings.GetConfig("altDB"))["Content"];
      }
   }</script>
```

The code in Examples 20-19 and 20-20 shows two equivalent ways of displaying the contents of the key value. One way is to assign the value to a string, then assign the string to the Text property of a label. The other way is to assign the value directly to the Text property. Although the latter technique is more concise, the former is often easier to debug.

In either case, notice the highlighted code in Examples 20-19 and 20-20. These are the calls to the GetConfig method. They are different for VB.NET and C#, and a bit confusing in both.

The GetConfig method takes a configuration section name as a parameter and returns an object of type NameValueCollection. The desired value in the collection is retrieved by using the key as an offset into the collection, using the get property syntax. In VB.NET, a property is retrieved by enclosing the property name in parentheses, and in C#, the property is retrieved using square brackets.

Notice that the C# code first casts, or converts, the value returned by GetConfig to type NamedValueCollection, while VB.NET does not. This is because C# does not support late binding, while VB.NET does by default. You can disable late binding in VB.NET (almost always a smart move) by setting the Strict attribute to true in the Page directive. You must then explicitly cast the object returned by GetConfig, just as in C#. This is shown in Example 20-21.

Example 20-21. Reading custom configuration values in VB.NET using early binding, vbConfig-02b. aspx

```
<script runat="server">
   sub Page_Load(ByVal Sender as Object, _
              ByVal e as EventArgs)
      if not IsPostBack then
         dim strTest as string
         dim strContent as string

         strTest = _
            CType(ConfigurationSettings.GetConfig("altDB"), _
               NameValueCollection)("Test")
         lblTest.Text = strTest

         lblContent.Text = _
            CType(ConfigurationSettings.GetConfig("altDB"), _
               NameValueCollection)("Content")
      end if
   end sub
</script>
```

Objects

appSettings and custom configuration sections are very useful. However, they both suffer from the same limitation of only being able to return a name/value pair. Sometimes it would be very useful to return an object.

For example, suppose you have a standard query into a database. You could store the query string in an appSettings tag, then open a database connection after retrieving the string. However, it would be much more convenient to store the query string in *web.config* and then have the configuration system return a DataSet directly.

To do this, you must add a <section> tag and a configuration section to the designated configuration file, just as with the custom section returning name/value pairs, described in the previous section.

Edit the *web.config* file used in the previous example and shown in Example 20-18, adding the lines of code highlighted in Example 20-22.

Example 20-22. Custom sections returning objects in web.config

```
<?xml version="1.0" encoding="utf-8" ?>
<configuration>

    <configSections>
        <section name="altDB"
              type="System.Configuration.NameValueSectionHandler, System" />
        <sectionGroup name="system.web">
            <section name="DataSetSectionHandler"
                    type="ProgAspNet.Handlers.DataSetSectionHandler,
                            vbSectionHandlers">
            </section>
        </sectionGroup>
    </configSections>

    <appSettings>
        <add key="appDSN"
            value=" SERVER=Zeus;DATABASE=Pubs;UID=sa;PWD=secret;" />
        <add key="appTitle" value="Programming ASP.NET" />
    </appSettings>

    <altDB>
        <add key="Test"
            value=" SERVER=Zeus;DATABASE=Test;UID=sa;PWD=secret;" />
        <add key="Content"
            value=" SERVER=Zeus;DATABASE=Content;UID=sa;PWD=secret;" />
    </altDB>

    <system.web>

    <!-- Custom config section returning an object -->
    <DataSetSectionHandler  str="Select BugID, Description from Bugs"  />


    </system.web>
</configuration>
```

In the <sectionGroup> section within the <configSections> section, a handler declaration is created for the DataSetSectionHandler within the system.web group. This specifies that elsewhere within the file, there will be a custom configuration section called DataSetSectionHandler within the system.web custom section. Furthermore, it also specifies that the class that will handle that configuration section is called Prog-AspNet.Handlers.DataSetSectionHandler, and that the class will be found in an assembly file called *vbSectionHandlers.dll* in the *\bin* directory.

Further down in the file, within the <system.web> section, there is in fact a section called DataSetSectionHandler. It has a single attribute, str. This is a string containing the SQL statement you wish to pass to the database.

Next you must create the ProgAspNet.Handlers.DataSetSectionHandler class and place it in a file called *DataSetSectionHandler.vb*. To do this, create a VB.NET source code file as shown in Example 20-23.

Example 20-23. Source code for section handler in VB.NET, DataSetSectionHandler.vb

```
Imports System
Imports System.Data
Imports System.Data.SqlClient
Imports System.XML
Imports System.Configuration

Namespace ProgAspNet.Handlers
   public class DataSetSectionHandler : _
        Implements IConfigurationSectionHandler

      public Function Create(parent as Object, _
                             configContext as Object, _
                             section as XmlNode) as Object _
         Implements IConfigurationSectionHandler.Create

         dim strSql as string
         strSql = section.Attributes.Item(0).Value

         dim connectionString as string = "server=Ath13; uid=sa; " & _
                     "pwd=password; database=Bugs"

         ' create the data set command object and the DataSet
         dim da as SqlDataAdapter = new SqlDataAdapter(strSql, _
                     connectionString)

         dim dsData as DataSet = new DataSet( )

         ' fill the data set object
         da.Fill(dsData,"Bugs")

         return dsData
      end Function
   end class
end NameSpace
```

Be sure to set the connection string to match your specific database. The server name and password are certainly different than that shown in Example 20-23.

The database aspects of the code in this example are covered thoroughly in Chapter 11 and won't be covered here in detail.

At the beginning of the Example 20-23 are several Imports statements (if written in C#, these would be using statements). Next a namespace is declared to contain the class. This is to prevent any ambiguity when calling the class.

In order for a class to be used as a configuration section handler, it must be derived from the IConfigurationSectionHandler interface. In VB.NET, this is implemented by using the Implements keyword. (In C#, this would be indicated with a colon between the class or method name and the class or interface being inherited.)

A full discussion of object-oriented concepts such as inheritance, base classes, and interfaces is beyond the scope of this book. For now, you should just know that an interface acts as a contract that the implementing class must fulfill. The interface may, for example, dictate the signature of methods that the implementing class must implement, or it may dictate which properties the class must provide.

The IConfigurationSectionHandler interface has only a single method, Create. Therefore our implementing class must implement the Create method with the specified signature. The three parameters are dictated by the interface. The first two parameters are rarely used and will not be further discussed here. The third parameter is the XML data from the configuration file.

The XML node is parsed and the value of the first item in the Attributes collection is assigned to a string variable in this line:

```
strSql = section.Attributes.Item(0).Value
```

Once the SQL string is in hand, the connection string is hard-coded, a SqlDataAdapter object is instantiated and executed, and the DataSet is filled. Then the DataSet is returned.

Before this class can be used it must be compiled. Open a command prompt by clicking on the Start button, then Microsoft Visual Studio .NET → Visual Studio .NET Tools → Visual Studio .NET Command Prompt. Use the cd command to make the application virtual root the current directory. This assumes that the virtual root directory already has a child directory called \bin. If not, you'll have to make one. Then enter the following command line:

```
vbc /t:library /out:bin\vbSectionHandlers.dll /r:system.dll,System.data.dll,System.xml.dll
DataSetSectionHandler.vb
```

Using command-line compilers is explained in some detail in Chapter 16. Here the target type of output is set to be library, i.e., a DLL. The name of the output file to be placed in the bin directory will be *vbSectionHandlers.dll*. Notice that three DLL files are referenced. The input source file is *DataSetSectionHandler.vb*. When the source file is compiled, you will have the output DLL in the \bin directory, where the classes it contains will automatically be available to the application.

The web page shown in Example 20-24 (in VB.NET) shows how to utilize this configuration section.

Example 20-24. Section handler demonstration in VB.NET, vbConfig-03.aspx

```
<%@ Page Language="vb"  %>
<%@ Import namespace="System.Data" %>
<%@ Import namespace="System.Data.SqlClient" %>

<script runat="server">
   sub Page_Load(ByVal Sender as Object, _
               ByVal e as EventArgs)
      if not IsPostBack then
         CreateDataGrid( )
      end if
   end sub

   sub CreateDataGrid( )
      dim dsGrid as new DataSet
      dsGrid = _
         ConfigurationSettings.GetConfig( _
            "system.web/DataSetSectionHandler")
      dg.DataSource=dsGrid.Tables(0)
      dg.DataBind( )
   end sub
</script>

<html>
   <body>
   <form runat="server">

      <h1>Configuration</h1>

      <asp:DataGrid
         id="dg"
         runat="server"/>

   </form>
   </body>
</html>
```

The page in Example 20-24 first imports two namespaces necessary for working with the SQL Server database. The interesting work is done in the CreateDataGrid method. There, rather than supply a DSN and SQL query string, a call is made to the

GetConfig method of the ConfigurationSettings class, which returns a DataSet object directly. Then the DataSet object is set as the DataSource of the DataGrid control, and the control is data bound. The parameter of the GetConfig method is a string containing the name of the section containing the configuration settings. Notice the syntax with the section name (system.web) separated from the subsection name (DataSetSectionHandler) by a slash.

Deploying the Application

It is very simple to deploy an ASP.NET application, especially when compared to classic ASP. There is no registering of components in the Registry, no need to stop and start the server or the operating system, no problem with multiple versions of the same DLL for different applications, and no more DLL hell.

That's the good news. There is no bad news, especially if you do not need to deploy assemblies globally.

ASP.NET derives all this deployment bliss by virtue of being part of the .NET Framework. The deployment features mentioned earlier are common to all applications developed under the .NET Framework.

There are actually two different ways to deploy applications. The first, *XCOPY deployment*, is so simple as to cause experienced developers to ask, "Is that all there is to it?" It provides all the deployment benefits of .NET except for the ability to deploy assemblies globally (i.e., to use application code modules for multiple applications). In order to implement globally available code modules, you will use *global deployment*. Both deployment methods are described in more detail in the following sections.

Assemblies

An *assembly* is the .NET unit of versioning and deploying code modules. Strictly speaking, an assembly consists of Portable Executable (PE) files. PE files can be either DLLs or EXEs. These PE files are in exactly the same format as normal Windows PE files.

In ASP.NET, an assembly will typically consist of a single DLL, although it may consist of multiple files. Assemblies appear to the user to be a single file.

Assemblies are *self-describing* because they contain *metadata* that fully describes the assembly and the classes, methods, and types it contains. One of the files in the assembly contains a *manifest* as part of the metadata, which details exactly what is in the assembly. This includes identification information (name, version, etc.), a list of the types and resources in the assembly, a map to connect public types with the implementing code, and a list of assemblies referenced by this assembly.

An application consists of all the files and resources in an application virtual root directory and in all the subdirectories underneath the virtual root. One of the standard subdirectories found in nearly all applications is the \bin directory, sometimes called the *application assembly cache*. All the assemblies for the application are typically placed in this directory.

If an assembly file is placed in the application assembly cache, then all the classes contained in that assembly are automatically registered with the application. There is no developer or user action required for this registration to occur. Any class, method, or type defined in the \bin directory is available to the rest of the application.

Assemblies are not loaded into memory unless and until they are needed. When an assembly is needed, the CLR does not actually load the assembly itself into memory. If it did, then that assembly would be locked until the application was stopped. This would require the application to be stopped and restarted every time a new version of the assembly was to be installed. Instead, a *shadow copy* of the DLL is created in memory. This shadow copy is then locked, leaving the original assembly file unlocked.

The CLR constantly monitors the assembly cache to see if any new assemblies have been added or if any of the existing assemblies have changed. If a new assembly is detected, the classes it contains are automatically registered with the application. If a change to an existing application is detected, than all pending requests to the old version of the assembly are allowed to complete but all new requests are handled by the new version. When the last request to the old version is finished, then the shadow copy of that version is allowed to expire and the transition is complete.

Note that ASP.NET is configured to prohibit access to the \bin directory. This prevents anyone from tampering with your assemblies.

XCOPY Deployment

All that is necessary to deploy most ASP.NET applications—in fact, to deploy most .NET applications—is to copy the new files to the proper directories on the proper machine, overwriting any previous versions of files if they exist. This is referred to as *XCOPY deployment*.

XCOPY is a command-prompt command that originated in the DOS days and has been enhanced for use in modern networks. It is used to copy files and directories from one location to another. The basic syntax is:

```
XCOPY source destination switches
```

Both *source* and *destination* can be either filenames or directories. There is full support for wildcards. There are a multitude of switches available that control such things as resetting (or not) the archive bit, copying (or not) any empty subdirectories, controlling the screen display during copying, and copying (or not) security information about the files. For a full list of the switches available, go to a command prompt and enter:

```
XCOPY /?
```

 All command-prompt commands (known colloquially as DOS commands, even though DOS is no more) are case-insensitive.

It is not required to actually use the XCOPY command to copy the files. You can copy the files in any manner you wish, including DOS commands from the command prompt, dragging and dropping in Windows Explorer, or FTP over the Internet. It is called XCOPY deployment to convey the essential fact that all that is required to deploy is to copy the application virtual root and all its subdirectories.

The CLR automatically handles any changes to application files seamlessly and invisibly to the user. If either the *global.asax* or *web.config* file (or their code-behinds) changes, the application is automatically restarted. If a page, web service, or custom or user control file changes, the next request to come in to the application just gets the new version. If an assembly file changes, the CLR handles the transition from old version to new for any pending requests. It doesn't get much easier than this.

Since all the files necessary to the application are contained within the application virtual root and its child directories, this implies that if two different applications on a server use a DLL of the same name, they are two independent copies of the file. They may be identical copies, but they don't have to be. It is possible to have two or more different versions of a DLL on the same machine, each in its own application directory structure, with no conflict between applications. This relegates DLL Hell to something that old programmers will tell war stories about, like 64k byte boundaries or running out of conventional memory in DOS.

Global Deployment

In the previous section "XCOPY Deployment," it was stated that most applications are deployed by simply copying files to the proper directory. The exception occurs when you wish to use the same assembly in more than one application. In this case, you use *global deployment*.

There are many scenarios in which it might be desirable to have a common assembly file accessible to multiple applications. A firm might have two different web sites on a server, both providing access to the same database. One web site is free of charge and open to the public but of limited functionality, while the other is fully functional, requiring a paid subscription. Since both sites access the same database, they will have common database query routines. They might also have common login routines. Using the same assembly to contain those common routines will enhance maintainability. Another scenario might be a web-hosting firm that has many web sites running on a server. They might want to offer some functionality to all their client web sites. Encapsulating this functionality in a globally available assembly would make this easy to offer and maintain.

Another consideration is versioning. When assemblies are local to an application, then each application can have its own version of common assemblies. The .NET Framework also allows for global assemblies to have multiple versions. Each application making use of the global assembly can either specify the version it wants to use or take the latest version. By specifying the version, an application will not break if a newer version of the assembly introduces signature changes or bugs.

In order to provide global availability of an assembly, it must be installed to the *global assembly cache*, or GAC. The GAC is a machine-wide location for code that is to be shared among multiple applications on that machine. Typically, it is physically located at *c:\winnt\assembly*. However, you cannot just copy an assembly file to that directory and have it be made available to all the applications. The assembly needs to be registered with the GAC, using the .NET command-line utility *GacUtil.exe*.

In order to make an assembly file suitable for inclusion in the GAC, it needs to have assembly information compiled into it. This is done using `Assembly` attributes. These `Assembly` attributes can either be included in the same source code file as the class(es) being compiled into the assembly, or in a separate source code file that is compiled into the assembly along with the class source code file(s). The format of the attributes is dependent on the language used. In VB.NET they look like this:

```
<Assembly:attributeName(attributeValue)>
```

and in C# the `Assembly` attribute looks like:

```
[Assembly:attributeName(attributeValue)]
```

where *attributeName* is the name of the `Assembly` attribute, and *attributeValue* is the string value assigned to the attribute. So, for example, if assigning the `AssemblyVersionAttribute`, it would look like the following in VB.NET:

```
<Assembly: AssemblyVersionAttribute ("1.0.3.101")>
```

and like this in C#:

```
[Assembly: AssemblyVersionAttribute ("1.0.3.101")]
```

If the project was developed using Visual Studio .NET, then this assembly information is contained in a file called *AssemblyInfo.cs* if the project was developed in C#, or *AssemblyInfo.vb* if the project was developed in VB.NET.

Table 20-17 lists the available `Assembly` attributes with a brief description.

Table 20-17. Assembly attributes

Attribute	Description
AssemblyCompanyAttribute	String containing company name.
AssemblyConfigurationAttribute	String configuration, such as Retail or Debug. Not used by CLR
AssemblyCopyrightAttribute	String containing copyright information.
AssemblyCultureAttribute	Field indicating culture supported by the assembly.
AssemblyDefaultAliasAttribute	String containing default alias for the assembly. Can contain a friendly name.
AssemblyDelaySignAttribute	Boolean indicating delayed application of digital signature.
AssemblyDescriptionAttribute	String containing short description of the assembly.
AssemblyFileVersionAttribute	String containing Win32 file version number. Defaults to assembly version.
AssemblyFlagsAttribute	Flag indicating the kind of side-by-side execution allowed.
AssemblyInformationalVersionAttribute	String containing version information not used by the CLR.
AssemblyKeyFileAttribute	String containing name of file with either public key signature if using delayed signing, or both public and private keys. Filename is relative to output file path, not source file path.
AssemblyKeyNameAttribute	String containing key container.
AssemblyProductAttribute	String containing product information.
AssemblyTitleAttribute	String containing friendly name for the assembly.
AssemblyTrademarkAttribute	String containing trademark information.
AssemblyVersionAttribute	A numeric version representation, in the form *major.minor.build.revision*.

If you are using Assembly attributes in a source file, you must also reference the System.Reflection namespace, using the Imports keyword in VB.NET or the using keyword in C#.

In order for an assembly to be included in the GAC, it must have a *strong name*. This is a cryptographically secure name that identifies an assembly by its name, version number, and a public key. A strong name can be generated using the .NET command-line utility *sn.exe*. To use this utility, enter at a command prompt:

```
sn -k outputDirectory\strongNameFile.snk
```

where outputDirectory is the path to the application virtual root directory, and strongNameFile.snk is the name of the file that will contain the public and private keys comprising the digital signature.

Having generated the strong name, you would add an Assembly attribute providing that strong name. In VB.NET, it appears as follows:

```
<Assembly: AssemblyKeyFileAttribute ("outputDirectory\strongNameFile.snk ")>
```

and in C#, it takes the form:

```
[Assembly: AssemblyKeyFileAttribute ("outputDirectory\strongNameFile.snk ")]
```

Once all this is in place, you can use *GacUtil.exe* to add the assembly to the GAC. The syntax is:

```
gacutil /i pathToDLL\myDLL.DLL
```

where *pathToDLL* is the path to the directory containing the assembly file, and *myDLL.DLL* is the name of the assembly file.

The *GacUtil.exe* utility has several command-line switches. For a complete list, enter at a command prompt:

```
gacutil /?
```

Some of the more common switches are described in Table 20-18.

Table 20-18. Some common switches to GacUtil.exe

Switch	Description
/i	Installs an assembly to the GAC.
/u	Uninstalls an assembly from the GAC. Note that if the name of the assembly to be uninstalled has no qualifying information, such as version, then all assemblies of that name will be uninstalled.
/l	Lists all the assemblies installed in the GAC.

In order to use a global assembly in applications, it must be registered in the *machine.config* file. To add the above assembly to the *machine.config* file, add the following line to the <configuration><system.web><compilation><assemblies> section:

```
<add assembly="myDLL, Version=1.0.3.101, Culture=neutral, PublicKeyToken=nnnnnnnn"/>
```

where *nnnnnnnn* is obtained from GacUtil by running:

```
GacUtil /l
```

from the command line, finding myDLL in the listing, and copying the public key token into place.

Relational Database Technology: A Crash Course

ADO.NET can be used to access data from any data source: relational databases, object databases, flat files, and text files. The vast majority of web applications, however, will access data from a relational database such as SQL Server. While one can certainly write an entire book on relational databases and another on SQL, the essentials of these technologies are not hard to understand.

 All of the examples in this appendix assume you are working with SQL Server and that the flavor of SQL you are using is T-SQL. Users of other relational databases will find that the lessons learned here transfer well to their environment, but be especially careful with applications like Access that use a different variation of SQL.

A *database* is a repository of data. A *relational database* organizes your data into tables that are "related" to one another. For example, one table might contain a customer's information and a second table might contain information about orders. The tables are related to one another because each customer has certain orders, and each order is owned by an individual customer.

Similarly, you might have a table of cars and a second table of car parts. Each part can be in one or more cars, and each car is made up of parts. Or you might have a table for bugs and a table for developers. Each bug is owned by one developer, and each developer has a list of bugs he owns.

Tables, Records, and Columns

The principal division of a database is into tables. Tables, like classes, should describe one logical entity and all of what you know about that entity.

Every table in a relational database is organized into rows, where each row represents a single record. The rows are organized into columns. All the rows in a table have the same column structure. For example, the Bugs table described in Appendix B (and used in Chapter 11) might have columns for the bugID, the ID of the person reporting the bug, the date the bug was reported, the status of the bug, and so forth.

It is common to make an analogy between tables and classes, and between rows and objects. The Bugs table, for example, tells you a great deal about the contents of a Bug, just as a Bug class tells you about the state and structure of a Bug. Each row in the Bug table describes a particular Bug, much as an object does.

This analogy is compelling, but limited. There is only an imperfect match between relational databases and objects, and one of the challenges facing an object-oriented programmer is overcoming the design differences between the object model, on the one hand, and the database model, on the other.

Relational databases are very good at defining the relationship among objects, but are not good at capturing the behavior of the types described in the table. The "impedance mismatch" between relational databases and object-oriented programs has led some developers to try to create object databases. While this has met with some success, the vast majority of data is still stored in relational databases because of their great flexibility, performance, and ability to be searched quickly and easily.

Typically, the interface between the back-end relational database and the objects in the application is managed by creating a database interface layer of objects that negotiate between the creation of objects and the storage of information in the database tables.

Table Design

To understand the issues in table design, consider the Bug database described in Chapter 11. You need to know who reported each bug, and it would be very useful to know the email address, phone number, and other identifying information about each person as well.

You can imagine a form in which you display details about a given bug, and in that detail page you offer the email address and phone number of the "reporter" so that the developer working on the bug can contact that person.

You could store the identifying information with each bug, but that would be very inefficient. If John Doe reported 50 bugs, you'd rather not repeat John Doe's email address and phone number in 50 records. It's also a data maintenance nightmare. If John Doe changes his email address and phone number, you'd have to make the change in 50 places.

Instead, you'll create a second table called People, in which each row represents a single person. In the People table there will be a column for the PersonID. Each person will have a unique ID, and that field will be marked as the *primary key* for the Person table. A primary key is the column or combination of columns that uniquely identifies a record in a given table.

The Bugs table will use the PersonID as a *foreign key*. A foreign key is a column (or combination of columns) that is a primary (or otherwise unique) key from a different table. The Bug table uses the PersonID, which is the primary key in People, to identify which person reported the bug. If you need later to determine the email address for that person, you can use the PersonID to look up the Person record in the People table and that will give you all the detailed information about that person.

By "factoring out" the details of the person's address into a Person table, you reduce the redundant information in each Bug record. This process of taking out redundant information from your tables is called *normalization*.

Normalization

Normalization not only makes your use of the database more efficient, it reduces the likelihood of data corruption. If you kept the person's email address both in the People table and also in the Bug table, you would run the risk that a change in one table might not be reflected in the other. Thus, if you changed the person's email address in the Person table, that change might not be reflected in every row in the Bugs table (or it would be a lot of work to make sure that it was reflected). By keeping only the PersonID in Bugs, you are free to change the email address or other personal information in People, and the change will automatically be reflected for each bug.

Just as VB and C# programmers want the compiler to catch bugs at compile time rather than at runtime, database programmers want the database to help them avoid data corruption. A compiler helps avoid bugs by enforcing the rules of the language. For example, in C# you can't use a variable you've not defined. SQL Server and other modern relational databases help you avoid bugs by enforcing constraints that you create. For example, the People database marks the PersonID as a primary key. This creates a primary key constraint in the database, which ensures that each PersonID is unique. If you were to enter a person named Jesse Liberty with the PersonID of LIBE, and then you were to try to add Stacey Liberty with a PersonID of LIBE, the database would reject the second record because of the primary key constraint. You would need to give one of these people a different, and unique, personID.

Declarative Referential Integrity

Relational databases use *Declarative Referential Integrity* (DRI) to establish constraints on the relationships among the various tables. For example, you might declare a constraint on the Bug table that dictates that no Bug may have a PersonID unless that PersonID represents a valid record in People. This helps you avoid two types of mistakes. First, you cannot enter a record with an invalid PersonID. Second, you cannot delete a Person record if that PersonID is used in any Bug. The integrity of your data and the relationships among records is thus protected.

SQL

The language of choice for querying and manipulating databases is *Structured Query Language*, often referred to as SQL. SQL is often pronounced "sequel." SQL is a declarative language, as opposed to a procedural language, and it can take a while to get used to working with a declarative language if you are used to languages like VB or C#.

Most programmers tend to think in terms of a sequence of steps: "Find me all the bugs, then get the reporter's ID, then use that ID to look up that user's records in People, then get me the email address." In a declarative language, you declare the entire query, and the query engine returns a set of results. You are not thinking about a set of steps; rather, you are thinking about designing and "shaping" a set of data. Your goal is to make a single declaration that will return the right records. You do that by creating temporary "wide" tables that include all the fields you need and then filtering for only those records you want. "Widen the Bugs table with the People table, joining the two on the PersonID, then filter for only those that meet my criteria."

The heart of SQL is the *query*. A query is a statement that returns a set of records from the database. For example, you might like to see all of the BugIDs and Bug Descriptions in the Bugs table whose status is Open. To do so you would write:

```
Select BugID, BugDescription from Bugs where status = 'open'
```

SQL is capable of much more powerful queries. For example, suppose the Quality Assurance manager would like to know the email address for everyone who has reported a high-priority bug that was resolved in the past 10 days. You might create a query such as:

```
Select emailAddress from Bugs b
join People p on b.personID = p.personID
where b.priority='high'
and b.status in ('closed', 'fixed','NotABug')
and b.dateModified < DateAdd(d,-10,GetDate())
```

 GetDate returns the current date, and DateAdd returns a new date computed by adding or subtracting an interval from a specified date. In this case, you are returning the date computed by subtracting 10 days from the current date.

At first glance, you appear to be selecting the email address from the Bugs table, but that is not possible because the Bugs table does not have an email address. The key phrase is:

```
Bugs b join People p on b.personID = p.personID
```

It is as if the join phrase creates a temporary table that is the width of both the Bugs table and the People table joined together. The on keyword dictates how the tables

---

are joined. In this case, the tables are joined on the personID: each record in Bugs (represented by the alias b) is joined to the appropriate record in People (represented by the alias p) when the personID fields match in both records.

Joining Tables

When you join two tables you can say either "get every record that exists in either," (this is called an *outer join*) or you can say, as I've done here, "get only those records that exist in both tables (called an *inner join*).

 Inner joins are the default, and so writing join is the same as writing inner join.

The inner join shown above says: get only the records in People that match the records in Bugs by having the same value in the PersonID field (on b.PersonID = p. PersonID).

The where clause further constrains the search to those records whose priority is high, whose status is one of the three that constitute a resolved Bug (closed, fixed, or not a bug), and that were last modified within the past ten days.

Using SQL to Manipulate the Database

SQL can be used not only for searching for and retrieving data but also for creating, updating, and deleting tables and generally managing and manipulating both the content and the structure of the database. For example, you can update the Priority of a bug in the Bugs table with this statement:

```
Update Bugs set priority = 'high' where BugID = 101
```

For a full explanation of SQL and details on using it well, take a look at *Transact SQL Programming*, by Kevin Kline et al., O'Reilly & Associates.

Bug Database Architecture

The Bug database consists of three primary tables (Bugs, BugHistory, and People) and four secondary (lookup) tables (lkProduct, lkRoles, lkSeverity, and lkStatus). To keep the examples as simple as possible, these tables have been stripped down to the absolute essentials.

Table B-1 shows the structure of the Bugs table and Table B-2 shows the structure of the BugHistory table. Table B-3 shows the structure of the People table.

Table B-1. Structure of the Bugs table

Column	Type	Notes
BugID	int (identity)	Uniquely identifies each bug in the database.
Product	int	Foreign key into lkProducts (identifies the unique product).
Version	varChar	Text description of the version number (e.g., 0.1.2).
Description	varChar	Text description of the bug as entered by the person recording the bug.
Reporter	int	Foreign key into People (ID of the person reporting the bug).

Table B-2. Structure of the BugHistory table

Column	Type	Notes
BugHistoryID	int (identity)	Uniquely identifies each bug history record.
BugID	int	Foreign key into Bugs table. This column combined with BugHistoryID is sufficient to track all the updates for a given bug.
Status	int	Foreign key into lkStatus—identifies the current status of the bug (e.g., open, closed, etc.).
Severity	int	Foreign key into lkSeverity—identifies the current severity of the bug (e.g., high, medium, low, etc.).
Response	varChar	Text description of the action taken at this step in the progress of the bug resolution.
Owner	int	Foreign key into People—identifies the current "owner" of the bug (typically a developer while bug is unresolved).
DateStamp	dateTime	Date and time stamp for the current entry.

Table B-3. People

Column	Type	Notes
PersonID	int (identity)	Uniquely identifies each person's record.
FullName	varChar	Text of person's full name (title, first, last and suffix: e.g., Mr. John Galt, Jr.).
eMail	varChar	Optional text field for email address. Cannot be null, can be blank.
Phone	varChar	Optional text field for telephone number. Cannot be null, can be blank.
Role	int	Foreign key into lkRoles, designates the person's current role within the organization (e.g., QA, Developer, etc.).

Each record in the BugHistory table has a Status value. The possible values for the Status field are captured in lkStatus, as shown in Table B-4.

Table B-4. Possible status values

Status	Notes
Open	The bug has been reported but not yet assigned to anyone to fix.
Assigned	Assigned (typically to a developer) but not yet accepted by that developer.
Accepted	Accepted (typically by a developer) but not yet resolved.
NYD	**Not Yet Deployed**: the developer thinks he has fixed it but has not yet deployed it for testing.
NAB	**Not A Bug**: the developer alleges that this is the intended behavior or is otherwise to specification.
NR	**Not Reproducible**: the developer cannot reproduce the behavior.
NPTF	**No Plan To Fix**: the developer agrees that the bug is as shown, but believes that the organization ought not fix it.
Defer	Without commenting on whether the bug is real or not, the developer suggests deferring all future action on the bug.
Fixed	The developer has deployed a fix for the bug but it has not yet been closed by QA.
Closed	Closed by QA.

You can certainly imagine other status values, but these will get you started. The work flow envisioned is that a bug is reported by entering the bug in the system. QA reads through the Open bugs and assigns a bug to a developer. The developer asks for all the bugs with his ID as owner and the status of Assigned and accepts the bugs. He then works on the bugs and marks them one of NYD, NAB, NR, NPTF, Defer, or (ideally) Fixed. QA then checks the results and either resets the status (e.g., marks a bug from Defer back to Assigned), reassigns the bug, or marks it Closed.

Table B-5 illustrates the lkStatus table structure.

Table B-5. lkStatus

Column	Type	Notes
StatusID	int (identity)	Uniquely identifies each status record.
StatusDescription	VarChar	One of the values shown in the left column in Table B-4.

Table Relationships

With these tables, you are able to create a working bug database.

Any two tables will typically have one of the following relationships:

One to Many
> Each developer may "own" multiple bugs

Many to One
> The reciprocal relationship of one to many. The developer is in a one-to-many relationship with bugs, and bugs are in a many-to-one relationship with developers

Many to Many
> You can imagine a system that allows more than one person to own a bug. Perhaps the bug is owned by a developer and also a marketing person. Each of these people may also own more than one bug. Thus, bugs and people would be in a many-to-many relationship. In the current design, we do not allow this relationship between bugs and people.

The relationships among the tables is shown in Table B-6.

Table B-6. The relationship among the tables

Primary	Key	Foreign	Key	Relationship
BugHistory	BugID	Bugs	BugID	One bug to many history records.
BugHistory	Status	lkStatus	StatusID	Each BugHistory has one status.
BugHistory	Severity	lkSeverity	SeverityID	Each BugHistory has one severity.
BugHisotry	Owner	People	PersonID	Each BugHistory has one owner.
Bug	Reporter	People	PersonID	Each Bug has one Reporter.
Bug	Product	lkProduct	ProductID	Each Bug has one Product.
People	Role	lkRoles	RoleID	Each person has one Role.

Index

Symbols

@ (at sign), creating verbatim strings, 503
= (equal sign) and attribute/value pairs, 237
> (greater-than) default value for
      NextMonthText property, 248
≥ (greater-than-or-equal-to) navigation
      symbol, 148, 150
≥ ≥ (greater-than-or-equal-to twice)
      navigation symbol, 151
< (less-than) default value for
      PrevMonthText property, 248
≤ (less-than-or-equal-to) navigation
      symbol, 148
? (question mark)
    conditional operator, 578
    query strings and, 389
<%# syntax, 388

Numbers

{0} symbol (substitution parameter), 371

A

<a> tag, 46
    HyperLink controls and, 71
AboveNormal value (CacheItemPriority
      enumeration), 787
AbsBottom value (ImageAlign property), 137
AbsMiddle value (ImageAlign property), 137
absolute URLs and ImageUrl property, 137
AbsoluteExpiration parameter (Add/Insert
      methods), 784–786

AcceptChanges()
    DataRow class, 433
    DataSet class, 431
    DataTable class, 432
AcceptChangesDuringFill property
      (DataAdapter class), 433
Accepted value (Status field), 905
Access Control Lists (ACLs) and file
      authorization, 830
Access database, using bug database
      with, 438–441
access modifiers, 201
AccessKey property, 55
ACID test, requirements of transactions, 505
ACLs (Access Control Lists) and file
      authorization, 830
<Ad> tag (AdRotator control), 143
AdCreated event (AdRotator control), 142,
      146
AdCreatedEventArgs class, 146
Add Reference/Add Web Reference options
      (Solution Explorer), 740
<add> section of <httpHandlers>
      section, 877
Add()
    adding columns to DataTable
      objects, 469, 471
    Cache class method, 774
      CacheItemRemovedCallback
      parameter, 787
      scavenging via Priority parameter, 786
      time dependencies, 784
    overloading, 90, 474

We'd like to hear your suggestions for improving our indexes. Send email to *index@oreilly.com*.

NameValueSectionHandler class, 872, 886
NavigateUrl property
    AdCreateEventArgs class, 147
    HyperLink control, 69, 375
<NavigateUrl> tag (AdRotator control), 143
navigating pages and DataGrid control, 422
Nested property (DataRelation class), 461
.NET Framework, 2–3
_new value
    Target property (AdRotator control), 142
    Target property (HyperLink control), 69
NewPageIndex property (DataGrid
        control), 423
NewRow() (DataTable class), 432, 472
NextMonthText property (Calendar
        control), 149, 247
    avoiding syntax problems using character
        entities, 248
NextPrev mode, 423
NextPrevFormat property (Calendar
        control), 149, 247
NextPrevStyle property (Calendar
        control), 152, 248
NextResult() (DataReader class), 434
NoCache value (HttpCacheability
        enumeration), 796
/nologo parameter (WSDL utility), 725
None value
    authentication mode, 808, 881
    CalendarSelectionMode
        enumeration, 150
    OutputCacheLocation enumeration, 759,
        796
    Rule enumeration, 476
Normal value (CacheItemPriority
        enumeration), 787
normalization process for databases, 901
NotRemovable value (CacheItemPriority
        enumeration), 787
NotSet value (ImageAlign property), 137
NotSupported value (TransactionOption
        enumeration), 690
NPTF (No Plan To Fix) value (Status
        field), 905
NR (Not Reproducible) value (Status
        field), 905
NTFS file system, 806
    file authorization and, 830
    Windows authentication and, 811
NTLM (NT Lan Manager)
        challenge/response (Integrated
        Windows authentication), 815

NumericPages mode, 423
NYD (Not Yet Deployed) value (Status
        field), 905

O

object caching, 754, 767–794
    Cache class functionality, 774
    cached item dependencies, 779–784
    callback methods, support for, 787–794
    file change dependencies, 776–779
    scavenging, 786
    time dependencies, 784–786
object databases vs. relational databases, 900
object model, ADO.NET, 429–434
objects
    binding to controls, 336–338
    declaring in global.asax file, 863
    examining value of, 285
    overloading methods, 90
    returning, using custom configuration
        sections, 888–893
    vs. rows, 900
Off value (mode attribute of
        <sessionstate>), 231, 232
OLE DB managed providers, 438–441
OleDbCommand class, 433
    invoking stored procedures with explicit
        parameters, 490
OleDbCommandBuilder, 564
OleDbConnection class, 433
OleDbDataAdapter class, 433, 439
OleDbDataReader class, 434, 454
    enhancing performance with, 804
OnAdCreated attribute, 146
    event handler for, 143
OnBubbleEvent attribute, 21
OnCancelCommand attribute (DataGrid
        control), 590
    implementing event handler for, 594, 599
OnCheckedChanged attribute, 21, 76, 79
OnClick attribute, 21, 51
    Button control and, 67
    vs. OnServerClick attribute, 40
OnClick(), 646
onCompletedGetHistory(), 750
onCompletedGetName(), 750
onCompletedGetPrice(), 750
OnDataBinding attribute, 21
OnDeleteCommand attribute (DataGrid
        control), 602

RadioButtonList control, 71, 80, 98–102
  binding ArrayLists to, 339–348
  in bug reporting form, 302–304
  C# code example, 99, 343
  code-behind source file (C#), 344–348
  font samples, setting attributes of, 113
  font sizes, setting, 125–128
  non-postback event, 26
  RequiredFieldValidator control and, 303
  Table control and, 120
  transactions, choosing, 509
  VB.NET code example, 100
RaisePostBackEvent(), 236
RaisePostDataChangedEvent(), 236
RangeValidator control, 299, 322–324
  code example, 323
rbl_SelectedIndexChanged event
          handler, 227
ReadOnly property (TextBox control), 64
read-write application state, use with
          caution, 222
ReadXML() (DataSet class), 431
ReadXMLSchema() (DataSet class), 431
record locking to prevent data
          corruption, 549
RedirectFromLoginPage(), 820, 826
Redirection status codes, 271
redirectUrl attribute of
          <passport> section, 882
/reference: command-line switch, 237
Reference directive, 241
/reference:<file list> parameter for compiling
          DLLs, 711
reformatting code, disabling option for, 247
Register directive, 241
  custom controls, registering with web
          pages, 633
  user controls, registering with web
          pages, 610, 615
Registers window, 289
RegularExpressionValidator control, 299,
          324–326
  code example, 325
RejectChanges()
  DataRow class, 433
  DataSet class, 431
  DataTable class, 432
relational data
  for Bugs, BugHistory, and People
          tables, 906
  code-behind page, source code
          for, 462–468

creating objects to model
          relationships, 458–468
  database technology for, 899–903
  displaying in data grid, 442–444
Relations property (DataSet class), 431, 458
relative URLs and ImageUrl property, 136
RemoteOnly value of mode attribute, 294,
          875
<remove> section of <httpHandlers>
          section, 877
Remove() (Cache class), 773
RemoveAt() (Cells collection), 385
Removed (CacheItemRemovedReason
          enumeration), 793
RemovedCallback(), 787–793
Render(), 235
  composite controls and, 657, 661–664
  custom controls and, 636–638
RenderBeginTag(), 637, 663
RenderEndTag(), 637, 663
RepeatColumns property
  CheckBoxList control, 84
  DataList control, 578
RepeatDirection property
  CheckBoxList control, 84
  DataList control, 578
Repeater control, 53, 349–351, 569–576
  binding data to, 568, 574–576
  postback event, 26
  templates, 569–576
  vs. Table control, 113
RepeaterItem objects, 351
RepeatLayout property (CheckBoxList
          control), 84
requestEncoding attribute of <globalization>
          section, 876
requestLimit property of
          <trace> section, 276, 879
Request.QueryString collection, 389, 392
Required value (TransactionOption
          enumeration), 690
RequiredFieldValidator control, 299–309
  adding to control comparison code, 315
  HTML source example, 305–307
RequiresNew value (TransactionOption
          enumeration), 690
responseEncoding attribute of
          <globalization> section, 876
Response.Write(), 219, 857
.resx files, 714
Right value (ImageAlign property), 137
role-based security, 812

About the Authors

Jesse Liberty is the author of a dozen books, including the best-selling *Programming C#* from O'Reilly, now in its second edition. Jesse is the president of Liberty Associates, Inc. (*http://www.LibertyAssociates.com*), where he provides .NET training, contract programming, and consulting. He is a former vice president of electronic delivery for Citibank and a former Distinguished Software Engineer and architect for AT&T, Ziff Davis, Xerox, and PBS.

Dan Hurwitz has been a software entrepreneur, developer, and trainer specializing in database applications for more than fifteen years. He is the principal in Sterling Solutions, a provider of database and PC consulting services, now focusing on .NET web and Windows training and application development. When not working on software projects or books or spending time with his family, he loves riding his mountain bike.

Colophon

Our look is the result of reader comments, our own experimentation, and feedback from distribution channels. Distinctive covers complement our distinctive approach to technical topics, breathing personality and life into potentially dry subjects.

The animal on the cover of *Programming ASP.NET* is a stingray. The stingray is a cartilaginous fish, distinguished from other types of rays by the saw-edged, venomous spines that adorn its whip-like tail. Stingrays have flat, disk-shaped bodies without distinct heads. They have well-developed pectoral fins, which undulate to propel their bodies through the water. Stingrays' eyes are on the top sides of their bodies, while their mouths are on their undersides. Because of this, they cannot see what they are eating and sometimes leave "hickeys" on scuba divers.

Stingrays live in shallow bays, sounds, and in-shore waters with sandy bottoms. They usually keep to the ocean floor and will flatten themselves against the ground to hide from predators. Despite their venomous tail spines, stingrays are not aggressive and will flee from danger whenever possible. They feed on mollusks, crustaceans, and some types of small fish. Sharks often prey on them, even though the two are closely related.

Catherine Morris was the production editor for *Programming ASP.NET*. Jane Ellin, Sue Willing, and Catherine Morris were the proofreaders. Emily Quill, Judy Hoer, and Claire Cloutier provided quality control. David Chu, Julie Flanagan, Matt Hutchinson, and Darren Kelly provided production assistance. Judy Hoer wrote the index.

Emma Colby designed the cover of this book, based on a series design by Edie Freedman. The cover image is a 19th-century engraving from the Dover Pictorial Archive. Emma Colby produced the cover layout with QuarkXPress 4.1 using Adobe's ITC Garamond font.

David Futato designed the interior layout. Mihaela Maier converted the files from Microsoft Word to FrameMaker 5.5.6 using tools created by Mike Sierra. The text font is Linotype Birka; the heading font is Adobe Myriad Condensed; and the code font is LucasFont's TheSans Mono Condensed. The illustrations that appear in the book were produced by Robert Romano and Jessamyn Read using Macromedia Free-Hand 9 and Adobe Photoshop 6. The tip and warning icons were drawn by Christopher Bing. This colophon was written by Linley Dolby.